T0320823

Britain's Political Economies

The Glorious Revolution of 1688–9 transformed the role of Parliament in Britain and its empire. Large numbers of statutes resulted, with most concerning economic activity. Julian Hoppit here provides the first comprehensive account of these acts, revealing how government affected economic life in this critical period prior to the industrial revolution, and how economic interests across Britain used legislative authority for their own benefit. Through a series of case studies he shows how ideas, interests, and information influenced statutory action in practice. Existing frameworks such as 'mercantilism' and the 'fiscal-military state' fail to capture the full richness and structural limitations of how political power influenced Britain's precocious economic development in the period. Instead, finely grained statutory action was the norm, guided more by present needs than any grand plan, with regulatory ambitions constrained by administrative limitations and some parts of Britain benefiting much more than others.

Julian Hoppit is Astor Professor of British History at University College London, where he has taught for more than thirty years. He is a Fellow of the British Academy and of the Royal Historical Society, and he has held visiting fellowships at the Huntingdon Library in California and the École des Hautes Études en Sciences Sociales in Paris. Previous publications include *Risk and failure in English business, 1700–1800* and *A land of liberty? England 1689–1727*. He edited the *Historical Journal* from 2008 to 2012, and he is the recipient of a Leverhulme Trust Major Research Fellowship (2016–19) to research 'Public finances and the Union, 1707–1978'.

Britain's Political Economies

Parliament and Economic Life, 1660–1800

Julian Hoppit

University College London

CAMBRIDGE
UNIVERSITY PRESS

CAMBRIDGE
UNIVERSITY PRESS

University Printing House, Cambridge CB2 8BS, United Kingdom

One Liberty Plaza, 20th Floor, New York, NY 10006, USA

477 Williamstown Road, Port Melbourne, VIC 3207, Australia

4843/24, 2nd Floor, Ansari Road, Daryaganj, Delhi – 110002, India

79 Anson Road, #06-04/06, Singapore 079906

Cambridge University Press is part of the University of Cambridge.

It furthers the University's mission by disseminating knowledge in the pursuit of education, learning, and research at the highest international levels of excellence.

www.cambridge.org
Information on this title: www.cambridge.org/9781316649909
DOI: 10.1017/9781139057875

First published 2017

Printed in the United Kingdom by Clays, St Ives plc

A catalogue record for this publication is available from the British Library.

ISBN 978-1-107-01525-8 Hardback
ISBN 978-1-316-64990-9 Paperback

Contents

Figures

Tables

Maps

Preface

Adam Smith, the first great student of Britain's political economies, devoted more than a quarter of *The wealth of nations* (1776) to explicating its forms, dynamics, and consequences. But by political economy Smith meant less bodies of ideas than the actions of those at the pinnacle of political society regarding economic life.

> Political œconomy, considered as a branch of the science of a statesman or legislator, proposes two distinct objects; first, to provide a plentiful revenue or subsistence for the people, or more properly to enable them to provide such a revenue or subsistence for themselves; and secondly, to supply the state or commonwealth with a revenue sufficient for the public services. It proposes to enrich both the people and the sovereign.[1]

This book follows Smith's definition, looking at why and how a key institution, the Westminster parliament, sought to affect economic life: of its concerns, efforts, and effects, in the context of the interests, ideas, and information available to it. Political economy as modes of thinking and specific ideas has its part in what follows, but the primary focus is on legislative action in the economic sphere.

Political economy emerged hand in hand with the development of the competitive 'European states system' from the late fifteenth century. After all, nobody doubted that a buoyant economy would ensure plenty of men and money with which to wage war. Yet while many in Tudor and Stuart Britain proposed ways to strengthen the economy, realizing those aims was hindered by repeated political breakdowns, including major revolutions centring on the execution of King Charles I in 1649 and the flight of his son James II in the Glorious Revolution of 1688–9. As revolutions, however, some of the obstacles to realizing economic reasons of state were cleared away. Critically, the Westminster parliament became a major arena for debating proposals and ideas and turning them

---

[1] Smith, *Wealth of nations*, vol. 1, p. 428.

into action. Parliament's legislative activity, the majority of which was directed at economic matters, grew markedly after 1688.

This book explores how the authority of a profoundly altered polity was applied to economic ends via the Westminster parliament's legislative efforts. More than 7,500 acts were passed affecting economic life between 1660 and 1800, along with more than 4,000 failed attempts to obtain acts. This was an extraordinary effort, speaking of enormous ambition, but a highly varied one, emanating from many different sources, for very different ends, and justified by widely varying ideas. Fundamentally, this book explores this huge legislative effort to bring out both the enormous scale and heterogeneous nature of Britain's political economies.

Relatively little legislation influencing the economy was devised centrally, and that which did often had ambiguous aims: power and plenty; stability and sustenance; welfare and wealth. Most legislation affecting the economy emanated locally, from individuals and interests, not centrally from ministers or departments. Consequently, little economic legislation related to systematic policies or programmes. Moreover, while statutes embodying imperial regulation and protectionism certainly existed, they were less coherent or dominant than is often thought and sat alongside many other general economic acts with very different aims. It follows that it is very misleading to tell a simple story of Britain's political economies in this period in terms of protectionism and regulation, often labelled 'mercantilism', giving way to laissez faire and free trade after the publication of Smith's *The wealth of nations* in 1776.

A fundamental limitation was that throughout this period many Britons were doubtful that central government should become more powerful at home: they cherished a limited executive, a balanced constitution, cheap government, local administration, and individual liberty. Central government lacked the wherewithal to manage the economy in ways we take for granted today: it collected plenty of taxes and built up a gigantic national debt to wage frequent wars, but it otherwise had very limited resources directly under its control. Consequently, not only were economic statutes many and varied, but there was a very uncertain relationship between prescription and practice. Britain's political economies were thereby highly flexible from one perspective, but from others variously arbitrary, oppressive, incoherent, and ineffective.

I need to make clear at the outset that while I believe political decisions significantly affected economic life in seventeenth- and eighteenth-century Britain, I am not much concerned with what their contribution was to the early industrial revolution or the 'great divergence'.[2] While

---

[2] 'The industrial revolution' is usually taken to mean the establishment of self-sustained economic growth. On the evolution of the concept see D. C. Coleman, *Myth, history and*

many contemporaries were confident that economic life could be 'improved' – a key concept developed in the seventeenth century – sustained and reasonably rapid economic growth was thought to be impossible by Adam Smith and his heirs.[3] No one at the time looked to alter political arrangements so as to produce an industrial revolution. Some decisions had strategic objectives in view, some were reactive, but most were finely grained. Moreover, if some political decisions clearly changed aspects of the economic order in this period, some did not have the desired outcome. Disentangling the effects of political action from other factors affecting economic lives is possible only in some specific instances and aggregating the effects of all economic statutes to produce a single measure would not be remotely meaningful. My aim, rather, has been to try to recover what people at the time tried to do and to gain some sense of whether they felt their ambitions had been met. As will become clear, many were very ambivalent on that second point. I appreciate that this produces a complex account without clear object lessons. But doing so avoids the distortions that beset accounts stressing the exceptional and exemplary nature of Britain's political economies. What was remarkable about Britain's political economies was the enormous effort at Westminster to produce huge numbers of laws. The dominant preoccupation was to produce modest, tailored legislation, whether for central government, interests, or individuals. Parliament was a vital tool both to central government and propertied interests across society. Britain's economic development would have been different without it.

This book is divided into two parts. The first is mainly concerned with establishing quantitatively the contours of economic legislation. Simple, systematic, and comprehensive counts of acts and failed attempts to obtain acts are provided in terms of patterns over time and by subject, scope, and place. To this framework is added a chapter that considers in broad terms the information, interests, and ideas that framed economic legislation. Part One establishes the huge scale and richness of Britain's political economies. Those patterns are brought to life in Part Two through four case studies, while also foregrounding facets of economic legislation which have too often been passed over. Yet they are themselves surveys across the whole period covered by this book, rather than an in-depth enquiry into particular measures. That is to say, in the

---

the industrial revolution (1992), ch. 1. The 'great divergence' is the point at which the macro-economic fortunes of Europe or the West markedly outstripped those of Asia. For an overview see Peer Vries, State, economy and the great divergence: Great Britain and China, 1680s–1850s (2015).

[3] Paul Slack, The invention of improvement: information and material progress in seventeenth-century England (Oxford, 2015); E. A. Wrigley, Energy and the English industrial revolution (Cambridge, 2010), pp. 10–13.

end this book provides a structured overview of economic legislation to be set alongside more detailed studies of particular measures that already exist or which others might write in the future. It aims to be wide ranging and systematic, with an emphasis placed on providing original research and using parliamentary legislation as a lens through which to view Britain's political economies. Although the scope of this book is wide, a particular perspective is adopted.

Acknowledgements

This book has been in my mind for many years, but had to be put aside until relatively recently because of other commitments. I regret that, but it does mean that even more students and colleagues at UCL have stimulated my thinking. Especially important in recent years, when most of this book was written, were discussions with my former doctoral students Daisy Gibbs and Philip Loft. I must also thank Philip for commenting with characteristic speed and insight on an earlier draft.

Two seminars of the Institute of Historical Research in London have also been influential, not least by working closely with my fellow convenors: Arthur Burns, Pene Corfield, the late John Dinwiddy, Negley Harte, Tim Hitchock, Alejandra Irigoin, Anne Murphy, David Ormrod, and Nuala Zahedieh. Many others have helped over the years with aspects of this project, including the late Donald Coleman, Martin Daunton, Nick Draper, Mark Goldie, Joanna Innes, Renaud Morieux, Philip Rössner, and Koji Yamamoto. Philippe Minard kindly arranged a month-long fellowship at École des Hautes Études en Sciences Sociales in Paris, where some of the ideas in this book were trialled. John Morrill has, as ever, been continuously supportive of me and my work. In the early stages I was fortunate to be able to call on the expertise of David Hayton and his colleagues at the History of Parliament. Many more still have inspired me, as my footnotes attest, though I particularly want to state how much I owe to the work of the late Paul Langford. I worked through some of the research in this book in earlier articles, putting me much in debt to plenty of editors and referees. Chapter 8 is a revised version of 'Bounties, the economy and the state in Britain, 1689–1800', in Perry Gauci, ed., *Regulating the British economy, 1660–1850* (2011), 139–60. I am grateful to the publisher, Ashgate, for permission to use it here.

Some of the original research in this book, undertaken with Joanna Innes, was funded by a grant from the Leverhulme Trust. In part this built on unpublished work by the late Sheila Lambert which she kindly made available to us. Further funding was generously provided by the

UCL history department, the British Academy, and the Huntington Library. At a very early stage Edmund Green, Simon Renton, and Nyani Samarasinghe acted as research assistants. I have also depended on many librarians and archivists, in Britain and the United States. I am very grateful to them all, but must particularly acknowledge the extraordinary help of James Collett-White, formerly of the Bedfordshire Archives, and the staff of the Sutro Library, San Francisco.

Richard Fisher welcomed this book on board Cambridge University Press. I owe him a lot, and not just for the faith he placed in this book. Michael Watson has seen this book through the press, and I am grateful for his help when things did not always go as smoothly as we hoped. I must also thank in the warmest terms the comments of the Press's wonderful reader of a complete draft. This book is very much the better for her efforts.

My friends at Shelford Bottom have been remarkably tolerant of my academic obsessions, helping me to keep this book in due perspective. And my wife, Karin, has had to live with this book for too long, but her love and support have helped to keep me going.

A Note on Sources and Dates

The two key sources of this book are: Acts of Parliament, conveniently listed in the table of contents of Owen Ruffhead, ed., *The statutes at large* (18 vols., 1769–1800); and failed attempts ('fails') to obtain an act in Julian Hoppit, ed., *Failed legislation, 1660–1800, extracted from the Commons and Lords journals* (1997).

Counts of acts and fails are not referenced in the text, but specific acts and fails are. Statutes, public unless specified as private – a distinction explained on p. 52 – are referred to by regnal year – a year running from the date of the monarch's accession – and chapter number, e.g. 3 George II, c. 4. Some acts were passed in sessions that straddled two regnal years, e.g. 8 & 9 George III, c. 8. The numbering of acts in Ruffhead is unreliable before 1714 and I have preferred those in *The statutes of the realm* (vols. 5–9, 1819–22). Failed attempts are referred to by the reference numbers in Hoppit, *Failed legislation*, e.g. 28.031.

Detail about the handling of legislation in nine sessions has been collected from the *JHC* and *JHL*: 1660, 1674, 1694–5, 1708–9, 1724–5, 1740–1, 1753, 1772–3, and 1795–6. Parliament's business was conducted within fairly discrete 'sessions' that varied in length and frequency and so for sake of clarity sessions are referred to by the calendar (rather than regnal) year or years in which they occurred.

The New Year is taken to begin on 1 January not, as was usual at the time, 25 March. Place of publication is London unless stated otherwise.

Abbreviations

Add Mss	Additional Manuscripts
Beds. Archives	Bedfordshire Archives and Records Service
BL	British Library
BPP	British Parliamentary Papers
Clements Library	Williams L. Clements Library, Ann Arbor, Michigan
Cobbett, *Parl. Hist.*	W. Cobbett, ed., *The parliamentary history of England, from the earliest times to the year 1803*, 36 vols. (1806–20)
ESTC	*English short title catalogue*, an online resource at 'estc.bl.uk'
HofP online	The History of Parliament – online edition at 'historyofparliamentonline.org'. This contains all of the printed volumes for the House of Commons for the period, comprising introductory surveys, constituency accounts, and political biographies of MPs.
Hoppit, *Failed legislation*	Julian Hoppit, ed., *Failed legislation, 1660–1800: extracted from the Commons and Lords journals* (1997) – the Introduction, pp. 1–24, co-authored with Joanna Innes
HMC	Historical Manuscripts Commission
JHC	*Journals of the House of Commons*, vols. 8 (1660–7) to 55 (1799–1800)
JHL	*Journals of the House of Lords*, vols. 9 (1660–6) to 42 (1798–1800)
Lambert, *Sessional papers*	Sheila Lambert, ed., *The House of Commons session papers of the eighteenth century* (147 vols., 1975).
Mss	Manuscripts
NAS	National Archives of Scotland

ODNB	*Oxford Dictionary of National Biography* – online edition at 'oxforddnb.com'
Sample sessions	Database of legislative activity in sessions 1660, 1674, 1694–5, 1708–9, 1724–5, 1740–1, 1753, 1772–3, and 1795–6, compiled from the *JHC* and *JHL*
Smith, *Wealth of nations*	Adam Smith, *An inquiry into the nature and causes of the wealth of nations*, ed. R. H. Campbell and A. S. Skinner (2 vols., 1976)
Sutro, Banks	The papers of Sir Joseph Banks, Sutro Library, San Francisco
TNA	The National Archives, Kew

Part One

Contours

The chapters in Part One provide overviews of the legislative dimensions of Britain's political economies and the contexts within which they should be placed. Chapter 1 introduces this book, looking at the strengths and weaknesses of key concepts, notably mercantilism and the fiscal-military state, before considering major trends in the historiography of Britain's political economies. Often employing simple counting, the following three chapters rest on a comprehensive and systematic exploration of the statute book and the *Journals* of the Commons and Lords. Chapter 2 considers how Parliament came to pass many more acts after the Glorious Revolution of 1688–9, pointing up the difficulties of the preceding period and the surge in the number of all acts passed between 1689 and 1714 as well as after 1760. Attention turns in Chapter 3 to considering the incidence and subject matter of economic legislation alone. Most of these concerned the local, regional or personal spheres, with only a minority dealing with the national or international spheres. It is shown that some types of measures were much more likely to be enacted than others. This has important implications for how the relationship between political power and economic life is conceived, particularly the meaning and significance of economic policy and the nature of property rights. Building on this, Chapter 4 explores the geographical incidence of economic legislation, identifying important differences between Britain's three nations, as well as within England. Consideration is also given to some important features of imperial economic legislation, especially the different layers of statutes that applied. Finally in Part One, Chapter 5 turns to some of the broad influences on Parliament as it considered economic measures: the often voluminous information it sought out or was put before it; the myriad interests that expressed themselves to it, especially via petitioning; and the broader context of a vibrant print culture concerning Britain's political economies.

Taken together, Part One shows the main legislative patterns concerning economic life in Britain at the time, with each chapter building on the last. The purpose is to map the key contours. What follows in Part Two are four case studies designed to bring some of the generalizations within Part One to life, as well as to begin to address the fundamental issue of the relationship between prescription and practice.

1 Introduction

'But what is government itself, but the greatest of all reflections on human nature? If men were angels, no government would be necessary. If angels were to govern men, neither external nor internal controuls on government would be necessary.'

James Madison, 1788[1]

Across Europe, from the middle of the sixteenth century economic matters gradually became what they have since remained, a major 'reason of state'. Given their quest for order, prosperity, and power governments had not previously ignored economic considerations, but they now attained much greater significance. Four related factors were critical to this: developing European interstate rivalry for souls, territory, trade, and empire; intensified crises of funding central government, mainly because of ever-rising military costs; mounting worries about the scourge of poverty and social disorder; and a developing optimism in the prospects for improvement, not least that aided by political authority. Thus the potent concept of the sovereign 'state' developed which in turn fed the emergence of 'political economy' as a discourse, a term first coined (in France) in 1615 though used only occasionally before the 1760s.[2] As Thomas Mun put it in the 1620s, 'well-governed states' cherished foreign trade, nurturing and protecting it 'because they know

---

[1] Alexander Hamilton, James Madison, and John Jay, *The federalist*, ed. Terence Ball (Cambridge, 2003), p. 252.

[2] Quentin Skinner, 'A genealogy of the modern state', *Proceedings of the British Academy*, 162 (2009), pp. 325–70; Hendrik Spruyt, *The sovereign state and its competitors: an analysis of systems change* (Princeton, NJ, 1994), pp. 3–7; Otto Hintze, 'Calvinism and raison d'etat in early seventeenth-century Brandenburg', in *The historical essays of Otto Hintze*, ed. Felix Gilbert (New York, 1975), p. 92; Jean-Claude Perrot, *Une historire intellectuell de l'économie politique, XVIIe–XVIIIe siècle* (Paris, 1992), p. 63; Mary Poovey, *A history of the modern fact: problems of knowledge in the sciences of wealth and society* (Chicago, IL, 1998), p. xvii; Steve Pincus, 'From holy cause to economic interest: the study of population and the invention of the state', in Alan Houston and Steve Pincus, eds., *A nation transformed: England after the Restoration* (Cambridge, 2001), pp. 271–98.

it is a Principle in reason of state to maintain and defend that which doth support them.'[3]

It was one thing for central governments to aspire to enhance economic activity, quite another to realize those hopes. In seventeenth-century Britain a dysfunctional constitution, epitomized by the execution of one king in 1649 and the exile of another in 1688, profoundly limited what could be done. But gradually at first, more swiftly after the 'Glorious Revolution' of 1688–9, a new political order was built that overcame some key limitations. This allowed Britain to become a major European power, a transformation related to its growing economy, military, and, until American independence in 1776, empire. At the heart of these relationships was a significantly heightened role for Westminster's legislation in both national government and local life. Parliament was used very successfully to hew men and money from national resources to wage repeated wars through the eighteenth century. But more directly moulding economic life often frustrated central government, with ambitious statutes and loud exhortations often encountering indifference, evasion, and resistance. After all, there were periodically loud complaints that smuggling and fraud were rife, or that key statutes were simply being ignored. Often enough, new laws were passed in the vain hope of making old ones effective; layer upon layer resulted. In contrast, numerous, more modest proposals to use political power for economic ends, mainly local and personal, collectively proved highly significant.

From the middle of the seventeenth century legislation on economic matters was sought in very much greater numbers than ever before at Westminster. But in the Restoration era (1660–88) of more than 700 attempts there to legislate about the economy only 166 succeeded (24 per cent). The Glorious Revolution of 1688–9 opened the floodgates. Between 1688 and 1800 more than 7,000 acts were passed directly concerning economic life, while there were nearly 3,000 failed attempts to do so – together consuming more than a half of Westminster's total legislative effort.[4] In contrast, the 'government', 'religion', and 'armed services' subject categories together accounted for only 11 per cent of all acts passed, and 17 per cent of failed attempts. It may be that spirited encounters over foreign policy, religion, and the constitution bulk large in the very incomplete records of parliamentary debates available, but the bread and butter of Parliament's work was legislating about the likes of infrastructure, property rights, market standards, domestic and

---

[3] Quoted in J. H. Shennan, *The origins of the modern European state, 1450–1725* (1974), p. 90.

[4] 'Economic' is an anachronism for the period studied here and is certainly not a clear-cut category. These issues, and the underlying sources, are discussed in Chapters 2 and 3.

overseas trade, and debtor–creditor relations.[5] This book provides the first systematic and comprehensive assessment of this effort.

This book considers political economy particularly in terms of legislative action (and inaction), including the influence of ideas and interests on the Westminster parliament. Centrally it explores the impact of political power on economic life using the terms employed at the time. Doing so makes clear the importance of recognizing the plurality of Britain's political economies in four main senses. Firstly, a single British national experience was limited to fairly specific areas. In particular, it is vital to appreciate the composite nature of the British state in this period, especially of the differing experiences of England and Scotland after the 1707 Union. Secondly, if today central government closely controls economic policy, in this period it did not. It developed some proposals, but major initiatives were also developed outside of central government and, critically, many thousands of statutes applied to particular people and places, invariably at the behest of specific, not national interests. In this way, relations were redrawn between London and the localities, especially England's. Thirdly, while national measures were devised to try to affect the economy, these were certainly not just 'mercantilist'. The subject matter of economic legislation was much richer than that label implies. Finally, the gap between prescription and practice was sometimes very large; what politicians and their administrators devised was far from always what was actually experienced. As former Prime Minister Shelburne put it: 'It requires experience in Government to know the immense distance between planning and executing. All the difficulty is with the last. It requires no small labour to open the eyes of either the public or of individuals, but when that is accomplished, you are not got a third of the way. The real difficulty remains in getting people to apply the principles which they have admitted, and of which they are now so fully convinced. Then springs the mine composed of private interests and personal animosity.'[6]

In turn, those four variants are linked to three key paradoxes in Britain's political economies. First, that while contemporaries were sure that political action might aid economic life, there was uncertainty about how much power central government should exercise to that end. The

[5] Doohwan Ahn and Brendan Simms, 'European great power politics in British public discourse, 1714–1763', in William Mulligan and Brendan Simms, eds., *The primacy of foreign policy in British history, 1660–2000: how strategic concerns shaped modern Britain* (Basingstoke, 2010), p. 84. This is an interesting but rather unpersuasive attempt to gauge the importance of certain themes in public discourse.
[6] Lord Fitzmaurice, *Life of William Shelburne afterwards first Marquess of Lansdowne* (2nd edn., 2 vols., 1912), vol. 1, p. 18.

authoritarianism of Charles I, Oliver Cromwell, and James II at home and of Louis XIV in France loomed large in the public consciousness, both immediately and long after, linking to ideas about ensuring the executive did not overbalance (and so corrupt) the constitution and that the costs of government did not escalate unreasonably.[7] Consequently, policy aspirations often lacked sufficient political and administrative capacity, a tension that was often unresolved. That said, secondly, contemporary obsessions with liberty – to Voltaire England was a 'land of liberty' – sat alongside the fact that people were increasingly heavily taxed, subject to rising numbers of capital statutes, contributed to global warfare and empire building (including the massive Atlantic slave trade), and prey to the enforced redistribution of numerous property rights.[8] The language of liberty was in important respects at odds with the practice of liberty. Indeed, finally, there was a largely unspoken tension between claims for the supremacy of Parliament on the one hand and those for the sanctity of property on the other. If Parliament was supreme, it could do anything; but if property was sacred, it was untouchable.

Such paradoxes might be taken to mean that contemporaries were hypocritical, especially in according liberty and property such totemic significance. Certainly like us they were capable of saying one thing and doing another. Certainly in part liberty and property were celebrated to justify or mask extreme inequalities. But this book also stresses the difficulties contemporaries faced in creating and implementing political economy, especially because of the challenges of reconciling very different interests (personal, local, sectional, and national), the absence of an agreed paradigm of economic discourse, the shortages or imperfections of information about some areas of economic life (all the more important given rapid change in some parts), and the problems of balancing legislative ambition and administrative realism. Such difficulties were real and substantial, making it very hard for contemporaries to act consistently.

Arguing for the plurality and paradoxes of Britain's political economies might seem rather obvious. But, particularly through resort to the anachronistic concept of 'mercantilism', too many previous accounts have exaggerated the coherence, cogency, consistency, and effectiveness of 'economic policy' in the period. Just what was aimed at and what was achieved has been unduly simplified, leading to misleading conclusions

---

[7] An important survey of related issues is Joanna Innes, 'Central government "interference": changing conceptions, practices, and concerns, c. 1700–1850', Jose Harris, ed., *Civil society in British history: ideas, identities, institutions* (Oxford, 2003), pp. 39–60.

[8] *Voltaire's correspondence*, ed. Theodore Besterman (107 vols., Geneva, 1953–65), vol. 2, p. 37.

about issues as fundamental as the nature of the regime, property rights, and the extent of economic regulation – as well as the general effect of political power on economic life. Such simplifications particularly arise from focusing on the origins and progress in Britain of the first industrial revolution, though also from a concern to explain the origins of American independence and alleged Western exceptionalism. On the former, it is understandably tempting to argue that the nature of political institutions was or was not a key determinant of Britain's macroeconomic performance in general or of the first industrial revolution more specifically. Many historians have been unable to resist the temptation. But it follows that an emphasis on the pluralities and paradoxes of Britain's political economies renders such arguments rather misleading. Certainly, establishing with some degree of quantitative accuracy the general effects of political power on economic performance is impossible. The evidence is just not there and no amount of statistical wizardry can fill that black hole convincingly.

That political power was applied to economic life in varied, confused, contradictory, and sometimes ineffective ways is emphatically not, however, to argue that contemporaries thought no effort was worth taking or that no effects can be discerned. Quite the opposite. Everyone in this period believed that political power could significantly affect economic life; they may often have exaggerated that belief, but they nonetheless held resolutely to it. Many thousands of Acts of Parliament, along with much else, bear unambiguous witness to that. Indeed, Adam Smith devoted a good part of *The wealth of nations* (1776) to criticizing such obsessions. From poor labourers and village shopkeepers to great merchants and rich landowners, no one could risk ignoring how that power might be used, while to a significant minority statutory power might be called on to help improve their own economic position, and occasionally that of others. That alone makes the subject an important one to work into accounts of British political and economic history in this period. It is what people at the time wished and feared, valued and discounted, initiated and opposed, that this book studies.

Thematically this book contributes to understanding both state formation in Britain and the relationship between the state and the economy. These are themes that have been explored not only by historians of various shades, but also by economists, political scientists, geographers, and sociologists. This book might therefore engage with a large number of meta-narratives, intellectual traditions, concepts, and methods. Certainly they are not ignored, though too many recent contributions read like political tracts or artificial abstractions. But so as not to spread myself too thinly I mainly engage more selectively with two main strands in the existing literature within political and economic history: that related to the architecture and authority of the state, of central and local governments generally and of Parliament particularly; and of the relationship between political power and economic life. One particularly important interpretation focuses on mercantilism, with an emphasis on regulation, protection, and empire. The next section explores this in the broad context of economic life at the time. Discussion then moves on to consider the political and constitutional tensions that the revolution constitution was slowly able to resolve. This leads to a discussion of arguments that emphasize, often contrary to the mercantilist approach, the question of liberty and property rights. This chapter concludes by considering the scope, sources, methods, and organization of the rest of this book.

Economic Hopes and Fears

By their very existence, governments affect economic life. Minimally they require resources with which to undertake the fundamental duties of defending lives and property, necessarily influencing the markets involved. Further basic steps, such as issuing money and setting standards of weights and measures, can have profound consequences, not least in helping to sketch the limits of the economy involved. But governments have often tried to do much more, seeking to aid economic life for, as Smith noted, both their own benefit and that of their peoples. These might relate to challenges or risks on the one hand, and those relating to opportunities on the other, or sometimes to both. A critical issue here is whether the fundamental general assumptions of society and its government about economic life are optimistic, pessimistic, or agnostic. Was there the potential to grow the economy, or was the best hope simply to stabilize what was already there? Put another way, should political power be used to guard, maintain, or enhance existing strengths, or should it try to create new ones, perhaps at the expense of the old?

The nature of economic life obviously influenced the answers to the questions just posed. But in Britain perceptions were as varied as the experiences. Between 1660 and 1750 population stagnated, because of fairly high age at marriage, significant emigration to North America between 1650 and 1680, the last visitation of the plague in 1665, famine or near famine in parts of Scotland in the 1690s, a major demographic setback in the late 1720s in England, and London's structurally high death rate.[9] But a lack of demographic growth before 1750 sat alongside

---

[9] E. A. Wrigley and R. S. Schofield, *The population history of England, 1541–1871: a reconstruction* (1981), ch. 7; Karen Cullen, *Famine in Scotland – the 'Ill Years' of the 1690s*

marked economic growth in some areas: agricultural output and productivity grew, especially in England; coal output, particularly from near Newcastle, soared; London boomed; overseas trade expanded, notably with the Caribbean, North America, India, and China; financial services developed and improved, mainly in banking, public finances, and insurance provision; significant investment in better rivers and roads also took place; and several industries grew markedly, including brewing, paper, and metal wares.[10]

Population rose after 1750, rapidly by the end of the eighteenth century, though significant emigration from Scotland took place in the 1770s in the context of a wider depopulation of the Highlands in the last quarter of the eighteenth century associated with the early 'clearances'.[11] Earlier improvements in agriculture, trade, services, and industries continued after 1750, but in places at a much quicker pace. Canals were dug, machines invented, and factories built. To many historians, this was the early part of an epochal change, the industrial revolution, where the limitations of traditional technologies and the division of labour were transcended, allowing population to break through the constraints linking population and resources that Malthus emphasized.[12] Certainly while London continued to be an economic powerhouse, Birmingham, Glasgow, Leeds, Liverpool, and Manchester, along with many other towns, were fast becoming industrial and commercial centres of global importance. By contrast Bristol, Exeter, and Norwich all struggled to keep pace, as did their industrial hinterlands.[13]

(Edinburgh, 2010); John Landers, *Death and the metropolis: studies in the demographic history of London 1670–1830* (Cambridge, 1993).

[10] Mark Overton, *Agricultural revolution in England: the transformation of the agrarian economy, 1500–1850* (Cambridge, 1996), ch. 3; M. W. Flinn, *The history of the British coal industry: vol. 2, 1700–1830, the industrial revolution* (Oxford, 1984), ch. 1; E. A. Wrigley, 'A simple model of London's importance in changing English society and economy, 1650–1750', *Past and Present*, 37 (1967), pp. 44–70; Ralph Davis, 'English foreign trade, 1660–1700', *Economic History Review*, 7.2 (1954), pp. 150–66; Ralph Davis, 'English foreign trade, 1700–1774', *Economic History Review*, 15.2 (1962), pp. 285–303; Anne Murphy, *The origins of English financial markets: investment and speculation before the South Sea Bubble* (Cambridge, 2009); Eric Pawson, *Transport and economy: the turnpike roads of eighteenth-century Britain* (1977), p. 13; D. C. Coleman, *The economy of England, 1450–1750* (Oxford, 1978), ch. 9.

[11] Wrigley and Schofield, *Population history of England*, ch. 7; Bernard Bailyn, *Voyagers to the West: a passage in the peopling of America on the eve of revolution* (New York, 1986).

[12] For introductions: E. A. Wrigley, *Energy and the English industrial revolution* (Cambridge, 2010); Joel Mokyr, *The enlightened economy: an economic history of Britain, 1700–1850* (2009); Roderick Floud, Jane Humphries, and Paul Johnson, eds., *The Cambridge economic history of modern Britain: vol. 1, 1700–1870* (Cambridge, 2014).

[13] John Langton, 'Urban growth and economic change: from the late seventeenth century to 1841', in Peter Clark, ed., *The Cambridge urban history of Britain: vol. 2, 1540–1840*

Such economic changes did not readily translate into economic contentment. Everywhere, huge inequalities meant that poverty was experienced by many, and threatened more still. The contemporary label 'the labouring poor' says it all. Moreover, the evolving economy was becoming more complex and interdependent, allowing extensions of the division of labour, but heightening the perceived risks of bad weather and disease, including to livestock – cattle distemper was a major problem in the period (and one the government tackled).[14] The frequent swings from war to peace and back again disrupted markets for labour, capital, and provisions, quite apart from the death and destruction involved. And rapid economic growth often came to rest on shaky foundations, leading in the late eighteenth century to major financial crises and the early stirrings of the business cycle.[15]

At the time, people were naturally struck by the vicissitudes and uncertainties in economic life. Short-term issues weighed heavily, to the extent that disentangling them from longer-term developments was very difficult. One key factor was that the information available to contemporaries was patchy, notably through the absence of a census until 1801. But another was pure perception. For example, the woollen and worsted industries had long been seen as critical to economic life, to both domestic and overseas trade, and peculiarly well-suited to Britain's natural circumstances. Thus any threat to them was looked on with pathological unease. Considerable ire was directed at any perceived challenges, especially from imports of cottons and silks. It was moreover impossible for anyone in Britain before the late eighteenth century to imagine that a cotton industry could flourish on Britain's own soil to the extent of profoundly affecting the lives of free and unfree in India, Egypt, and America. Yet that was just what started to happen by 1800.

The awkward term 'economic life' has been used so far because the idea of 'the economy' is a twentieth-century concept that has become a commonplace because we accept Keynes' argument from 1936 that national governments can influence aggregate demand to a meaningful degree. By contrast, in the period covered by this book 'œconomy' was an Aristotelian concept limited to household frugality or management; politicians struggled to imagine that there was a collective thing,

---

(Cambridge, 2000), pp. 473–4; Pat Hudson, ed., *Regions and industries: a perspective on the industrial revolution in Britain* (Cambridge, 1989).

[14] John Broad, 'Cattle plague in eighteenth-century England', *Agricultural History Review*, 31.2 (1983), pp. 104–15.

[15] T. S. Ashton, *Economic fluctuations in England, 1700–1800* (Oxford, 1959); Julian Hoppit, *Risk and failure in English business, 1700–1800* (Cambridge, 1987), chs. 7–8.

'the economy', which they could direct as a whole.[16] In the sixteenth century the terms 'commonweal' or 'commonwealth' came close to our meaning of 'the economy', but after the collapse of the republican Commonwealth in 1660 the restored royalist regime and its loyal subjects naturally turned their backs on such terminology.[17] In the late seventeenth century Sir William Petty and Gregory King did, through their inventive estimates of national income, see the economy as a whole, but in rather static terms.[18] In any case, their conceptualization was not widely adopted. Rather, resort was made to vague terms such as 'trade', 'commerce', or 'wealth' – and the first two often meant both domestic and overseas, not simply the latter.

That said, the importance of economic factors to the well-being of society was proclaimed more often and with increasing force in this period. Usually this was put in terms of national strength. To an anonymous author from 1695 commerce or exchange was 'the Soul of the Universe … the Fountain of Wealth, the true Foundation of all real Greatness'.[19] There were, however, rival views of just what it was that ultimately produced wealth. For some it was natural resources; to others (Petty and Smith for example) it was labour productivity, that is the way economic life was organized and its intensity; to others it was exchange, most commonly overseas trade.

There were certainly those who believed strongly that 'the home trade is the foundation of the Foreign.'[20] At the heart of the home trade was agriculture and the woollen and worsted industries, such that any threats to them, including diseases (to crops and livestock), the 'decay of rents', and imported calicoes and silks, led to significant action: compensating those affected by cattle disease, placing bounties on corn exports, and heaping duties, and sometimes complete prohibitions, on some imports. To others overseas commerce was a desirable end in its own right and a readier route to prosperity, with Dutch success in the European carrying trade in its seventeenth-century golden age being held up in

---

[16] Margaret Schabas, *The natural origins of economics* (Chicago, IL, 2005), pp. 1–3. 'Oeconomy, the prudent Conduct, or discrete, frugal Management of a Man's Estate, or that of another.' E. Chambers, *Cyclopædia: or, an universal dictionary of arts and sciences* (2 vols., 1728), vol. 2, p. 655.

[17] Early Modern Research Group, 'Commonwealth: the social, cultural, and conceptual contexts of an early modern keyword', *Historical Journal*, 54.3 (2011), pp. 659–87.

[18] Paul Slack, *The invention of improvement: information and material progress in seventeenth-century England* (Oxford, 2015), pp. 120–1; P. Studenski, *The income of nations, part 1, history* (New York, 1958), pp. 26–36; Tony Aspromourgos, 'The mind of the oeconomist: an overview of the "Petty papers" archive', *History of Economic Ideas*, 9.1 (2001), p. 50.

[19] Anon., *Angliae tutamen: or, the safety of England* (1695), p. 3.

[20] Carew Reynell, *The true English interest* (1674), pp. 35–6.

exemplary terms.[21] But it was also widely appreciated that Britain had a 'double Motive' for heightened trade, 'our Security, as well as our Prosperity depends upon it' because it provided plenty of seamen and naval resources to be called on in wartime: 'your Fleet, and your Trade, have so near a relation, and such mutual influence upon each other, they cannot well be separated'.[22]

Britain was certainly not alone in placing a heightened value on trade in this period. One stimulus was the widely held belief that prosperity was fickle, moving from one place to another. Both ancient and more recent examples bore that out to everyone's satisfaction. But in the sixteenth and seventeenth centuries the expansion of European trade and dominion across the Atlantic and into the Indian and Pacific Oceans introduced a major new consideration and heightened national economic rivalries: 'All the Nations of *Europe* seem to strive who shall outwit one another in point of Trade.'[23] This manifested itself in numerous ways, both pacific and not, often labelled 'mercantilism', by which is usually meant an alliance of politics and ideology in favour of protectionism and militarism. The concept was a late nineteenth-century adaptation of Adam Smith's 'mercantile system', though involving an important (if neglected) shift in meaning.[24] For many years its utility was heavily criticized, but recently it has enjoyed something of a renaissance, though often without much effort at defining it carefully.[25] If anything, the term

---

[21] Jonathan I. Israel, 'England's mercantilist response to Dutch world trade primacy, 1647–1674', in S. Groenveld and M. Wintle, eds., *Britain and the Netherlands, vol. 10: government and the economy in Britain and the Netherlands since the Middle Ages* (Zutphen, 1992), pp. 50–61; Erik S. Reinert, 'Emulating success: contemporary views of the Dutch economy before 1800', in Oscar Gelderblom, ed., *The political economy of the Dutch republic* (Farnham, 2009), pp. 19–39.

[22] Anon., *The fisheries revived: or, Britain's hidden treasures discovered* (1750), p. 1; Lord Haversham in Cobbett, *Parl. Hist.*, 6 (1702–14), col. 598.

[23] [Sir Theodore Janssen], *General maxims in trade, particularly applied to the commerce between Great Britain and France* (1713), p. 19.

[24] Smith detailed the mercantile system at length, arguing that it aimed at producing a positive balance of trade, paying particular attention to customs duties, bounties, and the navigation acts. By contrast, a century later Schmoller, who did so much to develop the concept of mercantilism, argued that 'The essence of the system lies not in some doctrine of money, or of the balance of trade; not in tariff barriers, protective duties, or navigation laws; but in something far greater: – namely, in the total transformation of society and its organisation ... in the replacing of a local and territorial economic policy by that of the nation state.' Gustav Schmoller, *The mercantile system and its historical significance* (1896), pp. 50 and 77. On the evolution of the concept see Lars Magnusson, *Mercantilism: the shaping of an economic language* (1994), ch. 2.

[25] D. C. Coleman was a fierce critic of the concept. See the collection he edited, with an important introduction, *Revisions in mercantilism* (1969), and his essay 'Mercantilism revisited', *Historical Journal*, 23.4 (1980), pp. 773–91. A recent important collection tellingly failed to define the term: Philip J. Stern and Carl Wennerlind, eds., *Mercantilism reimagined: political economy in early modern Britain and its empire* (Oxford, 2014).

has become vaguer as Britain's success in raising money to wage war between 1689 and 1815 has been hitched to older arguments about protectionism to argue that consequently brute force contributed significantly to Britain's economic precocity in this period.[26]

Mercantilism is commonly seen as a form of national economic policy. To many at its core was the view that commerce was a zero-sum game, that gain by some meant loss by others, in which the ultimate aim was a positive balance of trade. Policies supposedly centred on the granting of monopolies of one sort or another, such as the East India Company (1600), the establishment of a fairly closed imperial economy through the navigation acts (from 1651), and other types of regulation and protection to enhance exports and restrict imports. Certainly on the eve of American independence prohibitions were in place against the import of 175 and the export of 39 different goods.[27] This is often linked to a simple narrative whereby, in Hume's phrase, the 'jealousy of trade' among European powers was dominant until liberal ideas were developed in both France and Scotland in the mid-eighteenth century, most famously in Adam Smith's *The wealth of nations* in 1776. By this account, such new ideas gradually came to have a significant impact in Britain such that, aided by the altered circumstances wrought by the American, French, and industrial revolutions, it adopted free trade in the first half of the nineteenth century and left mercantilism behind.[28]

Unquestionably Smith's great book was pivotal to the development of economics and he was not to know how politically charged his ideas were to become, but a number of weaknesses with this simple transitional narrative must be grasped. The concept of mercantilism is useful to understanding some but far from all of Britain's political economies in this period and, given its popularity as a concept, some of its less well known features and limitations need setting out.

First, enthusiasm for free trade and hostility towards monopolies was expressed loudly and sometimes effectively from the early seventeenth century, albeit sometimes in the context of special interest pleading. For example, in 1674 it was exclaimed that 'The chief thing that

---

[26] P. K. O'Brien, 'Political structures and grand strategies for the growth of the British economy, 1688–1815', in Alice Teichova and Herbert Matis, eds., *Nation, state and the economy in history* (Cambridge, 2003), p. 32; Ronald Findley and Kevin H. O'Rourke, *Power and plenty: trade, war, and the world economy in the second millennium* (Princeton, NJ, 2007), p. 351. For the wider context see James D. Tracey, ed., *The political economy of merchant empires: state power and world trade, 1350–1750* (Cambridge, 1991).

[27] Anon., *A list of goods prohibited to be imported into or exported from Great Britain* (1775).

[28] On the move to free trade see Anthony Howe, 'Restoring free trade: the British experience, 1776–1873', in Donald Winch and Patrick K. O'Brien, eds., *The political economy of British historical experience, 1688–1914* (Oxford, 2002), pp. 193–213.

promote Trade and make it flourish, are that it be free', in 1704 that 'All Prohibitions seem to be a sort of Violence upon the very Nature of Trade, in that they limit and restrain what should be in its nature free', and in 1720 'Trade is never in a better condition, than when it's natural and free'.[29] Such sentiments were often tied to political battles over monopoly companies, dating back at least as far as the establishment of the East India Company, and in the generation or two before 1714 were sometimes caught up with wider constitutional battles giving them a party political edge.[30] A major assault on industrial monopolies was made in the 1640s and 1650s and, in the face of arguments for freer trade, the century after 1660 saw a whittling away of exclusive rights such that by 1760 only the East India and Russia Companies had maintained the substance of their original powers: among a host of others, the Royal African, Levant, and Framework Knitters Companies had all been undermined or abolished.[31] At home too, an important committee of the House of Commons in 1751 criticized guilds, arguing that 'the most useful and beneficial Manufactures are principally carried on, and Trade most flourishing, in such Towns and Places as are under no such local Disabilities'.[32] The merits of internal free trade were barely questioned in the eighteenth century.

Joan Thirsk, with enormous expertise in seventeenth-century economic history, was certain that 'no one denies that in the long term a

---

[29] Reynell, *True English interest*, p. 6; P. Paxton, *A discourse concerning the nature, advantage, and improvement of trade* (1704), p. 47; Isaac Gervaise, *The system or theory of the trade of the world* (1720), p. 3.

[30] Theodore K. Rabb, 'Sir Edwin Sandys and the parliament of 1604', *American Historical Review*, 69.3 (1964), pp. 646–70; Robert Ashton, 'The parliamentary agitation for free trade in the opening years of the reign of James I', *Past and Present*, 38 (1967), pp. 40–55; Pauline Croft, 'Free trade and the House of Commons, 1605–6', *Economic History Review*, 28.1 (1975), pp. 17–27. The advocacy of free trade in the late seventeenth century is discussed in George L. Cherry, 'The development of the English free-trade movement in parliament, 1689–1702', *Journal of Modern History*, 25.2 (1953), pp. 103–19 and William A. Pettigrew, *Freedom's debt: the Royal African Company and the politics of the Atlantic slave trade, 1672–1752* (Chapel Hill, NC, 2013), ch. 3. On the link between party politics and economic regulation see Henry Horwitz, 'The East India trade, the politicians and the constitution, 1689–1702', *Journal of British Studies*, 17.2 (1978), pp. 1–18; Steve Pincus, *1688: the first modern revolution* (New Haven, CT, 2009), ch. 12.

[31] Margaret James, *Social problems and policy during the Puritan revolution, 1640–1660* (1930), pp. 131–3; K. G. Davies, *The Royal African Company* (1957), ch. 8; Glyndwr Williams, 'The Hudson's Bay Company and its critics in the eighteenth century', *Transactions of the Royal Historical Society*, 20 (1970), pp. 149–71; Alfred C. Wood, *A history of the Levant Company* (Oxford, 1935), p. 156; D. S. Macmillan, 'The Russia Company of London in the eighteenth century: the effective survival of a "regulated" chartered company', *Guildhall Miscellany*, 4 (1971–3), pp. 222–36; J. D. Chambers, 'The Worshipful Company of Framework Knitters (1657–1778)', *Economica*, 27 (1929), pp. 320–4.

[32] *JHC*, 26 (1750–4), p. 292 (21 June 1751).

shift can be discerned between 1600 and 1700 in the weight of opinion supporting a policy of *laissez-faire* and turning away from the idea of the regulated economy.'[33] That may be pushing things a bit too far, but certainly *The wealth of nations* did not invent arguments for free trade, but systematized and developed them, very much in the context of a negative conceptualization of what Smith called 'the mercantile system'.[34] Moreover, as has been noted, parts of that mercantile system were being dismantled well before he published his great work. But such was the influence of Smith that political economists before him have often been neglected or caricatured; the ideas he attacked were supposedly not worth exploring on their own terms. For example, it is worth recalling that Charles Davenant, who ended his days as Inspector General of Customs (1703–14) and wrote widely on political economy, could argue both that trade 'must be suffered to take its own natural course' and that the monopoly rights of the likes of the Royal African Company provided greater trading security and a 'far greater probability of producing many national advantages, than private persons trading separately can do'.[35] It is too easy to dismiss such arguments as political or self-serving. Risk sharing, including guilds, open field agriculture, and trading companies, was an important response to common fears of economic uncertainty, slow rates of return on investments, the difficulties of the period of overcoming local shortages through regional or international trade, and less-developed financial markets, including for insurance.

It must secondly be noted that the balance of trade, and presumptions that economic life was a zero-sum game, was only one of a number of valued economic ideas influencing policy at the time. In particular, from the early seventeenth century there developed powerful arguments that England, and at that stage attention was focused on England, had considerable scope for 'improvement' which political power could nurture; plenty questioned whether economic life was indeed a zero-sum game. Natural resources were said to be especially abundant in Britain, comprising 'incomparable benefits' both on land and in the surrounding seas, but whose fuller exploitation was supposedly being held back by a combination of conservatism and idleness.[36] That is, some looked

---

[33] *The Restoration* (1976), p. xix.

[34] The intellectual context has been extensively discussed. But see, for example, Terence Hutchison, *Before Adam Smith: the emergence of political economy, 1662–1776* (Oxford, 1988); Istvan Hont, *Jealousy of trade: international competition and the nation-state in historical perspective* (Cambridge, MA, 2005).

[35] *The political and commercial works of that celebrated writer Charles D'Avenant*, ed. Sir Charles Whitworth (5 vols., 1771), vol. 5, pp. 140, 387.

[36] [J. Keymor], *A cleare and evident way for enriching the nations of England and Ireland* (1650), p. 10.

positively towards an unknown but much more prosperous future. This large and influential strand of thinking has been set out fully by Slack, who has shown how this enthusiasm for improvement arose from the same quest for knowledge, order, and understanding espoused by Francis Bacon and his followers in the early and mid-seventeenth century and which led to the formation of the Royal Society in 1660.[37] Moreover, this was associated with new ideas about the efficacy of higher levels of consumption, which was something Adam Smith also argued, though unlike the 'improvers' he was much less optimistic about long-term prospects of growth.[38] While some proponents of improvement argued like Smith that freer trade was desirable, others believed that the state had to seek to mould economic life, such as encouraging fisheries or establishing land registries.

Thirdly, it must be stressed that thinking about economic life was often not seen in solely material terms. Debates over mercantilism have recognized this in the discussion of the roles of power and plenty, but the issues went further and deeper. They are hinted at by the fact that Adam Smith would have described himself not as a political economist, but as a moral philosopher. Thinking about economic life was intimately bound up with politics, philosophy, history, and religion, not least because of the difficult task of reconciling notions of equity with a common belief in the inevitability (and to some the rightness) of profound inequalities. Notions of a 'just price' were, for example, periodically aired, in the context of the gradual disuse of old statutes regulating wages and the price of bread.[39] Customary expectations were certainly a part of this, though it is wrong, because it misunderstands Smith, to argue that E. P. Thompson's brilliant elaboration of a popular 'moral economy' faced an amoral Smithian one. Smith certainly understood (even if he sometimes criticized) the importance of culture, morality, and equity to everyday life, including the role in that of popular providentialism.[40]

Finally, the concept of mercantilism places a heavy emphasis on the structural, strategic, and proactive, rather than the contingent, tactical,

---

[37] Slack, *The invention of improvement*.
[38] Wrigley, *Energy and the English industrial revolution*, pp. 11–12.
[39] Sidney Webb and Beatrice Webb, 'The assize of bread', *Economic Journal*, 14.54 (1904), pp. 196–218; W. E. Minchinton, ed., *Wage regulation in pre-industrial England* (Newton Abbot, 1972); Joanna Innes, 'Regulating wages in eighteenth- and early nineteenth-century England: arguments in context', in Perry Gauci, ed., *Regulating the British economy, 1660–1850* (Farnham, 2011), pp. 195–215.
[40] E. P. Thompson, *Customs in common* (1988); Brodie Waddell, *God, duty and community in English economic life, 1660–1720* (Woodbridge, 2012). The literature on Smith is vast, but a very fine modern introduction is provided by Nicholas Phillipson, *Adam Smith: an enlightened life* (2010).

and reactive. Put another way, it foregrounds general economic policy as a response to a broad assessment of challenges and opportunities, viewing policy as fairly coherent. Doing so makes sense in some areas of Britain's political economies, such as the imperial economy, though even there the 'old colonial system' was rather unsystematic.[41] But it somewhat neglects the importance attached at the time to agriculture and industry, and emphasizes long-term challenges rather than short-term dislocations such as disease, bad weather, war, and financial crises.

The economic outlook of people in Britain in this period was far too mixed to be put under the single banner of 'mercantilist'. Certainly there was a strong belief in the need to protect the foundations of the national economy, especially land and the woollen trades, and to corral as much of the imperial economy as possible, in part for reasons of national defence. Certainly this was driven by anxieties about the strength of international competitors. But this existed alongside a belief that Britain was unusually well resourced such that significant material betterment was a realistic prospect, which some believed could best be achieved by freer trade. In any case, interventions in economic life were also prompted by short-term dislocations and non-economic factors, including national security and social order. Political economy in Britain in this period was heterogeneous and keenly debated, operating within structures of political power which need briefly setting out.[42]

The Nature and Limits of Political Power

Understanding how political power was applied to economic life requires considering the distribution, availability, and form of that power, how decisions were reached, what resources for implementing decisions were available, and the degree of compliance among people subject to those

---

[41] 'Historians refer to the "Old Colonial System" but in fact there was little that was systematic about the organization of the First British Empire. Based largely on a patchwork mosaic of measures adopted through expediency or accident, the imperial structure had little coherence or uniformity. If there was any organizing principle at all behind the resultant arrangements it was to be found, not in consciously defined systems, but rather in the unconscious assumptions [with] which the average Englishman of two or three centuries ago approached the day-to-day problems of empire.' Thomas C. Barrow, *Trade and empire: the British customs service in colonial America, 1660–1775* (Cambridge, MA, 1967), p. 1.

[42] Debates within mercantilism have recently been re-emphasized by Steve Pincus, 'Rethinking mercantilism: political economy, the British empire, and the Atlantic world in the seventeenth and eighteenth centuries', *William and Mary Quarterly*, 3rd series, 69.1 (2012), pp. 3–34. For earlier summaries to the same effect see: George Clark, *The seventeenth century* (2nd edn., Oxford, 1972), p. 21; John Brewer, *The sinews of power: war, money and the English state, 1688–1783* (1989), pp. 169–70.

decisions. In the first place that depends on the nature of the constitution, which in seventeenth-century Britain suffered recurring crises. Their nature and of how they were addressed, both before and after the Glorious Revolution of 1688–9, forms a vital preliminary to the subject of this book because gradually a new constitutional balance became accepted by most, resting on revolutionary levels of parliamentary legislation. This profoundly altered relations within political society. Parliament became the main site for negotiating between different and dispersed propertied interests that claimed to be acting for the common good. Importantly, a majority of this legislation concerned the economy fairly directly – and a sizeable minority indirectly. Resolving the constitutional crises consequently led to important changes in the relationship between political power and economic life.

The trial and execution of King Charles I on 30 January 1649 was at the heart of the greatest constitutional crisis in early modern Britain. Charged in the name of the 'Commons of England', he was accused of having 'a wicked design to erect and uphold in himself an unlimited and tyrannical power to rule according to his will, and to overthrow the rights and liberties of the people'. During his eleven-year 'personal rule' without Parliament (1629–40), he had denied people the usual means by which they could deal with 'misgovernment'. Finally, to get his way, he 'traitorously and maliciously levied war against the present Parliament and the people therein represented'.[43] Such extraordinary charges were the culmination of years of political conflict, of huge bloodshed in civil wars across Britain and Ireland, and the failure to reach a political settlement between the defeated crown and the victorious parliamentary army. There was not, of course, the slightest chance of Charles being acquitted.[44]

In court and on the scaffold, Charles I argued his case forcefully. Critically, he contended, 'I have a trust committed to me by God, by old and lawful descent', that is an authority both divine and long established. To be tried by a court otherwise authorized was, he urged, illegal, something which was bad not only for himself, but for everyone else too: 'for if the power without law may make laws, may alter the fundamental laws of the kingdom, I do not know what subject he is in England that can be sure of his life or anything that he calls his own.' Charles denied that he

---

[43] *The trial of Charles I: a documentary history*, ed. David Lagomarsino and Charles T. Wood (Hanover, NH, 1989), p. 61.

[44] As with almost every aspect of the political history of mid-seventeenth-century Britain, there is controversy about how to understand the trial. A simpler conventional reading seems best to me, as to Clive Holmes, 'The trial and execution of Charles I', *Historical Journal*, 53.2 (2010), pp. 289–316.

had acted arbitrarily, for he had been fulfilling his sacred responsibilities. Indeed, he insisted, an arbitrary power had defeated him in battle and was about to chop his head from his body. If such a power could do that to a king, what might it do to 'any free-born subject of England'?[45] At heart, the civil wars, the execution of the king, and the establishment of the republic were, therefore, about where sovereignty ultimately lay. Was it in the crown alone, or among 'the people' (variously defined), or some mix of the two? And what did it mean to be free?

Rightly, the trial and execution of Charles I resonated loudly through succeeding generations, with 30 January central to the annual calendar of public memory long after the monarchy was restored in 1660.[46] To many the tragedy of that king served as a reminder of mankind's fallen state, capacity for violence, and predilection for disorder. Yet, exceptional though it was, it was but one of a series of crises of monarchy experienced in Britain between the death of the childless Elizabeth I in 1603, through the Glorious Revolution of 1688–9 when a Dutch invasion led by the future William III forced James II into exile, to the military defeat of the 'young pretender' (James II's grandson) in the Jacobite rising of 1745–6. It is right and proper to emphasize the particular personalities and specific disagreements in these successive crises. That one followed the other was not inevitable; contingency mattered. Yet they do all speak to the inevitable difficulties hereditary monarchy has of providing good government: of the perils of producing legitimate heirs; of the crown sometimes landing on the head of a fool – or worse, a haughty half-fool; of legitimizing royal supremacy by resort to cultic, mystical, and discriminatory ideals; and of highly centralized authority struggling to keep abreast of societies becoming more intricate.[47] The first two of those factors are timeless, but the other two became increasingly important in the seventeenth century because Britain was now a composite state, new thinking developed about the nature of political authority and reasons of state, economic life became more complex (and therefore harder to oversee in a highly centralized political system), and rivalry among European states drove up their costs and, hence, imprint on society.

---

[45] *Trial of Charles I*, ed. Lagomarsino and Wood, pp. 65, 140–2; *The Stuart constitution, 1603–1688: documents and commentary*, ed. J. P. Kenyon (2nd edn., Cambridge, 1986), pp. 292–5.

[46] Helen W. Randall, 'The rise and fall of martyrology: the sermons on Charles I', *Huntington Library Quarterly*, 10.2 (1947), pp. 135–67; Byron S. Stewart, 'The cult of the royal martyr', *Church History*, 38.2 (1969), pp. 175–87.

[47] For some interesting reflections on related themes see Hugh Trevor-Roper, 'The general crisis of the seventeenth century', *Past and Present*, 16 (1959), pp. 31–64 and Mancur Olson, *The rise and decline of nations: economic growth, stagflation, and social rigidities* (New Haven, CT, 1982), pp. 157–9.

Addressing the crises of monarchy was no easy matter. In the first place, Charles I was not alone in believing that monarchy's ideological edifice was non-negotiable. Famously, Filmer, in a work written before 1642 but only published in the middle of another crisis of monarchy in 1680, denied that 'Mankind is naturally endowed and born with freedom from all subjection' on the grounds that it contradicted the Bible, the experience of all ancient monarchies, and 'the very principles of the law of nature'.[48] Many believed that profound inequalities were right and proper, ultimately deriving from God's will. Indeed, the obvious alternative to monarchy, a republic, had been established in 1649, but was compromised within a decade (evidenced by the offer of the crown to the lord protector Oliver Cromwell and the succession of his son as lord protector in 1658) and collapsed completely in 1660. The monarch was restored with relief then, but despite the permanent changes that the Republic had wrought and the affection with which Charles II was received, the weaknesses of monarchical government soon reared their head again, centring on the issues of religion and public finances.

In early modern Britain religious divisions within Protestantism were deep and fraught, but as nothing to the hostility most Protestants felt towards Catholics. In the end, the Catholic James II lost the domestic support necessary to sustain his authority because his overwhelmingly Protestant people would not allow him to aid his co-believers, few though they were.[49] His subjects were determined to countenance only a Protestant monarch and state; on this the crown had to follow the people, not vice versa, leading to passive disobedience, the Dutch invasion in 1688, the flight of James II to France, and the striking of a new constitutional balance between the crown and Parliament in 1689. Profound religious divisions remained after 1689, but they were rarely divisions between monarchs and subjects. The second key change, to public finances, arrived at a similar conclusion by building on the excise introduced in 1643, by bringing in house the collection of revenues from 1671, drip feeding funding to the executive one year at a time from 1689, instituting a permanent national debt after 1693, and separating off the wider costs of government from those of the crown's civil list. Together, these two broad changes in religion and public finance (though there were others) meant that from 1689 no British monarch could mimic

---

[48] Robert Filmer, *Patriarcha and other writings*, ed. Johann P. Somerville (Cambridge, 1991), pp. 2–3. The 'exclusion crisis' of 1679–81 saw 'whig' attempts to remove the succession from James, heir and brother of Charles II. Supporters of the crown were 'tories'.

[49] An ecclesiastical census in 1676 established that less than 2 per cent of England's population was Catholic. Anne Whiteman, ed., *The Compton census of 1676: a critical edition* (Oxford, 1986).

Louis XIV's alleged earlier boast that he was the state ('*l'état, c'est moi*'). After 1688 the emergence of cabinet government and the relative decline of the Privy Council and proclamations evidence crucial changes in executive decision making and authority. The disappearance of the impeachment of ministers also reflected wider constitutional developments. When Robert Harley, Earl of Oxford, was subsequently impeached on party-political grounds for the treaty of Utrecht (1713), he was defended by noting that he had worked in association with his monarch, Anne, through council discussions, and via Acts of Parliament. Consequently, if this 'be not sufficient justification for ministers ... acting against no known law, nor charged with any corruption, whose life, whose property is safe in Great Britain?'[50] Much greater political stability was thus carved out in the first quarter of the eighteenth century.[51]

At the centre of these developments was the heightened role of the Westminster parliament in general, and its legislative efforts in particular.[52] Aside from foreign policy, which remained a precious preserve of crown prerogative, major political decisions came to be formulated as Acts of Parliament. Parliament and its legislative efforts had been vital before, but irregularly so as it met at the behest of monarchs who often sought to avoid it. As Chapter 2 shows, after 1689 Parliament now met regularly, leading to a legislative revolution, but the crucial point here is that acts required the agreement of crown, peers (lay and spiritual), and commons. All three were needed. Parliament thereby became the forum for negotiating paths through the disagreements that had consumed so much blood, sweat, and tears over the previous century. That took time, but by setting out clear stages and procedural conventions for deliberation and resolution, parliamentary supremacy acquired a legitimacy amongst political society that was ferociously defended ever after.

Under the post-1688 'revolution constitution', Parliament was not what it is now. Though it met regularly and at sufficient length to allow it to undertake much more business, not much of that effort was directed by the executive. This gave considerable scope to MPs and peers to engage and disengage at will (absenteeism could reach alarming proportions), and for it to be approached by individuals and interests across the

---

[50] Quoted in Clayton Roberts, *The growth of responsible government in Stuart England* (Cambridge, 1966), p. 405.

[51] J. H. Plumb, *The growth of political stability in England, 1675–1725* (1967).

[52] For a fine overview of the nature of central government in this period see Peter Jupp, *The governing of Britain, 1688–1848: the executive, Parliament and the people* (Abingdon, 2006). For a similarly rich overview directed more to the rule of law see David Lemmings, *Law and government in England during the long eighteenth century: from consent to command* (Basingstoke, 2011).

nation, provided they had the money and connections to do so. Its composition was highly exclusive. MPs and peers were male, Protestant, and generally rich. The House of Lords was mainly comprised of great landowners in the form of hereditary peers, bishops, and, after 1707, sixteen Scottish representative peers. Elections to the House of Commons (there were 513 MPs before 1707, 558 thereafter) were erratic before 1688, but took place at least every three years from 1694 to 1716 and every seven years thereafter. MPs were elected to counties and to boroughs, usually two each. The right to vote varied from place to place, but was generally restricted to men of some property. In the eighteenth century between 17 and 24 per cent of the adult male population had the right to vote, but far from all seats were polled, with a nadir reached in the general election of 1761 when only 19 per cent of seats were formally contested. Two-member seats were commonly divided between rivals so as to avoid the danger of increasingly costly contests, while a rising proportion of seats, reaching two-thirds after 1750, was under a reasonable degree of control of peers, great landowners, and executive government.[53] Unquestionably, Parliament was a key component of an oligarchical and socially exclusive government.

Historians have emphasized two major features of the impact of Parliament on the nature of the state in Britain as it relates to political economy.[54] First that through it central government became very much better resourced, enabling it to wage frequent wars. Statutory authorization of much higher levels of taxation provided both greater immediate income and the security on which to accumulate national debts. Britons became very heavily taxed and public debts reached extraordinary proportions, not only funding greater military effort, but also creating new social forces, such as the monied interest, and changing the relationship between the present and the future as debts were often repaid over many decades.

Because most of the increase of central government income after 1688 was spent on the military and war debts, it has become common to label the state as 'fiscal-military' or a 'Leviathan'.[55] This sees the state very

---

[53] Frank O'Gorman, *Voters, patrons and parties: the unreformed electorate of Hanoverian England, 1734–1832* (Oxford, 1989), pp. 108–9, 179; J. A. Phillips, 'The structure of electoral politics in unreformed England', *Journal of British Studies*, 19.1 (1979), pp. 76–100.

[54] For surveys see Michael Braddick, 'State formation and the historiography of early modern England', *History Compass*, 2.1 (2004), pp. 1–17; Simon Devereaux, 'The historiography of the English State during "the long" eighteenth century: Part I – decentralized perspectives/Part II – fiscal-military and nationalist perspectives', *History Compass*, 7.3 (2009), pp. 742–64; 8.8 (2010), pp. 843–65.

[55] Brewer, *Sinews of power*; P. G. M. Dickson, *The financial revolution in England: a study in the development of public credit, 1688–1756* (1967); Peter Mathias and Patrick K. O'Brien,

much from its inner core at Whitehall as directed by leading ministers
and key departments, the Treasury especially, but backed by an unusually efficient tax administration, all told making the British state more
Weberian and robust than absolutist France: 'Suddenly Britain looks
rather more German or Prussian than we realized.'[56] Yet while the money
raised for central government was highly impressive in the eighteenth
century, Chapters 7 and 9 show that its power was in fact much more
patchy.

   In Chapter 3 it is established that legislation relating to central government finance was just a small part of all economic legislation, much of
which emanated from local administrators, economic interests, and private individuals. More generally, an important body of work has emphasized the extent to which the British state in the eighteenth century was
open to pressures from without, 'by those outside the traditional confines
of the English ruling class, most notably among an increasingly recogniz-
able urban middle class'. From this perspective the state tended not to
take the initiative in dealing with social and economic issues, but reacted
to information and initiatives from this rising class.[57] In certain respects
this is an updated variant of older Marxist accounts of capitalist classes
capturing the state – though Adam Smith said much the same – hitched
to Habermas' thesis of the growth of the 'public sphere' in England from
the mid-seventeenth century.[58] As can be seen, this emphasizes another

---

'Taxation in Britain and France, 1715–1810: a comparison of the social and economic
incidence of taxes collected for the central government', *Journal of European Economic
History*, 5.3 (1976), pp. 601–50; Patrick K. O'Brien, 'The political economy of British
taxation, 1660–1815', *Economic History Review*, 41.1 (1988), pp. 1–32. For a review of
the concept see Christopher Storrs, 'Introduction: the fiscal-military state in the "long"
eighteenth century', in Christopher Storrs, ed., *The fiscal-military state in eighteenth-
century Europe: essays in honour of P. G. M. Dickson* (Aldershot, 2009), pp. 1–22, and
Rafael Torres Sánchez, 'The triumph of the fiscal-military state in the eighteenth century: war and mercantilism', in Rafael Torres Sánchez ed., *War, state and development: fiscal-military states in the eighteenth century* (Pamplona, 2007), pp. 13–44.

[56] John Brewer and Eckhart Hellmuth, 'Introduction: rethinking Leviathan', in Brewer and
Hellmuth, eds., *Rethinking Leviathan: the eighteenth-century state in Britain and Germany*
(Oxford, 1999), p. 9.

[57] Lee Davison, Tim Hitchcock, Tim Keirn, and Robert B. Shoemaker, 'The reactive
state: English governance and society, 1689–1714', in Davison, Hitchcock, Keirn, and
Shoemaker, eds., *Stilling the grumbling hive: the response to social and economic problems in
England, 1689–1750* (Stroud, 1992), pp. xi–liv, quotes at xv.

[58] For a survey of Marxist ideas of the state see Bob Jessop, *The capitalist state: Marxist
theories and methods* (Oxford, 1982). Jürgen Habermas, *The structural transformation
of the public sphere: an inquiry into a category of bourgeois society*, translated by Thomas
Burger with the assistance of Frederick Lawrence (Cambridge, 1989; original German
edn., 1962). For an introduction to the extensive debate about the 'public sphere', see
James Van Horn Melton, *The rise of the public in Enlightenment Europe* (Cambridge,
2001). For some reservations about the idea of a 'reactive state' see Joanna Innes,
Inferior politics: social problems and social policies in eighteenth-century Britain (Oxford,

form of the participatory nature of government in England, this time the link between central government and social groups (rather than local governments), which had already been set out as a crucial aspect of Langford's outstanding study, as well as many other essays.[59]

Certainly in understanding the influence of political power on economic life in this period the fundamental starting point is to avoid assuming that the nation-state then was much as it is now. It was not. Three general features need particularly to be stressed. First, the crowns of England and Scotland were merged in 1603, and the parliaments of Edinburgh and Westminster in 1707, but Britain remained in many respects a composite state with substantial differences between its two main parts – quite apart from the treatment of Ireland. Both nations retained separate and distinctive legal systems after 1707; propertied interests in England and Scotland engaged very differently with Parliament as a legislative body; there were much clearer central attempts in Scotland (and Ireland) than in England to use public funding to stimulate certain avenues of economic development; and although the Union of 1707 did create the largest single market in Europe, the economic integration of the two nations was far from complete even by 1800.

Secondly, the size and functions of central government in Britain in this period were much smaller and less ambitious than in modern states. Before 1870, central government did not provide education, health care, or welfare, nor imagine that it could manage aggregate demand counter-cyclically or redistribute wealth and income structurally. The modern central state is therefore very much larger than its early modern antecedents. For example, in recent years, government spending in Britain has been between 40 and 45 per cent of GDP, whereas around 1750 it may have been about 11 per cent.[60] Put another way, today central government employs 2.8 million people compared to 8,000 in 1750, or forty-five times more when differences in total population at those dates are accounted for.[61] In the seventeenth and eighteenth centuries, central government mainly comprised a tiny 'civil service' to develop and oversee policies and rather more revenue officers. Though because of poor

2009), pp. 7–8. I would add that the concept of the 'reactive state' is underspecified by its authors.

[59] Paul Langford, *Public life and the propertied Englishman, 1689–1798* (Oxford, 1991); Stuart Handley, 'Local legislative initiatives for economic and social development in Lancashire, 1689–1731', *Parliamentary History*, 9.1 (1990), pp. 14–37; Innes, *Inferior politics*, ch. 3.

[60] O'Brien, 'The political economy of British taxation', p. 3.

[61] Respectively 4.5 and 0.1 per cent of the population. www.ons.gov.uk/ons/rel/pse/civil-service-statistics/2012/index.html: accessed 23 November 2012; Brewer, *Sinews of power*, p. 66; B. R. Mitchell, *British historical statistics* (Cambridge, 1988), p. 7.

accounting conventions the figures are a little misleading (see Chapter 9), it is nonetheless striking that between 1700 and 1799 only 9 per cent of central government spending was on civil administration, with 56 per cent on the military and 35 per cent on war debts.[62] This meant, as Jacob Viner neatly put it, that in the field of economic legislation England 'was something like a police state without official policemen; a meddlesome government without a bureaucracy'.[63]

Not only was central government tiny, but responsibility for economic legislation was scattered among various offices and departments, especially the Treasury, but also the advisory Board of Trade (formed in 1696, abolished in 1782, but reborn in new form in 1786), the Admiralty, and, after its creation in 1782, the Home Office. The revenue services, especially for customs and excise, were also important sources of information and ideas about political economy. But government lacked a central focal point in all of this (and much else), save in Parliament. It speaks volumes that efforts from the 1780s to develop an agricultural policy were non-governmental and resulted in a semi-official Board of Agriculture that survived only from 1793 to 1822. The introduction of the census in 1801, it is worth noting, was a non-governmental initiative.[64] Moreover, recalling an earlier point, throughout this period central government usually approached economic issues in tandem with other priorities, especially generating revenue, maintaining domestic order, and increasing Britain's international authority.

Those limitations to the scope of central government must constantly be borne in mind. Nevertheless, the executive and legislature were active. Much of the rest of this book deals with the latter, but it is worth noting here some of the avenues open to the former. Both the Privy Council and cabinet might choose or be forced to take an interest in a range of economic factors, including the state of the coinage, harvests, quarantine, imperial trade, and public order. Key departments

---

[62] Mitchell, *British historical statistics*, pp. 578–80, 587. I am unpersuaded by the attempt of Steve Pincus and James Robinson to argue otherwise, mainly because they ignore debt repayments and exaggerate the net effects of drawbacks (the repayment of duties under certain conditions) – though they are right to point out, as others have already done, that there was some direct spending on economic development projects. See their 'Challenging the fiscal-military hegemony: the British case', in Aaron Graham and Patrick Walsh, eds., *The British fiscal-military states, 1660–c. 1783* (2016), pp. 229–61.

[63] Jacob Viner, *Essays on the intellectual history of economics*, ed. Douglas A. Irwin (Princeton, NJ, 1991), p. 51.

[64] Rosalind Mitchison, 'The old Board of Agriculture (1793–1822)', *English Historical Review*, 74.290 (1959), pp. 41–69; Stephen John Thompson, 'Census-taking, political economy and state formation in Britain, c. 1790–1840' (University of Cambridge PhD thesis, 2010), ch. 2.

of state, the Treasury, Board of Trade, and revenue services provided one way in which those efforts were developed and effected by the executive before they reached Parliament. As executive government–developed proposals and policies, they were liable to be sent expressions of extra-governmental information and opinions, public and private, via petitions, memorials, pamphlets, and less-visible lobbying. A good example was the ways in which executive government negotiated with public creditors to accumulate national debts, especially from the 1690s. The Treasury was the key department of this, gradually becoming more expert and experienced at developing proposals to tax and borrow. Much of its legislative drafting was done out of the public gaze, but involved negotiating with key private-sector players in the City of London before bills were introduced into Parliament.[65] Additionally, while the executive played a role in developing some laws, it could exert its authority in other ways: proclamations might be issued – indeed, 'orders in council' became much more numerous after the outbreak of war against Revolutionary France in 1793 – and central judges, colonial governors, and revenue officers exhorted to act on certain matters.[66]

Third is the issue of how central government sought to enforce its decisions. France was 'ruled by thirty Intendants' according to John Law, the Scot who rose to be Controller General of Finances there in 1720, 'on whom depends the prosperity or wretchedness of their provinces, their abundance or their sterility'.[67] That was an exaggeration, but intendants were direct representatives of the centre across the nation and might develop and implement distinctive economic policies – most famously Turgot, a future Controller General of Finances, in Limoges between 1761 and 1774. Britain's central government lacked such figures who moved routinely between centre and localities doing the former's bidding, though circuit judges were an important way in which centre and provinces were kept in touch judicially. Central government

---

[65] Relations between Whitehall, Westminster, and the City were central to the work of Lucy Sutherland, *Politics and finance in the eighteenth century*, ed. Aubrey Newman (1984); then to Dickson, *The financial revolution in England* and Henry Roseveare, *The Treasury: the evolution of a British institution* (1969).

[66] Earl of Crawford, *A bibliography of royal proclamations of the Tudor and Stuart sovereigns and of others published under authority, 1485–1714* (2 vols., Oxford, 1910) and *Bibliotheca Lindesiana: vol. VIII, handlist of proclamations issued by royal and other constitutional authorities, 1714–1910* (Wigan, 1913); Leonard Woods Labaree, *Royal instructions to British colonial governors* (2 vols., New York, 1935); George S. Lamoines, ed., *Charges to the Grand Jury, 1689–1803*, Camden, Fourth Series, 43 (1992).

[67] Quoted in Colin Jones, *The great nation: France from Louis XIV to Napoleon* (2002), p. 113.

did, though, appoint to local offices responsible for both justice and administration.[68] At the county level, lord lieutenants, sheriffs, and Justice of Peace (JPs) were centrally appointed in England and Wales through the period. In Scotland, such central appointments developed during this period – sheriffs after the failed Jacobite rising of 1745–6 (which also led to the abolition of heritable jurisdictions), and lord lieutenants only in the 1790s. At the county level, in England and Wales JPs were key figures administering legislation, but in Scotland it was sheriffs depute. Such men were mainly drawn from the ranks of the gentry (medium landowners, including in England and Wales the clergy), with JPs being amateurs and volunteers, but increasing numbers of Scottish sheriff deputes had legal education and experience.[69] Naturally they shared many of the fundamental beliefs and assumptions of those in central government, and early in the period JPs in England and Wales were sometimes purged on political grounds, but throughout many cherished their autonomy and distinct sense of place.[70] Some statutes they embraced, but others were ignored by some or all, while attempts to encourage prosecutions by paying informants often ran into popular opposition.[71]

Local administration at the borough and parish levels, involving many thousands of offices, was also an important element in the implementation or not of Britain's political economies. While parishes covered every part of Britain, and had considerable responsibility for the administration of the poor law and road maintenance, corporations provided critical focal points for economic life, for both towns and their hinterlands.[72] Urbanization was a key development in eighteenth-century England and

---

[68] Lemmings, *Law and government*; Vivian R. Gruder, *The royal provincial intendants: a governing elite in eighteenth-century France* (Ithaca, NY, 1968).

[69] Ann E. Whetstone, *Scottish county government in the eighteenth and nineteenth centuries* (Edinburgh, 1981), p. 8.

[70] David Lemmings, 'The independence of the judiciary in eighteenth-century England', in Peter Birks, ed., *The life of the law: proceedings of the tenth British legal history conference Oxford 1991* (1993), pp. 125–49.

[71] For example, under a statute of 1692, 3 William & Mary, c. 12, repealed only in 1827, JPs were annually to set land carriage rates, but many never did so. T. S. Willan, 'The justices of the peace and the rates of land carriage, 1692–1827', *Journal of Transport History*, 5.4 (1962), pp. 197–204. On informers and popular opposition: Maurice Beresford, 'The common informer, the penal statutes and economic regulation', *Economic History Review*, 10.2 (1957), pp. 222–38; Stephen Banks, *Informal justice in England and Wales, 1760–1914: the courts of public opinion* (Woodbridge, 2014), ch. 5; Jessica Warner and Frank J. Ivis, '"Damn you, you informing bitch": vox populi and the unmaking of the gin act of 1736', *Journal of Social History*, 33.2 (1999), pp. 299–330.

[72] Joanna Innes and Nicholas Rogers, 'Politics and government, 1700–1840', in Peter Clark, ed., *The Cambridge urban history of Britain, vol. 2, 1550–1840* (Cambridge, 2000), pp. 529–74.

Scotland, indirectly enabling Westminster's legislation to have more of an influence.[73]

More broadly, the courts left a very patchy imprint on economic life.[74] Sometimes this could be considerable, as in notable cases, such as Sandys' attempt to break the monopoly of the East India Company in the 1680s or the Scottish Court of Session's decision in 1778 that slavery was illegal under Scots law.[75] Note must also be made of Lord Mansfield's wide-ranging efforts to update various aspects of commercial law in the late eighteenth century.[76] But notoriously lawyers and judges could also put obstacles in the way of change. Thus although in 1772 a statute legalized the market practices of forestalling, regrating, and engrossing, at the end of the century Lord Kenyon told jurors that they remained offences under common law, throwing in criticisms of Adam Smith's views for good measure.[77] (It is worth recalling that because of its confused common law heritage Weber saw Britain as very remote from a modern rational state, though recently it has been argued the 'Common law was fully engaged with multiple contemporary trends, and played a key role in the emergence of an enlightened society in eighteenth-century England.'[78])

From Whig History to the New Institutional Economics

In the eighteenth and nineteenth centuries Britain's constitution was lauded at both home and abroad for being perfectly balanced to secure liberty and property, supposedly the very springs of prosperity. To one

[73] In 1700 around 13 per cent of England's population lived in towns of at least 10,000 people, while for Scotland the proportion was 5 per cent. By 1800 the respective figures were 24 and 17 per cent. Julian Hoppit, 'The nation, the state, and the first industrial revolution', *Journal of British Studies*, 50.2 (2011), p. 314.

[74] An important context here is the relationship of legal, political, and economic history. See Ron Harris, 'The encounters of economic history and legal history', *Law and History Review*, 21.2 (2003), pp. 297–346.

[75] Philip J. Stern, *The company-state: corporate sovereignty and the early modern foundations of the British empire in India* (New York, 2011), pp. 46–58; J. W. Cairns, 'Knight v. Wedderburn', in David Dabydeen, John Gilmore, and Cecily Jones, eds., *The Oxford companion to Black British history* (Oxford, 2007), pp. 244–6.

[76] David Lieberman, *The province of legislation determined: legal theory in eighteenth-century Britain* (Cambridge, 1989).

[77] 12 Geo III, c 71; Douglas Hay, 'The state and the market in 1800: Lord Kenyon and Mr Waddington', *Past and Present*, 162 (1999), pp. 101–62; George T. Kenyon, *The life of Lloyd, first Lord Kenyon* (1873), p. 371.

[78] Joshua Getzler, 'Theories of property and economic development', *Journal of Interdisciplinary History*, 26.4 (1996), pp. 645–6; D. d'Avray, 'Max Weber and comparative legal history', in A. Lewis and M. Lobban, eds., *Law and history: current legal issues 2003*, vol. 6 (2004), pp. 189 and 197; Max Rheinstein, ed., *Max Weber on law in economy and society* (Cambridge, MA, 1954); the quote is from Julia Rudolph, *Common law and enlightenment in England, 1689–1750* (Woodbridge, 2013), p. 267.

Briton, 'The freedom of this nation, is the true parent of its grandeur', while to another the Glorious Revolution established a 'universal liberty' and rendered property 'perfectly secured'.[79] Abroad, Anglophiles praised the emergence of stable, mixed government, the extent of entrepreneurialism, and the flexible and open nature of British thought.[80] Thus Johann Archenholz, a Prussian soldier and historian who lived in England between 1769 and 1779, thought that 'Great Britain, which cannot naturally be considered, in the balance of Europe, but as belonging to the second order of kingdoms, has been elevated to the rank of one of the first powers in the world by bravery, wealth, liberty, and the happy consequences of an excellent political system.'[81] This led easily enough to the view that England or Britain (many at the time, including some Scots, used the two interchangeably) were exemplary and worth copying.[82]

Celebrating the revolution constitution of 1688–9, the Whig interpretation, was never as dominant domestically as is often supposed. Clarendon had powerfully defended his Stuart masters in the seventeenth century and in the middle of the eighteenth century Hume (a Scot) in his great and long-lived history of England famously sought to restore objectivity to accounts of the constitutional battles of the previous century.[83] Nor was Britain the only nation praised for its love of liberty: Sweden was held up in that regard.[84] Moreover, British exhortations on that score were also criticized as superficial and self-serving: 'perfidious Albion' was inclined to kill its kings, abandon its

---

[79] [Joseph Harris], *An essay upon money and coins* (1757), p. 27, note; James Anderson, *Observations on the means of exciting a spirit of national industry; chiefly intended to promote the agriculture, commerce, manufactures, and fisheries of Scotland* (Edinburgh, 1777), p. ix.

[80] Paul Langford, 'Introduction: time and space', in Paul Langford, ed., *The eighteenth century: 1688–1815* (Oxford, 2002), p. 9; Giorgio Riello and Patrick K. O'Brien, 'The future is another country: offshore views of the British industrial revolution', *Journal of Historical Sociology*, 22.1 (2009), pp. 1–29.

[81] J. W. Archenholz, *A picture of England* (2 vols., 1789), vol. 2, p. 190. Britain's constitution is analyzed very positively by the Swiss Jean Louis de Lolme, *The constitution of England*, ed. David Lieberman (1784 edn., Indianapolis, IN, 2007).

[82] Gabriel B. Paquette, *Enlightenment, governance, and reform in Spain and its empire, 1759–1808* (Basingstoke, 2008), esp. pp. 38–41; Sophus A. Reinert, *Translating empire: emulation and the origins of political economy* (Cambridge, MA, 2011); Sophus A. Reinert, 'Blaming the Medici: footnotes, falsification, and the fate of the "English model" in eighteenth-century Italy', *History of European Ideas*, 32.4 (2006), pp. 430–55.

[83] Philip Hicks, *Neoclassical history and English culture: from Clarendon to Hume* (Basingstoke, 1996); Mark Knights, 'The Tory interpretation of history in the rage of parties', *Huntington Library Quarterly*, 68.1–2 (2005), pp. 353–73; J. A. G. Baverstock, '"A chief standard work": the rise and fall of David Hume's *History of England* 1754–c.1900' (University of London PhD, 1997).

[84] Michael Roberts, *Swedish and English parliamentarianism in the eighteenth century* (Belfast, 1973), p. 3.

allies, bully its neighbours, and posture hypocritically.[85] Nonetheless, the Whig account reached its apogee with Britain's economic and imperial zenith in the second half of the nineteenth century. But soon enough the professionalization of history led to its sustained critical scrutiny, culminating in Butterfield's detailing of its questionable assumptions and methodological flaws in 1931. He particularly cautioned against viewing history as a progressive and inexorable unfolding, and of the dangers of teleologically determined selectivity. If such a work was directed mainly at a scholarly audience, it is worth recalling that just a year before the glib pieties of the Whig account had been mercilessly mocked in *1066 and all that*.[86] Namier and his followers buried the Whig account even deeper over the next four decades by piling up archival minutiae to emphasize the selfish, unprincipled, and non-partisan nature of the politics of the period – and in the process viewing Parliament mainly in terms of the contest for power rather than the uses to which that power was put.[87] Further limitations of Whig England were brilliantly developed in the 1970s, though also reacting against narrow Namierism, by exploring the exclusive and oppressive nature of the Hanoverian regime, as well as its ideological complexities.[88] More recently, several have rightly noted that there is no logical reason why Britain's exceptional experience in becoming the first industrial nation should be considered exemplary.[89] Indeed, just the opposite seems as likely, while wider experience has shown that there is no one right path from poverty to prosperity.

[85] H. D. Schmidt, 'The idea and slogan of "perfidious Albion"', *Journal of the History of Ideas*, 14.4 (1953), pp. 604–16; David A. Bell, *The cult of the nation in France: inventing nationalism, 1680–1800* (Cambridge, MA, 2001), ch. 3; Frances Acomb, *Anglophobia in France, 1763–1789: an essay in the history of constitutionalism and nationalism* (Durham, NC, 1950); Norman Hampson, *The perfidy of Albion: French perceptions of England during the French Revolution* (Basingstoke, 1998).

[86] H. Butterfield, *The Whig interpretation of history* (1931); W. C. Sellar and R. J. Yeatman, *1066 and all that* (1930).

[87] Linda Colley, *Lewis Namier* (1989); John Brooke, 'Namier and Namierism', *History and Theory*, 3.3 (1963–4), pp. 331–47.

[88] John Brewer, *Party ideology and popular politics at the accession of George III* (Cambridge, 1976); E. P. Thompson, *Whigs and hunters: the origin of the Black Act* (Harmondsworth, 1977); Quentin Skinner, 'The principles and practice of opposition: the case of Bolingbroke versus Walpole', in Neil McKendrick, ed., *Historical perspectives: studies in English thought and society in honour of J. H. Plumb* (1974), pp. 93–128.

[89] Patrick K. O'Brien, 'The Britishness of the first industrial revolution and the British contribution to the industrialization of "follower countries" on the mainland, 1756–1914', *Diplomacy and Statecraft*, 8.3 (1997), esp. pp. 50–1; Robert H. Bates, 'Lessons from history, or the perfidy of English exceptionalism and the historical significance of France', *World Politics*, 15.4 (1988), pp. 499–516; Jeff Horn, *The path not taken: French industrialization in the age of revolution, 1750–1830* (Cambridge, MA, 2006), ch. 1.

If most historians have moved beyond the presumptions and preoccupations of Whig history, in the past quarter of a century a number of leading economists, political scientists, and economic historians have refused to follow them. Reminted celebratory accounts of the relation between Britain's revolution constitution and its economic precocity have become something of the stock in trade of a certain type of general discussion of the conditions alleged to explain why some nations are rich and others are poor. We might take with a pinch of salt one recent prime minister's identification of a 'golden thread' of liberty running through British history, as well as the view of a former chairman of the Federal Reserve that the most 'free' of the leading modern economies 'all have roots in Britain', but such views have serious scholarly backing.[90] David Landes explained why Britain experienced the first industrial nation in part by stressing that it had an ideal institutional framework, securing property rights and contracts, with an 'honest government' that economic actors could not exploit for private advantage (or rent seeking in the jargon).[91] To Niall Ferguson, 'It was in the eighteenth century that the British state developed the peculiar institutional combination ... that enabled Britain at once to empire-build and to industrialize.'[92] Finally, one major survey from 2005 concluded that the civil wars and Glorious Revolution in Britain significantly redistributed political power, bringing about 'major changes in economic institutions, strengthening the property rights of both land and capital owners and spurred a process of financial and commercial expansion. The consequence was rapid economic growth, culminating in the Industrial Revolution'.[93]

In significant measure such views are the product of the development from the 1960s of the 'new institutional economics' (NIE) and more specifically follow or build on a much-cited article by North and Weingast from 1989. The NIE was a product of reactions to the unrealistic

---

[90] Gordon Brown noted this 'golden thread' through British history since Magna Carta in speeches in 2006 and 2007. It is restated in his introduction to Gertrude Himmelfarb, *The roads to modernity: the British, French and American Enlightenments* (2008), p. xii. For a critical view of Brown's motives: Tom Nairn, *Gordon Brown: bard of Britishness* (Cardiff, 2006). Alan Greenspan, *The age of turbulence: adventures in a new world* (New York, 2007), p. 276.

[91] David S. Landes, *The wealth and poverty of nations: why some are so rich and some so poor* (New York, 1998), pp. 217–19.

[92] *The cash nexus: money and power in the modern world, 1700–2000* (2002), p. 20.

[93] Daron Acemoglu, Simon Johnson, and James A. Robinson, 'Institutions as a fundamental cause of long-run growth', in Philippe Aghion and Steven N. Durlauf, eds., *Handbook of economic growth*, vol. 1a (Amsterdam, 2005), p. 393; reiterated in Daron Acemoglu and James A. Robinson, 'Paths of economic and political development', in Barry R. Weingast and Donald A. Wittman, eds., *The Oxford handbook of political economy* (Oxford, 2006), p. 673.

assumptions about market efficiency of neoclassical economics, as well as its failure to account for change over time. Building on points made in the 1930s that perfect competition is impossible and that markets involve 'transaction costs' and can 'fail', it was argued that 'institutions' could affect their costs significantly.[94] Political systems are especially important to determining the nature of institutions. Some institutions lower costs and/or risks, especially by better securing property rights and ensuring that current decisions are held to in the future ('credible commitment'), thereby raising efficiency and competitiveness. Some polities are therefore held to be better than others at producing economic growth. An important aspect of this approach is not simply to argue that 'institutions' matter, but that they can be systematically analyzed.[95]

Douglass North, Nobel Prize–winning economist, has been the key figure applying such thinking to early modern Britain (as well as developing the approach more generally). His seminal article co-authored with Weingast stressed how the Glorious Revolution led to more secure property rights, fundamentally because previous monarchs had not credibly committed to such rights but thereafter a newly supreme, but not unlimited, Parliament did.[96] Self-confessedly in the style of Whig history, a simple contrast was drawn between a pre-1689 era when monarchs were predatory and provided limited opportunities to use political power effectively for economic growth, and the constructive and well-balanced nature of parliamentary government thereafter. Oft repeated by other new institutional economists, this has now become conventional in the field. A key subject matter considered in this has been the growth of the national debt, though areas such as duties and road improvements have also been brought into the discussion.[97]

---

[94] Seminal works were Joan Robinson, *The economics of imperfect competition* (1933) and R. H. Coase, 'The nature of the firm', *Economica*, 4 (1937), pp. 386–405. It is important to note that 'institutions' are technically defined as 'the rules of the game; organizations are the players': Douglass C. North, *Understanding the process of economic change* (Princeton, NJ, 2005), p. 62. In practice, this technicality is often forgotten.

[95] For overviews see John N. Drobak and John V. C. Nye, 'Introduction' to Drobak and Nye, eds., *The frontiers of the new institutional economics* (San Diego, CA, and London, 1997), pp. xv–xx; L. J. Alson, 'New institutional economics', in Steven N. Durlauf and Lawrence E. Blume, eds., *The new Palgrave dictionary of economics* (2nd edn., 8 vols., 2008), vol. 6, pp. 32–9; Oliver E. Williamson, 'The new institutional economics: taking stock, looking ahead', *Journal of Economic Literature*, 38.3 (2000), pp. 595–613.

[96] Especially important has been Douglass C. North and Barry R. Weingast, 'Constitutions and commitment: the evolution of institutions governing public choice in seventeenth-century England', *Journal of Economic History*, 49.4 (1989), pp. 803–32.

[97] See for example, David Stasavage, *Public debt and the birth of the democratic state: France and Great Britain, 1688–1789* (Cambridge, 2003); John V. C. Nye, *War, wine, and taxes: the political economy of Anglo-French trade, 1689–1900* (Princeton, NJ,

In part, such findings rest on different disciplinary practices, especially a determination to test theoretically informed hypotheses and models by quantifying. Historians proceed very differently.[98] But a further key limitation of such approaches is their teleological nature, extracting certain features from the past held to lead to those later (and often present-day) conditions requiring explanation and emphasis, commonly liberty, representative government, and secure property rights. Institutions, moreover, are considered (and measured) mainly in terms of functional relationships to modern economic criteria, not to ideas, culture, and politics of the time. Such selectivity makes the approach often markedly ahistorical, as Epstein brought out especially well in relation to anachronistic conceptions of the state, and involve a good deal of wishful thinking.[99] More historically informed studies have noted that the Glorious Revolution in fact heightened the insecurity of property rights in key respects and created new opportunities for rent seeking.[100] The political economy of the revolution constitution depicted in the new Whig accounts would, ironically, have been unrecognizable to Adam Smith given the weight he accorded to rent seeking within the 'mercantile system'.

Conclusion

Some historians deny the importance of politics to the economic history of Britain in this period, consigning it to the very margins of their

---

2007); Dan Bogart, 'Did the Glorious Revolution contribute to the transport revolution? Evidence from investment in roads and rivers', *Economic History Review*, 64.4 (2011), pp. 1073–112.

[98] As John Habakkuk observed: 'Economic theory characteristically proceeds by building a model, a simplified, abstract version of the real world. A model is more than a hypothesis; it is a series of functional relations between the various elements of which the economy is composed. ... To use theory effectively in order to quantify, one has to limit the equations to a manageable number and include in them only those factors for which some sort of quantification is possible. ... But the need to limit the variables for these reasons may compel one to include an assumption that greatly limits the utility of the model to someone interested in explaining actual events.' 'Economic history and economic theory', *Daedalus*, 100.2 (1971), pp. 305 and 312.

[99] S. R. Epstein, *Freedom and growth: the rise of states and markets in Europe, 1300–1750* (Abingdon, 2000), especially pp. 5–7; Francesco Boldizzoni, *The poverty of Clio: resurrecting economic history* (Princeton, NJ, 2011), generally, but on this specific point, p. 18.

[100] Julian Hoppit, 'Compulsion, compensation and property rights in Britain, 1688–1833', *Past and Present*, 210 (2011), pp. 93–128; Nuala Zahedieh, 'Regulation, rent-seeking and the Glorious Revolution in the English Atlantic economy', *Economic History Review*, 63.4 (2010), pp. 865–90; William A. Pettigrew, 'Constitutional change in England and the diffusion of regulatory initiative, 1660–1714', *History*, 99.338 (2014), pp. 839–63.

accounts.[101] But by this is meant only that they believe that the effect of governmental action on aggregate economic activity was trivial. Such a conclusion often tends to reflect a predilection for mono- rather than multi-causality and, more importantly for this study, ignores the fact that at the time very many people took the relationship between economic and political power very seriously. At the very least, 7,000 Acts of Parliament relating to economic life show that clearly enough. But this book also seeks to negotiate between two very different arguments made by those who do see politics and economics as interrelated: between those who argue for the importance of mercantilist regulations and those who argue for the significance of liberty and property.

This book is not a study of the causes of the industrial revolution, nor of the determinants of the riches and poverty of nations. Rather, it seeks to recover what was desirable and possible to those at the time regarding the relationship of political power and economic life, resting heavily on original research and viewing the state and the economy in their own terms. Contemporaries had no notion of an industrial revolution, but they did ruminate on why some nations were richer and more powerful than others. In this it is important to stress that in their attitudes and prescriptions they might look in two very different directions. One was optimistic, imaginative, and positive: that untapped resources could be exploited, productivity enhanced, new types of property created, and the world of goods expanded. But the other was less sanguine and more backward looking, seeking to restore an order believed to have been more prosperous and harmonious than the present: that woollens should be encouraged (and its competitors discouraged), old skills cherished, customary rights respected, risks shared, and inequalities preserved.

The perspective adopted by this book is to explore economic legislation as it was sought from and provided by the Westminster parliament. But the sources available are badly skewed, mainly because almost all of the manuscript records of the House of Commons were destroyed by fire in 1834. Consequently, this book rests heavily on the printed *Journals* of both houses, as well as the statute book. These have been explored systematically and comprehensively, but it does mean that it is often impossible to get official accounts of how legislation was developed

---

[101] Gregory Clark, 'The political foundations of modern economic growth: England, 1540–1800', *Journal of Interdisciplinary History*, 26.4 (1996), pp. 563–88; Robert C. Allen, *The British industrial revolution in global perspective* (Cambridge, 2009), pp. 4–5; Deirdre N. McCloskey, *Bourgeois equality: how ideas, not capital or institutions, enriched the world* (Chicago, IL, 2016).

and deliberated on. Manuscript sources that can help and have been used, especially in Part Two, but only some of what is available has been looked at because they are so voluminous and widely scattered. Finally, the non-parliamentary printed sources of the period are especially rich and these have been accessed pretty widely.

The rest of Part One of this book focuses on patterns of parliamentary legislation. Parliament was the supreme focal point for the British state and it was through bills and acts that political power sought to affect economic life. The period covered runs from the Restoration of the monarchy in 1660, which also involved the restoration of Parliament, to the Union of Britain and Ireland, enacted in 1800 and taking effect at the start of the following year. Sometimes discussion drifts into the nineteenth century, but while consideration is given to the impact of the Union of England and Wales with Scotland in 1707, that of Britain and Ireland is not – because to do so would be a very large job. Chapter 2 explores the general context, of the transformational impact of the Glorious Revolution of 1688–9 and the great growth of legislation after 1760. This is related to attitudes at the time towards such frequent law making, especially of the perils involved. Chapter 3 homes in on legislation relating to the economy, setting out its incidence over time and in relation to its broad types. While a good deal of space is given over to governmental legislation relating to public finances and overseas trade, a much larger volume of legislation was local and specific in scope. It is essential to grasp this duality within Britain's political economies: there was much more to the 'state' than central government alone. Chapter 4 elaborates on this by considering the geography of economic legislation, pointing up important differences between England and Scotland and that Westminster existed alongside legislative bodies elsewhere within the British empire. Finally in Part One, Chapter 5 focuses on the general features of the information, interests, and ideas involved in Britain's political economies.

Part One rests on quite a bit of counting, seeking to be comprehensive and systematic: attention is directed wholly at what legislative proposals were considered and acts passed, overwhelmingly at the aggregate level. That leaves little room for seeing how Britain's political economies were constructed or worked in practice. Part Two, therefore, presents four case studies seeking to show how legislation was sought and implemented, at both the local and national levels. In Part One it is shown that economic acts affecting particular people, places, and interests outnumbered more general measures by two to one. Moreover, some types of such 'specific' legislation were much more easily enacted than others. Chapter 6 concentrates on such issues by reference to economic legislation that affected the Fens. It shows that some apparently minor Acts of Parliament were believed to have had wide-ranging consequences, leading to often fraught contests over the best ways of balancing particular and public interests. The rest of Part Two considers national legislation because of its importance in understanding policy considerations. Chapter 7 examines a classic piece of 'mercantilist' legislation and interest group politics, the ban on the export of raw wool, to show what was aimed at, why the legislation was often felt to have been ineffective, and what this says about the gap between prescription and practice. The next two chapters similarly concentrate on general legislation, but begin to think more about its effects, using patterns of expenditure and income as a means of indicating some critical matters of scale. Chapter 8 looks at one of the features that Adam Smith identified as central to the mercantile system, bounties (or subsidies). It shows an important way in which central government sought to aid some areas of economic life and of the inherent difficulties involved. Then in Chapter 9 the focus switches fully to considering the consequences of a key aspect of public finance legislation, the raising of taxes. It points up some striking regional features that have hitherto been unappreciated, casting fresh light on just how 'British' even national economic legislation often was. Chapter 10 provides conclusions for this book as a whole, introducing some comparisons between Britain and other European nations.

What follows covers a good deal of material, but it leaves relatively untouched a number of aspects of Britain's political economies. The role of executive proclamations and orders barely features, though the papers of a number of leading ministers have been trawled. Nor is attention paid to the ways in which the courts interpreted legislation. This book looks at only parts of the governmental process and from a Westminster-centred perspective.[102] And throughout the concern is to see the period as a whole, identifying key general features and moments of change. Consequently, the specific contexts and causes behind measures get very little attention, producing an account that is light on individual action

---

[102] 'Historians should therefore think less of *government* as an institution or as an event, than of *governance* as a process, a series of multilateral initiatives to be negotiated across space and through the social order. ... In this analysis, therefore, parliamentary legislation, conciliar order or royal proclamation were not the end of the law-making process but merely its beginning; litigation, indictment or violent self-assertion were not the end of the disputing process but merely its beginning.' Steve Hindle, *The state and social change in early modern England, c. 1550–1640* (Basingstoke, 2000), p. 23.

and specific circumstances. Further, the social impact of economic legislation is only touched on here and there, not because it was unimportant, but because to have done so would have made any already very large project impossibly big.[103] My hope is that setting out the main features of the legislative basis of Britain's political economies will provide a better context in which to place more detailed studies (both those already available and those that might be produced in the future).

---

[103] See Lemmings, *Law and government*, for a different and often complementary approach to this book.

2   The Legislative Revolution

'The basis of the English Constitution, the capital principle on which
all others depend, is that the Legislative power belongs to Parliament
alone; that is to say, the power of establishing laws, and of abrogating,
changing, or explaining them.'

Jean de Lolme, 1784[1]

'Some [acts] are vigorous, and live long; others sicken in their Infancy,
and see not half their Days. Some are begot to live Seven Years: Others,
as soon as they are born, either for some ugly Features they have, or
some mischievous Disposition they shew, are wisely knock'd on Head
by their own Parents. Some live long, indeed, but sleep all the Time, and
are never heard of, 'till they are awaken'd for some particular Occasion,
and then they sleep again. Some will make People Swear: Some have
a Spite at one particular Person: Some are not brought forth without
great Struggles: And others, tho' very good Children, have their Hands
tied behind them, sometimes for Six Months together, sometimes for
Twelve Months.'

Duke of Wharton, 1723[2]

'An ancient land in ancient oracles is called "law-thirsty": all the struggle there was after order and a perfect state.'

George Eliot, 1871–2[3]

Great events need not have great causes, but they must have great
consequences. In fact both the origins and outcomes of the Glorious
Revolution of 1688–9 were momentous in three different ways. Firstly,
it was part of a crisis in European interstate rivalry, largely prompted
by perceptions of the ambitions of France's Sun King, Louis XIV.
Britain was a prized jewel in that competition, won by the boldness

---

[1] Jean Louis de Lolme, *The constitution of England*, ed. David Lieberman (Indianapolis, IN, 2007), p. 55. At the time, foreigners especially, but also the English and the Scots, used 'England' and 'Britain' interchangeably. De Lolme was Swiss; the first French edition of his work was published in 1771.

[2] [Philip Wharton], *The True Briton* (2 vols., 1723), vol. 2, p. 620.

[3] *Middlemarch: a story of provincial life* (1871–2, serial publication), ch. 9.

and bravery of the Dutch republic and its leader, William of Orange. Yet remarkably, over the next quarter century Britain managed to transform itself from an object of desire into a great power in its own right. Secondly, the crisis of 1688–9 was a further painful consequence of the Reformation, establishing quite clearly that a Protestant nation would only countenance Protestant monarchs. Consequently, no longer could the crown claim the unlimited and unconditional loyalty of subjects. The Glorious Revolution was also, finally, a critical stage by which an increasingly complex society circumvented the structural limitations of hereditary monarchy as the mainspring of central government.

The institutionalization and regularization of Parliament within many aspects of everyday life in Britain was a momentous outcome of the Glorious Revolution, providing the means by which its main causes were addressed in the new order. Very quickly, the events of what some at the time called the 'happy revolution' morphed into the 'Glorious Revolution'. In the eighteenth century the Revolution constitution was frequently celebrated both at home and abroad as being beautifully balanced for the good of liberty and property. Quite what this meant in practice has not always been clear. The work of the Westminster parliament was for long misunderstood, mainly because it was explored within the narrow compass of 'high politics'. But this seriously misrepresents what Parliament did between the Glorious Revolution and Union with Ireland.[4] Most of its efforts were given over to handling revolutionary levels of legislation, a majority of which concerned economic matters. It is by recognizing the full extent of Parliament's legislative effort that the richness and variety of Britain's political economies in the eighteenth century becomes possible.

This chapter sets out the general dimensions of the growing torrent of legislation from 1660 to 1800. Two broad explanations are then developed: in terms of Parliament's institutional development; and a dramatically heightened willingness to seek legislation by individuals and interests across the country. This second development was vital to the transformation of British political society and of Britain's political economies. But this flood of legislation was not without problems. After all, if floods can irrigate and enrich, they can also drown and erode; serious

---

[4] Paul Langford, *Public life and the propertied Englishman, 1688–1798* (Oxford, 1991); Joanna Innes, *Inferior politics: social problems and social policies in eighteenth-century Britain* (Oxford, 2009); Julian Hoppit, 'Patterns of parliamentary legislation, 1660–1800', *Historical Journal*, 39.1 (1996), pp. 109–31; Hoppit, *Failed legislation*, introduction. As the footnotes in following chapters show, there is rich literature on some aspects or parts of the legislative revolution.

doubts were raised at the time about the value of all this legislation, individually and collectively, especially after 1750.

Counting Legislation

In the late seventeenth century the empire of quantification expanded impressively, particularly through Sir William Petty's 'political arithmetic', by which he meant assessing policy considerations in terms of number, weight, and measure. The potency of counting was such that in 1711 even Richard Steele, a man of impeccable urbanity and politeness, could exclaim that 'Numbers are so much the Measure of every thing that is valuable, that it is not possible to demonstrate the Success of any Action or the Prudence of any Undertaking without them.'[5] In that spirit, counts of legislative activity provide the building blocks of this and the following two chapters, and crop up occasionally thereafter. In this chapter the aim is to explore legislation generally, comprehensively, and systematically to show how Parliament's legislative business was transformed. Once that basis is established, attention can then turn in the next chapter to looking at legislation that affected the economy, then in Chapter 4 to where economic legislation applied.

It is easy enough to identify all of the Acts of Parliament passed in this period. Their date of enactment and their short titles are all readily available. This allows various types of categorization to be undertaken, of their timing, subject matter, and where geographically they applied. Not that there is one agreed way of defining categories, while borderline cases, including multipurpose acts, can be tricky to deal with.[6] Additionally, the short titles of acts might be rather misleading, a problem that could only be overcome by reading the texts of the acts. Because of the huge numbers involved that has been done fairly rarely in the research for this book. Furthermore, interpreting counts of acts may not be straightforward. Joel Hurstfield nicely hinted at the dangers involved when questioning G. R. Elton's enumeration of Thomas Cromwell's legislative fertility under Henry VIII: 'I am myself reluctant to attempt to measure the quality of parliamentary government by weight'.[7] That is certainly a caution that needs to be borne in mind throughout this book.

---

[5] *The Spectator*, ed. Donald F. Bond (5 vols. Oxford, 1965), vol. 2, p. 188. Steele and Addison were the central figures in this pivotal periodical, so influential in the history of manners and taste in the English-speaking world of the eighteenth century.

[6] For some questions about the categories employed see Henry Horwitz, 'Changes in the law and reform of the legal order: England (and Wales) 1689–1760', *Parliamentary History*, 21.3 (2002), pp. 314–15.

[7] *Freedom, corruption and government in Elizabethan England* (1973), p. 32.

Acts of Parliament warrant counting because, even if they varied considerably (some were great, others small, some permanent, others temporary, some new, others renewals, refinements, or rejections – see Wharton's observation at the head of this chapter), they were generated by a common procedure and they show where Parliament was putting so much of its effort. Some 14,217 were passed at Westminster from 1660 to 1800. All were the result of bills, draft acts, being introduced into one or other of the Houses of Parliament, scrutinized and refined there (especially at the second reading committee stage) before being passed to the other house for consideration. When that house had finished its work – essentially by repeating the stages of the other house – and both houses had agreed to a text, the bill would be passed to the monarch for approval as an act. That approval was formally withheld only twelve times after 1660, lastly by Queen Anne in 1708.[8] Bills had to become acts within a single parliamentary session, of which there were 143 in the period, albeit of differing lengths. If by the end of a session a bill had not progressed through all the stages, and many did not, then to become an act they would have to go back to stage one in a succeeding session and try again.[9]

There were three broad phases of numbers of Acts of Parliament in this period. As Figure 2.1 shows, most sessions in the Restoration era saw few enactments, but soon after 1688 fifty acts per session became the usual minimum number until 1750 when a rise began; there were often more than 200 per session after 1763 and three sessions in the 1790s saw more than 300, though interrupted by a significant trough in 1783–4. In the first thirty years of our period Parliament passed 620 acts, but in the last thirty years more than 6,600 acts, an extraordinary increase of revolutionary significance. Which of these concerned the economy is considered in the next chapter.

Three general qualifications to this legislative fertility must be noted immediately, however. Firstly, before 1707 Britain had parliaments

---

[8] Fails 2.041, 2.129, 2.134, 17.003, 27.034, 28.031, 28.066, 29.005, 30.053, 31.035, 36.043, 44.012 in Hoppit, *Failed legislation*. Additionally, in 1663 a bill that had passed both houses was stolen from the table of the House of Lords, perhaps by order of Charles II, and so could not be passed. In 1681 another bill that had passed both houses was not presented to Charles II because he said he would veto it. C. E. Fryer, 'The royal veto under Charles II', *English Historical Review*, 32.125 (1917), pp. 103–11.

[9] For a discussion of procedure in the Commons see P. D. G. Thomas, *The House of Commons in the eighteenth century* (Oxford, 1971), ch. 3. A contemporary insider's view is provided in Anon., *The Liverpool tractate: an eighteenth century manual on the procedure of the House of Commons*, ed. Catherine Strateman (New York, 1937). For the Lords, Anita Jane Rees, 'The practice and procedure of the House of Lords, 1714–1784' (University of Aberystwyth PhD thesis, 1987).

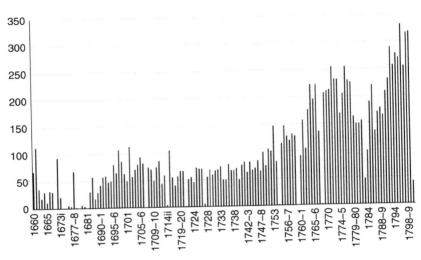

Figure 2.1 Numbers of acts by session, 1660–1800.

separately legislating at Edinburgh for Scotland and at Westminster for England, Wales, and the British empire. Their amalgamation in 1707 meant that Westminster's legislative responsibilities were extended to a further million persons and 20 million acres (respectively about 20 and 54 per cent of the numbers for England and Wales) – and as will be seen Chapter 4, the Edinburgh parliament passed plenty of acts before the Union. Similarly, the extent of the British empire grew considerably until American independence, declared in 1776 and recognized in 1783.[10] Even so, Britain's empire in 1800 was much larger than it had been in the Restoration era, especially through expansion in Canada and India. This necessarily confronted Westminster with new peoples, interests, responsibilities, and opportunities which might have resulted in more legislation.

Aggregate counts of acts also need, secondly, to recognize that some were wholly new, while others amended, continued, explained, or repealed existing legislation, numbers of which might be expected to rise as a share of all legislation over time. Distinguishing these types of acts is not always straightforward, but some counts can be attempted. Across the whole period, 82 per cent of acts were apparently new,

[10] There was one colony in 1607, twenty-five in 1713, and thirty-three in 1763: Charles M. Andrews, *The colonial background of the American Revolution* (New Haven, CT, 1931), p. 69.

albeit often relating to existing legislation, but the proportion did indeed decline a little over time. In the 1660s, 91 per cent of acts were apparently new, but in the 1790s 76 per cent. Numbers of acts repealing existing legislation increased from the 1760s, but across the whole period numbered only 148, or just 1 per cent of the total. More significant was the increase in the numbers of acts continuing, explaining, or amending existing legislation (distinguishing between them is often impossible). As will be seen, many of these related to turnpike trusts, for their initial statutory basis usually lasted for twenty-one years only. For trusts to continue after that time required further legislation. Even so, while numbers of all acts increased by eleven fold between 1660–89 and 1771–1800, those of new acts increased by a still impressive nine fold.

A third factor crucial to understanding the scale of changes in the volume of legislation was patterns of parliamentary sessions. As has been noted, sessions were the fundamental units for the consideration of legislative initiatives. But they varied both in length and frequency. Longer and more predictable sessions ought to have allowed a higher proportion of attempts at legislation to succeed: proposers would know the sorts of timescales involved and become more expert at generating well-drafted bills, and Parliament should have been better able to manage the complex work of turning legislative proposals into acts. Unquestionably, profound changes to the patterns of sessions occurred as a consequence of the Glorious Revolution, though there were occasionally still very short sessions when little business was completed.[11] Charles II (1660–85) and James II (1685–8) frequently sought to avoid Parliament, preferring to dismiss than to summon it. On seven occasions in their reigns intervals between sessions exceeded 400 days (two of which were more than 1,000 days). But after 1688 the longest interval was 279 days and the median interval was 181 days. Similarly, in the Restoration period 11 of the 22 sessions lasted less than fifty days, compared to just 8 of the 121 sessions from 1689 to 1800. After 1688, Parliament's careful control of public finances established annual sessions and a predictable parliamentary calendar; sessions usually began in the autumn or winter, lasting for an average of 100 days. Unsurprisingly, of the seven sessions that passed no acts in our period, only two of them were after 1688.[12] As Sir Thomas Meres noted in 1675, 'Five or six times, Bills have been cut to

---

[11] Such very short sessions explain most of the markedly anomalous numbers in almost all of the post-1688 sessions in Figures 2.1, 2.2, 2.4, and 2.5.

[12] The sessions were 1669, 1673ii, 1674, 1679i, 1681, 1707, 1760.

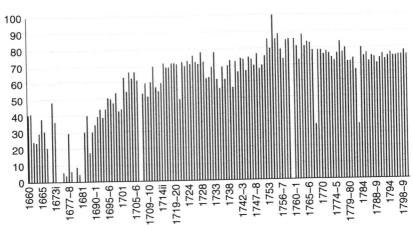

Figure 2.2 Success rate of legislation by session, 1660–1800.

pieces by prorogations ... [which] destroy all we can do by Bill.'[13] Such crude political violence followed James II into exile, never to return.

How the regularization of the meetings of Parliament affected the handling of legislation is made clear when the number of acts passed is compared to the numbers of attempts to obtain an act. Because almost all of the manuscripts of the House of Commons were destroyed by fire in 1834, those attempts have to be identified by a detailed and difficult trawl of more than 63,000 double-column pages of the printed *Journals* of both houses.[14] That effort has identified 7,026 failed attempts to obtain an act in Parliament, including not only bills, but also less concrete attempts, allowing a success rate of attempts at legislation to be calculated (see Figure 2.2).[15]

In the Restoration era, the success rate averaged just 28 per cent and was declining on trend, being only 17 per cent from 1674–88. It rose after the Glorious Revolution, reaching 70 per cent for the first time

---

[13] Anchitell Grey, ed., *Debates of the House of Commons, from the year 1667 to the year 1694* (13 vols., 1769), vol. 3, p. 346. Very similar was Mr Vaughan's comments in debate in 1681. Cobbett, *Parl. Hist.*, 4 (1660–88), col. 1312.

[14] For the period there are forty-eight volumes of *JHC* and thirty-two volumes of *JHL*, comprising 40,619 and 22,732 pages respectively.

[15] The Introduction to Hoppit, *Failed legislation* discusses problems of definition and identification. Of the 7,026 fails, 3,710 (53 per cent) had at least a first reading, giving a minimum number of bills involved. The success rate is defined as acts as a percentage of the sum of acts and failed attempts.

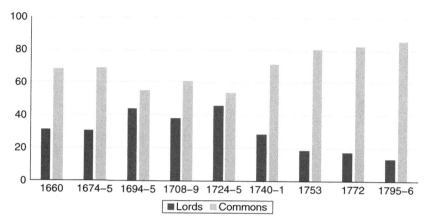

Figure 2.3 Share of acts and fails originating in both houses by sample sessions, 1660–1800.

in 1711–12 and being around 75 per cent for most of the rest of the eighteenth century. As is clear from Figure 2.2, the improvement in the success rate after 1688 was gradual, suggesting a process of learning and development both within and without Parliament.[16] But by 1700 it was clear enough for one foreigner to note that 'One can infer that it is the frequent Parliaments which England has enjoyed during this reign that has given rise to an infinity of Acts made for the public good.'[17]

Shouldering the Burdens of Legislative Business

Clearly the legislative revolution placed enormous workloads on both houses, but in fact much more on the Commons than the Lords. Some 75 per cent of all acts in nine sample sessions began in the Commons, and 80 per cent of all 7,026 fails began there.[18] But there was some change in this proportion over time, as Figure 2.3 shows.

More legislation than average originated in the Lords between about 1689 and 1730 (with a peak share in 1724–5 of 46 per cent), but by the middle of the century it was decidedly the second house, and in 1795–6

[16] Well discussed in D. W. Hayton, 'The House of Commons 1690–1715, introductory survey: the business of the house – legislation', *HofP online*. Also useful is Kathryn M. Ellis, 'The practice and procedure of the House of Commons 1660–1714' (University of Aberystwyth PhD thesis, 1993).

[17] Quoted in Ellis, 'House of Commons', p. 91.

[18] Hoppit, *Failed legislation*, p. 13.

the Lords was the first house for only 14 per cent of the total of acts and failed legislation. Yet with its legal expertise, the Lords had a particular role to play in the scrutiny of legislation, though in fact it amended only 15 per cent of bills passed to it by the Commons, compared to the Commons amending 32 per cent of bills arriving from the Lords. The Commons was also more heavily involved in failed legislation. If 80 per cent of failed legislation began in the Commons, only 12 per cent of these passed to the Lords to fail there. By contrast, 49 per cent of fails originating in the Lords were passed to the Commons and failed there. Put another way, the Commons had a hand in 5,829 fails, the Lords only 2,099.

Whichever way one looks at it, the Commons had a more significant role in handling legislation than the Lords. In part this arose from the convention that all measures that taxed or charged the public had to originate in the Commons because of its representative role, while the Commons could also draw on more manpower to help in this work. There were 513 MPs until Union with Scotland added a further forty-five. The Lords had a constant composition of twenty-six spiritual peers and, from 1707, sixteen Scottish peers, but a variable number of other peers – 173 in 1700, 181 in 1760, and 267 in 1800.[19] Doubtless that accounts for some of the imbalance in their roles, not simply in the amount of work they could undertake, but also in terms of the numbers of points of contact they afforded to the rest of society. Some peers did make themselves available in these ways, such as the dukes of Bedford, but many did not – for some because their estates were scattered and they were largely absent. MPs by contrast were more consistently active in that regard.

With the relative importance of the two houses established, their handling of business needs to be explored. Critically, more regular sessions helped Parliament pass more legislation, but that explains only part of the legislative revolution. After all, regular sessions were quickly established, yet increasing numbers of acts took place gradually over the next twenty years, and was dwarfed by the increases after 1750. Parliament's improved handling of legislative proposals was eventually very disproportionate to the increase in its meetings. That is, in terms of the time available to it, the weight of legislative business increased, and increased significantly. A crude measure of that is to divide the number of days Parliament sat by the number of acts it passed. On that basis, as Figure 2.4 shows, there is no question that Parliament turned out many more acts,

---

[19] John Cannon, *Aristocratic century: the peerage of eighteenth-century England* (Cambridge, 1984), p. 15.

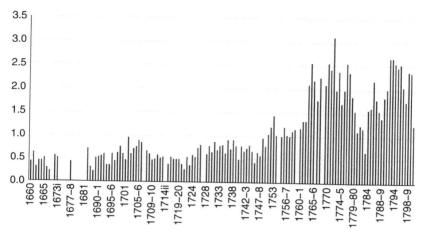

Figure 2.4 Acts per day by session, 1660–1800 (excluding sessions with fewer than ten acts).

especially after 1750, with a marked rise in the late 1760s, followed by a fall to a nadir in 1785 and then another rise and fall.

By this simple measure, after session lengths are accounted for Parliament processed five times as many acts in the 1790s as in the 1660s.[20] While number of working days in a session is a crude unit of measure in this instance, the change is too great to be ignored. Figure 2.4 suggests that the Glorious Revolution indeed ushered in a new era of legislative productivity, with further growth taking place from the late 1740s, followed by a marked rise, fall, and rise in the last third of the eighteenth century. Three broad explanations are possible: that Parliament became less conscientious; that Parliament increasingly used its time better; and that bills became better drafted. It is impossible to address these possibilities systematically, not least because so many parliamentary archives were destroyed in 1834, but there is some good evidence.[21]

The most important piece of evidence is the orders made by both houses about bills and their work on them. Some of those orders were more or less repeated in each session, notably that private bills could

[20] This is a count of days in all sessions on which the Commons sat taken from the *JHC*, excluding days given over wholly to the swearing of oaths and election disputes – a total of 13,735 days. For a sample of thirty-four sessions across the period, the Lords sat on 87 per cent of the days the Commons sat.

[21] More thorough discussion of these issues is in Thomas, *House of Commons*, and Sheila Lambert, *Bills and acts: legislative procedure in eighteenth-century England* (Cambridge, 1971), especially ch. 4.

not be submitted after a certain date (to allow adequate time for their consideration before the end of the session) and were to be heard at certain times of the parliamentary day and week. Others were standing orders, which set out requirements for the submission and consideration of private business. There had been some developments here in the Restoration period: in 1685 it was required for private bills to originate as petitions. But between 1697 and 1707 a raft of standing orders established a basic framework for handling private bills that remained in place for the rest of our period, including: a restatement that they had to originate with a petition to Parliament; committees had to report on the allegations made in bills; they had to be printed; and there had to be at least three days between each of the three readings of a bill. Mainly these orders were designed to improve the quality of legislative proposals, but they also looked to ensure reasonable transparency so that different interests would not be caught unawares. For a while these orders were sufficient to cope with the volume and type of legislative proposals, but in 1774 new ones were adopted to help with the rising tide of turnpike, drainage, river, canal, and enclosure legislation.[22]

These orders may have encouraged further requests for legislation, but they were mainly a part of wider changes in coping with heightened demand for legislation. In 1701 the Commons established the fees on private business that remained in place until the nineteenth century.[23] These itemized the costs of sixty-six potential payments, many of them to the different officers involved in handling legislation, including the speaker, serjeant, clerk, doorkeepers, and housekeepers, or at different formal stages of the legislation process. Administrative functionaries were vital in ensuring procedures were followed, and that parliamentarians dealt at the right stage with the petitions, pamphlets, and counsel involved in any attempt at legislation. This was a complex juggling act which put considerable strains on resources. Little wonder that clerical support in the Commons expanded in this period. The system of four under-clerks, so important to organizing committee work, becomes visible in 1696; a clerk of the ingrossment dates from about 1727; a clerk of the papers was first appointed in 1740 (becoming a clerk of the journals and papers in 1754); and a clerk of

---

[22] Orlo Cyprian Williams, *The historical development of private bill procedure and standing orders in the House of Commons* (2 vols., 1948–9), vol. 2, pp. 262–7; Betty Kemp, *Votes and standing orders of the House of Commons: the beginning* (1971); Anon., *Remembrances: or, a compleat collection of the standing orders of the House of Lords in England* (1744).

[23] *JHC*, 13 (1699–1702), pp. 356–7 (26 Feb. 1701).

the fees from 1774.[24] Arthur Onslow's long tenure as speaker from 1728 to 1761 also transformed the handling of legislation through his attention to procedural propriety and the political independence of the office.

One sign of the effect of all these changes is that before 1710 only 55 per cent of legislative proposals were raised in Parliament before mid-session point, but thereafter it was 82 per cent, an important development that enhanced the chances of bills completing all the necessary stages before the end of the session.[25] It is also possible that the parliamentary day lengthened or increased in intensity, including by better use of the space available for committee work. The length of the parliamentary day is occasionally glimpsed, often by the *Journals* recording the ordering of candles to allow business to continue after dusk or in terms of usual orders to keep the approaches to Parliament clear at certain times of the day. But such evidence is rather imprecise. Just after our period, we do know that on average in each session from 1806–10 the Commons sat for 746 hours over ninety-four days, that is, nearly eight hours a day on average, to pass 408 acts.[26] Even this gives a fairly crude indication, as much of Parliament's legislative work took place away from the floor of the houses, in committees whose business is largely hidden from historians.[27] One thing is clear: by 1730 they did so without the need usually to sit on Saturdays, allowing parliamentarians to enjoy London life at the weekend – Parliament never sat on Sundays (see Figure 2.5).

Success rates have already provided some indication of the quality of legislative proposals and how contentious they were. Two other pieces of information cast some light on these important issues in a general way. The first is the frequency with which legislation was amended, given that well-drafted and uncontroversial legislation would be less likely to be amended than poorly drafted legislation. In fact, of the 1,498 acts and fails in the sample sessions, 67 per cent were amended, with the

---

[24] W. R. McKay, *Clerks in the House of Commons, 1363–1989: a biographical list* (House of Lords Record Office occasional publications, no. 3, 1989), pp. 120, 122–3; Orlo Cyprian Williams, *The clerical organization of the House of Commons, 1661–1851* (Oxford, 1954).

[25] This uses the same data as in the sample sessions data. It is the mid-point of days on which business was conducted.

[26] 'Report from select committee on public petitions, with the minutes of evidence', BPP, 639 (1831–2), p. 18. I am grateful to Joshua Civin for this reference. For a discussion of the day in the Commons see Thomas, *House of Commons*, ch. 9.

[27] More evidence has survived of committee work in the Lords, available at the Parliamentary Archives; Maurice F. Bond, *Guide to the records of Parliament* (1971), p. 45. 'The minute book of James Courthope', ed. Orlo Cyprian Williams, *Camden Miscellany*, 20 (1953) is a committee clerk's notebook, but it does not record some basic information such as who attended committees or how long they sat.

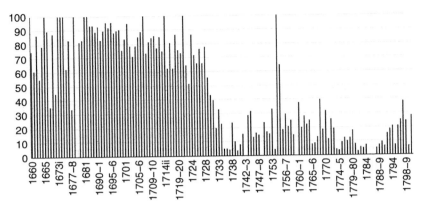

Figure 2.5 Saturday sittings of the House of Commons, as % of available Saturdays by session, 1660–1800.

Commons responsible for three times as many amendments as the Lords. This figure is somewhat misleading, as many bills were submitted with blanks to be filled in, that is amended, during its passage through the first house. But as 10 per cent of legislation was amended in its second house, after blanks had usually been filled in, a higher proportion still must have been significantly amended. The evidence of divisions in the Commons is more robust as these were formal votes, usually when the question was finely balanced. Evidence of amendments in the second house and divisions in the Commons for both acts and fails is presented in Figure 2.6.[28]

Increasingly, most legislation was not amended in the second house, nor subject to a division in the Commons. A clear sense is gained from this evidence of the continued political stresses and strains of the post-Revolution era. A marked change happened between the sessions of 1708–9 and 1740–1; subsequent changes were fairly insignificant.

An attempt can now be made to piece together this evidence to provide a parliamentary explanation of the legislative revolution. The first phase, lasting from the Revolution to about 1708, was the most critical: regular sessions were established; relevant standing orders agreed; and administrative support developed. These allowed legislation to be

---

[28] Divisions in the Lords were much less frequent. See J. C. Sainty and D. Dewar, *Divisions in the House of Lords: an analytical list 1685 to 1857* (House of Lords Record Office occasional publications, no. 2, 1976). Details of divisions have sometimes survived. See G. M. Ditchfield, David Hayton, and Clyve Jones, eds., *British parliamentary lists, 1660–1800: a register* (1995); Donald E. Ginter, *Voting records of the British House of Commons, 1761–1820* (6 vols., 1995).

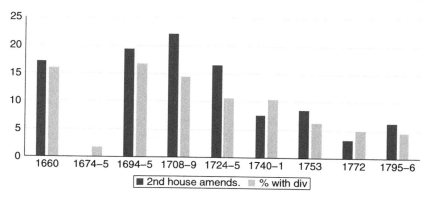

Figure 2.6 Per cent of acts and fails subject to a division and amendment in second house by sample sessions, 1660–1800.

handled more effectively, but one consequence, probably intentional, was to stem the flow of proposed legislation, the combined numbers of acts and fails clearly falling on trend from about 1700 to about 1727. This was the main period of the 'growth of political stability' analyzed by Plumb. Certainly, the evidence of second house amendments and Commons' divisions supports this broad view, as does the fact that the success rate of legislation clearly if subtly improved with the advent of Whig one-party rule in 1714.[29] Before long the good ordering of business enabled Parliament largely to give up sitting on Saturdays. Yet soon it was faced with an increasing volume of proposals, barely perceptible at first, but by the 1760s clear and visible. By then legislation was less contested within Parliament, helping Parliament to manage this work. Cynically this might be ascribed to institutional sclerosis. After all, 1760 marked the apogee of unrepresentative politics under the Hanoverians: of uncontested elections, bought votes, and peerage influence. Yet some legislation continued to be controversial and the poverty of the Namierite view of Parliament as an ideology-free zone was established long ago.[30] The Commons in particular remained capable of rousing itself. Probably more important, therefore, were the efforts of Onslow and his successors. The handling of legislation was taken to another administrative level by 1760, just as a huge new wave of demand for acts began to sweep in. Explaining who wanted legislation is therefore the essential next step to understanding the legislative revolution.

[29] J. H. Plumb, *The growth of political stability in England, 1675–1725* (1967).
[30] John Brewer, *Party ideology and popular politics at the accession of George III* (Cambridge, 1976).

Categories of Legislation

Today central government dominates Westminster's legislative programme. Proposed legislation, usually a couple of dozen per session, is worked out in detail at departmental level, and, supposedly mandated by general elections, is very rarely defeated outright (though is commonly amended). This was emphatically not the case before the twentieth century. Most acts were sought from beyond government, local or central, with the latter having very limited legislative needs. Consequently, the origins of the legislative revolution were widely scattered, and from strikingly varied interests. To assess that requires in the first instance that legislation be categorized.

Contemporaries distinguished between public and private acts until 1798, when the category of local public act was introduced. But those distinctions rested neither on whether legislation was sought by those inside or outside central government, nor on whether it affected private or public interests. Legislation for turnpike roads, for example, was public because of the tolls involved; but the parliamentary enclosure of land was private, because its costs were not held to be a charge on the public. Many private acts affected the public, though in particular places rather than nationally.[31] Further, some measures introduced as private bills were passed as public acts. One difference was that private bills paid fees whereas public ones did not.[32] As fees on private bills were fixed in 1701, changes in external market conditions obviously affected calculations as to whether to seek legislation. Structurally, moderate inflation after 1750, but rapid in the 1790s, lowered somewhat the real costs of private legislation, though the many other expenses of seeking legislation were unfixed.[33] But economic fluctuations would also likely have more of an effect on numbers seeking, for example, private enclosure acts than public turnpike acts. Finally, Parliament handled public and private bills differently. The former were introduced by motion or from major committees, such as Ways and Means which dealt with public finances. Such bills might be handled in select committees or committees of the whole house. By contrast, private bills originated in petitions and were considered only in select committees.

---

[31] The distinction is well discussed in Langford, *Public life*, p. 164.

[32] Frederick C. Clifford, *A history of private bill legislation* (2 vols., 1885–7), is mainly concerned with the nineteenth century.

[33] From the 1750s to the 1790s numbers of private acts rose by 160 per cent, but combined agricultural and industrial prices by 54 per cent. P. K. O'Brien, 'Agriculture and the home market for English industry, 1660–1820', *English Historical Review*, 100.397 (1985), pp. 787–95.

Across the whole period 52 per cent of acts were public, 48 per cent private (7,414 to 6,803). There were two main periods when these proportions diverged. Firstly, the growth of numbers of acts in the generation after the Glorious Revolution was especially because more private acts were passed, particularly from 1697 to 1714. Private estate acts were particularly numerous then, until the Lords established standing orders in 1705 and 1706 to manage the flow.[34] Secondly, there was a sudden collapse of numbers of private acts in the late 1770s such that through the 1780s public acts were much more common. As will be seen in the next chapter, this was mainly because the volume of enclosure legislation shrank.

Distinguishing between public and private legislation is of limited analytical value. The categories were not consistently applied and do not distinguish governmental from non-governmental legislation. Much more helpful is to distinguish legislation which appears to have been 'general' in intended reach from that which was 'specific', a distinction some at the time effectively made.[35] Put most simply, general measures affected the national and international levels, while specific legislation concerned regional, local, and personal levels. Some general legislation was governmental, but some was not, while specific legislation emanated locally, from individuals, interests, institutions, and administrators. Crucially, while all private acts were 'specific', so were 47 per cent of the 7,414 public acts; specific acts thereby accounted for 72 per cent of all legislation. In part, this was because the success rate of general legislation was significantly lower than for specific legislation. Consequently, as Table 2.1 shows, there were nearly as many failed attempts at general as at specific legislation.

Differences in the success rate for general and specific legislation were fundamental to the legislative revolution. After 1688 that for specific legislation rose quickly, passing 75 per cent for the first time in 1698–9. By contrast, general legislation did not reach that level until 1722–3, even then entering a period of prolonged decline during the years of Walpole's supremacy to a nadir in 1741–2. Parliament generally found it easier to pass specific than general legislation because the smaller scale of issues and interests involved limited the scope and effects of controversy, though as will be seen governmental measures relating to public finances

---

[34] *JHL*, 18 (1705–9), pp. 20 (16 Nov. 1705), 70 (18 Jan. 1706), 105–6 (16 Feb. 1706), 183–4 (18 Dec. 1706).

[35] Ferdinand Pulton and Thomas Manby, *A collection of statutes now in use* (1670). The title page distinguished acts that related to the whole 'Common-Wealth' from those affecting 'Private Persons, Places, or Things'.

Table 2.1 *General and specific legislation, 1660–1800*

	Number	%	Success rate %
General acts	3,927	28	56
Specific acts	10,290	72	73
General fails	3,128	45	
Specific fails	3,897	55	

and external trade came to enjoy very high success rates. Political society in general, and Parliament in particular, had been badly scarred by the revolutions and civil wars of the seventeenth century. For many decades the risks involved in pursuing general legislation acted as a brake on some political ambitions.

This argument can be developed in a final general way by considering the broad subject matter of legislation – the scheme employed is reproduced in Appendix 1.

Table 2.2 shows that the first three categories accounted for nearly two-thirds of the total and of these 86 per cent were specific and only 14 per cent general. By contrast, general legislation was especially dominant in the finance and the armed services categories, giving some sense of the importance of fiscal-military matters to central government, though general legislation also clearly predominated in the categories of law and order and government.

Vital to the legislative revolution, therefore, was the quest for acts from particular persons, places, and interests. Efforts were widely dispersed and largely free of any central initiative – though they had to pass over hurdles arranged centrally. Such legislation was in many respects uncoordinated, a product of the assumptions, imagination, desires, and calculations of individuals and small groups that could vary from place to place and year to year. Even general legislation might emanate from beyond central government, while the distinction between governmental and non-governmental legislation is problematic.[36] It was not simply that government, central and local, had a narrower sense of responsibility then than now, but that its competence and capacity was also fairly circumscribed. Thus, for example, when in 1741 efforts were yet again made to help the woollen industry by regulating trade in its raw material, the

---

[36] Innes, *Inferior politics*, ch. 1; Richard Connors, '"The grand inquest of the nation": parliamentary committees and social policy in mid-eighteenth-century England', *Parliamentary History*, 14.3 (1995), pp. 285–313.

Table 2.2 *Subject matter of acts and fails, 1660–1800 – by numerical rank order*

	Acts and fails	% general	Success rate %
Personal	5,135	1	77
Economy	4,964	32	66
Communications	3,500	6	74
Finance	2,188	87	72
Social issues	1,403	30	51
Law and order	1,242	74	49
Government	1,134	70	49
Religion	800	52	47
Armed services	739	90	73
Misc.	138	70	41
Total	21,243	33	67

Board of Trade, unable to devise effective proposals itself, publicly advertised for help from the public, receiving more than two dozen schemes.[37] Local interests, moreover, could play an important role in consideration of national legislation.[38] In many respects, the eighteenth-century 'state' was dispersed and disaggregated, a flexibility that was a source of great strength, but that caused some developing problems.

That said, the ability to seek legislation was limited by access to time, literacy, information, expertise, connections, and money. Few, whether individuals or groups, had all those to hand and for most people obtaining legislation was unthinkable; unquestionably legislation arose from but also perpetuated and produced profound inequalities. Much legislation had to have a willing MP or peer to introduce the measure into Parliament. As representatives, many, though not all, felt obliged to do so if asked. Even more of a barrier was drafting a bill. It was easy enough to sketch the heads of a bill, but to turn those into credible measures framed in the necessary legal language required a high level of particular and costly expertise. Given the volumes of bills and acts, it was unsurprising that specialist parliamentary draftsmen emerged in the eighteenth century to help with this. Through Sheila Lambert's efforts, Robert Harper is the best known, responsible as he was for 37 per cent of all private acts

[37] *Journal of the Commissioners for Trade and Plantations*, vol. 7 from January 1734–5 to December 1741 (1930), p. 394. See Chapter 7.
[38] Innes, *Inferior politics*, ch. 3; Stuart Handley, 'Local legislative initiatives for social and economic development in Lancashire, 1689–1731', *Parliamentary History*, 9.1 (1990), pp. 14–37.

passed between 1732 and 1762. (His forte was private estate acts, drafting more than a half of those passed in that period.[39]) Almost certainly, the quality of bills improved significantly by 1760, by which point well-established conventions and forms could be drawn on in drafting the numerous bills considered over the rest of the century.

Why Acts?

There were often alternatives to acts. Notably, the crown, church, courts (civil, criminal, and ecclesiastical), and local administrators (especially county, corporation, and parish) were sites of authority used both from within and without; and their authority might do nicely. For example, in Scotland, the Court of Session and the Convention of the Royal Burghs both provided different ways of managing disputes and administering change. In England and Wales, Chancery decrees could amend strong contracts binding estates and robustly endorse enclosure agreements.[40] Similarly, quarter sessions and assizes might require the maintenance of roads and bridges under existing legislation.[41] Likewise, commissioners of sewers had responsibility for maintaining drainage systems. Yet frequently in our period there was a shift to using Acts of Parliament to attain these ends, usually at the behest of local initiatives, albeit sometimes involving the creation of new bodies to administer matters, including enforcement and dispute resolution. Such developments may have been associated for a time with the decline of royal proclamation and civil litigation from the late seventeenth century – though both grew again later in the eighteenth century when numbers of Acts of Parliament surged.[42] An important element of the legislative revolution, therefore, to remove business or responsibility from some older institutions such as Chancery, manor courts, and courts of sewers, but to create some new

[39] Lambert, *Bills and acts*, p. 11.
[40] M. W. Beresford, 'The decree rolls of Chancery as a source for economic history, 1547–c. 1700', *Economic History Review*, 32.1 (1979), pp. 1–10; E. M. Leonard, 'The enclosure of common fields in the seventeenth century', *Transactions of the Royal Historical Society*, 19 (1905), pp. 101–46.
[41] William Albert, *The turnpike road system in England, 1663–1840* (Cambridge, 1972), pp. 14–16; Sidney Webb and Beatrice Webb, *English local government: the story of the king's highway* (1913), chs. 2–3.
[42] C. W. Brooks, 'Interpersonal conflict and social tension: civil litigation in England, 1640–1830', in A. L. Beier, David Cannadine, and James M. Rosenheim, eds., *The first modern society: essays in English history in honour of Lawrence Stone* (Cambridge, 1989), pp. 357–99; Henry Horwitz and Patrick Polden, 'Continuity or change in the court of Chancery in the seventeenth and eighteenth centuries?', *Journal of British Studies*, 35.1 (1996), pp. 24–57.

ones, temporary or permanent. The landscape of authority was considerably complicated in the process.

Part of the attraction of acts was their omnipotence. Famously, in the late seventeenth century John Locke wrote that 'This *Legislative* is not only *the supream power* of the Common-wealth, but sacred and unalterable in the hands where the Community have once placed it'. It was in Parliament, Blackstone later asserted, where 'that absolute despotic power, which must in all governments reside somewhere, is entrusted by the constitution of these kingdoms'.[43] Theoretically, therefore, acts provided the most powerful instruments for the management of society; they could do or require anything, providing the authority to allow, encourage, exempt, prevent, and require. Such authority was certainly not monolithic; it might be imposed on all, or be a device to be used by some. And as we have seen, acts might operate from the national and imperial level to the personal and familial level, and all points in between. In such ways, acts were a potent tool to be variously used in many different settings.

What gave acts power was partly a deep reverence for parliamentary supremacy and the rule of law, partly that the processes of turning bills into acts involved publicly negotiating private rights and public interests. Those negotiations mattered hugely in building legitimacy. Proposals were often opposed, at least in part, in many cases leading to their amendment or rejection; as Langford demonstrated, Parliament was highly sensitive to the potential abuse of its power.[44] Scrutiny did not take place only inside Parliament. The requirement that the intention to seek some types of legislation be advertised in advance, or that bills be published, was meant to ensure that interested parties outside Parliament would be not caught unawares and could actively contribute to the legislative process by petitioning, corresponding, meeting, publishing, or giving evidence. As we will see, many did so, to a remarkable extent. Consequently, acts were considered outcomes, having survived a degree of wider examination that heightened their legitimacy. Moreover, even if a bill was wrecked in Parliament, at least that happened within a session usually lasting no more than a few months. Going to court was almost bound to take longer and involve more expense. The situation in Chancery appears to have worsened in the eighteenth century,

[43] John Locke, *Two treatises of government*, ed. Peter Laslett (Cambridge, 1991), p. 356; William Blackstone, *Commentaries on the laws of England* (4 vols., Oxford, 1765–9), vol. 1, p. 156.
[44] Langford, *Public life*, pp. 156–66, though I see Parliament as much less willing to rubber stamp legislative initiatives.

giving substance to Dickens's mid-nineteenth-century depiction in *Bleak house*.[45] By comparison, an act was cheap in time and money.

A final desirable aspect of legislation was that an addition to the statute book had a significant and enduring physicality about it. Acts not only established legal requirements, they announced them. In their work, assize judges, JPs, and grand juries might all note public acts. Copies of bills and acts were pinned to doors and added to libraries. In an era when the press expanded hugely, legislation provided plenty of topics for discussion, in newspapers, periodicals, pamphlets, and books. Sometimes the issues were new, but often they were old, with a new act helping to revive or re-establish an existing position. If many felt that old laws tended to get forgotten, a new one hardly could be. Everyone, including those without property, ignored what Parliament was doing at their peril.[46] Two examples hint at the extent of that. In 1770 Henry Hindley, a textile merchant at Mere, Wiltshire, wrote to a London correspondent requesting a copy of a recent act about a linen bounty. For him, given the potential implications for his business, the fine detail of that act warranted close scrutiny. But this was only part of keeping abreast with what Parliament did; four years later he requested copy of some evidence at a Commons' committee.[47] Doubtless, given his economic and social position, legislation intruded at other times, conversationally at inns and privately via the press. But prospective and actual legislation was highly visible to all. In 1727, the Bristol turnpike trust, just established by act, faced complaints and violence from local colliers who objected to the trust's power to take materials from the commons to repair highways, viewed tolls straightforwardly as a tax that would benefit trustees alone, and believed that the act had simply been bought. They compared unfavourably the new act with still current general Tudor legislation for parish road maintenance, 'an Act of Parliament well grounded with Experienced Actions and Good Authority'.[48] Legislation, past and present, seeped deep into Britain's economic and social landscape.

---

[45] Horwitz and Polden, 'Continuity or change', pp. 53–6.

[46] Innes, *Inferior politics*, ch. 2.

[47] Julia de L. Mann, ed., *Documents illustrating the Wiltshire textile trades in the eighteenth century* (Wiltshire Archaeological and Natural History Society, 19, for 1963 (1964)), pp. 89, 134. Mere is 100 miles from London.

[48] Albert, *Turnpike road system*, pp. 27–8 – and pp. 14–15 for the Tudor legislation; 13 George I, c. 12. The case is explored in detail in Robert Malcolmson. '"A set of ungovernable people": the Kingswood colliers in the eighteenth century', in John Brewer and John Styles, eds., *An ungovernable people: the English and their law in the seventeenth and eighteenth centuries* (1980), pp. 85–127.

Of Acts Few and Many

If it might be argued that what was happening by passing so many acts was a 'progressive refinement' of existing legislation to altered conditions, others doubted this.[49] A central paradox of the legislative revolution was that the proliferation of statutes, slowly after 1688, rapidly after 1750, ran in the face of commonplace sentiments of the benefits of few laws: 'The Happiness of a State, consists in a regular Form of Government, by just and equal Laws, few and plain. ... But such is the Fate of *England*, that the *Laws* are almost *numberless*'.[50] A group of five closely related points questioned the wisdom of too many acts.

A crucial concern was the awareness that to be enforceable laws had to be sufficiently consensual and credible. As Sir William Petty put it, 'Things will not be ill governed'; the natural order (physical and human) was incapable of being bent out of shape by government for long.[51] One MP, objecting to the proposed census in 1753 was clear that

There is a certain limit, beyond which human authority can never be obeyed; to exceed this bound is always to bring authority into contempt, and an effort still to enforce laws, by multiplying penalties, can only provoke indignation and endanger the state. Let the laws therefore be few, such as human power can furnish sufficient motives to keep; the legislature will then preserve its dignity, and the people their independence.[52]

At heart, this was a point about the power of self-interest, in turn often the product of passions, including the pursuit of gain.[53] This was a point made often enough, even before Smith's *The wealth of nations*. In 1769 George Whatley was certain that 'no Laws the Art of Man can devise, will, or can, hinder, or entirely stop the Current of, a gainful Trade.'[54] Legislators were caught in something of a trap here, exclaiming the need for the rule of law or the potential of enactments to develop society, but conscious of the limitations on their authority. A sense of those limitations could be taken to extremes, as in Rousseau's point that 'the first duty of a legislator

---

[49] T. W. Williams, *A compendious digest of statute law, comprising the substance and effect of all the public acts of Parliament in force, from Magna Charta ... to the twenty-seventh year of ... George III* (1787), p. v.

[50] [Thomas Sheridan], *A discourse of the rise and power of parliaments* (1677), p. 37.

[51] Susan Dale, 'Sir William Petty's "ten tooles": a programme for the transformation of England and Ireland during the reign of James II' (Birkbeck College London PhD thesis, 2011), p. 215.

[52] *Gentleman's Magazine*, 23 (1753), p. 501; Hoppit, *Failed legislation*, 91.018.

[53] Albert O. Hirschman, *The passions and the interests: political arguments for capitalism before its triumph* (Princeton, NJ, 1977).

[54] [George Whatley], *Reflections on the principles of trade in general* (1769), p. 4.

is to make laws conform to the general will', but certainly Parliament could not ignore the 'prejudices as well as the interests of a nation'.[55] In eighteenth-century Britain, hostile as most were to the idea of a 'police' (the term was used more generally then than now), unenforced acts were dead letters. As Sir Joseph Banks, President of the Royal Society put it, 'if the will of the legislature cannot be carried into execution, it had better to have never been declared, since futility never fails to beget contempt.'[56]

A second problem of a bloated statute book was that layer upon layer of acts and precedents could generate inconsistencies and confusions. There were long-standing concerns on this score, going back through the frustrated movement for law reform in the mid-seventeenth century to at least Francis Bacon's plans as Lord Keeper to consolidate statutes.[57] From the middle of the eighteenth century there was increasing doubt about the wisdom of having laws that were ignored or administered partially and inconsistently. In 1751 the House of Commons established three committees to try to bring some order to the statute book, without success.[58] Intellectual challenges were also mounted, notably prompted by Beccaria (an English translation was published in 1767) and developed by Bentham from 1776.[59] In 1772 an English version of ideas from the Société Œconomique de Berne stressed that legislation should be harmonious, 'clear, fixed, small in number, and their violation unpardonable. Indulgence or partiality mixing with them, throw the whole into disorder.'[60]

Less government and less legal restraint might also be lauded in certain walks of life. In 1696 Charles Davenant noted that 'They say few laws in a state are an indication of wisdom in a people; but it may be more truly said, that few laws relating to trade are the mark of a nation that thrives by traffic'.[61] This was building on a long-standing suspicion of economic monopolies, whether established by the crown or Parliament, which was

---

[55] Jean Jacques Rousseau, 'Political economy', in *The social contract*, ed. Christopher Betts (Oxford, 1994), p. 12; Lord Holland, in Cobbett, *Parl. Hist.*, 34 (1798–1800), col. 187.

[56] [Joseph Banks], *The propriety of allowing a qualified exportation of wool discussed historically* (1782), p. 67.

[57] David Lieberman, *The province of legislation determined: legal theory in eighteenth-century Britain* (Cambridge, 1989), ch. 9; Alan Cromartie, *Sir Matthew Hale 1609–1676: law, religion and natural philosophy* (Cambridge, 1995); Barbara Shapiro, 'Law reform in seventeenth-century England', *American Journal of Legal History*, 19.4 (1975), pp. 280–312.

[58] Lambert, *Sessional papers*, vol. 1, p. 39. The areas considered were trade, highways, and felonies and the poor law.

[59] [Cesar Beccaria], *An essay on crimes and punishments* (Italian edn., 1764; 1767).

[60] [Jean Bertrand, Benjamin Samuel Georges Carrard, and Gabriel Seigneux de Correvon], *Essays on the spirit of legislation, in the encouragement of agriculture, population, manufactures, and commerce* (1772), p. 18.

[61] Charles Davenant, *The political and commercial works of that celebrated writer Charles D'Avenant*, ed. Sir Charles Whitworth (5 vols., 1771), vol. 1, p. 99.

occasionally important, as in the failure to pass legislation to continue the monopoly of the Royal African Company beyond 1712.[62] More generally, this adds to the points made in Chapter 1 about the prevalence of free trade ideas in the century and a half before Smith's *The wealth of nations*.

Fourthly, the mounting volume of acts posed obvious challenges in terms of ensuring that they were well worded. Those which were not might lead to unintended consequences, or create terrible headaches for courts. The expectation that bills would be carefully scrutinized was fully in place at the start of the Restoration, but was occasionally reiterated in the next century or so.[63] In 1756 Lord Chancellor Hardwicke, as might be expected, decried the increasing role of the Commons in generating public acts. He was sure that the Lords, with its 'learned judges', would not have allowed the current mess to have developed. Allegedly destitute of good advice, the Commons was 'too apt to pass laws, which are either unnecessary, or ridiculous, and almost every law they pass stands in need of some new law for explaining and amending it'.[64] In fact, there were about thirty barristers in the Commons when Hardwicke made his complaint (and there had been seventy-four lawyers in the previous Parliament), but he was right about how many acts were subject to subsequent amendment and clarification, stimulating Sheridan later to mock those bills for 'an act to remedy the defects of the act for explaining the act that amended' the original act.[65]

Finally, the flood of acts raised important questions about keeping abreast of the statute book. One aspect of this was the haphazard promulgation of new acts until the very end of the period. This was critical because so much depended on the work of unpaid, amateur, and unmanaged JPs. As Charles Abbot, MP, noted in 1796, 'The plain fact is this, that the magistrates, who are entrusted with the execution of the laws, have not any correct and speedy means of knowing the laws which they are required to enforce'.[66] This was no small matter, for an enquiry he

---

[62] William Pettigrew, 'Free to enslave: politics and the escalation of Britain's transatlantic slave trade, 1688–1714', *William and Mary Quarterly*, 3rd Series, 64.1 (2007), pp. 3–38.

[63] [Edward Chamberlayne], *Englands wants: or several proposals probably beneficial for England* (1668), p. 45.

[64] Cobbett, *Parl. Hist.*, 15 (1753–65), cols. 728, 740. In 1781 Lord Chancellor Thurlow made a similar complaint: Cobbett, *Parl. Hist.*, 22 (1781–2), cols. 59–60.

[65] John Brooke, 'The House of Commons 1754–1790, introductory survey: members – the lawyers and professional men', *HofP online*; Romney Sedgwick, 'The House of Commons, 1715–1754, introductory survey: appendix 7', *HofP online*; *Edinburgh Monthly Review*, 5 (1821), p. 183.

[66] Quoted in Simon Devereaux, 'The promulgation of statutes in late Hanoverian Britain', in David Lemmings, ed., *The British and their laws in the eighteenth century* (Woodbridge, 2005), p. 80.

chaired identified 4,119 active resident JPs across Britain. It was proposed that less than half of these should receive copies of public general acts, but then nearly 400 copies were to be sent to cities, boroughs, and corporations and more than 1,000 to central authorities, making 3,550 in total.[67] How helpful this reform was might be doubted.

For most of the period, knowledge of new statutes was derived by other means. It was, further, one thing to learn about a new act, quite another to grasp its relationship to previous acts, including those recently expired, and case law. Moreover, given their length acts might also need to be abbreviated or indexed. No one thought that any of this was easy. An important response, and much more numerous than treatises analyzing the law, was to sell collections, digests, abridgements, manuals, and guidebooks.[68] One centuries-old practice was to produce editions of statutes, which necessarily had frequently to be updated. Another which flourished in our period was selections of legislation and other relevant information for particular officers heavily involved in the law, mainly JPs or revenue officers. Burn's manual for JPs, which eventually went through thirty editions after publication in 1755, is the best known of these, but there were many others.[69] Selections might also be made relating to particular areas or questions. These might be major matters, such as the collection of 112 acts relating to the East India Company first published in 1786, or much smaller, such as the eight acts concerning Rochester bridge.[70] By these means, a range of guides to legislation was available through our period, though where their acquisition depended on unpaid individuals obviously some were more willing purchasers than others.

Overwhelmingly, these concerns related to general legislation, understandably so as specific legislation often did not need to be known about beyond a restricted circle. For personal acts, only the individuals or families involved needed to be kept aware. For enclosure, it was the particular community affected who had to be informed of a new act. Many other

---

[67] 'Report from the committee for the promulgation of statutes' (1796), in Lambert, *Sessional papers*, vol. 105, pp. 53–6, 62–3.

[68] For an introduction to the legal treatise, see A. W. B. Simpson, 'The rise and fall of the legal treatise: legal principles and the forms of legal literature', *University of Chicago Law Review*, 48.3 (1981), pp. 632–79.

[69] Richard Burn, *The justice of the peace, and the parish officer* (2 vols., 1755). John Scott, a turnpike trustee, produced a guide to general highway legislation because he found a key act confusingly arranged, indeed contradictory in places: *Digests of the general highway and turnpike laws* (1778), Advertisement.

[70] Anon., *A collection of statutes concerning the incorporation, trade, and commerce of the East India Company* (1786) – an updated edition, acknowledged as being compiled by Francis Russell, was published in 1794; Anon., *A collection of statutes concerning Rochester bridge* (1733).

specific acts similarly posed few problems of promulgation or explanation. But some specific acts had wider consequences. Notably, numerous acts relating to road and river improvement affected many different communities through which they passed, and even more users from wider afield. As has been noted, these improvements often involved passing a series of acts, at least to continue, amend, or explain prior legislation. That is, the growth of the statute book posed problems not simply for those active in central government or local administration, but more widely across society.

Despite worries, the statute book continued to grow into the 1790s and beyond. One factor was the common belief among the political elite that natural tendencies towards disorder – especially because of the power of passions and interests – had to be restrained. Where developing circumstances limited the capacity of the common law to do that, statute law had to step in. More positively, it was widely recognized that certain opportunities could only be seized by providing key actors with the necessary authority. Yet there was general suspicion of the growth of central powers domestically – of the standing army, general excise, census, and police. To take just one broad example, in a debate in the Commons in 1763 two future prime ministers, Pitt the elder and Grenville, both described the excise as 'odious' because of its intrusive nature, despite the fact that it provided central government with so much revenue.[71] Much more palatable was for authority to be strengthened or expanded locally, through both governmental and non-governmental means. Parliament thus passed hundreds of turnpike acts and thousands of enclosure acts in preference to general legislation. The bespoke tailoring of legislation to particular circumstances inflated the statute book enormously, but it was a vital means of keeping central government in check.

Conclusion

Hitherto, our view of the growth of the state after 1688 has been especially influenced by fiscal-military, mercantilist, and nation-state considerations, all of which emphasize the development of central government. But important though they were, they are very misleading when they are privileged for anachronistic or teleological reasons. The growth of the state in the eighteenth century arose from the dynamics of that and earlier periods, not because of what the state was to become in the middle of the twentieth century. Examining the broad dimensions and features

---

[71] Cobbett, *Parl. history*, 15 (1753–65), cols. 1307–8.

of the legislative revolution has brought home the fertility of that society, of a willingness to develop positively in certain directions, and negatively away from others. It is vital that we follow Langford and others to appreciate the full extent of changes wrought to political society after 1688, especially the de-centring of uses of political power, even if we should not be as categorical as Sir John Bowring's observation to Tocqueville in 1833 that 'Decentralisation is the chief cause of the substantial progress we have made in civilisation.'[72]

A fundamental cause of the divisions and destruction of the seventeenth century was the absence of effective lines of communication between central and local powers. Regular meetings of Parliament after 1688 dealt conclusively with that structural flaw, with elections occasionally important, legislation much more so. Legislation provided a key means for addressing problems and seizing opportunities, from the very particular to the impressively general. Proposals often involved organizing and negotiating locally, of defining and cohering interests in ways fundamental to economic and social identity. But a request to Parliament also opened up a connection to London that often drew in many others, especially through petitions and the press. MPs and peers were crucial to those connections, to an extent acting as representatives of often rather differing views. Sometimes those connections were brief, but many acts were links in long chains of legislation, passed over many years. Frequently, such legislation added new institutions to the landscape of governance. If legislation bridged the central-local divisions that had proved so destructive in the seventeenth century, this was because most agreed that Parliament was the best place to settle differences. Increasing numbers of acts, therefore, need to be seen not only in terms of expansion, but in terms of connection and containment.

The legislative revolution did, however, also erode and sometimes swamp. Other forms of authority often sank in stature, utility, and authority. Most obvious was the reduction of monarchical independence and power, including of the court and Privy Council. Certainly this was under way before 1688, as the Restoration of Charles II in 1660 had been far from complete: the French ambassador had noted that the English form of government was 'very far from being a monarchy'.[73] Yet as pensioners of France, Charles II and his brother retained sufficient independence frequently to thwart parliamentary government. But with the flight of James II to France in 1688, prerogative power began to shrink

[72] Alexis de Tocqueville, *Journeys to England and Ireland*, ed. J. P. Mayer (1958), p. 62.
[73] Quoted in Christopher Hill, *Reformation to industrial revolution: a social and economic history of Britain, 1530–1780* (1967), p. 107.

considerably. Nor was the monarchy alone in suffering under the weight of growing legislative power. For example, turnpike acts removed some authority from parishes, and enclosure acts from both central and manorial courts. Crucially, however, the growth of legislation did not usually extinguish existing institutions, leading to an even more complex picture that, from the era of the American Revolution, became a key concern of reformers. In our period, however, those concerns made only limited practical headway. The legislative revolution made the state even more multi-layered and many-headed than before. It is in that context that we need to consider in more detail legislation that particularly affected the economy.

3   Legislating Economically

'Trade is the General Concern of this Nation, but every distinct Trade has a distinct Interest. The Wisdom of the Legislative Power consists, in keeping an even hand, to promote all, and chiefly to Encourage such Trades, as increase the Publick Stock, and add to the Kingdoms Wealth, considered as a Collective Body.'

Charles Davenant, 1696[1]

'Sir William Yonge reported from the Committee, who were appointed to enquire into the Laws relating to Trade and Manufactures [that they] have very frequently met and made a considerable Progress in the Enquiry ... but they have found it a much more voluminous Work than they had imagined, though, at the same Time, a very useful and necessary Employment.'

JHC, 1751[2]

If the legislative revolution was unplanned, it nonetheless voiced the hopes, fears, and beliefs of political society, especially its economic preoccupations. While Parliament's patchy and uncertain existence in the Restoration era limited how much could be done by statute to affect economic life, in the legislative revolution which followed the 'economic' predominated, though admittedly that anachronistic category resists precise definition. Drawing the boundaries tightly, between 1689 and 1800 53 per cent of acts, some 7,545, were 'economic'; but including private estate acts raises it to 72 per cent. Either way, Parliament's legislative efforts in the period were mainly given over to economic questions.

Hitherto, historians have explored only aspects of this huge effort. Counts of economic bills and acts between 1660 and 1714 were made by Julian in an unpublished thesis; Bogart and Richardson, building on my earlier work, have surveyed in general terms numbers of acts relating to property rights; and there are excellent studies of some major

[1] *An essay on the East-India-trade* (1696), p. 25.
[2] *JHC*, 26 (1750–4), p. 292 (21 June 1751).

categories of legislation for the whole period.[3] But in the absence of a general quantitative survey of all acts and fails relating to the economy across the whole period, considerable weight has previously been put on examples, raising obvious enough questions about their typicality. Thus, for example, the statutory basis of imperial trade has usually been considered in relation to a few foundational 'navigation acts' in the seventeenth century and a handful of amending acts in the eighteenth, despite the fact that, as will be seen, hundreds of other acts also played a part. If this is understandable, it has led to important features of economic legislation being under-valued or entirely missed. Initially, therefore, this chapter establishes the very broad quantitative contours of all economic legislation – of acts, failures, and success rates. Some attention is then given to the vital distinction between economic legislation that was general (i.e., national or imperial) in scope from that which was specific (i.e., local or personal). This leads in turn to a consideration of the sub-categories of economic legislation, five of which are found to have been especially important. Two of those, public finance and external trade, were mainly general, and their dimensions and main features are then established. This chapter then moves to consider the three main types of specific economic legislation relating to enclosures, turnpikes, and waterways.

What is clear from such statistics is that politics and the economy met at many different points in this period, sought a wide range of ends, and were promoted by a wide array of people, some in government, but most outside. Governmental legislation that can be called 'economic' grew much more numerous after 1760. A surge in economic legislation from private interests began earlier and reached greater heights. In both cases, Parliament did not rubber-stamp proposed legislation; it weighed and judged to accept some and reject others, though with important patterns according to the types of legislation involved.

As with the previous chapter, the aim here is to approach economic legislation comprehensively and systematically, providing some broad contexts and lines of thought within which to place the more detailed studies later in this book. Little attempt is made to judge the importance of economic legislation except in terms of their numbers so as to establish some of the key patterns of success, failure, and subject matter.

---

[3] M. R. Julian, 'English economic legislation, 1660–1714', (London School of Economics MPhil thesis, 1979); Dan Bogart and Gary Richardson, 'Property rights and Parliament in industrializing Britain', *Journal of Law and Economics*, 54.2 (2011), pp. 241–74. Studies of categories of economic legislation will be noted later as appropriate.

Counting Economic Legislation

Sifting and sorting the statute book and journals to identify 'economic' legislation is laborious and somewhat imprecise.[4] But employing the subject scheme described in Appendix 1 there are three major categories of legislation that are obviously economic: 'Economy' includes legislation directly affecting the land, farming, mines, manufactures, and internal and external trade; 'Communications' relates to the road and water infrastructure through which economic activity passed; and 'Finance' includes that concerning money, banking, and public finance. To these three large categories can be added two other small groups of legislation: forty acts from the 'labour' sub-category within 'Social Issues' because of their important labour market implications; and fifty-nine acts about property rights from the 'Law and Order' category because they looked to structure aspects of exchange.[5]

It is important to stress what is not included in the definition of economic legislation employed throughout this book. One especially important omission is legislation regarding the armed services, which did have an economic dimension to it: substantial public expenditure was directed towards the armed forces, affecting economic life directly, while such expenditure partly sought to secure economic life, partly to expand Britain's overseas and imperial economies. But legislation about the military was also concerned with many other matters, including dynastic security and the European balance of power, which is why they do not warrant categorizing as economic. Other areas of legislation also had an economic dimension which has been thought to be mainly a secondary consideration: tithes, building regulation, water supply, and the poor law.[6] Private 'Estate' legislation comprise a distinctive and voluminous category with rather more of an economic dimension to them as they usually related to the transmission of property between generations and at marriage, via settlements, wills, and trusts.[7]

---

[4] The definition here differs somewhat from that employed by Julian, who put the number of economy acts 1660–1714 at 638, whereas my total is 645. Julian, 'Economic legislation', pp. 175–6, 201. More importantly, Julian counted as failed attempts at legislation only bills, i.e., measures which obtained at least a first reading in Parliament, whereas the category of 'fails' used in this work is broader. For a discussion, see Hoppit, *Failed legislation*, pp. 2–3.

[5] These are categories 301–3 and 610–19 in Appendix 1. All acts and fails have been given a primary subject code and, where necessary, a secondary one, but in identifying economic legislation only primary codes have been used.

[6] Together these numbered 189 acts, or 1.3 per cent of the total.

[7] S. Lambert, *Bills and acts: legislative procedure in eighteenth-century England* (Cambridge, 1971), ch. 6. I provided a quantitative overview in 'The landed interest and the national interest, 1660–1800', in Julian Hoppit, ed., *Parliaments, nations and identities in Britain*

Table 3.1. *Economic and estate legislation, by sub-period, 1660–1800*

	1660–85	1689–1714	1714–60	1760–1800	1660–1800
Acts					
Economic	165	480	1,546	5,354	7,545
Estates	182	667	813	908	2,570
Other	217	605	1,190	2,090	4,102
All	564	1,752	3,549	8,352	14,217
Annual average number of acts					
Economic	6.3	18.5	41.8	130.6	53.5
Estates	7.0	25.7	22.0	22.1	18.2
Other	8.3	23.2	32.2	51.0	29.1
% Acts					
Economic	29	27	44	64	53
Estates	32	38	23	11	18
Other	38	35	34	25	29
Fails					
Economic	536	683	549	1,597	3,365
Estates	190	249	253	79	771
Other	710	750	480	950	2,890
All	1,436	1,682	1,282	2,626	7,026
% Fails					
Economic	37	41	43	61	48
Estates	13	15	20	3	11
Other	49	45	37	36	41
Success rate, %					
Economic	24	41	74	77	69
Estates	49	73	76	92	77
Other	23	45	71	69	59
All	28	51	73	76	67

The rather large Table 3.1 sets out some of the broad dimensions of economic and estate legislation, both in their own right and in relation to other legislation.

Leaving aside estate legislation, some 10,910 pieces of economic legislation were considered in Parliament in this period (7,545 acts and 3,365 fails), or 51 per cent of the total. But this was unevenly spread

and Ireland, 1660–1850 (Manchester, 2003), pp. 85–90. The most complete survey is now Dan Bogart and Gary Richardson, 'Making property productive: reorganizing rights to real and equitable estates in Britain, 1660 to 1830', *European Review of Economic History*, 13.1 (2009), pp. 3–30, but see also Michael McCahill, 'Estate Acts of Parliament, 1740–1800', in Clyve Jones, ed., *Institutional practice and memory: parliamentary people, records and histories. Essays in honour of Sir John Sainty* (Chichester, 2013), pp. 148–68.

over the whole period: before 1714 less than 30 per cent of all acts were economic, but after 1760 it was 64 per cent. In the Restoration era on average just six economic acts per annum were passed; in the last four decades of the eighteenth century, with the early industrial revolution under way, it was 130, or more than twenty times higher. That is, 71 per cent of economic acts passed between 1660 and 1800 were enacted after 1760. By contrast, in relative terms estate acts peaked markedly in the generation after the Glorious Revolution, but accounted for just 11 per cent of legislation after 1760.

Such counts of economic acts are a little misleading, however, for whereas across the whole period 91 per cent of non-economic acts were 'new', for economic acts it was only 73 per cent – with 27 per cent explicitly amending, continuing, explaining, or repealing prior legislation. As will become clear, such chains of legislation were especially important to a number of different sub-categories of economic acts, and not just those concerned with turnpike roads which were initially established for twenty-one years.

The success rate of economic legislation was close to that for 'Other' legislation for all sub-periods save the last when so much economic legislation was not 'new'. But it is also notable that the success rates for estate legislation rose sharply after the Glorious Revolution, but much less so for economic acts. Why that should have been requires considering different types of economic legislation, beginning by distinguishing the general from the specific (see Table 3.2).

Across the whole period specific economic acts outnumbered general acts by two to one, but before 1714 those proportions were reversed. The share of economic legislation that was general was high in the Restoration era, peaked in the 1690s, frequently being more than 80 per cent, but fell away thereafter, usually to be in the range of 20–35 per cent after 1750. Figures 3.1 and 3.2 set out the underlying numbers here.

Absolute numbers of general economic acts grew significantly in the 1690s, to reach a peak of thirty-one in the session 1697–8, a level not surpassed until 1765 (thirty-two). Numbers of such acts began to grow noticeably from the late 1740s, with a spurt in the early 1760s, a surge in the three sessions 1784–6, and very large numbers in the late 1790s, peaking at seventy-six in 1798–9. Strikingly, 61 per cent of all general economic acts passed between 1660 and 1800 came after 1760.

Specific economic acts were generally not passed in great numbers before the 1740s, with the session of 1748–9 the first to have more than thirty such acts – a level reached for general economic acts in 1697–8. A very significant surge in numbers followed, to reach a peak in 1776–7 of 145, followed by a marked falling away in the American war to a nadir

Table 3.2. *General and specific economic acts, by sub-period, 1660–1800*

	1660–85	1689–1714	1714–60	1760–1800	1660–1800
General economic acts	116	316	520	1,490	2,442
Specific economic acts	49	164	1,026	3,864	5,103
% general	70	66	34	28	32
Annual average number					
General economic acts	4.5	12.2	11.1	36.3	17.3
Specific economic acts	1.9	6.3	21.8	94.2	36.2
General economic fails	356	469	252	344	1,421
Specific economic fails	180	214	297	1,253	1,944
% general	66	69	46	22	42
Success % general economic	25	40	67	81	63
Success % specific economic	21	43	78	76	72

Note: 'general' means measures applying nationally or internationally; 'specific' means personal, local, or regional.

in 1783–4 of only twenty-one, followed by an even more spectacular recovery to another peak in the 1790s when seven sessions had more than 120 such acts each. Seventy-five per cent of all specific economic acts passed between 1660 and 1800 came after 1760. All told, some 75 per cent of the overall growth of economy acts between 1714–60 and 1760–1800 was because the dramatic growth of numbers of specific acts outstripped the significant growth of general acts.

Changing success rates are a part of this picture. Overall, the success rate for specific legislation was significantly higher than for general, mainly because a high success rate was achieved earlier. But in the final sub-period, 1760–1800, when so much general and specific legislation was passed, the former had a higher success rate (81 and 76 per cent, respectively). Overall, numbers of both general and specific economy acts grew somewhat after the Glorious Revolution, but spectacularly in the last four decades of the eighteenth century, when nearly two-thirds of all acts related to the economy (or three-quarters including estate acts). Both national and specific economic interests were seeking legislative authority in huge numbers in the eras of the American, French, and industrial revolutions. To understand why requires exploring just what types of economy acts were involved (see Table 3.3).

Five sub-categories provided 89 per cent of all economic acts: two, external trade and public finance, were overwhelmingly general in scope; the other three were very largely specific acts: land (mostly enclosure),

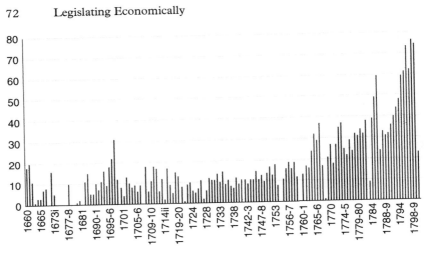

Figure 3.1 General economic acts by session, 1660–1800.

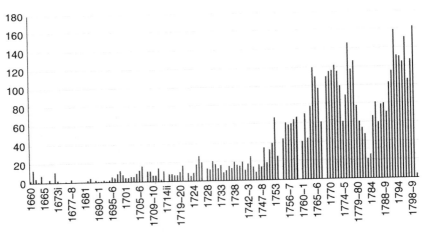

Figure 3.2 Specific economic acts by session, 1660–1800.

road transport (mostly turnpikes), and water transport (mostly river improvement and canals). It should not be forgotten that if not especially numerous, other types of economic legislation might have had especially important implications for Britain's economy – for example, about weights and measures or creditor–debtor relations – but the following discussion will concentrate on the five most numerous sub-categories,

Table 3.3 *Numbers of economic acts by sub-categories and scope, 1660–1800*

Sub-category	General	Specific	Total	% general	% economic acts
Agricultural production	102	21	123	83	2
External trade	477	35	512	93	7
Food and drink	34	3	37	92	0
Internal trade	98	60	158	62	2
Labour	36	4	40	90	1
Land (mainly enclosure)	20	2,307	2,327	1	31
Manufactures*	88	20	108	81	1
Mines and quarries	6	7	13	46	0
Money and banking	205	74	279	73	4
Property law	40	24	64	63	1
Public finance	1,229	62	1,291	95	17
Road transport	77	1,895	1,972	4	26
Water transport	30	591	621	5	8
Grand Total	2,442	5,103	7,545	32	100

* Manufactures includes all areas except food and drink, e.g., textiles, leather, metals, and candles.

beginning with the public finance and external trade legislation before considering the three most common types of specific acts.

Public Finance and External Trade Legislation

At first glance, that nearly 70 per cent of general economy legislation concerned public finances and overseas trade confirms established views about the importance of these areas to both central government and the wider political nation, specifically about the financial revolution in government after the Glorious Revolution and of mercantilist legislation, at least before American independence in 1776. Central government's concerns with power and plenty, well-worn watchwords by 1700, certainly meant that it was active in these areas. But on closer inspection their legislative history suggests modifications to usual accounts, for though rates of such legislation both doubled after 1688, later increases were greater still, while important contrasts in the timing of rising success rates between the two categories hints at differences both in the priorities accorded to each by the executive and the different challenges involved in obtaining legislation in these areas.

Distinguishing between public finance and external trade legislation is inevitably difficult, indeed at times downright artificial: a high customs duty might seek to raise revenue, to reduce imports of a commodity, or a bit of both. As Ralph Davis showed, the 'rise of protection' under the Revolution constitution sometimes reflected contemporary anxieties about domestic manufacturing, the balance of trade, and bullion flows, but it was mainly driven by the revenue needs of the state.[8] While such ambiguities also afflicted other categories of legislation, they were especially important to external trade legislation. Because of this, legislation has where necessary been given both a primary and secondary subject code. Thus, looking only at general economic acts there were 1,229 public finance acts with a primary coding, but another 89 with it as a secondary code. For external trade the numbers were 477 and 170, respectively. By including secondary codes numbers of public finance acts are increased by 7 per cent and external trade acts by 36 per cent – though at the cost of some double counting. In the rest of this section the discussion of these sub-categories is based on these increased numbers.

Even when secondary codes are included, twice as many acts were passed relating to public finance as to external trade. It is clear from Table 3.4 that it was very difficult to obtain enactments in both areas before the Glorious Revolution, but especially regarding external trade where only a quarter of attempts succeeded. After then the success rates for both categories improved. This was earlier and more quickly for public finance, though by the final sub-period around 90 per cent of attempts at legislation in both areas were successful. Indeed, by the end of the eighteenth century both areas enjoyed significantly higher success rates than specific economic legislation.

Table 3.5 provides a more detailed view of changes in numbers of public finance and external trade acts.

Broadly, numbers of general public finance and external trade acts followed similar paths, with a surge in the 1690s followed by a falling off, and then by renewed growth from around 1750. Given the overlap which existed between the two areas this is unsurprising and thus only a little weight should be put on differences in specific timings suggested in Table 3.5, especially of the greater growth of external trade acts from the 1750s to the 1760s, and of public finance acts from the 1770s to 1780s. A little surprisingly, numbers of acts in both of these categories did not clearly rise and fall in relation to periods of war and peace, though clearly the impact of the Nine Years War (1688–97) led to a surge in numbers of

[8] Ralph Davis, 'The rise of protection in England, 1689–1786', *Economic History Review*, 19.2 (1966), pp. 306–17.

Table 3.4. *General public finance and external trade legislation, by sub-period, 1660–1800, using primary and secondary codings*

	1660–85	1689–1714	1714–60	1760–1800	1660–1800
Public finance					
Acts	54	179	279	806	1,318
Acts per annum	2.1	6.9	7.5	19.7	9.3
Fails	76	97	36	66	275
Success rate %	42	65	89	92	83
External trade					
Acts	21	59	104	463	647
Acts per annum	0.8	2.3	2.8	11.3	4.7
Fails	60	95	54	67	276
Success rate %	26	38	66	87	70

Note: the use of primary and secondary codings means that some acts are counted twice, under both public finance and external trade headings. Numbers should not, therefore, be summed.

Table 3.5 *Decennial numbers of general public finance and external trade acts, 1660–1800, using primary and secondary codings*

	Public finance	External trade
1660–88	54	21
1689–99	90	31
1700–9	56	20
1710–19	62	15
1720–9	57	16
1730–9	52	21
1740–9	59	22
1750–9	74	36
1760–9	118	76
1770–9	125	95
1780–9	238	110
1790–9	287	157

Note: the use of primary and secondary codings means that some acts are counted twice, under both public finance and external trade headings. Numbers should not, therefore, be summed.

public finance acts, while later and ever more expensive wars required new taxes, all with a statutory basis. Similarly, the British defeat of the French in North America and India by 1763 led to realignments of external trade regulations, as did the recognition of American independence in 1783.

Table 3.6 *Percentage of general public finance and external trade acts continuing, amending, explaining, or repealing existing acts, by sub-period, 1660–1800 using primary and secondary codings*

	Public finance		External trade	
	Continue, amend, explain	Repeal	Continue, amend, explain	Repeal
1660–85	6	0	20	0
1689–1714	18	0	22	5
1714–60	21	2	20	1
1760–1800	23	4	37	4
1660–1800	21	3	32	3

Note: the use of primary and secondary codings means that some acts are counted twice, under both public finance and external trade headings. Numbers should not, therefore, be summed.

Tables 3.1–3.5 treated all acts as simple additions to the statute book. Yet 'Repeals, Alterations, Amendments and Explanations' afflicted many of them, as Table 3.6 shows.[9]

In both sub-categories, few acts were straightforward repeals. But continuing, amending, and explanatory acts grew significantly for public finance legislation after the Glorious Revolution and surged for external trade legislation in the late eighteenth century. Between 1760 and 1800 there were 184 public finance and 171 external trade acts of these types, suggesting the tentative, piecemeal, and tinkering nature of much legislation in these areas. Thus, for example, seventy-three 'corn laws' were passed between 1660 and 1800, even excluding those simply suspending exports and/or bounties, meaning most fine-tuned prior legislation rather than setting the corn laws on a very different path to the foundational acts of 1673 and 1689.[10] Consequently, much public finance and external trade legislation comprised long chains or involved networks of acts, seeking to modify existing laws but at the danger of creating further complexity, even at times contradiction and confusion. As one Scottish excise commissioner put it in 1790, 'the Revenue Code of this country [Britain], now contains more absurdities and contradictions, than almost any publick record in the world'.[11]

[9] James Earnshaw, *An abstract of various penal statutes relating to the revenue of customs* (2 vols., 1793), vol. 1, pp. v–vi.
[10] Donald Grove Barnes, *A history of the English corn laws, 1660–1846* (1930), pp. 295–6.
[11] [Andrew Hamilton], *An enquiry into the principles of taxation* (1790), p. 211.

Table 3.7 *British population, public finances (using primary and secondary codes), and public finance acts, 1700–1709 to 1790–1799 – percentage growth*

Population	67
GDP	98
Taxes	134
Expenditure	185
Debt	430
Acts	413

Note: Constant prices are used for GDP, taxes, expenditure, and debt. Britain was at war in 1702–13 and 1793–1802.

Source: B. R. Mitchell, *British historical statistics* (Cambridge, 1988), pp. 575–80, 600–1; Julian Hoppit, 'The nation, the state and the first industrial revolution', *Journal of British Studies*, 50.2 (2011), p. 313; P. K. O'Brien, 'Agriculture and the home market for English industry, 1660–1827', *English Historical Review*, 100.397 (1985), pp. 788–9; Steve Broadberry, Bruce M. S. Campbell, Alexander Klein, Mark Overton, and Bas van Leeuwen, *British economic growth, 1270–1870* (Cambridge, 2015), pp. 239–42.

It is helpful to put such trends in a wider context, first of the scale of Britain's public finances and then of overseas trade. Much has rightly been made of the ability of Britain's central government to increase its tax take between 1689 and 1800 to meet the costs of frequent and increasingly expensive wars – through direct expenditure on the military and the support of a national debt that spread the costs of war over time. It is useful, therefore, to compare the scale of changes across the century which were underwritten by public finance acts (Table 3.7).

The figures in Table 3.7 are suggestive of relative changes in general terms only, quite apart from the tentative nature of the underlying statistics. But it is safe to conclude that public finances in the eighteenth century, and of the legislative edifice that supported it, grew much more quickly than population or the economy: people were shouldering a much greater burden on both accounts by the 1790s. It was clearly also the case that numbers of public finance acts grew much more quickly than the tax take and public expenditure, though not of the national debt. These patterns can be refined a little by looking at decade-by-decade figures, though they must be read as doing no more than pointing at broad changes over time, not as changes of a precise or unambiguous 'ratio'.[12] But relating numbers of general public

---

[12] Relating figures in this way is rather artificial, not least because it only considers numbers of acts passed in each decade, not the number of acts that were 'active', which was usually much more.

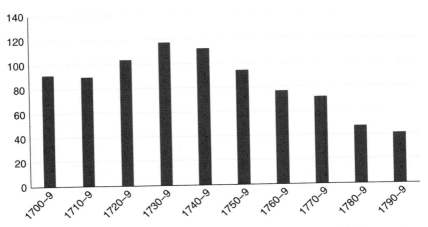

Figure 3.3 Public revenue (£000 constant prices) divided by numbers of general finance acts, 1700–1799.
Source: Mitchell, *British historical statistics*, pp. 575–7

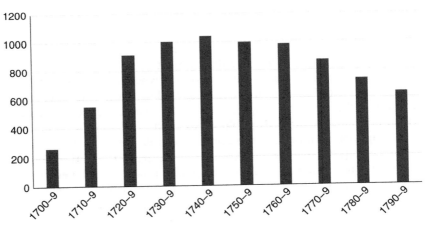

Figure 3.4 Unredeemed national debt (£000 constant prices) divided by numbers of public finance acts.
Source: Mitchell, *British historical statistics*, pp. 600–1

finance acts, again using primary and secondary codes, to amounts of taxes collected and the unredeemed national debt is revealing, as Figures 3.3–3.4 show.

Figures 3.3–3.4 together suggest that public finance legislation passed in the early eighteenth century raised relatively more money than that raised later. That is, the early years of Dickson's 'financial revolution'

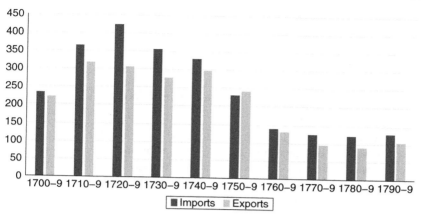

Figure 3.5 Official trade values (£000) divided by numbers of general external trade acts.
Source: note 14

or of Brewer's 'fiscal-military state' required relatively little legislative effort.[13] But after 1760, rising numbers of public finance acts outstripped the amounts raised. Put in questionable terms, the 'productivity' of public finance legislation reached a peak in the period 1730–50, but declined markedly thereafter. In the second half of the eighteenth century there is a clear suggestion that public finance legislation struggled to meet its objectives; 'diminishing returns' had set in.

A similar exercise can be done by relating numbers of general external trade acts, using primary and secondary codes, to the official values of exports and imports into England and Wales – figures for the whole of Britain are unavailable on a consistent or market price basis decade by decade.[14] Between the first and last decades of the eighteenth century imports grew by 333 per cent, exports by 271 per cent, and general external trade acts by 538 per cent. But, as Figure 3.5 shows, decade-by-decade changes were similar to those regarding public finances.

Numbers of public finance and external trade acts grew markedly across the eighteenth century, especially from 1760, both absolutely and in relation to the growth of taxes, national debts, and trade – and much more quickly than Britain's population and economy. In both cases, these

[13] P. G. M. Dickson, *The financial revolution in England: a study in public credit, 1688–1756* (1967); John Brewer, *The sinews of power: war, money and the English state, 1688–1783* (1989).
[14] Elizabeth Boody Schumpeter, *English overseas trade statistics, 1697–1808* (Oxford, 1960), pp. 15–16. Because figures are missing for 1705 and 1712 I have used average figures per decade. The 'official values' applied to goods traded changed little across the period, so are best thought of as reflecting changes in the volume of trade.

vital areas saw a 'thickening' of their statutory basis, albeit one that had usually begun between about 1730 and 1750. Much of this thickening involved extending already intricate networks of acts. The next section offers some explanations for the patterns that have been uncovered.

Understanding Public Finance and External Trade Legislation

Both public finance and external trade legislation raised major questions over the source and direction of key areas of public policy. Because no one doubted their importance, or that they usually had to be considered in national terms, the potential for disagreements between the executive and legislature and between central government and society could never be ignored. To control legislative proposals in these areas was in important respects to control fundamental aspects of the central state, such that the success rate for legislative proposals in these areas provides something of an index both of political tensions in general and of those between the executive and Parliament in particular. Yet clearly, legislative efforts were made at different levels and with different degrees of success between the two areas. How might that be explained?

Passing public finance legislation was usually a more pressing concern of central government than changing the statutory basis of external trade. Money simply had to be found to pay the military as Britain waged its frequent wars, including the repayment of war debts. By contrast, tweaking the navigation laws, a key area of external trade legislation, was rarely a matter of life and death. Moreover, many enactments relating to taxes usually remained in force for only a year or so, in significant part so as to ensure the crown and its ministers had to make annual recourse to Parliament.

Money bills always began in the Commons and the Lords could reject but not amend them. Further, supply bills were never printed so as to minimize pressure from without, while petitions against money bills gradually became prohibited by the early eighteenth century. Business in the Commons was concentrated in two committees of the whole house: Supply and Ways and Means. The former first voted for the money needed by central government, the latter then for the means by which it was to be raised. Chairs of these committees undertook considerable work. Usually holding the post for many years, they gained considerable expertise, acting as important mediators between the Commons and the ministry.[15]

---

[15] P. D. G. Thomas, *The House of Commons in the eighteenth century* (Oxford, 1971), ch. 4. Sir Charles Whitworth was a very well informed and productive chairman of Ways and Means; see pp. 148–9.

Despite such factors, initially the Treasury lacked good control over public finance legislation – though the success rate in this area was consistently higher than other legislation. That was unsurprising in the Restoration era, given the suspicions of mismanagement of crown finance, considerable experimentation in this area (much of it directed by Sir George Downing), and wider political tensions, but it sits awkwardly with current views of the rise of the fiscal-military state from the Revolution.[16] It was certainly important that William III initially refused to appoint a lord treasurer, keeping the department in commission.[17] This allowed proposals for public finance legislation to emanate from various sources, including the floor of the House of Commons, with major problems of co-ordination and control arising. Although in the 1690s some seventy-two public finance acts were passed, including those establishing the Bank of England in 1694 and the national debt, there were forty-five failures (ten in the 1697–8 session alone). This prompted the executive to increase its control over public finance legislation. By 1698 petitions against taxes were disallowed, but it was Godolphin's appointment as lord treasurer for much of Anne's reign (1702–14) that led to the Treasury's grip over this legislative area becoming much firmer.[18] In 1706 the Commons decided to receive money bills only from the executive, turning this into a standing order in 1713; and parliamentary scrutiny of public finance legislation became formulaic.[19] Tellingly, the language of the 'budget', perhaps coined during the excise crisis of 1733, entered common usage in the 1760s.[20] The success rate of general public

[16] Pre-1688 developments are set out in C. D. Chandaman, *The English public revenue, 1660–1688* (Oxford, 1975); Michael Braddick, *The nerves of state: taxation and the financing of the English state, 1558–1714* (Manchester, 1996); Henry Roseveare, 'Prejudice and policy: Sir George Downing as parliamentary entrepreneur', in D. C. Coleman and Peter Mathias, eds., *Enterprise and history: essays in honour of Charles Wilson* (Cambridge, 1984), pp. 135–50. Brewer, *The sinews of* power, emphasized post-1688 developments in tax collection. The birth of the national debt in the 1690s is set out in Dickson, *The financial revolution*. A very good synthesis is Henry Roseveare, *The financial revolution, 1660–1760* (Harlow, 1991).

[17] On the Treasury see S. B. Baxter, *The development of the Treasury, 1660–1702* (1957) and Henry Roseveare, *The Treasury: the evolution of a British institution* (1969). On the pivotal importance of Godolphin's tenure as lord treasurer the best study remains J. G. Sperling, 'Godolphin and the organization of public credit, 1702 to 1710' (University of Cambridge PhD, 1955).

[18] John Hatsall, *Precedents and proceedings in the House of Commons: under separate titles, with observations* (4 vols., 1818), vol. 3, p. 235. A useful discussion of the development of public finance legislation after the Glorious Revolution is D. W. Hayton, 'The House of Commons 1690–1715, introductory survey: the business of the house – the "grand inquest"', *HofP online*.

[19] Many useful points are made in Thomas, *House of Commons*, ch. 4.

[20] [William Pulteney], *The budget opened. Or an answer to a pamphlet intitled, a letter from a Member of Parliament to his friends in the country* (1733); [David Hartley], *The budget* (1764).

finance legislation consequently rose from 62 per cent between 1689 and 1714 to 91 per cent after 1750. Treasury management of public finance legislation came to constitute, therefore, a rare clear area of ministerial and departmental policy making where very few bills were not enacted.[21]

By contrast, it is notable how little general external trade legislation was passed before 1760, just 184 acts in all: annual averages rose from under two before 1760 to eleven thereafter. Ten of the twenty-two sessions in the Restoration era, supposedly a key period of enacting mercantilism, had no general external trade legislation, and even in the 1720s only six of the eleven sessions saw any at all. In fact, this was a complex area of legislation where not until the 1760s did the executive exercise strong control over turning bills into acts.[22] Three major factors help explain this: that what is often put under the umbrella of 'mercantilism' actually comprised parts that might clash; the uncertain place of external trade within executive and legislative government; and the ways in which overseas trade became embroiled in both party politics – though the same was also true of much public finance legislation before 1714 – and interest group politics.

It is a well-worn commonplace that overseas trade became a major concern of central government in the seventeenth century, with some emphasizing within this the executive's development of 'mercantilist' economic policies aiming at bullion inflows via a positive balance of trade: supposedly exports, domestic manufacture, fisheries, and the carrying trade were to be promoted – sometimes in association with colonies; but obstacles were to be put in the way of imported manufactures and exported raw materials. However, if mercantilist policies had been coherent, cogent, executive led, and consistent with the beliefs of propertied society, then statutes should have been generated relatively easily. Yet the success rate rose more gradually than that for public finance legislation, not reaching high levels until the late eighteenth century. One explanation is, as Coleman repeatedly argued, that mercantilist ideas were less reasoned and hegemonic than is often assumed, such that even if certain objectives were generally acknowledged there was considerable disagreement about how they were to be attained and the different interests involved weighed.[23] Increasingly, contemporaries were confronted

---

[21] Historians have not focused on the legislative history of public finances, but I provide an overview in Julian Hoppit, 'Checking the leviathan, 1688–1832', in Donald Winch and Patrick K. O'Brien, eds., *The political economy of British historical experience, 1688–1914* (Oxford, 2002), pp. 267–94.

[22] For a discussion of mercantile legislation before 1714 see Perry Gauci, *The politics of trade: the overseas merchant in state and society, 1660–1720* (Oxford, 2001), pp. 220–32.

[23] D. C. Coleman, 'Mercantilism revisited', *Historical Journal*, 23.4 (1980), pp. 773–91; D. C. Coleman, 'Editor's introduction', in D. C. Coleman, ed., *Revisions in mercantilism* (1969), pp. 1–18.

by the complexities inherent to legislating on such matters. For example, if merchants wielded the sword of free trade to attack the monopolies of the East India and Royal African Companies, especially between about 1670 and 1714, then landowners and farmers might wonder why the export of raw wool was restricted.

Secondly, the high failure rate of external trade legislation before 1714 suggests that it was not well controlled by central government. Part of the problem was that some aspects fell outside the interests or concerns of the Treasury and Admiralty; departmental responsibility was certainly much clearer in the area of public finances. For example, in the 1740–1 sample session four general external trade acts were passed. Two were driven by worries over domestic food shortages – one halted the export of corn, the other eased the import of food into Scotland from Ireland. These were introduced by the Attorney General and Scottish interests (via Lindsay, MP for Edinburgh), respectively. A third act about silk imports was submitted to the Commons by a Treasury lord (Winnington), but the final act regarding trade with Persia via Russia came from a London alderman (Perry).[24] This gives a good sense of the varied origins, mixed nature, and wide implications of external trade legislation – and it might be noted how none directly related to colonial trade.

Had central government taken more of an initiative with external trade legislation, then perhaps different patterns might have resulted. But it struggled to find the institutional forms with which to approach this vital area. There was significant chopping and changing in the executive committees that considered trade matters before the establishment of the Board of Trade in 1696, the same year that the Inspector General of Customs was created.[25] But that the Board was created by the crown to pre-empt a parliamentary competitor hints at the tensions surrounding the management of overseas trade, while the Commons' own grand committee on trade, formally established at the start of each session, appears not actually to have met after the 1660s.[26] Tellingly, a separate committee to survey economic legislation appointed in March 1751 was overwhelmed by the task (see the quote at the head of this chapter). One reason the Commons may have undertaken this enquiry – probably at

---

[24] 14 George II, c. 3, c. 4, c. 7, and c. 36.

[25] Charles M. Andrews, *British committees, commissions, and councils of trade and plantations, 1622–1675* (Baltimore, 1908); Brian Weiser, *Charles II and the politics of access* (Woodbridge, 2003), ch. 5.

[26] R. M. Lees, 'Parliament and the proposal for a Council of Trade, 1695–6', *English Historical Review*, 54.213 (1939), pp. 38–66; Thomas, *The House of Commons*, p. 268; Kathryn M. Ellis, 'The practice and procedure of the House of Commons, 1660–1714' (University of Aberystwyth PhD thesis, 1993), p. 264. External trade legislation was usually handled by committees of the whole house: Gauci, *The politics of trade*, pp. 227–8.

the behest of Pelham's administration – was because the Board of Trade was mainly concerned with procedural rather than policy matters after 1714, though there were also attempts to refine other areas of the statute book about then.[27]

A third explanation for the difficulties of legislating in the area of external trade is that it became entwined with wider political divisions between 1660 and 1714. One aspect of this was its foreign policy implications, but it also became embroiled in debates over monarchical powers and monopoly rights. In the 1680s, crown support for some companies with monopoly rights, notably the East India and Royal African Companies, made them more attractive to Tories and objects to be attacked by Whigs. These types of divisions remained especially significant until 1714; indeed, if anything their intensity grew, climaxing in debates over the commercial aspects of peace with France in 1713.[28] In such an environment, passing external trade legislation was often painfully difficult. Most significantly, the Royal African Company tried hard but unsuccessfully to obtain statutory authority for its monopoly, its failure aiding the development of the British slave trade.[29] The East India, Hudson's Bay, and Eastland companies all similarly struggled with the legislature in this period.[30] It is notable that with the advent of Whig one-party rule at the accession of George I the number of failed attempts at general external trade legislation fell away dramatically: in the thirteen sessions of Queen Anne's reign (1702–14) there were thirty-one fails, but in the fourteen sessions of George I (1714–27) just six. Here we sense Walpole, prime minister from 1721–42, seeking to avoid confrontation and division by letting sleeping dogs lie.[31]

---

[27] Lambert, *Sessional papers*, vol. 1, p. 39.

[28] D. C. Coleman, 'Politics and economics in the age of Anne: the case of the Anglo–French trade treaty of 1713', in D. C. Coleman and A. H. John, eds., *Trade, government and economy in pre-industrial England: essays presented to F. J. Fisher* (1976), pp. 187–211.

[29] Well discussed in Tim Keirn, 'Monopoly, economic thought, and the Royal African Company', in John Brewer and Susan Staves, eds., *Early modern conceptions of property* (1995), pp. 427–66 and William A. Pettigrew, *Freedom's debt: the Royal African Company and the politics of the Atlantic slave trade, 1672–1752* (Chapel Hill, NC, 2013). There are still points to be gleaned from K. G. Davies, *The Royal African Company* (1957).

[30] There is a large literature here. A good crisp account is provided in Gary Stuart de Krey, *A fractured society: the politics of London in the first age of party, 1688–1715* (Oxford, 1985), pp. 22–5. The party nature of the political contests around overseas trade is very heavily stressed in Steve Pincus, *1688: the first modern revolution* (New Haven, CT, 2009). A more complex picture, stressing the fluid nature of party positions and the importance rather of interests than parties, is offered in Gauci, *The politics of trade*, ch. 6 and Shinsuke Satsuma, *Britain and colonial maritime war in the early eighteenth century: silver, seapower and the Atlantic* (Woodbridge, 2013).

[31] Edward Hughes, *Studies in administration and finance, 1558–1825 with special reference to the history of salt taxation in England* (Manchester, 1934), p. 291.

After 1760 there was a rapid growth in numbers of public finance and external trade acts, with both now experiencing very high success rates. There had been no surge in numbers with the end of the War of the Austrian Succession in 1748, but there was with the end of both the Seven Years War in 1763 and the American War in 1783, along with another surge in the 1790s. Looking initially at public finance legislation, by usual accounts the critical phase of their development lay earlier, reaching a degree of maturity under Walpole's premiership in the 1720s and 1730s. Later developments have by contrast often been ignored.[32] But the difficulties of managing public income and expenditure during and after the Seven Years War (1756–63) were of a wholly new order of magnitude, as were the associated problems of dramatically increased imperial responsibilities. These generated deep worries amongst the political classes, of the imminence of national bankruptcy, of a powerful eruption of smuggling, and of key offices increasingly being turned into sinecures. Critically, pressures were rising both within and outside of central government, sometimes outside of Parliament.

In explaining these patterns it is helpful to pick out key developments that occurred from around the middle of the eighteenth century, looking first at public finance and then at overseas trade. Following Walpole's fall in 1742, Pelham successfully modified key elements of the fiscal state, notably regarding the competitive tendering for loans and the introduction of consols. But he oversaw no great growth in numbers of revenue acts (he died in office in 1754). From 1763, however, numbers grew markedly, to peaks of twenty in the session 1766–7 and thirty-nine in 1785. In the 1750s an average of nearly seven general public finance acts was passed in each session; by the 1790s it was twenty-eight. In the eleven sessions 1790 to 1799–1800, 326 public finance acts were passed, or 25 per cent of the total for the whole period 1660–1800. The sheer volume of such enactments must be stressed, for, quite apart from the enormous strain it put on Parliament, Pitt the younger (prime minister, 1783–1801), the Treasury, and the revenue services, it meant that much of it was very finely grained, if driven by the huge pressure to exploit old sources of revenue better and find new ones. In the session 1795–6, for example, fourteen separate acts were passed relating to inland duties alone, including distinct acts regarding levies on malt, hats, and

---

[32] But not by J. E. D. Binney, *British public finance and administration, 1774–1792* (Oxford, 1958) or Patrick K. O'Brien, 'The political economy of British taxation, 1660–1815', *Economic History Review*, 41.1 (1988), pp. 1–32; P. K. O'Brien, 'Public finance in the wars with France, 1793–1815', in H. T. Dickinson, ed., *Britain and the French Revolution, 1789–1815* (Basingstoke, 1989), pp. 165–87.

dogs. Somehow, duties on horses required four separate acts in this session.[33] Yet these inland duties acts clearly originated from the pinnacle of government; George Rose, Pitt's right-hand man, introduced twelve of them into the Commons, and reported from the committee stage for the other two.[34]

Public finance legislation accumulated mainly in small bits and pieces, often through modifying some existing measure in the hope of allowing taxes to be raised more easily and fully. Britain's central government may have been unusually successful at collecting taxes and contracting national debts, but the legislative effort involved was huge. After 1760 the legislative history of public finances has the air of frantic effort until the introduction of the income tax in 1799 provided a very different solution to funding problems. The growth of the fiscal state did not always overcome its problems readily, and its shortcoming after 1763, not least in terms of widespread evasion and struggles to make ends meet, should be integral, not marginal to its characterization.[35] Thus to try to stamp out smuggling in the Irish Sea in 1765 the British government paid the Duke of Atholl £70,000 to bring the Isle of Man squarely within the British customs system; in his short-lived ministry in 1782–3 Shelburne initiated reforms into several branches of government, including the revenue services; in 1783–4 the House of Commons issued three major reports into revenue fraud and evasion; and in 1787 because of the efforts of Rose, Pitt managed to consolidate many customs and excise duties, significantly simplifying the statute book.[36]

After the end of the Seven Years War in 1763 numbers of external trade acts grew even more quickly. In the four sessions from 1763–4 to 1766–7 there were fifty-three acts passed, whereas in the previous twenty sessions (1745–6 to 1762–3) just forty-nine acts found their way into the statute book. Interpretations of this exceptional legislative effort have

---

[33] 36 George III, c. 1, c. 13, c. 14, c. 15, c. 16, c. 17, c. 19, c. 52, c. 80, c. 84, c. 117, c. 123, c. 124, and c. 125. Similar was the introduction and evolution of the tax on servants. John Chartres, 'English landed society and the servants tax of 1777', in N. Harte and R. Quinault, eds., *Land and society in Britain, 1700–1914: essays in honour of F. M. L. Thompson* (Manchester, 1996), pp. 34–56.

[34] Sample session database.

[35] In this context, we lack adequate studies of smuggling and fraud in the eighteenth century. But see Paul Muskett, 'English smuggling in the eighteenth century' (Open University PhD thesis, 1997) and William J. Ashworth, *Customs and excise: trade, production, and consumption in England, 1640–1845* (Oxford, 2003), parts 3 and 4.

[36] Rupert C. Jarvis, 'Illicit trade with the Isle of Man, 1671–1765', *Transactions of the Lancashire and Cheshire Antiquarian Society*, 58 (1947 for 1945–6), pp. 245–67; 5 George III, c. 26; John Norris, *Shelburne and reform* (1963), especially ch. 12; 'Reports from the committee on illicit practices used in defrauding the revenue', *Reports from Committees of the House of Commons 1715–1800*, vol. 6 (1782–1802); 27 George III, c. 13.

generally focussed on ministers addressing the challenges of managing a significantly enlarged empire, especially because of the defeat of France in Canada and India, and the heavy debts incurred in doing so. As such, within the context of external trade attention has overwhelmingly been on key changes to the navigation system, including their better enforcement. Immediately at the close of the Seven Years War in 1763 pressures mounted from economic interests in Britain and its empire regarding rice, indigo, beaver furs, and whale, seeking modifications to existing regulations and duties.[37] These fed in to the wider constitutional issues raised by attempts by central government in London to raise revenue in the colonies. This surge in legislative activity regarding Britain's imperial economy took place, it is worth noting, just when Smith wrote *The wealth of nations*.[38] Certainly there was important legislation in this area from 1763–7, and one that executive government directed, even if 'Government policy ... lacked consistency of direction.'[39] But a heavy preoccupation with the Atlantic perspective and the origins of the American Revolution has obscured other vital considerations.[40]

It is too easily forgotten that Westminster and Whitehall sought trade and empire not as ends in themselves, but as means of maximizing both plenty at home and Britain's weight within the European balance of power. It is in those contexts that some important changes in the subject matter of general external trade legislation across the period should be noted (see Table 3.8).

The two most significant changes in this table are the rise in the proportion of acts relating to the trade in food and drink (which includes

---

[37] R. C. Simmons and P. D. G. Thomas, eds., *Proceedings and debates of the British parliaments respecting North America, 1754–1783* (6 vols., Millwood, NY, 1982–7), vol. 1, pp. 457–84; Davis, 'The rise of protection', p. 314. A general view is taken in Judith Blow Williams, *British commercial policy and trade expansion, 1750–1850* (Oxford, 1972). See also Stephen Conway, 'British governments, colonial consumers, and continental European goods in the British Atlantic empire, 1763–1775', *Historical Journal*, 58.3 (2015), pp. 711–32.

[38] Smith returned to his hometown of Kirkcaldy in 1766 and probably began writing *The wealth of nations* in earnest then, though some of its key points had been developed in the early 1750s.

[39] J. H. Elliott, *Empires of the Atlantic world: Britain and Spain in America, 1492–1830* (New Haven, CT, 2006), p. 306. Elliott contrasts this with the 'greater coherence of Iberian reformist policy in America'.

[40] Again, the secondary literature on this topic is vast. A standard account is Oliver M. Dickerson, *The navigation acts and the American Revolution* (Philadelphia, PA, 1951). While valuable, it is notable that, in common with many other historians, Dickerson isolates the American colonial component from the wider body of London's efforts to govern trade. His discussion of bounties, for example, ignores the most important, the corn laws, and only briefly notes the second most important relating to sugar, because they were largely irrelevant to colonial North America. See Chapter 8 in this volume.

Table 3.8 *Subjects of general external trade acts, 1660–1800 – per cent in sub-periods*

	1660–1760	1760–1800
General import-export regulations	22	26
Food and drink	29	42
Textiles	25	13
Other raw materials	16	9
Other	8	9
	100	100

tobacco and sugar) and the decline in the proportion of acts about textiles. In significant part the first reflected growing worries over food supplies, both in the short-term context of harvest failure and, with hindsight, the longer-term context of rising population from 1750 beginning to strain domestic agriculture's capacity. The corn laws were a particular bone of contention, but trying to improve food supplies in crisis years required other efforts to be made, which could be legislatively complex and involved. Thus, for example, the session following the terrible harvest of 1766 passed ten external trade acts dealing with different aspects of food supplies, including but not limited to corn.[41] The second major change in Table 3.8 is particularly a function of the shrinking efforts to stimulate the domestic woollen industry, especially by prohibiting or limiting the export of its key raw materials, wool and fuller's earth. As will be seen in Chapter 8, these were especially numerous before 1760, much less common thereafter as legislators became more realistic about what might be attempted, perhaps sensing that the wool industry was of declining relative significance.

An important feature of the growth of external trade legislation is that it came increasingly under the control of the ministry, leading to very high success rates after 1760. In the 1795–6 session, for example, thirteen external trade acts were passed, with seven of them being introduced by George Rose, three by Dudley Ryder, Vice-President of the Board of Trade, and two by the chairman of the Ways and Means Committee which oversaw public finance measures. Only one act appears not to have been governmental, relating to a cotton contract between the East India Company and a businessman.[42] Moreover, as with public finance acts

---

[41] 7 George III, c. 1, c. 3, c. 4, c. 5, c. 7, c. 8, c. 11, c. 12, c. 22, c. 30.
[42] 36 George III, c. 120.

in this session, some of those relating to overseas trade overlapped to a greater or lesser extent: three acts dealt with corn imports (the 1795 harvest had been terrible) and two acts dealt with bounties and drawbacks on re-exported sugar.[43]

Heightened control by the executive over public finance and external trade legislation took place alongside a proliferation of statutes. This was a crucial feature of Britain's political economies, of repeated attempts not only to raise more money and regulate trade better, but to fine-tune existing legislation. Such refinements were necessary both because earlier legislation was not having the desired effect, but also because of the cast of mind of key legislators, anxious not to be too bold or cavalier. Thus a hostile witness polemically said of George Rose, who had such a hand in so many general economic acts at the end of the eighteenth and start of the nineteenth centuries, that 'It was quite absurd that in a country which has produced such a work as the Wealth of Nations, a man of such limited views should have so great an influence upon almost every branch of the economy'.[44]

To conclude this section, six main factors can be identified as crucial to the great growth of public finance and external trade legislation after 1760. Firstly, to provide the funding for increasingly costly wars, through raising taxes and managing the national debt – including measures to tackle smuggling and fraud which successive ministers felt were major problems. Secondly, there were related attempts at reform so as to clarify the statute book in these vital areas, enabling laws to be better known and more easily enforced. These became increasingly necessary as the statute book grew, and such efforts were pushed hard by Shelburne, briefly, and Pitt the younger more significantly. Thirdly, to restructure imperial relations, with regard to both revenue and trade relations. It must be stressed that this was not limited to problems in the Caribbean and North America, but also to those associated with the empire in Asia and, much closer to home, Ireland. Fourthly, population growth from 1750 began to strain domestic food supplies, requiring major legislative efforts following poor harvests. Fifthly, increasing product innovation, both with exports and imports, required frequent redefinitions of commodities to try to ensure public finances did not suffer and that trade regulations remained reasonably meaningful: as Hume noted, 'The continual fluctuations in commerce require continual alterations in the nature of the

---

[43] Corn: 36 George III, c. 3, c. 21, c. 56. Sugar: 36 George III, c. 18, c. 106.
[44] Brian Murphy and R. G. Thorne, 'Rose, George (1744–1818), of Cuffnells, Hants', *HofP online*.

taxes'.[45] Finally, fundamental to the character of legislation in these areas was that it was almost always particular and limited, including temporary acts that were repeatedly revived. In significant part this was an attempt to avoid bitter opposition and division, along with the associated loss of legitimacy that reached its zenith with American independence.

General public finance and external trade acts grew more numerous in two main waves: initially between 1689 and 1714, and then on an even larger scale after 1760. Each wave reflected the growth of executive influence in these legislative areas, to reach exceptionally high levels by the end of the eighteenth century. Even so, it is striking that the executive sought so many acts, such that if general, they were often also narrowly directed and tightly defined. Minor changes of circumstance might thereby create the need for further legislative refinement. Similarly, the navigation laws that structured colonial trade were the subject of frequent minor alterations – such as a new bounty here, a revised duty there – rather than wholesale reconsideration. Part of the reason for such tinkering was because of suspicions of executive authority, but also important was that new acts often sought to improve old ones. Much legislation about public finances and external trade needs, therefore, to be seen in terms of extended chains of statutes, with new links being forged according to changing circumstances, effectiveness, and ambitions. If certainly the product of some general ideas and hopes, much such legislation is better viewed as frequently indulged refinements, a groping towards something that would work.

Specific Economic Legislation

A key feature of the general economic legislation just considered was its success rate of around 90 per cent from 1760. This is hardly surprising given the difficulties of defeating a measure the executive was committed to – which is one reason why the excise crisis of 1733, the cider tax controversy of 1763, and the Anglo–Irish trade treaty of 1785 stand out as exceptional moments of successful domestic opposition.[46] Party loyalties, patronage, political arithmetic, and propaganda might all

---

[45] David Hume, *Essays, moral, political, and literary*, ed. Eugene F. Miller (Indianapolis, IN, 1987), p. 358.

[46] Paul Langford, *The excise crisis: society and politics in the age of Walpole* (Oxford, 1975); Patrick Woodland, 'Political atomization and regional interests in the 1761 parliament: the impact of the cider debates 1763–1766', *Parliamentary History*, 8.1 (1989), pp. 63–89; David R. Schweitzer, 'The failure of William Pitt's Irish trade propositions 1785', *Parliamentary History*, 3.1 (1984), pp. 129–45; Paul Kelly, 'British and Irish politics in 1785', *English Historical Review*, 90.356 (1975), pp. 536–63.

be exploited by the executive to gain their legislative way. By contrast, the powers available to those seeking specific economic legislation were more limited, and their rates of success were lower after 1760, sometimes markedly so. Necessarily, such measures had to be organized and promoted in very different ways, while Parliament's determination that its power not be abused ensured that the plentiful opportunities for opposition were often seized.

As Table 3.2 and Figure 3.2 showed, numbers of specific economy acts grew especially rapidly after 1760, averaging just two a year in the Restoration era, but more than ninety-four from 1760–1800, causing their share of economic legislation to rise from 30 to 72 per cent. In turn, much of this transformation was due to acts about the land, overwhelmingly enclosure, and infrastructure, mainly relating to turnpikes, river improvements, and canal building. But legislating in these three areas did not conform to a common pattern.

Unlike general economic legislation, historians have carefully quantified two of the main aspects of specific economic legislation.[47] In particular, Tate and Turner published definitive studies of enclosure legislation, as did Albert and Pawson of turnpike legislation.[48] Only legislation about waterways has been less systematically studied, though Willan and others have gone much of the way.[49] Even so, some summary statistics must be presented of specific economic legislation to allow meaningful comparisons to be made with figures for general economic legislation.

Obviously, numbers of land and road acts were very much greater than those relating to waterways. However, 54 per cent of road acts continued, amended, explained, or, very occasionally, repealed prior acts. Mainly this was because turnpikes were usually established for only twenty-one years, requiring further legislation even just to prolong them. In clear contrast, only 29 per cent of waterways acts and a trivial 2 per cent of land acts were of this type. It follows that apparently new acts relating to

---

[47] There is a useful count of English road and canal acts for 1701–1830, broken down by regions, in W. T. Jackman, *The development of transportation in modern England* (3rd edn., 1966), p. 743.

[48] W. E. Tate, *A domesday of English enclosure acts and awards*, ed. Michael Turner (Reading, 1978); Michael Turner, *English parliamentary enclosure: its historical geography and economic history* (Folkestone, 1980); William Albert, *The turnpike road system in England, 1663–1840* (Cambridge, 1972); Eric Pawson, *Transport and economy: the turnpike roads of eighteenth century Britain* (1977).

[49] T. S. Willan, *River navigation in England, 1600–1750* (Oxford, 1936); J. R. Ward, *The finance of canal building in eighteenth-century England* (Oxford, 1974); D. Swann, 'The pace and progress of port investment in England, 1660–1830', *Yorkshire Bulletin of Economic and Social Research*, 12.1 (1960), pp. 32–44; David Harrison, *The bridges of medieval England, 1300–1800* (Oxford, 2004).

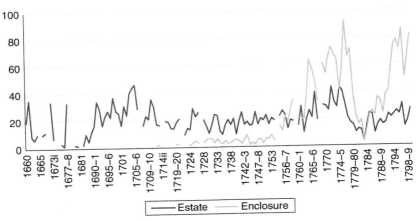

Figure 3.6 Numbers of estate and enclosure acts by session, 1660–1800.

the land (2,253) were nearly double the number of the combined total for roads (876) and waterways (418).

A difficulty in analyzing general economic legislation was the significant overlap between the public finance and external trade subcategories. Though ambiguities were much less significant regarding specific economic legislation, they were not entirely absent. Thus certain river improvement acts, falling under the 'waterways' heading, might have a drainage dimension (which is within the general category of 'land') which only detailed research could identify.[50] (There were in fact 591 specific waterways acts and a further 114 specific acts concerned mainly with issues of land drainage and flooding.) A less obvious overlap may have existed between enclosure and estate legislation, as numbers of acts in these areas after 1760 shown in Figure 3.6 suggests.

What Figure 3.6 shows is that after 1760 ups and downs in numbers of estate acts were similar to the well-known chronology of enclosure enactments – and 34 per cent of all acts (not just economic acts) were either estate or enclosure acts. Private estate acts mainly concerned the webs of contracts which frequently bound landed estates. They dealt with strict settlements, marriage agreements, wills, trusts, and guardianships, often looking to alter legally binding inter-generational arrangements which had been made in increasing numbers since the Restoration. Often they related to indirect inheritances, or allowing sale or reorganization of an estate so as to tackle heavy debts. Critically, they were an alternative to a

[50] These issues are explored in the case study about the fens in Chapter 6.

suit in Chancery, being cheaper, quicker, and more predictable in their outcomes; certainly they enjoyed a very high success rate (see Table 3.1). As Defoe put it, 'an Act of Parliament is *Omnipotent* with respect to Titles and Tenures of Land'.[51] Enclosure, the redistribution of property rights to land within villages usually in pursuit of agricultural improvement and higher rents, had taken place through Chancery in the seventeenth century, but appears to have mainly been undertaken through Parliament from 1750.[52] Likely some enclosure acts were driven by the same causes as estate acts – a need to recast holdings because of altered circumstance – and vice versa – and some estate acts were driven by the desire for lands to be reconfigured so as to extract higher rent, which depended on attaining increased yields. But probably more significant was that both were affected by changes in investor confidence, interest rates, prices, and rates of return that Turner carefully detailed.[53]

Bearing these points in mind, the chronology of enclosure and infrastructure legislation needs briefly to be set out. It is clear from Table 3.9 that relatively little legislation was passed relating to either before 1688 – and not much by 1714. New turnpike legislation briefly became common in the mid-1720s, but the main phase was between 1750 and 1770 (with a century-high peak of thirty-nine acts in 1753), though with another peak in the 1790s (and around 1810 and 1825).[54] Enclosure legislation came later than that for turnpikes. Little was passed before 1750, but a major wave followed, peaking in the 1770s – more than 600 acts were passed in that decade. A deep trough was then reached in the early 1780s, before the second and larger wave set in, with three ever greater peaks about a decade apart from the mid-1790s. By the 1820s the major phase of parliamentary enclosure was past.

Much less waterways legislation was passed, and the category was less homogenous than land and road acts. As Table 3.10 shows, by subject 25 per cent dealt with river navigation, 30 per cent with canals, 20 per cent with bridges and other crossings, and 23 per cent with ports, harbours, and docks.

---

[51] [Daniel Defoe], *An essay upon projects* (1697), p. 109.
[52] Maurice Beresford, 'Habitation versus improvement: the debate on enclosure by agreement', in F. J. Fisher, ed., *Essays in the economic and social history of Tudor and Stuart England in honour of R. H. Tawney* (Cambridge, 1961), pp. 40–69; J. R. Wordie, 'The chronology of English enclosure, 1500–1914', *Economic History Review*, 36.4 (1983), pp. 483–505.
[53] *English parliamentary enclosure*, ch. 5.
[54] The first turnpike was established by act in 1663, the second in 1696. Of the eventual total mileage of turnpike roads, 15 per cent was in place by 1750, but 55 per cent by 1770. Pawson, *Transport and economy*, p. 114.

Table 3.9 *Main types of specific economic legislation, 1660–1800*

	1660–85	1689–1714	1714–60	1760–1800	1660–1800
Land (mainly enclosure)					
Acts	12	6	276	2,013	2,307
Acts p.a.	0.5	0.2	5.9	49.1	16.4
Fails	45	12	47	609	713
Success %	21	33	85	77	76
Roads (mainly turnpikes)					
Acts	2	33	523	1,337	1,895
Acts p.a.	0.1	1.3	11.1	32.6	13.4
Fails	11	33	88	220	352
Success %	15	50	86	86	84
Waterways					
Acts	17	44	139	391	591
Acts p.a.	0.7	1.7	3	9.6	4.2
Fails	45	62	83	261	451
Success %	27	42	63	60	57

Table 3.10 *Numbers of main types of specific waterways acts, by sub-period, 1660–1800*

	1660–85	1689–1714	1714–60	1760–1800	1660–1800
Rivers	10	16	61	58	145
Canals	0	0	2	168	170
Bridges and crossings	1	5	34	76	116
Ports, harbours, and docks	6	19	38	75	138
Total	17	40	135	377	569

Numbers of acts for both crossings and ports increased gradually over the sub-periods, but were still not large by the end of the eighteenth century. Those for rivers grew somewhat, from about one every two years before 1714 to one or two a year thereafter. But it was the well-known explosion of canal legislation that was especially striking, rising rapidly in the 1790s.

As ever, in looking to understand the chronology of specific economic acts it is helpful to distinguish demand-side factors from those affecting Westminster's willingness or ability to turn out acts. For the former, four general elements were crucial: problems associated with the status quo; the financial environment; the challenges of organizing a legislative proposal; and expectations of the likelihood of bills becoming acts.

Problems with the status quo were often most apparent and urgent in the case of deteriorating roads. Under Tudor legislation parishes had a duty to maintain their roads, but this burden could become unbearable with rising use, especially where major roads passed through heavy, ill-drained land. In those cases, parishes could easily feel all the costs and none of the benefits of growing interregional carrying. Similar problems could also lead to the need for new bridges and docks. Slower natural changes could also play a part, most obviously silting could gradually increase pressure for a new navigation or drainage – while drainage could also create new problems through land shrinkage. In all these cases, the limits of the status quo were being reached. Another type of pressure, however, related to the inefficiencies of existing arrangements, a consideration that was especially important in relation to enclosure.

To its proponents enclosure was a means of raising agricultural yields: land and labour could both be used more productively, especially by redistributing land to carve out more compact farms that could integrate arable and pastoral farming better. Fundamental to enclosure was the belief that the existing order was riddled with inefficiencies and hindered potential improvements. Importantly, in the seventeenth century the old association of enclosure with depopulation was refuted by a new wave of writers on agriculture, coinciding with a considerable amount of enclosure by agreement.[55] It is then important to note that the success rate for parliamentary enclosure was 86 per cent between 1714–60, well before it became common; attitudes amongst political society had clearly shifted such that while there was a revival after 1750 of worries that enclosure depopulated, these were passionately rebutted by 'expert' agriculturalists such as Arthur Young and the efforts of the agricultural societies emerging in England.[56]

---

[55] Beresford, 'Habitation versus improvement'.

[56] Goldsmith's attack in his poem 'The deserted village' (1770) was more against the effects of landscape gardens than enclosure. Richard Price made the most important arguments for depopulation. S. J. Thompson, 'Parliamentary enclosure, property, and the decline of classical republicanism in eighteenth-century Britain', *Historical Journal*, 51.3 (2008), pp. 621–42; D. V. Glass, *Numbering the people: the eighteenth-century population controversy and the development of census and vital statistics in Britain* (Farnborough, 1973); Nicholas Goddard, 'Agricultural literature and societies', in G. E. Mingay, ed., *The agrarian history of England and Wales, 6: 1750–1850* (Cambridge, 1989), pp. 361–83. The first agricultural society in England dates from 1772, but by then eleven had been

It need hardly be said that specific economic acts were usually sought for financial reasons, though sometimes also because of a vaguer attachment to the quest for 'improvement' or to keep up with the times. But there were significant costs in obtaining and implementing acts. Bills often required considerable preparation and expense, with costs rising sharply if they encountered opposition, especially in Parliament. Drafting and printing bills, along with parliamentary fees, might be the least of these.[57] Petitions, witnesses, and counsel might need to be organized for the committee stage of a bill. Pamphlets, advertisements, and handbills could all be judged necessary to attempt to sway opinion generally and parliamentarians specifically. Once enacted, much specific economic legislation required the compulsory sale or exchange of property, with infrastructural legislation especially challenging in this regard. Infrastructure and enclosure legislation also entailed significant surveying, building, and maintenance costs. For example, a proposal in the early eighteenth century to make navigable seventeen miles of the River Nene in Northamptonshire was costed at £1,800, to be spent on eight sets of locks, two bridges, the removal of 681 trees, the purchase of land for paths, and dredging.[58]

Expenses were only worth incurring if it was anticipated that they would be outweighed by future income streams. Market conditions obviously affected this, both in terms of the costs involved in implementing an improvement and the prices that could then be charged, such as tolls and rents. Increasing population and prices from about 1750, along with wider economic growth, was clearly important to this. Opportunity costs, the alternative uses to which money might be put rather than investing in a piece of specific economic legislation, were also a consideration. Here the low interest rates of the middle of the eighteenth century may have been especially significant in encouraging investment outside of the usual safe havens for savings.[59] That said, while some of those thinking about specific economic legislation had good market data to hand, others

---

established in Scotland: Brian Bonnyman, 'Agrarian patriotism and the landed interest: the Scottish "Society of Improvers in the Knowledge of Agriculture", 1723–1746', in Koen Stapelbroek and Jani Marjanen, eds., *The rise of economic societies in the eighteenth century: patriotic reform in Europe and North America* (Basingstoke, 2012), p. 50.

[57] Even these could spiral. For example, printing costs for four iterations of a Trent-Mersey canal bill cost £125 in 1766 (6 George III, c. 96), or about ten times the annual wages of an agricultural labourer, according to Joseph Massie: BL, Add Mss 4880, Strahan papers, f. 146v; Peter Mathias, *The transformation of England: essays in the economic and social history of England in the eighteenth century* (1979), p. 187. This was admittedly unusually expensive: Lambert, *Bills and acts*, p. 48.

[58] Northamptonshire Record Office, W(A) Box 4/parcel XIII, no. 9, 'A survey of the river Nine als Nen from Oundle to Allerton mill', n.d.

[59] T. S. Ashton argued for the importance of this to the timing of enclosure legislation in *An economic history of England: the eighteenth century* (1972), pp. 40–1, a thesis considered

surely did not. In any case, limitations of accounting practices gave cost-benefit analyses a fairly speculative element at the time, such that those contemplating such legislation were more likely to be persuaded by evidence of their success elsewhere – the demonstration effect; emulation is always easier than innovation.[60]

The third general factor influencing the demand for specific economic legislation was the capacity of individuals or groups to organize a legislative proposal. While the text of bills was certainly crucial, the wording of many turnpike and enclosure acts became formulaic, with plagiarism no sin. Much more difficult was gathering together the local support – financial, political, and social – to give the measure a good chance of success. This was not as easy for propertied society as might be assumed: identifying potential allies was a challenge, while realizing that potential might require negotiation and treating, as well as guarding against free riders. For parliamentary enclosures, where small numbers of owners were usually involved, who might or might not be an ally was easy enough to discern. For road, bridge, and port improvements, parish, borough, and county obligations also helped to set limits fairly easily. Much harder was organizing groups to take forward schemes which cut across such boundaries and obligations, especially for river improvements, canals, or drainage. A lead might be provided by major landowners, merchants, inland traders, and manufacturers. Towns and cities could also easily see how their well-being depended on better communications. But because such 'improvements' had wide implications, geographically and in terms of the interests involved, many others had to be considered. Nor could they be ignored, for through its standing orders Parliament stood against bills being submitted previously unannounced. Consequently, letters, dinners, and meetings had to be organized and advertisements, plans, and reasons published, all costing plenty of time and money.

In contemplating whether to develop a legislative proposal, specific economic interests had carefully to consider potential opposition, and how Parliament might react should such opposition be voiced there. Such opposition involved conflicts of interest – the canal should run there, not here – or conflicts of principles – canals are a waste of precious land and capital, or some mix of the two. The former were more likely to be expressed in Parliament than the latter. Petitioning Parliament for a specific economic act usually meant that success was expected, but

---

in detail in Turner, *English parliamentary enclosure*, ch. 5. For interest rates and turnpike legislation see Albert, *Turnpike road system*, ch. 6.

[60] For a useful discussion distinguishing phases of turnpike diffusion see Pawson, *Transport and economy*, pp. 111–15. Also Albert, *Turnpike road system*, pp. 117–18.

significant differences in success rates show that those expectations were met much more easily with some types of legislation than with others, as Table 3.11 makes clear.[61]

These figures immediately give the lie to the idea that Parliament always rubber-stamped legislative proposals to advance particular economic interests. Even for road and enclosure, where so many acts were passed, there were more than 900 fails in total. Between 1730 and 1838 Parliament received nearly 5,500 enclosure bills, of which 10 per cent were the subject of counter petitioning and 26 per cent were dropped.[62]

Crudely put, Table 3.11 suggests that it was much more difficult to obtain specific economic legislation involving water than land. Important studies by Willan and Knights have established that river improvement bills were frequently highly controversial, but it is clear that legislating about navigation and drainage more generally was difficult.[63] A key point in explaining this is that in these areas higher numbers of individuals and types of rights were involved. Enclosures, for example, on average redistributed land within just 2.3 square miles.[64] Numbers of landowners involved were often fairly limited – though many other villagers were also bound to be affected, usually adversely, by the changes.[65] Moreover,

---

[61] Occasionally Parliament was formally approached in one session to give notice of a concerted attempt to obtain an act in a later session. In 1795 William Vaughan, who led ultimately successful efforts for an act to build new docks in London, stated that it was intended to introduce but then withdraw a bill 'in order to give a fair discussion to all parties and all interests' so that a better drafted bill could be submitted subsequently. [William Vaughan], *Reasons in favour of the London-docks* (1795), p. 3. This appears to relate to Hoppit, *Failed legislation*, 138.031, which was indeed highly controversial, involving forty-nine petitions.

[62] Michael Turner and Trevor Wray, 'A survey of sources for parliamentary enclosure: the House of Commons' Journal and commissioners' working papers', *Archives*, 19.85 (1991), p. 261; W. E. Tate, 'Members of parliament and their personal relations to enclosure: a study with reference to Oxfordshire enclosures, 1757–1843', *Agricultural History*, 23.3 (1949), pp. 213–20; J. M. Neeson, *Commoners: common right, enclosure and social change in England, 1700–1820* (Cambridge, 1993) is an important study, concentrating on one major area of opposition.

[63] Willan, *River navigation*, pp. 28–51; T. S. Willan, *The early history of the Don navigation* (Manchester, 1965); Mark Knights, 'Regulation and rival interests in the 1690s', in Perry Gauci, ed., *Regulating the British economy, 1660–1850* (Farnham, 2011), pp. 63–81. Between 1700 and 1730 there were 156 petitions against twenty-two river bills: Pawson, *Transport and the economy*, p. 118.

[64] Calculated from Turner, *English parliamentary enclosure*, pp. 176–9 – excluding enclosures under nineteenth-century general enclosure acts.

[65] For a summary of the rich literature about the concerns of villagers (those with common rights and not) see Douglas Hay and Nicholas Rogers, *Eighteenth-century English society: shuttles and swords* (Oxford, 1997), pp. 99–102. Tithe owners were also a potential source of opposition to enclosure. See E. J. Evans, 'Tithes', in Joan Thirsk, ed., *The agrarian history of England and Wales, vol. 5.2, 1640–1750: agrarian change* (Cambridge, 1985), pp. 389–405.

Table 3.11 *Success rate of selected types of specific economic legislation, 1660–1800 – by rank order of success rate*

	Acts	Fails	Success rate %
Road, specific (mainly turnpikes)	1,840	324	85
Enclosure and wastes	2,185	610	78
Bridges and crossings	116	58	67
Canals	170	105	62
Ports, harbours, and docks	138	109	56
Drainage and flooding	114	96	54
Rivers	145	159	48

in enclosure the costs and benefits had little or no indirect consequences for those beyond the area immediately concerned. In contrast, measures for roads, rivers, and canals crossed many miles, involving not only those directly affected, but those further up and down the route.[66] With many people affected, the chances of opposition would have escalated.

Yet had that been all that was at issue, the success rates of road and river legislation should have been similar. One explanation for the marked difference may lie with the greater role of parish and county governments in the turnpike movement, ensuring that before entering Parliament measures were often effectively negotiated by an authority already possessing a reasonable degree of legitimacy. For river improvements and canals, however, newly formed interests, constituted for the purpose, took a leading role, which might indeed be seen as a threat by those in local government. But also critical was that changes to improve navigation could adversely affect water use (riparian rights) for many others, including farmers, millers, fowlers, and fishermen.[67] Parliament could fairly easily judge the probable negative consequences of the route of a turnpike, but river improvements, canals, and drainage usually raised vaguer worries of droughts and floods. As will be seen in Chapter 6, the tortured history of the draining of the fens, stretching from before the 1640s and involving many bills and acts thereafter, may have been especially important here. Initially, even while there was considerable opposition, drainage could be celebrated within the rhetoric of improvement, but it soon led to serious unintended consequences, including land shrinkage, occasional catastrophic flooding, and challenges to the internal navigations on which

---

[66] From 1741–70, new turnpikes averaged around twenty-eight miles in length: Pawson, *Transport and economy*, p. 96.
[67] Joshua Getzler, *A history of water rights at common law* (Oxford, 2004).

the ports of Wisbech and King's Lynn depended.[68] Thus while both road and river legislation experienced success rates of only 25 per cent in the Restoration era, by 1714–60 that for roads was 84 per cent, but for rivers only 57 per cent, levels maintained for both for the rest of the century.

Conclusion

The majority of all statutes passed in this period concerned the economy. In turn, most of these were specific in scope, being sought by particular individuals and interests so as to do something at the personal or local level, sometimes to make money, sometimes to make some improvement of wider benefit, sometimes a bit of both. Collectively numbers of such acts were so great that they profoundly affected society, especially landownership and infrastructure, and while they emanated from across society they might prompt central action, as in Sir John Sinclair's efforts to pass a general enclosure act from the 1790s.[69] For many, enclosure changed once and for all the relationship between villagers and the land and between farmers and landlords, not only economically or financially, but also socially, culturally, and politically. John Clare's poetic laments in the early nineteenth century make that plain enough, all centred on what he called the tyranny of the 'parish state'.[70] Statutes for roads and waterways, by contrast, introduced hundreds upon hundreds of new institutions within society as the communications network developed to serve trade and commerce and further enable its growth, not least interregional and international trade. The politics of local economic life were redrawn through thousands of Acts of Parliament.

Although less numerous there were still thousands of general acts that directly affected economic life, mainly regarding public finances and overseas trade. A key finding of this chapter is that numbers of both came under a high degree of executive control – around 1700 for public finances, but after 1760 for overseas trade – with numbers for both surging dramatically after 1760. Yet though these acts were very numerous, many of them were short-term and/or finely grained measures, while others sought to correct failings in earlier acts – because of poor drafting, altered circumstances, or unsatisfactory compliance. Thus a good deal of effort was of a piecemeal sort, driven by exigencies as much as policy. Still, structural considerations were important, mainly as executive government sought to maintain or

---

[68] H. C. Darby, *The draining of the fens* (2nd edn., Cambridge, 1956); Dorothy Summers, *The great level: a history of draining and land reclamation in the fens* (Newton Abbot, 1976).

[69] Rosalind Mitchison, *Agricultural Sir John: the life of Sir John Sinclair of Ulbster, 1754–1835* (1962), pp. 156–7, 181.

[70] John Clare, *The parish: a satire*, ed. Eric Robinson (Harmondsworth, 1986), p. 62.

improve Britain's place within the European states system. This was a feature through the whole period, but it is notable how many more general economic acts were being passed after 1760, in response to important developments within empire – of gain (in Canada and India) and of loss (America) – as well as changes within Europe. The remarkable surge of such acts in the 1790s bears witness to the efforts of Pitt the younger to meet the challenge posed by Revolutionary France. When he had become prime minister in 1783, Pitt had tried hard to rationalize public finances, including its statutory basis. But the exigencies of war after 1793 overwhelmed the improvements that had been made by a tidal wave of new legislation, culminating in the introduction of the income tax in 1799.

This chapter has concentrated on what Parliament did, through passing acts or rejecting proposed acts. But it is also worth noting areas where little legislation was considered. There was in fact relatively little directly concerning manufacturing or extractive industries. Certainly there was some, notably with regard to the woollen and worsted industries, but generally efforts were few and far between. Various factors were at play here, notably a belief that central government should be little involved in internal affairs, linked to ideas about liberty and that what could best be done was structure overseas trade so as to ensure manufacturers had ready supplies of raw materials and secure access to overseas markets.

Plainly, Parliament was highly responsive to the needs of propertied society generally and executive government particularly. It was capable of handling a vastly increased amount of business to create laws that underwrote taxes, commerce, agriculture, and inland trade. Such openness to the needs of propertied society did not, however, mean that it was uncritical in its handling of legislation. A key finding of this chapter is that it did not simply rubber-stamp such proposals. There were many fails, notably within certain categories of specific economic legislation. Moreover, Parliament was usually cautious about dispensing powers to others: because no general enclosure act was passed in this period landowners had to resort to more expensive bespoke measures; turnpikes were established for twenty-one years, requiring renewal and amendment acts to continue them; and many acts about public finances lapsed after a year, ensuring that the Treasury was a key body seeking general economic acts. That is, while parliamentarians were certain of the supremacy of statutes to the ordering of society, at both the general and specific levels, they preferred to see long chains or involved networks of particular acts to be made rather than clear policies buttressed by a reasonably small number of broader acts that fitted together, sometimes in a rough-and-ready way, to create a greater whole.

4   The Local, National, and Imperial

'The laws ought to vary with the country, and form in their assemblage a system adapted to the circumstances of the times, places, and persons. It is the code of national rules, which ought to be relative to the diversity of soil, climate, productions, character of the inhabitants, nature of the government, to various relations of the state with its neighbours, the extent of the territory, and more or less to the facility of transportation, whether interior or exterior.'

Société Œconomique de Berne, 1772[1]

'The parliament unquestionably possesses a legal authority to *regulate* the trade of Great Britain, and all her colonies. Such an authority is essential to the relation between a mother country and her colonies; and necessary for the common good of all. ... We are but parts of a *whole*; and therefore there must exist a power somewhere, to preside, and preserve the connection in due order. This power is lodged in the parliament; and we are as much dependent on *Great Britain*, as a perfectly free people can be on another.'

John Dickinson, 1767[2]

'[T]he benefit of equal laws has been extended alike to all quarters of the Empire. Compare the series of the Acts of the British Legislature during the progress of this eighteenth century, with the statutes enacted during the seventeenth, by the respective Parliaments of Scotland and England!'

Robert Heron, 1797[3]

A crucial distinction identified in the previous chapter is that in this period only 32 per cent of economic statutes, some 2,442, were general in scope, applying at the 'national' or imperial level. This was a

---

[1] [Jean Bertrand, Benjamin Samuel Georges Carrard, and Gabriel Seigneux de Correvon], *Essays on the spirit of legislation, in the encouragement of agriculture, population, manufactures, and commerce* (1772), p. 5.
[2] *Letters from a farmer in Pennsylvania* (New York, 1768), pp. 8–9.
[3] [Robert Heron], *A letter from Ralph Anderson, esq. to Sir John Sinclair* (Edinburgh, 1797), p. 25.

substantial effort for sure, but 68 per cent of economic legislation, 5,103 acts, were specific, relating to particular places and people. Collectively this was an extraordinary undertaking and an essential component of Britain's political economies. It was not, though, one that was randomly scattered. The key aim of this chapter is to pin down just where economic legislation applied – or what might be called its 'reach'. Doing so makes clear how some parts of Britain were much more heavily involved than others in economic legislation; there was a marked 'patterning' to Britain's political economies. In turn, this leads to several key points: an emphasis on the importance of particular dynamics to the production of so much legislation; rethinking the meaning of 'nation' to Britain's political economies, including the consequences of the Union of 1707; and an appreciation of how particular areas of Britain and its empire could be influenced by legislation generated for different places and under different pressures.

Because economic considerations had become a major 'reason of state' by the early seventeenth century, the application of political power to influence economic life has understandably enough often focused on the nation-state. As the quote from the Société Œconomique de Berne at the head of this chapter shows, the relationship was naturally to be understood as one between the nation-state and the national economy, if one that was also, in the spirit of Montesquieu, influenced by natural circumstances. Adam Smith too, despite building on Hume's criticism of international rivalry in trade, was concerned with establishing the determinants of the wealth of nations.[4] Modern historians have followed these leads. For example, Smith's critique of the 'mercantile system' has usually been rewritten as an attack on 'mercantilism', vaguely defined as an expression of economic nationalism. More widely, works abound about why some nations are rich and others poor, with nations often being viewed as a natural unit for economic analysis, especially when measuring economic growth.[5]

---

[4] '... the narrow malignity and envy of nations, which can never bear to see their neighbours thriving, but continually repine at any new efforts towards industry made by any other nation. We desire, and seem by our absurd politics to endeavour to repress trade in all our neighbours ... the consequence of which must be, that we would have little more than domestic trade, and would have nobody either to sell or buy from us. ... This narrow spirit of nations, as well as individuals, ought carefully to be repressed'. David Hume to Lord Kames, 5 January 1753, *The letters of David Hume*, ed. J. Y. T. Greig (2 vols., Oxford, 1932), vol. 1, p. 272.

[5] Simon Kuznets, 'The state as a unit in the study of economic growth', *Journal of Economic History* 11.1 (1951), pp. 25–41. Work within the regional and global frameworks in recent decades has pointed out the limitations of an exclusive use of the nation as the unit of assessment and analysis. A very useful summary of the regional approach

If many have argued that nation-states have often significantly influenced the performance of national economies, this is because, as Barry Supple observed, it is commonly held that 'Frontiers are more than lines on a map: they frequently define quite distinctive systems of thought and action. The state is, of course, pre-eminently such a system'.[6] Such thinking has fed into several types of explanation of Britain's early industrialization. Particularly relevant here is that some have lauded the early formation of nationhood and national identity in Britain as providing an especially encouraging environment for economic growth.[7] Others have more directly seen the emergence of the British state as especially well-suited to promoting such growth, as in arguments about the large size of the home market, secure property rights, and the use of military might to expand the imperial economy.[8]

Such approaches usually operate at a high level of generalization where, as Ogilvie has observed, clear and verifiable lines of causation are often hard to discern.[9] Moreover, they are invariably concerned with governmental measures only and are usually untroubled by whether the experiences of England and Britain were one and the same under the revolution constitution. Yet nationhood in Britain was very unsettled in this period. In the first place, Britain was developing from a composite monarchy to a composite state of unequal parts.[10] The union of the crowns of England and Scotland in 1603 and of their parliaments in 1707 certainly did not end fundamental differences between the two nations and for most of the period Ireland was looked on rather fearfully

is provided in Pat Hudson, ed., *Regions and industries: a perspective on the industrial revolution in Britain* (Cambridge, 1989). For a recent global approach see Robert C. Allen, *The British industrial revolution in global perspective* (Cambridge, 2009).

[6] Barry Supple, 'The state and the industrial revolution, 1700–1914', in *The Fontana economic history of Europe, vol. 3*, ed. Carlo M. Cipolla (1971), p. 301.

[7] David S. Landes, *The wealth and poverty of nations: why some are so rich and some so poor* (New York, 1998), p. 219; Liah Greenfeld, *The spirit of capitalism: nationalism and economic growth* (Cambridge, MA, 2001), pp. 22–4.

[8] Thomas Sowell, *Conquests and cultures: an international history* (New York, 1998), pp. 32 and 87; Douglass C. North, 'The paradox of the West', in R. W. Davis, ed., *The origins of modern freedom in the West* (Stanford, CA, 1995), p. 8; Douglass C. North and Barry R. Weingast, 'Constitutions and commitment: the evolution of institutions governing public choice in seventeenth-century England', *Journal of Economic History*, 49.4 (1989), pp. 803–32; Niall Ferguson, *The cash nexus: money and power in the modern world, 1700–2000* (2002), p. 20; Ronald Findlay and Kevin H. O'Rourke, *Power and plenty: trade, war, and the world economy in the second millennium* (Princeton, NJ, 2007), pp. xviii–xix.

[9] Sheilagh Ogilvie, '"Whatever is, is right"? Economic institutions in pre-industrial Europe', *Economic History Review*, 60.4 (2007), pp. 649–84. For further reflections on such arguments see Julian Hoppit, 'The nation, the state, and the first industrial revolution', *Journal of British Studies*, 50.2 (2011), pp. 308–13.

[10] J. H. Elliott, 'A Europe of composite monarchies', *Past and Present*, 137 (1992), pp. 48–71.

in England because of its lower labour costs, the strength of its pastoral economy, and supposed higher volume of illicit trade.[11]

National identity was also very uncertain in Britain, and perhaps varied between its nations: certainly in 1750 Sir James Lowther was clear that the Irish and the Scots 'are both more national than the English.'[12] How true that was is impossible to say, but the situation was confused by the fact that 'Britain' and 'England' were often used indiscriminately. For example, copies of the Act of Union of 1707 were quickly distributed to colonial governors, who were told that 'Scotchmen are ... to be looked upon for the future as Englishmen to all intents and purposes whatsoever.'[13] But this was not simply English arrogance and presumption. Many in Europe and America did the same – and still do – and even David Hume, the great Scottish philosopher and historian, thought of himself mainly as Scottish (and a citizen of the world), but in a sense also as English.[14] Self-identification as 'British' made very limited headway in our period, and it is notable that the attempt after 1750 to overcome such difficulties by resorting to the new terminology of North and South Britain made little headway before fizzling out.[15]

Certainly, understanding the great explosion after 1688 of Westminster's statutes affecting economic life must recognize that where these were felt varied considerably, complicated by the fact that on the one hand, Westminster acquired new responsibilities, especially in Scotland after the 1707 Union and in North America and Asia, but then lost some with American independence. It was also the fact that while Westminster was an imperial parliament, confident in its legislative supremacy, it sat alongside other legislative bodies and powerful institutions beyond England, and occasionally within. To some, such as the future 'Founding Father' John Dickinson (at the head of this chapter), Westminster was

---

[11] There is a very large literature here, but see particularly: J. G. A. Pocock, *The discovery of islands: essays in British history* (Cambridge, 2005); Linda Colley, *Britons: forging the nation, 1707–1837* (New Haven, CT, 1992); Steven G. Ellis and Sarah Barber, eds., *Conquest and union: fashioning a British state, 1485–1725* (Harlow, 1995); Glenn Burgess, ed., *The new British history: founding a modern state, 1603–1715* (1999); David Eastwood and Laurence Brockliss, eds., *A union of multiple identities, the British Isles c. 1750–c. 1850* (Manchester, 1997).

[12] Quoted in Christopher A. Whatley, *Scottish society, 1707–1830: beyond Jacobitism, towards industrialization* (Manchester, 2000), p. 118.

[13] *Calendar of state papers, colonial series, 1706–1708, June*, ed. Cecil Headlam (1916), pp. 426–7, 431.

[14] *The letters of David Hume*, vol. 1, p. 470.

[15] Colin Kidd, 'North Britishness and the nature of eighteenth-century British patriotisms', *Historical Journal*, 39.2 (1996), pp. 361–82; Ellen Sallie Filor, 'Complicit colonials: border Scots and the Indian empire, c. 1780–1857' (UCL PhD thesis, 2014), p. 219.

the exactly the place to coordinate the complex and multi-layered nature of applying political power imperially. If he was right about Parliament's importance in expressing and legitimating attempts at the provision of such coherence, he glossed over the fact that the bills to that effect came from various branches of executive government and that this was often done rather haphazardly.[16] The rather chequered history of the Board of Trade brings out well the lack of a clear and consistent line of policy.

In the Restoration period various executive committees had been tried to provide oversight of colonial and overseas trade matters, but with patchy results. In 1696 the crown hurriedly established the Board of Trade to do this, prompted by the fear that Parliament was about to do the same. The Board was notably active in its first decade, when Locke was among its members, but thereafter much of its work was routine rather than strategic; it acted mainly as a clearing house for the correspondence of colonial government. From 1748–61 Lord Halifax provided it with clearer and more ambitious leadership, but its powers were circumscribed in the 1760s and in 1782 it fell victim to Burke's calls for economic reform and was abolished. Only when it was reborn in 1784–6 and led by Charles Jenkinson, committed with Pitt the younger as prime minister to reforming trade laws, did its strategic role become more prominent.[17]

If general economic legislation was often the product of a complex interweaving of various parts of the executive government and different interest groups, specific economic legislation naturally emerged from very varied circumstances, prompted by personal, local, and sometimes regional considerations – there was no English equivalent to the role played by Scotland's Convention of the Royal Burghs, for example. There was no national coordination involved, save the common parliamentary process of turning bills into acts. At the levels of both general and specific legislation, therefore, broad-brush arguments about the relationship between Parliament, nation, and empire are untenable. This

[16] Jacob M. Price, 'Who cared about the colonies? The impact of the thirteen colonies on British society and politics, circa 1714–1775', in Bernard Bailyn and Philip D. Morgan, eds., *Strangers within the realm: cultural margins of the first British empire* (Chapel Hill, NC, 1991), pp. 395–436.

[17] Charles M. Andrews, *British committees, commissions, and councils of trade and plantations, 1622–1675* (Baltimore, 1908); R. M. Lees, 'Parliament and the proposal for a Council of Trade, 1695–6', *English Historical Review*, 54.213 (1939), pp. 38–66; Arthur Herbert Basye, *The Lords commissioners of trade and plantations, commonly known as the Board of Trade, 1748–1782* (New Haven, CT, 1925); Denis Stephen Klinge, 'Edmund Burke, economical reform and the Board of Trade, 1777–1780', *Journal of Modern History* (1979), 51.3 on demand supplement, D1185-1200; Vincent T. Harlow, *The founding of the second British empire, 1763–1793* (2 vols., 1964), vol. 2, chs. 4–5.

chapter, therefore, seeks to build from the bottom up, firstly by examining the record of legislative activity at Westminster affecting the economy relating to England, Scotland, and Wales. This is done by considering both specific and general legislation, but also legislation passed by the Edinburgh and Dublin parliaments before their abolition in 1707 and 1801, respectively. The second main objective of this chapter is to consider economic legislation which sought to influence Britain's empire. Two key points emerge: that the role of central government varied considerably in relation to economic life in England, Scotland, and empire; secondly, that in part this was because of the strength or weakness of local interests in driving forward economic development, in part because of the importance of strategic considerations.

Economic Legislation in England, Scotland, and Wales

Pinning down where economic legislation passed at Westminster applied is much easier for that which was 'specific', relating to particular places, than that which was 'general', relating to nations or internationally. For the 5,103 specific economic acts, 99 per cent stated clearly where they applied; but for the 2,442 general economic acts only 33 per cent did so. That is, only some 804 general economic acts can certainly be said to apply to Africa, America, Britain, England, Scotland, and so on. The 'reach' of the remaining 1,638 general economy acts is uncertain. Reading the text of the acts would reduce this number somewhat, but the fact is that most were held to apply to England and Wales before 1707 and to the whole of Britain after the Union of the Edinburgh and Westminster parliaments. Even so, the situation was not so clear-cut.

Unspoken assumptions – or sloppy drafting – complicated matters. It says much that in 1746, just as Scottish Jacobitism was defeated, it was enacted that statutes said to apply to England alone should actually be read as applying to England, Wales, and Berwick-upon-Tweed.[18] But general legislation apparently applying to the whole of Britain did not necessarily do so. Thus one well-informed survey identified 457 public statutes passed between 1707 and 1754 that were 'in force and use relative to Scotland', out of 1,552 public acts passed at Westminster in that period.[19] That is, 70 per cent of those public acts, many of them seeming

---

[18] 20 George II, c. 42, § 3.

[19] John Swinton, *An abridgment of the public statutes in force and use relative to Scotland* (2 vols., Edinburgh, 1755). This surveyed all public acts, not just those relating to the economy. It has been claimed that between 1727 and 1745 Westminster passed only nine acts dealing 'solely with problems of Scotland as a whole'. But that seems a bit misleading. John Stuart Shaw, *The management of Scottish society 1707–1764: power, nobles,*

to apply across Britain, were not judged actually to do so, presumably because of continuing national differences between the legal systems rendered them irrelevant in Scotland. As has been observed, after 1707 Scotland developed a 'coherent and integrated set of structures, which were often able to shrug off or isolate themselves from London influence'.[20]

National differences in the implementation of legislation are another matter. Chapter 9 explores this in relation to tax collection, but it was also the case that if the Union created the largest free-trade area in Europe, its requirement that English standards of weights and measures be applied across Britain was often ignored until the introduction of the 'imperial system' in 1824. For example, in Scotland corn often continued to be measured not by the Winchester bushel, but by the boll, which varied considerably between Scotland's counties.[21] In a related vein, some legislation that was British in scope might particularly favour English or Scottish economic interests. Bounties, discussed further in Chapter 8, provide several telling examples here. Those on corn were very largely dispensed in southern and eastern England, very little in Scotland; as one informed Scottish commentator complained, the corn laws were poorly adapted to Scotland's environment and circumstances.[22] Rather the reverse was true with regard to bounties on fishing, which again the Union had sought to equalize across Britain: 'British fisheries legislation seems to have privileged Ireland and Scotland through what amounted to regional fiscal subsidies.'[23] Another significant area of difference, albeit arguably more social than economic in its implications, was the poor laws. There were well-known distinctions between England and Wales on the one hand and Scotland on the other, with Anderson judging in this case the advantage lay with Scotland, the poor rates being in his view expensive and productive of idleness.[24] But there was also some

---

lawyers, Edinburgh agents and English influences (Edinburgh, 1983), p. 126. A number of other authors have repeated Shaw's claim.

[20] S. J. Connolly, R. A. Houston, and R. J. Morris, 'Identity, conflict and economic change: themes and issues', in S. J. Connolly, R. A. Houston, and R. J. Morris, eds., *Conflict, identity and economic development: Ireland and Scotland, 1600–1939* (Preston, 1995), p. 2.

[21] Julian Hoppit, 'Reforming Britain's weights and measures, 1660–1824', *English Historical Review*, 108.426 (1993), pp. 82–104.

[22] James Anderson, *Observations on the means of exciting a spirit of national industry: chiefly intended to promote the agriculture, commerce, manufactures, and fisheries of Scotland* (Edinburgh, 1777), p. 372.

[23] Anna Gambles, 'Free trade and state formation: the political economy of fisheries policy in Britain and the United Kingdom, circa 1750–1850', *Journal of British Studies*, 39.3 (2000), p. 292.

[24] Anderson, *Observations*, p. 460. Adam Smith made similar points: *Wealth of nations*, vol. 1, p. 156.

Table 4.1 *National distribution of specific economic acts, 1707–1800*

	Specific acts	Success %	% of specific	% Britain's population	% Britain's territory
England	4,615	74	94	78	56
Scotland	171	74	3	16	35
Wales	118	69	2	6	9

Source: B. R. Mitchell, *British historical statistics* (Cambridge, 1988), pp. 7, 11; R. A. Houston, *The population history of Britain and Ireland, 1500–1750* (Basingstoke, 1992), pp. 29–30; J. Williams, *Digest of Welsh historical statistics* (2 vols., Cardiff, 1985), vol. 1, 6. National shares of Britain's population changed relatively little between 1700 and 1800. Average figures have been used.

variation between parts of Wales and England. In 1770 Welsh circuit judges complained to the Treasury that in the counties of Anglesey and Caernarvon local magistrates were refusing to implement the poor laws, despite 'repeated admonitions'.[25]

Such limitations are crucial to what follows: the reach of general economic acts is very uncertain, but that of specific economic acts is much clearer. Thus counts of economic acts will focus initially on the latter; general acts will be brought back into the discussion subsequently.

As Table 4.1 shows, clearly there was a much greater resort to Westminster by English than by Scottish or Welsh interests, even when taking population or territorial size into account. Low numbers of specific economic acts relating to Scotland and large numbers relating to England stand out particularly clearly. England's population was about five times that of Scotland, but its interests obtained twenty-seven times more specific economy acts. Nor was this the product of Westminster rejecting a higher share of attempts at legislation from Scotland. This is the more striking when the legislative efforts of Edinburgh and Westminster between 1660 and 1707 are compared in Table 4.2.

Before the Union specific economic interests in Scotland made considerable use of the Edinburgh parliament, even if nearly one-half of such acts related to the particular category of the rights to hold markets. If in a sense this confirms the view of the pro-Union Sir John Clerk that 'The grand business of [the Edinburgh] Parliament was generally very

---

[25] TNA, T1/487, f. 314; Joanna Innes, 'The state and the poor: eighteenth-century England in European perspective', in John Brewer and Eckhard Hellmuth, eds., *Rethinking Leviathan: the eighteenth-century state in Britain and Germany* (Oxford, 1999), pp. 225–80; Peter M. Solar, 'Poor relief and English economic development before the industrial revolution', *Economic History Review*, 48.1 (1995), pp. 1–22.

Table 4.2 *Economic acts passed at Edinburgh and Westminster, 1660–1707*

	Economic acts	% general	% all acts
Edinburgh	709	29	32
Westminster	496	69	27

Sources: The acts of the parliaments of Scotland, (12 vols., Edinburgh, 1820–75). See also the online 'Records of the parliaments of Scotland prior to 1707' at www.rps.ac.uk.

triffling', the collective effort involved was clearly considerable.[26] Yet after the Union, Scottish interests made relatively little resort to Westminster.[27]

Nearly all specific economic acts relating to Scotland after 1707 concerned roads and waterways (67 and 26 per cent, respectively). Two features of this need stressing. First, very little such legislation was passed before 1770. Notably, by 1750 237 specific road acts had been passed for England since the Union, but only one in Scotland.[28] This might reflect the fact that Scottish interests were slow to discover the benefits of turning to Westminster for authority, though in fact Scottish appeals to the House of Lords mounted quickly after the Union.[29] But more likely it reflects the weaker local demand for improved road links in Scotland, or possibly of the availability of capital there, though as will be seen there were also variations between England's regions. Growth in parts of Scotland's economy that began to be evident in the 1740s led to a rise in such road acts, numbering fifty-eight in the 1790s (compared to 378 for England). But a second key feature of economic legislation that was specific was the complete absence of enclosure acts in Scotland, whereas in England there were more than 2,000 (including many passed after 1800). Crucial here was that Scottish landowners, 'the most absolute in Britain', could use general enclosure acts passed at Edinburgh in the seventeenth century because the Union left Scottish law largely untouched.[30] English

[26] 'Sir John Clerk's observations on the present circumstances of Scotland, 1730', ed. T. C. Smout, *Miscellany of the Scottish History Society*, 10 (1965), p. 184.

[27] For a wider and more thorough discussion of this point see Joanna Innes, 'Legislating for three kingdoms: how the Westminster parliament legislated for England, Scotland and Ireland, 1707–1830', in Julian Hoppit, ed., *Parliaments, nations and identities in Britain and Ireland, 1660–1850* (Manchester, 2003), pp. 15–47.

[28] 23 George II, c. 17; Henry Hamilton, *An economic history of Scotland in the eighteenth century* (Oxford, 1963), pp. 222–3. See also Ann E. Whetstone, *Scottish county government in the eighteenth and nineteenth centuries* (Edinburgh, 1981), pp. 80–9.

[29] Philip Loft, 'Peers, parliament, and power under the Revolution constitution, 1685–1720' (UCL PhD thesis, 2015), chs. 1–2.

[30] The quotation is from T. C. Smout, 'Scottish landowners and economic growth, 1650–1850', *Scottish Journal of Political Economy*, 9.3 (1962), p. 218; Julian Hoppit, 'The

landowners had no such laws to turn to before the nineteenth century, being required to obtain bespoke legislation. Scottish landowners had far less need to turn to Westminster to reorder their estates than their English counterparts.[31]

Leaving enclosure acts out of counts of specific economic acts narrows the gap in numbers relating to England and Scotland passed after the Union, but it does not close it. On that basis England's share reduces from 94 to 89 per cent of all such acts, still well above its share of Britain's population (see Table 4.1). Obviously English interests had older and closer ties to Westminster, but fundamentally this is to be explained by lower levels of productivity and trade (internal and external) in Scotland and by the availability there of alternative institutions through which to resolve disputes and try to stimulate its economic life, particularly the Convention of the Royal Burghs and the central Court of Session in Edinburgh. In the mid-eighteenth century Lord Kames stressed the benefits of judge-made rather than Parliament-made law to societal development.[32] Before moving on to consider these, a few points should be made about two categories of general economic legislation that were important to Scotland before considering the local distribution of economic acts in sub-national terms.

From the statute book some seventy-six general acts relating to the economy appear to have been directed at Scotland alone between 1707 and 1800, 70 per cent of them after 1760 – 45 per cent in the 1790s alone. In those last four decades, three-quarters of all such acts related to the major category of 'Finance', of which twenty-one were within the sub-category 'Public finance' and seventeen within 'Money and banking'. Although such numbers are not large, this is nonetheless a significant clustering of legislative activity relating to Scotland. Those concerning public finance mainly sought to increase the tax take in Scotland, discussed in more detail in Chapter 9. But those relating to money and banking bear witness to distinctive aspects of the growth of financial services in Scotland, to the growing integration of financial

---

landed interest and the national interest', in Hoppit, ed., *Parliaments, nations, and identities*, pp. 94–5; T. M. Devine, 'The great landowners of lowland Scotland and agrarian change in the eighteenth century', in Sally Foster, Allan Macinnes, and Ranald MacInnes, eds., *Scottish power centres from the early Middle Ages to the twentieth century* (Glasgow, 1998), pp. 147–61.

[31] A 'Committee of Gentlemen' in Scotland pushed forward a general act regarding entailed estates in 1769 and 1770, 10 George III, c. 51. Brian Bonnyman, *The third Duke of Buccleuch and Adam Smith: estate management and improvement in enlightenment Scotland* (Edinburgh, 2014), p. 70.

[32] John Finlay, *The community of the College of Justice: Edinburgh and the Court of Session, 1687–1808* (Edinburgh, 2012), pp. 93–4; David Lieberman, *The province of legislation determined: legal theory in eighteenth-century Britain* (Cambridge, 1989), pp. 162–3.

markets across Britain, to the burgeoning Scottish economy in the last third of the eighteenth century, and to the associated challenges of dealing with the many severe financial crises which occurred after 1763 – the failure of the Ayr bank in 1772 was a key cause of the crisis in that year and took years to clear up.[33] There were, for example, several acts to increase the capital of the Bank of Scotland and to improve the payment of creditors.[34] Following the suspension of cash payments in 1797 three acts were passed in a single parliamentary session regarding note issuing by Scottish banks, a somewhat disorganized effort that was continued and amended by later legislation.[35]

Local Economic Legislation

Though patterns of specific and general economic legislation varied between Britain's three nations, the former also varied within them, sometimes markedly so. This can be explored by looking at the distribution of specific economic acts by counties.[36] At one extreme, some thirty-four counties, all of them in Scotland or Wales, had less than ten each for the whole period. That is, nearly 40 per cent of Britain's counties accounted for only 134 specific economic acts in all, or under 3 per cent of the total. Six Scottish counties had no specific economic acts at all (and five of these had no fails either).[37] At the other extreme, nineteen counties had more than 100 each, all of them in England, as Table 4.3 and Map 4.1 show.

These nineteen counties, under a quarter of all counties, accounted for 3,404 specific economic acts, or 67 per cent of the total of such acts. While all were in England, they were widely scattered: only the far northern counties are absent among England's regions.

Obviously, counties varied in terms of area and population, making simple county totals of specific economic acts of limited use. In

---

[33] S. G. Checkland, *Scottish banking: a history, 1695–1973* (Glasgow, 1973); Richard Saville, *Bank of Scotland: a history, 1695–1995* (Edinburgh, 1995); Julian Hoppit, 'Financial crises in eighteenth-century England', *Economic History Review*, 39.1 (1986), pp. 39–58; Paul Kosmetatos, 'The winding-up of the Ayr bank, 1772–1827', *Financial History Review*, 21.2 (2014), pp. 165–90.

[34] 24 George III, stat. 2, c. 12; 30 George III, c. 5; 32 George III, c. 25, c. 33 George III, c. 74, 34 George III, c. 19; 39 George III, c. 53.

[35] 37 George III, c. 40, c. 62, c. 137. These were followed by 38 George III, c. 2 and 39 George III, c. 10, c. 25, c. 48.

[36] England had forty counties – and London (the contiguous urban area) has also been called a county here; Scotland had thirty-three; and Wales twelve; so a total of eighty-six, including London.

[37] The counties of Banff, Dunbarton, Nairn, Orkney, Shetland, and Sutherland. Dunbartonshire had a solitary fail.

Map 4.1 Map of counties with more than 100 specific economic acts, 1660–1800.

Table 4.3 *Counties in Britain with more than 100 specific economic acts, 1660–1800, in rank order*

Hampshire	106	Somerset	149
London	106	Wiltshire	150
Middlesex	116	Norfolk	155
Oxford	120	Gloucestershire	180
Staffordshire	120	Warwickshire	183
Kent	121	Northamptonshire	184
Worcestershire	129	Leicestershire	191
Nottinghamshire	135	Lincolnshire	305
Devon	148	Yorkshire	657
Lancashire	149		

Note: Yorkshire comprises: West Riding, 262; East Riding, 148; North Riding, 89; whole 158.

particular, it is sensible to take population into account, largely on the grounds that it provides a rough proxy for relative economic size which was obviously an important factor influencing resort to Parliament for specific economic acts. However, this can only be done for England and Scotland, as Wales was treated as a whole in the original source for population estimates before the first census in 1801.[38] Relating numbers of acts (from 1707–1800 only to ensure comparability in the treatment of counties in England and Scotland) to population size puts a rather different complexion on the geography of specific economic acts, for although it confirms that their incidence was indeed very low in the majority of Scottish counties, it also shows that London, Essex, Devon, Middlesex, and Cornwall had less than half the average numbers of acts when related to population size. (Detailed figures are given in Appendix 2.) Low population totals in a number of Scottish counties helped to boost their place in this ranking, such that on this basis Selkirkshire with two acts is above Lancashire with 149. Similarly, Linlithgowshire, the highest ranking

[38] E. A. Wrigley, 'Rickman revisited: the population growth rates of English counties in the early modern period', *Economic History Review*, 62.3 (2009), pp. 711–35; James Gray Kyd, *Scottish population statistics, including Webster's analysis of population 1755* (Edinburgh, 1952). County population figures before the first census in 1801 are imprecise and error margins can only be speculated on. For the English figures see also E. A. Wrigley, *The early English censuses* (Oxford, 2011) and for the Scottish figures Michael Anderson, 'Guesses, estimates and adjustments: Webster's 1755 "census" of Scotland revisited again', *Journal of Scottish Historical Studies*, 31.1 (2011), pp. 26–45. Population figures for English counties are for 1750 and those for Scottish ones 1755. Obviously, this is a snapshot only and the populations of some counties changed significantly between 1660 and 1800.

Table 4.4 *Eleven counties with the highest numbers of specific economic acts relative to population, 1707–1800*

	Population	Acts	Index
	1750	1707–1800	
Huntingdonshire	32,004	66	336
Leicestershire	97,088	190	319
Lincolnshire	163,607	301	300
Rutland	13,251	22	271
Bedfordshire	53,102	85	261
Northamptonshire	116,079	184	258
Nottinghamshire	88,427	135	249
Derbyshire	105,261	148	229
Warwickshire	132,472	183	225
Oxfordshire	94,893	119	204
Yorkshire	521,188	648	203

Note: The index is acts/population expressed as a per cent of the figure for England and Scotland as a whole.
Source: population see note 38.

Scottish county, sat between Staffordshire and Suffolk, though they had 120 specific economic acts each compared to Linlithgowshire's 13.

It is at the extremes that the ranking of an index of acts related to population by county can be read fairly straightforwardly. At the bottom, with under 25 per cent of the average, were twenty-one Scottish counties and, strikingly, London. At the top, with more than 200 per cent of the average, were eleven counties, all in England, listed in Table 4.4.

Differences in success rates played a small part in explaining the markedly uneven geographical spread of specific economic legislation. Most counties had rates close to the average of 78 per cent for the period 1707–1800, but some were notably higher, such as Suffolk with 93 per cent and Buckinghamshire with 90 per cent. But a success rate of 100 per cent, experienced by nine Scottish counties, was not so significant overall as only fifty-five acts were involved in total.

As the previous chapter showed, specific economic acts were mainly given over to enclosures and turnpikes. For economy acts which can be located within particular counties of England and Scotland, 47 per cent concerned enclosure, 37 per cent turnpikes, and 11 per cent water communications, a sub-total of 95 per cent – though it must be repeated that there was no bespoke enclosure legislation for Scotland. Thus the counties in Table 4.4 were those with large numbers of

Table 4.5 *Ten counties with the highest numbers of specific economic acts,
excluding enclosure acts, relative to population, 1707–1800*

	Population	Acts	Index
	1750	1707–1800	
Linlithgowshire	16,829	13	243
Bedfordshire	53,102	40	237
Derbyshire	105,261	69	206
Huntingdonshire	32,004	20	197
Kent	183,701	114	195
Warwickshire	132,472	80	190
Worcestershire	109,703	66	189
Berkshire	92,162	54	185
Sussex	98,376	57	182
Westmoreland	35,468	20	178
Hertfordshire	84,099	45	169

Note and sources: as for Table 4.4.

enclosure and turnpike acts. Tate and Turner have conclusively established the spread of the former, which was particularly concentrated in
a broad area running south and west from Lincolnshire to Oxfordshire.
Just over 20 per cent of England's surface area was enclosed by Acts
of Parliament, some after 1800, and all of the counties in Table 4.4
were above this level, and significantly so save Derbyshire (23 per cent
of which was enclosed by act).[39] For turnpikes, Pawson has shown
that mileage was especially concentrated around London, including a
marked northward 'spur' through Hertfordshire and into Bedfordshire
and Cambridgeshire.[40]

Given the geographical concentration of enclosure legislation, including its complete absence from Scotland, it is worth recalculating the indices in Table 4.4 by leaving enclosure acts out of the counts.

Four counties appear in both Tables 4.4 and 4.5: Bedfordshire,
Derbyshire, Huntingdonshire, and Warwickshire. But the differences
between the tables are more striking, particularly the inclusion of both
Linlithgowshire and Westmoreland. If that largely reflects their relatively small populations, it nonetheless shows that distant counties did

[39] Michael Turner, *English parliamentary enclosure: its historical geography and economic history* (Folkestone, 1980), pp. 180–1.
[40] Eric Pawson, *Transport and economy: the turnpike roads of eighteenth century Britain* (1977),
p. 147.

sometimes turn to Westminster. More striking, though, is that four of the counties in Table 4.5 were close to London: Kent, Berkshire, Sussex, and Hertfordshire and two others, Bedfordshire and Huntingdonshire, had major roads out of London pass through them. All six of those counties had largely agricultural economies, though with rural domestic industry in places (such as lace making in Hertfordshire and Bedfordshire). If they were heavily involved with developments in farming practices, they were certainly not heavily involved in industrial developments. Indeed, only two counties, Derbyshire and Warwickshire, were the site of significant new industrial growth.

If London appears to have exerted some influence on patterns of specific economic legislation in counties nearby, it did not itself turn much to Westminster for legislation relative to population size. It had under a quarter of the average number of acts when population is accounted for; even when enclosure acts are excluded, it had under a half of the average. This is not what one would expect given its economic vitality and importance.[41] In part, but only in part, this was because the success rate of legislation was so low there. Across the whole period 1660–1800 it had 106 acts and 187 fails, and thus a 36 per cent success rate.[42]

Six factors likely explain the capital's distinctive experience of specific economic legislation: that it had a vibrant culture of local, participatory, and often oppositional politics (including linkages between national and local levels); that, related, it had a large number of well-established and articulate interest groups (e.g., guilds, corporations, and charities) who were watchful for any threat to their position; that, similarly, local institutions provided means of acting, thereby reducing the need to turn to Parliament, most obviously the ability of the Court of Common Council to pass acts (essentially by-laws); that it was easier to establish new oppositional interest groups there because of the concentration of people, facilities, and other resources; that opposition in London could more easily utilize the power of the press and lobbying in making its case – not least because of proximity to Westminster and the social haunts of parliamentarians; and, finally, that the subject matter of specific economic legislation in London diverged somewhat from the rest of England, not only in the obvious absence of enclosure legislation, but in a significant amount of failed legislation relating to bankruptcy and debt (usually

---

[41] E. A. Wrigley, 'A simple model of London's importance in changing English society and economy, 1650–1750', *Past and Present*, 37 (1967), pp. 44–70.

[42] For the period 1707–1800 London had ninety-five acts and 117 fails, and thus a success rate of 45 per cent. An index relating population to the sum of acts and fails shows that London still had only 40 per cent of the average for England and Scotland.

imprisoned debtors), company and business law, and that relating to the capital's infrastructure, especially crossing the Thames (bridges and ferrying) and port facilities.[43] Put most simply, London's distinctive economy – its size, structure, complexity, flexibility, and roles (local, regional, national, and international) – melded with a distinctive political culture to produce fewer attempts at legislation than might have been expected and a notably low success rate for those that were.

Managing Scotland's Economy

It is clear that patterns of economic legislation varied notably between and within England and Scotland, with regard to both general and specific measures. In particular, relatively few economic acts applied to Scotland. Yet this underplays the use of political power there to try to increase plenty and wealth. Indeed, the importance of central direction to such efforts marked Scotland's experience as rather different to that of England and Wales. Certainly its integration into the British state after the Union made limited headway until the 1740s, not least because the abolition of the Scottish Privy Council in 1708 removed a body that might have generated policies in London towards Scotland, while in the 1720s and 1730s Walpole made only limited efforts to intervene directly in Scottish affairs. (It also appears that its economy was still struggling within the Union state.[44]) Such relative inaction changed in the 1740s: Walpole's successor, Pelham, made greater efforts to improve central government's oversight of Scotland and Britain's empire. But it was Jacobitism, especially the rising of 1745–6, which really made Westminster and Whitehall take notice of Scotland. Major acts regarding Scotland were passed, but no less important were new ideas for promoting Scotland's economy that emerged from within Scotland and were realized through existing or new Scottish institutions.

In Phillipson's cogent account, the Union initially caused something of a void within Scottish political society through the removal to London of key members of its elite.[45] But social forces were already at work

---

[43] A good overview in this respect remains George Rudé, *Hanoverian London, 1714–1808* (1971). For its local politics, see Nicholas Rogers, *Whigs and cities: popular politics in the age of Walpole and Pitt* (Oxford, 1989). Suggestive points are made in A. G. Olson, 'Parliament, the London lobbies, and provincial interests in England and America', *Historical Reflections*, 6.2 (1979), pp. 367–86.

[44] Philipp Robinson Rössner, 'The 1738–41 harvest crisis in Scotland', *Scottish Historical Review*, 90.1 (2011), pp. 27–63.

[45] He set out his views in a series of essays, summarized in Nicholas Phillipson, *Adam Smith: an enlightened life* (2010), ch. 4. A fine overview of his work, with references to the essays, is Colin Kidd, 'The Phillipsonian Enlightenment', *Modern Intellectual History*, 11.1 (2014), pp. 175–90.

there, building on pro-union sentiments expressed since before 1707, which sought to promote Scotland's economy within a greater British whole. By 1740 'Edinburgh's cultural life was exactly what one would expect to find in a western provincial capital possessing a vigorous, self-consciously modern-minded elite.'[46] A key expression of this, providing fora in which ideas of improvement were generated, were numerous associations, including the Honourable Society of Improvers in Knowledge of Agriculture, founded in 1723, and the Select Society, which included Hume and Smith among its members, founded in 1754.[47] The first of these was ambitious for Scotland to catch up with England economically: 'If we are far behind, we ought to follow the faster'.[48] Yet important though such efforts were, their calls to improve Scotland's economy had to be mediated through interests and institutions to be registered as legislative initiatives at Westminster.

Scottish pro-union sentiment before 1707 focused heavily on the economic benefits of closer links with English markets, but particularly on being able to trade within imperial markets.[49] Terrible harvests in the 1690s and the disastrous attempt of the Darien scheme to establish a colonial presence in Central America exposed major limitations of Scotland's economy.[50] Yet although the Union created a British free-trade zone and allowed Scotland access to imperial markets, its economy struggled for several decades. Some initial difficulties of adjustment had been anticipated. Thus Article 15 of the Union provided £2,000

---

[46] Nicholas Phillipson, 'Towards a definition of the Scottish Enlightenment', in Paul Fritz and David Williams, eds., *City and society in the eighteenth century* (Toronto, 1973), p. 132.

[47] D. D. McElroy, 'The literary clubs and societies of eighteenth-century Scotland, and their influence on the literary productions of the period from 1700 to 1800' (University of Edinburgh PhD thesis, 1952); Davis D. McElroy, *Scotland's age of improvement: a survey of eighteenth-century literary clubs and societies* (Washington DC, 1969); Brian Bonnyman, 'Agrarian patriotism and the landed interest: the Scottish "Society of Improvers in the Knowledge of Agriculture", 1723–1746', in Koen Stapelbroek and Jani Marjanen, eds., *The rise of economic societies in the eighteenth century: patriotic reform in Europe and North America* (Basingstoke, 2012), pp. 26–51.

[48] Robert Maxwell, *Select transactions of the Honourable Society of Improvers in the Knowledge of Agriculture in Scotland* (Edinburgh, 1743), p. 1.

[49] Colin Kidd, *Union and unionisms: political thought in Scotland, 1500–2000* (Cambridge, 2008), ch. 2.

[50] T. C. Smout, 'The Anglo–Scottish Union, 1707, 1: the economic background', *Economic History Review*, 16.3 (1964), pp. 455–67; C. A. Whatley, 'Economic causes and consequences of the Union of 1707: a survey', *Scottish Historical Review*, 68.2 (1989), pp. 150–81; T. M. Devine, 'The Union of 1707 and Scottish development', *Scottish Economic and Social History*, 5.1 (1985), pp. 23–40. The tercentenary of the Union prompted a number of major works, which are well surveyed in Bob Harris, 'The Anglo–Scottish Treaty of Union, 1707 in 2007: defending the revolution, defeating the Jacobites', *Journal of British Studies*, 49.1 (2010), pp. 28–46.

annually for seven years to encourage the woollen industry, fisheries, and other manufactures.[51] This was pretty paltry, but it set the tone for a greater willingness in Scotland than in England to consider centrally funded economic projects.

In such an environment, and with Scotland's economy struggling to grow after 1707, it was hardly surprising that schemes proliferated there for how its economy might be stimulated. In 1718 a further annuity of £2,000 was created, and after 1724 the surplus yield on the malt tax was also to be made available for investment in the economy. This prompted the Convention of the Royal Burghs, which was developing into an important lobbyist for Scottish economic interests, to argue for the funds to be administered by an independent body, leading to the statutory creation of a Board of Trustees for Fisheries and Manufactures in 1727, with an initial budget of £6,000 per annum.[52] Attention soon focused on the linen industry, whose fortunes were significantly enhanced with the introduction of an export bounty in 1742 for British linens, in place (with a brief hiatus in the 1750s) until 1832. The Board expended £236,000 on the linen industry and £150,000 on flax production between 1727 and 1815.[53] Scotland's linen industry prospered under this 'fervent zeal', its output doubling every twenty years from 1730 to 1800.[54]

The considerable attempts to encourage the Scottish fishing industry were rather less successful. Governmental enthusiasm in Scotland for this trade was very apparent between the Restoration and the Union, with several acts passed at Edinburgh, though the Royal Fishery Company established in 1670 was dismantled in 1690. In 1711 the Convention of the Royal Burghs and the Board of Trade in London investigated the Scottish fishing industry, but to little significant effect. From 1727 the Board of Trustees gave out premiums to encourage the Scottish fisheries,

---

[51] It should be remembered that the Union was agreed as a treaty between the two nations, endorsed through acts in both of their parliaments. For the financial aspects of the Union see Douglas Watt, *The price of Scotland: Darien, Union and the wealth of nations* (Edinburgh, 2007).

[52] 13 George I, c. 30; R. H. Campbell, ed., *States of the annual progress of the linen manufacture, 1727–1754* (Edinburgh, 1964), pp. v–vii. We badly need a study of the work of the Convention of the Royal Burghs after the Union, but for some important thoughts see Bob Harris, 'The Scots, the Westminster parliament, and the British state in the eighteenth century', in Hoppit, ed., *Parliaments, nations and identities*, pp. 124–45 and his *Politics and the nation: Britain in the mid-eighteenth century* (Oxford, 2002), p. 63.

[53] A. J. Durie, *The Scottish linen industry in the eighteenth century* (Edinburgh, 1979), pp. 29, 164.

[54] A. M'Donald, *An essay upon the raising and dressing of flax and hemp* (Edinburgh, 1784), p. 2; Alastair J. Durie, ed., *The British Linen Company, 1745–1775* (Edinburgh, 1996), pp. 1–5.

but gave this up in 1742 because of the losses incurred.[55] In 1750 the Free British Fishery Society was created by statute as a public-private venture to try to re-start fisheries, long lauded as a 'great Nursery of Seamen', across Britain, but Scotland particularly.[56] The Society's capital came from private subscriptions, but which were underwritten by bounties for building shipping busses and exporting herring paid out of customs revenue. Initially successful, the Society ran into serious difficulties with the advent of war in 1756.[57] But £647,000 was spent in bounties for the herring fisheries in Scotland between 1765 and 1796.[58]

Both before and after the Union Scottish burghs often gained statutory authority to impose further duties on the sale of beer to help fund urban improvements of various sorts, thereby gaining 'less tightly constricted additions to their disposable funds than English corporations ever did by their local acts'.[59] Not all such funds were spent on projects to improve local economies, notably markets and infrastructure, but a significant amount appears to have been. Moreover, other sources of public funds might be accessed. Thus, for example, the port of Greenock, developed by Sir John Schaw, and opened in 1710 at a cost of £5,555, was paid for via a local tax on ale for thirty years.[60] Rather differently, the Board managing Scottish forfeited estates in the wake of the failed Jacobite rising of 1745–6 loaned money to a number of infrastructure schemes in the second half of the eighteenth century, including £50,000 to the Forth–Clyde canal, becoming thereby something of a regional development agency.[61]

Using confiscated resources to aid economic development points towards an important area of overlap in Scotland between issues of security and economic development. The fundamental point was the challenge posed to central government by Jacobitism, especially among Highland clans. Such opposition involved warfare immediately after the

[55] Bob Harris, 'Scotland's herring fisheries and the prosperity of the nation, c. 1660–1760', *Scottish Historical Review*, 79.1 (2000), pp. 39–60.
[56] 23 George II, c. 24; Huntington Library, Ellesmere papers, EL9609, f. 3.
[57] Bob Harris, 'Patriotic commerce and national revival: the Free British Fishery Society and British politics, c. 1749–58', *English Historical Review*, 114.456 (1999), pp. 285–313.
[58] 'Report respecting the British fisheries' (1798), pp. 218–25, reprinted in Lambert, *Sessional papers*, vol. 118, pp. 506–13.
[59] Joanna Innes, *Inferior politics: social problems and social policies in eighteenth-century Britain* (Oxford, 2009), p. 102. But unlike England and Wales, Scottish towns rarely established improvement commissions by Act of Parliament before the nineteenth century: Bob Harris and Charles McKean, *The Scottish town in the age of the Enlightenment, 1740–1820* (Edinburgh, 2014), pp. 86–7.
[60] David Wilkinson, 'Sir John Schaw, 3rd bt. (?1679–1752)', *HofP* online, 1690–1715; Eric J. Graham, *A maritime history of Scotland, 1650–1790* (East Linton, 2002), p. 319.
[61] Annette M. Smith, *Jacobite estates of the forty-five* (Edinburgh, 1982), p. 211.

Glorious Revolution, two major risings in 1715 and 1745–6, numerous other plots, and a significant resistance to and independence from London. Central government certainly met such challenges with brute force – to persons, property, and ways of life. But such measures could be linked to ambitions to improve Scottish economic life: heightened trade was hoped to render society more pacific and compliant. As is well known, General Wade oversaw the building of 250 miles of military roads in the Highlands before the 1745–6 rising, but less well known is the fact that central government spent £169,000 on Highland roads between 1760 and 1800, well after their military purpose became secondary.[62]

Other measures also melded considerations of security and prosperity with regard to the Highlands, notably in the abolition of heritable jurisdictions in 1748.[63] These were Scottish courts and offices granted by the crown to individuals and effectively owned by them as freeholds to be passed on by inheritance, gift, or sale as they chose. Critics of the jurisdictions asserted that they placed people under a 'slavish Subjection' – the language of liberty was very important here.[64] They argued that there were limited inherent differences between England and Scotland, but that Scots were 'like men with their hands tied behind them'. Once freed from the 'slavish tenures', their natural 'prudence, diligence and frugality' would bear fruit: 'A prospect of wealth and plenty would naturally create industry, which having once taken root, would flourish in that climate.'[65]

Abolishing heritable jurisdictions sought to increase government's control over the machinery of justice in Scotland, cutting the ground from under feudal authorities so as to provide better security for the Hanoverian regime on the one hand and the market economy on the other. Critically, however, abolition was not simply imposed on Scotland. Rather, many owners were compensated, the total bill to British taxpayers amounting to £152,000. If the executive government in London, Lord Chancellor

---

[62] Patrick Colquhoun, *A treatise on the wealth, power, and resources, of the British empire* (1814), p. 228; BPP, 35 (1868–9), p. 448.

[63] 20 George II, c. 43. For a fuller discussion see Julian Hoppit, 'Compulsion, compensation and property rights in Britain, 1688–1833', *Past and Present*, 210 (2011), pp. 108–15. The abolition of heritable jurisdictions was one of a number of acts seeking to pacify the Highlands. See Byron Frank Jewell, 'The legislation relating to Scotland after the Forty-Five' (University of North Carolina PhD thesis, 1975).

[64] Anon., *Superiorities display'd: or, Scotland's grievance, by reason of the slavish dependence of the people upon their great men* (Edinburgh, 1746), p. 11. Similarly, Anon., *An ample disquisition into the nature of regalities and other heretable jurisdictions* (1747), p. 10. For a discussion of such arguments, see Colin Kidd, *Subverting Scotland's past: Scottish Whig historians and the creation of an Anglo-British identity, 1689–c. 1830* (Cambridge, 1993), pp. 150–61.

[65] Anon., *An ample disquisition*, preface, pp. 10, 38–9.

Hardwicke especially, was determined to bring Scotland into line with England in this regard, it was appreciated that such a fundamental redefinition of property rights had to be paid for.

It is clear that the relationship between legislation and economic life differed markedly between England and Scotland, despite the fact that the Union created a single market and put both nations on an equal footing with regard to overseas and imperial trade. In England, thousands of individuals or small interests gained legislation to aid their quest for profit; in Scotland, very few did. But in Scotland direct funding by central government of schemes for economic improvement, loosely defined, was much more significant than in England – though as will become clear in Chapter 8, expenditure on corn bounties in England dwarfed combined expenditure by the government in Scotland on economic development. National and local differences were a critical element of Britain's political economies.

Economic Legislation and Britain's Empire

A vast literature exists about how Westminster and Whitehall sought to manage the development of Britain's overseas empire in this period. Five especially important, long-running, and often interlocking debates have often stimulated this effort: of the nature of the imperial constitution, the utility of the concept of 'mercantilism', the causes of the American Revolution, the contribution of slavery and the slave trade to Britain's early industrialization, and the evolution of the East India Company from a trading enterprise into a territorial power in India.[66] A common feature to these approaches is to look selectively at the role of legislation. Yet it is worth remembering that Adam Smith referred to 255 Acts of Parliament in *The wealth of nations*. With a family background in the customs service, in touch with leading ministers, and himself a Commissioner of Customs in Edinburgh from 1778 until his death in 1790, Smith was well aware of the volume of statutes that had been amassed, especially relating to overseas trade in general, and that of the imperial economy in particular.[67] In that spirit, what follows looks at Westminster's legislative activity as a whole and how that helps in understanding the imperial dimension of Britain's political economies.[68]

---

[66] For an overview see Robin W. Winks, *The Oxford history of the British empire, vol. 5 Historiography* (Oxford, 1999), although much has been published since then, including on important new themes.

[67] Smith, *Wealth of nations*, vol. 2, pp. 1006–8. Far from all of those 255 acts related to overseas and/or imperial trade, but many did.

[68] The value of a more comprehensive view of Westminster legislation regarding empire was briefly considered by Ian K. Steele, 'The British parliament and the Atlantic colonies

As with Scotland, it is far from straightforward trying to identify legislation relating to the imperial economy. A key consideration is that central
government expenditure, all of it based on statutory authority, was fundamental to the use of Britain's military power to gain and guard empire,
formal and not. It should be remembered, therefore, that although public
finance legislation has been categorized as 'economic', that relating to
the army and navy has not. This is further complicated by the fact that it
is impossible to say how much central government expenditure – which
was dominated by spending on the military and the repayment of war
debts – was directed at either imperial or non-imperial ends.[69] Thus if
it is impossible to weigh British military effort in Europe on one side of
the balance, and that on empire on the other, it is also impossible to say
how far the management of public credit, some of it via the East India
Company and the South Sea Company, both certainly imperial enter-
prises, was directed at imperial ends. It is nonsensical, for example, to see
legislation addressing the aftermath of the South Sea Bubble that burst
in 1720 as 'imperial'.

It has long been recognized that the ambitions of power and plenty
were inextricably linked in this period, not least because contemporaries
often stressed it.[70] An editor of Joshua Gee, for example, thought that the
increase of shipping and seamen, so as to be available to the Royal Navy
in wartime, was a more important objective of much legislation regarding
overseas commerce than trying to improve the balance of trade.[71] It is,
then, inevitably a simplification to treat the one without the other. With
that in mind, the title of some economy acts made clear that they applied
to particular parts of Britain's empire, almost all of it general in scope.

It must be stressed that Table 4.6 excludes those general economic
acts that applied to Britain's empire without reference to a particular
area or place, including the key navigation acts. Even so, for reasons
that will become clear, the figures in the first column of Table 4.6 are
rather misleading, but those in the second and third are not. Enhanced

---

to 1760: new approaches to enduring questions', *Parliamentary History*, 14.1 (1995),
especially pp. 37–8.

[69] In any case, Europe and empire were closely linked issues to the British government.
As Pitt the elder famously put it at the end of the Seven Years War, with Britain now
supreme in North America, 'America had been conquered in Germany'. Cobbet, *Parl.
Hist.*, 15 (1753–65), col. 1267.

[70] Jacob Viner, 'Power versus plenty as objectives of foreign policy in the seventeenth and
eighteenth centuries', in D. C. Coleman, ed., *Revisions in mercantilism* (1969), pp. 61–91.

[71] Joshua Gee, *The trade and navigation of Great-Britain considered: a new edition with many
interesting notes and additions, by a merchant* (1767), pp. 195–6. An edition of this work
was published in Glasgow in the same year, raising the interesting possibility that the
editor was a merchant there.

Table 4.6 *General economic acts directed at particular parts of Britain's empire, 1660–1800*

	Acts	Of which External trade	% External trade
Africa	20	18	90
America	96	61	63
Asia	1	1	90
Canada	23	10	43
India	42	17	40
Ireland	56	48	86
South America	3	2	66
West Indies	42	34	81
Total	282	191	68

overseas trade, which grew rapidly in the eighteenth century, was crucial to Britain's imperial ambitions. In the 1660s, empire took 11 per cent of England's exports; but by the late 1790s that had increased to 40 per cent, within a much larger absolute total.[72] This only enhanced the importance of empire within political economy. If there was undoubtedly a 'cult of commerce' as a consequence, this was in good measure because politicians and interests invested a lot of effort in developing the legislative framework within which it operated.[73] In Joseph Massie's extensive library of works of economics, 27 per cent concerned trade, 23 per cent policy (many of which would have included trade considerations), and 9 per cent colonies.[74]

An important fact is that three-quarters of all the acts in Table 4.6 were passed between 1760 and 1800: forty-two in the 1760s, sixty in the 1770s, forty-three in the 1780s, and sixty-six in the 1790s.[75] In other words, relatively few acts were needed in the seventeenth century to define the limits, participants, and commodities of the imperial

[72] Ralph Davis, 'English foreign trade, 1660–1700', *Economic History Review*, 7.2 (1954), p. 165; Ralph Davis, *The industrial revolution and British overseas trade* (Leicester, 1979), p. 89.

[73] The term is Colley's, *Britons*, p. 56; Jack P. Greene, *Evaluating empire and confronting colonialism in eighteenth-century Britain* (Cambridge, 2013), ch. 1; David Armitage, *The ideological origins of the British empire* (Cambridge, 2000), ch. 6; Nancy F. Koehn, *The power of commerce: economy and governance in the first British empire* (Ithaca, NY, 1994), ch. 3.

[74] Julian Hoppit, 'The contexts and contours of British economic literature, 1660–1760', *Historical Journal*, 49.1 (2006), p. 88.

[75] The rise of imperial economic legislation probably began in the 1750s. See P. J. Marshall, *The making and unmaking of empires: Britain, India, and America, c. 1750–1783* (Oxford, 2005), p. 78.

economy.[76] By contrast, the amendment of the statutory basis of the imperial economy after 1760, including after American independence, saw many more bills drafted, considered, and enacted. The legislative basis of the imperial economy evolved across the period, but at an accelerating rate from the 1760s, its nature inevitably becoming rather different in the process. Put another way, ministers and Parliament were expending increasing amounts of effort on commercial legislation at just the time that Adam Smith was writing the lengthy section on the 'mercantile system' in *The wealth of nations* (1776) and revising it in 1784, where merchants and manufacturers were savaged for pulling the wool over the eyes of legislators.[77]

In many respects, these numbers sit comfortably with the well-known fact that there were major attempts to revise the imperial economy both before and after the American War of Independence (1775–83) – especially through aiming at the better enforcement of existing acts, raising more revenue, and containing the growth of the East India Company as a territorial power.[78] Even so, the numbers are sometimes very striking. Thus although historians have provided a richly detailed account of Westminster's attempts to refashion the relationship between Britain and the North American colonies after the end of the Seven Years War in 1763, it is still startling to see that this involved passing forty-two general economic acts specifically aimed at the American colonies from then until the Declaration of Independence in 1776 – by contrast there were only four directed at the West Indies and six at Canada. It is also striking to see how much legislation was being enacted during the 1790s, much of it after war broke out with Revolutionary France in 1793. If some of this legislation was the product of strategic thinking about the evolution of Britain's empire in America, the sheer numbers involved also point to the importance of acts that were reacting to circumstances. Complex patchworks of legislation resulted.

The West Indies provides a good example of the webs of legislation that framed Britain's imperial economy, a 'plenitude of her legislation' ordering the 'compact' between the islands and mother country.[79]

---

[76] Smith, *Wealth of nations*, Book 4; Charles M. Andrews, *England's commercial and colonial policy* (New Haven, CT, 1938); Lawrence A. Harper, *The English navigation laws: a seventeenth-century experiment in social engineering* (New York, 1939).

[77] Adam Smith, *Additions and corrections to the first and second editions of Dr. Adam Smith's Inquiry into the Nature and causes of the wealth of nations* (1784).

[78] For introductions see various essays in P. J. Marshall, ed., *The Oxford history of the British empire, vol. 2, the eighteenth century* (Oxford, 1998); and for more recent views Marshall, *The making and unmaking of empires*, esp. pp. 78–80; P. J. Marshall, *Remaking the British Atlantic: the United States and the British empire after American independence* (Oxford, 2012).

[79] Anon., *The legal claim of the British sugar-colonies to enjoy an exclusive right of supplying this kingdom with sugars, in return for sundry restrictions laid upon these colonies in favour*

Foundational were the general navigation acts of the seventeenth century, limiting the destination of many exports to Britain alone, to be carried on British-built ships, manned by mainly British crews. The first act that specifically focused on the West Indies was the so-called Molasses Act of 1733: 'An act for the better securing and encouraging the trade of His Majesty's sugar colonies in America'.[80] Forty-one acts followed before 1801, thirty-seven of them after 1760. Most of these amended trade regulations in one way or another, such as by establishing 'free ports', or otherwise allowing trade outside the strict boundaries of the navigation acts. A common feature was for such amendments initially to be introduced for only a few years, but then later extended by further acts. Thus an act established free ports in Jamaica and Dominica in 1766, whose life was extended by further acts in 1774 and 1781.[81] (Later, free ports were also established by act in Tobago and Curaçao.[82]) In the mid- and late 1790s, seven acts were passed indemnifying officers who had allowed imports into the islands on foreign ships in contravention of the navigation acts – presumably because of wartime circumstances.[83]

Renewing acts did not require as much legislative effort as passing wholly new ones, but there was certainly more to legislating about the economy of the West Indies than the forty-two acts clearly directed towards them. In the first place was legislation surrounding the African slave trade, which began in 1698 with the statutory redefinition of the powers of the Royal African Company, which had been established by crown charter in 1672. Later the Company tried but failed to obtain an act extending its powers.[84] Three acts were passed in the mid-eighteenth century formally winding up the Company, including the payment of £110,000 in compensation to its stockholders.[85] A flurry of acts followed from 1788, often the product of anti-slavery agitation. Typically,

---

of the products, manufactures, commerce, revenue, and and [sic] *navigation, of Great-Britain; demonstrated by proofs extracted from the statute-book* [1792], p. 15.

[80] 6 George II, c. 13; Richard B. Sheridan, 'The Molasses Act and the market strategy of the British sugar planters', *Journal of Economic History*, 17.1 (1957), pp. 62–83.

[81] 6 George III, c. 49; 14 George III, c. 41; 21 George III, c. 29. The last of these continued many other acts as well. Memorials to the Treasury in support of the 1774 extension were sent from Manchester (sixty signed) and Lancaster (forty), on the grounds that it would secure cotton supplies: TNA, T1/506/52. Generally see Frances Armytage, *The free port system in the British West Indies: a study in commercial policy, 1766–1822* (1953).

[82] 36 George III, c. 55; 41 George III, c. 23.

[83] 34 George III, c. 35; 35 George III, c. 57; 36 George III, c. 32; 37 George III, c. 64; 38 George III, c. 72; 39 George III, c. 57; 39 & 40 George III, c. 76. The short title of these acts was the same.

[84] K. D. Davies, *The Royal African Company* (1957); William A. Pettigrew, *Freedom's debt: the Royal African Company and the politics of the Atlantic slave trade, 1672–1752* (Chapel Hill, NC, 2013); 9 William III, c. 26; Hoppit, *Failed legislation*, 48.008, 49.007.

[85] 23 George II, c. 31; 24 George II, c. 49; 25 George II, c. 40.

Dolben's act of that year, regulating how slaves were carried from Africa across the Atlantic, expired after a year, requiring further renewal acts.[86] But some acts that applied to Britain also affected the West Indies pretty significantly, particularly the duties, drawbacks, and bounties regarding the sugar trade. A thoroughgoing attempt to amend these required five acts in the 1790s, prompted by concerns over the high price of sugar.[87] Consideration of the proposed West India dock in London's East End also consumed a large amount of legislative effort in the 1790s.[88] To try to ensure the financial viability of the dock, the act passed in 1799 gave it a monopoly for twenty-one years for ships arriving in London from the West Indies.

Five layers of statutes directly affected Britain's economic relationship with the West Indies: the foundational navigation acts of the seventeenth century and those that generally amended them; refinements to those laws relating specifically to the West Indies; the management and protection of the African trade, the slave trade particularly; duties in Britain on goods imported from the West Indies; and even some specific legislation within Britain. Together this was highly complex, the interlocking of many dozens of acts, some permanent, some temporary, some general, some particular. Moreover they had different points of origin, from central government, colonial governments in the West Indies, and business interests. Nor did the statutory complexity end there, for colonial legislatures, overseen by the Privy Council in London, were also often active lawmakers.[89] Unsurprisingly, in London the 'West India interest' was substantial, if heterogeneous, comprising on the eve of American independence eight 'West Indian' MPs among a wider block of up to sixty MPs judged 'West India voters', ten agents formally representing the islands in London, dozens of merchants trading to the West Indies from Glasgow, Liverpool, Bristol, and London, acting alone and as an

---

[86] 28 George III, c. 54.

[87] 32 George III, c. 43; 33 George III, c. 56; 35 George III, c. 110; 36 George III, c. 106; 38 George III, c. 61.

[88] 39 George III, c. 69 (public local and personal acts); Walter M. Stern, 'The first London dock boom and the growth of the West India docks', *Economica*, 19 (1952), pp. 59–77; Stephen Porter, ed., *Survey of London*, vol. 43: *Poplar, Blackwall and Isle of Dogs* (1994), ch. 10.

[89] Alison G. Olson, 'Eighteenth-century colonial legislatures and their constituents', *Journal of American History*, 79.2 (1992), pp. 562–3; Peverill Squire, *The evolution of American legislatures: colonies, territories, and states, 1619–2009* (Ann Arbor, MI, 2012), ch. 2. Constitutional arrangements are well discussed in Jack P. Greene, *Peripheries and center: constitutional development in the extended polities of the British empire and the United States, 1607–1788* (New York, 1990) and Mary Sarah Bilder, *The transatlantic constitution: colonial legal culture and the empire* (Cambridge, MA, 2004).

organized lobby, and perhaps 2,000 to 3,000 absentee planters or slave owners living in Britain.[90]

Legislation produced within Britain's empire is a neglected dimension of political economy in practice in this period. The Privy Council in London considered 8,563 acts from colonial assemblies between 1700 and 1783, with a significant rise in numbers in the years before 1776.[91] Much more work needs to be done on this, especially on assemblies in the Caribbean, but some of the factors can be illustrated by looking briefly at the acts of the Dublin parliament. Obviously Ireland and its parliament was in a very different relationship to Westminster than colonies in the Caribbean and North America, but what went on there was certainly more immediately important to legislators in London. Under Poynings' Law (1495), acts passed at Dublin were subject to some control by the Privy Council in London, even after its independence in 1782, while in 1720 a Westminster statute confirmed its authority to legislate towards Ireland.[92] Westminster had indeed long been doing this (though mainly in relation to its economic and external affairs), in part because Ireland was perceived as a major economic threat. Irish cattle and woollens were considered especially dangerous to English interests, leading to their exclusion from England and Wales.[93] As one author observed, 'Ireland is subject to *England*, and as

---

[90] Lewis Namier and John Brooke, 'The House of Commons, 1754–1790: introductory survey; West Indians and North Americans', *HofP online*; Lillian M. Penson, *The colonial agents of the British West Indies: a study in colonial administration, mainly in the eighteenth century* (1924), p. 228; Andrew Jackson O'Shaughnessy, *An empire divided: the American Revolution and the British Caribbean* (Philadelphia, PA, 2000), p. 15; Andrew J. O'Shaughnessy, 'The formation of a commercial lobby: the West India interest, British colonial policy and the American revolution', *Historical Journal*, 40.1 (1997), 71–95; Perry Gauci, 'Learning the ropes of sand: the West India lobby, 1714–1760', in Perry Gauci, ed., *Regulating the British economy, 1660–1850* (Farnham, 2011), pp. 107–21; M. W. McCahill, ed., *The Correspondence of Stephen Fuller, 1788–1795: Jamaica, the West India Interest at Westminster and the Campaign to Preserve the Slave Trade, Parliamentary History*, Special Issue: Texts and Studies Series 9, 33, Supplement 1 (2014), pp. 49–50. The estimate of absentees has been kindly provided by Nick Draper, but is provisional.

[91] Edward White, *Law in American history: vol. 1, from the colonial years through the civil wars* (Oxford, 2012), p. 82.

[92] 10 Henry VII, c. 22; 6 George I, c. 5; James Kelly, *Poynings' law and the making of law in Ireland, 1660–1800* (Dublin, 2007); Isolde Victory, 'The making of the 1720 Declaratory Act', in Gerard O'Brien, ed., *Parliament, politics and people: essays in eighteenth-century Irish history* (Dublin, 1989), pp. 9–29.

[93] Carolyn A. Edie, 'The Irish cattle bills: a study in Restoration politics', *Transactions of the American Philosophical Society*, 60.2 (1970), pp. 1–66; H. F. Kearney, 'The political background to English mercantilism, 1695–1700', *Economic History Review*, 11.3 (1959), pp. 484–96; Patrick Kelly, 'The Irish woollen export prohibition act of 1699: Kearney revisited', *Irish Economic and Social History*, 7 (1980), pp. 22–44; Chapter 7 in this volume. The import of Irish cattle into Britain was allowed on a temporary basis in 1759 (32 George II, c. 11), but effectively made perpetual through continuing acts.

such is ruled *Provincially*, and accordingly should be made useful and profitable to *England*'.[94] English authority was not unlimited in this regard, as shown by the furore over Wood's halfpence in 1722 in which Swift was highly active, but it was considerable.[95] Nor did Westminster ever attempt to raise taxes in Ireland in this period. Ireland thus fell under one crown, but unlike Britain's three nations after 1707, two parliaments.

The Dublin parliament passed more than 2,300 acts between 1660 and 1800, of which a half concerned economic matters. This was a fraction of the number of economic acts passed at Westminster (7,545), and lower than might be expected given the rapid growth of Ireland's population in the eighteenth century – which was about half that of Britain in 1801.[96] But the Dublin parliament met far less often and acted under much greater constraints for most of the period. It is notable that more than a half of all of Dublin's economic acts were passed after it attained independence in 1782 and that their character was also different, with 80 per cent 'general' in scope, compared to just 32 per cent at Westminster.

Low numbers of economic acts passed at Dublin that were 'specific' in import is reminiscent of the few efforts made by Scots to obtain statutory authority at Westminster after 1707. Just as in Scotland, what little specific economic legislation there was in Ireland was dominated by infrastructure (149 road acts, 41 waterways).[97] Ireland, though, was subject to a lot of general economic acts of its own making. Of these 917 acts, 343 (37 per cent) concerned public finance, and 109 (12 per cent) external trade, though the varied nature of general economic legislation is also striking. Three points can be stressed here. First, that Ireland's trade relations with Britain and its empire were largely structured by legislation passed at Westminster, but were also ordered by legislation passed at Dublin. Second, that public finance legislation from Dublin raised a lot of money by the middle of the eighteenth

---

[94] P. Paxton, *A discourse concerning the nature, advantage, and improvement of trade* (1704), p. 48.

[95] Patrick McNally, 'Wood's halfpence, Carteret, and the government of Ireland, 1723–6', *Irish Historical Studies*, 30, no. 119 (1997), pp. 354–76.

[96] Hoppit, 'The nation', p. 313; *The statutes at large, passed in the parliaments held in Ireland* (21 vols., Dublin, 1786–1804). Short titles of both public and private acts prior to 1799 are listed in the index volume, vol. 8. Private acts for 1799 and 1800 have been taken from the *Journals of the Commons ... of Ireland*, vols. 18–19 (1796–1800). See also the 'Irish legislation database' at www.qub.ac.uk/ild.

[97] The form of Irish turnpike legislation 'was borrowed directly from the Westminster parliament': David Broderick, *The first toll-roads: Ireland's turnpike roads, 1729–1858* (Cork, 2002), p. 43.

century. Third, that such funds encouraged legislators in Dublin to fund various economic projects, often through direct subsidies. This last point is worth stressing. The efforts made via the Linen Board (1711–1828) are the best known of these. Established with funds arising from the excise on tea, it also received effectively annual grants from 1721, totalling £247,340 by 1800.[98] The Linen Board was to encourage an industry judged well suited both to Irish conditions and, in the main, to English interests, and if not entirely successful was in a way 'a remarkably progressive achievement for an eighteenth-century government', an 'undeniable triumph'.[99] A similarly constituted and funded body to aid river improvement, canal building, and agricultural development began life in 1729, and spent some £900,000 of public money on canals by 1787.[100] Many other grants were also made, proliferating from mid-century. For example, in a two-week period in the autumn of 1755 the Irish House of Commons received fifty petitions seeking 'encouragement' for various projects, including twenty-six relating to manufactures and thirteen to infrastructure. Grants totalling £55,800 were awarded. Moreover, a raft of bounties was also provided to encourage various areas of economic activity. As Conrad Gill nicely put it, '"Parliamentary Colbertism" had become as strong a force in Ireland as in any country in Europe'.[101] As yet no overall figure is available for the amount of direct public finance into the domestic Irish economy in the eighteenth century by the Dublin parliament, but it was certainly very substantial, apparently dwarfing what was attempted in England and Scotland. Though, as Barnard has remarked, 'how far into society the benefits reached, may be questioned'; certainly in the end such funds were unable to make up for the lack of private capital.[102]

---

[98] T. J. Kiernan, *History of the financial administration of Ireland to 1817* (1930), pp. 165–79; Harry Gribbon, 'The Irish Linen Board, 1711–1828', in Marilyn Cohen, ed., *The warp of Ulster's past: interdisciplinary perspectives on the Irish linen industry, 1700–1920* (Basingstoke, 1997), pp. 71–91.

[99] Edith Mary Johnston-Liik, *History of the Irish parliament, 1692–1800* (6 vols., Belfast, 2002), vol. 1, p. 307; T. C. Barnard, *Improving Ireland? projectors, prophets and profiteers, 1641–1786* (Dublin, 2008), p. 168. Some in England complained that Ireland was unduly advantaged by governmental support for its linen industry: J. Gee, *Observations on the growth of hemp and flax in Great Britain* (1765), pp. 4–8.

[100] Toby Barnard, *The kingdom of Ireland, 1641–1760* (Basingstoke, 2004), p. 88; Eoin Magennis, 'Coal, corn and canals: Parliament and the dispersal of public moneys 1695–1772', *Parliamentary History*, 20.1 (2001), p. 74.

[101] Magennis, 'Coal, corn and canals', p. 81; Conrad Gill, *The rise of the Irish linen industry* (Oxford, 1925), p. 197.

[102] Barnard, *Kingdom of Ireland*, p. 82; Magennis, 'Coal, corn and canals', p. 86.

The Limits of Westminster

Plainly the statutory framework for both the domestic and overseas elements of the British economy was substantial, multi-layered, and evolving. Hundreds upon hundreds of acts of many different shapes, sizes, and aims, each seeking to affect how people behaved, were heaped on top of each other. But if this was not challenging enough, the complexity was compounded by the considerable variations which existed between the letter of the law and how people actually behaved. Laws were certainly more respected and better enforced in some parts of Britain, and some parts of Britain's empire, than others. Crudely put, it is generally thought that observance and enforcement declined quickly beyond England, though, as is well known, the West Indies and the Thirteen Colonies reacted differently to measures such as the Stamp Act, while smuggling and evasion may well have been as rife in Irish as in western Atlantic waters.[103]

In part, such a situation arose because the authorities made more efforts to enforce laws in some places than others. If they expected obedience to laws from all subjects of the British crown wherever they might be, much the greatest efforts at enforcing Westminster's statutes were made in England, though such efforts were certainly not always successful (see Chapter 7). As is well known, the application of imperial trade laws was very lax for much of the first half of the eighteenth century – what seemed with hindsight to be a 'salutary neglect'.[104] This began to change in the 1740s and attempts after 1763 at greater enforcement, by beefing up the Vice Admiralty courts and colonial customs service, provoked considerable resistance, passive and active.[105]

Behind such considerations lay the supremacy or not of the Westminster parliament across the British empire. Parliament itself was certain of its

---

[103] Donna J. Spindle, 'The Stamp Act crisis in the British West Indies', *Journal of American Studies*, 11.2 (1977), pp. 203–21; O'Shaughnessy, *An empire divided*. For an overview of smuggling in the New World, Wim Klooster, 'Inter-imperial smuggling in the Americas, 1600–1800', in Bernard Bailyn and Patricia L. Denault, eds., *Soundings in Atlantic history: latent structures and intellectual currents, 1500–1830* (Cambridge, MA, 2009), pp. 141–80; on smuggling nearer to Britain see L. M. Cullen, *Anglo-Irish trade, 1660–1800* (Manchester, 1969), ch. 8. Trading with the enemy was an element of this, for which see Thomas M. Truxes, *Defying empire: trading with the enemy in colonial New York* (New Haven, CT, 2008).

[104] The term was first used by Edmund Burke in 1775. James A. Henretta, *'Salutary neglect': colonial administration under the Duke of Newcastle* (Princeton, NJ, 1972); Andrew D. M. Beaumont, *Colonial America and the Earl of Halifax, 1748–1761* (Oxford, 2014).

[105] Oliver M. Dickerson, *The navigation acts and the American Revolution* (Philadelphia, PA, 1951); Michael Craton, 'The role of the Caribbean vice admiralty courts in British imperialism', *Caribbean Studies*, 11.2 (1971), pp. 5–20.

right to legislate everywhere under the crown, confirming this by statute specifically with regard to Ireland in 1720 and American colonies in 1766.[106] The preamble to the latter noted how colonial assemblies were denying the right for Parliament to legislate over them. Such opposition had not simply arisen in response to recent measures like the Sugar and Stamp Acts. A high degree of colonial autonomy was clear in the late seventeenth and early eighteenth centuries.[107] In 1756 the Earl of Loudoun wrote from America to London that it was 'very common for the people' there to say that 'they would be glad to see any Man durst Offer to put an English Act of Parliament in Force in this country.'[108]

Views such as those that Loudoun reported arose from very different views of the nature of the British imperial constitution and of the applicability of acts passed at Westminster to different parts of the imperium. In those views there were different spheres and levels of sovereignty within Britain's empire, doubts expressed both near and far. As is well known, Molyneux had raised similar views with regard to Ireland at the end of the seventeenth century.[109] Jacobites in both Ireland and Scotland naturally doubted the sovereignty of the Revolution constitution tout court. And American independence was, at heart, a relegation of the sovereignty of Parliament beneath natural rights.

In practice, ideas of sovereignty overlapped with those of legitimacy, the extent to which Westminster statutes were perceived as reasonable and just. As E. P. Thompson observed, in practice this tied the hands of lawmakers to a degree that is easy to overlook: 'If the law is evidently partial and unjust, then it will mask nothing, legitimize nothing. ... The essential precondition for the effectiveness of law, in its function as ideology, is that it shall display an independence from gross manipulation and shall seem to be just.'[110] It was also the case that less formalized views and different cultural norms also played on the reception of Westminster's statutes. For example, in his tour of the Scottish Highlands in 1773, Samuel Johnson reflected on the difficulties governments had of

---

[106] See note 92; 6 George III, c. 12. H. T. Dickinson, 'The eighteenth-century debate on the sovereignty of parliament', *Transactions of the Royal Historical Society*, 5th series, 26 (1976), pp. 189–210.

[107] J. M. Sosin, *English America and imperial inconstancy: the rise of provincial autonomy, 1696–1715* (Lincoln, NE, 1985).

[108] Quoted in Greene, *Peripheries and center*, p. 58.

[109] William Molyneux, *The case of Ireland's being bound by Acts of Parliament in England stated* (Dublin, 1698); Jacqueline Hill, 'Ireland without Union: Molyneux and his legacy', in John Robertson, ed., *A union for empire: political thought and the British Union of 1707* (Cambridge, 1995), pp. 271–96; Marie Léoutre, 'Contesting and upholding the rights of the Irish parliament in 1698: the arguments of William Molyneux and Simon Clement', *Parliaments, Estates, and Representations*, 34.1 (2014), pp. 22–39.

[110] *Whigs and hunters: the origin of the Black Act* (Harmondsworth, 1977), p. 263.

exercising authority in remote and mountainous regions, believing that 'Law is nothing without power'. As has been seen, such views had been crucial to the abolition of heritable jurisdictions in Scotland. Even so, Johnson believed that the 'common people' in the Highlands might interpret acts as they preferred, for example quite wrongly believing that the law against the wearing of tartan lapsed with the death of its author, Lord Hardwicke, in 1764 – the ban was actually lifted in 1782.[111] In Cornwall, the prosecution of smugglers was severely hampered by the difficulty of finding jurors willing to countenance the possibility of guilty verdicts, hostile as all were to the revenue laws.[112] Similarly it was reported in 1764 that 'Smugglers of molasses instead of being infamous are called patriots in North America.'[113] Custom and convention was certainly an important element within which to place the acts considered both in this and the previous chapter.

Conclusion

In 1770 General Conway, MP, told the House of Commons that 'the people of England [he meant Britain] till our legal dissolution can possibly have no existence but within these walls. ... The nation has chosen us as its agents for a term of years: during that term therefore we are virtually the nation.'[114] But the legislative record shows that this was a complex 'nation', with marked geographical patterning, at both the general and the specific levels. At the general level, there was confusion well into the eighteenth century as to whether acts passed applied to all parts of Britain. At the specific levels some parts of Britain were heavily involved in economic legislation, but some hardly at all. And legislation affecting empire, both direct and not, grew very voluminous from around 1760, in the context of heightening legislative activity in colonial assemblies.

Disparities in the distribution (by time, subject, and place), application, and reception of the acts considered in this and the previous chapter were vital variants within Britain's political economies. Necessarily the discussion of such heterogeneity has so far been very general. More

---

[111] *Johnson's journey to the western islands of Scotland and Boswell's journal of a tour to the Hebrides with Samuel Johnson, LL.D*, ed. R. W. Chapman (Oxford, 1978), pp. 40, 46; 22 George III, c. 63.

[112] Peter King and Richard Ward, 'Rethinking the bloody code in eighteenth-century Britain: capital punishment at the centre and on the periphery', *Past and Present*, 228 (2015), pp. 204–5.

[113] R. C. Simmons and P. D. G. Thomas, eds., *Proceedings and debates of the British parliaments respecting North America, 1754–1783* (6 vols., Millwood, NY, 1982–7), vol. 1, p. 490.

[114] Cobbett, *Parl. Hist.*, 16 (1765–71), col. 892.

detail is provided in the case studies later to show some of the particular dynamics at work. But three points can usefully be made here.

The first is the simple but crucial point that Parliament considered vast numbers of legislative initiatives that aimed at directly affecting economic life in Britain and its empire. Using quite a narrow definition, more than 7,400 acts were passed, comprising more than half of all acts passed at Westminster. Chronologically, there was a small surge after the Glorious Revolution, but a much larger one after 1760, especially associated with the two classes of general legislation, public finance and external trade, and two of specific legislation, enclosure and infrastructure. Increasingly strained public finances, a refashioning of the imperial economy, before and after American independence, and the rapid development of the agricultural and service sectors from about 1760 were all associated with many more Acts of Parliament. This was a huge undertaking.

Specific economic acts obviously had fairly narrow implications when considered individually, but collectively they were critical to changes in landownership, farming, and internal trade. Because such acts were sought by individuals and small interests, they were not the product of central policy making, though the conventions Westminster used to assess bills required such efforts (and opposition) to be regularized to an extent. The patterns that can be found in their number, distribution, and subject matter are, rather, mainly to be explained by reference to the nature of the profit motive among propertied society (including ideas of improvement), price changes affecting margins, the availability and cost of capital and expertise, and the nature of opposition. This was a very complex and fluid set of considerations, which will later be explored in some detail through the case study of the fens in Chapter 6.

This chapter has shown secondly, however, just how differently specific economic legislation was sought in England than in Scotland, and thus of the need to understand the internal regional and national dynamics of Britain's political economies. In part, that may be explained by the factors just noted, but it also reflected the different legal systems of the two nations and the institutions to which propertied society could turn for help. On that latter point, it is important to stress that direct economic investment by central government was much greater in Scotland (and Ireland) than in England. It was developments at Edinburgh and Dublin that were crucial to this, though Westminster and Whitehall sometimes intervened, and underwrote expenditure by raising taxes across Britain. Even then, as Chapter 9 shows, tax collection was geographically skewed, with little raised directly in Scotland and huge amounts in and around London – though the capital sought little specific economic legislation and obtained less still.

All told, it is important to heed Epstein's cogent warning against projecting 'backwards in time a form of centralised sovereignty and jurisdictional integration that was first achieved in Continental Europe during the nineteenth century'.[115] It is tempting to see nationhood and state formation in Britain between 1660 and 1801 as involving marked consolidation and centralization, with England coming to exercise increasing authority over Ireland, Scotland, and Wales, especially through the efforts of the sovereign Parliament.[116] Certainly some such developments took place, especially in the 1740s and 1790s, but this chapter has shown that the Glorious Revolution generated both centrifugal and centripetal forces. The legislative activity of the Dublin, Edinburgh, and Westminster parliaments was significantly invigorated after 1688, marking an important step in the evolution of Britain and Ireland from a 'multiple kingdom' to a 'composite state' of unequal parts.[117] Britain emphatically did not conform to the aphorism of Count Duke Olivares, 'many kingdoms, but one law'.[118]

Thirdly, this and the previous chapter have shown how voluminous yet finely grained even general economic legislation was. This raises the fundamental question of the extent to which it constituted a system, or was at least the product of a clear line of policy making. It could be hypothesized that some of this general legislation was indeed systematic and strategic, the rest contingent and tactical. Certainly, important efforts were made in the seventeenth century to delimit the economic relationship between Britain and its empire, notably through the 'navigation acts'. A key aspect of that was to confine that relationship to subjects of the British crown and to ensure that empire complemented and did not compete with the economy of Britain, England especially. This can reasonably be called a policy. But as is now clear it was one that accounted for only a fraction of general economic legislation, was much more fluid than is often appreciated, and was frequently ignored or subverted. It took Adam Smith's analytical imagination and rhetorical brilliance to construe this as a general 'mercantile system', which was later morphed

[115] S. R. Epstein, *Freedom and growth: the rise of states and markets in Europe, 1300–1750* (2000), p. 6. Also Jack P. Greene, *Negotiated authorities: essays in colonial political and constitutional history* (Charlottesville, VA, 1994), pp. 11, 23.

[116] Michael Hechter, *Internal colonialism: the Celtic fringe in British national development 1536–1966* (1975).

[117] J. H. Elliott, 'A Europe of composite monarchies', *Past and Present*, 137 (1992), pp. 48–71; H. G. Koenigsberger, 'Composite states, representative institutions and the American revolution', *Historical Research*, 62.148 (1989), pp. 135–53; David Hayton, 'Constitutional experiments and political expediency, 1689–1725', in Ellis and Barber, eds., *Conquest and union*, pp. 276–305.

[118] Cited in Elliott, 'Composite monarchies', p. 63.

into 'mercantilism'. Whichever term is used, it is clear that it can only be applied to a corner of Britain's political economies in this period.

The timing of Smith's conception of the 'mercantile system' is telling in two major regards. First, it further spurred efforts by leading ministers to reform general efforts to apply political power to economic life. It was in the 1780s that they – Shelburne, Jenkinson, and Pitt particularly – sought to make coherent hundreds of statutes that had emerged over the preceding century and a half. They did this, moreover, fully aware that many of those laws were redundant, unenforced, or disobeyed. Further, they came to feel the full weight of new forms of interest group politics, notably through the emergence of chambers of commerce. This made painfully clear the difficulties of maintaining a 'system' which required balancing increasing numbers and types of give and take. Put more plainly, the heaping of statute upon statute that was such a marked feature of the 'old colonial system' was so great that it broke its foundations through sheer weight of numbers. The political effort to sustain those modes of proceedings became increasingly unworkable. It was dismantled in stages over the following decades – key strides were made in the 1820s, but protectionism and the navigation system were not fully exorcised until 1849 – not simply because of the triumph of free trade ideas, but because it was politically and legally unsustainable.

Secondly, an important finding of this and the previous chapter is that *The wealth of nations* was brought to fruition when there was a wholly remarkable growth in the numbers of economic acts. Much of Book IV of Smith's great work was informed by this, including many of the revisions he added in 1784. On the one hand, the surge of interest group politics after 1763 was one major factor he saw at work, another was the efforts of executive government to extract some revenue from the crown's overseas subjects and, no less important, to make the legislative framework for the imperial economy more effective – such efforts were far from entirely successful. The piling up of general economic acts was a marked feature of Britain's political economies in the final four decades of the eighteenth century as ministers and legislators struggled to give statutes form, consistency, and force, including adapting the navigation acts to the new imperial order consequent upon success in North America in 1763, defeat there in 1783, and the challenge of confronting Revolutionary France after 1789. This was a major undertaking and if empire and its legislative framework was certainly very important to the development of the British economy in this period, it is worth stressing the speed with which trade between Britain and an independent United States recovered after 1783. Path-dependency arguments might help explain something of that recovery, but only a part. Just as important was that Britain's trade laws provided only a general frame that was frequently honoured as much in the breach as in the observance.[119]

A significant limitation of general economic legislation through the period remained the unwillingness of most to see an expansion of central government's ability to ensure its will was obeyed. By contrast, specific economic legislation saw power delegated to those usually determined to see through their ambitions. In this way, a significant part of the landscape of England and the infrastructure of Britain was changed. General economic legislation has understandably caught the eye of most historians; but the collective significance of thousands upon thousands of specific economic acts was so great that it too needs to be placed centre stage in our understanding of Britain's political economies.

---

[119] Attempts to establish the effects of political power on the imperial economy have struggled to distinguish coincidence from causation. For a brief introduction see Nuala Zahedieh, *The capital and the colonies: London and the Atlantic economy, 1660–1700* (Cambridge, 2010), Introduction.

5   Information, Interests, and
       Political Economy

'[T]he ideas of economists and political philosophers, both when they
are right and when they are wrong, are more powerful than is commonly understood. Indeed the world is ruled by little else. Practical
men, who believe themselves to be quite exempt from any intellectual
influence, are usually the slaves of some defunct economist. Madmen
in authority, who hear voices in the air, are distilling their frenzy from
some academic scribbler of a few years back. I am sure that the power
of vested interests is vastly exaggerated compared with the gradual
encroachment of ideas.'

John Maynard Keynes, 1936[1]

'[H]e that would make himself useful to his own state, with regard to its
policy and government, should first furnish himself amply with as much
real matter, concerning the condition of the trading interest of his own
state, as he can.'

Malachy Postlethwayt, 1749[2]

To become an act, proposed legislation had (and has) to obtain the consent
of the Commons, Lords, and crown. But as the previous three chapters
showed, in this period that was often not forthcoming: nearly one-third
of proposals were rejected or stillborn, and in becoming acts many bills
were heavily amended. An important factor in this was that Parliament
itself generated relatively few proposals: some came from the executive,
but most came from widely scattered sources elsewhere. Yet Parliament,
conscious of the potency of statutes, was wary that such proposals might
be inconsistent with the public good. Far from rubber-stamping proposals, it had to be persuaded to turn them into acts. It sought out a large
amount of information to help with this, but also received suggestions
and criticism from outside, by lobbying, petitioning, and publication.

---

[1] *The general theory of employment, money, and interest*, ed. Donald Moggridge (Cambridge,
1979), p. 383.
[2] [Malachy Postlethwayt], *A dissertation on the plan, use, and importance, of the universal dictionary of trade and commerce* (1749), p. 26.

A key aspect of the legislative process was that Parliament was delibera-tive and, to a degree, sensitive to pressures from without. To gain some sense of this, this chapter explores in general terms the types of infor-mation sought by Parliament, the nature of some of the pressures put on it from external interested parties via petitioning, and the general climate of thinking about political economy evidenced from the record of published works.

It would be naïve to believe that Parliament was a neutral and disinter-ested umpire in weighing legislative proposals. After all, its membership was in no sense representative of society as a whole. Most parliamen-tarians were landowners, though some MPs were drawn from the law, armed services, commerce, finance, and manufacturing.[3] Given their narrow origins, parliamentarians undoubtedly shared some values that predisposed them to react in certain ways to legislative proposals. Almost all were united in their Protestantism (most were Anglicans) and sure that profound inequalities of income, wealth, sex, age, and ethnicity were right and proper; unsurprisingly they believed that they and their like were best able to judge what was and what was not best for the public good. Yet a patrician outlook was qualified by notions of paternalistic responsibility, if limited by the belief that political power could adjust the 'natural order' to only a very limited extent, that the liberty of individu-als should not be eroded, that the balance of the constitution should be maintained, and that government expenses should be minimized. Where almost all agreed action might be directed was at correcting supposed distortions of the 'natural order', such as rooting out insubordination, idleness, and vice, or increasing exploitation of natural resources, includ-ing the quest for empire.

Shared assumptions and beliefs may have underwritten much decision making in Parliament, but it is easy to exaggerate this, as the large num-bers of failed attempts at economic legislation suggest. After all, most parliamentarians may have been landowners who prided themselves on their general or 'liberal' interests, but most were conscious of the need to engage with ideas and information from far and wide and readily rec-ognized the value of manufacturing and trade to national well-being. In part this was because Parliament, despite its reputation for being remote,

---

[3] For the background of MPs crucial sources are the 'Introductory surveys' to the rel-evant parts of the *HofP online*. See also Gerrit P. Judd, *Members of Parliament, 1734–1832* (New Haven, CT, 1955). The composition of the House of Lords has been less carefully explored, but some points are made in John Cannon, *Aristocratic century: the peerage of eighteenth-century England* (Cambridge, 1984). A useful synthesis is Peter Jupp, *The gov-erning of Britain, 1688–1848: the executive, Parliament and the people* (2006), chs. 3 and 4, and the references therein.

exclusive, and blinkered, was in key respects open, informed, and deliberative. All bills were liable to close scrutiny and parliamentarians often elicited information with which to help them in this. Unfortunately, the destruction of so many of its records makes this hard to assess, but this chapter explores three aspects that give some sense of the extent to which Parliament was very much more than an assembly of the bewigged and the befuddled. First, attention is directed at how Parliament itself elicited information, then at petitions sent to Parliament on economic matters, before finally considering the huge literature published on economic matters in the period, much of it specifically directed at legislative proposals.

As the patterns of economic legislation explored in the previous three chapters have suggested, Britain's political economies in this period involved a dynamic arrangement of numerous interests, large and small. Moreover, they employed a rapidly changing arsenal of ideas and information seeking to persuade Parliament of the consistency of their proposals with the wider public interest. Parliament was not inert in this, handling legislation within frameworks of standing orders and conventions so as to ensure a reasonable (for the period) due process and transparency, while also seeking information with which to aid its deliberations. This chapter provides a general sense of the interactions between Parliament and wider society in the making of economic legislation, looking first at its own efforts, then at cases made specifically to it, and finally at a key aspect of the wider culture. It establishes some of the contours of information gathering, pressure from without, and the wider print culture of political economy which will be seen in action in the case studies in Part Two.

Informing Parliament

To a much greater extent than is usually thought, Parliament actively sought out or pondered information either to help judge bills under consideration or to prompt the executive to act: as Lord Hervey put it, there was a 'natural propensity of Parliaments to Inquiry'.[4] This might be done collectively or by individual members, though influenced by the efforts of the executive and opinion out of doors.

Formally, both houses were required as a minimum to scrutinize in committees all bills at the second reading stage, assuming they reached that far – which 7,545 economic acts and 1,042 economic fails did. In total, in this period 16,316 committees of some or all members were

---

[4] Quoted in A. A. Hanham, 'Whig opposition to Sir Robert Walpole in the House of Commons, 1727–1734' (University of Leicester PhD thesis, 1992), p. 311.

established to consider economic legislation, where witnesses might be quizzed, legal counsel heard, petitions considered, and information and ideas exchanged.[5] Certainly some bills were much more lightly scrutinized than others at this stage, for lack of interest, opposition, time, and energy by parliamentarians. On this last point, Moore and Horwitz found that in the late seventeenth century much of the work in the Commons was done by one-third of MPs, the other two-thirds being pretty inactive.[6] But the destruction of the manuscript records of the Commons in the fire of 1834 makes it impossible to know with any certainty how most committees were conducted, though bits of information can be found in scattered archives.[7] For the Lords, whose records have survived, Loft has shown them to have been fairly assiduous in their committee work.[8] Perhaps this was less true in the Commons, but it seems unlikely.

Investigative committees, rather than those on bills, were also sometimes established, especially in the Commons. Hayton estimates that between 1689 and 1714 the Commons established twenty such committees on average a year.[9] Between 1714 and 1800 some 952 reports of Commons' committees were published, many of them not directly related to a bill then under consideration. This was not a trivial effort, sometimes dealing with major issues of economic policy.[10] Private citizens struggled to gather good information about many areas of economic life, but Parliament, the Commons in particular, could call for 'persons, papers, and records'.[11] In the wake of the establishment of the Commission of Public Accounts in 1780 many major committees were instituted in the late eighteenth century, alongside non-parliamentary commissions, including royal commissions.[12] This constituted a much more thorough

---

[5] Of the 1,042 economic fails which reached the second reading committee stage, 184 also reached the same stage in the second house, a total of 1,226. The 7,545 economic acts were obviously considered in twice that number of committees, i.e., 15,090.

[6] T. K. Moore and H. Horwitz, 'Who runs the house? Aspects of parliamentary organization in the later seventeenth century', *Journal of Modern History*, 43.2 (1971), pp. 205–27. In the Restoration era, only a half of peers appointed to select committees actually attended: Andrew Swatland, *The House of Lords in the reign of Charles II* (Cambridge, 1996), p. 63.

[7] 'The minute book of James Courthope', ed. Orlo Cyprian Williams, *Camden Miscellany*, 20 (1953), pp. 47–90, gives an insider's view of committee work in the 1690s. But entries are very general and matter of fact.

[8] Philip Loft, 'Peers, parliament and power under the Revolution constitution, 1685–1720' (UCL PhD thesis, 2015), chs. 3 and 4.

[9] D. W. Hayton, 'The House of Commons 1690–1715, introductory survey: the business of the house – the "grand inquest"', *HofP online*.

[10] Lambert, *Sessional papers*, vols. 1 and 2.

[11] Arthur Young, *Political arithmetic* (1774), p. 314.

[12] John Torrance, 'Social class and bureaucratic innovation: the commissioners for examining the public accounts, 1780–1787', *Past and Present*, 78 (1978), pp. 56–81.

investigation of governmental matters, many with an economic dimension, especially relating to public finance. Thus the Commons' Finance Committee of 1797 published thirty-six reports and minutes of its proceedings, and so 'cleared away much of the mystery or incomprehension concerning the government's financial operations, mainly by obliging the executive to present more information to parliament and to cast it in an intelligible form'.[13]

To aid Parliament's deliberations, reports, known as 'accounts and papers', were also frequently requested, especially by the Commons, which ordered 10,508 between 1714 and 1800. By any standards this was a major effort to be better informed, though as is clear from Figure 5.1 and Table 5.1, numbers were roughly stable before 1750 before growing markedly thereafter.[14]

The last quarter of the eighteenth century saw a dramatic surge in numbers of accounts and papers ordered by the Commons, largely in response to the huge costs and disruptions of three major wars. The greatest number produced in a single session was in fact in 1786 (328) – which coincided with a marked peak in general economic acts.[15] But the driver here was not simply establishing more clearly the resources available to pay for increasingly expensive wars or reconstituting the mercantile system after the loss of America, but of wider efforts to 'reform', a word which now began to take on its modern meanings.[16] That said, while numbers of accounts and papers more than trebled between 1714–24 and 1792–1800, this lagged the fivefold rise in numbers of all acts and the fourfold rise in the number of failed attempts at legislation, a lag better explained by the finely grained and repetitive nature of much legislation, even that which was general, than by Parliament being slow in seeking to inform itself about critical matters.

Commissioners for examining public accounts had been appointed briefly early in the eighteenth century, but they made far less headway. J. A. Downie, 'The Commission of Public Accounts and the formation of the Country Party', *English Historical Review*, 91.358 (1976), pp. 33–51.

[13] The quote is from J. E. Cookson, *The friends of peace: anti-war liberalism in England, 1793–1815* (Cambridge, 1982), p. 59. The Finance Committee reports are conveniently available in Lambert, *Sessional papers*, vols. 107–13. They were bound together and published in more than 3,600 pages with an index in 1803. More generally see Julian Hoppit, 'Checking the leviathan, 1688–1832', in Donald Winch and Patrick O'Brien, eds., *The political economy of British historical experience, 1688–1914* (Oxford, 2002), especially pp. 277–8.

[14] Very short sessions account for the absence or low numbers in Figure 5.1.

[15] See Chapter 3, p. 72.

[16] Joanna Innes, '"Reform" in English public life: the fortunes of a word', in Arthur Burns and Joanna Innes, eds., *Rethinking the age of reform: Britain 1780–1850* (Cambridge, 2003), pp. 71–97.

Table 5.1 *Numbers of 'accounts and papers' ordered by the Commons, 1714–1800*

	Numbers	Annual averages
1714–50	2,413	65
1751–75	2,735	109
1776–1800	5,360	206

Source: Lambert, *Sessional papers*, vols. 1 and 2.

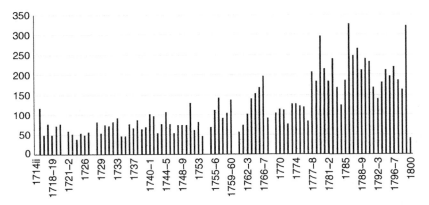

Figure 5.1 Numbers of 'accounts and papers' requested by House of Commons by session, 1714–1800.
Source: Lambert, *Sessional papers*, vols. 1 and 2.

A majority of accounts and papers related to economic matters, especially the closely connected categories of public finances and overseas trade, and most were 'general' rather than 'specific' in scope.[17] Most usually they provided particular information to guide decision making, sometimes comprising tabulations of data, sometimes qualitative assessments. A flavour of what was involved is suggested by looking at those requested from late April to mid-May 1770: a report from the Commissioners for annexed estates in Scotland, two reports from the Customs Commissioners assessing a petition and a memorial from linen manufacturers, a statement of public debts at the Exchequer, an estimate

---

[17] Julian Hoppit, 'Political arithmetic in eighteenth-century England', *Economic History Review*, 49.3 (1996), p. 522.

of Highland road-building costs, savings in the hands of the Paymaster General, four tables of figures of linens exported over the previous fifteen years, an account of compensation payments for the cattle distemper, and transfers of certain public debt annuities.[18] Alternatively, taking the long-run view, between 1699 and 1792, the Commons received, for example, twenty-seven reports from the Admiralty about the state of the Newfoundland fishery. At that last date reports stretching back to 1699 were utilized.[19] Usually such information was sought to help judge the merits of bills and petitions submitted to Parliament, but the nature of the request depended in part on the ways in which the issues involved were understood and the sources from which reasonably meaningful information might be supplied.

As the previous three chapters made clear, even general economic legislation was often finely grained. Much of the information that Parliament sought on such matters was consequently of particular runs of data about overseas trade (often of specific commodities), the output of certain industries (usually by resort to excise data), and public income and expenditure. Here it is worth remembering that, despite the efforts between 1660 and 1714 of Sir William Petty and other early political arithmeticians, contemporaries struggled to conceive of 'the economy' – the term is certainly anachronistic – and conceived of macroeconomic management in much more limited terms than modern governments.[20] Evidence of overseas trade, which had become centralized and regularized with the end of the farming of customs duties in 1671 and the establishment in 1696 of both the Inspector General of Customs and the General Register of Shipping, was the best data available with which to assess general economic conditions, though occasionally the output of the Mint or the burdens of poor rates were also turned to. Even then, the existence of very different guesses about what was happening to numbers of people before the first census in 1801 meant that absolute figures could not be put in relative context.[21] Overwhelmingly, Parliament accessed information about economic life with reference to specific issues rather than general assessments.

Most of the information supplied to Parliament via accounts and papers came from the revenue services, Treasury, Exchequer, Board of Trade, and

---

[18] Lambert, *Sessional papers*, vol. 2, p. 61.
[19] *JHC*, 47 (1792), p. 695 (5 April 1792); Lambert, *Sessional papers*, vols. 1–2.
[20] See p. 11.
[21] D. V. Glass, *Numbering the people: the eighteenth-century population controversy and the development of census and vital statistics in Britain* (Farnborough, 1973), chs. 1 and 2; Andrea A. Rusnock, *Vital accounts: quantifying health and population in eighteenth-century England and France* (Cambridge, 2002).

Admiralty. Often this was done with impressive speed, though sometimes requests for information went unanswered, probably because of the burdens of extracting details from the underlying sources, especially those kept by the customs service. Thus the two requests on 27 April 1770 for data on the export between 1757 and 1770 of British and Irish linens on the one hand and those of foreign linens on the other were not complied with. But on 1 May two new requests were submitted for export data between 1765 and 1770 of foreign linens, distinguishing England and Wales from Scotland. These were provided on 7 and 15 May, respectively.[22] Seemingly Parliament was quickly told that its original request was too onerous and a new more realistic request was issued. In other words, it had a close relationship with the revenue services and though the relationship was akin to that of master and servant, Parliament had to be realistic in its demands.

If bureaucratic capacity set limits to the information Parliament could elicit, it was sometimes able to transcend them by turning to proxy evidence. For example, the quantity and quality of harvests profoundly influenced employment, prices, and well-being and so an appreciation of corn markets would have been crucial to a governing class that was highly sensitive to the fragility of the social order. But because agricultural production figures were not collected at the time the Commons turned to evidence of the import and export of corn provided by the customs service. This began in the 1730s and lasted until the mid-1770s, with reports submitted often every other session. Between 1714 and 1750 there were thirteen reports on corn exports and three on imports; between 1751 and 1800 the numbers were twenty-two and twenty-two, respectively. Many of these provided data for just two or three years, but occasionally more extensive surveys were undertaken. That in 1766–7 stands out when, amidst anxiety about the very bad harvest and extensive food rioting, twenty-three reports were submitted providing, amongst other things, export data back to 1670 and evidence of the starch and distilling industries, both of which depended on corn as a raw material.[23] Soon enough such reports were overtaken by the institution of a remarkably thorough county-by-county collection of corn price data, with prices published weekly in the official *London Gazette*.[24] At the end

[22] Lambert, *Sessional papers*, vol. 2, p. 61.
[23] Lambert, *Sessional papers*, vol. 2, pp. 38–43.
[24] 10 George III, c. 39. D'Maris Coffman and David Ormrod, 'Corn prices, corn models and corn rents: what can we learn from the English corn returns?', in Martin Allen and D'Maris Coffman, eds., *Money, prices, and wages: essays in honour of Professor Nicholas Mayhew* (Basingstoke, 2014), pp. 196–210; Liam Brunt and Edmund Cannon, 'The truth, the whole truth, and nothing but the truth: the English corn returns as a data source in economic history, 1770–1914', *European Review of Economic History*, 17.3 (2013), pp. 318–39.

of the eighteenth century, under extreme pressures of wartime, national crop surveys were also undertaken.[25]

The development of an effective system for collecting corn prices in 1770 was the latest in a long line of such bureaucratic developments that increased the information that Parliament might access, stretching back particularly to the end of the 'farming' of customs and excise collection in the late seventeenth century. Inevitably, as the years passed longer runs of official data became available, allowing historical views to be drawn, somewhat reinforced by the introduction in the last quarter of the eighteenth century of 'statistics' from Germany.[26] Such views were a critical development, allowing the exigencies of the moment to be set within a wider framework. The building blocks for these were official sources, which were beginning to be systematized from around the middle of the eighteenth century, as in the work of Treasury official James Postlethwayt. His compendium systematically and comprehensively arranged on an annual basis public income and expenditure for more than half a century.[27] Such sources were exploited both within and outside government; indeed, there was significant cross-over between the two. Among the outsiders, note might be made of William Playfair's brilliant invention in the 1780s of graphs showing the growth of overseas trade, the national debt, and public expenditure, or George Chalmers' major work of 1782 arguing that Britain's long-run economic and demographic performance was much better than pessimists such as Richard Price had argued.[28] This, and Chalmers' knowledge of imperial trade,

---

[25] W. E. Minchinton, 'Agricultural returns and the government during the Napoleonic wars', *Agricultural History Review*, 1.1 (1953), pp. 29–43.

[26] 'Statistics are that comprehensive Part of municipal Philosophy, which states and defines the Situation, Strength, and Resources of a Nation, and is a Kind of political Abstract, by which the Statesman may be enabled to calculate his Finances, as well as guide the Œconomy of his Government.' Benjamin Pitts Capper, *A statistical account of the population and cultivation, produce and consumption, of England and Wales, compiled from the accounts laid before the House of Commons, and the Board of Agriculture* (1801), p. vii. An influential work was E. A. W. Zimmermann, a professor at Brunswick (Braunschweig), *A political survey of the present state of Europe, in sixteen tables* (1787). For background see J. van der Zande, 'Statistik and history in the German Enlightenment', *Journal of the History of Ideas*, 71.3 (2010), pp. 411–32.

[27] James Postlethwayt, *The history of the public revenue, from the revolution in 1688, to Christmas 1753* (1759). This was supported by around 360 subscribers, including leading politicians, lawyers, and clerics. This built on the much briefer Anon., *A view of the taxes, funds and public revenues of England … from the year 1702, to the year 1712 inclusive* (1743). James was brother to Malachy, author of *The universal dictionary of trade and commerce* (2 vols., 1751–5), who had been an economic advisor to Sir Robert Walpole. See R. J. Bennett, 'Malachy Postlethwayt: genealogy and influence of an early economist and spin doctor', *Genealogists' Magazine*, 31 (June 2011), pp. 1–7.

[28] William Playfair, *The commercial and political atlas; representing, by means of stained copperplate charts, the exports, imports, and general trade of England; the national debt, and other*

was such that he became chief clerk to the reconstituted Board of Trade in 1786, working alongside its president, Charles Jenkinson MP, who himself had a keen interest in better understanding developments since the mid-seventeenth century.[29] But nobody was more important to better informing government, including Parliament, in the late eighteenth century than Sir Joseph Banks, President of the Royal Society. Though never an MP, he pondered many economic issues, including such thorny issues as smuggling, weights and measures, and the money supply, personally accumulating a large amount of information, much of it historical, and seeking to influence government, the executive especially but, as will be clear in Chapter 7, sometimes the legislature as well.[30]

Parliamentarians too were involved in this effort at building a statistically informed historical view of Britain's economic developments, most notably Sir Charles Whitworth, chairman of the key Commons committee of Ways and Means in the ten years prior to his death in 1778. In 1763, building on James Postlethwayt's synthesis, he published an important survey of public finances since 1688. In 1776 he presented annual statistics of British overseas trade since 1697.[31] There followed a short-lived quarterly account of the trade of the Port of London, and in the following year additions to Cunningham's major history of customs duties originally published in 1764.[32] Alongside such efforts he also produced editions of works by earlier political economists, including in five volumes the works of Charles Davenant (1656–1714), a political arithmetician, party propagandist, and Inspector General of the Customs.[33] In these ways, Whitworth brought long runs of data into the heart of parliamentary decision making, while reviving the importance

public accounts (1786); Ian Spence, 'William Playfair (1759–1823)', *ODNB*; George Chalmers, *An estimate of the comparative strength of Britain during the present and four preceding reigns* (1782). In 1785 Chalmers asked Adam Smith, a Scottish Customs Commissioner since 1778, for trade data. *The correspondence of Adam Smith*, ed. Ernest Campell Mossner and Ian Simpson Ross (Oxford, 1987), p. 289.

[29] Julian Hoppit, 'Economical reform and the Mint, 1780–1816', *British Numismatic Journal*, 84 (2014), p. 183.

[30] John Gascoigne, *Joseph Banks and the English Enlightenment: useful knowledge and polite culture* (Cambridge, 1994); John Gascoigne, *Science in the service of empire: Joseph Banks, the British state and the uses of science in the age of revolution* (Cambridge, 1998).

[31] Charles Whitworth, *State of the trade of Great Britain, in its imports and exports* (1776).

[32] [Charles Whitworth], *A collection of the supplies, and ways and means, from the Revolution to the present time* (1763) and *A register of the trade of the Port of London* (1777). Timothy Cunningham, *The history of the customs, aids, subsidies, national debts, and taxes … The third edition corrected. With several improvements suggested by Sir Charles Whitworth* (1778).

[33] *The political and commercial works of that celebrated writer Charles D'Avenant*, edited by Sir Charles Whitworth (5 vols., 1771); Charles Whitworth, ed., *Select dissertations on colonies and plantations. By those celebrated authors, Sir Josiah Child, Charles D'Avenant, LL. D. and Mr. William Wood.* (1775); Charles Whitworth, ed., *Scarce tracts on trade and commerce, serving as a supplement to Davenant's works* (2 vols., 1776).

of long-dead authors. Doubtless this irked Adam Smith, and indeed may have prompted him to heighten his criticisms of the advocates of the 'mercantile system'. But in terms of both data and ideas, a sense of the past was critical to how Parliament assessed economic matters.

Whitworth was far from alone amongst parliamentarians who researched economic problems themselves or supported the researches of others, often by subscribing to the publication of major works. This stretched from leading ministers anxious to frame and justify better policies, to MPs and peers who developed particular concerns. For the former, close connections with leading bankers and traders in the City of London were a key part of this, but only a part. Robert Harley, who rose to head the Tory administration of 1710–14, turned to the great political arithmetician Gregory King and made use of political and economic reports produced by Daniel Defoe.[34] Most of his successors similarly valued good economic intelligence, but this was taken to a new level by the advent of wide-ranging efforts at reform from around 1780. Thus Shelburne, briefly prime minister in 1782–3, had 'calculating people about him' and elicited reports into, for example, the revenue services and the Mint, in the latter case from the Birmingham businessman Samuel Garbett.[35] Shelburne's successor, Pitt the younger, often working with Jenkinson and Banks, sustained this effort, directly to introduce the income tax in 1799 and indirectly the census in 1801.[36]

A critical feature of the relationship between Parliament, economic legislation, and information was also the efforts of non-governmental members in both houses. Just as some developed expertise in welfare matters detailed by Innes, some sought the same in the sphere of economic life.[37] Those of London's leading merchants and bankers who became MPs, such as Sir John Barnard or Micajah Perry, were always liable to be especially important, but there were many other MPs from different backgrounds, such as the early cotton lord Robert Peel, father of the future prime minister, who published on the national debt and actively intervened in many commercial and industrial matters, or Sir John Sinclair, a major landowner in the far north of Scotland who

---

[34] Joan Thirsk and J. P. Cooper, eds., *Seventeenth-century economic documents* (Oxford, 1972), pp. 790–98; BL, Harleian Mss, 7021, ff. 46–50; J. A. Downie, *Robert Harley and the press: propaganda and public opinion in the age of Swift and Defoe* (Cambridge, 1979).

[35] Harold B. Carter, ed., *The sheep and wool correspondence of Sir Joseph Banks, 1781–1820* (New South Wales and London, 1979), p. 76; Hoppit, 'Economical reform and the Mint', pp. 180–1; John Norris, *Shelburne and reform* (1963).

[36] Stephen John Thompson, 'Census-taking, political economy and state formation in Britain, c. 1790–1840' (University of Cambridge PhD thesis, 2010).

[37] Joanna Innes, *Inferior politics: social problems and social policies in eighteenth-century Britain* (Oxford, 2009), ch. 1.

became committed to improving information gathering in the service of economic development.[38]

Any government, of whatever complexion, directs its efforts in response to beliefs it has formed about the nature of what it is trying to affect, often seeking to make the complex both comprehensible and amenable to governmental action.[39] And any institution, such as Parliament, works with regard to a mix of conventions and rules, learning and forgetting.[40] What is clear is that in Britain a large amount of information gathering in Parliament or by parliamentarians was an essential part of the history of economic legislation. The scale of this effort was very considerable, and gives quite a different impression to faded pictures of complacent oligarchical politics. But this was not a one-way relationship of Parliament acting and others reacting. Parliament was also subjected to a torrent of expressions of points of view, especially via petitioning and the press.

Petitions, Interest Groups, and Economic Legislation

If Parliament accessed very large amounts of information, it was also subjected to considerable efforts from those outside to persuade it this way or that.[41] Many of those efforts were highly targeted, making claims about legislation in one way or another. This might be done by many routes, including correspondence, lobbying, pamphleteering, and petitioning. In this section, attention focuses on the last of these, while the next section turns to consider the general character of published political economy that framed so much of Parliament's efforts to influence economic life.

Focusing on petitions has the advantage of showing a key means by which the wider nation engaged with economic legislation, in particular the types of 'interests' at work. Understanding their nature is in fact critical to analyzing Britain's political economies. The language of 'interests' had grown markedly in the seventeenth century and by the eighteenth was much more important than party, oppositional politics, and class as a means by which contemporaries understood the working out of the

---

[38] R. G. Thorne, 'Peel, I (1750–1830), of Drayton Manor, Staffs', *HofP online, 1790–1820*; Rosalind Mitchison, 'Sinclair, John (1754–1835), of Ulbster and Thurso Castle, Caithness', *HofP online, 1754–1790*.

[39] James C. Scott, *Seeing like a state: how certain schemes to improve the human condition have failed* (New Haven, CT, 1998).

[40] Mary Douglas, *How institutions think* (1987).

[41] A fuller discussion of the material in this section is in Julian Hoppit, 'Petitions, economic legislation and interest groups in Britain, 1660–1800', in Richard Huzzey, ed., *Pressure on Parliament* (Oxford, 2017).

relationship between economic and political power.[42] As one commentator noted, 'No human ties are so binding as those founded in interest.'[43] Moreover, because large societies were inevitably composed of 'jarring interests', these were liable to 'endanger the public peace or liberty' if left unconstrained.[44] A key function of Parliament was believed to be judging between different interests, some of which were governmental, and harmonizing them as far as possible.

In his famous *Dictionary*, Samuel Johnson defined an interest as a 'concern; advantage; good', associated with a 'Regard to private profit'.[45] Hirschman has stressed how conceptualizations of 'interests' developed from the sixteenth century as an alternative to viewing human motivation solely in terms of passions, defining them as a 'disciplined understanding of what it takes to advance one's power, influence, and wealth'.[46] Interests can involve needs, desires, concerns, and fears, with people having many interests, not just one.[47] When the interests of at least a few people cohere, historians have applied various anachronistic labels, including 'lobbies', 'pressure groups', and 'interest groups' – to Johnson a 'lobby' meant only an antechamber. In this period the term 'interest' was often used rather loosely on its own, but reasonably often with a qualifying adjective, as in 'landed interest', 'mercantile interest', 'monied interest', and 'manufacturing interest' – according to Hirschman, the language of interests took a marked economic turn in the 1690s.[48] The key issue for Parliament, however, was whether the preoccupations of individuals or groups were compatible with the public good, or 'national interest'. Through the period many doubted it, seeing particular interests as corrosive of a well-ordered society.

---

[42] J. A. W. Gunn, ' "Interest will not lie": a seventeenth-century political maxim', *Journal of the History of Ideas*, 29.4 (1968), pp. 551–64; J. A. W. Gunn, *Politics and the public interest in the seventeenth century* (Toronto, 1969).

[43] [Joseph Galloway], *Cool thoughts on the consequences to Great Britain of American independence* (1780), p. 18.

[44] Thomas Day, *A letter to Arthur Young, esq. on a bill now depending in Parliament to prevent the exportation of wool* (1788), pp. 25–6.

[45] *A dictionary of the English language* (1755), s.v. 'interest'.

[46] Albert O. Hirschman, *The passions and the interests: political arguments for capitalism before its triumph* (Princeton, NJ, 1977), p. 38.

[47] Lawrence Susskind, 'Arguing, bargaining, and getting agreement', in Michael Moran, Martin Rein, and Robert E. Goodin, eds., *The Oxford handbook of public policy* (Oxford, 2006), p. 272.

[48] For a useful typology of interest groups in the period see Alison Gilbert Olson, *Making the empire work: London and American interest groups, 1690–1790* (Cambridge, MA, 1992), pp. 2–4. Also useful is Michael Kammen, *Empire and interest: the American colonies and the politics of mercantilism* (Philadelphia, PA, 1970), especially pp. 11–12. Hirschman, *Passions and interests*, p. 36.

Criticisms of self-interest gradually came to be contested, as in Mandeville's argument that private vices could produce public virtues, elaborated on by Smith's emphasis that the operation of the market mechanism – the 'invisible hand' – naturally harmonized the selfish with the social.[49] But alongside that Smith argued that consumers, whose interests he thought ought to be preeminent, invariably suffered through the power of interest groups, especially of merchants and manufacturers swaying Parliament to legislate the conditions with which to reap higher profit margins. This suspicion of interest groups has proved very resilient, and with good reason. But in an unduly neglected essay Charles Wilson rightly pointed out the positive functions they served when, as in Britain in this period, central government had limited means both to be informed of crucial developments and to act to address them.[50] And petitioning was a key weapon in the armoury of interests.

Petitioning Parliament was well established before 1660, gaining in potency in the troubles of the 1640s and 1650s.[51] But the considerable unpredictability in the meetings of Parliament in the Restoration period limited the opportunities for petitioning it. That changed quickly after the Glorious Revolution. The institutionalization and regularization of Parliament within government revolutionized its legislative work, leading to more bills and acts and greater occasion for petitioning.[52] Interests immediately realized this, with significant petitioning activity becoming established in the 1690s, even though legislation in 1661 had sought to prevent the submission of 'tumultuous' petitions and petitions could not be submitted on money bills.[53]

Petitions were submitted to Parliament for various reasons, especially to seek legislation, to influence the passage of bills under consideration, to raise a more general matter for Parliament to consider, to appeal a

---

[49] Though in *The wealth of nations* Smith referred to the 'invisible hand' and 'self-interest' rarely. Emma Rothschild, 'Adam Smith and the invisible hand', *American Economic Review*, 84.2 (1995), pp. 319–22; Pierre Force, *Self-interest before Adam Smith: a genealogy of economic science* (Cambridge, 2003).

[50] Charles Wilson, 'Government policy and private interest in modern British history' in his *Economic history and the historian: collected essays* (1969), ch. 9. Modern lobbies have also been defended as important parts of the political process, e.g., S. E. Finer, *Anonymous empire: a study of the lobby in Great Britain* (2nd edn., 1966).

[51] David Zaret, 'Petitions and the "invention" of public opinion in the English revolution', *American Journal of Sociology*, 101.6 (1996), pp. 1497–555; Derek Hirst, 'Making contact: petitions and the English republic', *Journal of British Studies*, 45.1 (2006), pp. 26–50.

[52] Petitions were used in other parts of society, to local government, various institutions, and private individuals. See, for example, R. A. Houston, *Peasant petitions: social relations and economic life on landed estates, 1600–1850* (Basingstoke, 2014).

[53] Mark Knights, *Representation and misrepresentation in later Stuart Britain* (Oxford, 2005), ch. 3. 13 Charles II, stat. 2, c. 5. For an outline of the parliamentary procedures involved

legal decision to the Lords, and to contest an election return. Ignoring legal and election appeals, there were 2,412 petitions submitted to Parliament in nine sample sessions studied in detail across the period, of which 1,281 (53 per cent) related to economic issues. If these sessions were reasonably representative, then Parliament might have received around 38,000 petitions in total between 1660 and 1800, with perhaps 20,000 concerning economic matters. As with legislation, there was a pronounced growth in numbers of petitions from the 1760s, with 880 presented between 1785–9 and 1,026 from 1801–5.[54] One way of making sense of some of this voluminous yet varied petitioning is to focus on specific topics or issues (overwhelmingly particular bills) that each attracted at least five petitions in each of the sample sessions – using this as a crude filter by which to focus on issues involving interest groups.[55] Obviously this has the negative effect of drawing attention away from certain types of issues that might have been very significant either in their own right or collectively. But the importance of disputes over political economy was well recognized at the time. As Malachy Postlethwayt put it, 'nothing is more common than for traders to differ widely among themselves, in regard to measures proper to be taken by the legislature for the due encouragement or regulation of peculiar branches. Whence arise those opposite and contradictory petitions to parliament from traders, which often tend to mislead, and even confound the legislature itself.'[56]

Some forty-eight occasions (or 'issues') elicited at least five petitions in nine sample sessions studied in detail, involving 759 petitions in all – 701 were presented to the Commons (92 per cent), just 58 to the Lords. A little more than a half of the occasions related more or less to national concerns, and unsurprisingly attracted more petitions on average than specific issues (19.8 as against 10.7). If a majority of legislation in the period concerned economic matters, this was even truer of issues attracting at least five petitions, accounting for 85 per cent of the issues and 68 per cent of the petitions (see Table 5.2).[57] The remaining discussion of

in petitioning see P. D. G. Thomas, *The House of Commons in the eighteenth century* (Oxford, 1971), pp. 17–19.

[54] 'A return of the number of petitions presented in each of the five years ending 1788–9 … 1832', BPP, 83 (1852–3), pp. 2–3. A useful overview of the character and development of petitioning regarding 'public grievances' from the late eighteenth century is Joanna Innes, 'Legislation and public participation, 1760–1830', in David Lemmings, ed., *The British and their laws in the eighteenth century* (Woodbridge, 2005), pp. 112–21.

[55] These measures were also subject to a disproportionate number of divisions.

[56] Malachy Postlethwayt, *The universal dictionary of trade and commerce* (2 vols., 1751–5), vol. 1, p. vi.

[57] Some economic issues were certainly not just that, such as those relating to overseas trade or the quartering of troops. The seven non-economic issues were: the general

Table 5.2 *Issues with at least five petitions to Parliament within sample sessions, 1660–1800*

Session	Economic issues	Numbers of petitions on economic issues	Non-economic issues	Numbers of petitions on non-economic issues
1660	2	10	1	6
1674	0	0	0	0
1694–5	1	12	0	0
1708–9	7	126	0	0
1724–5	6	57	2	21
1740–1	7	100	0	0
1753	8	94	0	0
1772–3	6	46	2	17
1795–6	4	73	2	197
All	41	518	7	241

Note: 1674 was a short session, like many others in the Restoration era.
Source: Sample sessions.

petitions considers those relating to the forty-one economic issues alone (hereafter 'the sample').

On average, topics in the sample attracted an average of 12.6 petitions each, with only seven attracting more than twenty petitions, with the case of the building of the London docks in 1795–6 attracting the most, forty-nine.

The forty-one economic issues in Table 5.2 related to twenty-one public acts, one private act, fifteen failed attempts at legislation, and four other matters. Of the fifteen failed attempts, six were specific or local in their intended reach and nine were general. By subject matter, some seventeen of the forty-one economic issues (41 per cent) dealt with infrastructural developments – turnpike roads, river navigations, canals, and docks – and nine others (22 per cent) dealt with matters of overseas trade, some of which related to exclusive rights, such as the Royal Africa (in both 1694–5 and 1708–9) and the Levant Companies. There was a

pardon, 1660; the building of London's fifty new churches and regulating the city's elections, 1724–5; the relief of Protestant dissenters and a proposal to change charities, 1772–3; and the enormous reactions to the two acts on seditious meetings and treasonable practices, 1795–6. Stuart Handley has shown that 87 of the 111 petitions sent from Lancashire relating to general legislation between 1689 and 1731 concerned economic matters: 'Provincial influence on general legislation: the case of Lancashire, 1689–1731', *Parliamentary History*, 16.2 (1997), pp. 172–3.

small amount of petitioning relating to industry, such as regulating the West Riding cloth manufacture in 1724, and to the Framework Knitters Company in 1753 (about its monopoly rights),[58] though other measures that mainly concerned overseas trade might have a marked industrial dimension: the twenty-seven petitions about the failed bill regarding the clandestine export of wool in 1740–1 clearly need in part to be considered in terms of an industrial raw material and a long history of attempts at its regulation, which are discussed in Chapter 7. Notably, little petitioning on economic issues related to agriculture: there were just two such issues in the sample (5 per cent), regarding corn exports in 1740–1 and enclosure in 1795–6.

More than 96 per cent petitions in the sample were submitted to the Commons, 94 per cent came from groups rather than individuals, and 87 per cent were submitted from within England. Given that 7 per cent of the sample cannot be placed geographically, obviously few petitions came from other parts of Britain and its empire – just 3 per cent from Scotland, 1 per cent from Wales, and 1 per cent from the West Indies and North American colonies. These non-English shares were roughly in line with the patterns of specific legislation enacted, though somewhat less than the patterns of population distribution and economic activity.[59] Some explanations for that emerge by exploring more generally what types of groups generated petitions.

Because the *Journals* routinely record who submitted petitions, it is possible to categorize the type of person or body sending them, with a particular aim of distinguishing petitions sent by groups with established and often formal connections from those sent by groups appearing to have cohered specifically for the occasion (albeit probably usually based on previous informal connections of various sorts) – hereafter these are 'established' and 'ad hoc' groups.[60] As Table 5.3 shows, about 53 per cent of the petitions came from ad hoc groups created for the purpose, about 42 per cent from established groups.

Clearly, it is important that so many petitions came from ad hoc groups.[61] Established groups had many advantages in terms of preparing

---

[58] J. D. Chambers, 'The Worshipful Company of Framework Knitters (1657–1778)', *Economica*, 27 (1929), pp. 322–3.

[59] It is worth noting how, from this perspective, the secondary literature has given disproportionate attention to colonial lobbying.

[60] This categorization rests on the summary details provided by the *Journals* and so may be wrong in a few cases.

[61] Gauci has calculated that more than three-quarters of groups petitioning the Commons on mercantile matters in the period 1690–1714 were not from chartered companies or civic corporations. Perry Gauci, *The politics of trade: the overseas merchant in state and society, 1660–1720* (Oxford, 2001), p. 212.

Table 5.3 *Type of petitioners in sample*

	Number	Per cent
Ad hoc groups	276	53
Established groups:		
Local law, politics, and administration	75	15
Central law, politics, and administration	9	2
Companies, guilds, etc.	55	11
Imprisoned debtors	77	15
Others:		
Personal	25	5
Unknown	1	0
Grand Total	518	101

Note: 'Local law, politics, and administration' includes JPs, grand juries, civic corporations, and agents for Caribbean and American colonies; 'Central law, politics, and administration' includes mainly those working at the central courts.
Source: Sample sessions.

petitions, most obviously organizational, but also in terms of drawing on an existing, if not necessarily well worked out interest and identity. Ad hoc groups lacked those advantages, depending on the energy of key individuals to mobilize opinion: common aims needed to be specified, possible adherents identified and pursued. Even so, certain issues were more likely to be the subject of petitioning from ad hoc rather than established groups. For example, ad hoc groups sent 86 of the 101 petitions in the sample on the subject of the monopolies or privileges of the Royal Africa, Levant, and Framework Knitters Companies. With their exclusive rights targeted by those outside the companies, few other established groups than the companies themselves were likely to join the petitioning fray. Infrastructural developments, on the other hand, tended to engage both ad hoc and established groups, generally local. The nature of both established and ad hoc groups can be explored a little further.

Looking first at the types of established groups, debtors were highly distinctive and numerous. The contemporary law was such that debtors could find themselves imprisoned by their creditors, and if they lacked the means to pay their debts, their release depended on either a parliamentary amnesty or creditors' goodwill. Parliament legislated for such amnesties about every other year, and debtors, accustomed to this pattern, played their part in reminding them almost ritualistically of their need. Their petitions bear witness to a structural limitation in credit-debt laws at the time, but one Parliament failed fundamentally to reform, despite significant pressure, until the nineteenth century.[62]

Local government, law, and administration provided the second most petitions (seventy-five) from amongst established groups within the sample. A little more than 80 per cent of these came from urban corporations, just 12 per cent from county administration (usually JPs and/or grand juries), with the rest, 7 per cent, from colonial agents. The importance of urban centres to petitioning was more considerable still, as 55 per cent of all petitions in the sample were submitted by groups within parliamentary boroughs (112 ad hoc, 54 established), and 19 per cent of the sample came from London. It was certainly easier for townspeople to organize petitions than those in the counties and colonies. Civic office-holders of various sorts, such as mayors, aldermen, and burgesses, had a responsibility throughout their term to look after the interests of their jurisdiction – to be watchful of potential sources of damage and to aid the development of proposals to help their towns.[63] This was less true at the county level, where lord lieutenants, sheriffs, and JPs often played more ceremonial, electoral, and judicial roles, though gatherings might be held in association with quarter sessions and the assize, along with ad hoc 'county meetings'.[64] Arguably political society generally was also more likely to be able to cohere and act at the specific urban level than the wider county level. As locales with concentrated economic interests, legislative proposals were, similarly, more likely to emanate from the urban rather than the county level.

Three types of groups dominated petitions submitted by established companies, guilds, and the like: nineteen of the fifty-five came from business companies; sixteen from those directing infrastructure projects; and fourteen from 'guilds'. The distinction between businesses and infrastructure is arguably insignificant, but even so it is the small number of petitions from such groups which is striking. Plainly they might easily petition, arguably more easily than town corporations given they were probably less likely to be politically or ideologically riven. Yet if corporate and collective enterprise and regulation caught the eye of both contemporaries and historians, they played only a small role in total economic activity in Britain and consequently were unlikely to figure much in terms

---

[62] Paul H. Haagen, 'Eighteenth-century English society and the debt law', in Stanley Cohen and Andrew Scull, eds., *Social control and the state* (Oxford, 1983), pp. 222–47.

[63] An important overview of civic government in the period is provided in Joanna Innes and Nicholas Rogers, 'Politics and government, 1700–1840', in Peter Clark, ed., *The Cambridge urban history of Britain: vol. 2, 1550–1840* (Cambridge, 2000), pp. 529–74.

[64] B. Keith-Lucas, 'County meetings', *Law Quarterly Review*, 70 (1954), 109–14.

Table 5.4 *'Leading' ad hoc petitioners in sample*

	Number	Per cent
Clothiers	38	14
Gentlemen	49	18
Inhabitants	33	12
Innkeepers	13	5
Merchants	64	23
Sub-total	197	72
Total	276	

of pressure on Parliament as measured by simple counts of numbers of petitions submitted.

It is harder to categorize types of petitioners constituting ad hoc groups, not least because the summary in the *Journals* might give only a broad sense of who they were. Additionally, they were often composite groups, comprising a number of different elements, such as 'gentlemen, clergy, merchants, tradesmen and others'. However, by looking only at the first category of person mentioned in ad hoc petitions, on the grounds that they were likely judged by those managing the petition locally to be the most important, a very tentative summary can be provided. As Table 5.4 shows, using this method five types of people were especially prominent, leading nearly three-quarters of ad hoc petitions.

Gentlemen and inhabitants, that is, people essentially distinguished by status and locale, led nearly one-third of ad hoc groups petitioning. More widely, twenty-nine petitions were sent by groups claiming to be the 'principal' members of their group, often of inhabitants, merchants, or tradesmen.[65] Such groups suggested their importance and authority less because of what they did than where and who they were. It is notable that nearly one-quarter of ad hoc groups was merchants. Some of these appear to have been inland merchants, or merchant manufacturers, but the majority were engaged in overseas trade, mainly petitioning about such matters. It was difficult for working people to involve themselves actively with Parliament. But with sufficient encouragement and connections they were sometimes able to do so. In 1755 poor weavers in the Gloucestershire woollen industry petitioned successfully for an act

---

[65] The characteristics of 'chief inhabitants' of localities are discussed in H. R. French, 'Social status, localism and the "middle sort of people" in England 1620–1750', *Past and Present*, 166 (2000), pp. 66–99.

confirming the principle of wage assessment by justices, catching the clothiers unawares.[66]

Petitions to Parliament doubtless helped to cohere many interest groups for the first time. Even so, obviously this involved building on existing similarities of circumstance, aspirations, and beliefs. Three aspects were crucial. First, place, locale, and circumstance were especially important in petitioning, in part because of organizational considerations, but also mainly because of local or regional economic specialization. This could mean, second, that divisions expressed via petitions might also involve a sectoral or sectional element, notably when one region saw its interests as different to those of another. In 1708–9, for example, a proposed duty on imported Irish woollen yarn was favoured by seventeen petitions from Devon and Cornwall, but opposed by nine petitions mainly from Gloucestershire, Somerset, and Wiltshire. Thirdly, as has been seen, social status was important in some petitions.

Petitions alone were rarely, if ever, decisive. The impression is that the petitioners felt it important to express their views, that they thought they would be taken seriously, but that it was possible that their aim would not be met. Among the advantages of a petition was that it had a degree of formality about it. A case had to be prepared and agreed to, helping thereby to confirm or (re)constitute the interest involved and to clarify its arguments. Moreover, because petitions were public expressions, they perhaps reduced the extent to which the interests they expressed were viewed as narrow and particular. And because petitions were formally presented to Parliament, they could not be ignored completely: the claims were usually taken seriously and the information welcomed, even if ultimately Parliament decided against them.[67] A range of factors affected that decision, but in terms of interest group formation obtaining signatures was crucial.

Signatories gave the arguments of petitions an unambiguous weight; it is clear that both the number of petitions and the number of signatories was seen to matter. That said, an important feature of petitions is that they were very largely just lists of signatories (very few signed

---

[66] W. E. Minchinton, 'The petitions of weavers and clothiers of Gloucestershire in 1756', *Transactions of the Bristol and Gloucestershire Archaeological Society for 1954*, 73 (1955), pp. 216–27. The act was 29 George II, c. 33. See also Joanna Innes, 'Regulating wages in eighteenth and early nineteenth-century England: arguments in context', in Perry Gauci, ed., *Regulating the British economy, 1660–1850* (Farnham, 2011), especially pp. 201–3.

[67] 'The stream of petitions from clothiers, merchants, poor weavers, gilds and companies and the like did not only represent an exercise of constitutional rights; they also represented the best and often the only source of information the government could obtain on complex economic problems.' Wilson, *Economic history*, p. 143.

with a mark), overwhelmingly male, lacking addresses, occupations, and titles.[68] Such details were presumably not thought to add weight to the petition, or might distract attention away from what was being sought. Yet if weight of numbers was obviously meaningful, that weight might look different when conceived of in terms of the numbers of possible signatories. Patterns here were not always what might be expected. Local interests might be fairly extensive, for example, involving all those affected along the route of a proposed canal or turnpike. More than 700 signed a petition regarding a forty-five-mile stretch of the River Nene in Northamptonshire in 1725, for example.[69] By contrast, Gauci has found that for fifty petitions from West India interests between 1670 and 1720 usually only between fifteen and twenty-five signed.[70] Moreover, apparently smaller groups might be able to imply a higher concentration of expertise: that is, that their lack of numbers was significant. Kim has argued that some merchants may have sought to limit the number of petitioners to heighten 'the authenticity of their applications, at the same time avoiding the undesirable impression that they tried to exercise an unsolicited collective power to force their wills on decision-makers'.[71]

As is clear, petitions were important weapons to interests, not least because they could be used by such different types of groups. But they had limitations as a means of applying pressure on Parliament. They required a degree of organization, literacy, funding, and connection that many lacked. An MP, peer, or sheriff of the City of London had to be willing to present them; when presented they might be heard by very few in a thin house; even then, they might quickly be forgotten, especially if they were ordered to lie on the table amongst many other petitions and papers; and it was difficult to make an elaborate argument, or present much factual detail, within the constraints of the genre – even the number of signatories was probably only glanced. As one guide put it, 'all Petitions ought to be drawn as short and in Terms as general as can

---

[68] Most petitions I have examined have no female signatories – both first and second names are usually signed, with marks very rare. An exception is that seventeen women were among the seventy-four signatories (23 per cent) to a petition from London calico retailers in February 1721: Parliamentary Archives, HL/PO/JO/10/3/213/37.

[69] Parliamentary Archives, HL/PO/JO/10/3/218/8. In the same session a petition was submitted to the Commons from the coachmen, carriers, waggoners, salesmen, drovers, hagglers, and others of eastern England who used the main London-to-York road. How many signed is unknown, but it was potentially thousands. *JHC*, 20 (1722–7), p. 409 (13 Feb. 1725).

[70] Perry Gauci, 'Learning the ropes of sand: the West Indies lobby, 1714–60', in Perry Gauci, ed., *Regulating the British economy, 1660–1850* (Farnham, 2011), p. 110.

[71] Daeryoon Kim, 'Political convention and the merchant in the later eighteenth century', in Gauci, ed., *Regulating the British economy*, p. 131.

possibly be conceived'.[72] But there was a further significant structural consideration, for if petitioners were notionally informed, they were certainly not disinterested. They sought a particular advantage, and their claims that such advantages would serve the wider good could not be taken on trust.[73] Ultimately, petitioners expressed specific interests. Part of the job of parliamentarians was to be alert to that, to make judgements supposedly from a disinterested point of view so that the public good would be maximized.

Weaknesses in petitioning Parliament obviously encouraged interests to present their cases by other means, though at the risk of further undermining the legitimacy of petitions. One way was to petition less publicly, in the hope of swaying important decision makers and, perhaps, reducing or eliminating the chances of counter-petitioning. Thus, for example, between 1698 and 1803 the Bristol Society of Merchant Venturers sent 100 petitions to Parliament, but additionally twenty-three to the Privy Council, thirteen to the Treasury, and six to the Board of Trade.[74] Other, related, modes of lobbying also existed. Much of that would have been unstructured and sometimes even opportunistic. Some bodies, however, gained considerable expertise in expressing themselves via a number of routes, such as Scotland's Convention of the Royal Burghs, who eventually had an agent in London to act for it, lobbying and keeping abreast of political developments of concern to it. The appointment of agents for many of the West Indian and American colonies was an important development attempting to address imperial coordination problems within Britain's political economies.[75]

It is also significant that a number of bodies emerged in the eighteenth century in part to represent the economic interests of their members politically, most commonly of societies of merchants or manufacturers, but also including some agricultural societies.[76] Most long-lived were the chambers of commerce, with the first being formally established in Jersey

---

[72] Anon., *The Liverpool tractate: an eighteenth century manual on the procedure of the house of commons*, ed. Catherine Strateman (New York, 1937), p. 28.

[73] Roey Sweet, 'Local identities and a national parliament', in Julian Hoppit, ed., *Parliaments, nations and identities in Britain and Ireland, 1660–1850* (Manchester, 2003), pp. 48–63, provides a telling discussion of the types of arguments employed to make compatible local and national advantage.

[74] W. E. Minchinton, ed., *Politics and the port of Bristol in the eighteenth century. The petitions of the Society of Merchant Venturers, 1698–1803* (Bristol Record Society, 23, 1963), p. xviii.

[75] Bob Harris, 'The Scots, the Westminster parliament and the British state in the eighteenth century', in Hoppit, ed., *Parliaments, nations and identities*, 124–45; Lillian M. Penson, *The colonial agents of the British West Indies: a study in colonial administration, mainly in the eighteenth century* (1924); Olson, *Making the empire work*.

[76] Three can be found once in the sample, petitioning unsuccessfully for a general enclosure act in the 1795–6 session: the Bath and West of England Society, the Agricultural

in 1767. Manchester had one of sorts in 1774 and those established at Glasgow, Dublin, Belfast, and Birmingham in 1783 still survive, if not always continuously since their foundation. Such organizations grew markedly in number after 1770, mainly because of economic growth in those places and possible changes in Britain's commercial relations with France, Ireland, and the United States in the aftermath of American independence.[77] They might also adopt rather different tactics. Dietz has argued that by the end of the eighteenth century manufacturers were more often submitting 'memorials' to departments of state, where the emphasis was on an exclusive capacity to comment than on numbers of signatories. As such, they may have been seeking to distinguish themselves from the growth of mass petitioning to Parliament from the late eighteenth century.[78] Certainly, interest groups always have a nice decision to make as to whether they speak for a very wide body, in which case dangers of expressing the lowest common denominator come into play, or whether they were exclusive, with a high degree of specific expertise.

Print and Political Economy

A second major way in which Parliament was confronted with ideas about economic life was by the printed word, ranging from large, long, and costly tomes, through pamphlets, periodicals, and newspapers to very brief 'cases', 'reasons', and the like, often distributed gratis to parliamentarians. As Sharpe remarked, 'politics involved, at all levels, negotiations with texts and the process of interpreting and constituting meaning from texts.'[79] Bills and acts were central texts in this process, but surrounded by many others that framed or commented on them.

Numbers of all publications had surged in the 1640s and 1650s, quickly falling back after the Restoration and the re-imposition of a significant degree of state censorship. But the lapse of the Licensing Act in 1695 removed many of those restrictions, allowing the press to flourish.[80]

Society of Manchester, and the Berkshire Agricultural Society. This relates to Hoppit, *Failed legislation*, 138.023, which was promoted by Sir John Sinclair, president of the recently formed Board of Agriculture.

[77] V. E. Dietz, 'Before the age of capital: manufacturing interests and the British state, 1780–1800' (Princeton University PhD thesis, 1991), ch. 3; Robert J. Bennett, *Local business voice: the history of chambers of commerce in Britain, Ireland, and revolutionary America, 1760–2011* (Oxford, 2011), pp. 14–16, 121–7.

[78] Dietz, 'Before the age of capital', p. 292; Peter Fraser, 'Public petitioning and Parliament before 1832', *History*, 46.158 (1961), pp. 195–211.

[79] Kevin Sharpe, *Reading revolutions: the politics of reading in early modern England* (New Haven, CT, 2000), p. ix.

[80] Raymond Astbury, 'The renewal of the Licensing Act in 1693 and its lapse in 1695', *The Library*, 5th series, 33.4 (1978), pp. 296–322; James Raven, *The business of books: booksellers and the English book trade* (New Haven, CT, 2007), Introduction.

The liberty of the press in Britain was consequently often remarked on in this period. Yet numbers of publications changed little in the first half of the eighteenth century, only growing markedly thereafter. Numbers of imprints in Britain and Ireland for which evidence survives rose from 1,916 in 1703 to 2,566 in 1753 and 6,801 in 1793.[81] It is impossible to say just how many of these were concerned with economic matters, let alone those which related specifically to economic legislation, but the proportion collectively given over to 'Agriculture, almanacs and other practical matters', 'Business and finance', and 'Politics, government and law', was 33, 35, and 44 per cent at those dates.[82]

Published works about economic life began to become common in the 1620s, linked closely to the emergence of economic considerations as a reason of state. By 1670 it was claimed with good reason that 'Trade is now become the Lady, which in this present Age is more Courted and Celebrated than in any former by all the Princes and Potentates of the World.'[83] Unquestionably there was an extraordinary outpouring of works addressing the relationship between politics and the economy in Britain after 1660, with perhaps 10,000 published from 1701 to 1775.[84] This was a very mixed genre. When Joseph Massie pitched for a public mercantile library in London in 1754, he identified six main types of works to be included: statutes, histories, legal judgements, official reports, and the guides to the revenue services, along with 'A Collection of whatever has been written in any Language, on Navigation, Commerce, Manufactures, Plantations, Fisheries, Mines, Metals, Minerals, Gems, Fossils, Drugs, Agriculture, Gardening, Mannual-Arts, & c'.[85] Similarly, a little earlier a compendium of key sources on the woollen industry drew on 'Books of Records and Antiquity, the Statute Books (English, Scottish, and

---

[81] Michael F. Suarez, 'Towards a bibliometric analysis of the surviving record, 1701–1800', in Michael F. Suarez and Michael L. Turner, eds., *The Cambridge history of the book in Britain: vol. 5, 1695–1830* (Cambridge, 2009), p. 43.

[82] Suarez, 'Towards a bibliometric analysis', p. 46.

[83] Roger Coke, *A discourse of trade* (1670), preface.

[84] L. W. Hanson, *Contemporary printed sources for British and Irish economic history, 1701–1750* (Cambridge, 1963); Henry Higgs, *Bibliography of economics, 1751–1775* (Cambridge, 1935). The latter contains many works published outside of Britain and Ireland, which have been excluded from this total. Both contain some works published in Ireland, producing a total of 10,779. Both of these bibliographies were compiled before the ESTC became available and so certainly understate the actual number, hence my conclusion that at least 10,000 were published in Britain, 1701–75. Numbers of works of economic literature published in the final quarter of the eighteenth century have yet to be produced.

[85] [Joseph Massie], *An essay on the many advantages accruing to the community from the superior neatness, conveniences, decorations and embellishments of great and capital cities* (1754), pp. 19–20. There are some echoes here of the Royal Society's uncompleted 'history of trades' project from the late seventeenth century: Walter E. Houghton, 'The history of

Irish) Rymer's *Foedera*, State Papers, Debates, and Votes in Parliament; History, ancient and modern; Dictionaries, Atlases: All the best Books of Trade, general and particular; Foreign as well as English'.[86] Works of or relevant to political economy ranged from huge folios, 'which nobody thinks of reading, down to small ephemeral pamphlets, which few readers take the trouble of preserving'.[87]

The sheer scale and variety of economic literature published in Britain in this period helps explain why it has been considered so selectively, usually by identifying the evolution of key ideas by key thinkers, with the publication of Smith's *The wealth of nations* in 1776 often pivotal in such accounts. However, amongst other things this often exaggerates the novelty and impact of some of Smith's arguments and, teleologically, privileges certain types of works. For example, it is worth repeating an earlier point that there had periodically been loud calls for freer trade since the early seventeenth century.[88] In the late seventeenth century these were revived, when they were successfully ranged against the Royal African Company.[89] And such calls were renewed in the 1750s. Take, for example, Charles, 3rd Viscount Townshend, father of the Chancellor responsible for the 'Townshend duties' of 1767 that so inflamed colonial Americans. In 1751 he attacked in print, as Smith later did in *The wealth of nations*, bounties on corn exports and two years later introduced into Parliament a bill to liberalize labour markets, employing the ideas of one of his correspondents, Josiah Tucker, a clergyman and prolific author on economic matters.[90] Writing more than a quarter of a century before Smith, Tucker opined that monopolies, public companies, and

---

trades: its relation to seventeenth-century thought, as seen in Bacon, Petty, Evelyn and Boyle', *Journal of the History of Ideas*, 2.1 (1941), pp. 33–60.

[86] John Smith, *Chronicon rusticum-commerciale; or, memoirs of wool* (2 vols., 1747), vol. 1, p. ix.

[87] John Sinclair, *Memoirs of the life and works of the late right honourable Sir John Sinclair* (2 vols., Edinburgh, 1837), vol. 1, p. 116.

[88] See pp. 13–14.

[89] George L. Cherry, 'The development of the English free-trade movement in Parliament, 1689–1702', *Journal of Modern History*, 25.2 (1953), pp. 103–19; Tim Keirn, 'Monopoly, economic thought, and the Royal African Company', in John Brewer and Susan Staves, eds., *Early modern conceptions of property* (1995), pp. 427–66.

[90] [Charles Townshend], *National thoughts, recommended to the serious attention of the public: with an appendix, shewing the damages arising from a bounty on corn* [1751]; Hoppit, *Failed legislation*, 91.023, 'A bill, intituled, An act for encouraging industry in the kingdom, by removing certain disabilities and restraints contained in several former acts'. The bill sought the repeal of the 'Statute of Artificers' (5 Elizabeth I, c. 4), which regulated apprenticeship and wages, and the settlement requirement to receive poor relief introduced in 1662 (14 Charles II, c. 12), aims which were finally achieved in 1813 and 1834, respectively. HMC, *Eleventh report, appendix, part 4. The manuscripts of the Marquess of Townshend* (1887), especially pp. 371–82.

corporate charters were 'the *Bane and Destruction* of a *free Trade*'.[91] It is also notable that the original Royal African Company was wound up in 1752 and the Levant Company's monopoly was effectively ended by statute in 1753, following pamphleteering and forty-seven petitions to Parliament.[92] Whatever he suggested, Smith's calls for free trade in *The wealth of nations* built on a long tradition of such arguments and, critically, no little action.

It has long been recognized that it is very misleading to group economic ideas before Smith under the anachronistic heading of 'mercantilist'.[93] Certainly Parliament was faced by economic ideas that were numerous and varied. Importantly, political economy as a branch of intellectual enquiry was in its infancy – even the term had made limited headway by 1800.[94] Moreover there was a striking degree of disagreement over fundamentals: arguments for free trade sat alongside those for regulation; some viewed agriculture as the foundation of the economy, others trade; a labour theory of value was employed by some, a land theory by others; and to some a greater population was crucial, for others a positive balance of trade. Such was this richness that attempts in the 1750s and early 1760s by Massie, Postlethwayt, and Tucker to reduce matters to a coherent and integrated whole were notably unsuccessful.[95] To borrow from Thomas Kuhn, this was very much a pre-paradigmatic situation, and one which *The wealth of nations* did so much to resolve.[96] Even so, to a greater extent than Smith acknowledged, his work rested on the ideas of others and certainly did not instantly sweep all before it.[97]

[91] [Josiah Tucker], *A brief essay on the advantages and disadvantages which respectively attend France and Great Britain, with regard to trade* (1749), p. 25.

[92] Alfred C. Wood, *A history of the Levant company* (Oxford, 1935), p. 156; Michael Wagner, 'The Levant Company under attack in Parliament, 1720–53', *Parliamentary History*, 34.3 (2015), pp. 295–313; 26 George II, c. 18.

[93] Major surveys include Terence Hutchison, *Before Adam Smith: the emergence of political economy, 1662–1776* (Oxford, 1988).

[94] James Steuart, *An inquiry into the principles of political oeconomy* (2 vols., 1767) was the first work in English to use the term in its title.

[95] J. Massie, *A representation concerning the knowledge of commerce as a national concern; pointing out the proper means of promoting such knowledge in this kingdom* (1760); Postlethwayt, *The universal dictionary of trade and commerce*; Josiah Tucker, *The elements of commerce and theory of taxes* [Bristol?, 1755].

[96] Thomas Kuhn, *The structure of scientific revolutions* (3rd edn., Chicago, IL, 1996), pp. 15–16; T. W. Hutchison, *On revolutions and progress in economic knowledge* (Cambridge, 1978), ch. 1.

[97] Salim Rashid, 'Adam Smith's acknowledgements: neo-plagiarism and *The wealth of nations*', *Journal of Libertarian Studies*, 9.2 (1990), pp. 1–24; Kirk Willis, 'The role in Parliament of the economic ideas of Adam Smith, 1776–1800', *History of Political Economy*, 11.4 (1979), pp. 505–44; Richard F. Teichgraeber, '"Less abused than I had reason to expect": the reception of *The wealth of nations* in Britain, 1776–1790', *Historical Journal*, 30.2 (1987), pp. 337–64.

One way of beginning to appreciate the nature of economic ideas published in this period is to explore some of their bibliographical characteristics, using the fairly comprehensive modern listings of Hanson and Higgs, and the selection of 2,180 works of 'commercial knowledge' collected by Joseph Massie for the years 1660–1759.[98] Firstly, it is clear that numbers of such works published grew significantly at the end of the seventeenth century. Massie listed 267 works published in the thirty years 1660–89, but 704 in the thirty years 1690–1719. The structural causes of this were the growth of parliamentary activity following the Glorious Revolution and the lapse of the Licensing Act in 1695. An outpouring of works of economic literature followed – as will be seen many of these were very short and better thought of as copies rather than publications. From Hanson, 10,080 works were published in the first half of the century, whereas a seemingly comparable study of French economic literature arrives at a count of just 1,518 for the same period.[99] Tellingly, whereas numbers of works listed by Massie grew by 164 per cent between 1660–89 and 1690–1719, in France the growth was just 28 per cent.[100] The structures of French government did not warrant as many printed interventions on matters of political discussion, while the presence of state censors – seventy-nine in 1741, nearly 200 by 1789 – speaks to a very different print culture in France.[101]

Not only structural features drove forward economic literature in Britain. Charting annual numbers in Massie's collection (Figure 5.2) shows that some years saw very large numbers of works.

Most of these peaks can be associated with well-known controversies: the re-coinage of 1695–6; Union of England and Scotland in 1707; peace with France in 1713; the South Sea Bubble of 1720; the Excise scheme of 1732–3; and Anglo–Spanish commercial rivalry in 1739–40.

---

[98] Hanson, *Contemporary printed sources*; Higgs, *Bibliography of economics*. Massie probably had experience of mercantile matters in London. R. D. Sheldon, 'Joseph Massie (d. 1784)', *ODNB*; the catalogue to Massie's collection is BL, Lansdowne Mss. 1049. A printed edition, omitting Massie's subject scheme, is William A. Shaw, ed., *Bibliography of the collection of books and tracts on commerce, currency, and poor law (1557 to 1763) formed by Joseph Massie* (1937). Shaw's edition misses one title, number 2024, Anon., *Account of nature, &c. of oil from beech-tree* (1714), p. 32. Missing bibliographical information to Massie's catalogue has been supplied in many cases from the ESTC. For further details on this, and other methodological considerations, see Julian Hoppit, 'The contexts and contours of British economic literature, 1660–1760', *Historical Journal*, 49.1 (2006), pp. 84–91.

[99] Christine Théré, 'Economic publishing and authors, 1566–1789', in Gilbert Faccarello, ed., *Studies in the history of French political economy: from Bodin to Walras* (London and New York, 1998), p. 11.

[100] Massie's collection was almost entirely of English-language works.

[101] Colin Jones, *The great nation: France from Louis XIV to Napoleon* (2002), p. 116.

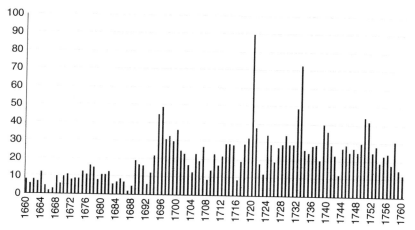

Figure 5.2 Annual numbers of works in Massie's catalogue, 1660–1760.
Source: BL, Lansdowne Mss. 1049.

Only the last peak, that of 1750–1, cannot be ascribed to a clear politico-economic controversy – it may be linked to developing post-war concerns about the level of the national debt and the extent of luxury, but it may also be a peak because Massie began to collect works around then and was fired by initial enthusiasm. Either way, as a rule these peaks suggest just how many works on economic matters were connected to policy at particular moments, prompted by the significantly heightened legislative role of Parliament after the Glorious Revolution.

Plainly Massie's collection was a subset of works listed by Hanson and Higgs. In particular, he avoided very short works: though about 80 per cent were under 100 pages long, few of these were less than ten pages (under 5 per cent of the total) and he listed only one single-side work. His was, therefore, a collection mainly of pamphlets and short books, but not of the broadsheets, handbills, and flyers that were produced in great numbers in the period.[102] For example, more than 40 percent of works relating to the South Sea Bubble published between 1719 and 1722 were under ten pages long, but for the same period only 5 per cent of works from Massie's collection were that short.[103] A large amount of

[102] 'Between the mid-sixteenth century and the end of the seventeenth, pamphlets became part of the everyday practice of politics, the primary means of creating and influencing public opinion.' Joad Raymond, *Pamphlets and pamphleteering in early modern Britain* (Cambridge, 2003), p. 26. See also Kevin Sharpe, *Reading revolutions*.
[103] J. G. Sperling, *The South Sea Company: an historical essay and bibliographical finding list* (Boston, MA, 1962). About 80 per cent of 198 tracts on the African trade published

printed economic literature of the period was very short and addressed
particular practical issues under consideration by politicians. Some of
these were indeed 'publications', but many are better thought of as 'copies', produced to be given to parliamentarians and other key political and
administrative figures.

A few points can be made about the broad subject matter of economic
literature. A little more than 40 per cent of the works in Massie's list
addressed issues associated with overseas trade and nearly 18 per cent
with public finance questions. These two main categories dominate his
collection and 77 per cent of the collection dealt with the tertiary sector.
The significance of mercantile matters compared to works on agriculture
or industry is striking –together just 12 per cent of the whole. Probably
this reflected Massie's mercantile background and interests. In Hanson's
catalogue, covering the half century to 1750, 30 per cent of works dealt
with 'finance', 21 per cent with 'commerce' (inland and overseas), and
12 per cent with 'agriculture'. But, as might be expected, overseas trade,
especially regarding the colonies, was a growing concern from the middle
of the eighteenth century, accounting for 23 per cent of works listed by
Higgs for 1751–5, 29 per cent for 1761–5, and 38 per cent for 1771–5.[104]

An important feature of economic literature was that much of it was
anonymous. In Massie's collection only 31 per cent were published
under an author's name between 1660 and 1759, and even then, in keeping with the times, sometimes clearly fictitious names.[105] Another 126,
6 per cent, were published under an author's initials only. But a very clear
majority, some 61 per cent, were anonymous, though the proportions
changed significantly over time, as Figure 5.3 shows.

After the Restoration, just one-third of works were anonymous, but
by the 1730s it was nearly three-quarters, a substantial and counterin-
tuitive change. This might be because for older works Massie was more
inclined to seek out those of a particular author, but probably it reflects
real changes, that anonymity became more frequent in economic literature from the late seventeenth century, probably because of several complex reasons.[106] Indeed, across Europe in the middle of the eighteenth

---

between 1689 and 1714 were one or two pages long. Keirn, 'Monopoly, economic
thought, and the Royal African Company', p. 437.

[104] This is a count of those he classed as 'Colonies', 'Commerce', and 'Shipping'.

[105] 'In the whole history of literature there is not a more fantastical group of whimsicalities
than that of English pseudonyms which abounded between 1688 and 1800.' Quoted in
Samuel Halkett and John Laing, *A dictionary of the anonymous and pseudonymous literature of Great Britain* (4 vols., Edinburgh, 1882–8), vol. 1, p. 1.

[106] Only 24 per cent of works from 1719–22 on the South Sea scheme were published
under an author's name or initials. Sperling, *The South Sea company*, pp. 56–78.

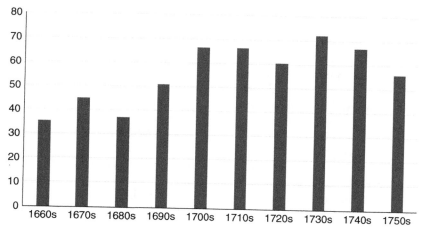

Figure 5.3 Proportion of anonymous works in Massie's catalogue by decade, 1650–1759.
Source: BL, Lansdowne Mss. 1049.

century 'anonymity in political economy was still the rule.'[107] Amongst the reasons for this might be 'an aristocratic or gendered reticence, religious self-effacement, anxiety over public exposure, fear of prosecution, hope of an unprejudiced reception, and the desire to deceive'.[108] Dudley North's main contribution to the field of economic literature was published anonymously allegedly 'to avoid the Fatigue of digesting and polishing his Sentiments into such accurate Method, and Clean Style, as the World commonly expects from Authors'.[109] Anonymity certainly changed the perceived personality of the work, a change authors might positively seek for some or all of their works to lend them particular credibility and authority via a certain depersonalization.[110] Perhaps also

---

[107] Richard S. Howey, *A bibliography of general histories of economics, 1692–1975* (Lawrence, KS, 1982), p. 7.

[108] Robert J. Griffin, 'Introduction', to Griffin, ed., *The faces of anonymity: anonymous and pseudonymous publication from the sixteenth to the twentieth century* (Basingstoke, 2003), p. 7.

[109] [Dudley North], *Discourses upon trade: principally directed to the cases of interest, coynage, clipping, increase of money* (1691), Preface, unpaginated. This work was actually published posthumously in 1692, edited by his brother Roger. Richard Grassby, 'Sir Dudley North (1641–1691)', *ODNB*.

[110] Literary scholars have done most in this area. For example, both Swift and Pope sometimes adopted anonymity, sometimes not. See Michael J. Conlon, 'Anonymity and authority in the poetry of Jonathan Swift', in Howard D. Weinbrot, Peter J. Schakel, and Stephen E. Karian, eds., *Eighteenth-century contexts: historical inquiries in honor of Phillip*

the rise of anonymity was related to the lapsing of the Licensing Act in 1695 as licensing had in part been about ensuring that authors and publishers were known and accountable for their works. Certainly anonymity could irritate some and there were attempts to legislate against it.[111] As one anonymous author put it, 'Authors without Names are like *Vagrants*, who strole up and down the Country without a Pass, and ought to be employed, not in writing, but in working for the Good of their Country'.[112] It is notable in this regard that a peak in the rate of anonymity was reached in the 1730s when Sir Robert Walpole often oppressed the press, though if anonymity was tied to oppositional politics, it arguably heightened the risks of being tarred with the brush of sedition.[113] Whichever, it suggests another way in which much writing on economic matters in this period needs to be located politically.

A final feature of Massie's collection to note is that only 10 of the 2,418 titles were in French, and there were no other foreign-language works. Linguistic incompetence may explain this, but Massie was courting the good opinion of potential patrons, men of high status and some education, who may well have been on the grand tour and probably knew French. Moreover, it was at just this time that developments in economic thinking in France were being held up as a challenge and a model to Britons.[114] Crucially, French authors were addressing economic questions in particularly concerted and intellectually imaginative ways as he was assembling his collection – with numbers of published works of economics in France rising from eighty-five in the 1740s to 489 in the 1750s.[115] That, therefore, Massie aspired to build a collection with

Hart (Madison, 2001), pp. 133–46; Pat Rogers, 'Nameless names: Pope, Curll, and the uses of anonymity', *New Literary History*, 33.2 (2002), pp. 233–45. For some important general reflections, Michel Foucault, 'What is an author?' in his *Language, counter-memory, practice: selected essays and interviews*, ed. Donald F. Bouchard (Oxford, 1977), pp. 113–38.

111 See Conlon, 'Anonymity', p. 136, which appears to relate to Hoppit, *Failed legislation*, 49.005.

112 [William Webster], *The draper confuted; or, a candid and impartial, but full answer to the consequences of trade: humbly offer'd to the consideration of both houses of Parliament* (1740), p. 1. Similarly, 'anonymous Publications cannot be supposed to carry that conviction with them, as those which are avowed by a person'. John Anstie, *To the land-owners, wool-growers, and wool-dealers, in the county of Sussex* ([n.p.], 1786).

113 'Under arbitrary governments the circulation of anonymous pamphlets, secretly printed, involves serious risk to the writers if they are discovered.' James Kennedy, W. A. Smith, and A. F. Johnson, eds., *Dictionary of anonymous and pseudonymous English literature* (9 vols., Edinburgh and London, 1926–62), vol. 1, p. xi. On Walpole and the press see Michael Harris, 'Print and politics in the age of Walpole', in Jeremy Black, ed., *Britain in the age of Walpole* (Basingstoke, 1984), especially pp. 196–203.

114 Bob Harris, *Politics and the nation: Britain in the mid-eighteenth century* (Oxford, 2002), ch. 6.

115 Théré, 'Economic publishing and authors', p. 11; Jean-Claude Perrot, *Une histoire intellectuelle de l'économie politique: XVIIe-XVIIIe siècle* (Paris, 1992); Antoine Murphy,

virtually no engagement with non-English literature is striking. In this context it is telling that translations of works of economic thought did not become numerous in the major European countries until after 1750 and that until around then national insularity was not much challenged.[116]

This quantitative analysis has established several important general points about the contours of economic literature in the period. First, there was clear growth in the number of works, especially after the Glorious Revolution – the lapsing of the Licensing Act in 1695 and the growth of legislative politics made marked differences. Numbers of works published in Britain were very much higher than in France, its main and much larger competitor. This reflected the heightened opportunities for debate brought about by the legislative revolution. Consequently, the number of works published was liable to significant short-term variations because so many addressed current policy options under consideration in Parliament. That in turn meant, thirdly, that many works were short, often a side or two, and pamphlets of up to a few dozen pages significantly outnumbered books. Often these were not sold to readers, but given out to interested parties, especially MPs and peers. Almost all of these were paid for by extra-parliamentary interests, but sometimes the executive government took the lead. There is evidence among Walpole's papers of longer runs for pamphlets justifying his policies, which were distributed among MPs, peers, the clergy, collectors of customs and excise, and other government supporters.[117] Fourth, a minority of authors owned up to their work. Most writings could not easily be put at the door of particular individuals and their success depended not on authorial reputation, but on the force of the printed words alone. Finally, the subject matter of works relating to

---

'Le développment des idées économiques en France (1750–1756)', *Revue d'histoire Moderne et Contemporaine*, 33.4 (1986), pp. 521–41; Judith A. Miller, 'Economic ideologies, 1750–1800: the creation of the modern political economy?', *French Historical Studies*, 23.3 (2000), pp. 497–511; Robin Ives, 'Political publicity and political economy in eighteenth-century France', *French History*, 17.1 (2003), pp. 1–18.

[116] Kenneth E. Carpenter, *Dialogue in political economy: translations from and into German in the eighteenth century* (Boston, MA, 1977), p. 6; Sophus A. Reinert, *Translating empire: emulation and the origins of political economy* (Cambridge, MA, 2011); Sophus A. Reinert, 'The empire of emulation: a quantitative analysis of economic translations in the European world, 1500–1849', in Sophus A. Reinert and Pernille Røge, eds., *The political economy of empire in the early modern world* (Basingstoke, 2013), pp. 105–28. The significance of the erosion of national insularity in political economy after about 1750 was marked. For example, David Hume, James Steuart, and Adam Smith all spent a considerable amount of time in mainland Europe.

[117] Some 10,000 copies of *Some considerations concerning the publick funds* (1735) were distributed: Hanson, *Contemporary printed sources*, p. xviii. Charles King's *British merchant; or commerce preserv'd* (3 vols., 1721), was distributed to all parliamentary boroughs, the costs being met by the Exchequer. See E. A. J. Johnson, *Predecessors of Adam Smith: the growth of British economic thought* (1937), pp. 146–7.

economic issues was dominated by the service sector, especially commerce and finance, areas where the executive and the legislature could make a significant impact on economic practices. Agriculture and industry were surprisingly little attended to, though the whole body of the literature cannot be characterized as 'mercantilist' or mercantile in its concerns.

Quantitatively, economic literature at the time was overwhelmingly short, ephemeral, anonymous, and politically orientated. Much of it addressed a world of shifting problems, arguments, and solutions, often those under consideration in Parliament. Yet if we can be certain both as to its volume and political intent, it is much less obvious what its effect was.[118] Certainly parliamentarians could hardly be unaware of much of the print literature issued in relation to economic legislation, but judging issues of readership and reception is very difficult for this genre in this period.[119] Very little information has survived of the print runs of works of economic literature, how they were distributed, who acquired them, or how they were used. From the accounts of Strahan, a major printer, it is clear that short pamphlets often had a print run of several hundred, sometimes of 1,000.[120] Given their ephemeral purpose, it was doubtless true that many quickly fell into oblivion. But Gauci has shown that Charles Cooke (d. 1721), a merchant, member of the Board of Trade from 1714, and an MP from 1715, had a pamphlet collection of 315 titles, which comprised for him a set of 'working papers'.[121] Cooke may have been unusual in preserving, binding, and indexing his collection, but pamphlets, broadsheets, and cases certainly made their impact on MPs and peers. Private libraries tended to hold longer works, often including supposed past masters of the genre, such as William Petty and John Locke. It is telling, for example, that Child's best-known work began as an anonymous work in 1663 and existed in nine textually and seventeen bibliographically distinct versions by 1804, and that a complete edition of Davenant's works from the late seventeenth and early eighteenth centuries was published in five volumes in 1771.[122]

---

[118] In part because of the need to study the particular circumstances of production and reception. For an example see Kwasi Kwarteng, 'The political thought of the recoinage crisis of 1695–7' (University of Cambridge PhD thesis, 2000).

[119] For an introduction to the methodological and historiographical issues see James Raven, 'New reading histories, print culture and the identification of change: the case of eighteenth-century England', *Social History*, 23.3 (1998), pp. 268–87.

[120] E.g., BL, Add Mss, 4880, Strahan papers, ff. 69v, 146v; 4881, f. 33v.

[121] Perry Gauci, 'The clash of interests: commerce and the politics of trade in the age of Anne', *Parliamentary History*, 28.1 (2009), pp. 115–25, quote at 118. George Bowes, MP for Co. Durham under George II, also had a collection: Paul Langford, *Public life and the propertied Englishman, 1688–1798* (Oxford, 1991), p. 186.

[122] T. H. Bowyer, 'The published forms of Sir Josiah Child's *A new discourse of trade*', *The Library*, 5th series, 11.2 (1956), pp. 95–102; Charles Davenant, *The political and commercial works of D'Avenant*, ed. Charles Whitworth (5 vols., 1771).

Conclusion

Parliament's information gathering and the impact on it of petitioning and political economy from outside strengthened its relationship to
British society. Although an exclusive body and remote from working
people, it was very much part of society, though it played a distinctive
role, as co-ordinator, adjudicator, and stimulator. As Furner and Supple
argued, 'the state's accumulation of information and application of models are related to the performance of functions that no private interest can
adequately undertake, namely, adjusting or at least recognizing different
sectional interests, pursuing general objectives, and assessing particular
policies in light of their consequences for society as a whole. The state,
after all, *is* different.'[123] In eighteenth-century Britain Parliament rather
than the executive government was the crucial site of that difference.

From this and the previous chapters it is now very clear just how much
effort was expended on political economy in Britain in this period. In
Parliament economic matters involved more than 7,500 acts, 3,300
failed attempts at acts, 5,000 accounts and papers, and perhaps 20,000
petitions. Outside Parliament, the press produced more than 10,000
works of political economy between 1700 and 1775, and so, guessing
wildly, perhaps 15,000 for the whole of the period under discussion. All
told, this was a huge expression of political economy. But it was also a
highly varied one, for if bills and acts in Parliament provided the focal
point, much of the effort was made by widely scattered interests, small
and large, acting within an unusually vibrant culture of improvement
and debate. Also striking in this regard was the permeability of borders
between the executive and the legislature on the one hand and the legislature and opinion outdoors on the other. This allowed different views
to be presented, feeding into active debates about economic legislation,
both general and specific.

In the context of this chapter, the information, interests, and ideas
that Parliament engaged in, and that engaged with Parliament, were not
just very numerous, but very varied. Some structure was provided by
executive policy and key departments of state, the Treasury and revenue
services especially, but much arose in response to particular interests
and authors seeking to express their views. If not really spontaneous, this
was structured only loosely by very mixed motives, especially those of
financial betterment and a wider sense of political culture. This fertility

[123] Mary O. Furner and Barry Supple, 'Ideas, institutions, and state in the United States
and Britain: an introduction', in their eds., *The state and economic knowledge* (Cambridge,
1990), p. 11.

was very marked and indeed constituted a key characteristic of Britain's political economies.

A critical feature of the political culture within which economic legislation was proposed and considered was that many outside Parliament had a voice, a voice that had first been potently expressed in the 1640s and 1650s and, after a hiatus, became embedded in the Restoration era, in print and coffeehouses particularly, receiving a fillip with the end of pre-publication censorship in 1695.[124] Much of this was centred on London, though developments took place against a backdrop of increasing scientific enquiry into social and economic phenomena, such as the Royal Society's 'history of trade' project and the emergence of political arithmetic.[125] Yet if this vibrant culture of enquiry, publication, and debate certainly advanced knowledge and understanding, it also involved plenty of misinformation and miscomprehension. As always, local and sectional views were commonly said to be consistent with the national interest, but the period was particularly marked by wild guesses about fundamental issues such as population size and fierce satires. This was a culture where fact and reason battled plenty of headwinds.[126]

Developments in Britain's political culture after 1700 were heavily affected by the foundations laid down in the previous fifty years or so. But new influences came into play, especially from around 1750, notably the new thinking criss-crossing Europe about the determinants of the wealth of nations, a key aspect of which was the role of the state and its relationship to natural rights, including the extent of liberty. Continental connections were common here, and flowed in both directions. As a matter of course British intellectuals and politicians crossed the Channel, mentally if not physically. And there were flows the other way, especially from France, including Voltaire, Montesquieu, Rousseau, Morellet, and, later, de Tocqueville. Unquestionably, aspects of Britain's political economies fed off wider European developments, of exploration, experimentation, quantification, reasoning, and a developing 'public sphere'. But what happened in Britain was influenced by its particular institutional arrangements. Thus there was virtually no influence in Britain of, let alone anything comparable to, 'Cameralism', a supposed science of administration which became important in parts of Germany early in the eighteenth century – in part as an academic discourse about

---

[124] Peter Lake and Steve Pincus, 'Rethinking the public sphere in seventeenth-century England', *Journal of British Studies*, 45.2 (2006), pp. 270–92.

[125] Houghton, 'The history of trades'; G. N. Clark, *Science and social welfare in the age of Newton* (Oxford, 1937); Paul Slack, 'Government and information in seventeenth-century England', *Past and Present*, 184 (2004), pp. 33–68.

[126] Knights, *Representation and misrepresentation*.

the nature of government, including chairs in the subject, in part as the administration of sovereign finances. 'German Cameralists existed at the nexus between science and economic development' mediated through government action, specifically princely courts.[127] The complexity both of Parliament itself and of its relations with society precluded any such programme in Britain.

---

[127] Keith Tribe, *Strategies of economic order: German economic discourse, 1750–1950* (Cambridge, 1995), ch. 2; T. C. W. Blanning, *The culture of power and the power of culture: old regime Europe, 1660–1789* (Oxford, 2002), pp. 210–11. The quote is from Andre Wakefield, *The disordered police state: German Cameralism as science and practice* (Chicago, IL, 2009), p. 25. He stressed the inadequacies and limitations of the Cameralists, challenging Marc Raeff, *The well-ordered police state: social and institutional change through law in the Germanies and Russia, 1600–1800* (New Haven, CT, 1983).

Part Two

Cases

Part One set out the broad legislative dimensions of Britain's political economies. The emphasis on patterns and trends left little room for exploring the particular types of action undertaken – the reasoning involved, the types of controversies engendered, and the consequences. Part Two begins to explore such considerations. The following four chapters are case studies designed to show key aspects of Britain's political economies in action in this period.[1] The first is a regional study as a means of better understanding the nature of specific economic legislation in the period. As has been seen, such types of acts were very numerous and very different to general economic legislation. How local economic interests operated politically and economically is a key consideration. The remaining case studies, however, concentrate on general economic legislation as a means of better understanding the nature of economic policy, including the gap between prescription and practice. Chapters 7 and 8 consider aspects of the 'mercantile system', Chapter 9 an aspect of the 'fiscal state'. Chapter 7 explores a long-lived attempt to aid Britain's most important industry, the manufacture of woollen goods, through a ban on the export of raw wool. Yet while the ban was in place until 1824, it was often believed to have been evaded. It shows up, therefore, important issues about enforcement, as well as competition between large interest groups within economic society: landed, industrial, and mercantile. Both Chapters 6 and 7 concentrate on the nature of the legislation involved. The final two case studies, however, use the scale of financial consequences of key types of general economic legislation as a means of gauging their varied impacts. Chapter 8 considers bounties,

---

[1] Other case studies I have published include 'Reforming Britain's weights and measures, 1660–1824', *English Historical Review*, 108.426 (1993), pp. 82–104; 'Checking the leviathan, 1688–1832', in Donald Winch and Patrick K. O'Brien, eds., *The political economy of British historical experience, 1688–1914* (Oxford, 2002), pp. 267–94; 'Compulsion, compensation and property rights in Britain, 1688–1833', *Past and Present*, 210 (2011), pp. 93–128; and 'Economical reform and the Mint, 1780–1816', *British Numismatic Journal*, 84 (2014), pp. 177–90.

which Adam Smith placed at the heart of the mercantile system, to see what commodities were involved, the scale of payments made, and the limits to this form of state action. Chapter 9 considers taxes, specifically how their collection varied markedly between Britain's three nations, as well as within England. To an extent that is not well appreciated, the British state's financial prowess depended to a considerable degree on exploiting the importance of London and south-east England to economic life across the island.

'"If this country had been drained intelligently and all of a piece,"
remarked Wimsey, "by running all the canals into the rivers instead of
the rivers into canals, so as to get a good scour of water, Walbeach might
still be a port and the landscape would look rather less like a crazy quilt.
But what with seven hundred years of greed and graft and laziness, and
perpetual quarrelling between one parish and the next, and the mis-
taken impression that what suits Holland must suit the Fens, the thing's
a mess. It answers the purpose, but it might have been a lot better."'
Dorothy L. Sayers, 1934[1]

'We spoke of our fears for the future, as all Fenmen do.'
Alan Bloom, 1953[2]

In Chapter 3 it was shown that two-thirds of acts relating to the economy were specific rather than general in scope (5,103 to 2,442), applying to particular places and people. None of this was sought by central
government and little by local government; the overwhelming majority
was the product of the efforts of individuals and interests, constituting
an enormous if very scattered effort. General legislation was more widely
important, potentially or actually affecting many, many people – which
is why they are the focus of the following three chapters. But specific
economic legislation was a vital part of Britain's political economies and
a key objective of this chapter is to delve into the dynamics involved by
focusing on the relationship between place and economic legislation via a
case study, the fens. Certainly the nature of the fens sits well with the fact
that 94 per cent of specific economic legislation concerned agriculture
and infrastructure. But this region has not been chosen because it experienced unusual amounts of legislation – it did not – but because it helps
to develop two key findings from Chapters 3 and 4: that localities and
regions came to bear the imprint of different types of specific economic

---

[1] *The nine tailors* (1934), pp. 154–5.
[2] *The fens* (1953), p. 24.

legislation and that these were sometimes pretty easily enacted, but sometimes not. In particular, it was shown that attempts at road and enclosure
legislation had a high success rate, but those involving water did not.

The purpose of this chapter is to explore how local and regional interests mobilized themselves regarding specific legislation – both for and
against – and how that legislation affected local economic life. Fen legislation was not meaningfully the product of policy, but rather of the quest
for profits by individuals and groups. They were not always successful in
that, but even so resort to Parliament continued through the eighteenth
century. Through these efforts the landscape and economy of the fens
was changed, with the effects sometimes felt miles away.

This chapter begins by sketching how the fens might be defined and
what their state was in 1660. Consideration then turns to the numbers
of acts and fails relating to the region, over time and by subject. As most
fen legislation was sought for financial gain, it is important then to have
some sense of the monetary costs and benefits that were envisaged.
Others, though, were affected by such plans and a rich range of interest groups was involved in fen legislation. What they were and how they
expressed themselves need then to be considered. Though it is impossible to establish in a general quantitative way the economic costs and
benefits involved, this chapter closes by piecing together evidence of the
effects of this regional legislative effort.

Fens are a particular type of wetland found around the world. But
'the fens' was recognized as a distinctive region of Britain even before
Hereward made it his base to resist the Norman conquest of 1066.[3] The
region is mainly the basin surrounding the Wash, comprising around
1,300 square miles, mostly lying in the counties of Cambridgeshire,
Huntingdonshire, Lincolnshire, and Norfolk, though also taking in small
parts of Suffolk and even Northamptonshire, see Map 6.1. At heart,
its regional coherence was environmental and ecological, arising from
a distinctive interplay of land and water.[4] Hybrid words captured the
special qualities of this hybrid world, part land, part water: this was the
'fen-country' or 'fen-land', inhabited by distinctive 'fen-landers' using
'fen-poles' and vulnerable to 'fen-fever'. Its flora too stood out, with its
'fen-berries' (cranberries), 'fen-cress', and 'fen-whort'.[5]

[3] 'The [664] charter of King Wolfere to the Abbey of Peterborough ... makes the first mention of the Fens.' Neil Walker and Thomas Craddock, *The history of Wisbech and the fens*
(1849), p. 88.
[4] Harry Godwin, *Fenland: its ancient past and uncertain future* (Cambridge, 1978) is a good
introduction to the region's natural characteristics.
[5] *The Oxford English Dictionary* lists twenty-five compound words of 'fen'. On the rich
local dialect, Samuel H. Miller and Sydney B. J. Skertchly, *The fenland, past and present*
(Wisbech and London, 1878), pp. 126–31.

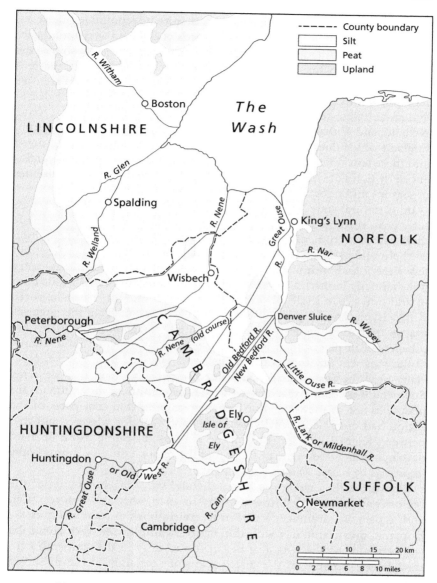

Map 6.1 Map of the fen region

If certainly a region, the fens was not, despite its reputation, unvaried. Although low lying and generally flat, islands of dry land were found here and there – the cathedral sitting atop the Isle of Ely, the great ship of the fens, can be seen for miles around. Moreover, while parts of the fens were naturally classic peat wetlands, the region also included extensive silt lands around the Wash, through which four main rivers struggled to find an outfall to sea: the Great Ouse (much the most important), Nene, Welland, and Witham. As Defoe put it, 'all the water of the middle part of England which does not run into the Thames or the Trent, comes down into these fens.'[6] The fens were, indeed, a region that was unusually influenced by flows of both freshwater and saltwater, through the regularities of seasons and tides as well as the shocks of floods and surges.

In its natural state, the fens was rich in fish, fowl, osier (willow), pasture, peat, reed, and sedge, though in many places the landscape made these resources difficult to exploit intensively. Unenclosed and common land abounded; large landowners hovered on the edge of the fens, but few were found within. Pockets of dry land were farmed, but industry was distinctly limited. The region's rivers allowed the flow of goods both in and out, yet in itself this brought prosperity only to the main ports, King's Lynn especially, but also Wisbech and Boston. All of this suggests that in its natural state the fens was relatively stagnant, if a little more prosperous in places than is commonly thought. Yet 'the natural state' of the fens was far from constant, as rivers changed their course, especially near the sea, and silt aggregated, especially along the coastline. Such changes, taking place over decades or centuries, were difficult for people to see at the time. But evidence accumulated that parts of the region had once been heavily wooded – and therefore dryer – and that between Kings Lynn and Boston the sea was retreating. Both of these developments lured many to think that the region could be dramatically improved by better water management.

Bits of the fens were in a 'natural state' by 1660, but much of the region had already felt the imprint of man, through deforestation and, especially, drainage. This can be traced back at least as far as the Romans, most famously with the eighty-five-mile Car dyke along the western edge of the fens, but began to intensify in the sixteenth century, partly because of the distribution of the lands of the dissolved monasteries at Croyland, Ramsey, and Thorney.[7] No less important, in

---

[6] Daniel Defoe, *A tour through the whole island of Great Britain*, ed. Pat Rogers (Harmondsworth, 1971), p. 101.

[7] The classic account is H. C. Darby, *The draining of the fens* (2nd edn., Cambridge, 1956). Also very useful is Dorothy Summers, *The great level: a history of drainage and*

1532 powerful Commissioners of Sewers were established to oversee drainage matters.[8] But increasing efforts were also made by entrepreneurs to drain large parts of the fens, especially from 1630, usually via the exercise of crown prerogative. Most spectacularly, the Earl of Bedford and his fellow 'Adventurers' tackled some 344,000 acres of the 'Great Level', mainly in Cambridgeshire and Huntingdonshire, while in south Lincolnshire the Earl of Lindsey and others attempted the drainage of 36,000 acres. Huge resources were expended and the landscape bent to the will of the entrepreneur and the engineer. By any standard, this was an impressive mobilization of labour, capital, and expertise. Thus, for example, the Old and New Bedford rivers, effectively massive drainage canals, ran almost dead straight and closely parallel for twenty miles from Earith to Denver, taking much of the waters of the Great Ouse from its old course.

Yet extraordinary though these efforts certainly were, their results were very ambiguous. Many denied that they effectively drained the land; some thought they created problems elsewhere; in places, especially in Lincolnshire, the loss of common lands led to considerable and often effective resistance; and ownership of the drained lands was everywhere thrown into doubt by the civil wars of the 1640s and political turmoil of the 1650s. At the Restoration in 1660, therefore, large parts of the fens were clearly in a state of considerable natural, economic, and legal uncertainty. That was one cause of Parliament's subsequent legislative efforts towards the region. But those efforts were also prompted by the view that the region was rich in potential, that the land could become much more productive (and valuable) if adequately drained and protected from flood and surge.[9] It was also a region whose rivers were vital conduits to the inland trade of its neighbouring regions, including as far inland as Northamptonshire and Buckinghamshire. The health of those rivers, and the ports through which the trade they carried passed, had at the very least to be maintained. What, then, were the legislative efforts made?

---

land reclamation in the fens (Newton Abbot, 1976) and Richard L. Hills, *Machines, mills, and other uncountable costly necessities: a short history of the drainage of the fens* (Norwich, 1967). For an early account, though a pro-draining one, see William Dugdale, *The history of imbanking and drayning of divers fens and marshes* (1662).

[8] 23 Henry VIII, c. 5. G. R. Elton, *Reform and renewal: Thomas Cromwell and the common weal* (Cambridge, 1973), pp. 121–2. The best account of the considerable powers of the Commissioners is Sidney Webb and Beatrice Webb, *Statutory authority for special purposes, with a summary of the development of local government structure* (1922), ch. 1.

[9] For example, Walter Blith, *England's improver, or a new survey of husbandry* (1649).

Counting Fen Legislation

Before 1642 efforts to improve the fens were usually authorized by the crown. This proved highly controversial, leading to widespread and often violent opposition. But as soon as Charles I lost his head in 1649 improvements usually became sanctioned by Parliament and opposition seemingly more peaceful. With its greater legitimacy, it was at Westminster, not Whitehall, that the political economy of the fens was ultimately determined in our period.[10]

Legislation, attempted or enacted, dealt not with the whole of the fens, but with its parts. However, identifying them cannot be done with absolute precision.[11] The region's borders were never formally determined and some legislation, notably for roads, rivers, and drains, might cross its informal limits. Moreover, it is a big job to isolate fen legislation from all the 21,000 acts passed and fails identified between 1660 and 1800. Even when that has been done it must be remembered that neither 'acts' nor 'fails' are a consistent unit of account. Thus, for example, an act of 1767 to enclose Holland Fen in Lincolnshire led ultimately to the award of 18,000 acres, while another passed in the same session for Yaxley in Huntingdonshire involved only about 1,000 acres.[12] Similarly, the act establishing the Bedford Level Corporation in 1663 created an authority responsible for the drainage of more than 300,000 acres, whereas the commissioners for the Haddenham Level, established by an act of 1727, were responsible for the drainage of 7,500 acres.[13] The numbers which follow (Table 6.1), therefore, should be treated cautiously.

In the century after 1660 only fifty-five acts were passed relating directly to the fens, but in the last forty years of the eighteenth century there were 174; that is a rise from an act every two years or so to more than four acts a year. Over that first century, fails outnumbered acts, being highest in the Restoration era but still numerous even after the Glorious Revolution, the success rate taking a long time to improve significantly. In fact, the success rate of fen legislation, which was all

---

[10] C. Holmes, 'Drainers and fenmen: the problem of popular political consciousness in the seventeenth century', in Anthony Fletcher and John Stevenson, eds., *Order and disorder in early modern England* (Cambridge, 1985), pp. 166–95.

[11] I ignore legislation that affected the region but that was aimed elsewhere, as in that relating to the upper reaches of the rivers that later passed through the fens.

[12] 7 George III, c. 14 & 112 (both private); W. E. Tate, *A domesday of English enclosure acts and awards*, ed. M. E. Turner (Reading, 1973), pp. 169 and 141.

[13] 15 Charles II, c. 17; 13 George I, c. 18; www.hlowidbs.org.uk/Haddenham.html, accessed 11 July 2014.

Table 6.1 *Legislation relating to the fen region, 1660–1800*

	Acts	Fails	Success rate %
1660–85	10	34	23
1689–1714	6	14	30
1714–60	39	14	74
1760–1800	174	62	74
Total	229	124	65

Table 6.2 *Percentage success rate of fen legislation and all specific legislation, 1660–1800*

	Fen	All specific
1660–85	23	38
1689–1714	30	63
1714–60	74	79
1760–1800	74	77
1660–1800	65	73

Table 6.3 *Fen legislation share of all specific legislation, 1660–1800, per cent*

	Acts	Fails
1660–85	2.8	5.8
1689–1714	0.5	2.0
1714–60	1.5	2.0
1760–1800	2.8	3.3

'specific', was consistently below the national average, if not significantly so by the middle of the eighteenth century (see Table 6.2).

Put another way in Table 6.3, fen legislation was a larger share of all specific legislation in the first and the last sub-periods; those in the middle were relatively quiet.

Explaining these patterns has to begin by considering just what legislation was being attempted and enacted. As ever, this is not straightforward and a particular difficulty about fen legislation was the considerable overlap in the objectives of acts about drainage and enclosure, about drainage

Table 6.4 *Primary subject of legislation relating to the fen region,*
1660–1800. By rank order of numbers of acts

	Acts	Fails	Success rate %
Drainage	83	68	55
Enclosure	71	21	77
Road	35	4	90
Rivers	14	12	54
Canals	3	4	43
Ports	3	2	60
Others	20	13	61
Totals	229	124	65

and river navigation, and about embanking and roads. (Such problems also troubled Parliament as it had to ensure relevant standing orders were applied.[14]) Given the scale of the task, I have not worked through all of the acts and fails to untangle such ambiguities, so the following figures, once again, are indicative only. Table 6.4 shows that drainage and enclosure legislation accounted for two-thirds of all acts affecting the fens, and infrastructural matters another quarter – the limited impact of turnpike roads in the region is unsurprising given the relative shortage of naturally dry land. All of this legislation was specific in scope.

Unsurprisingly, the fens accounted for 72 per cent of all drainage acts passed at Westminster in this period. By contrast, the region witnessed less turnpike and enclosure legislation than elsewhere, because of the natural difficulties of finding routes in the region and because enclosure often depended on land first being adequately drained and the large size of some of the enclosures.

[14] In 1778 it was complained that a bill that had been introduced as a drainage bill was actually a navigation bill, and so liable to different standing orders governing how bills were to be handled in the Commons. Beds. Archives, R Fens (uncatalogued), Box 2, Bundle 20: Anon., *Bedford Level* [1778] and Anon., *Answer to the observations on, intitled Bedford Level* [1778]. Neither of these are in the ESTC and the dates come from internal evidence. Sir Joseph Banks, who from the 1780s was a key figure in legislation affecting the Lincolnshire fens, had an interesting count of acts where those regarding drainage and enclosure were lumped together to be compared with those relating to canals. Sutro, Banks: F10:19 'An account of the number of bills which have passed from session 1786 to session 1797/8 inclusive, relating to drainage, inclosure and canals'. The figures also contrasted periods of war and peace. Michael Chisholm, 'Navigation and the seventeenth-century draining of the fens', *Journal of Historical Geography*, 32.4 (2006), pp. 731–51.

Table 6.5 *Drainage and enclosure legislation in the fen region by sub-period, 1660–1800*

	1660–85	1689–1714	1714–60	1760–1800
Drainage				
Acts	6	0	19	58
Fails	28	5	7	28
Success %	18	0	73	67
Enclosure				
Acts	1	0	4	66
Fails	1	0	3	17
Success %	50	n.a.	57	80
Drainage and enclosure				
Acts	7	0	23	124
Fails	29	5	10	45
Success %	19	0	70	73

An important feature of Table 6.4 is to confirm the finding from Chapter 3 concerning the great difficulties of passing acts where water was involved, with an average success rate of just 54 per cent for the region, compared to 77 per cent for other fen legislation. Explaining that is an important objective of this chapter. That said, clearly drainage and enclosure legislation was especially important for the region, accounting for more than two-thirds of both acts and fails and so worth detailing a little in Table 6.5.

A key finding from Table 6.5 is the very large numbers of failed attempts at drainage legislation in the Restoration era and that it was not until the advent of the Hanoverians in 1714 that drainage acts began to be passed in any number. It was particularly in the 1760s that numbers of such acts grew, with forty-three drainage and enclosure acts passed in the seven sessions to 1776–7 – fourteen in the session 1772–3 alone, the greatest number in any one session in the period covered by this book. The American War, 1775–83, led to a collapse of such legislation for the fens, with only four such acts being passed in six sessions 1779/80–1784. But whereas the American War led to the drying up of such acts, the Revolutionary War, 1793–1802, did not, with thirty-six being passed between 1793 and 1800.

There were some important local dynamics at work in drainage and enclosure acts for the fens. Table 6.6 gives a broad overview, but two detailed developments are worth noting here. First, eighteen of the twenty-eight failed attempts at drainage legislation in the Restoration

Table 6.6 *Success rates of drainage and enclosure legislation in the four main counties of the fen region, 1660–1800*

	Drainage	Enclosure
Cambridgeshire	59	60
Huntingdonshire	100	78
Lincolnshire	38	81
Norfolk	63	80

Note: legislation relating to the 'Great Level' or 'Bedford Level' has been counted as Cambridgeshire.

era related to Lincolnshire. Yet, second, acts relating to the county were especially numerous in the surge just before the American War – twenty-four of the forty-three.[15]

It must be remembered that 'fen legislation' was very largely aimed at specific locales and, given the small numbers involved, many places were rarely directly concerned with the legislative process in this period. Nowhere was as troubled as King's Lynn, the largest town in the fens, but it was directly involved in only twelve acts and seven fails, or an average of one about every seven years.[16] But what distinguished the low-lying fens was that statutory changes to drains and watercourses in one place might have, or be believed to have, effects many miles away, especially on the Witham from Boston to Lincoln, the Nene from Wisbech to Northampton, and the Great Ouse from King's Lynn to Bedford. Consequently many different communities and interests were drawn indirectly into dealing with relatively small numbers of acts and fails. Reconciling such various views was often difficult, helping to explain the low success rate of fen legislation in general, and that relating to water in particular.

Counting legislation directly affecting the fens helpfully pinpoints certain major developments. In particular, before 1714 the large number of failed attempts and small number of acts stands out, as does the dramatic surge in numbers of acts from the middle of the eighteenth century. This chronology was particularly the product of drainage and enclosure legislation, which accounted for two-thirds of fen legislation, though drainage

[15] Bearing out T. W. Beastall, *The agricultural revolution in Lincolnshire* (Lincoln, 1978), p. 7.
[16] 12 & 13 William III, c. 6 (private); 18 George II, c. 3; 24 George II, c. 19; 10 George III, c. 20, c. 27, c. 85, c. 86; 13 George III, c. 30; 31 George III, c. 112, c. 113; 35 George III, c. 77; 36 George III, c. 33; Hoppit, *Failed legislation*, 2.085, 5.030, 32.030, 110.040, 133.007, 135.053, 136.011.

legislation often had an enclosure element to it, and vice versa. The success rate of legislation involving water was generally low, and especially so in the Lincolnshire fens.

Put very simply, these patterns were mainly (but certainly not completely) the product of three developments: the considerable difficulties of sorting what might be called the fen dimension of the Restoration land settlement; the difficulties of maintaining the drainage of the Great Level; and finally the lure of rising agricultural prices from 1760 encouraging the risking of substantial monetary and political capital. It will be helpful to set out briefly these three developments before turning to three main structural considerations that were crucial to most fen legislation: the costs and benefits of local legislation; the nature of interest groups within the fens; and the ways in which proposals were assessed and determined.

Between 1660 and 1685 there were eleven attempts to legislate for the Lindsey Level in Lincolnshire, all of them unsuccessful.[17] Sir William Killigrew, one of the original adventurers and an MP from 1664 to 1679, was a leading advocate of these efforts until his death in 1695.[18] This was indeed a 'great business', and a bitter one, involving five divisions in the Commons (the first in 1670, the last in 1685) and a torrent of briefs, reports, and cases – by 1705 the clerk of the House of Commons had 109 documents in six bundles of papers relating to the case.[19] Despite all this effort, the original drainers, who had invested heavily, lost everything, without gaining any compensation. In those circumstances, it would have been brave for anyone quickly to have suggested further schemes for improvement. Tellingly not until the 1760s were further legislative efforts made to drain and enclose the Lincolnshire fens, becoming notably common in the 1790s.

For the Great Level there were fourteen attempts at legislation between 1660 and 1685, only four of them successful.[20] In this case the

[17] Hoppit, *Failed legislation*, 2.114, 7.045, 8.040, 9.008, 10.007, 13.033, 14.039, 15.029, 16.006, 16.074, 22.014, 35.075, 36.054. The Lindsey Level ran in an arc from Bourne, northwards and eastwards, to Boston. It is now known as the Black Sluice Level.
[18] W. H. Wheeler, *A history of the fens of south Lincolnshire* (2nd edn. Boston, 1896), pp. 143, 252–3; Keith Lindley, *Fenland riots and the English revolution* (1982); P. A. Bolton and John P. Ferris, 'Killigrew, Sir William (1606–95), of Westminster', *HofP online*; J. P. Vander Motten, *Sir William Killigrew (1606–1695): his life and dramatic works* (Gent, 1980).
[19] *Diary of John Milward, esq. Member of Parliament for Derbyshire September 1666 to May 1668*, ed. Caroline Robbins (Cambridge, 1938), p. 246; William Killigrew, *The property of all English-men asserted, in the history of Lindsey Level* (1705), pp. 22–4.
[20] Hoppit, *Failed legislation*, 1.051, 1.082, 2.003, 2.004, 2.155, 4.010, 5.032, 7.054, 8.070. Acts: 15 Charles II, c. 17; 15 Charles II, c. 9 (private), 19 & 20 Charles II, c. 13, 1 James II, c. 2 (private). The opposition is well summarized by Darby, *Draining the fens*, pp. 49–64; Julie Bowring, 'Between the Corporation and Captain Flood: the fens and drainage after 1663', in Richard W. Hoyle, ed., *Custom, improvement and landscape in early modern Britain* (Farnham, 2011), pp. 235–61.

original drainers had their ownership and responsibilities for maintenance confirmed. An act of 1663, essentially confirming an earlier 'act'
of 1649, established the Bedford Level Corporation and gave it powers
of Commissioners of Sewers for the Level, operating within an elaborate
constitution of a governor, six bailiffs, and twenty-four conservators, to
be elected annually at a public meeting of the owners of 100 acres or
more of Corporation land. The act also provided for the paid offices of
surveyor, register, treasurer, auditor, engineer, and superintendents. And
it gave the Corporation the right to tax the land under its authority to pay
for maintenance works. It says much that the Corporation's 'Fen Office'
was in London's legal quarter.[21]

Establishing such a novel commercial, financial, and political authority within the fens was bound to be contentious – more on this later.
It had to work with other local authorities, while its land was mixed
in amongst 'free lands'. Moreover, some thought that key aspects of its
drainage works caused floods elsewhere or damaged navigations, especially at Wisbech and King's Lynn, leading to some major legislative
battles. Even within the Corporation's jurisdiction, many thought that its
drainage works were becoming hopelessly ineffective, including through
lack of routine maintenance, and local interests sought legislative authority to rectify matters. This began with Haddenham, six miles south-west
of Ely, in 1727, to be followed by a number of other parishes through the
eighteenth century, gradually undermining the supposed coherence of
the Bedford Level drainage scheme.[22] Unsurprisingly, the Corporation
itself occasionally sought legislation, sometimes with far-reaching implications. For example, in 1754 it printed 150 copies of a bill to reorder its
perilous finances, followed by 600 copies of the act, which were quickly
sent into the fens.[23]

Enclosure and drainage legislation exploded in the fens after 1760, especially in Lincolnshire, coinciding there with the highest land prices of the
century.[24] Partly this followed national trends, but an important stimulus
was the improvement of the River Witham between Lincoln and Boston,
both for drainage and navigation. Against stiff resistance this gained statutory
authority in 1762, which created six new administrative drainage districts,

---

[21] The laws relating to the Corporation are brought together in Charles Nalson Cole, *A
collection of laws which form the constitution of the Bedford Level Corporation* (1761; 2nd
edn., 1803).

[22] For a study of one such local body see John G. A. Beckett, *The urgent hour: the drainage
of the Burnt Fen district in the South Level of the fens, 1760–1981* (Ely, 1983).

[23] Beds. Archives, R Fens (uncatalogued), Box 2, Bundle 16: two bills for printing and letter from H. Reade to F. Tregale, 8 June 1754.

[24] B. A. Holderness, 'The English land market in the eighteenth century: the case of
Lincolnshire', *Economic History Review*, 27.4 (1974), p. 576.

covering nearly 128,000 acres.[25] This provided a spur and a framework for many subsequent enclosure acts for particular parishes or manors within the districts, sometimes containing a local drainage element. Other parts of Lincolnshire also followed, such developments climaxing with acts passed in 1801, but set in motion several years earlier, for the enclosure and drainage of Wildmore Fen (8,000 acres) and East and West Fen (16,000 acres).[26]

To begin to understand how particular individuals, communities, and interests generated and considered all of this fen legislation, it is helpful to look closely at three factors: the costs and benefits of legislative action in the fens; how interests there formed, acted, and reacted; and what ideas and information was presented by interests when making their case.

The Finances of Fen Legislation

The overwhelming majority of fen legislation was sought by small groups for their own financial betterment. Its proposers certainly weighed the costs and benefits involved, both financial and not, though usually in a rough-and-ready way. For the especially important categories of drainage and enclosure legislation, it was obviously usually hoped that improved land would raise yields, leading to substantially higher land prices and rentals. For example, in 1791, after nearly half a century of rising prices, it was estimated that it would cost nearly £18,000 to embank 4,370 acres of profitable land in South Holland in Lincolnshire, or £4 an acre, but leading to land prices rising more than fivefold, 'which is unquestionably a very sufficient inducement.'[27] A decade later, Sir Joseph Banks was making similarly optimistic calculations about the proposed drainage and enclosure of 60,000 acres in the East, West, and Wildmore Fens in Lincolnshire.[28] Gradually, evidence of actual costs accumulated. Arthur Young, certainly not a dispassionate observer, using figures for 43,000 acres of land drained and enclosed in Lincolnshire in the half century to 1813, calculated that their average value increased seven fold. Whether this was really true is unknown, but certainly that was a much greater increase than followed enclosure specifically or improvements in yields from land more generally in the eighteenth century. Cereal yields in Lincolnshire almost doubled between 1700 and 1830 while nationally rents quadrupled in real terms in the eighteenth century.[29]

[25] 2 George III, c. 32. Wheeler, *South Lincolnshire*, ch. 6.
[26] 39 & 40 George III, cc. 135, 241, 242; Tate, *Domesday of enclosures*, p. 170.
[27] Joshua Peart, Henry Boulton, and Nathaniel Kent, *South Holland embankment* (1791).
[28] Sutro, Banks, F10:12.
[29] Arthur Young, *General view of the agriculture of Lincolnshire* (2nd edn. 1813), p. 280; Mark Overton, *Agricultural revolution in England: the transformation of the agrarian*

The first cost to be borne was that of attempting to obtain an act. What was aimed at would have to be firmed up through advertised meetings with others who might join the venture, by commissioning surveys and reports, and by drafting and printing a bill. Managing a bill through Parliament also involved various costs, including clerical fees and perhaps the presence of counsel and witnesses and the free distribution of printed statements in support. MPs and peers would also have to be engaged to support a measure. If the bill passed, then copies of the act would often have been printed and circulated. All of this even before the costs of the actual works involved began to be felt.

The wording of turnpike and enclosure legislation became fairly routine as their numbers rose, with perhaps some fall in their real cost. But most other categories of local legislation needed highly bespoke and more costly preparation. Moreover, where a large and sophisticated opposition to proposed legislation was anticipated or encountered, costs inevitably rose: more supporting petitions, pamphlets, and handbills might be needed; and more expensive legal support bought in. Thus when the bankrupt Bedford Level Corporation sought an act to put its finances on a new footing in 1753–4, in part by adjusting its tax rates, considerable opposition was bound to materialize. It prepared the ground by printing off a plan of the act being sought, had elaborate and well-supported petitions compiled, 500 copies of a statement of its financial position printed, and retained the services of a range of expensive legal expertise, including Robert Yeates, a clerk in the Commons with considerable experience as a parliamentary agent who was to become 'the first Parliamentary Counsel to the Treasury'.[30] Expenses of £900 were paid for all of this, which was certainly only a part of expenditure on obtaining the act.[31] The costs of obtaining the even more controversial act for making the Eau Brink cut in 1795 were officially put at £11,944.[32] This was certainly very exceptional, but the general principle is that obtaining drainage and other water-related legislation was more costly because of the greater preparation that was necessary and opposition that was encountered.

economy, 1500–1850 (Cambridge, 1996), p. 77; M. E. Turner, J. V. Beckett, and B. Afton, Agricultural rent in England, 1690–1914 (Cambridge, 1997), p. 207.

30 Sheila Lambert, Bills and acts: legislative procedure in eighteenth-century England (Cambridge, 1971), p. 45.

31 Anon., A plan for obtaining an Act of Parliament for the better draining the North-Level, part of the Great Level of the fens [1753?]; Anon., A state of the revenue and debt of the Corporation of Bedford-Levels [1753?]; Beds. Archives, R Fens (uncatalogued), Box 2, Bundle 7 for the petition and Bundle 16 for expenses; 27 George II, c. 19.

32 Christopher Pemberton, Eau Brink accounts: copy of statement of account made up to the 25th August, 1817 (1817), p. 1; 35 George III, c. 77.

It was one thing to spend money on obtaining an act, quite another thing to implement it. Critically, the fens were a difficult landscape to improve, with drainage often a prerequisite for other changes, especially enclosure. The labour-intensive digging of deep ditches and mounding of tall banks was physically demanding and rarely straightforward. In the first place, the low-lying land often made it hard to find a sufficient gradient in the rivers and drains to ensure a good outfall to sea. This became harder as the natural build-up of silt near the coast compromised many of the channels. Moreover, the draining of peatlands caused a dramatic fall in their level (through drying and wasting), by up to four metres in places – sometimes taking the land beneath mean sea level. When that happened, water had to be taken off the land through wind-mills, which gradually infested the fen landscape until replaced by steam pumps in the nineteenth century. Even then the peat fens were more vulnerable to persistent flooding, whether caused by tidal surges or heavy rains, both on the fens themselves or on the surrounding uplands which drained through the region. To try to manage this required expensive locks, sluices, and the like.[33] Yet these might compromise the river navigations that were so important to the towns and cities of the fens and beyond.

Generally drainage legislation was especially costly to implement. For example, at Wimblington in Cambridgeshire, the enclosure of 800 acres in 1791 cost £1,200, but the associated drainage £2,000, respectively £1.50 and £2.50 an acre.[34] Many drainage schemes were in fact very expensive, raising huge challenges of capital mobilization, exacerbated by the fact that returns usually took several years to materialize. In current prices, the Great Level may have cost about £370,000 before the Bedford Corporation was established in 1663; the Witham drainage £48,000 in 1763–7; the Black Sluice drainage £34,000 in 1765–9; Kinderley's cut at Wisbech £9,000 in 1773–6; Witham Fens drainage £14,000 in 1785–93; and the drainage of the East, West, and Wildmore Fens £430,000 in 1802–10.[35] Plainly, these were sometimes very substantial and capital-intensive projects. Enclosure was less 'lumpy', but could still involve significant expenditure on surveying, fencing, ditching,

[33] Michael Chisholm, 'Locks, sluices and staunches: confusing terminology', *Transactions of the Newcomen Society*, 75.2 (2005), pp. 305–16.

[34] W. E. Tate, 'The cost of parliamentary enclosure in England (with special reference to the county of Oxford)', *Economic History Review*, 5.2 (1952), p. 261.

[35] A. W. Skempton et al., eds., *A biographical dictionary of civil engineers in Great Britain and Ireland, vol. 1: 1500–1830* (2002), appendix 2. Often these figures are estimates. The costs of draining the Great Level are not really known (key papers were destroyed in the Great Fire of London), but have been put at more than £500,000 by Summers, *The great level*, p. 77.

and tithe commutation.[36] Enclosure legislation (i.e., ignoring drainage legislation with an enclosure element) affected more than 150,000 acres in the fens in this period. Nationally, costs have been estimated at about £0.63–0.84 an acre in the 1760s and £1.55–1.96 in the 1790s. That is to say, the total cost of implementing enclosure legislation in the fens by 1800 may have been about £150,000 in 1770s prices, or an average of about £2,100 for each of the seventy-one enclosure acts concerned.[37]

Enclosure was not only less financially stressful to implement, but maintenance costs were also less than drainage. 'Floods and Tempests will have their Turn, level the strongest Banks, and in a Moment, as it were, lay waste whole Countries, and leave not the least Traces of the Industry and Improvement, which have been exerted and made by Generations. These melancholy Events to which all flat Countries are liable'.[38] This might involve new capital expenditure. Thus the Middle Level had 250 windmills by 1748, at a total cost of perhaps £100,000.[39] Initially, maintenance costs in the Great Level were estimated at £10,000 per annum, at only 3 per cent of the capital expenditure surely well short of the actual rate of depreciation, let alone the costs of dealing with unanticipated consequences of the initial drainage, such as peat shrinkage. This was a key reason why the finances of the Bedford Level Corporation were so perilous before 1754: its costs were higher than anticipated and the frequently flooded land was unable to pay anything like full taxes.[40] But it was still faced with major challenges after those finances were put on a new footing. In November 1770 a breach in one of its drainage banks required 33,000 tons of gault clay to repair.[41] In Lincolnshire, annual

---

[36] Tithe commutation has often been underestimated, but for Sir Joseph Banks it was a crucial reason for undertaking enclosure. Banks to Thomas Foster, 30 December 1796: Sutro, Banks, F8:34. Eric J. Evans, *The contentious tithe: the tithe problem and English agriculture, 1750–1850* (1976).

[37] Total acreage has been taken from Tate, *Domesday of enclosures*, of amount awarded where possible, of amount anticipated where not. Figures are missing for a few enclosures, so the actual figure will be a bit higher. Costs of enclosure are from Michael Turner, *English parliamentary enclosure: its historical geography and economic history* (Folkestone, 1980), p. 133.

[38] Cole, *Collection of laws*, p. lii.

[39] Thomas Neale, *The ruinous state of the parish of Manea in the Isle of Ely, with the causes and remedy of it* (n.p., 1748), p. 14; Frances Willmoth, *Sir Jonas Moore: practical mathematics and Restoration science* (Woodbridge, 1993), p. 101.

[40] Anon., *State of the revenue and debt of the Corporation of the Bedford-Levels*. The debts were put at nearly £50,000, and annual revenues at a little more than £6,000. The Burnt Fen drainage commission, established in 1759, also found that its taxes generated far too little, requiring further acts to allow more money to be raised in 1772, 1796, and 1807. Beckett, *Urgent hour*, pp. 9, 18–20.

[41] Beds. Archives, R Fens (uncatalogued), Box 1, Bundle 13, John Wing, Thorney Abbey, to Robert Palmer, 28 November 1770.

maintenance costs between 1748 and 1764 were £304 for twelve miles of the Deeping Bank and £288 for six miles of the Country Bank.[42] In the Bedford Level there were more than 200 miles of banks to maintain, as well as fifty other 'great works'.[43]

Much fen legislation required considerable finance, both for construction and maintenance. This was a question both of how money should be raised and of who should be required to contribute. Because enclosure was both cheaper and usually undertaken on a smaller area, this was achieved relatively easily through savings and private credit markets. For drainage, the challenge was much greater. Charles I often granted drainers a share of the land involved – 95,000 acres in the case of the Great Level. Such an easy solution was also an unpopular one leading to claims that the Adventurers privileged their own land and had prematurely claimed that drainage was complete to get their hands on it. It was also clear that such an arrangement generated far too little revenue to undertake maintenance. Thus when the Bedford Level Corporation was established in 1663 it was given powers to tax. Such powers were usually granted to subsequent drainers, but it was obvious that, because drainage schemes benefitted some more than others, a flat tax across an authority's jurisdiction would be inequitable. Sometimes complex graduated schemes had to be proposed based on categorizing different types of lands and the degree to which they were expected to benefit from schemes, which were always liable to be met with complaints that certain pockets of land were already well drained or that the works that were proposed were too distant or expensive.

Improvements to roads and navigations were usually paid for by tolls, with published rates. These could be mortgaged to pay for the initial capital expenditure and provide the revenue stream to pay for maintenance.[44] This seemed clear enough, but navigations were sometimes also drains and vice versa, and the banks of drains sometimes used as roads or paths. Thus, when the Eau Brink cut was being discussed, some expected it to be paid for by tolls on those using the river, others by taxing landowners across the whole of the Middle and South Levels. Unsurprisingly, this was hotly contested and a compromise of sorts decided on: a tax was laid on 300,000 acres for fifteen years, as well as tolls on the completed

---

[42] Sutro, Banks, F6:31. These are similar to the costs of maintaining the River Cam between Cambridge and the Ouse. Cambridgeshire Archives, Accounts of Conservators of the River Cam, Q/S9/1 (1751–92), 2 (1793–1824).
[43] George Maxwell, General view of the agriculture of the county of Huntingdon (1793), p. 44.
[44] William Albert, The turnpike road system in England, 1663–1840 (Cambridge, 1972), chs. 5–6; J. R. Ward, The finance of canal building in eighteenth-century England (Oxford, 1974).

navigation – which provided security for borrowings of £35,000.[45] Freeriding was always a danger on drainage banks and one drainers and landowners – threatened by floods from damaged banks – became very sensitive to.

Necessarily the acts and fails studied in this chapter resulted from their promoters anticipating that their investment of time and money would prove profitable. They certainly were not always correct in that belief, but it was crucial to driving forward their projects. But occasionally what seemed initially a profitable idea might on reflection look too risky or uncertain. Some proposals at Westminster were abandoned, while some never even got there, such as the idea of a canal linking Cambridge to Bishop's Stortford so as to provide a continuous inland navigation from King's Lynn to London, free from the threat of storms and wars.[46] Quite a bit of effort was put into developing this idea, but the obstacles were simply too expensive to overcome given projections of likely traffic on the route.

Clashing Interests

All told, much legislation in the fens committed its promoters to undertake heavy capital expenditure and substantial maintenance costs. Yet though they sought private profit, these projectors often needed statutory authority to overcome opposition. In such circumstances they had to justify themselves in terms of the public rather than self-interest. Relatively little ink was spilt on this. Sometimes this was done in very general terms, with the assertion of the compatibility of private and public interest: 'I sing heaps of Water turn'd to Land. … I sing heaps of Gold and Indian ore, Of private Profit, and Publick Store'.[47] Particular arguments for the benefits of drainage, enclosure, and river improvements

---

[45] Pemberton, *Eau Brink accounts*, pp. 1–2. For comments on the proposed tax: Anon., *Free and candid remarks on the plan of taxation, as resolved on by the Eau-Brink Cut Committee* (Kings Lynn, [1794?]); Anon., *The claim of taxing the navigations and free lands for the drainage and preservation of the fens* (1793).

[46] Anon., *Calculations on the navigation proposed to be made in order to extend the communication between London and Cambridgeshire, by water carriage* [1788?]; Anon., *A short state of facts; tending to shew the utility of the proposed plan of navigation from the town of Bishops Stortford, to join the Cambridge River* (1788); Anon., *Calculations and remarks, shewing the utility of extending the Cambridge navigation, so as to communicate with the City of London* (n.d.). This last work is not in the ESTC and may be found at the Beds. Archives, R Fens (uncatalogued), Box 1, Bundle 12. An even more ambitious stillborn plan looked to cut a canal through the heart of East Anglia, linking London to Norwich, to King's Lynn: John Phillips, *A treatise on inland navigation: illustrated with a whole-sheet plan, delineating the course of an intended navigable canal from London to Norwich and Lynn* (1785).

[47] Jonas Moore, *The history or narrative of the Great Level of the fenns* (1685), p. 72.

built more specifically on the optimism for 'improvement' that developed in the 1640s and 1650s, associated with Hartlib and his circle – and so separate from those authors who argued for overseas trade as offering the best source for economic growth.[48]

It was easy enough to argue that draining land led to greater output and productivity, supporting a larger population, increased public revenues, and reduced imports of crops such as flax. Much the same was said of enclosure, but in both cases this could be linked to criticisms of idleness and ungodliness in the fens and on the commons. This moral reform dimension was periodically expressed across the period: Nehemiah Grew lambasted commoners as 'Lazy Lubbers' while Arthur Young lamented that the wild fens produced a wild 'race ... and thus the morals and eternal welfare of numbers are hazarded or ruined for want of an enclosure.'[49] Relatedly it was also complained that the sodden fens loaded sickness onto their people and livestock, such that draining them improved both 'health and wealth'.[50] As for navigation, the cheapness of shipping goods by water rather than land – at one-twelfth the cost by one estimate – created larger markets and, applying Adam Smith's reasoning, a greater division of labour.[51]

Such arguments were certainly important, but did little to disarm the numerous and varied opponents of fen legislation that existed. Indeed, it is striking just how passionately some fen legislation was debated. Pamphlet wars, letters to the press, petitions to Parliament, and vicious satires can often be found. Sometimes this clearly involved fierce personality clashes, but the structural issue was that fen legislation was liable to involve several competing groups. These virtually never expressed themselves in party-political terms, almost always in terms of the contemporary language of 'interest'. An important feature of the political economy of the fens was, indeed, the distinctive nature of some of its

---

[48] Paul Slack, *The invention of improvement: information and material progress in seventeenth-century England* (Oxford, 2015); Paul Warde, 'The idea of improvement, c.1520–1700', in Hoyle, ed., *Custom, improvement and landscape*, pp. 127–48.

[49] Julian Hoppit, ed., *Nehemiah Grew and England's economic development* (Oxford, 2012), p. 18; Maurice Beresford, 'Habitation versus improvement: the debate on enclosure by agreement', in F. J. Fisher, ed., *Essays in the economic and social history of Tudor and Stuart England in honour of R. H. Tawney* (Cambridge, 1961), pp. 40–69. Young, *Lincolnshire*, p. 254. A good brief discussion of such ideas is Robin A. Butlin, 'Images of the Fenland region', in Edward Royle, ed., *Issues of regional identity in honour of John Marshall* (Manchester, 1998), especially pp. 29–30.

[50] W. Pennington, *Reflections on the various advantages resulting from the draining, inclosing, and allotting of large commons and common fields* (1769), p. 9.

[51] The figure of one-twelfth was Robert Southwell's, a friend of Sir William Petty. It was reproduced in Thomas Birch, *The history of the Royal Society of London* (4 vols., 1756–7), vol. 3, p. 208. Smith, *Wealth of nations*, vol. 1, pp. 31–6.

interest groups and understanding them is essential to understanding the patterns of legislation set out earlier.

Most interests in the fen were non-institutional. Crudely speaking there were those who used water – such as millers and navigators – and those who used land. Landowners were especially important and had to be alert to the potential effects and costs of works being undertaken near and far. They might co-ordinate their actions via manor courts, quarter sessions, and ad hoc meetings, as well as socially at key points in the local calendar (Joseph Banks timed his visits to Lincolnshire to coincide with the races there). But the 'landed interest' in the fens was usually deeply divided, and along shifting fault lines: uplanders against lowlanders, resident landowners against absentees, large against small landowners, and tax payers against non-taxpayers – i.e., those who did and did not pay for works. What united them were property rights which, classically, was most obviously exposed in their contests with commoners, both those with and without legally enforceable rights.[52]

To commoners drainage and enclosure often threatened a way of life, cultural as well as economic, social as well as political. The poet John Clare (1793–1864), who lived much of his life near the fens, thought the quest for gain scarred the landscape, producing productive fields, but a lifeless plain.[53] In 1783 105 commoners on the East Fen in Lincolnshire petitioned against the 'rage for drainage' that threatened their livelihood of fishing, keeping a cow or two, and cutting thatch.[54] Such resistance was essentially conservative in its aims, but could be expressed dramatically and directly. For example, in 1699 a crowd of perhaps 1,000 attacked forty houses and twenty 'water engines' at Pinchbeck in Lincolnshire, allegedly drowning 30,000 acres.[55] In 1722 a similar number destroyed navigation works at Wisbech being undertaken by the Bedford Level Corporation.[56] And in 1769–70 the enclosure of Holland Fen met

---

[52] With regard to drainage the best work is Lindley, *Fenland riots*, though he focuses on the seventeenth century; and for enclosure J. M. Neeson, *Commoners: common right, enclosure and social change in England, 1700–1820* (Cambridge, 1993).

[53] 'With gain the merchandise of farms ... Gain mars the landscape every day ... Change cheats the landscape every day ... And all is nakedness and fen ... A picture dreary to behold ... But all is level cold and dull'. John Clare, '[The fens]', in Clare, *The major works*, ed. Eric Robinson and David Powell (Oxford, 2004), p. 240.

[54] Quoted in David N. Robinson, 'Sir Joseph Banks and the East Fen', in Christopher Sturman, ed. *Lincolnshire people and places: essays in memory of Terence R. Leach* (Lincoln, 1996), p. 99.

[55] William Bunyon, ... *or, strange news from the fenns. Being a full and true account of a [p]owerful and tumultuous riot, near Spalding in Lincolnshire* (1700). The ESTC lists only one copy of this work, at the Sutro, Banks F7:76, which unfortunately is badly cropped and tightly bound. It is dated January 1699 on p. 2, i.e., 1700, and signed by Bunyon on p. 8. Lindley, *Fenland riots*, p. 232.

[56] Summers, *Great level*, pp. 107–8.

spectacular resistance against a 'Rogish Act of Parleyment to take poors Right from them by Force and fraud'.[57]

Threats such as these led Parliament to pass a general act in 1754 clearly establishing the death penalty for those guilty of 'destroying turnpikes, locks, or other works'.[58] Sometimes this was invoked, as in 1768 by the Commissioners of Sewers at Wisbech against 'several ill disposed, and evil minded Persons [who] have openly threatened that they will riotously and forcibly oppose the said Commissioners and their Servants'.[59] Even so, potential violence understandably preyed on the minds of those thinking of obtaining fen legislation. As John Parkinson of Asgarby in Lincolnshire wrote in 1779,

No gentleman on the spot cares to be the entire Promoter of so extensive an Improvement [the proposed enclosure of the East fen], particularly on account of seeing the Holland Fen Inclosure executed, in which those who were called Advocates either suffered by having their Stacks fired or such other Private damages which might be as injurious as the Advantages any Individual might Receive.[60]

Eye-catching though such direct action is to the historian, rioting in the fens appears to have been much more frequent in the seventeenth than in the eighteenth century.[61] Moreover, it is important to bear in mind the varied nature of 'commoners' in the fens. Certainly many were labourers, but some were landlords and farmers: a meeting in 1795 of owners of common rights in the 'Marshlands' district between King's Lynn and Wisbech was headed by the bishop of Bangor, followed by two baronets (one of them an MP for King's Lynn), sixteen esquires, two clergymen, and eleven plain 'misters', i.e., 'gentlemen'.[62] Further, in Lincolnshire especially, some commons were very large and owned by a number of parishes – eleven in the case of Holland Fen, for example. It was, therefore, not only poor

---

[57] Quoted in E. P. Thompson, 'The crime of anonymity', in Thompson et al., *Albion's fatal tree: crime and society in eighteenth-century England* (Harmondsworth, 1977), p. 276. On opposition to Holland Fen enclosure see: Charles Brears, *Lincolnshire in the seventeenth and eighteenth centuries* (1940), pp. 135–6; Betty Brammer, 'The Holland Fen: social and topographical changes in a fenland environment, 1750–1914' (University of Leicester PhD thesis, 2009), ch. 2; Steve Hindle, 'Power, poor relief, and social relations in Holland Fen, c. 1600–1800', *Historical Journal*, 41.1 (1998), p. 78.

[58] 27 George II, c. 16.

[59] Anon., *A result of a meeting at Wisbech, December 17, 1768* (1768).

[60] TNA, DL 41/1159/8 Jun 1779, quoted in Brammer, 'Holland Fen', p. 69.

[61] It makes little showing in the eighteenth-century parts of Andrew Charlesworth, ed., *An atlas of rural protest in Britain, 1548–1900* (1983).

[62] Sutro, Banks, F8:95. Leigh Shaw-Taylor estimates from a sample study that 80 per cent of common right owners were landlords and farmers: 'Labourers, cows, common rights and parliamentary enclosure: the evidence of contemporary comment c. 1760–1810', *Past and Present*, 171 (2001), p. 104.

labourers who were concerned with the fate of the commons. At the end of the seventeenth century some 'considerable comoners' [*sic*] were key drivers in an attempt to drain Deeping Fen, while some common rights were exploited as a commercial resource, perhaps increasingly so as food prices rose in the second half of the eighteenth century.[63] A striking case of this was the use of the West Fen common pastures in Lincolnshire by the Birtwhistle family in the late eighteenth century. John Birtwhistle was a major drover of Scottish cattle to London, sending perhaps 10,000 animals a year. Though based in Yorkshire, he owned property in Galloway and bought land and the advowson at Skirbeck in Lincolnshire, installing his son Thomas as rector.[64] This allowed his droving business to put an average of nearly 600 cattle a year from 1775–84 onto the commons nearby on their way south – no one else put on more than sixty. Other commoners damned this as a type of free-riding over-exploitation that was certainly wrong and probably illegal. A fund was established so that a legal challenge to the Birtwhistles could be mounted.[65]

Such matters could be bound up with wider divisions. As a local clergyman commenting on the Birtwhistle case put it, 'The East-Hollanders I deem not friendly to the interests of the Soke of Bolingbroke and think they wish to take every step to drive the Soke into an inclosure: but on the contrary could we turn the tables upon them and obtain a limited common: would there be so beneficial a common in Great-Britain?'.[66] In fact, the church was often concerned with fen legislation, as a land and tithe owner, but also because of the need to create parishes in some drained lands, in part to manage poor relief and migration.[67] In Lincolnshire, the Rev. Edward Walls, JP, locked horns with Joseph Banks on such issues, and the Rev. James Ashley with George Maxwell, Lord Eardley's land agent and a very active enclosure and drainage commissioner.[68]

---

[63] Lincolnshire Archives, Spalding Sewers/500/101. Joan Thirsk, *English peasant farming: the agrarian history of Lincolnshire from Tudor to recent times* (1957), pp. 112–17 for the earlier origins of the 'shortage of commons'.

[64] Tony Stephens, 'The Birtwhistles of Craven and Galloway: "the greatest graziers and dealers in the kingdom?"', *North Craven Heritage Trust Journal*, no vol. (2008), pp. 13–17.

[65] Sutro, Banks, F8:48, 49, 52; F9:89. 'Abuses' and 'infringements' were also taking place on commons in the Norfolk Marshlands in 1795, leading to pressure to enclose. Sutro, Banks, F8:94. The Birtwhistle case is an interesting example of the 'tragedy of commons' debated by economists. See Leigh Shaw-Taylor, 'The management of common land in the lowlands of southern England circa 1500 to circa 1850', in Martina de Moor, Leigh Shaw-Taylor, and Paul Warde, eds., *The management of common land in north west Europe, c. 1500–1850* (Turnhout, 2002), pp. 59–85, especially p. 80.

[66] Sutro, Banks, F8:53.

[67] For example, Anon., *Case of the commoners in the Soke of Bolingbroke* (1810).

[68] On Walls, Edward Walls, *A letter to the right honourable Sir Joseph Banks* (1803; 2nd edn., 1804); Anon., *A refutation of the charges brought forward by Mr. Coltman, at a meeting*

If the Church was one prominent existing interest group that had to be alert to the implications of fen legislation, important towns were another. King's Lynn, the largest in the fens with a population of 5,000–7,000 in 1700, stands out in this regard.[69] As an incorporated town it had its mayor and burgesses; it was parliamentary borough, returning two MPs to Westminster (Robert Walpole from 1702–42); and it was a regional centre for the collection of both customs and excise. Trade was its lifeblood, mainly of agricultural produce flowing out, and coal, wine, groceries, and timber flowing in.[70] This depended very heavily on the River Ouse and its tributaries: the inland 'verge of the Lynn Trade, was now very large', extending as far as Bedford, seventy miles away; Lynn was 'at the Door of this River, as it were the Turnkey of it'.[71] In the first half of the eighteenth century its coastwise shipping fleet surpassed in size those of all other English outports save for those centring on the north-east coal trade: Newcastle, Scarborough, Sunderland, and Whitby.[72]

If King's Lynn was proud of its regional importance, it was very nervous about the effects of fen drainage on the Ouse navigation in general and its haven in particular. Its merchants and corporation well knew that vibrant ports, including Boston on the north side of the Wash, had withered as their rivers had shifted and silted and were very fearful that the same was happening at King's Lynn. Even before works on the Great Level were finished the corporation was complaining, especially that the building of a £7,000 sluice to control tidal flows at Denver, fourteen miles upstream, would restrict the natural scour of the haven, leading to silting up and the need to use smaller and less cost-effective vessels. Supposedly the sluice was built 'In Contempt of *Magna Charta*, and Ten

held at Spilsby, against Sir Joseph Banks, and his steward, Mr. Parkinson (1803). Ashley published letters against Maxwell between 1797 and 1802, culminating in *A seventh letter from the Rev. James Ashley, Rector of Fleet, to Mr. George Maxwell, respecting the Fleet inclosure* (Wisbech, 1802). Maxwell replied via letters to papers. Maxwell and Sir Joseph Banks were also at loggerheads from the mid-1790s, though mainly on financial and engineering matters.

[69] David Harris Sacks and Michael Lynch, 'Ports, 1540–1700', in Peter Clark, ed., *The Cambridge urban history of Britain, vol. 2, 1540–1840* (Cambridge, 2000), p. 384.

[70] Fiona Jean Wood, 'Inland transportation and distribution in the hinterland of King's Lynn, 1760–1840' (University of Cambridge PhD thesis, 1992).

[71] Beds. Archives, Franklin papers, FN1255, f. 515, Henry Ashley, 'Some thoughts on the case of Lynn Regis, in relation to their port and trade', n.d.; Thomas Badeslade, *The history of the ancient and present state of the navigation of the port of King's Lyn, and of Cambridge* (1725), preface.

[72] T. S. Willan, *The English coasting trade, 1600–1750* (1938), pp. 220–2. But John M. Barney, 'Shipping in the port of King's Lynn, 1702–1800', *Journal of Transport History*, 20.2 (1999), p. 128, states that its fleet ranked tenth amongst England's outports in 1702.

or more *Statutes* of this *Realm*'.[73] The initial complaint made in 1649 was followed by others, sometimes to the Bedford Level Corporation, sometimes to Parliament, including failed bills in 1665 and 1696–7.[74] Nature then took its course, the sluice being largely destroyed by a powerful tide in 1713, though in 1732 it was reported that the trade of King's Lynn was 'much decayed of late years'.[75] Plans to rebuild the sluice, only achieved in 1750, periodically revived the controversy. The Bedford Level Corporation consistently argued that the sluice was innocent of King's Lynn's charge, pointing the finger instead at the growth of a large bend in the river near the town and more extensive tidal flats in the Wash, leading to the Ouse becoming slower and unable to provide an effective scour. The remedy it supported, though it had no authority for that part of the river, was to shorten and narrow the river by making the Eau Brink cut straight across the five-mile bend. King's Lynn Corporation held out strongly against this until the end of the eighteenth century. Both thought that there was a problem, but both thought it needed to be addressed (and paid for) by someone else.

King's Lynn was not the only town worried about the consequences of statutory engineering works being undertaken miles away. It often found allies in Cambridge, the town, the university, and the conservators of the River Cam (charged with its improvement and maintenance by act in 1702), perhaps mindful of the decline of the nearby Stourbridge fair, once one of Europe's greatest marts.[76] Wisbech was similarly 'obsessed with the idea that any improvement of the drainage of the neighbourhood would react unfavourably on the port and Nene Outfall'.[77] Like King's Lynn, it petitioned the Bedford Level Corporation and Parliament. It says much of the depth of the divisions that the Bedford Level Corporation alleged that the riot there in 1722 against its works had the tacit support of local JPs and Commissioners of Sewers. It took up the matter with Lord Townshend, a Secretary

---

[73] Anon., *An abstract of the ancient and present state of the navigation of Lynn, Cambridge, &c* [1775?], p. 2.

[74] Hoppit, *Failed legislation*, 5.032 and 32.030. There were two divisions on the latter, 95:94 and 117:71. A good summary of the efforts made by King's Lynn towards the Bedford Level Corporation down to 1725 is Badeslade, *History of the navigation of King's Lynn*, pp. 50–108.

[75] From the diary of Edward Harley, quoted by H. L. Bradfer-Lawrence, 'The merchants of Lynn' in Clement Ingleby, ed., *A supplement to Blomefield's Norfolk* (1929), p. 158.

[76] 1 Anne stat. 2, c. 11; Honor Ridout, *Cambridge and Stourbridge fair* (Cambridge, 2011), ch. 10.

[77] Anon., 'Wisbech: charters of incorporation', in R. B. Pugh, ed., *A history of the county of Cambridge and the Isle of Ely: volume 4: City of Ely; Ely, N. and S. Witchford and Wisbech hundreds* (2002), p. 257.

of State but also a local landowner and Lord Lieutenant of Norfolk, and petitioned the Privy Council. In return, Wisbech challenged the Corporation in the court of Chancery.[78] This was an extraordinary trial of strength between an old and a new institution, but almost any town in the region could be a focal point for similar anxieties that were fundamental to so much fen legislation: that the consequences of works could be felt far and wide, often unpredictably so.

Oftentimes towns looked to the established authority of Commissioners of Sewers in Lincolnshire and Norfolk to aid them in their confrontations with the new institutions set up to drain and embank. These were potentially powerful local bodies, somewhat akin to JPs and quarter sessions. They heard complaints, held courts with juries, and had powers to fine and to imprison. They also employed surveyors, keepers, and bailiffs to manage works, levied taxes to pay for them, and could impress labour and materials. But they also passed statutes, ordinances, and provisions – dozens in the case of those at Spalding, Lincolnshire.[79]

Some waxed lyrical that

Commissioners of Sewers are created *pro Bono Publico*; and amongst the largeness of their Powers, they are constituted a Court of Equity, to stop Sutes, and to prevent the Peevishness of a few, from prejudicing the great Advantages of much the major part: And a Decree of their Inspired with *Le Roy Assent a ceo*, is by Parliament declared an Establishing of a Right no ways reversible but by Parliament.[80]

(This last point helps to explain why some contests ultimately played out in Parliament.) If therefore the Commissioners of Sewers were an important and powerful component of institutions in the fens, they did not go uncriticized. Because they were established by a pro-drainage crown, they were caught up in the wider political and constitutional disputes of the seventeenth century.[81] Through the period they were sometimes accused of exceeding their powers, sometimes of not meeting their legal obligations. As local bodies, moreover, they also naturally looked at only parts of drainage systems.

---

[78] Cambridgeshire Archives, R59/31/11/20, ff. 1–2.
[79] Anon., *The laws of sewers; or the office and authority of Commissioners of Sewers* (2nd edn., 1732). Lincolnshire Archives Office, Spalding Sewers 488/A-E and 493–6.
[80] Anon., *Reasons humbly offered, to bring in a bill to confirm the decrees for draining of Lindsey-level, in the county of Lincoln* [1660?].
[81] Joan Thirsk, 'The crown as projector on its own estates from Elizabeth I to Charles I', in R. W. Hoyle, ed., *The estates of the English crown, 1558–1640* (Cambridge, 1992), pp. 297–352; Mark E. Kennedy, 'Fen drainage, the central government, and local interest: Carleton and the gentlemen of South Holland', *Historical Journal*, 26.1 (1983), pp. 15–37.

Such complaints lay behind the extensive range of new authorities introduced into the fens in this period. The Bedford Level Corporation was the most notable of these – being 'the Guardians of the Country' to one of its supporters – but other drainage and navigation commissions were established, along with turnpike trusts.[82] Most of these operated for at least a century, the Bedford Level Corporation lasting until 1914; some even survive today, albeit in amended form, for the Haddenham Level, Black Sluice Level, and River Cam, for example. A key feature of such bodies was that statutes defined fairly precisely what they were to do, how they were to be funded, and what their constitution was. This gave them considerable authority, allowing them to cut across existing local bodies. But it could burden them with obligations they struggled to meet. This was certainly true of the Bedford Level Corporation, which was bombarded by petitions and memorials from landowners and farmers about faults in the drainage works, both through lack of routine maintenance and exceptionally heavy rain.[83] Sometimes this led such bodies to return to Parliament to enhance their powers, give them more time, or allow them to raise more money. Whenever they did so, opposition was always possible.

A rich constellation of interests promoted, opposed, and implemented fen legislation. But they were constantly evolving, and if they sometimes acted independently, they sometimes acted in concert with others. Such alliances might come and go. For example, while the King's Lynn and Bedford Level Corporations often were at loggerheads, they sometimes worked together, as in 1753 when they 'fully debated' and unanimously agreed a scheme for improving the navigation of the River Nene.[84] It was also the case that it cost time and effort for interests to clash. Compromise was sometimes worth it, as when both drainers and commoners agreed to the use of a 'referee' to adjudicate on several contentious issues between them in 1699.[85] That is to say, those interested in fen legislation obviously weighed the costs and benefits involved, including some assessment of the likelihood of them being able to establish their position. Again this was liable to some particular considerations in the fen context.

---

[82] Beds. Archives, R Fens (uncatalogued), Box 2, Bundle 11, letter from Rev Thomas Neale, Great Gidding, 17 January 1740.
[83] There were 790 submitted and dated between 1660 and 1800, and more not dated but clearly from that period, though certainly not all concerned faults with the drainage and navigation. Cambridgeshire Archives, S/B/SP/1–790.
[84] Beds. Archives, R Fens (uncatalogued), Box 2, Bundle 11, mss dated 12 July 1753.
[85] Lincolnshire Archives, Spalding Sewers/500/77–8. John Rennie was called in to arbitrate in a dispute between Sir Joseph Banks and George Maxwell over engineering works in Lincolnshire. Sutro, Banks, F6:5, 11.

Claiming and Knowing

The highly varied origins, purpose, and size of interests was a crucial factor in the history of fen legislation. But it was one thing for them to exist, another for them to be influential; it was never enough simply to assert what their interest was. Claims might easily be made, but substantiating them persuasively was also crucial. It was particularly difficult to make authoritative statements about the effects of works to improve drainage and navigation. One problem was that it was well known that those effects could be felt an uncertain number of miles away. For example, improving draining in one area might simply put more water into insufficient drains in a neighbouring district. A further problem was distinguishing the effects of such works from those of natural forces without good records of rainfall, temperature, tides, and silting. Finally, plenty of times competing schemes for improvement were advanced, each supposedly superior. How was the best to be determined?

Competing interests employed the usual range of methods to make their case: lobbying, petitioning, pamphleteering, and calling on supposedly expert knowledge or judgement. Two features stand out in the case of fen legislation, especially relating to drainage and navigation: the attempt, mainly through petitions, to determine the key localities; and the use of engineers and surveyors to make claims and counterclaims. The examples of Denver sluice and the Eau Brink cut help to bring out these features well.

When in 1696–7 King's Lynn promoted a bill for the removal of Denver sluice, seven petitions were submitted to the Commons supporting it and nine against.[86] Four of those in favour of the bill came from towns up to fifty miles away, on or near tributaries of the Great Ouse – including Bury St Edmunds, Cambridge, and Thetford – complaining that the sluice was causing the decay of their river link to King's Lynn. Three of the others came from groups of landowners and occupiers, mainly in the area around Denver sluice, bemoaning the flooding it had supposedly caused. The nine petitions in favour of retaining Denver sluice came from a wider range of interests and sometimes from further afield: from the counties of Bedfordshire, Buckinghamshire, and Huntingdonshire (usually the Deputy Lieutenants and JPs); the borough corporation of Bedford; Ely cathedral; merchants, traders, and others at St. Ives on the Ouse in Huntingdonshire; independent landowners on the Great Level; and the Bedford Level Corporation. They emphasized the importance of

[86] *JHC*, 11 (1693–7), pp. 653 (7 Jan. 1697), 655 (9 Jan. 1697), 657–8 (11–12 Jan. 1697), 670 (23 Jan. 1697), 672–3 (26–7 Jan. 1697), 680 (28 Jan. 1697), and 689 (4 Feb. 1697).

the sluice to the inland limits of the navigation of the Great Ouse and the extent of trade that depended on that.

Such petitioning was clearly coordinated by the King's Lynn Corporation on the one hand and the Bedford Level Corporation on the other. In doing so, webs of connection were spun across the fens, linking different communities together to support two different causes concerning just one engineering work. Such petitioning can be found on many other occasions. For example, in preparing a case to rebuild Denver sluice after its destruction in 1713 (for which a new act was not required), the Bedford Level Corporation received, presumably at its behest, six petitions in 1723 (with 201 signatories in total, 29 using a mark), and ten in 1741 (with 394 signatories in total, 63 using a mark).[87] These landowners, mainly from across the South Level, complained at the incessant flooding they had suffered since 1713 and of the urgent need to rebuild the sluice and to undertake some dredging. Drowned lands were unable to pay full taxes, damaging the Bedford Level's cash flow. But the corporation also received petitions in the 1740s against rebuilding the sluice, including from Cambridge University, Cambridge Corporation, and the Commissioners of Sewers for Norfolk at Wiggenhall, just seven miles from Denver.[88]

Petitioning was obviously an important expression of opinion, giving some sense of the scope and scale of interested parties. A notably comprehensive example of this was in 1753–4 when a petition was drawn up, preparatory to a bill for improving the drainage of the North Level, which specified the acreages of those in favour and those against.[89] But petitioning could not, because of the limitations of the genre, do more than assert positions. Thus when Ely Cathedral petitioned the Commons for the retention of Denver sluice in 1697, it damned King's Lynn's case as no better than 'a bare Suggestion'. [90] It was a commonplace at the time that new proposals often met unthinking opposition – which might be justified as a guard against 'wild and delusive theories'.[91] A scheme for improving the North Level in 1752 was thought bound to encounter opposition, 'like all other things that must depend at first on matter of

---

[87] Cambridgeshire Archives, S/B/SP/292, 294–8, 417–26.

[88] Cambridgeshire Archives, S/B/SP/442–5.

[89] Beds. Archives, R Fens (uncatalogued), Box 1, Bundle 7, 'An abstract of the proprietors of Corporation lands in the North Middle & South Levels also of free lands in the North Level and lands in Porsand'. This was part of the complex renegotiation of the Corporation's debts to the Duke of Bedford and Earl of Lincoln, culminating in the act of 27 George II, c. 19.

[90] *JHC*, 11 (1693–7), 11 January 1697, p. 657.

[91] Anon., *Reasons attempting to shew the necessity of the proposed cut from Eau Brink to Lynn* (1793), p. 30.

opinion, and presumption only'.[92] Consequently, 'It is an invidious task for any man to stand forward to promote such improvements. He is sure to be Blackened and Wited as it suits the interest of scheming men which reside in the country. ... He is sure to bring on him the resentment of all the tennants, who are always jealous of their rents being raised whenever improvements are mentioned.'[93]

Actually proving that certain works would have or had had certain effects was in fact very difficult. One way of trying to establish a case was to call on older people to testify to the changes they had seen in their lifetime. In preparing its failed bill of 1696–7 to demolish Denver sluice, King's Lynn gathered eyewitness testimony from fourteen men with an average age of sixty-five and an average of forty-six years' experience of its navigation – that is, mainly from those who began to work just before the sluice was built.[94] Nearly a century later, a Commons select committee considering a bill to make the Eau Brink cut similarly often heard from older witnesses whose experience was deemed especially valuable.[95] This was notable, but ultimately somewhat limited. People might identify a suggestive coincidence from their lifetime, but obviously had not witnessed earlier developments or could not really prove cause and effect. Such circumstantial evidence counted for something, but increasingly the protagonists put more faith in surveyors and civil engineers.

Seemingly, King's Lynn unexpectedly achieved a key goal with the natural destruction of Denver sluice in 1713. Yet problems with silting in its port did not ease and, as has been seen, the destruction led to calls for the sluice to be rebuilt so as to prevent flooding in the South Level – sometimes from areas which had petitioned against the sluice in 1697. In 1721 the King's Lynn Corporation complained to the Bedford Level about silting up, but plainly the case could not simply be made on the old terms. Consequently, the town commissioned the highly experienced John Armstrong, a Fellow of the Royal Society and the Chief Engineer (i.e., military engineer) of England, to report on the drainage and navigation. He was supported by Thomas Badeslade, 'Gent. Surveyor and Proffesor of Mathematics', who surveyed the port, including its

---

[92] Beds. Archives, R/4508/13. Several authors quoted Sir Clement Edmonds from 1619 that 'he that would do good in draining, must do it against the will of such as have profit by it.' Neale, *Ruinous state of Manea*, p. 22; Sir Joseph Banks, 'Reply to queries relating to labour in Lincolnshire', *Annals of Agriculture*, 19 (1793), p. 188.

[93] Sutro, Banks, F5:32, James Creasy to Banks, St John St, Smithfield, 30 July 1793.

[94] Badeslade, *History of the navigation of King's Lynn*, pp. 61–2. Keith Thomas, 'Age and authority in early modern England, *Proceedings of the British Academy*, 62 (1976), pp. 205–48.

[95] 'Minutes of evidence taken ... on the second reading of the ... Eau Brink [drainage bill]', Lambert, *Sessional papers*, vol. 94, pp. 1–470.

channels.[96] Recourse to such expertise was hardly new – Vermuyden, a key figure in fen drainage, famously published a major work in 1642 – but King's Lynn obviously hoped that Armstrong's expertise constituted a novel, disinterested, and weighty intervention in a long-running debate.[97] They were quickly disappointed. The Earl of Lincoln, a senior figure in the Bedford Level Corporation, immediately commissioned a counter-report from Charles Bridgeman, best known as a landscape gardener (including for Robert Walpole at Houghton Hall in west Norfolk).[98] Just as quickly, this was answered paragraph by paragraph.[99]

Such reports and counter-reports, which were often printed, became a common feature of debates over fen drainage and navigation through the rest of the period, drawing in some of Britain's most notable civil engineers, including Smeaton and Rennie.[100] This injected an important level of professional and scientific expertise, albeit one that was gradually finding its feet methodologically and institutionally, including through the foundation of the Society of Civil Engineers in 1771.[101] By such means the 'rules' or 'laws of draining' were gradually refined, to the extent that the engineers could be mocked as 'Demi-gods'.[102] Nevertheless, disagreements among engineers continued to feed the fraught nature of much fen legislation.[103] One reason was that the reports were invariably commissioned and so took their lead from interested positions. Another complaint was that although engineers used 'science' or 'speculative knowledge' to pierce the thick fog of misunderstanding,

[96] *Colonel Armstrong's report, with proposals for draining the fenns and amending the harbour of Lynn, 1724* (1724). Skempton, *Biographical dictionary*, pp. 19–20.
[97] Cornelius Vermuyden, *A discourse touching the drayning the great fennes* (1642); Willmoth, *Moore*, ch. 3.
[98] Charles Bridgman [i.e., Bridgeman], *A report of the present state of the Great Level of the fens, called Bedford-Level, and of the port of Lynn; and of the Rivers Ouse and Nean* (1724).
[99] Anon., *An answer, paragraph by paragraph, to A report of the present state of the great level of the fens* [1724]. Skempton, *Biographical dictionary*, p. 27, says this is 'certainly written by Badeslade'.
[100] A. W. Skempton, *British civil engineering, 1640–1840: a bibliography of contemporary printed reports, plans and books* (1987).
[101] Mike Chrimes, 'Society of Civil Engineers', *ODNB*; Penelope J. Corfield, *Power and the professions in Britain, 1700–1850* (1995), pp. 181–2.
[102] Nathaniel Kinderley advanced a plan that was 'natural, easy, and rational; so agreeable to the Laws of Drainage, and reconcileable with the Principles of Mathematics and Philosophy'. *The ancient and present state of the navigation of the towns of Lyn, Wisbeach, Spalding, and Boston* (2nd edn., 1751), p. ix. For an example of reference to the 'rules' see Thomas Badeslade, *A scheme for draining the great level of the fens, called Bedford-Level* (1729), p. 4. For the mocking reference to 'Demi-gods', Anon., *A word or two to the South Holland proprietors, and the Fleet commoners* (1796), p. 10.
[103] A good case study of disagreements between engineers concerning the harbour at Wells on the north Norfolk coast is in Tal Golan, *Laws of men and laws of nature: the history of scientific expert testimony in England and America* (Cambridge, MA, 2004), ch. 1.

they often lacked practical experience or 'Mechanick Practice' to construct plausible plans.[104] Either way, engineers were very important, but rarely decisive figures in debates over fen legislation, as the case of the Eau Brink cut at the end of the eighteenth century brings out.

In 1721 Nathaniel Kinderley had proposed shortening the course of the Great Ouse near King's Lynn as a means of draining the fens more quickly and increasing the power of the river to deepen the port.[105] The Bedford Level Corporation embraced the idea, but the King's Lynn Corporation did not. The idea was periodically revived, but was only purposefully pursued in the early 1790s. Significantly, in 1790 the Norfolk Commissioners of Sewers (thirty-seven strong, with one of them an MP for King's Lynn) consulted with John Rennie, a leading engineer and FRS, and, with the sanction of juries, began to take forward the Eau Cut proposal. A sub-committee was formed, including again one of the MPs for King's Lynn. Support in principle was obtained from the Bedford Level Corporation, who were later encouraged by a petition signed by 329 landowners asking for their support.[106] Further surveys and engineers' reports were obtained and general meetings held, including one at March attended by 400 landowners. Emboldened, a further committee was established to seek statutory authority to make the cut. Two bills failed in 1793 and 1794, but a third was passed in 1795.[107]

With five interests involved, the proposed Eau Brink cut was hugely controversial, with opposition particularly coming from landowners in the South Level, the gentry and others both in Bedford and Bedfordshire (more than sixty miles away), navigators on some of the tributaries of the Ouse, and the corporation and inhabitants of Thetford.[108] The particular issues were whether the cut would have the desired effects and how it was to be paid for. There were numerous petitions and pamphlets and at

---

[104] Badeslade, *A scheme for draining*, p. 3; T. Pownall, *A memoir entituled drainage and navigation but one united work ... addressed to the corporations of Lynn-Regis and Bedford Level* (1775), pp. 1–3. Pownall had been a colonial governor and was an early critic of Adam Smith in *A letter from Governor Pownall to Adam Smith* (1776).

[105] [Nathaniel Kinderley], *The present state of the navigation of the towns of Lyn, Wisbeech, Spalding, and Boston* (Bury St Edmunds, 1721). The ESTC wrongly gives the author as Charles Kinderley: Skempton, *Biographical dictionary*, p. 386.

[106] Anon., *Reasons Eau Brink cut*; Cambridgeshire Archives, S/B/SP/776; Skempton, *Biographical dictionary*, pp. 346, 558, 766.

[107] Hoppit, *Failed legislation*, 135.053, 136.011; 35 George III, c. 77.

[108] The five interests were said to be: the Middle Level; the South Level; the Marshlands; King's Lynn; and the inland navigations and 'Countries interested therein'. Anon., *View of the conduct of parties, respecting the proposal of accommodation offered by the merchants of Lynn, to the promoters of the bill for making the cut from Eau Brink to Lynn* (1794), p. 6. 'Minutes of evidence ... on the second reading of the ... Eau Brink [drainage bill]', p. 3 in Lambert, *Sessional papers*, vol. 94, p. 3.

least eight engineers published reports, including from Sir Thomas Hyde Page, FRS, a leading military engineer.[109] The Commons select committee on the second failed bill spent more than a dozen days on the business, hearing from many witnesses, the evidence from whom is spread over 470 printed pages.[110] This was followed by another select committee on the bill that was enacted, working over twenty days, again with many witnesses and whose minutes of evidence comprise 263 pages.[111] It was, indeed, ultimately MPs and peers who had to weigh such evidence, and it is striking that they took such pains over their work and decided in favour of the cut. Thus while the Eau Brink cut was obviously a local measure, it was also a matter of wide concern, requiring considerable care.

Several factors were crucial to the passage of the Eau Brink act in 1795. The first was that Norfolk landowners and King's Lynn abandoned decades of opposition and fell in behind the idea. Doubtless that was in part because of the weight of professional advice and its growing credibility. In this regard it was important that a similar cut at Wisbech in 1773 – following through on the plan that had provoked rioting in 1722 – had been pretty successful. Further, very rapidly rising agricultural prices in the 1790s, associated with the exigencies of wartime, provided plenty of encouragement for such schemes, especially as the draining of the Marshland was associated with enclosing common land. And the finance and administration of the Eau Brink proposal nicely balanced the interests of King's Lynn, of navigators on the Ouse, and landowners across the Marshlands and Middle and South Levels. The cut was to be paid for by both taxes on landowners (of 300,000 acres) and tolls on navigators. Dozens of commissioners were appointed to oversee the works, including many landowners (some of them peers), the President of the Royal Society (Banks), King's Lynn's MPs, the corporations of Bury St Edmunds, Cambridge, King's Lynn, and Thetford, the Conservators of the River Cam, and the Vice-Chancellor of Cambridge University.[112] All this for just a few miles of river. That

---

109 The eight engineers were: James Golborne, Joseph Hodskinson, John Hudson, Robert Mylne, Joseph Nickalls, Thomas Hyde Page, John Rennie, John Watté. Mylne and Nickalls were founding members of the Society of Civil Engineers.

110 'Minutes of evidence ... on the second reading of the ... Eau Brink [drainage bill]', Lambert, *Sessional papers*, vol. 94, pp. 1–470. For reasons that are unclear, this does not include the evidence of Hyde Page, which was printed separately in seventy-six pages: *Minutes of the evidence of Sir Thomas Hyde Page, Knight, on the second reading of the Eau Brink drainage bill* (1794).

111 'First report from the committee appointed to take the residue of the evidence which may be thought proper to be adduced in support of the bill for improving the drainage of the Middle and South Levels', Lambert, *Sessional papers*, vol. 96, pp. 17–279.

112 35 George III, c. 77, § 3.

said, although the act was passed in 1795, difficulties of finding the capital and the need to solve further engineering problems meant that the Eau Brink cut took five further acts, nearly £150,000, and twenty-five years to complete.[113]

Ultimately, key judgements about fen legislation were made in Parliament or the courts. Rarely can these have been easy to arrive at. If both had to take due account of evidence and precedence, Parliament was a political as well as a legal institution.[114] It may have been 'an established maxim in policy ... that a great and general benefit should not be obstructed, through fear of a small and partial evil', but as Langford has stressed, in some circumstances Parliament often found matters to be more finely balanced, making it nigh on impossible to weigh the different cases and their supporters.[115] For example, in 1749 hauliers on the Great Ouse sought an act giving them the right for their horses to use the banks. This was vigorously opposed by the landowners, fearful that the banks would quickly be damaged and heighten risks of their land being flooded. They stressed the sanctity of property – that allowing hauliers to use their land was contrary to fundamental principles of justice 'by which the property of all the subjects of this Kingdom is so happily protected and secured'. That was a very important consideration for Parliament to weigh. On the other hand, the Commons was impressed by the fact that the bill was advantageous to trade and would benefit the five counties through which the river passed. Compensating landowners was the obvious way to reconcile such clashing principles, but it is notable that the bill was dropped, perhaps because of the difficulties of determining proper levels of 'satisfaction' and ways of raising the money.[116]

Conclusion

Everywhere people work within the constraints and the opportunities of the natural environment. The belief that environment affects politics is similarly ancient, while environmental history has a long heritage. In those ways, the case study of the fens is simply that, a particular English

---

[113] Pemberton, *Eau Brink accounts*; Walker and Craddock, *Wisbech and the fens*, p. 164; Samuel Wells, *The history of the drainage of the great level of the fens, called Bedford Level* (2 vols., 1828–30), vol. 1, p. 766.

[114] A good discussion of the rules of evidence and the impact of professional and scientific expertise in the period is Golan, *Laws of men*.

[115] Anon., *Gephyralogia: an historical account of bridges, antient and modern* (1751), p. 71; Paul Langford, *Public life and the propertied Englishman, 1689–1798* (Oxford, 1991), pp. 166–75.

[116] Beds. Archives, Franklin papers, FN1265/1275, 1319–22, 1327–9. Hoppit, *Failed legislation*, 87.017.

case study.[117] After all, major drainage projects can be found within very different political societies, including early modern France and the Dutch Republic.[118] Certainly ideas and expertise about drainage readily crossed borders, as the impact of Dutch engineers in seventeenth-century Britain attests. But Rosenthal has argued that more land was drained in England than in France, in significant part because its institutions were better at defusing and overcoming opposition.[119] Although relatively more land was drained in seventeenth- and eighteenth-century England than France, whether it was institutional arrangements that were the vital distinguishing element is impossible to say with any certainty – other obvious contenders would be the economic and financial climate (especially prices, patterns of landholding, the availability of capital). But it is helpful to think about the particular role that Parliament played.

The execution of Charles I in 1649 ensured that so long as the republic survived, Parliament, not the crown, was the ultimate site of political authority in the nation. In fact, the Restoration of Charles II in 1660 challenged but did not reverse this, as the 1663 act for the Bedford Level Corporation hints. Through the period covered by this book the sovereign Parliament was where local interests usually went to try to obtain the authority they needed to drain, enclose, turnpike, pave, and more. Parliament provided the ultimate means of solving local or regional coordination problems, providing the authority to overcome sticking points and opposition to change. Sometimes this involved instituting temporary bodies to do the work, most obviously with enclosures. But often permanent bodies were created, to undertake and manage drainage and turnpikes, for example.

A striking feature of the creation by Parliament of authorities to undertake economic projects was the public and advertised nature of the processes involved. Proposals could not be sprung on communities; they had to be advertised and justified. Opponents had clear opportunities to express their views. Rival interests naturally often sought to reconcile

---

[117] For some interesting comparisons see Andrew Gritt, 'Making good land from bad: the drainage of West Lancashire, c. 1650–1850', *Rural History*, 19.1 (2008), pp. 1–27.

[118] G. P. van de Ven, ed., *Man-made lowlands: history of water management and land reclamation in the Netherlands* (Utrecht, 1994); Raphaël Morera, *L'assèchement des marais en France au XVIIe siècle* (Rennes, 2011); Hugh D. Clout, 'Reclamation of coastal marshland', in Hugh D. Clout, ed., *Themes in the historical geography of France* (1977), pp. 184–213.

[119] Jean-Laurent Rosenthal, *The fruits of revolution: property rights, litigation, and French agriculture, 1700–1860* (Cambridge, 1992), ch. 9. Comparisons are also made in Piet van Cruyningen, 'Dealing with drainage: state regulation of drainage projects in the Dutch Republic, France, and England during the sixteenth and seventeenth centuries', *Economic History Review*, 68.2 (2015), pp. 420–40.

their differences before matters reached such a head, but they knew that in the end Parliament would decide, heavily informed by the cases that they made. Sovereignty, transparency, and negotiation went hand in hand to produce legitimacy, at least for the propertied. The landless certainly struggled to make their voice heard in Parliament, but they sometimes succeeded while the lack of police powers constrained the ambitions of the propertied.

Much specific legislation dealt with property rights, seeking to redistribute them to those who felt that they could enhance their value. This was most obviously the case with enclosure, but it was clearly also a point behind much drainage, navigation, and turnpike legislation. As such, what the Glorious Revolution led to was, contra North and Weingast, not the enhanced security of property rights, but rather a greater means to compel some to surrender them on payment of compensation where the losers could produce legal title.[120] Fen drainage statutes did not always involve such compulsory sale, but they did frequently legally require landowners or tenants within given jurisdictions to contribute to the common good. Compulsion was crucial, as was the exclusion of those who had previously made a living from marshy and swamped land. Ultimately, on such occasions Parliament decided to subjugate particular interests to those of a wider good.[121] In the battle between parliamentary sovereignty and the sanctity of property the former usually won out.

Legislation made a huge difference to the economy of the fens in this period, even if nothing like as much as the original promoters had hoped for. Obviously a large amount of land was enclosed, improvements to river navigations made in many places, some turnpike roads built, and significant efforts made at drainage and reclamation. Just how much this improved the output and productivity of the region is impossible to say as no regional figures of economic performance exist. It may be notable that the share of the national population in the four main counties of the region shrank steadily across the eighteenth century, from 10 to 7 per cent, but whether this was caused by changes in the fens, or was the result of significant improvements in productivity, is impossible to tell.[122]

---

[120] Douglass C. North and Barry R. Weingast, 'Constitutions and commitment: the evolution of institutions governing public choice in seventeenth-century England', *Journal of Economic History*, 49.4 (1989), pp. 803–32. Their argument is contextualized earlier, pp. 29–33.

[121] For a fuller discussion of the points in this paragraph see Julian Hoppit, 'Compulsion, compensation and property rights in Britain, 1688–1833', *Past and Present*, 210 (2011), pp. 93–128.

[122] E. A. Wrigley, 'Rickman revisited: the population growth rates of English counties in the early modern period', *Economic History Review*, 62.3 (2009), p. 724.

There are some small signs of the tax take in the region growing a little in the late eighteenth century, though this was from a very small base.[123]

What is clear is that despite all of the legislative efforts that were made, in 1800 many parts of the region were still very vulnerable to flooding, often compromising improvements already made. At that date parts of the region still seemed ripe for further improvement. Most obviously, the drainage of the Bedford Level was highly imperfect, producing a very 'uncertain country', while in the Lincolnshire fens Joseph Banks and Arthur Young thought a lot remained to be done.[124] Given this, it is the more striking that such efforts were put into obtaining fen legislation through the period. This speaks loudly to the strength of regional economic and legislative entrepreneurialism, especially amongst medium and large landowners, even if this waxed and waned. They used Parliament to increase their grip on property, often at the expense of small owners and users of commons and wastes. Critically, statutes were a means to grapple with both nature and property rights, less successfully with the former than the latter. But it was not only many commoners who were adversely affected, for drainage and enclosure legislation took power away from manor courts and Commissioners of Sewers and turnpike acts from parish vestries. In these ways, fen legislation subtly but profoundly affected the distribution of economic as well as political power, producing even more complexity.

The century or more before 1660 had seen the evolution of very ambitious plans for fen drainage. In that period the crown dispensed the political authority to undertake such schemes and, as such, a central organizing dynamic.[125] But after 1660 it was Parliament, not the crown, which was the key sovereign power. An important consequence was that no grand plan structured fen legislation. It was always non-governmental and sought by small interests preoccupied by their own bottom line. Yet in 1660 the ambitious attempt to drain the Great Level still seemed realizable and at the end of the eighteenth century it was hoped that the Eau Brink cut and associated improvements would make much of that drainage effective. In between, statutory powers were granted for particular local solutions to some of the problems being encountered. Their limited effectiveness and the realization that a solution in one area could create problems elsewhere led to increasing weight being given to the wider resolutions suggested by engineers. If usually commissioned to consider

---

[123] TNA, PRO 30/8/288; BL Add Mss, 8133, Musgrave papers.
[124] Beds. Archives, R Fens (uncatalogued), Box 2, Bundle 20, William Finch to Robert Palmer, 10 January 1778.
[125] Holmes, 'Drainers and fenmen'.

particular problems, they had to grapple with the broader potential of the main districts within the wider region.

Fen legislation requires, therefore, a rethinking of what is usually meant by 'political economy'. Far from being the preserve of central government and informed by discourses concerning national well-being, political economy in Britain in this period was often taken forward locally by those with very little interest in mercantilist notions. Individually some of the efforts were very small and others pretty large, but cumulatively the effects were very considerable, leading to major changes in the nature of land use and the available infrastructure. But it was not just that in these ways Westminster affected villages and towns across Britain, for a large amount of Westminster's work was given over to considering local initiatives. In doing so it had to be sure of its information, made increasing resort to outside expertise, and had to firm up the principles on which it acted. Those were challenges it slowly if imperfectly rose to meet, but which nonetheless were a critical element in Britain's political economies.

7   The Political Economy of Wool, 1660–1824

'[I]f you were to ask a manufacturer of Halifax, for instance, what was the greatest crime upon earth, was it felony, was it murder, was it parricide? he would answer, no, none of these; it was the exporting of wool.'
Marquis of Lansdowne, 1785[1]

Specific economic legislation was a critical feature of Britain's political economies. But the efforts of the individuals and interests involved did not really constitute a policy. As a whole the effort involved was huge and important, but it reflected more the assumptions of propertied society and its quest for improvement and income, leading to national economic betterment only indirectly. Parliament provided a key point of coordination and negotiation, but in only a minimal sense directed developments towards particular ends. Specific economic legislation mattered a lot, locally and in the aggregate, but understandably it played little part in Smith's analysis of political economy. For him, 'policy' was to be found in the 'mercantile system', or what has come to be called 'mercantilism'. Smith argued that what drove that system was a common desire to produce a positive balance of trade, because of, in his view, an erroneous belief that wealth consisted of money.[2] This involved, he contended, encouragements to export (considered in the next chapter) and re-exports, as well as restrictions or prohibitions on imports.

This chapter explores one such prohibition, the ban on the export of raw wool, to see how a cornerstone of the mercantile system was instituted, the sorts of arguments that were employed for and against it, and difficulties encountered in making the ban effective. It shows up the experimental or aspirational nature of the mercantile system, including that ambition might clash with economic interests that central

---

[1] Cobbett, *Parl. Hist.*, 25 (1785–6), col. 857. Lansdowne is better known as Lord Shelburne, Prime Minister, 1782–3.
[2] Eight of the nine chapters of Book 4 of the *Wealth of nations* were devoted to the 'mercantile system'. Only one chapter was devoted to the 'agrarian system', which mainly considered French Physiocracy.

government lacked the administrative wherewithal to contain – because the complexity and costs of effectively enforcing the ban were too great, in monetary, administrative, and political terms. It also sheds important light on the evolution of large interests within Britain, as in the 1780s leading landowners failed in their battle with manufacturers to have the ban lifted.

In early modern Britain all agreed that the manufacturing of wool provided an essential foundation on which much of society rested. From poor spinners to great landowners, wool was a national resource of enormous importance. Contemporaries declaimed on its significance long and loud. If Spain extracted bullion from its mines in South America, Britain had its 'growing Gold', 'the jewel and *Indies of England*'.[3] Moreover, golden fleeces were catalytic and fertile, not inert and impotent, bringing employment, wages, and profits to many. Raw wool fuelled the clothing trades that were 'the great Engine that turnes about all Trades of this Realm, which sets our Poore at Work, Inriches the subjects, and setts a better price upon Wool, which causeth Lands to be at higher Rates'.[4] National economic might and prestige was held to depend heavily on wool and its manufacture. Plenty would have agreed that they were 'the Richest Treasure in his Majesties Dominions, the flower, strength, and sinews of this Nation'.[5] Little wonder that lord chancellors had for centuries sat on a rather grand woolsack in the House of Lords.

Wool was not quite that important, but modern historians agree that its manufacture – into a huge variety of types – was the largest industry in Britain until supplanted by cotton early in the nineteenth century.[6] Quite what its importance was around 1700 is hard to pin down, though it certainly provided an extraordinary 69 per cent of exports from England then.[7] Over the eighteenth century the output of the industry

---

[3] John Dryden, *King Arthur* (1691), in *The works of John Dryden, vol. 16*, ed. Vinton A. Dearing (Berkeley, CA, 1996), p. 61; *JHC*, 13 (1699–1702), p. 570 (26 May 1701).

[4] O. Albin to Board of Trade, 15 July 1696: TNA CO389/14/9.

[5] [William Carter], *England's interest asserted: in the improvement of its native commodities; and more especially the manufacture of wool* (1669), p. 2.

[6] We still depend heavily on Phyllis Deane, 'The output of the British woolen industry in the eighteenth century', *Journal of Economic History*, 17.2 (1957), pp. 207–23; a very important recent overview is Pat Hudson, 'The limits of wool and the potential of cotton in the eighteenth and early nineteenth centuries', in Giorgio Riello and Prasannan Parthasarathi, eds., *The spinning world: a global history of cotton textiles, 1200–1850* (Oxford, 2009), pp. 327–50. Types of manufactured wool are defined in Florence M. Montgomery, *Textiles in America, 1650–1870* (New York, 1985). In this chapter I mean by 'woollens' any textile where raw wool provided the majority of the yarn. I do not distinguish between 'woollens' and 'worsteds', or 'old' or 'new' draperies.

[7] Ralph Davis, 'English foreign trade, 1660–1700', *Economic History Review*, 7.2 (1954), p. 165. In about 1700 one guess was that England produced 66 per cent of British wool, Wales 15 per cent, and Scotland 19 per cent. BL Stowe 354, f. 158r.

rose, but estimates of by how much vary from nearly 50 per cent to 200 per cent.[8] Either way this was slower than the growth of cotton, iron, and coal production. Critically, consumers were increasingly preferring lighter fabrics. As Josiah Tucker observed in 1782, 'Silks, Cottons, and Linens, combined in a thousand Forms, and diversified by Names without Number, are now almost the universal Wear'.[9] Consequently, if in 1770 woollens accounted for perhaps 30 per cent of value added in British industry, this had fallen to 19 per cent by 1801 and 14 per cent by 1830. It was being overtaken by cotton as Britain's leading textile industry, providing 42 per cent of exports of British produce by 1804–6, with wool now contributing only 16 per cent.[10]

Obviously the growth of wool production and manufacture was not without its challenges. In particular, it was mainly experienced in England's West Riding and West Country (straddling Gloucestershire, Somerset, and Wiltshire). Elsewhere, notably in Devon and Norfolk, there was struggle and retreat.[11] In part this helps to explain why contemporaries were frequently very anxious about the sector. Recurring laments were voiced about 'decay', 'decline', and 'distemper'.[12] Mostly, this was based on a belief that foreign producers were gaining ground with their more attractive textiles (lighter woollens, calicos, linens, and silks), helped by lower labour costs. Such anxieties were far from new, having been especially potent in the 1620s, leading to analyses of trade usually labelled 'mercantilist'.[13] The response was a near universal belief that wool and its industries ought to be watched carefully by central government and regulations introduced to ensure its vitality.

[8] Stephen Broadberry, Bruce M. S. Campbell, Alexander Klein, Mark Overton, and Bas van Leeuwen, *British economic growth, 1270–1870* (Cambridge, 2015), p. 112; Deane, 'Output', p. 220. Wool was unquestionably a vital raw material, though it does not feature in E. A. Wrigley's classic article, 'The supply of raw materials in the industrial revolution', *Economic History Review*, 15.1 (1962), pp. 1–16.

[9] *Reflections on the present low price of coarse wools* (1782), p. 9.

[10] N. F. R. Crafts, *British economic growth during the industrial revolution* (Oxford, 1985), p. 22; Ralph Davis, *The industrial revolution and British overseas trade* (Leicester, 1979), p. 15.

[11] R. G. Wilson, 'The supremacy of the Yorkshire cloth industry in the eighteenth century', in N. B. Harte and K. G. Ponting, eds., *Textile history and economic history: essays in honour of Miss Julia de Lacy Mann* (Manchester, 1973), pp. 225–46.

[12] John Haynes, *Great Britain's glory, or an account of the great numbers of poor employ'd in the woollen and silk manufactures ... with the reasons for the decay of those trades* (1715); [Daniel Webb], *An enquiry how far the declining state of the British woollen manufactures for exportation does affect the English landed interest* [1732?]; [William Webster], *The consequences of trade, as to the wealth and strength of any nation; of the woollen trade in particular, and the great superiority of it over all other branches of trade* (1740), p. 2.

[13] B. E. Supple, *Commercial crisis and change in England, 1600–1642* (Cambridge, 1959).

Lobbyists and the press ensured that central government was always well aware of any problems being faced by the woollen industries. In fact, they often found themselves knocking at an open door, with bills and acts the stock in trade of this relationship. In 1806 a parliamentary committee investigating the woollen manufactures in England calculated that seventy acts actively and directly applied to the sector, which they divided into three categories: those regulating masters and workmen in manufacture; those regulating masters in the sale of cloth; and those preventing the export of 'certain materials and implements'.[14] In all three, complex systems of regulation had been constructed.

This chapter is concerned only with a part of one of those areas, the complete ban on the export of raw wool, viewed by Wilson as the very epitome of 'mercantile system'.[15] The ban was proclaimed and enacted in 1660 and not lifted until 1824. It was, though, subject to considerable legislative reconsideration. In summary, between 1660 and 1824 some twenty-four different acts were passed about wool exports, or about one every five years (see Table 7.1). Some of these acts were no more than minor adjustments to the regulations, but with many of them Parliament sought to forge a powerful new link that would make the whole chain capable of securing within Britain all of the domestic wool clip. Yet almost always the new link was soon believed to have broken under the slightest of strains. Moreover, there were even more failed efforts to pass legislation.

---

[14] *JHC*, 61 (1806), p. 697 (Appendix 23). Some efforts had previously been made directly to increase consumption of woollen textiles. In the Restoration era bodies were meant to be wrapped in woollen cloth when buried: 18 & 19 Charles II c. 4, 30 Charles II c. 3, and 32 Charles II c. 1. But observance was probably very patchy at best. As Charles Davenant put it, 'The Natural Way of promoting the Woollen Manufacture, is not to force its consumption at Home, but by wholsome Laws to contrive, That it may be wrought cheaply in England, which consequently will enable us to command the Markets abroad.' *An essay on the East-India trade* (1696), pp. 26–7.

[15] C. H. Wilson, 'Trade, society and the state', in *The Cambridge economic history of Europe, vol. 4. The economy of expanding Europe in the sixteenth and seventeenth centuries*, ed. E. E. Rich and C. H. Wilson (Cambridge, 1967), p. 496. For previous discussion of the ban, see: James Bischoff, *A comprehensive history of the woollen and worsted manufactures* (2 vols., 1842); Peter J. Bowden, *The wool trade of Tudor and Stuart England* (1962), pp. 194–212; E. Lipson, *A short history of wool and its manufacture* (1953), pp. 21–30, 97–116; J. de L. Mann, *The cloth industry in the west of England from 1640 to 1880* (1971), ch. 9. The ban usually also extended to the export of fuller's earth, an important raw material in wool manufacture. Historians have looked at other areas of regulation of woollen manufacture. A sense of the range of legislative efforts is provided by Raymond L. Sickinger, 'Regulation or ruination: Parliament's consistent pattern of mercantilist regulation of the English textile trade, 1660–1800', *Parliamentary History*, 19.2 (2000), pp. 211–32. For a recent deeply considered work, referencing many others, see John Styles, 'Spinners and the law: regulating yarn standards in the English worsted industries, 1550–1800', *Textile History*, 44.2 (2013), pp. 145–70.

Table 7.1 *Wool export legislation, 1660–1824*

Period	Acts	Fails	Success %	General economic legislation success %
1660–85	2	14	13	25
1689–1714	6	20	23	40
1714–60	8	4	67	67
1760–1800	4	3	57	81
1800–24	4	n.a.	n.a.	n.a.

The relatively low success rate of legislation in this area bears witness to the contentions involved. Initially the concern was with identifying the best means to enforce the ban. From the middle of the eighteenth century, however, the ban came to be seen by many important and powerful figures as distorting at best and damaging at worst. It took, however, decades for such voices to triumph and only then in very different circumstances.

This chapter considers the ban not to explain the fortunes of the woollen industries, but to tease out further the ideas and interests involved in the making of political economy in practice. A second concern is to consider contemporary perceptions of the gap that existed between prescription and practice. As such, it sheds light on the tension between mercantilist aspirations and a reluctance to empower central government sufficiently to realize those hopes. Exploring the ban on the export of wool sheds a powerful light on some important limits to the 'mercantile system' and 'mercantilism'. Discussion is arranged in five sections, the first four of which focus on developments over time. The first explores the advent of the statutory ban in 1660 and its evolution before the Hanoverian succession in 1714. In this period, efforts at enforcement turned first to the death penalty, then to greater policing. Contemporaries thought that both provided at best only temporary compliance. In the second period, from 1714 to the onset of the American war in 1775, various efforts were made to enforce the law, especially through attempts to institute a national register of wool. But no such register was ever established. The next section looks first at highly controversial and unsuccessful attempts made in the early 1780s to allow wool export under certain conditions. The effort in part prompted a new law in 1788 consolidating existing legislation regarding the ban, in the hope that it might then be more easily enforced. These efforts involved bitter battles between landed and manufacturing interests, prefiguring those over the repeal of the corn laws by half a century. The fourth section looks briefly at the reasons why the ban on the export of wool was lifted in 1824. Finally, the chapter considers the general implications of this case study for our understanding of Britain's political economies.

Establishing the System, 1660–1714

In part, the vitality of the woollen industries depended on the quantity, quality, and price of raw wool. Until the end of the eighteenth century it was believed that the whole of the national wool clip could be consumed by manufacturers in Britain. Some imports might be needed from time to time, but supposedly there was no excess that might be exported. English wool was also believed to be of unrivalled quality internationally, such that from the fourteenth century there had been worries that some were exporting it, lured by higher prices on the continent. Consequently, its export from England had long been restricted and regulated, for example, by directing the trade through the Staple merchants. But a complete ban was first instituted by proclamation as part of the Cockayne project of 1614.[16] Soon after his Restoration in 1660, Charles II reiterated the ban, again by proclamation, which was almost simultaneously placed on a statutory footing that remained in place until 1824.[17]

The reasons for the ban were set out clearly in the 1660 proclamation:

Whereas the making of woollen cloth, and other manufactures of wool, which hath been, and is the great staple of this kingdom (whereby the commerce of this kingdom, and many thousand families therein have been, and are principally maintained and upheld) hath nevertheless of late years been much impaired and decayed; and whereas it is apparent, that the exportation of wools, wool fells, yarn made of wool, fullers earth, and other scouring earths, are a great means and occasion of such decay of the said trade, by enabling the foreign making of cloth, and thereby hindering the vent of our clothes made within this our realm of England.

Such thinking was central to the retention of the ban for over 150 years. It was supposed, Anglo-centrically, that England was naturally able to produce plentiful superior-quality wool that was coveted by its major competitors, France especially, though initially also the Dutch Republic. (Scotland too was counted as foreign before the Union in 1707.) The ban was also justified on the ground of the importance of the value added in the manufacturing of wool, especially through employment, to national wealth: 'The *Riches* of a Nation arise out of the *Labour* of

---

[16] Bowden, *Wool trade*, pp. 164, 180.
[17] Robert Steele, ed., *Tudor and Stuart royal proclamations, 1485–1714* (2 vols., Oxford, 1910), vol. 1, p. 391; 12 Charles II, c. 32.

the People *exported* to *foreign* Markets.'[18] Frequent calculations of this value sought to turn superlatives into substance, if never very convincingly – in 1702 it was extravagantly claimed that illegal wool exports to France meant that employment for 1.9 million people (35 per of the population) was lost.[19] All agreed that such a wonderful raw material had to be manufactured domestically to maximize this gift from God. Moreover, allegedly cloth producers in France and the Low Countries were uncompetitive without English wool because their own wool was of poor quality. That danger was bad enough, but lower labour costs on the continent also threatened cheaper cloths that would drive England's from its major markets, perhaps even at home.[20] One nation's loss would inevitably be the other's gain: 'the Exportation of our Wool to France is the chief Cause of their Strength and our Weakness.'[21] If that happened, England's woollen industries would be doomed to a painful death, with terrible consequences for the whole nation.

In many respects such arguments were mercantilist, viewing the European market for woollen textiles as fixed, that plenty and power went hand in hand, and that national action was needed. Maximizing labour inputs, through the manufacture of wool, tackled the twin evils of poverty and idleness while also heightening the value of exports. Balance of trade arguments were not much stressed, presumably because they were so self-evident, though as we have seen wool was likened to precious metals. But the ban also rested on a belief in England's comparative advantage in raw wool production and its manufacture, a type of argument refined by Ricardo as classical economics took shape in the early nineteenth century. As the Board of Trade noted in a report on the state of the woollen manufactures in 1702, 'the nature of Trade is such, that it depends upon the mutual Conveniency which every Nation finds in the Barter and Exchange of the commodities of their own Growth for those of the Growth of other Countries'.[22]

Such arguments were dominant before 1745, though not completely unchallenged, mainly because two major limitations to the ban quickly became apparent. The first was that the ban was very hard to enforce. The 1660 act assumed that its provisions would be met with general

---

18 [Webster], *Consequences of trade*, p. 7; Thomas Manly, *A discourse shewing that the exportation of wooll is destructive to this kingdom* (1677), p. 3.

19 Anon., *The deplorable case of the chief and other agents or officers that have been deputed and concerned in the preventing the carrying away and the exportation of wool of this kingdom* [1702].

20 Anon., *The ancient trades decayed, repaired again* (1678), p. 8.

21 John London, *Some considerations on the importance of the woollen manufactures* (1740), p. 12.

22 TNA, PC1/1/171.

acceptance and acquiescence, with JPs and revenue officers readily bringing malefactors to justice, punishing them with specified fines and forfeitures. But that the combined will of crown and Parliament did not produce the desired outcome quickly became apparent, for in 1662 new teeth were added to the ban by making the export of wool a felony punishable by death.[23] If this new terror was meant to rein in smuggling by the 'owlers' – so named because of their night-time call – it clearly failed. Canterbury quickly became something of an entrepôt of the smuggling trade, allegedly handling £100,000 of smuggled wool annually in the early 1660s.[24] It was claimed that in 1669 an organized trade had sent 10,000 packs of wool from Sussex across the channel. The revenue officers in the front line of attempts to enforce the ban were overwhelmed by the numbers of armed smugglers, who in any case easily avoided being caught in the act.[25]

In the 1670s especially there was active debate and discussion of the wool export ban, concentrating on how to make it work, including suggesting that its administration be delegated to Christ's Hospital.[26] In that decade there were eleven failed bills (but no acts), with a good deal of related discussion in pamphlets. (With Parliament hardly meeting between 1681 and 1689 debate abated, though in 1685 the Commons considered how to keep up the price of wool and corn, including some sumptuary measures.[27]) One dispute, relatively minor at this stage, concerned the question of whether the ban was in the national interest, or whether it only served sectional interests. In 1677, for example, it was noted that arguments were being aired that the ban damaged landowners by depressing prices for wool and, thereby, rents that they could charge.[28] To one anonymous pamphleteer, such a consequence of the ban was incompatible with the fact that landowners were 'the greatest concern and Interest of the Nation'. Making policy to advantage those few who used wool otherwise surplus to home manufacture was to put the cart before the horse. It was landowners, nobody else, who were the 'Masters and proprietaries of the foundation of all the wealth in this Nation'.[29] Such a view of interests was challenged by William Carter,

---

[23] 14 Charles II, c. 18.
[24] BL Egerton Mss 2985, ff. 74, 77.
[25] HMC, *Eighth report* (1881), pp. 127–8, 137.
[26] HMC, *Eighth report*, p. 138. It was thought that Christ's would be disinterested and had some knowledge of the trade because of their role as governors of Blackwell Hall, a market for woollen manufactures in London. A few years later, in 1673, the Royal Mathematical School was founded at Christ's.
[27] *JHC*, vol. 9 (1667–87), p. 734 (12 June 1685).
[28] Manly, *Discourse*, p. 1.
[29] Anon., *Reasons for a limited exportation of wooll* (1677), p. 5.

who was highly active both in this debate and in trying to enforce the ban in Sussex and Kent. In the main he asserted the unity of interests between merchants, mariners, and artificers on the one hand and landowners on the other.[30] Essentially he thought that landowners who said otherwise were blind to facts and to reason, imprisoned as they were by a false consciousness. It was an argument that won out, as it would again in the 1780s.

The second limitation to the wool export ban concerned England's changing economic relationship with Ireland. In particular, from the 1660s the Irish sheep flock was thought to be growing rapidly – in response to England's ban on the import of Irish cattle via acts of 1663 and 1666 (to protect English beef farmers and their landlords). With Irish wool now plentiful, it might either be sent to France or, just as bad, be used to develop woollen industries in Ireland. With their lower labour costs, the Irish threatened to out-compete English manufacturers.[31] On this score, as others, English interests were viewed as fundamentally incompatible with Irish interests. Little wonder that this prompted Thomas Southwell, the Irish peer and friend of William Petty, to remark a little later that 'It is a difficult task and next to impossible to please all interests & partys'.[32]

Despite all the huffing and puffing, between 1662 and the Glorious Revolution little was actually done to improve the effectiveness of the wool export ban. James II issued two proclamations, the first simply reiterating that of Charles II in 1660, the second calling for the laws to be enforced.[33] But no more acts were passed and no new administration instituted. By contrast, as Table 7.1 shows, the quarter century after James' deposition saw considerable legislative action relating to the ban – helped by frequent and long meetings of Parliament, but also by the institution of the Board of Trade in 1696 to provide oversight of commercial matters, including a report on woollen manufacture and trade.[34] Indeed, quickly after the Glorious Revolution Parliament passed a major new act, suggesting the importance and the urgency of improving the ban. It and five other acts, all but one passed before William's

[30] [William Carter], *The proverb crossed, or a new paradox maintained, (viz.) that it is not at all times true, that interest cannot lye* (1677), pp. 6–7. He had been employed by the Staple Company to prosecute owlers. Bowden, *Wool trade*, p. 180.

[31] 15 Charles II, c. 7; 18 & 19 Charles II, c. 2; Anon., *An account of the late design of buying up the wooll of Ireland in company. In a letter to J. L.* (1674); Carolyn A. Edie, 'The Irish cattle bills: a study in Restoration politics', *Transactions of the American Philosophical Society*, 60.2 (1970), pp. 1–66.

[32] Southwell to Charles Montague, n.d., BL Add Mss 4761, Milles collection, f. 186

[33] Steele, ed., *Royal proclamations*, vol. 1, pp. 465 and 468.

[34] *JHC*, 12 (1697–9), pp. 425–40 (18 January 1699).

death in 1702, established a framework for enforcing the ban.[35] The ten key elements were:

1. Commissioners were established to oversee enforcement of the ban;
2. Irish wool had to be exported to England from six specified ports, and imported into England through seven specified ports – trade outside of those ports, or direct from Ireland to other countries was forbidden and bonds were required of those involved in this trade;
3. The sale of colonial wool and wool products was significantly regulated, mainly to ensure their sale to British markets;
4. Wool had to be packed in a specific way, and clearly labelled as wool – even the size of lettering was specified;
5. Coastwise shipping of wool within England had to be declared to the authorities by the shippers; there was no unrestricted movement;
6. Limited amounts of wool could be shipped from Southampton to the Channel Islands, where the governor licensed its distribution;
7. Wool could not be moved at night within certain distances of the coast;
8. Newly shorn wool close to the coast in Kent and Sussex had to be declared and registered;
9. Cruisers were specifically assigned by statutes to patrol certain waters to stop smuggling;
10. The death penalty was replaced by fines and forfeitures.

Not all of these elements were in place down to 1824, and some were significantly modified, but they give a good sense of how wool exports from Britain were to be prevented, and the sale regulated of wool and woollen goods in other parts of Britain's empire. They clearly show that Parliament was determined that neither British nor Irish wool would go anywhere but to manufacturers in England and Wales (later extended to Scotland after Union in 1707). They also imply, correctly, that the greatest fear was that wool was being sent to France. Thus Irish wool was not to be sent to ports on England's south coast, Exeter notably, so as to hamper its illicit diversion to France on rounding Land's End. Devon's major textile region could only access Irish wool via ports in the Bristol Channel, incurring high land haulage charges.

As in the 1670s, these measures were associated with extensive and intensive debate, especially relating to how to prevent Irish wool reaching

---

[35] 1 William & Mary, c. 32; 7 & 8 William III, c. 28; 9 William III, c. 40; 10 William III, c. 16; 11 William III, c. 13; 4 & 5 Anne, c. 7. Anon., *A collection of all the statutes now in force, against the transportation of wooll* (1714) represents a drawing of breath after such legislative exertions.

markets in Europe and whether to allow it to be made into yarn or cloth in Ireland and, if so, where those products might be sold.[36] English assumptions were overwhelmingly that Ireland's economy should be supplementary and subservient to England's.[37] It must pose no threat. As Molyneux wrote to Locke, 'England, most certainly, will never let us thrive by the woollen trade; this is their darling mistress, and they are jealous of any rival.'[38] (Much the same was also said of New England.) A petition from Exeter, signed by more than 1,300, was typical: 'The woollen manufacture in England has been much lessened by the Irish, who are rivals in the trade, and by reason of the cheapness of their wool, wages and provisions, supplant the English in foreign markets, to the ruin of the trade and the diminution of the value of land in England.'[39] In 1699 high duties on the import into England and Wales of Irish woollen manufactures was effectively a ban on the industry in Ireland.[40]

A key point of the legislation of William's reign was to improve oversight of the shipping of wool, including extensive recordkeeping regarding wool from Ireland, Kent, and Sussex. Such bureaucratization could be onerous. For Irish wool, bonds were taken at a number of Irish and English ports, with the periodic reconciliation of accounts between the two to ensure that what was shipped out of Ireland was indeed received at its declared destination in England. That this was done is clear.[41] The registering of wool in Kent and Sussex placed new burdens on customs officers at the same time as they were trying to collect more and more revenue to help fund a very expensive war.

The legislation of William's reign also created new offices, or increased the responsibilities of existing offices. Especially noteworthy was the institution of Commissioners of Wool in 1689, though the real work was done by, at its peak in about 1701, seventeen surveyors of nineteen English counties, with 299 riding officers, all at an annual cost of nearly £21,000.[42]

---

[36] H. F. Kearney, 'The political background to English mercantilism, 1695–1700', *Economic History Review*, 11.3 (1959), pp. 484–96; Patrick Kelly, 'The Irish woollen export prohibition act of 1699: Kearney revisited', *Irish Economic and Social History*, 7 (1980), pp. 22–44.

[37] TNA, PC1/1/171.

[38] Quoted in Maurice Cranston, *John Locke: a biography* (1957), p. 407.

[39] HMC, *House of Lords manuscripts*, vol. 2 (new series). *The manuscripts of the House of Lords, 1697–1699* (1905), p. 131.

[40] L. M. Cullen, *An economic history of Ireland since 1660* (2nd edn., 1981), pp. 34–9.

[41] BL, Liverpool papers, Add Mss 38,339, ff.50–5. This report covers the period 1750–64, detailing wool and yarn shipped from Ireland to England annually. Similarly, in the Treasury papers are accounts of the bonds taken in English and Irish ports, 1739–43: TNA, T64/282/1–2.

[42] John Smith, *Chronicon rusticum-commerciale; or, memoirs of wool* (2 vols., 1747), vol. 2, pp. 166–7. Robert M. Lees, 'The constitutional importance of the "Commissioners for

These were police, not revenue officers, though their arrangement some-what echoed that used in the excise service. Additionally, after the peace of Ryswick in 1697 naval forces were stationed in home waters to keep watch, which cost nearly £30,000 per annum in 1700.[43] These two initia-tives required a significant financial investment, costing together about half that then being spent collecting the excise in England and Wales.[44] Whether this was money well spent is impossible to tell: the commissioners seized little wool, the cruisers none at all. That might be a sign that they provided an effective deterrent, such that smuggling withered away. But it could just as well mean that they caught very little of what smuggling there was and were hopelessly ineffective.[45] Either way, with the advent of the War of the Spanish Succession in 1702 both forms of action soon disappeared, though cruisers were periodically ordered to help out subsequently in peacetime. More telling is the fact that the commissioners were meant to be paid out of the value of what they seized. But this was totally inadequate, being about 5 per cent of total costs.[46] Little wonder that in 1702 the officers complained at their lack of pay and the Commission of Wool died.[47]

Unease and Inaction, 1714–1774

In 1710 war weariness overwhelmed Britain, leading to the election of a Tory government committed to seeking peace. That was no easy task, and one made more complicated by attempts to place Franco–British trade relations on a new footing.[48] The export of wool was a factor in this, such that in the general election of 1713 it became bound up with party con-siderations, probably for the first time. In Buckinghamshire Whigs wore a piece of wool in their hats, 'saying 'twas all going into France', whereas Tories, referencing Charles II's escape from the battle of Worcester in 1649, had oak leaves.[49] Still, soon after 1713 Queen Anne issued a

Wool" of 1689: an administrative experiment of the reign of William III' [in two parts], *Economica*, 40 and 41 (1933), pp. 147–68, 264–74.

[43] Smith, *Memoirs of wool*, vol. 2, p. 164. Costs of the cruisers were £22,000 in the year to July 1699. *JHL*, 16 (1696–1701), p. 569 (4 April 1700).

[44] Management charges for the excise in England and Wales were £115,000 in 1700: TNA, CO390/4, from the European State Finance Database, online.

[45] The Board of Trade thought that the system was effective: TNA, PC1/1/171. The offi-cers of the Commission of Wool did not: TNA, SP34/2/23.

[46] Smith, *Memoirs of wool*, vol. 2, p. 167.

[47] TNA, SP34/2/23.

[48] D. C. Coleman, 'Politics and economics in the age of Anne: the case of the Anglo–French trade treaty of 1713', in D. C. Coleman and A. H. John, eds., *Trade, government and economy in pre-industrial England: essays presented to F. J. Fisher* (1976), pp. 187–211.

[49] James J. Cartwright, ed., *The Wentworth papers 1705–1739: selected from the private and family correspondence of Thomas Wentworth, Lord Raby, created in 1711 Earl of Strafford* (1883), p. 351.

proclamation calling for the enforcement of the ban on the export of wool, and offering rewards of £40 to informants. By one later report this immediately broke the smuggling gangs of Kent and Sussex, as 'Happy was he who Could get in first to Impeach his Fellows.'[50] Perhaps the law looked settled, yet very quickly complaints about wool smuggling and proposed remedies were heard again.[51] Anxieties about the effectiveness of the ban recurred for more than a quarter of a century, prompting renewed efforts to make it work better. In the end, however, although there were several acts addressing smuggling in one way or another, wool running probably increased after 1714 exposing an important limit to mercantilism in practice.[52]

Walpole, prime minister from 1721 to 1742, took a very active interest in smuggling. Famously, he bought smuggled wines himself, but more importantly he was eager to reduce smuggling so as to boost the public revenues. His papers are littered with letters and reports on smuggling in all its forms, including the export of wool. He also received several schemes for tackling the smuggling of wool out of both Britain and Ireland.[53] Yet important though he was, the Board of Trade played a more significant role in seeking to improve the effectiveness of the wool export ban, producing reports or proposals in 1721, 1732, and 1742 (a day after Walpole resigned). On all three occasions it was simply assumed – not reasoned or evidenced – that the export of unmanufactured wool was pernicious and that smuggling was rife. The first two reports reflected on the nature of the ban and what might be done to improve its effectiveness. In 1742, by contrast, a fully worked-out proposal was offered to Parliament. No act resulted.

The Board of Trade was created in 1696 by William III as a branch of executive government, worried as he was that Parliament was about to constitute such a body itself. It is usually depicted as having been highly active and moderately effective for a decade or two, not least because it counted John Locke and William Blathwayt among its members,

---

[50] Cambridge University Library (CUL), Walpole papers, Ch(H) 80/486, 'The humble representation of the woollen manufacturers of Ipswich'. This is undated, but is certainly after 1720. For Queen Anne's proclamation, *London Gazette*, 5166, 20–4 October 1713.

[51] Haynes, *Great Britain's glory*. To enforce the wool export ban he proposed, pp. 69–74, twenty-two sloops to be stationed around Britain's coastline and 209 inland riding officers (under twenty-four supervisors), at an annual cost of nearly £32,000.

[52] Eveline Cruickshanks and Howard Erskine-Hill, 'The Waltham black act and Jacobitism', *Journal of British Studies*, 24.3 (1985), p. 362; Paul Monod, 'Dangerous merchandise: smuggling, Jacobitism, and commercial culture in southeast England, 1690–1760', *Journal of British Studies*, 30.2 (1991), p. 153.

[53] Especially relevant is CUL, Walpole papers, Ch(H) 41/1/1–64.

respectively real intellectual and administrative heavyweights.[54] But after they left office the Board inevitably fell into the hands of lesser mortals, while its business became increasingly one of routine, especially as a clearing house for correspondence about colonial governance. That the Board was repeatedly and heavily involved in discussion over the wool export ban – it had also produced a major report in 1699, part of which considered the ban – sits, therefore, a little uneasily with such depictions.[55] That it came up with suggestions or solutions that were not implemented certainly reflects on the impracticality of some of them, but rather more on the reluctance of parliamentarians to countenance a growth in the powers of central government domestically.

Strong feelings were expressed periodically in the 1720s and 1730s that Britain's woollen industries were in crisis and that something must be done, especially regarding the export of wool. In 1731 a controversial bill, supported by the ministry, made its way through the Commons before failing in the Lords.[56] As so often, in the Lords it was said that the bill would restore the nation's fortunes in the manufacture of wool. Its opponents claimed that the bill would only help Ireland.[57] Proceedings ground to a halt. Turning to the Board of Trade was presumably hoped to be a means of finding a way through the impasse. Certainly its 1732 report put its finger on the difficulties faced with the ban and the options that might be adopted to ensure its reasonable effectiveness. It noted that ideally wool should be tracked from the moment it was shorn to its final manufacture, which might be done by requiring all wool to be sold through public warehouses, by public purchase and resale, by a general register of wool shorn, or by putting the whole trade under the watchful eye of the excise. But all of those methods would produce a 'Multiplicity of Accounts, besides other Difficulties, and great Expence' and were impractical.[58]

The recommendations in 1732 were clear. It was not proposed, as the report of 1721 had, that the Commissioners of Wool be revived, but both reports recommended an extension of the system of registering wool near the coast of Kent and Sussex to the rest of Britain's coastline.[59] The report

---

[54] I. K. Steele, *Politics of colonial policy: the Board of Trade in colonial administration, 1696–1720* (Oxford, 1968); James A. Henretta, *"Salutary neglect": colonial administration under the Duke of Newcastle* (Princeton, NJ, 1972).

[55] The relevant part of the 1699 report is in *JHC*, 12 (1697–9), pp. 425–8 (18 Jan. 1699).

[56] Hoppit, *Failed legislation*, 69.010. A. A. Hanham, 'Whig opposition to Sir Robert Walpole in the House of Commons, 1727–1734' (University of Leicester PhD thesis, 1992), pp. 297–9.

[57] *Gentleman's Magazine*, 1 (1731), p. 213.

[58] *JHC*, 21 (1727–32), pp. 832–3 (6 Mar. 1732).

[59] *JHC*, 19 (1718–21), pp. 409–10 (25 Jan. 1721); *JHC*, 21 (1727–32), p. 833 (6 Mar. 1732).

also believed that unless Ireland's wool was fully monopolized by Britain, then any ban in Britain was bound to fail. A trade that was already limited to specific ports was now, it recommended, to be limited to specific ships. But such clear proposals were followed only by legislative inaction. A failed bill followed in 1735, but the relative silence on the matter probably reflects on the difficulty of forwarding realistic and realizable proposals.[60]

In the late 1730s and the early 1740s an especially profound sense of crisis in England's woollen industries was articulated. This began before, but was accentuated by, the start of the War of the Austrian Succession (1740–8). Bad weather in 1740–1 deepened the problems and spread them to other parts of the economy. We have no total output figures, but certainly the value of woollen exports, having generally risen for a decade, peaked in 1738 and then fell back 30 per cent to a nadir in 1744. Not that problems were felt everywhere as over that period the output of the Yorkshire industry, for which figures are available, rose.[61] Yet a campaign in 1741, calling for the wool export ban to be enforced, saw twenty-six petitions sent in from eleven counties, including Yorkshire, though half the petitions did emanate from the West Country. The feeling that something needed to be done was palpable. The cause of the decline of woollen textile exports was laid squarely at the door of prolific wool smuggling, from both Britain and Ireland.[62] Four failed efforts at legislation in the four years 1739–42 fed into and off of dozens of pamphlets or books on the topic.[63]

Although no act was produced as a consequence of this crisis, the Board of Trade did develop a full legislative proposal. This was the result of a remarkable joint effort by the Board and ideas sent in from the public. From the mid-1730s the Board had received several unsolicited proposals. The content of these is not always clear, but in November 1740 it received one clearly suggesting the institution of a national register of

[60] Hoppit, *Failed legislation*, 73.002.

[61] Elizabeth Boody Schumpeter, *English overseas trade statistics, 1697–1808* (Oxford, 1960), pp. 36–7; B. R. Mitchell, *British historical statistics* (Cambridge, 1988), p. 351. For an overview of these years see T. S. Ashton, *Economic fluctuations in England, 1700–1800* (Oxford, 1959), pp. 146–7.

[62] For example: 'that the Woollen Manufactory for Exportation out of Great Britain, is in a declining State, and owing principally to the Running of Wool from Great Britain, and Wool and Woollen Goods from Ireland'. Anon., *Some general observations on the petitions now before the honourable House of Commons, praying a remedy against the running of wool* [1741?], p. 1. The ESTC suggests a publication date of 1740, but it is more likely that the pamphlet related to the petitions submitted at the start of 1741 discussed later.

[63] Hoppit, *Failed legislation*, 78.002, 78.027, 79.020, 80.007. It is telling that among the publications was Anon., *Abstract of several Acts of Parliament, now in force, to prevent the exportation of wool, sheep, & c.* [1740?].

wool – that is some version of the Kent and Sussex registry extended not only around the coast of Britain, but also inland.[64] Following the petition campaign of 1741 and an address from the Commons to the king, the Board was instructed by Walpole's ministry to develop such an idea. Remarkably, it did so by asking for ideas via newspaper adverts in May 1741, soon setting aside each Wednesday to receive them.[65] This repeated efforts in 1720 and 1731, but on this occasion several dozen 'schemes' and 'proposals' flowed in, sometimes followed up by refinements and further explanations, including in person.[66] In January 1742 the Board drew up its plan, submitting it to the House of Commons, copying it to leading ministers and the speaker of the Commons.[67] Plainly it thought that its proposal should be turned into an act as a governmental measure.

What the Board proposed was nothing less than the registering of all British wool produced at both shearing and slaughter in Britain, then licensing its subsequent movement, inland and coastwise.[68] A new administrative department was to be created, comprising in England a central office of twenty-five (including eight commissioners and ten clerks), overlooking and synthesizing the returns collected by sixteen supervisors (each with two assistants), 157 riding officers, and 100 other officers 'to be constantly stationed in the principal ports and manufacturing Towns'. All 330 of these were salaried posts, though to extend the system to Scotland and Ireland (as was thought possible) would obviously increase the cost further, probably significantly so. Wool shearers and fell mongers were to be required to swear to officers what wool they had, obtaining a licence for its onward sale. Only wool with a licence could be sold, and wool dealers had to keep accurate accounts of their dealings, their books being sent to the officers for checking. Finally, the coastwise movement of wool was to be limited to vessels specifically registered for the trade, which had to be home built 'and navigated by the King's natural subjects only'. Various fines, penalties, and forfeitures

---

[64] *Journal of the Commissioners for Trade and Plantations*, vol. 7 from January 1734–5 to December 1741 (1930), p. 358. For note of the earlier schemes, pp. 3, 66, 248, 253, 270–1, 279.

[65] Ibid., pp. 381–2.

[66] *London Gazette*, no. 5883, 3–6 September 1720; no. 6995, 12–15 June 1731. What the Board received in 1741 is listed in *Journal of the Commissioners for Trade and Plantations*, vol. 7, pp. 393–414.

[67] *Journal of the Commissioners for Trade and Plantations*, vol. 8 from January 1741–2 to December 1749 (1931), pp. 1, 4–5, 7–8, 16, 22.

[68] 'Report from the commissioners for trade and plantations, in pursuance of the address of the honourable House of Commons to his majesty on the fifth of March last', Lambert, *Sessional papers*, vol. 19, pp. 1–11.

were specified for those guilty of non-compliance with any stage of this intricate web of regulation.

The Board produced exactly what had been requested, no more, no less. But it was an idealized solution, setting out just what it would take to register and track wool. They do not appear to have been asked to provide costings or funding. What they came up with appears to have been modelled on the excise administration, as had an earlier scheme in Walpole's papers where 380 riding officers were expected to cost £32,500 annually, rather more than the Commissioners of Wool had cost at the start of the century.[69] That was not a huge amount, but it would have been an unwelcome additional charge to contemplate in the middle of an expensive war being waged both in Europe and across the Atlantic. No less important, public sentiment stood firmly against the permanent expansion of the powers of central government at home, as Walpole had discovered to his cost in 1733 when he had sought to expand the excise so as to reap greater efficiencies in revenue collection. Arthur Young later put down the rejection of the proposed general register to the fact that 'it resembled an excise.'[70] (By contrast, central government was able to institute measures to contain the cattle plague at various times in the eighteenth century, including compulsory destruction of infected cattle, in part, perhaps, because of the temporary nature of such measures.[71]) Perhaps to some the resemblance with the excise meant that such a register was preparatory to levying a tax on wool, just as one was already levied on hides. This may well explain the fact that, although the report coincided with another petitioning campaign complaining about the export of wool, all the Commons did with the report was to order that it be printed and, nearly four months later, address the king asking him to enforce the current laws.[72]

No bill for a general register of wool was introduced into Parliament following the report of the Board of Trade in 1742. Petitions and pamphlets continued to keep the matter alive, but no obvious action followed. But there were two important developments. First, the Treasury took a more active role in the question of the ban from around 1742, soon receiving reports on the coastwise trade in England, shipments of wool to the Channel Islands

---

[69] CUL, Walpole papers, Ch(H) 41/1/41. In 1713 a universal registry administered by 1,136 officers was proposed, and costed at £59,000. Richard Carter and Peter Ellers, *A scheme for preventing the exportation of wool* (1713), p. 1.

[70] [Arthur Young], *The question of wool truly stated* (1788), p. 22. Paul Langford, *The excise crisis: society and politics in the age of Walpole* (Oxford, 1975).

[71] John Broad, 'Cattle plague in eighteenth-century England', *Agricultural History Review*, 31.2 (1983), pp. 104–15.

[72] *JHC*, 24 (1741–5), p. 272 (4 June 1742).

(suspected of being a centre for evading the ban), and Irish shipments to England.[73] (Similar or related reports can be found in the department's files periodically for the rest of the century.) This may have been part of a wider examination of the efficiency of the customs service, but it may also indicate that the Treasury was concerned with the costs of administering the wool export ban, whether in its current or some later expanded form. Consequently, though no bill for a registry was heard in Parliament, an act was passed in 1746 reintroducing the death penalty for organized gangs of wool smugglers and in 1753 the requirement that the trade in Irish wool be limited to certain ports was lifted.[74]

A second development that followed on not long after the failure to legislate in 1742 was the slow growth of a body of opinion increasingly hostile to the ban. Decker made a few reflections on this score in 1744, but it began in earnest with John Smith's important compendium of material about the industry, *Memoirs of wool*, published in two volumes in 1747.[75] One consequence of this major survey was to set out clearly just how much had been written on the subject of the ban over many decades, often concerning recurrent problems with it. But Smith did not merely extract and synthesize from the huge numbers of writings, he subjected them to some critical analysis. He mocked, for example, the crude calculations that some authors made to justify views that the export of wool robbed millions of employment, quoting approvingly from a 1744 pamphlet that if 'we could enrich the Nation by a Dexterity in Computation, it would be a pretty easy Way of doing it'.[76] Reviewing copious evidence about wool prices and exports of woollen manufactures, he concluded that the landed interest and its dependents were suffering under a 'Yoke of Monopolish Abuse and Oppression'.[77]

Challenges, Confrontations, and Consolidation, 1774–1788

Smith was an invaluable source for discussion of the ban for the rest of the century, but his criticisms of it had no immediate effect – perhaps because they were somewhat buried within a richly detailed two-volume work. In fact, it was to be a generation before the ban came under sustained

---

[73] TNA: T64/278, 281; T1/332/41–2; T64/282/1–2.
[74] 19 George II, c. 34; 26 George II, c. 11.
[75] [Matthew Decker], *An essay on the causes of the decline of foreign trade* (1744), p. 31.
[76] *Memoirs of wool*, vol. 2, p. 389.
[77] Ibid., vol. 2, p. 472. Unsurprisingly, Smith became a darling of the classical economists: J. R. McCulloch, *The literature of political economy: a classified catalogue* (1845), pp. 237–8.

criticism. Tellingly, these initially came from Scotland, where the ban had never been of much importance. In 1774 Lord Kames, a leading lawyer with considerable experience in trying to stimulate Scotland's economy by centralized efforts, thought that the ban was not holding back France's textile industries, that it gave landowners too few incentives to improve sheep rearing, and that it was unenforceable because so profitable to avoid.[78] If Kames' language was moderate, Adam Smith's was not. He thought that no manufacturing interest group had been as influential with the legislature, obtaining not one, but two monopolies: the first against consumers by a ban on the import of woollen textiles; the second against sheep farmers through the wool export ban. Moreover, if the revenue laws were notoriously rigorous and invasive, those relating to wool 'Like the laws of Draco ... may be said to be all written in blood'.[79] The language of monopoly that Smith used was adroit, resurrecting as it did a key complaint about forms of economic regulation that had caused so many battles in the seventeenth century. But Smith also emphasized the practical effect of the export ban in depressing prices for wool in Britain. Those in Scotland had allegedly fallen by 50 per cent after the Union, and he cited John Smith, 'the very accurate and intelligent author', on the higher prices for wool at Amsterdam. Like Kames, he emphasized that this reduced incentives to produce wool within Britain. His proposed solution, however, was not for free trade, but that wool exports be allowed subject to heavy duties.[80]

It is usual to argue that *The wealth of nations* had only a slight impact on politicians and practical political economy before the end of the Napoleonic Wars in 1815.[81] Yet some of the language of his attack on the wool export ban, his emphasis on the price distortions, and his proposed remedy were soon taken up, creating a firestorm of controversy.[82] The spark came from Lincolnshire, where in October 1781 a meeting

[78] Henry Home, Lord Kames, *Sketches of the history of man*, ed. James A. Harris (3 vols., Indianapolis, IN, 2007), vol. 2, pp. 464–6.

[79] Smith, *Wealth of nations*, vol. 2, p. 648. These words were not in the original 1776 edition, but added in 1784.

[80] Ibid., vol. 2, pp. 652–3. Another Scottish critic of the ban was James Anderson, *Observations on the means of exciting a spirit of national industry; chiefly intended to promote the agriculture, commerce, manufactures and fisheries of Scotland* (1777), pp. 268–71.

[81] Richard F. Teichgraeber, '"Less abused than I had reason to expect": the reception of *The wealth of nations* in Britain, 1776–1790', *Historical Journal*, 30.2 (1987), pp. 337–64; Kirk Willis, 'The role in Parliament of the economic ideas of Adam Smith, 1776–1800', *History of Political Economy*, 11.4 (1979), pp. 505–44; Salim Rashid, 'Adam Smith's rise to fame: a re-examination of the evidence', *The Eighteenth Century: Theory and Interpretation*, 23.1 (1982), pp. 64–85.

[82] Well discussed in H. B. Carter, *His Majesty's flock: Sir Joseph Banks and the merinos of George III of England* (Sydney, 1964), ch. 2; Richard Wilson, 'Newspapers and

of the county was called to consider the 'low state of our wool trade'. (A key market for Lincolnshire's wool were manufacturers in the West Riding, where production had fallen back sharply between 1778 and 1781 after the American War hit exports hard.[83]) At the meeting, the depression of wool prices was agreed to be so acute that the temporary lifting of the ban should be sought.[84] Crucially, the key figures sought the aid of a fellow landowner from the county, Sir Joseph Banks, President of the Royal Society. He quickly threw his huge energy, expertise, connections, and money behind the venture, including circulating copies of a recent pamphlet calling for the end of the export ban written by Sir John Dalrymple, a Scot who well knew Kames and Smith.[85] Banks also sought out detailed information, including in January 1782 sending a researcher on a 2,000-mile tour to collect information about the demand for and prices of English wool in the Low Countries and northern Germany.[86] A thick web of correspondence quickly linked Dalrymple, Banks, and the Lincolnshire landowners.[87] Dalrymple suggested that Scotland was foursquare behind some easing of the ban, and that he had found widespread opposition to the ban on a round trip to London. Opinion in other 'wool counties' was also sought out. More meetings were held, including in London, of the Lincolnshire landowners, and Banks himself wrote a long pamphlet, including much statistical matter. He sought to establish quantitatively the damage the ban caused and whether smuggling was as rife as was commonly asserted.[88] Implicitly following John and Adam Smith, Banks placed immediately after the title page of his pamphlet an extract from a speech from Coke, the great lawyer, in 1621: 'freedom of

industry: the export of wool controversy in the 1780s', in Michael Harris and Alan Lees, eds., *The press in English society from the seventeenth to nineteenth centuries* (Cranbury, NJ, London, and Ontario, 1986), pp. 80–104.

[83] The volume of broad and narrow cloth milled in the West Riding fell by 27 per cent between 1778 and 1781: Mitchell, *British historical statistics*, p. 351. Exports of woollen goods from England fell 39 per cent between 1775 and 1780: Schumpeter, *English trade statistics*, pp. 39–40.

[84] Harold B. Carter, ed., *The sheep and wool correspondence of Sir Joseph Banks, 1781–1820* (New South Wales and London, 1979), p. 43. The case was soon fully outlined in print in Anon., *Considerations upon the present state of the wool trade, the laws made concerning that article, and how far the same are consistent with true policy, and the real interest of the state* (1781). The ESTC suggests the author was Henry Butler Pacey, FRS, and Recorder of Boston. This is doubted by a well-informed source in Carter, ed., *The sheep and wool correspondence of Banks*, p. 47.

[85] John Dalrymple, *The question considered, whether wool should be allowed to be exported, when the price is low at home, on paying a duty to the public?* (1781).

[86] Carter, ed., *The sheep and wool correspondence of Banks*, p. 69.

[87] Ibid., pp. 44–77.

[88] [Joseph Banks], *The propriety of allowing a qualified exportation of wool discussed historically* (1782).

trade is the life of trade and all monopolies and restrictions of trade do overthrow trade'. The language of monopoly and the language of interest went hand in hand. These were arguments that won over Sir William Musgrave, a notably active and effective customs commissioner, who in writing later in 1782 to the prime minister, Shelburne, proposed that that ban be lifted because it was depressing prices and was little more than a tax on landowners paid out to manufacturers.[89]

This was a huge effort, made in real earnest, but it came to nothing legislatively; not even a bill was presented to Parliament. Mainly this was because it quickly faced well-organized, well-financed, and widespread opposition from manufacturers of woollen goods. Having seen its advertisement, three members of the 'Worsted Committee' for Cheshire, Lancashire, and Yorkshire, founded in 1777 to inspect textile production in the region, attended the initial meeting of the Lincolnshire landowners. Clear in what that meeting intended, the committee 'Resolved to oppose the scheme of the Lincolnshire woolgrowers in every step', spending freely to do so from public monies collected for other ends.[90] Other groups of manufacturers were almost as quick off the mark, notably at Leeds, where in December a 'general meeting of merchants in woollens and of the woollen manufacturers of Yorkshire' resolved to oppose any law allowing the export of wool, that the 'Landed Interest ... would be materially prejudiced' by such a law, and that correspondence should be opened with merchants and manufacturers across the country.[91] Similar meetings at ten other towns were held in the next three months, from Halifax in the north to Potton in Bedfordshire in the south, and from Exeter in the west to Norwich in the east.[92]

In keeping with wider developments in associational politics from the late 1770s, the decisive encounters between the Lincolnshire landowners and the woollen merchants and manufacturers took place not in Parliament, but at three meetings in London taverns, culminating in

---

[89] Clements Library, Shelburne papers, 114, f. 16.

[90] West Yorkshire Archives Service, Bradford, Worsted Committee minute book, 56D88/1/1, 31 December 1781, 25 March 1782, 17 June 1782. More than £80 was spent by the committee opposing the Lincolnshire landowners' efforts. The committee had been established in 1777 by statute (17 George III, c. 11) to enforce production standards through a paid inspectorship, funded from a drawback on the soap excise. The place of its meetings moved around the three counties, but its main home was in the West Riding, Halifax particularly. See Herbert Heaton, *The Yorkshire woollen and worsted industries from the earliest times up to the industrial revolution* (2nd edn., Oxford, 1965), ch. 12.

[91] BL, Liverpool papers, Add Mss 38,217, f. 236.

[92] Most of the meetings are listed in [Edmund Turnor], *A short view of the proceedings of the several committees and meetings held in consequence of the intended petition to Parliament, from the county of Lincoln, for a limited exportation of wool* (1782).

one at the Thatched House on 2 February 1782.[93] About 200 attended, including fifty MPs, making 'many able Speaches'.[94] But, as Banks reported, 'Lincolnshire stood alone' and in small numbers. Nor were they well prepared, being mere 'Bablers' under questioning about possible causes of the decline of wool prices. (Increasing supply and diminishing quality were posited as alternative explanations of the fall in wool prices.[95]) 'The Manufacturers on the other hand attended in a well arrang'd body of members of the house of Commons headed by several good Business men who well [k]new how to arrange the Ideas of the whole proceeding.'[96]

Outmanoeuvred and out-argued, the Lincolnshire contingent stormed out of the Thatched House meeting. If for a time there was relative quiet, the troubles of the landowners were far from over. In September 1784 the manufacturers began to agitate again for the better enforcement of the ban on the export of wool. This does not appear to have been prompted by a general collapse of export markets – production in Yorkshire was reasonably buoyant – nor were wool prices rising to new heights.[97] In fact, concern came from six counties in west and south-west England (though support was obtained from Yorkshire), directed through a general meeting at Bath that passed ten resolutions about the export of wool and sheep leading to high prices.[98] At first, progress was slow and halting, but a flurry of meetings in 1786 produced two compendiums of laws on the export ban. A Commons committee very quickly investigated the illicit export of wool, sheep, worsted, and yarn in June 1786, followed in short order by a proposed bill that faltered very quickly in the Commons.[99] That proposal may not have been very meaningful, perhaps

[93] E. C. Black, *The association: British extra-parliamentary organisation, 1769–1793* (Cambridge, MA, 1963).
[94] *The Oakes diaries: business, politics and the family in Bury St Edmunds, 1778–1827*, ed. Jane Fiske, Suffolk Records Society, 32 (2 vols., Woodbridge, 1990), vol. 1, p. 224.
[95] Using figures of Gregory King and Arthur Young, Banks himself showed that England's sheep population had increased from 12 million in the late seventeenth century to 26 million in 1774. [Banks], *The propriety*, pp. 76–7. Moreover, his evidence (pp. 84–5) of falling prices of raw wool was ambiguous. Some modern figures support his case more clearly, the price of Lincolnshire wool falling 58 per cent from 1774 to 1782. A. H. John, 'Statistical appendix' in G. E. Mingay, ed., *The agrarian history of England and Wales, vol. VI, 1750–1850* (Cambridge, 1989), p. 990.
[96] Carter, ed., *The sheep and wool correspondence of Banks*, p. 62.
[97] Schumpeter, *English trade statistics*, p. 39; Mitchell, *British historical statistics*, p. 351; John, 'Statistical appendix', p. 990.
[98] *Gloucester Journal*, 13 December 1784, p. 2; West Yorkshire Archives Service, Bradford, Worsted Committee minute book, 56D88/1/1, 27 September 1784.
[99] William Nicholson, *An abstract of such Acts of Parliament as are now in force for preventing the exportation of wool* (1786). Nicholson was secretary of the short-lived General Chamber of Manufacturers of Great Britain. The second compendium was William

being designed to flush out opposition. A new bill followed in late 1787, passing into law in the following year.[100] It sought to improve the ban by clarifying how it was to be enforced and what the penalties were, in part by repealing all prior legislation on the matter. Consolidation and codification, it was hoped, would underscore the ban's legitimacy and aid its enforceability.

As in 1781–2, a major debate erupted over the proposed new act, mainly outside Parliament but, in its later stages, inside as well. As in 1781–2 the main points contended were about who gained and who lost from the ban, the quality of the evidence underlying positions on those points, and whether smuggling wool was a major problem. But in 1787–8 the debate was wider, better funded, and more polemical. The involvement of Arthur Young, the great propagandist for agricultural improvement, was a key reason for that. He was notably active organizing opposition in Suffolk, struck up a strong working relationship with Banks (both gave evidence to Parliament), published pamphlets on the question, and gave over a good deal of his *Annals of Agriculture* to the matter.[101] Young's approach was to mix evidence with exhortation, reason with ridicule, and persuasion with polemic. The bill that led to the 1788 act was 'impudent', based on 'ignorance and falsehood', and a 'hodgepodge of tyranny and oppression'.[102] Like Banks and most other opponents of the bill, he called the manufacturers monopolists whose claims damaged both the landed and the national interest. Little wonder that in 1788 an effigy of him was burned at Norwich, a struggling centre of woollen manufacturing.[103]

Others followed Young's lead. A year after the first major effort had been made to end the slave trade, Thomas Day mocked the '*sacred rage of the monopolizers*' as being animated by the same 'merciful spirit' that moved Liverpool's slave traders. A century after the Glorious Revolution,

---

Holmes, *A digest of the Acts of Parliament (now in force) for preventing the exportation of sheep, wool, & c.* (Exeter, 1786). This is not in the ESTC, but may be found in the Sutro, Banks papers. 'Report from the committee appointed to consider of the illicit exportation of wool, live sheep, worsted, and yarn', *JHC*, 41 (1786), pp. 891–4 (12 June 1786). Hoppit, *Failed legislation*, 128.059.

[100] 28 George III, c. 38.
[101] *The autobiography of Arthur Young*, ed. M. Betham-Edwards (1898), pp. 165–74; *The question of wool*; [Arthur Young], *A speech on the wool bill, that might have been spoken in the House of Commons, Thursday, May the 1st, 1788* (1788). John G. Gazley, *The life of Arthur Young, 1741–1820* (Philadelphia, PA, 1973), pp. 198–9, 215–17.
[102] *Annals of Agriculture*, 6 (1786), pp. 508, 520.
[103] *The autobiography of Arthur Young*, p. 172. On hearing this news, Banks wrote to Young, p. 174, 'I give you joy sincerely at having arrived at the glory of being burned in effigy; nothing is so conclusive a proof of your possessing the best of the argument. No one was ever burned if he was wrong'.

he noted that claims for 'liberty and property' and a 'free constitution' sat ill with burdensome regulations that 'would shake the foundations of half the despotic governments of the world'.[104] But there were more moderate voices against the bill as well, Banks most obviously, but also Thomas Pownall, one-time governor of Massachusetts, and an early commentator in print on Smith's *Wealth of nations*.[105] Pownall placed the wool export ban within the wider context of economic and social evolution, especially the tendency for two 'general classes' to emerge 'As the community civilizes, and the arts of life refine'. Those classes were liable to bitter rivalry, 'envy, jealousy, and avarice' blinding them to their mutual dependence. That said, he was certain that the ban ought to be lifted, that now was the time for 'a new system of commercial policy' based not on general maxims, vague habits, or grafts onto authority, but on well-considered principles.[106]

Naturally, the manufacturers could not ignore these attacks on their position. John Anstie was an especially important figure, being behind the efforts, making links between the West Country and the West Riding, and publishing defences of the ban and the bill. He directly challenged the information and ideas of Banks, Young, and Pownall, doing so clearly and calmly, if not always convincingly.[107] Others contested the charge that the export ban constituted a monopoly and that the landed and manufacturing interests were in conflict. The ban was said to be a 'modern policy' that ensured the employment of millions, and in the previous century had raised the productivity of the land four fold and its rents three fold.[108] As in 1781–2, such words were backed up by well-drilled organization. The manufacturers met together, got committed and active support from a group of MPs, and took aside the prime minister, Pitt the younger, to ensure that he and his government would not be obstructive.[109] When the crunch came in the Commons, despite strong

---

[104] Thomas Day, *A letter to Arthur Young, esq. on a bill now depending in Parliament to prevent the exportation of wool* (1788), pp. 10, 19, 29.

[105] *A letter from Governor Pownall to Adam Smith* (1776).

[106] [Thomas Pownall], *Live and let live; a treatise on the hostile rivalships between the manufacturer and land-worker* [1787], pp. 14–15.

[107] John Anstie, *A general view of the bill presented to Parliament during the last session, for preventing the illicit exportation of British wool and live sheep* (1787); John Anstie, *A letter addressed to Edward Phelips, esq. member for the county of Somerset, containing general observations on the advantages of manufacturing the combing wool of England, which is smuggled to France* (1788).

[108] Anon., *An epitome of the bill now depending in Parliament, the better to prevent the exportations of live, sheep, wool, &c.* (1788), p. 3.

[109] Anon., *A narrative of the proceedings and resolutions of a general meeting of the delegates from the manufacturers of wool, held at the Crown and Anchor tavern, in the Strand, the 28th of November, 1787* (1787).

opposition to the bill, Pitt spoke in favour of its detailed consideration. Silent on the question of the principle of free trade, his substantive points were that laws should be enforced (which was the aim of the bill) and that the smuggling of wool was bound up with the smuggling of brandy, 'to the additional prejudice of the revenue'.[110]

Landowners were not passive in the face of the efforts of manufacturers. Agricultural societies joined chambers of commerce in the constellation of institutions representing sectional interests. A particularly important element of this were efforts to improve agriculture in general and sheep husbandry in particular. Sir John Sinclair was a leading figure here, particularly stimulated by a patrician concern with the sustainability of the Highland economy – of significant emigration in the 1770s, terrible harvests in the 1780s, and the early examples of 'clearances'. One expression of this was the foundation of the Highland Society in Edinburgh in 1784, but the institution of the Society for the Improvement of British Wool in 1791 had more British ambitions, with Banks among its founding directors.[111] Here Sinclair revived arguments about the unique permanence of land that had been aired in the 1690s and 1700s when a 'monied interest' seemed threatening to landowners: 'Our acres, when once improved, cannot be run away with; whereas the arts of manufacture ... may be filched from us by our neighbours. Our ships ... may be captured by the enemy in war, and even in peace are exposed to a thousand accidents.'[112] Such arguments lay behind his successful advocacy in 1793 for the establishment of a Board of Agriculture.[113] If practical improvements were central to such bodies, they also saw the importance of trying to harness political power, in doing so deepening the divide between landowners on the one hand and merchants and manufacturers on the other, prefiguring the post-1815 furore over the protectionist corn laws that often found expression in class terms.[114] The debate over the export of wool in the 1780s was with hindsight a notable contribution to the development of class politics in Britain.

---

[110] Cobbett, *Parl. Hist.*, 27 (1788–9), cols. 387–8.

[111] Sir John Sinclair, *Address to the Society for the Improvement of British Wool, constituted at Edinburgh, on Monday, January 31, 1791* (1791), appendix; John Sinclair, *Memoirs of the life and works of the late right honourable Sir John Sinclair* (2 vols. Edinburgh, 1837), vol. 1, p. 220.

[112] Sir John Sinclair, *Address to the landed interest, on the corn bill now depending in Parliament* (1791), pp. 9–10.

[113] Sir John Sinclair, *Plan for establishing a Board of Agriculture and internal improvement* (1793), p. 1; Rosalind Mitchison, 'The old Board of Agriculture (1793–1822)', *English Historical Review*, 74.290 (1959), pp. 41–69.

[114] Asa Briggs, 'Middle-class consciousness in English politics, 1780–1846', *Past and Present*, 9 (1956), pp. 65–74; Dror Wahrman, *Imagining the middle class: the political representation of class in Britain, c. 1780–1840* (Cambridge, 1995).

The End of the Ban

In 1788 woollen manufacturers had achieved a comprehensive victory. The ban was now clearer than ever, and the hope was that its enforcement would be easier. It was a hope that was never really tested because the outbreak of war with France in 1793, continued with little respite until 1815, changed priorities dramatically. Thus when the House of Commons investigated the state of the woollen industries in 1806 it simply acknowledged the existence of the ban. Its main interest was in the laws surrounding employment, quality, and the sale of cloth.[115]

The lifting of the ban in 1824 came within a decade of peace. Three broad factors were crucial. First, enthusiasm over the previous half century or so for selective breeding of sheep in England (and to a lesser extent Scotland), linked with the enclosure movement, managed to produce animals with more meat, but lower-quality wool. Mann's conclusion was that 'nearly all English wool grew somewhat coarser between 1600 and 1800.'[116] It might be expected that lower-quality wool would be less attractive in international markets and that pressures for its illicit export were declining. This was related, secondly, to the significant growth in imports of foreign wool, especially from Germany and Spain, to feed the needs of a domestic industry that was gradually adopting the factory system – the weight of raw wool imports into England and Wales rose nearly thirteen fold from 1773–5 to 1822–4.[117] The heightened efficiency of British wool manufacturing naturally reduced anxieties about overseas competition and weakened a little its dependence on domestic supplies of raw materials. Whatever incentives there may once have been to export British wool were on the wane. In those circumstances, prices of wool in Britain were on an upward trend until the late 1810s, helping woolgrowers to digest the effects of the ban.[118] As prices began to fall, so the landowners renewed their calls for a repeal of the export ban.[119]

Such evolving factors, thirdly, were joined in 1819 by a wholly new one when, with little consultation, the government raised the duty on imported wool from one to six shillings a pound. It was motivated by financial desperation, of the difficulties of servicing a massive national debt – it tripled between 1793 and 1815 – in the aftermath of the abolition

---

[115] *JHC*, 61 (1806), pp. 696–703 (Appendix 23).
[116] Mann, *Cloth industry*, p. 259.
[117] Mitchell, *British historical statistics*, p. 338; D. T. Jenkins and K. G. Ponting, *The British wool textile industry, 1770–1914* (Aldershot, 1982), ch. 2, esp. pp. 43–8.
[118] Prices are conveniently graphed in Hudson, 'The limits of wool', pp. 335–6.
[119] John Maitland, *Observations on the impolicy of permitting the exportation of British wool, and of preventing the free importation of foreign wool* (1818).

of income tax in 1816.[120] Opposition was quickly raised, in print and petitions, the latter leading the Board of Trade to investigate.[121] With the government having little room for financial manoeuvre, and pressed by the woolgrowers and their landlords, the duty was not changed. It was this which provided the lever by which the ban was finally lifted, for if, as the chancellor of the exchequer, Robinson, stressed in 1824, the import duty was solely a revenue not a protectionist measure, it then became difficult to argue for reducing or removing it on free trade grounds while simultaneously arguing against a free trade in wool exports.[122] As Robinson acknowledged, some manufacturers held to old views,

But a majority, – I may say a decided majority, – of the individuals interested in the woollen trade, were of opinion that it would be advantageous to them to accede to the proposed compromise, namely, that the duty on the importation of foreign wool should be repealed, and the free exportation of British wool permitted.[123]

Free trade in the wool trade was finally achieved. Economic ideas had played a part in this, but if they counted for anything in 1824, it was very much because of altered circumstances, of the sheep themselves, of how their fleeces were now being manufactured, of increasing overseas trade, and of the revenue needs of government. And as Robinson noted, free trade was, in this instance, viewed very much as a compromise. What was critical now was that the manufacturers did not all sing the same tune.

Conclusion

In 1825 William Huskisson, president of the Board of Trade, pondered aloud and at length in the Commons on the effects of centuries of political effort to aid the nation's woollen industries,

which has been most nursed and dandled by the legislature – a favourite child, which like other favourites, has, I suspect, suffered, rather than profited, by being spoilt and petted in rearing; whilst its younger brother of cotton, coming in to the world much later, has thriven better by being much more left to rough it, and make its own way in life. Some detailed and authentic history of the paternal

---

[120] Mitchell, *British historical statistics*, p. 601.

[121] A notable contributor against the new duty was James Bischoff, *Reasons for the immediate repeal of the tax on foreign wool* (3rd edn., 1820); 'Copy of the minutes of examination, taken before the committee of the Privy Council for the affairs of trade, regarding the wool tax', BPP, 56 (1820).

[122] Some landowners certainly welcomed the duty as protectionist: John Baker Holroyd, *Lord Sheffield's report at Lewes wool fair, July 26th, 1819* (1819), p. 2. Sheffield gave such annual reports for a number of years before his death in 1821.

[123] Hansard, *Commons debates*, 23 February 1824, col. 328.

and zealous solicitude with which our ancestors in this House interposed to protect the woollen manufacture (should such a history ever be written), will alone preserve future generations from incredulity, in respect to the extent to which legislative interference was once carried in this branch of internal industry. Within my own time, regulating acts, dealing with every minute process of the manufacture, have been repealed by the score; as have also heaps of other laws, equally salutary and wise, prescribing the mode of clipping wool, its package, the time to be allowed, and the forms to be observed, in removing it from one place to another – laws, the violation of which, in some instances, amounted to felony, but which now no longer disgrace the Statute-book. Fortunately for the cotton manufacture, it was never favoured with this species of protection, so abundantly lavished upon woollen, and which was only withdrawn last year from silk, by the repeal of the Spitalfields acts.[124]

Amongst other things, Huskisson reminds us that this chapter, by isolating the wool export ban from the wider body of laws seeking to improve woollens, rests on a conceit. But we cannot simply follow Huskisson in assuming the superiority of free trade. It may fast have been becoming the new orthodoxy, but it should not be assumed that in the context of the risks faced by producers, merchants, and politicians in the century and a half before the Vienna settlement in 1815 regulation and restriction did not 'pay'.

Judging quantitatively the economic consequences of the wool export ban is, alas, impossible. There are three related insuperable problems: the lack of good data; the impossibility of isolating the effects of the ban from those caused by the myriad of other regulations applied to the woollen industries; and the impracticality of comparing what happened with what might have happened had the ban not been in place. Such exercises in counterfactual history can be thought-provoking, but they are inevitably vague or speculative at key points. All that can be said is that at the time many, but far from all, thought that the ban was a significant aid to an industry threatened by powerful foreign competitors. The ban was part of their way of managing some of those challenges and risks. They may have been misguided in that – we cannot tell – but they were in earnest and their beliefs affected their behaviour.

Qualitatively, more can be said. There is no question that the ban on the export of wool was a major plank of national economic policy. Introduced in the high age of 'mercantilism', it sought to manage a supposedly especially precious natural resource for the national good. For

---

[124] Hansard, *Commons debates*, 25 March 1825, col. 1,199. A similar view had been expressed by Arthur Young when he noted how Birmingham, Manchester, Sheffield, and Etruria (Wedgwood's factory) prospered without prohibitions: 'The gigantic strides of their progress have been taken without treading on the neck of any other class of society.' *Annals of Agriculture*, 7 (1787), p. 165.

many years its potential utility was barely questioned, and even when questions became more forceful in the 1780s they made little political headway. The combined might of the President of the Royal Society, leaders of the Scottish enlightenment, a pre-eminent agricultural pro-pagandist, and sections of the landed interest was rebuffed, comprehen-sively if not easily. Only later was the ban lifted, amidst a general move towards freer trade.

Yet it is clear that periodically many contemporaries were certain that the wool export ban was being flouted, that the letter and practice of mercantilist regulation diverged. By such accounts, foreshores resounded to the calls of large, well-organized gangs of owlers. Certainly, it was one thing to pass new laws to direct economic life, quite another to enforce them. A key point of this chapter has been to show the repeated attempts to hit on the right balance of policing and punishment. If solutions were sometimes thought to work initially, they were always soon judged fail-ures. Critically, no one wanted to pay for a higher level of policing, or see the powers of central government in the localities grow further. It is telling that Walpole's son thought that to stop the smuggling of wool out of Ireland by military might would be prohibitively expensive, both abso-lutely and in relation to the 'national advantages' it might bring.[125] Often enough, many thought that the ban lacked meaningful teeth, while insti-gating the death penalty went too far, making juries and judges reluctant to convict. The wider implications of this are very important. Here was a measure in defence of a prized industry that was widely believed not only to be ignored, but unenforceable. If this was so at home, even in south-east England, how much more difficult was enforcing mercantilist regulations across the Atlantic?

It is clear that for the ban to be effective depended heavily on its being judged legitimate by those involved in the wool trade. Surely many factors fed into such judgements, but an important one involved a simple analy-sis of the costs and benefits of obeying or ignoring the law, set against a guess of the risks of disobedience. After all, when all is said and done, smuggling is, as Pitt and others well knew, a business that will disappear if it cannot be made to pay or the risks are too great. In fact, a recurring problem that the ban faced was that smuggling wool was, or appeared to be, highly profitable. But it was not simply that higher prices prevailed in Europe – most agreed on that – but that ships were not given over wholly to wool smuggling. Ships that had illicitly landed tea or brandy needed a

---

[125] He was responding to a report from the Commissioners of Revenue in Ireland in January 1755 about the extent of smuggling wool from Ireland's west coast. TNA, T1/361/21 and 38.

cargo for the return voyage to exploit the capital resource fully as well as to have the ballast to be seaworthy.[126] The ban on the export of wool was inescapably bound up with quite other areas of national financial policy, as Pitt acknowledged.

The rise in duties on imported goods in the two wars following the Glorious Revolution produced considerable incentives to smuggle tea, brandy, wine, silks, and other goods into Britain, southern England especially, their routes often overlapping with those used by wool smugglers.[127] Because of this, wool smuggling was liable to be linked closely with the economics of smuggling different goods, even perhaps to the extent that cross-subsidies may have helped the black economy along. A fundamental difference, was that smuggling tea, say, could be ended quickly by cutting the duty that was paid – as happened in 1784.[128] Smuggling wool, by contrast, was not liable to any such manipulation. In those circumstances, and given the failure of the Commissioners and cruisers at the start of the eighteenth century, the options to manage wool smuggling were limited.

Whether the export ban was ignored as much as was often claimed is impossible to know. Smuggling was periodically said to be common, usually on the basis of some encounters with revenue officers. But it could not and cannot be known either what proportion of smuggling was observed, or whether smuggling was intermittent or persistent, or small or large scale. Only in the 1780s was there a concerted effort to collect robust evidence on the matter. In 1786, the woollen manufacturers turned to sporadic reports from French ports about the numbers of English smugglers in harbour and to figures of wool that had been seized. Joseph Banks criticized such impressionistic and self-serving evidence, preferring to use official French figures of wool imports to argue that wool smuggling must have been very limited. Back came the manufacturers, asserting that such figures always tended to exaggerate imports.[129]

Political arithmetic could not resolve the debate over the extent of the smuggling of wool. Nothing could. More important was that its utilization

---

[126] As was recognized at the time, for example, by Stephen Theodore Janssen, a London merchant and MP, who developed an unrivalled expertise in the political economy of smuggling. See *JHC*, 25 (1745–50), p. 106 (24 March 1746); [Stephen Theodore Janssen], *Smuggling laid open, in all its extensive and destructive branches* (1763).

[127] Ralph Davis, 'The rise of protection in England, 1689–1786', *Economic History Review*, 19.2 (1966), pp. 306–17. The most thorough study of smuggling is Paul Muskett, 'English smuggling in the eighteenth century' (Open University PhD thesis, 1997).

[128] Hoh-Cheung Mui and Lorna H. Mui, 'William Pitt and the enforcement of the Commutation Act, 1784–1788', *English Historical Review*, 76.300 (1961), pp. 447–65.

[129] 'Report of the illicit exportation of wool'; Anstie, *A letter addressed to Edward Phelips*, pp. 5–12.

was part of a drawing of battle lines in the 1780s between representatives of the landed and manufacturing interests. As the Lincolnshire landowners were made painfully aware in 1782, this was not a battle between equals. Manufacturers were better organized, linking different regional blocs to present a united face nationally. In doing so, they were drawing on more than a century of such efforts, and not just within the woollen industries. The formation of the Worsted Committee for Yorkshire, Lancashire, and Cheshire in 1777 was part of a wider process of putting such efforts on a more permanent footing. Thus the era of the American War saw the institution of chambers of commerce in many towns and cities, in Britain, Ireland, and the Channel Islands.[130] To Shelburne, such developments threw up obstacles to change: 'Professor Adam Smith's principles have remained unanswered for about thirty years, and yet when it is attempted to act upon any of them, what a clamour!'[131]

It was very important that the manufacturers rather than the Lincolnshire landowners and their allies won in 1782 and 1788. It is very striking that a parliament of landowners failed to do what some of their number passionately believed in. But the power of the manufacturers unwittingly encouraged landowners to become more politically astute, agile, and organized. Gradually landowners also turned to associational activity, through local agricultural societies as well as the public-private national Board of Agriculture (1793–1822).[132] Such developments were important foundations on which was built the bitter and prolonged struggle over the corn laws that was so important to the development of class politics in early nineteenth-century Britain.

Finally, it is worth recalling that a long chain of legislation, attempted as well as enacted, related to the wool export ban. Not that this was in any way contemplated in 1660, when what was attempted was seemingly so simple. Yet quickly unforeseen complications set in. If these can all be labelled 'enforcement difficulties', they also included important jurisdictional considerations, especially how best to deal with Ireland's raw wool, yarn, and manufactures, but also the trade in wool to the Channel Islands. In doing so, the ban became entangled in colonialism, imperialism, and the very meanings of England and then Britain as a nation state. Policymakers in London may have hoped that the seas around Britain were a barrier that could be policed to ensure the

[130] Robert J. Bennett, *Local business voice: the history of chambers of commerce in Britain, Ireland, and revolutionary America, 1760–2011* (Oxford, 2011), p. 15.

[131] Lord Fitzmaurice, *Life of William Shelburne afterwards first Marquess of Lansdowne* (2 vols., 2nd edn., 1912), vol. 1, pp. 18–19.

[132] Nicholas Goddard, 'Agricultural literature and societies', in *The agrarian history of England and Wales*, vol. 6, ed. Mingay, pp. 361–83.

effectiveness of mercantilist policies. What they found, however, was that in the right circumstances those seas could be bridged too easily for comfort.[133]

Why, then, did legislators persist with the ban, even in the face of fierce opposition in the 1780s? After all, a similar ban on the export of leather did not last a decade after its statutory reintroduction in 1662.[134] Probably crucial was that an overwhelming majority of political society was behind the wool export ban in its early years, with a very high value put on the manufacture of woollens, especially to the labouring poor. For them, the woollen interest was the national interest. Landowners may have had doubts about it, but enough of them must have believed that it helped boost their rents and keep the poor rates down. Other landowners perhaps saw the bounty on the export of corn, made permanent in 1689, as a reasonable compensation. A further limitation was that many farms lacked sheep, and for those that did not, wool was only a part of their value. Moreover, problems caused by the ban seem to have fluctuated from year to year – perhaps in reality (allied to wider influences on smuggling), perhaps in perception – while as the decades passed and imports of wool mounted, the whole issue shrank in significance. Finally, in the last resort, landowners could significantly hinder the enforcement of the ban by turning a blind eye, but also by refusing in Parliament to countenance greater policing. Indeed, whether by the ban manufacturers gained as much as they hoped, or landowners lost as much as they feared, is very far from clear. J. P. Cooper's conclusion with regard to the seventeenth century can be extended to the eighteenth: the state 'was both too strong and too weak to pursue either centralized regulation or *laissez-faire* in its domestic economic and social policies'.[135]

Adam Smith devoted a large part of the *Wealth of nations* to describing and criticizing the mercantile system. In its modern form, mercantilism is a common way to view 'economic policy' in the period covered by this book. But this chapter has borne out Smith's acknowledgement towards the end of his discussion of systems of political economy that 'the natural effort which every man is continually making to better his own condition, is a principle of preservation capable of preventing and correcting, in many respects, the bad effects of a political œconomy, in some degree,

[133] Renaud Morieux, *The Channel: England, France and the construction of a maritime border in the eighteenth century* (Cambridge, 2016), ch. 7.

[134] 14 Charles II, c. 7; 19 & 20 Charles II, c. 10; Giorgio Riello, 'Nature, production and regulation in eighteenth-century France and England: the case of the leather industry', *Historical Research*, 81.211 (2008), pp. 75–99.

[135] 'Economic regulation and the cloth industry in seventeenth-century England', *Transactions of the Royal Historical Society*, 5th series, 20 (1970), p. 99.

both partial and oppressive.'[136] That is, even Smith acknowledged that the mercantile system was liable to be significantly diluted in practice. Unless that essential point is both grasped and emphasized, then continuing to argue for the potency of mercantilism seriously distorts characterizations of the already anachronistic notion of 'economic policy'.

[136] Smith, *Wealth of nations*, vol. 2, p. 674.

8   The Political Economy of Bounties, 1689–1800

'I was just informed, that the manufacturers of checks in Lancashire, had applied for a bounty upon the exportation of them; the Scotch upon printed linens; and in consequence of that, the manufacturers of cottons at Blackburn, &c. on printed cottons and that the business is now agitating before the house of commons.'

Joseph Wimpey, 1770[1]

Considering the ban on the export of wool has begun to bring key facets of the mercantile system into the light. Like all the earlier chapters, Chapter 7 did so by considering the aims and perceived limitations of the legislation involved. The aim now is to develop further an understanding of general economic legislation by beginning to explore more carefully its implementation. A focal point is provided by considering in this chapter and the next the financial consequences of two types of general economic acts: those establishing bounties and those for raising taxes. Attending to the amounts of money that were involved provides one way of quantifying some key features. After all, how and how much governments raised money and where they spent it offers another perspective on their priorities than the counting and categorization of legislation. Consequently, less consideration is now given to the passage, revision, or repeal of legislation.

Bounties to incentivize certain types of economic behaviour must initially be placed within the wider context of British public expenditure.[2] As Patrick O'Brien noted, 'Patrick Colquhoun's [1814] estimates imply that only 0.5 per cent of total public revenues collected during the long reign of George III was devoted to objectives that might nowadays be

---

[1] Joseph Wimpey, *Thoughts upon several interesting subjects, viz. on the exportation of corn, on the high price of provisions, on manufactures, commerce, &c.* [1770], p. 42.

[2] P. K. O'Brien, 'The political economy of British taxation, 1660–1815', *Economic History Review*, 41.1 (1988), p. 2; John Brewer, *Sinews of power: war, money and the English state, 1688–1783* (1989), pp. 39–40; B. R. Mitchell, *British historical statistics* (Cambridge, 1988), pp. 578–80.

defined as developmental.'³ Such figures buttress the view that economic regulation then depended overwhelmingly on prohibitions, obstructions, and legal requirements. They are similarly compatible with depictions of 'rent seeking', as well as of a 'reactive state', of the power of particular interests, private and corporate, seeking public authority, but rarely direct funding, for example, to reorder estates and form companies.

Although central government spent relatively little directly on stimulating the economy, it did spend some. A few projects received pretty heavy funding – such as the military roads in the Scottish Highlands (£185,000), the Levant Company (£77,000), the 'forts' in West Africa (£631,000), and Westminster Bridge (£223,000). As is well known, in 1714 an Act of Parliament instituted a prize to encourage a way of determining longitude at sea, with John Harrison receiving more than £20,000 for decades of efforts.⁴ More modest rewards were also sometimes handed out to inventors and entrepreneurs. Amongst others, Lombe got £14,000 for his silk machine, Stephens £3,000 for a method of making potash, Irving £5,000 for the distillation of salt water, Williams £3,000 for a green dye, and the Borells £2,500 for a red dye. Because such spending is listed in the standard reference source for British public revenues – a summary report produced in the mid-nineteenth century – it has sometimes caught the eye of historians and is a part of the civil expenditure of the period – which accounted for 9 per cent of all expenditure by central government.⁵ But that source does not unpick the odd accounting conventions employed before the late eighteenth century, meaning that a significant source of governmental spending on the economy via bounties is missing.

Bounties were paid out of tax receipts, overwhelmingly customs, not excise, and deducted with management and other charges from gross receipts. Because they were not formerly budgeted for, they have not been systematically studied by historians of mercantilism.⁶ Yet this is surprising as Adam Smith spent a substantive chapter within his discussion of the 'mercantile system' analyzing them. Historians studying

---

³ P. K. O'Brien, 'Political preconditions for the industrial revolution', in P. K. O'Brien and R. Quinault, eds., *The industrial revolution and British society* (Cambridge, 1993), p. 228.

⁴ 13 Anne, c. 14; 5 George III, c. 11. Humphrey Quill, *John Harrison: the man who found longitude* (1966), chs. 1 and 21.

⁵ BPP, 35, (1868–9).

⁶ For convenience, these are simply termed 'bounties' hereafter, though contemporaries sometimes called them 'allowances' or 'premiums'. Moreover, 'bounties' were also offered to attract soldiers and sailors into the armed forces, or to help them at demobilization, and were also paid as pensions or gifts, usually to public servants and their dependents, including the clergy (via both Queen Anne's bounty and other funds). These are not considered here.

particular instances have, though, made clear that a lot of money might be involved: more than £6 million was paid out in corn export bounties before 1764; £1.5 million on imported naval stores between 1705 and 1775; £2 million on whaling between 1733 and 1800; and £0.8 million on fisheries between 1771 and 1796.[7]

This chapter seeks to explore the scale, direction, and purpose of bounties more fully. It begins by looking at what bounties were intended to do, the commodities liable to bounties, and who was responsible for the acts that brought them into being. It then seeks to quantify patterns of spending, over time, place, and sector. A case study of a bounty on growing hemp and flax is then provided. Finally, the conclusion considers the utility of bounties to Britain's political economies, but also their limitations because of fraud and the pressures for them to be time limited.

The Objectives and Origins of Bounties

In the language of the time, bounties were a means to 'encourage' certain economic activities. But while no plan was followed in their creation, they were linked by some structural factors regarding control over public revenues by central government.

Bounties were usually paid on the quantity, not the value of the goods produced or shipped, most commonly on exported goods, which in turn were mainly funded from particular customs duties; only rarely were other revenue streams exploited.[8] Another type of payment made at ports, 'drawbacks', the repayment, in whole or in part, of a duty already paid, involved much larger sums, though their cost implications to the state were largely neutral.[9] The immediate task is to describe what bounties

---

[7] A. H. John, 'English agricultural improvement and grain exports, 1660–1765', in D. C. Coleman and A. H. John, eds., *Trade, government and economy in pre-industrial England: essays presented to F. J. Fisher* (1976), p. 59; Joseph J. Malone, *Pine trees and politics: the naval stores and forest policy in colonial New England, 1691–1775* (1964), p. 45; Gordon Jackson, *The British whaling trade* (1978), p. 264; Anna Gambles, 'Free trade and state formation: the political economy of fisheries policy in Britain and the United Kingdom circa 1780–1850', *Journal of British Studies*, 39.3 (2000), p. 314. Smith devoted ch. 5 of book 4 of the *Wealth of nations* to a discussion of bounties.

[8] In 1799 92 per cent of bounties paid in England and Wales were paid from customs receipts. 'Accounts presented to the House of Commons, respecting the public expenditure of Great Britain, for the year ending fifth of January 1800' (1800), Appendix E.1, p. 16 in Lambert, *Sessional papers*, vol. 129, p. 264.

[9] The English customs system paid out an annual average of £1.9 million on drawbacks and bounties between 1756 and 1766, 88 per cent on the former. TNA, T1/462/43–4. Drawbacks aimed to encourage re-exports, which were 31 per cent of all exports in 1699–1701, 35 per cent in 1772–4, and 18 per cent in 1804–6: Ralph Davis, 'English foreign trade, 1700–1774', *Economic History Review*, 15.2 (1962), p. 302; Ralph Davis, *The industrial revolution and British overseas trade* (Leicester, 1979), p. 33. They were

Table 8.1 *Commodities able to claim bounties (excluding re-exports), 1770*

Export bounties	Import bounties
Cordage	Hemp and flax*
Corn	Indigo*
Fish and flesh	Naval stores*
Fisheries and whaling	Portage
Gunpowder	Raw silk*
Linens	Tobacco, damaged
Sail cloth	Wine, damaged
Silk, manufactured	Wood
Sugar, refined	

Note: bounties limited to plantation goods are marked *.
Source: Samuel Baldwin, *A survey of the British customs* (1770), part 2, pp. 19–20, 19*.

were available, when they were introduced, how much they were worth, and where the money was claimed.

As we saw in Chapter 3, external trade regulations were extremely complicated in Britain in this period, making it difficult to identify all bounties. One informed overview of the customs 'system' noted in 1757 that bounties and drawbacks were not 'so immediately obvious to the officers of customs', not least because 'they are now become very numerous, and in regard to bounties and premiums a very extensive and formidable branch of the business of the customs'.[10] Such guides to duties provide, in fact, useful snapshots of bounties at particular moments, with a particularly clear summary being provided in 1770 (see Table 8.1).

Today, bounties or subsidies are thought of mainly as aids to infant industries, needed to help them only in their early years. Some certainly argued along such lines at the time, but bounties were rarely merely economic in aim, often also serving military and political purposes.[11] It was believed that improving hemp and flax supplies would simultaneously aid Britain's economic and military might, a point that was shared with a number of other bounties, such as naval stores, while fisheries and whaling aimed to ensure adequate supplies of sailors and shipwrights. The

particularly valuable to the growth of Glasgow: Philipp Robinson Rössner, *Scottish trade in the wake of the Union (1700–1760): the rise of a warehouse economy* (Stuttgart, 2008).
[10] H. Saxby, *The British customs* (1757), p. xiv; on the title page Saxby was accredited to 'the customhouse, London'.
[11] Wimpey, *Thoughts upon several interesting subjects*, pp. 42–3.

context here was the frequency of wars within the European states system. Indeed, in the 1770s Lord Kames argued in favour of corn bounties on strategic grounds, not least in reducing French agriculture to a 'languishing state', improbable though that seems. 'This bounty, therefore, is our palladium, which we ought religiously to guard, if we would avoid being a province of France.'[12] Nor were political objectives insignificant. Bounties were a means by which central government sought to improve links between Britain and its empire, including Ireland, as well as ties between central government and specific interests. The corn law of 1673 was in part justified in terms of making a new tax palatable to landowners, on whom it 'principally lyeth', and though it is unclear why it was revived in 1689, it seems likely that the new and vulnerable regime was looking to buy support from vital English interests, landed and commercial.[13]

If military and political considerations were important to creating bounties, economic reasons were especially powerful. Often they were aimed at new or vulnerable areas of the economy, effectively aiming to lower entry costs or risks.[14] Some also sought to develop a division of labour between the economies of Britain and her colonies as 'primarily militaristic conceptions of empire gradually gave way to commercial ones'.[15] Often this was associated with a desire to increase self-sufficiency by reducing dependence on European sources of supply, especially those that were vulnerable to the closure of the Baltic Sound in wartime. This might be framed in terms of import substitution and balance of trade. Some bounties were aimed more clearly at the internal economy, especially those relating to cordage, linens, silk, hemp, and flax. Job creation and the hope of increased exports were powerful motives here.[16] Additionally, price stabilization appears to have been one factor behind the corn law of 1689, the preamble asserting that exporting corn when the domestic price was low 'hath been a great Advantage, not only to the Owners of Land, but to the Trade of this Kingdom in general'.[17] The variability of harvests because of the weather was a risk not only to farmers and landlords, but also to corn merchants to whom, Josiah Tucker

---

[12] Henry Homes, Lord Kames, *Sketches of the history of man*, ed. James A. Harris (3 vols., Indianapolis, IN, 2006), vol. 2, p. 462.
[13] 25 Charles II, c. 1, § 31.
[14] Jacob Viner considered the 'infant industry problem' as part of one of the few overviews of bounties in eighteenth-century Britain: *Studies in the theory of international trade* (New York, 1937), pp. 69–72.
[15] Nancy F. Koehn, *The power of commerce: economy and governance in the first British empire* (Ithaca, NY, 1994), p. 65.
[16] See, for example, the arguments in 'Observations of London merchants on American trade, 1783', *American Historical Review*, 18.4 (1913), p. 779.
[17] 1 William & Mary, c. 12, § 1.

asserted, it 'is a kind of Lottery, in wch there are a few Prizes & many Blanks'.[18] In sum, bounties had multiple objectives in view: economic, military, and political.

Most bounties were enacted in the first half of the eighteenth century, including naval stores in 1705; herring fisheries in 1707 (based on earlier Scottish bounties); sailcloth in 1713; fish in 1719; manufactured silks in 1722; whale fisheries in 1733; linens in 1742; indigo in 1748; hemp and flax in 1764; and raw silk in 1769.[19] That bounties were introduced in a piecemeal fashion over many decades demonstrates that no grand plan lay behind them. But a structural factor at work was that only with the growth of customs and excise revenues after 1688 were public finances secure enough to contemplate such expenditure. Moreover, bounties might be offered up as part of negotiations between the state and different interests when duties were under consideration.[20] Often enough, 'What one Clause gives in Bounties, other Clauses take away in Duties, Excises, and expensive obligatory Conditions'.[21] As has been noted, corn bounties were linked in this way to the tax burdens on landowners, as were fish bounties to the salt tax.[22] In a similar vein, in 1713 it was argued that duties on imported hemp and flax made the domestic manufacture of sailcloth uncompetitive with international rivals, a wrong that could be righted through the introduction of a bounty.[23] This chapter considers bounties somewhat in isolation, but in practice they were part of dense networks of duties and regulations.

Because bounties entailed spending by central government, most of the legislation was categorized as supply measures, beginning life in the Commons. There, like other public finance measures, they were often guided by the Chairman of the Ways and Means Committee or Secretary to the Treasury and usually subject to little opposition, passing quickly through both houses. Even when government officers did not manage bills seeking to establish new bounties, such as the indigo bounty of 1748,

---

[18] HMC, *Eleventh report, appendix, part 4. The manuscripts of the Marquess of Townshend* (1887), p. 372.

[19] Naval stores, 3 & 4 Anne, c. 9; herring fisheries, 6 Anne, c. 29; sailcloth, 12 Anne c. 16; fish, 5 George I, c. 18; manufactured silks, 8 George I, c. 15; whale fishery, 6 George II, c. 33; linens, 15 George II, c. 29; indigo, 21 George II, c. 30; hemp and flax, 4 George III, c. 26; raw silk, 9 George III, c. 38.

[20] R. Davis, 'The rise of protection in England, 1689–1786', *Economic History Review*, 19.2 (1966), pp. 314, 316–17.

[21] 'Third report from the committee appointed to enquire into the state of the British fisheries' (1786), p. 97 in Lambert, *Sessional papers*, vol. 53, p. 139.

[22] Edward Hughes, *Studies in administration and finance, 1558–1825 with special reference to the history of salt taxation in England* (Manchester, 1934), p. 178.

[23] *JHC*, 17 (1711–14), p. 351 (14 May 1713).

it seems unlikely that those which were passed did so against the wishes of the Treasury.[24] Unfortunately, the sources are unclear or lacking here. Failed attempts to establish new bounties cannot be accurately identified because of the frequent use of the ambiguous term 'encouragement' rather than 'bounty' in their short titles in the journals.[25] It is equally unclear whether proposals for a particular bounty originated in society at large, within departments of central government such as the Treasury or Board of Trade, or in the policy deliberations of leading ministers – not least because records of behind the scenes lobbying are very patchy. A few bounties seemingly originated in petitions, though sometimes themselves clearly the product of earlier efforts at political mobilization. Petitions led to the bill for a bounty on sailcloth (1713), though it quickly became a governmental measure.[26] Similarly, the bounty on linen (1742) was prompted by petitions from London and fourteen Scottish towns, but clearly came under management of the Chairman of Ways and Means, who was also a member of the Board of Trade.[27]

Expenditure on Bounties

Although most bounties were governmental measures, outlining the cost of them is difficult. They did not begin to be formally noted in public accounts until the late eighteenth century, even then being sometimes bound up with wider categories of expenditure. But from time to time reports on some or all bounties were produced, under two stimuli. Firstly, because bounties often came up for renewal or revision, statistics were prepared to aid decision making. Secondly, Pelham in around 1750, Townshend in 1767, and Shelburne in 1783 all undertook more general surveys of expenditure on bounties, worried perhaps by their cost, perhaps by their efficacy. (Townshend's father had written against the corn bounty and Shelburne had taken on board some free trade ideas.)

---

[24] *JHC*, 25 (1745–50), pp. 617 (5 April 1748), 652 (4 May 1748). Lieutenant General Oglethorpe, with considerable experience in colonial affairs, played a leading role in managing this bill in the Commons, but he held no government office. *HofP* online. The idea for the bounty originated in South Carolina: C. Robert Haywood, 'Mercantilism and South Carolina agriculture, 1700–1763', *South Carolina Historical Magazine*, 60.1 (1959), pp. 18–20.

[25] Eight fails in the period explicitly proposed bounties: Hoppit, *Failed legislation*, 30.045, 85.023, 87.015, 90.005, 90.020, 97.015, 103.017, 143.011.

[26] *JHC*, 17 (1711–14), p. 432 (19 June 1713).

[27] *JHC*, 24 (1741–5), pp. 189 (29 April 1742), 190 (30 April 1742), 193 (3 May 1742), 194 (4 May 1742), 212 (5 May 1742), 256 (25 May 1742), 270–1 (3 June 1742), 272 (4 June 1742).

Table 8.2. *Selected annual averages spent on bounties from customs in Britain, 1712–1800*

	£	War or peace
1712–14	81,424	Both
1746–8	181,703	War
1799–1800	621,156	War

Source: see note 29.

Official data on annual spending on bounties from customs receipts is available for England and Wales from 1711 to 1770, 1777–81, and 1799–1800, for Scotland from 1707–48, 1788, and 1799–1800, and for Britain from 1786–90.[28] Obviously the lack of data for some years, especially for England after 1770 and Scotland after 1748, limits what can be said about developing trends. Moreover, the figures were not compiled on a consistent basis. The figures in Table 8.2 are, therefore, best treated as rough approximations.

Given that prices more than doubled over this period, the increase in real spending on bounties was a bit more than threefold – though this depends on the average figures for two very different years at the end of our period being roughly on trend.[29] As might be expected, the pattern of growth was far from smooth, as is clear by looking only at the figures for England and Wales in Figure 8.1.

Figure 8.1 and the sources on which it rests suggests two important points. Firstly, their cost was subject to closest ministerial consideration by Townshend in 1766–7 and Shelburne in 1782–3.[30] It is in their papers

---

[28] English figures are in: Clements Library, Townshend papers, 8/21/8 (1711–65); Clements Library, Shelburne papers, vol. 135i (1766–70 and 1777–81). Scottish figures are in: Clements Library, Shelburne papers, vol. 109, ff. 57–8 (1708–49). British totals for 1786–90 are in 'Report from the select committee on accounts and other papers, relating to the public income and expenditure' (1791), p. 90, in *Reports from the committees of the House of Commons 1715–1801*, vol. 6 (1782–1802). English and Scottish figures for 1799 and 1800 are in 'Accounts presented to the House of Commons, respecting the public expenditure of Great Britain, for the year ending the fifty of January 1800' (1800), Appendix E.1, in Lambert, *Sessional papers*, vol. 129, p. 264 and TNA CUST17/21. These are the sources for the following discussion.

[29] P. K. O'Brien, 'Agriculture and the home market for English industry, 1660–1820', *English Historical Review*, 100.397 (1985), pp. 773–800. Spending on bounties averaged more than £500,000 per annum in 1801–13: Patrick Colquhoun, *A treatise on the wealth, power, and resources, of the British empire* (1814), p. 231.

[30] Shelburne's papers provide annual figures for 1766–70 and 1777 to 1781, broken down by commodity and whether paid in London or the outports. He also had reports on Scottish customs and bounties, from the Union to 1749, perhaps compiled for Pelham,

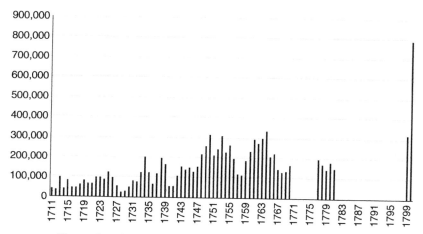

Figure 8.1 Annual bounties paid from customs, England and Wales, 1711–1800 (£).
Source: note 28

that the fullest official accounts of the annual costs of bounties have been found. It may simply be the chance failure of records to survive elsewhere, but Pitt the younger, in office from 1783 until 1801, appears to have taken much less interest, despite his deep immersion in public finance matters. If true, it seems likely that bounties were felt to be most costly and significant before 1783. In fact it is notable, secondly, that there were marked periods of growth in the costs of bounties around the ends of the War of the Austrian Succession in 1748 and the Seven Years War in 1763, periods when overseas trade was recovering, especially across the Atlantic. The American trade in general and some of the plantation bounties in particular were important drivers to the fluctuating cost of bounties.

Assessing the significance of the growth in spending on bounties is aided by employing a benchmark. Two might be offered, bounties expressed as a percentage of total public civil and military expenditure and customs revenue (Table 8.3). Neither of these benchmarks is ideal. The picture may be confused by the mixture of years of war and peace, which obviously could significantly affect flows of trade liable to bounties, and a British benchmark is being applied to figures

and kept at the Treasury until Shelburne became prime minister in 1782. Townshend's papers have a simple annual cost of bounties, 1711–65, but also an analysis by periods of war and peace, relating the cost of bounties to other charges and total receipts.

Table 8.3. *Expenditure from English and Welsh customs on bounties as a percentage of British civil and military expenditure and net customs revenue, 1712–1800*

	Civil and military expenditure	Customs revenue	War or peace
1712–14	2.0	5.4	Both
1746–8	2.2	14.6	War
1786–8	6.5	11.2	Peace
1799–1800	1.9	13.5	War

Sources: note 28; Mitchell, *British historical statistics*, pp. 575, 580.

Table 8.4 *Five main recipients of customs bounties, by commodity, 1740–1800: percentage share of totals by period*

1740–50		1766–70		1777–80		1800	
85	Corn	20	Linens	27	Corn	64	Refined sugar
6	Silk	17	Corn	22	Refined sugar	21	Linens
3	Refined sugar	15	Whale fishery	19	Linens	5	Corn/rice imports
2	Linens	15	Refined sugar	15	Whale fishery	5	Silk
1	Whale fishery	9	Silk	8	Silk	2	Whale fishery

Source: TNA, Cust37/62; Clements Library, Shelburne papers, vol. 135i; TNA, Cust17/21.

for England and Wales. There is no doubt, however, that bounties were only ever a small part of governmental spending as a whole. But they look bigger when set alongside the scale of customs revenue – from which most of them were paid. Some sense of the dynamics involved can be gained by considering on what commodities the money was spent.

Detailed figures of what bounties were spent on are available for 1740–50, 1766–70, 1777–81, and 1800, with important developments being revealed in Table 8.4.

Corn's early dominance is unsurprising, but it was liable both to short-term fluctuations caused by variable harvests, and structural changes as the nation's population grew from 1750, the rising corn prices making exporting it less profitable, even with bounties. It is well known that corn exports grew about four fold from 1700 to 1766, reaching a notable peak in 1749–51. After 1766, however, net imports became increasingly the norm and from 1793 bounties on corn exports had almost completely

Table 8.5. *Decennial annual averages of corn bounties, 1700–1799*

	£
1700–9	44,141
1710–9	59,745
1720–9	67,503
1730–9	102,204
1740–9	117,208
1750–9	131,867
1760–9	85,968
1770–9	22,694
1780–9	47,238
1790–9	11,637

Source: Henry Thornton, *Historical summary of the corn laws* (1841), p. 42. The underlying figures differ somewhat from others used in this chapter, even though both seem to be drawn from official sources, probably because different years have been used.

disappeared before their abolition in 1814.[31] Table 8.5 shows the pattern of payments of corn bounties that resulted, though it hides suspensions of the bounties on many occasions from 1765, especially in the years 1767–73.[32] In the eighteenth century 88 per cent of expenditure on corn bounties was before 1767.

In the 1740s corn generated 90 per cent of the increase of total spending on bounties. But in the next four decades corn bounties fell substantially, off-setting increases that must have been experienced by other bounties – which were growing in number. Moreover, just as bounties on the corn trade were on the wane, accounting for only 5 per cent of all bounties paid by 1790, American independence also significantly undermined a number of import bounties, especially naval stores, indigo, hemp, and flax.[33] Three other bounties were especially important in taking the place of those on corn and plantation goods in the last quarter of the eighteenth century: linen, whaling, and refined sugar.

Bounties on the export of British and Irish linens from Britain were enacted in 1742 and soon judged to have 'greatly increased' output, Harte concluding that 'between about 1740 and 1790 the English linen industry enjoyed a flowering.'[34] A total of nearly £500,000 was spent

---

[31] BPP, 16 (1826–7), pp. 487–8; John, 'English agricultural improvement'; David Ormrod, *English grain exports and the structure of agrarian capitalism, 1700–1760* (Hull, 1985).

[32] Donald Grove Barnes, *A history of the English corn laws, 1660–1846* (1930), pp. 38–45.

[33] Clements Library, Shelburne papers, vol. 135i.

[34] BL, Add Mss, 35,910, Hardwicke papers, f. 5v. N. B. Harte, 'The rise of protection and the English linen trade, 1690–1790', in N. B. Harte and K. G. Ponting, eds., *Textile*

on these bounties by 1771 when they cost around £37,000 per annum. Expenditure fell back during the American War, but in 1800 had surged to nearly £106,000, not including a further £72,000 on a printed cottons and linen bounty.[35] A second area of growth of bounties between 1766 and 1790 was in whaling, the annual average paid to the Greenland whaling rising from £17,573 in 1750–76 to £50,855 in 1787–92 despite a reduction in the rate of the bounty by 25 per cent between the two periods.[36] But figures for linen and whaling bounties were dwarfed by those for refined sugars, which were worth £217,000 in 1798 and £550,000 in 1800 (up from an average of only £4,500 in the 1740s), though Smith thought, not altogether convincingly given the importance of the processing stage, that the bounty 'may be considered as a drawback of the duties upon the [imported] brown and muscovado sugars, from which it is made'.[37]

The final stage of this statistical overview considers some geographical patterns in bounty payments, something that was bound to be significant because they applied to particular goods often produced or traded in certain regions and were usually paid at ports. For the years from 1707 to 1749 it is clear that 91 per cent of bounties paid out of the customs was distributed in England and Wales, 9 per cent in Scotland. Figures for the second half of the eighteenth century are hard to find and often appear to be somewhat doubtful, but by one official and well-constructed account those shares were much the same in 1800.[38] Scotland's share appears to have been much less than its population, but as will be seen in the next chapter much more than the customs collected there. Even so, Scotland was less able to take advantage of the corn laws, it being harder to grow wheat there for environmental reasons. Though corn bounties were available to the Scots from 1707, they were much less heavily involved in the corn trade than the English, as Table 8.6 shows.

Measured in crude volume terms, Scotland's share of corn exports was very small, being significant only in oatmeal, a crop not much exported;

---

history and economic history: essays in honour of Miss Julia de Lacy Mann (Manchester, 1973), p. 108.

[35] 'Report from the committee appointed to enquire into the present state of the linen trade, in Great Britain and Ireland' (1773), p. 46 in Lambert, *Sessional papers*, vol. 25, p. 436; Clements Library, Shelburne papers, vol. 135i; TNA, CUST17/21.

[36] Jackson, *Whaling*, p. 264.

[37] 'An account of the quantity of British-plantation sugar and rum imported into and exported from Great Britain' (1799), in Lambert, *Sessional papers*, vol. 121, p. 291; TNA, CUST37/62; TNA CUST17/21; Smith, *Wealth of nations*, vol. 1, p. 523. Smith's point was accepted by the well-informed Bryan Edwards, *The history, civil and commercial, of the British colonies in the West Indies* (2 vols., 1793), vol. 2, pp. 447–8, 458.

[38] TNA CUST17/21, 'Accounts of customs and excise, for year to 5 Jan 1801'.

Table 8.6. *Total English and Scottish corn exports, 1707–1766 – by quarters (a volume measure)*

	Barley	Malt	Oatmeal	Rye	Wheat and flour	Total
England	2,296,051	12,975,842	126,979	2,177,372	13,684,107	31,260,351
Scotland	155,264	495,854	383,095	16,093	108,595	1,158,901
Total	2,451,315	13,471,696	510,074	2,193,465	13,792,702	32,419,252
% Scotland	6	4	75	1	1	4

Source: TNA, T64/274/66, 68

by volume, English wheat exports were thirty-six times larger than those of Scottish oatmeal between the Union and 1766. Nonetheless, as Whatley has emphasized, bounties were one of the issues keenly considered at the Union in 1707. Recognizing that Scottish agriculture was unlikely to produce much surplus wheat, the corn bounties were extended to include oatmeal for the first time in the first session of the Union parliament.[39] But because Scottish exports of oatmeal were never large, corn bounties paid in Scotland totalled only £207,000 from 1707–49, but £3,731,000 in England and Wales. By one report, bounties paid in Scotland on exported oatmeal totalled only £5,583 between 1746 and 1753, albeit about twice the amount paid in the same period in England.[40] This raises the possibility that Adam Smith's attacks on corn bounties may in part have been stimulated by these national differences, though he did not convince all Scots.[41]

If the corn laws did not loom as large in Scottish as in English experience of bounties, three certainly did, much preoccupying the Convention of the Royal Burghs from at least mid-century. In descending order of cost these were to fisheries, whaling, and linens (though linens also received significant amounts of non-bounty subsidies). Each will be briefly considered.

[39] In an act passed soon after the Union: 6 Anne, c. 29, § 13. C. A. Whatley, 'Salt, coal and the Union of 1707: a revision article', *Scottish Historical Review*, 66.1 (1987), pp. 26–45.
[40] BL, Add Mss. 35,906, Hardwicke papers, ff. 41–2; TNA, T64/274/67; Clements Library, Shelburne papers, vol. 109, ff. 57–8. More than 98 per cent of Scottish oatmeal bounties were paid at Edinburgh.
[41] Smith, *Wealth of nations*, vol. 1, pp. 505–43; James Anderson, *Observations on the means of exciting a spirit of national industry: chiefly intended to promote the agriculture, commerce, manufactures and fisheries of Scotland* (Edinburgh, 1777), p. 309.

The same act at the Union which extended the corn laws to include oatmeal also brought England and Wales into line with Scottish encouragement for the herring fisheries – Scotland already had a bounty, which in the year before Union cost £28,452.[42] Bob Harris and Anna Gambles have both powerfully argued the need to view fisheries policies in relation to patriotic and national as well as economic and political themes.[43] What might be added here is a little statistical detail and context, though evidence from the first half of the eighteenth century has not been found. By one probably incomplete report, a little more than £600,000 was paid out in bounties to support the herring and cod fisheries between 1751 and 1782, a clear majority on Scotland.[44] By another comprehensive and consistently compiled report, just more than £1 million was provided in bounties to British herring fisheries between 1765 and 1797, with 63 per cent being paid out in Scotland (Table 8.7).

As the final row of Table 8.7 shows, Scotland's share of British herring fisheries bounties rose significantly in the second half of the eighteenth century to very nearly 70 per cent, giving weight to Gambles' conclusion that this appears to have constituted a regional subsidy.[45]

A bounty on whaling was introduced in Britain in 1733. None, however, was claimed in Scotland until 1750, when the bounty was doubled, its effects there being 'quite dramatic'.[46] By 1760 about £8,000 was being claimed there annually, certainly more than that being claimed for corn, but significantly less than for the fisheries. Nonetheless, in November 1766 a petition to the Convention of the Royal Burghs from Scottish Greenland whalers urged a renewal of bounties thereon for a trade asserted to be of 'the greatest advantage to Britain in general' and 'to those petitioners in particular'.[47] In fact, Scottish whalers received £304,187 in bounties on this trade in the second half of the eighteenth century, nearly 16 per cent

[42] 6 Anne, c. 29, § 7; Hughes, *Studies in administration and finance*, p. 243.
[43] Bob Harris, 'Scotland's herring fisheries and the prosperity of the nation, c. 1660–1760', *Scottish Historical Review*, 79.1 (2000), pp. 39–60; Bob Harris, 'Patriotic commerce and national revival: the Free British Fishery Society and British politics, c. 1749–58', *English Historical Review*, 114.456 (1999), pp. 285–313; Gambles, 'Fisheries policy'; also James R. Coull, 'Fishery development in Scotland in the eighteenth century', *Scottish Economic and Social History*, 21.1 (2001), pp. 1–21.
[44] 'Third report from the committee appointed to enquire into the state of the British Fisheries, and into the most effectual means for their improvement and extension' (1785), pp. 126–8 in Lambert, *Sessional papers*, vol. 53, pp. 171–3.
[45] Gambles, 'Fisheries policy', p. 292.
[46] G. Jackson, 'Government bounties and the establishment of the Scottish whaling trade, 1750–1800', in John Butt and J. T. Ward, eds., *Scottish themes: essays in honour of Professor S. G. E. Lythe* (Edinburgh, 1976), p. 50.
[47] *Extracts from the records of the Convention of the Royal Burghs of Scotland, 1759–79* (Edinburgh, 1918), pp. 220–1.

Table 8.7. *Bounties spent on British herring fisheries, 1765–1796 (£)*

	1765–70	1770–86	1787–96	Totals
England	151,310	151,104	85,168	387,582
Per annum	16,812	9,444	8,517	12,112
Scotland	172,545	277,682	197,710	647,937
Per annum	19,172	17,355	27,768	20,248
Total	323,855	428,786	282,878	1,035,519
Per annum	35,984	26,799	28,288	32,360
% England	47	35	30	37
% Scotland	53	65	70	63

Note: periods taken from original report; there is insufficient information to change them.
Source: 'Report respecting the British fisheries' (1798), pp. 218–25, in Lambert, *Sessional papers*, vol. 118, pp. 506–13.

of total British whaling bounties of £1.96 million. This was slightly disproportionate to Scotland's share of the tonnage of shipping clearing for that trade, and much larger than Scotland's share of British trade and customs receipts.[48] Much of the bounty went to Scottish east coast ports, stimulating their economies, though it was very heavily criticized by Adam Smith.[49]

Finally, note needs to be made of the impact of linen bounties on Scotland. Linen was certainly a favoured product there. The Board of Trustees for Fisheries and Manufactures instituted in 1727 spent £236,000 on Scotland's linen industry before 1815.[50] Additionally, bounties on linen exports were available from 1743, with Scots prominent advocates of the measure; by 1748 some £14,540 was dispersed in Britain, 40 per cent of it in Scotland.[51] Scotland's linen industry prospered under these stimulants, its output doubling every twenty years from 1730 to 1800, and its share of British linen output fluctuating about a rising trend to 31 per cent in 1790.[52] Perhaps £240,000 was provided

[48] TNA, BT6/230, f. 76; 'An account of the number of ships which have been employed in the whale fishery, to Davis's Streights, and the Greenland Seas' (1785), in Lambert, *Sessional papers*, vol. 53, pp. 509–11; Jackson, *Whaling*, p. 265.

[49] Jackson, 'Government bounties', p. 61; Smith, *Wealth of nations*, vol. 2, p. 578.

[50] R. H. Campbell, ed., *States of the annual progress of the linen manufacture, 1727–1754* (Edinburgh, 1964), pp. v–vii, 141; Alastair J. Durie, *The Scottish linen industry in the eighteenth century* (Edinburgh, 1979), p. 29.

[51] *JHC*, 24 (1741–5), p. 189 (29 April 1742), 270–1 (3 June 1742); 25 (1745–50), pp. 719 (7 Feb. 1749), 749 (20 Feb. 1749).

[52] Mitchell, *British historical statistics*, p. 352; Harte, 'English linen trade', p. 104; Alastair J. Durie, ed., *The British Linen Company, 1745–1775* (Edinburgh, 1996), pp. 1–5.

for the export from England and Wales of British linen between 1743 and 1771. If this was 70 per cent of the British total, then Scotland may have received £100,000, or about £3,400 per annum.[53]

Given their differing natural endowments, administrative organization, and political structures and expectations, there is some sense in distinguishing the experience of bounties in composite state terms. But obviously distinguishing an English and Welsh from a Scottish experience is relatively crude. In fact, there were significant differences in the distribution of bounties within those nations. After all, more than a half of Scottish customs was collected in Glasgow in this period and about a fifth at Leith.[54] There was even greater concentration in England and Wales, with more than two-thirds of customs being collected at London for most of the eighteenth century.[55] In fact, in the era of the American crisis some 78 per cent of bounties dispersed in England and Wales were paid at London, only 22 per cent in the 'outports'.[56] Earlier in the century, with the corn bounties much more prominent, there was a different geographical dispersion of such monies. Some corn flowed out through London, but much through other ports, especially in Norfolk (King's Lynn, Wells, Blakeney-Cley, and Yarmouth). In 1732 36 per cent of corn bounties were paid in that county and by 1752 it was more than 40 per cent.[57] With some justice, William Stout, a shopkeeper in Lancaster, complained in 1735 that £200,000 spent on corn exports from London and the south helped farmers and landowners there cope with low prices.[58]

This hurried statistical sketch of bounties has established four critical points: that their cost rose about a fluctuating trend – though details of growth after 1770 are few; that until the 1750s the growth was largely driven by the bounty on corn exports, thereafter especially by bounties on linens, refined sugar, whaling, and fisheries; that bounties were claimed across Britain, to the extent that with regard to Scotland they might be viewed as a regional subsidy, but became more concentrated on the port of London by the late eighteenth century; finally, bounties were part of Britain's imperial economy, explicitly seeking to stimulate the import of certain raw materials for processing or manufacture in Britain, both to aid national defence and the balance of payments.

---

[53] These estimates contain some assumptions which may prove unwarranted. 'Report into the present state of the linen trade', p. 46 in Lambert, *Sessional papers*, vol. 25, p. 436.

[54] From data very kindly provided by Dr Philip Rössner.

[55] BL Add Mss 8133, Musgrave papers.

[56] Clements Library, Shelburne papers, vol. 135i.

[57] TNA, CUST24/19. London's share of corn bounties in 1735 was 23 per cent and in 1752 21 per cent.

[58] *The autobiography of William Stout of Lancaster, 1665–1752*, ed. J. D. Marshall (Manchester, 1967), pp. 217–18.

A Case Study of the Encouragement of Hemp and Flax Production

The question of why bounties were created and how effective they were has only been touched on in passing so far. A case study of bounties for hemp and flax begins to answer those questions, before discussion is widened out in the conclusion.

Hemp and flax, whether as raw materials or semi-processed ('dressed'), had long been judged to be of national importance as the main raw material for the cordage and linen industries. The cordage industry was vital to Britain's naval power, both directly through the ropes that rigged and anchored its ships, and indirectly through fishing nets used by seamen whom the state might call on in time of war. Linen also provided the sailcloth for the Royal Navy, while a strong domestic linen industry was also believed to be vitally important as it would reduce imports and create substantial employment across Britain and Ireland. As William Playfair, the inventor of graphs and an early editor of Adam Smith, put it, 'A bounty for raising hemp is … partly political, partly commercial.'[59]

A bill to encourage hemp and flax growing was considered at Westminster in 1662, but failed. Further similar efforts in the seventeenth century also came to nothing, though duties on imported linen, initially to raise revenue, then to be prohibitory, encouraged the development of the British and Irish linen industries.[60] As has been seen, in Scotland state aid helped in this, something that was also the case in Ireland, where £234,000 was expended by the publicly funded Linen Board between 1711 and 1800.[61] Bounties on the export of certain types of British and Irish linens from Britain provided encouragement in another way. The growth of the shipbuilding industries in Britain was no less marked, with the state's active role being concentrated on the expansion of the Royal Navy and the naval stores bounties. Developments in the linen and cordage industries depended on adequate supplies of hemp and flax. While more was produced in Ireland than in England and Scotland, imports from overseas began to grow in the 1740s, leading to calls for more domestic production to avoid

[59] Adam Smith, *An inquiry into the nature and causes of the wealth of nations*, ed. William Playfair, introduction by William Rees-Mogg (3 vols., 1995), vol. 2, p. 291.
[60] Joan Thirsk, 'Agricultural policy: public debate and legislation', in Joan Thirsk, ed., *The agrarian history of England and Wales, V, 1640–1750: II, agrarian change* (Cambridge, 1985), pp. 339–41.
[61] Conrad Gill, *The rise of the Irish linen industry* (Oxford, 1925), ch. 4; T. J. Kiernan, *History of the financial administration of Ireland to 1817* (1930), pp. 165–79.

over-reliance on foreign supplies that were liable to be interrupted by inter-state competition.[62]

In Scotland the Board of Trustees had sought to stimulate the growth of flax through premiums, paid according to the acreage sown. But in 1749 the scheme was abandoned because the costs became unbearable, not least because of strong suspicions of widespread fraud.[63] For a while the market was left to its own devices, but in 1764, at the behest of American trading interests, a bounty was instituted for twenty-one years on imported hemp and flax from Britain's American colonies.[64] Probably the initial bounty provided insufficient inducement, while it was quickly thrown into doubt by deteriorating relations between Britain and the American colonies: only £5,560 in total was claimed on the bounty between 1766 and 1772.[65] Parliament quickly responded by passing in 1767 an act to establish a fund of £15,000 per annum to encourage British growing and processing of hemp and flax, to be paid for by increased duties on certain foreign imported linens – import substitution was clearly an aim.[66] This was an important development, not least because the funds were to be made available across Britain and led the state to attempt a new mode of economic support in England and Wales, though it eventually petered out in the 1790s. Why, then, was the fund instituted?

The first sight in Parliament of the idea of statutory support for domestic hemp and flax production is a petition submitted to the Commons on 31 January 1767 from the gentlemen, clergy, freeholders, growers, and dealers in hemp and flax of parts of Lincolnshire. Their concern was not that American supplies might be unreliable, but rather the opposite, that plentiful cheap supplies would render their own efforts uncompetitive, arguing that because Americans 'pay nothing for their lands' they needed no bounty. The petition was ordered to lie on the table, but seemingly out of the blue at the start of May it was referred to one of the Commons' main committees dealing with public revenue. Three days later the Commons received a second petition about supplies of hemp and flax, from Scotland's Convention of the Royal Burghs, arguing that

[62] Elizabeth Boody Schumpeter, *English overseas trade statistics, 1697–1808* (Oxford, 1960), pp. 52–5; Durie, *Scottish linen industry*, p. 35; W. Ellis, *The modern husbandman, or the practice of farming* (4 vols., 1744), vol. 3, pp. 93–5.

[63] Durie, *Scottish linen industry*, p. 69.

[64] 4 George III, c. 26; P. D. G. Thomas, *British politics and the Stamp Act crisis: the first phase of the American Revolution, 1763–1767* (Oxford, 1975), p. 67.

[65] 'Parliamentary diaries of Nathaniel Ryder, 1764–7', ed. P. D. G. Thomas, *Camden Miscellany*, 23 (1969), pp. 295, 298; *St James's Chronicle*, 12 December 1775, p. 1.

[66] 7 George III, c. 58.

importing raw materials from Europe cost the nation £1 million annually and made it dependent on foreign powers. Only a week later a bill was introduced by the Chairman of the Committee of Ways and Means (meaning it had ministerial approval) to establish a fund to encourage domestic hemp and flax production. Ten petitions against this proposal came into the Commons over the following month, from London, Bristol, Exeter, Norwich, Northamptonshire, Kidderminster, Tiverton, Wakefield, Halifax and Bradford, arguing that the new duties would raise their raw material costs – no comment was passed on the fund. But the bill passed in the Commons, though there was a division (28:39) on one amendment, and sailed through the Lords.[67]

As the record in the *Journals* hints, if notionally a governmental measure, the act arose from considerable non-governmental preparation.[68] Mostly this was in Scotland, particularly in the Convention of the Royal Burghs and the Board of Trustees. The Board had recently received a report from Lord Kames, one of its members and a leading figure of the Scottish enlightenment, on the need to improve domestic flax production. On the orders of the trustees this report was published anonymously in 1766, its arguments then being employed by the Convention in pursuit of statutory funding of a bounty.[69]

The Convention took up the issue when presented with a petition in July 1766 from the Edinburgh Linen Society suggesting an application to Parliament for a bounty on the culture of flax and hemp in Great Britain. The Convention consulted various Scottish counties and burghs in preparing a memorial, which was printed and distributed to the royal burghs, 'requiring them in the name of the convention to instruct their respective representatives to do all in their power to support the burrows' application to parliament for obtaining a parliamentary encouragement to promote the culture of flax & hemp in Great Britain'.[70] The memorial noted the importance of linen in its own right, and to the wool, cotton, sailcloth, and cordage industries. It claimed that imported raw materials would be more expensive than those domestically produced, and foreign sources were inherently 'uncertain and precarious'. Not only war might

---

[67] *JHC*, 31 (1766–8), pp. 98 (31 Jan. 1767), 334 (1 May 1767), 337 (4 May 1767), 345 (7 May 1767), 352 (11 May 1752), 368–9 (18 May 1767), 379 (21 May 1767), 385 (26 May 1767), 390 (1 June 1767), 398 (10 June 1767), 402 (11 June 1767), 403 (12 June 1767), 417 (30 June 1767).

[68] There was nothing new in this. For similar earlier activities see Trevor Griffiths, Philip Hunt, and Patrick O'Brien, 'Scottish, Irish, and imperial connections: Parliament, the three kingdoms, and the mechanization of cotton spinning in eighteenth-century Britain', *Economic History Review*, 61.3 (2008), pp. 625–50.

[69] [Henry Home, Lord Kames], *Progress of flax-husbandry in Scotland* (Edinburgh, 1766).

[70] *Records of the Convention of the Royal Burghs*, pp. 186, 205–8 (quote at 208).

interrupt supplies, but perhaps Russia, Holland, and other nations might in the future bar exports in line with the 'maxim of conduct firmly established amongst all commercial states to discourage the exportation of the materials for carrying on any manufacture in their rude state'. The costs to Britain of these raw material imports were put at £1.3 million per annum, saving which would advantage all, 'the labourer, the tenant, and the landholder'. Arguments were advanced as to why American supplies were unlikely to meet British needs adequately and of the practicability of extending hemp and flax cultivation in Britain. A bounty was 'no doubt the most effectual method that can be devised' to achieve the desired end.[71]

Meanwhile, the Edinburgh Linen Society had sent two representatives south to co-ordinate efforts from both English and Scottish interests, a move endorsed by the Convention. Probably they made a connection with the interests in Lincolnshire that presented the first petition to Parliament in 1767. Joseph Gee of Lincolnshire wrote a number of works at the time about hemp, flax, and linens, noting in 1766 the moves afoot in Scotland and in April 1767 issuing a broadsheet abstract of reasons for the legislation then under consideration.[72] To mobilize support, the Convention wrote to some English towns, to MPs and to Townshend, the Chancellor of the Exchequer – the Board of Trustees separately wrote to members of the ministry and Scottish parliamentarians. The Convention's London agent was instructed to wait on Townshend, presumably to discuss the proposal, and to present its petition to Parliament. Their letter to him developed some additional lines of thought, not least the potential cost of a bounty, judging that one proposal would involve expenditure of £120,000 annually, 'a sum which it's thought the parliament would not chuse to grant towards promoting any one species of manufacture however usefull and important'.[73] But they thought that Parliament might agree to an annual charge of £45,000, two-thirds to England (Wales was ignored or subsumed within England), one-third to Scotland. In Scotland the sum might be dispersed by a newly instituted board. No mention was made as to how the sum might be administered

---

[71] 'Memorial with respect to the state of the linen and hempen manufactures in Great Britain', 27 October 1766, *Records of the Convention of the Royal Burghs*, pp. 209–19.

[72] *Records of the Convention of the Royal Boroughs*, p. 222. J. Gee, *Considerations on the expediency of a bounty upon hemp and flax of home growth* [1767], p. 1; Gee had earlier complained that Ireland had passed many laws to support its linen industry, but this was inequitable because Ireland did not 'bear a proportionably *equal share* ... of the Publick Expence'. J. Gee, *Observations on the growth of hemp and flax in Great Britain* (1765), p. 4. J. Gee, *An abstract of reasons for encouraging the linen manufactory* ([1767]).

[73] *Records of the Convention of the Royal Burghs*, pp. 221–38, quote at 231.

in England. Funding was proposed to come from an additional duty on German and Russian linens.[74]

Townshend, who was well versed in free trade thinking, did not simply follow what the Convention proposed. He obtained information from the Scottish Trustees for Fisheries and Manufactures and the Irish Linen Board and had to fend off opposition. The proposal that the bounty be funded by a duty on imported linens led to howls of complaint from merchants trading to Russia and wholesale drapers.[75] In fact, the act established a much smaller fund of £15,000 per annum and made no provision for its administration. Even so, the Convention was grateful for an act 'so necessary for securing the independency of the British navy, as well as rendering the linen manufactory permanent', though Townshend's death in September 1767 may have disrupted preparations of ways to distribute the fund.[76] Certainly nothing appears to have been decided until 1770 when it was agreed to split the fund, £7,000 to go to Scotland via the Board of Trustees, £8,000 to England via means to be decided.[77] Durie has considered what was done in Scotland, with £127,000 being spent between 1773 and 1815, an annual average of nearly £3,000.[78] His view was that 'much better use of the Flax Fund was made in Scotland by the Board ... than was the case south of the Border, where it seems largely to have been frittered away.'[79] Certainly the English fund appears to have been untouched through the 1770s, but then, in the midst of the American War, with the 1764 bounty a dead letter, statutory provision was made for using the fund in England and Wales that led to significant and productive effort.[80] The key points were:

1. £8,000 annually was to be distributed by the Board of Trade.
2. The bounty was 3d a stone for hemp, 4d a stone for flax, both dressed.
3. Claims were to be made to a JP, to be forwarded to the next quarter sessions.
4. To counter fraud, two sureties were to be provided of treble the value of the claim.
5. Justices were to advertise the bounties at the Michaelmas quarter sessions.
6. Names of claimants were to be published by justices.

---

[74] *Records of the Convention of the Royal Burghs*, pp. 229–33.
[75] Clements Library, Townshend papers, 8/17/3–11, 16–17, 22.
[76] *Records of the Convention of the Royal Burghs*, pp. 272–3.
[77] 10 George III, c. 40.
[78] Durie, *Scottish linen industry*, p. 29.
[79] Ibid., p. 108.
[80] 21 George III, c. 58.

7. Justices were to submit yearly statements to the Board of Trade, who were to arrange payment with the Treasury.
8. The Board of Trade was to prepare annual summaries for Parliament.
9. The scheme was to run for five years from 1 August 1782.

The reasoning behind this scheme seems clear: using an existing local administrative framework would help keep costs down, the state small, and frauds difficult to commit unnoticed. Abolition of the Board of Trade in 1782 required administrative oversight to pass to a Privy Council committee. In 1786 management of the scheme passed to the Treasury and extended down to 1794.[81]

To establish the new system, in December 1781 the Board of Trade wrote to the clerks of the peace in English and Welsh counties, including copies of the act and *Directions for the raising of flax*, a twenty-four-page pamphlet authored by the Scottish Board of Trustees, first issued in 1744, with further editions in 1750, 1763, and 1772.[82] In total, 462 copies of the *Directions* were distributed, with most counties sent six, ten or fifteen copies, though Lincolnshire received twenty and Yorkshire as a whole fifty.[83] These efforts appear to have been successful, the first claims being made at the midsummer quarter sessions in 1783 and payments being agreed in London the following year. Annual summaries for the period 1783–94 are available, with a gap for the 1787 claims.[84] A total of £76,597 was paid out, an annual average of nearly £7,000, with a peak of more than £10,000 for the 1790 claims. Claims were submitted from twenty-six English counties and three Welsh (totalling just £153), but most came from just six counties (see Table 8.8).

Bounties were paid for the production of 451,229 cwt of flax, 164,267 cwt of hemp, respectively perhaps 19 per cent and 3 per cent of domestic needs.[85] Such levels of output were significantly greater than in Scotland. Moreover, if Scotland produced 17 per cent of British flax from 1787–93, it consumed 24 per cent of the monies spent on flax and hemp bounties.[86] Far from being frittered away, south of the border the money appears to have obtained the intended results for a while, rather more productively indeed than in Scotland.

---

[81] 26 George III, c. 43.

[82] *Directions for raising flax ... re-printed by order of the Lords Commissioners for Trade and Plantations* (1781). A similar pamphlet was published when the Irish Linen Board was established in 1711: *Directions for the sowing and preparing of flax* (Dublin, 1711).

[83] TNA, BT6/99, ff. 1–5.

[84] Parliamentary Archives, HL/PO/JO/10/7/681, 703, 740, 760, 849, 867, 894, 921, 945, 974, 1006.

[85] Using import of flax and hemp data in Schumpeter, *English trade statistics*, pp. 57–8.

[86] Durie, *Scottish linen industry*, p. 107.

Table 8.8. *Largest county shares of bounties for hemp and flax production in England and Wales, 1783–1794*

	%
Lincolnshire	20
Somerset	17
Yorks West Riding	14
Yorks East Riding	12
Dorset	8
Norfolk	7
Devon	5
Sub-total	83

Source: see note 85.

Though the total numbers of claimants is unknown, in any one year there were certainly many hundreds and at the peak perhaps a few thousand. For example, in 1784 about 200 claimed in Somerset and 340 in the East Riding.[87] Consequently, most of the claims were for small sums, usually a few pounds. Little wonder that the authorities in Somerset quickly observed that the new system 'was a work of much time, and consequently much trouble'.[88] Indeed, the expenses of the clerks of the peace were sometimes questioned at the centre. As the Privy Council committee pointed out to the East Riding, its clerk's expenses could render the bounty 'inadequate to the wise purposes for which it was intended' and reduced the clerk's charge.[89] Administration charges were recorded in the annual surveys from 1786, consuming thereafter nearly 12 per cent of the cost of the scheme.

The 1786 act expired in 1794 and a bill to continue it was introduced the following year by Rose, Pitt's right-hand man, and passed through the Commons. But it was rejected in the Lords, probably because in the same session an act to ease the importation of flax was passed.[90] Two broad factors were likely at work here. The first is suggested by the fact that in England and Wales the highpoint of claims was in 1790, hemp and flax production falling by 49 per cent between then and 1794. For

[87] TNA, PC1/16/11, ff. 3–6, 12–17, 38.
[88] TNA, PC1/16/11, f. 1v. Somerset's claims were the highest of all counties for 1783, but none appears in the summaries for the following two years.
[89] TNA, PC1/16/25, f. 22r. See also ff. 24–5 for similar letters to Sussex and Dorset. For the reduction, TNA, BT6/99, f. 17 – second foliation.
[90] The Lords rejected the bill on 26 June 1795: Hoppit, *Failed legislation*, 137.071. 36 George III, c. 4.

example, in the Lindsey part of Lincolnshire 507 claimed the bounty for the 1790 crop, but only 205 for 1794.[91] This implies that farmers responded positively to the advent of the bounty, but soon decided that other crops were more profitable to cultivate and/or that claiming the bounty was more trouble than it was worth. Ultimately the bounty was a relatively minor factor alongside broader market forces.[92] Secondly, while the bounty was attractive to many farmers, they mostly produced on a small scale, either because they were unwilling to turn over more of their land to these crops or because their farms were small – the bounty may well have been particularly attractive to smallholders.[93] Because each claim was subject to some fixed administrative costs, particularly to guard against fraud, overheads took up more of the fund than was usual or, probably, as was politically acceptable. Given these factors, with the scheme reaching the end of its life at the start of a major war, legislators may well have reasoned that it was better for Britain to produce food and depend on imported flax and hemp. The future was left to the market.

Conclusion

The case of hemp and flax supplies brings out clearly a number of important general features about trade bounties in eighteenth-century Britain relating to the types of effects they had and reactions they elicited. In particular, the limitations of bounties as a key weapon in the mercantile system need considering.

Judging the success or not of bounties is not straightforward, not least because they often had multiple objects in view: economic, military, and political. At one level the considerable sums expended indicate some success. But the uptake on some bounties was modest, usually because they offered relatively slight aid in relation to market forces. Thus they did not enable Britain to be consistently self-sufficient in corn after population began to rise significantly from 1750, while the indigo bounty of 1748 probably offered limited help to South Carolina producers, relative price swings as between it and rice being more important.[94] Further, bounties on imports of products from colonial America were rendered

[91] Lincolnshire Archives Office, LQS B/7/2–8. Payments are graphed in Charles Brears, *Lincolnshire in the seventeenth and eighteenth centuries* (1940), p. 127.

[92] David Grigg, *The agricultural revolution in south Lincolnshire* (Cambridge, 1966), p. 77.

[93] Joan Thirsk, *English peasant farming: the agrarian history of Lincolnshire from Tudor to recent times* (1957), pp. 41, 77, 137.

[94] R. C. Nash, 'South Carolina indigo, European textiles, and the British Atlantic economy in the eighteenth century', *Economic History Review*, 63.2 (2010), pp. 363, 375–6.

meaningless from 1775. A further weakness was the potential for fraud
that bounties offered – particularly of re-landing goods on which bounties had already been paid and adulteration of one sort or another.[95]
This was a stern test of the administrative capacity of the customs service, if not as dangerous one as tackling smuggling. Indeed, an official
view in 1783–4 was that 'bounties in general are open to fraud, and in
many instances operate to the support of illicit trade.'[96] Bounties strained
Britain's customs service in ways which the excise was largely free from.

Bounties were also liable to a self-generating problem, whereby their
aim to stimulate certain activities might succeed sufficiently to generate
unbearable calls on the public purse, a problem that was first manifested
in the corn laws. In 1748 the cost of the corn bounty exceeded £200,000
for the first time and two years later £300,000. Because most bounties
were meant to be paid out of customs receipts, this could mean that in
places insufficient funds were available. Payment systems came under
enormous strain, with significant arrears accumulating. This threatened not just the well-being of corn merchants because in some ports
and their hinterlands bounty payments had become important parts of
circuits of credit.[97] In the 1760s the same problem happened with the
herring fisheries bounties in Scotland which were 'thunder-struck' as a
consequence.[98]

Though the number and cost of bounties rose from the late seventeenth century, the problems they were associated with soon made them
vulnerable to criticism. In 1704 one author called bounties 'unnatural', strikingly putting his faith in free trade by arguing that profitability
depended 'upon the Nature of our Goods, and not our Laws'.[99] In 1712
Inspector General of Customs Charles Davenant suggested that the corn
bounty was more or less a tax paid by Britons to the benefit of consumers
overseas, an argument picked up on and developed by Matthew Decker

[95] For example, the bounty on exports of manufactured silk was abused by putting tiny amounts of silk in a fabric very largely made up of cotton, woollen, and linen. James Postlethwayt, *The history of the public revenue, from the revolution in 1688, to Christmas 1753* (1759), p. 154.
[96] 'Reports from the committee on illicit practices used in defrauding the revenue', *Reports from Committees of the House of Commons 1715–1800*, vol. 6 (1782–1802), p. 285.
[97] Barnes, *Corn laws*, pp. 23–4; TNA T1/351/47, 49, 59.
[98] 'Third report of the British fisheries', p. 81 in Lambert, *Sessional papers*, vol. 53, p. 123. Arrears on herring fishery bounties between 1766 and 1770 were more than £83,000. TNA, T36/13. For an early example of the role of fish bounties in local circuits of credit in Scotland see *The letter-book of John Steuart of Inverness, 1715–1752*, ed. William Mackay, Scottish History Society Publications, second series, vol. 9 (1915), pp. 32, 68, 237, and 239.
[99] P. Paxton, *A discourse concerning the nature, advantage, and improvement of trade* (1704), pp. 13–14.

in 1744.[100] Given the increasing numbers of bounties before 1750, such criticisms cannot have had much immediate effect, but they provided some of the ammunition used for the more concerted attacks that began in 1751.

From 1750 until the end of the century criticisms of bounties mounted. The strain on the massive corn bounty debentures in 1749 and 1750, pointing up total costs involved, was the immediate context of Townshend's attack on corn bounties in 1751, initiating a dispute that was to rage for a century.[101] He was soon corresponding with Josiah Tucker, dean of Gloucester and a well-known writer on commerce, both agreeing that bounties were liable to produce unwelcome distortions to economic life if left in place for too long.[102] In the 1760s pressures for new or heightened bounties provided a focus for such doubts. For some, bounties offered up a means of attaining competitive advantage. But one problem was that instituting a bounty encouraged some in other parts of the economy to press the case for similar treatment. In 1765, with three bounties proposed, the Treasury was warned from the London custom-house that these were a concerted effort by merchants 'to divide the Revenues amongst them'.[103] As the quote at the head of this chapter suggests, claims for bounties by one group could prompt others to do the same for fear of being disadvantaged; Adam Smith noted that bounties were 'frequently petitioned for'.[104] Part of the justification of such claims was that existing patterns of taxation rendered nationally important areas of the economy uncompetitive. Seen from another angle, these were calls for some relief from the exactions of the fiscal state. To Joseph Massie in 1767, bounties were really a means of 'UN-TAXING'.[105]

When Adam Smith subjected bounties to critical scrutiny in 1776 he was, it is clear, joining a growing chorus of complaint. But his intervention was also prompted by a major reconfiguration of the corn laws through acts passed from 1770–3, including the institution of systematic collection of corn price data.[106] To Smith the new 'system ... [was] in

---

[100] G. N. Clark, *Guide to English commercial statistics, 1696–1782* (1938), p. 58; [Matthew Decker], *An essay on the causes of the decline of foreign trade* (1744), pp. 30–1.

[101] [Charles Townshend], *National thoughts, recommended to the serious attention of the public. with an appendix, shewing the damages arising from a bounty on corn* [1751].

[102] HMC, *Eleventh report, appendix, part 4: the manuscripts of the Marquess of Townshend*, pp. 371–82.

[103] TNA, T1/425/286–7. This was from Henry Saxby, author of *The British customs* (1757).

[104] Wimpey, *Thoughts upon several interesting subjects*, p. 42; Smith, *Wealth of nations*, vol. 1, p. 505; Huntington Library, Ellesmere papers, EL9855.

[105] *Observations on the new cyder-tax* [1764?], p. 8.

[106] 10 George III, c. 39; 12 George III, c. 33 and c. 71; 13 George III, c. 1, 2, 3, 43. Richard Sheldon, 'Practical economics in eighteenth-century England: Charles Smith on the grain trade and the corn laws, 1756–72', *Historical Research*, 81.124 (2008),

many respects better than the ancient one, but in one or two respects perhaps not quite so good'.[107] There is no space here to detail the issues at stake: they tended to centre on the questions of who actually benefited and who actually paid, of their weight relative to market fundamentals, and of unintended consequences, including market distortions and fraud. Too few, however, have noted that Smith himself distinguished between different types of bounties, some of which, especially those motivated by considerations of national defence, were broadly acceptable.

Smith's criticisms of bounties were not very original, but they were timely in two main regards. More narrowly, as has been said, because they came after a major revision of the corn laws; more generally because of the huge challenges posed by American independence. For bounties, American independence had two notable consequences. One was to bring about the short-lived ministry of Shelburne in 1782–3, an enthusiast for the latest thinking and reform. In 1761 Shelburne and Smith shared a coach from Edinburgh to London, which was something of a road to Damascus for the future statesman.[108] In July 1782 he asked Sir William Musgrave, a customs commissioner, to examine the customs administration, clearly with a view to making considerable changes. Musgrave, who appears to have imbibed some of Smith's thinking, was categorical on bounties: they were beset by frauds, were a tax on the community for the benefit of a few, and contributed badly to the bewildering complexity of the system of duties.[109]

Secondly, several bounties had been specifically devised to encourage specialization or complementarities between Britain and her colonies. But if colonies could not be depended on to play their part, then the policy would have to be rethought. One consequence was to bring into focus Britain's economic relations with Ireland. Notably, some in Britain began to question the Irish parliament's voting of considerable sums to help its trade and industry, including subsidies to particular individuals and places.[110] Given that Ireland fell partly within Britain's

---

pp. 636–62. This provides a useful introduction to the nature of the debate between 1750 and 1776. For the new legislation, Barnes, *Corn laws*, pp. 41–4.

[107] Smith, *Wealth of nations*, vol. 1, p. 541.

[108] Dugald Stewart, 'Account of the life and writings of Adam Smith, LL.D', in Adam Smith, *Essays on philosophical subjects*, ed. W. P. D. Wightman, J. C. Bryce, and I. S. Ross (Oxford, 1980), p. 347; John Rae, *Life of Adam Smith* (1895), pp. 153–4.

[109] Clements Library, Shelburne papers, vol. 114, ff. 5, 13, 31; John Norris, *Shelburne and reform* (1963), pp. 211–13. Smith too viewed bounties as akin to taxes: *Wealth of nations*, vol. 1, p. 508.

[110] Eoin Magennis, 'Coal, corn and canals: Parliament and the dispersal of public moneys 1695–1772', *Parliamentary History*, 20.1 (2001), p. 74; Kiernan, *Financial administration of Ireland to 1817*, pp. 165–79.

trade regulations, benefitted from Britain's linen bounties, and had lower labour costs, British manufacturers began to argue that Ireland was being unduly favoured. This was clearly noted in 1751, but came to a head in 1785 when Pitt proposed the harmonization of British and Irish trade regulations. Robert Peel was sure that Irish manufacturers enjoyed too many advantages, but Josiah Wedgwood spoke particularly loudly. He thought it inevitable that Ireland would use its public funds to mount an attack on one of Britain's prime export trades and that Britain was in no position to win 'a Warfare of Bounties' with Ireland.[111] Though Pitt's measure failed, not least because of opposition in Ireland, sentiment in central government towards bounties was now at the very least cold and sometimes positively hostile.[112]

Bounties grew in scope and cost in eighteenth-century Britain, constituting a small but important element of public funding. That they have been rather hidden from view hitherto is due partly to a preoccupation on military spending and the corn laws, to the use by historians of figures of net revenue, and to their place within a complex system of duties encouraging a case-by-case approach. Yet if bounties were more important than has usually been appreciated, they were sometimes directed at non-economic ends, particularly in relation to national defence and encouraging connections within Britain and her empire. As such, they were often assessed by political, military, and imperial criteria as well as by general considerations of costs and benefits, helping to explain their survival well into the nineteenth century despite their often limited economic impact and the advent of concerted criticisms against them from the 1750s.

---

[111] 'Report from the committee appointed to examine ... several petitions of the manufacturers of, and traders and dealers in, the linen manufactury' (1751), pp. 25–44 in Lambert, *Sessional papers*, vol. 19, pp. 123–42; 'Minutes of the evidence taken before a committee of the whole House of Commons ... to consider ... the adjustment of commercial intercourse between Great Britain and Ireland' (1785), p. 184 in Lambert, *Sessional papers*, vol. 51, p. 185. V. E. Dietz, 'Before the age of capital: manufacturing interests and the British State, 1780–1800' (Princeton University PhD thesis, 1991), ch. 3; R. D. Collison Black, 'Theory and policy in Anglo–Irish trade relations', *Journal of the Statistical and Social Inquiry Society of Ireland*, 18.3 (1950), pp. 312–26.

[112] David R. Schweitzer, 'The failure of William Pitt's Irish trade propositions 1785', *Parliamentary History*, 3.1 (1984), pp. 129–45; Paul Kelly, 'British and Irish politics in 1785', *English Historical Review*, 90.356 (1975), pp. 536–63.

9   Refiguring the British Fiscal State, 1680–1800

'[T]axation, as a subject of knowledge, has never been duly cultivated; and therefore we need not wonder at the uncertainty in which it is involved, and the inconsistent, ever-varying, and ineffectual laws, which the Legislature are continually promulgating.'

Andrew Hamilton, 1790[1]

The largest category of general economic acts concerned public finances, with 1,229 passed between 1660 and 1800, nearly two-thirds of which were about taxation. There was a surge in the number of acts associated with the financial revolution in the late seventeenth and early eighteenth centuries, when the management of public finances came fully under parliamentary control, which, with the separation of the crown's civil list from the other costs of central government, enabled the nation to be increasingly heavily taxed and indebted. Later, from 1760 to 1800, an explosion of public finance legislation occurred, when 735 such acts were passed, or an average of eighteen a year. This was a key area of executive government action, with a high success rate from the early eighteenth century.

Public finance legislation was driven by the need to pay for frequent and costly wars and in revenue terms was highly successful. Taking inflation into account, between 1700 and 1800 per capita tax receipts rose more than fourfold and the national debt more than tenfold. So whereas taxes had been perhaps just 3 per cent of national income in 1700, they were 13 per cent in 1800; the national debt grew from only 28 per cent of national income in 1700 to 200 per cent in 1800.[2] While certainly resting on important experiments and developments since the 1640s, what

---

[1] *An enquiry into the principles of taxation* (1790), p. iii. Hamilton was an excise commissioner in Edinburgh, who must have known Adam Smith.
[2] Patrick K. O'Brien, 'The political economy of British taxation, 1660–1815', *Economic History Review*, 41.1 (1988), p. 3; B. R. Mitchell, *British historical statistics* (Cambridge, 1988), pp. 7–9, 600–1. We have good figures for revenue and the national debt, but national income estimates involve considerable guesswork.

happened to public finances after 1688 was of a truly revolutionary scale, permanence, and significance.[3]

Quite rightly, historians have carefully detailed how these changes took place and what they might mean. A major foundation was laid by Peter Dickson in 1967 when he published the most important single work on the topic by establishing how public credit was exploited between 1688 and 1756.[4] At the centre of his account was the institution and development of the permanent funded national debt, whereby loans raised by central government were secured on specific future taxes, with the administration of the loans also involving institutions such as the Bank of England (created in 1694). It mattered enormously that both the loans and the means for their payment had statutory authority: Acts of Parliament not only gave form to such measures, but usually provided enough legitimacy and power to ensure their success. Just as Addison allegorized, the national debt, taxes, and Revolution constitution were all of a piece: the beautiful virgin of public credit 'set an unspeakable Value' on such acts, fearing 'any thing approaching that might hurt them'.[5] All told, in Dickson's terminology this was truly a 'financial revolution', if initially an experimental, hesitant, and vulnerable one, that put central government on a very different financial and constitutional footing to its predecessors.

The main refinement made to Dickson's case has been to emphasize the importance of growing tax receipts, the excise especially, to underpinning the birth and development of the national debt. In the 1690s the excise produced about 26 per cent of total taxes, but from 1725 to 1790 it was usually 47 per cent.[6] Despite the power of such numbers, they were brought vividly to life and brilliantly placed within their administrative context by John Brewer in 1989. Consequently the excise has generally been depicted as remarkably efficient and effective, with its officers weaving strong and intricate webs of exaction over the whole country, with every effort empowered by Acts of Parliament.[7] Seemingly

---

[3] For a crisp and deeply informed survey, Henry Roseveare, *The financial revolution, 1660–1760* (Harlow, 1991).

[4] P. G. M. Dickson, *The financial revolution in England: a study in the development of public credit, 1688–1756* (1967).

[5] *The Spectator*, ed. Donald F. Bond (5 vols. Oxford, 65), vol. 1, p. 15.

[6] Mitchell, *British historical statistics*, pp. 575–7. See also P. K. O'Brien and P. A. Hunt, 'The rise of a fiscal state in England, 1485–1815', *Historical Research*, 66.160 (1993), pp. 129–76. An important earlier study was J. V. Beckett, 'Land tax or excise: the levying of taxation in seventeenth- and eighteenth-century England', *English Historical Review*, 100.395 (1985), pp. 285–308.

[7] John Brewer's key publication was *The sinews of power: war, money and the English state, 1688–1783* (1989). Much of the groundwork had been established by Selma E. Fine, 'Production and excise in England, 1643–1825' (Radcliffe College PhD thesis, 1937).

no corner of the land was untouched by tax laws and revenue officers. 'Dependent upon a complex system of measurement and bookkeeping, organized as a rigorous hierarchy based on experience and ability, and subject to strict discipline from its central office, the English excise more closely approximated to Max Weber's idea of bureaucracy than any other government agency in eighteenth-century Europe.'[8]

In Brewer's view, there is no question that the excise was especially important in providing the lavish resources that enabled Britain's central state to project its power more widely and successfully than its main competitor, 'absolutist' France.[9] Yet Brewer recognized that this argument should not be pushed too far, which was in any case restricted to England alone. Notably, his study concluded with the end of the American War, just when efforts at major reform of Britain's fiscal regime were renewed, efforts that went further than anything attempted since the 1690s.[10] A background cause was Britain's attempts to introduce the stamp and Townshend duties into America in the 1760s, attempts which had spectacularly failed, categorically exposing some of the limits of Britain's fiscal state.[11] Those failures came home to roost in a number of ways, including that in the 1780s the ministries of Shelburne and Pitt grappled with a dramatic surge of smuggling in British waters that had been fuelled by increased duties needed to fund a failed war effort (1775–83). There were, moreover, long-standing anxieties that the national debt was unsustainably large, anxieties Adam Smith unequivocally endorsed in 1776. Finally, in 1780 Burke and others launched the movement for 'economical reform', one of the many aims of which was to end sinecures

---

Important studies that developed Brewer's framework include: Lawrence Stone, ed., *An imperial state at war: Britain from 1688 to 1815* (1994); Miles Ogborn, *Spaces of modernity: London's geographies, 1680–1780* (New York, 1998), ch. 5; John Brewer and Eckhard Hellmuth, eds., *Rethinking Leviathan: the eighteenth-century state in Britain and Germany* (Oxford, 1999); and William J. Ashworth, *Customs and excise: trade, production, and consumption in England, 1640–1845* (Oxford, 2003).

[8] Brewer, *Sinews of power*, p. 68.

[9] This was a comparison which had been tellingly considered by Peter Mathias and Patrick O'Brien, 'Taxation in England and France, 1715–1810: a comparison of the social and economic incidence of taxes collected for central governments', *Journal of European Economic History*, 5.3 (1976), pp. 601–50.

[10] J. E. D. Binney, *British public finance and administration, 1774–1792* (Oxford, 1958). For an excellent overview of the reforms begun in the 1780s, with citations to much of the historiography, see Joanna Innes and Arthur Burns, 'Introduction', to Joanna Innes and Arthur Burns, eds. *Rethinking the age of reform: Britain, 1780–1850* (Cambridge, 2003), pp. 1–70. Not that these were the first reforms. Some efforts had been made by Walpole in the 1720s and early 1730s, followed by Pelham in the decade or so before his death in 1754.

[11] Tax resistance was not unknown in Britain, with strong opposition to the malt tax in Scotland in 1725, the excise scheme in 1733, and the cider tax in south-west England in 1763.

within the upper echelons of the revenue services. In short, contemporaries were often less sanguine about Britain's fiscal-military state than modern historians.

Such contemporary anxieties inform the perspective of this chapter, though they are initially approached by noting that existing interpretations focus heavily on England and usually treat it homogenously.[12] What, for example, is to be made of the view of one English MP who, having poured over some official statistics, exclaimed in the Commons in 1790 that they

contained the most extraordinary entries which he had ever read. His surprise was excited by observing the small return of Excise duties of Scotland. He had always understood, that in England the Excise was the best collected system of taxes in the country, and in Scotland, from what he had read … he feared it was the worst. … Surely there must be a neglect somewhere, or such a return could not have been made.[13]

Though such views reek of Scotophobia, this MP believed that British statutory taxation was implemented more vigorously in some parts than others. This was not a new or isolated view. In the late seventeenth century John Houghton and Charles Davenant both puzzled over issues of regional tax incidence. At the end of the eighteenth century Pitt the younger did the same. And there were others in between. Crucially, many of these efforts rested on producing figures, providing the key sources on which this chapter rests. Yet while such data were 'official' in nature, they provide only occasional snapshots and were not compiled on a consistent basis. Nor did most of the figures enter the public domain: the key sources used in this chapter are archival. Questions of tax incidence sometimes became central to wider political debate, famously in the American crisis, but often they were addressed much more privately.

As has already been seen in Chapter 4, there were certainly a number of important differences between England and Scotland regarding the volume and types of economic legislation. What the rest of this chapter does is to explore whether national and regional differences can also be found with regard to the impact of statutory taxation. John Brewer rightly noted that such legislation was national in conception and application.[14]

[12] This is acknowledged by Brewer, *Sinews of power*, pp. 22–3 and O'Brien, 'Political economy', p. 3. In studies of quite another topic O'Brien has attended to composite state considerations: Trevor Griffiths, Philip Hunt, and Patrick O'Brien, 'Scottish, Irish, and imperial connections: Parliament, the three kingdoms, and the mechanization of cotton spinning in eighteenth-century Britain', *Economic History Review*, 61.3 (2008), pp. 625–50.

[13] *Parliamentary Register* (1790), pp. 466–7 (19 April 1790).

[14] 'England's tax system was not only exceptionally centralized, it was also uniform in its legal incidence. No English county or region enjoyed special fiscal privileges. Though

But as will be seen, levels of exaction varied considerably from one part of Britain to another. Where government raised taxes from sheds a different light on the huge volume of public finance legislation. Consequently this chapter explores national and regional patterns of revenue raised, focusing largely on the excise and customs. By exploring the geography of exaction, a richer picture emerges of a key corner of Britain's political economies.

This chapter is in four main parts. The first and second are mainly descriptive, setting out regional patterns of gross revenue collection and where that money went before remittance to the Exchequer in London. The third and longest part considers the main causes of the patterns uncovered. Finally, the implications for our view of the British fiscal-military state and Britain's political economies are considered.

The Political Geography of Taxation

What follows sets out where revenue was raised within Britain's regions and nations. In doing so four key features must be borne in mind. Firstly, that what revenue officers collected always exceeded what the Exchequer received in London – a position often masked because contemporary accounting practices inadequately separated the income and the expenditure sides of public accounts. Gross receipts were liable not only to administration charges, but other costs before money was passed on to London. Such spending, which could be very considerable, is not immediately apparent in the standard sources used; this chapter will bring it fully into the light. Secondly, while it is fairly unproblematic to seek to distinguish national shares of the British whole, adopting a regional approach is much more difficult. In what follows Scotland and Wales (including Monmouthshire) are usually treated as regions in their own right with England divided into six regions, see Map 9.1.[15] But these distinctions are often only approximate because the underlying sources were differently arranged.[16] Thirdly, because the concern is with shares

there were regional disparities in the payment of the land tax ... indirect taxes ... which together were fiscally far more important, were levied at the same *national* rates.' Brewer, *Sinews of power*, p. 129.

[15] The regions are those used in Peter Clark, ed., *The Cambridge urban history of Britain: vol. 2, 1540–1840* (Cambridge, 2000). These are London, Wales, and Scotland, and for the rest of England: the North (Cheshire, Cumberland, Durham, Lancs, Northumberland, Yorks, Westmorland); Midlands (Derbs, Herefordshire, Leics, Lincs, Northants, Notts, Rutland, Shrops, Staffs, Warwickshire, Worcs); East Anglia (Cambs, Hunts, Norfolk, Suffolk); South East (Beds, Berks, Bucks, Essex, Hants, Herts, Kent, Middx, Oxon, Surrey, Sussex); and South West (Cornwall, Devon, Dorset, Glos, Soms, Wilts).

[16] Pitt the younger was warned that the boundaries of excise 'collections have no relation to the boundaries of counties; therefore no account can be rendered distinguishing the amount in each county.' TNA, PRO 30/8/288, f. 18.

Map 9.1 Map of the regions used in analyzing the geography of taxation in eighteenth-century Britain

at given moments, what follows makes no adjustments for price changes. Finally, because nations and regions varied in size, population estimates have sometimes been used to allow per capita comparisons. Such estimates are fairly good for England but rather mixed for Scotland and Wales.[17] Consequently, the figures produced are likely to be approximately rather than precisely correct.

It is best to begin with the excise given its importance within current depictions of the 'fiscal-military state'. This type of taxation began life in the 1640s and through the eighteenth century was the most important source of central government taxation. It was a tax mainly collected at point of production on commodities such as beer, candles, and soap, but which also came to include some services, such as auctions, and some imported goods, notably tea, tobacco, and spirits. Four reports have been found from across the period that allow regional levels of collection in England and Wales to be analyzed, while good figures for Scotland are available from 1707 to 1800 (see Table 9.1).

Despite the caveats, these statistics reveal huge differences that changed relatively little across the period. London's importance is very apparent, but even more so when added to south-east England, together providing 47 per cent of the excise collected in 1685 and consistently more than 50 per cent thereafter. At the other extreme, amounts collected in both Scotland and Wales were under a half of even the least productive of England's regions as late as 1796. In the years immediately after the Union of 1707 Scotland provided only 3 per cent of the gross excise collected in Britain; by the late 1790s this had risen to 7 per cent, still well short of its 16 per cent share of the island's population.

This regional approach can also be applied to the collection of the land tax, for which convenient figures are available for 1744 (regional patterns hardly changed in the eighteenth century). Crucial developments to the land tax had been made in the 1690s, the assessments made then remaining unchanged through the rest of the eighteenth century despite

---

[17] E. A. Wrigley, 'Rickman revisited: the population growth rates of English counties in the early modern period', *Economic History Review*, 62.3 (2009), p. 721; E. A. Wrigley, 'English county populations in the later eighteenth century', *Economic History Review*, 60.1 (2007), pp. 54–5; Phyllis Deane and W. A. Cole, *British economic growth, 1688–1959: trends and structures*, (2nd edn., Cambridge, 1969), p. 103; Leonard Schwartz, 'London 1700–1840', in Clark, ed., *Cambridge urban history*, p. 650; Vanessa Harding, 'The population of early modern London: a review of the published evidence', *London Journal*, 15.2 (1990), pp. 111–28; Mitchell, *British historical statistics*, pp. 8–9; R. A. Houston, *The population history of Britain and Ireland, 1500–1750* (Basingstoke, 1992), pp. 29–30; John Williams, *Digest of Welsh historical statistics* (2 vols., Cardiff, 1985), vol. 1, p. 6.

Table 9.1 *Per capita regional gross excise collected, selected years 1685–1796 – in £ by rank order 1783*

	1685	1741	1783	1796	% increase
					1741–96
London	1.10	1.41	2.86	4.15	194
South East	0.39	0.53	0.99	1.19	125
East Anglia	0.37	0.37	0.72	0.91	146
North	0.28	0.21	0.61	1.01	381
South West	0.22	0.28	0.58	0.76	161
Midlands	0.26	0.28	0.57	0.73	163
Wales	0.17	0.12	0.20	0.24	100
Scotland	n.a.	0.06	0.20	0.36	500

Note: Annual averages are used for 1684–6 and 1782–4.
Sources: For the excise BL Harleian Mss 4227; Sandon Hall, Harrowby Trust Mss 525; TNA PRO 30/8/288 ff. 18 and 56; NAS, E554/3. For population, see note 17

the fact, well known at the time, that some areas were more heavily taxed than others, south-east England particularly, while Scotland's land tax was capped at a low level at the Union – see Table 9.2.[18]

Whereas the excise and land tax were collected across Britain, customs could only be collected at certain designated ports, rendering a regional analysis less meaningful. Notably, in the scheme being used the midlands region had only one coastal county, Lincolnshire, and only one customs port, Boston.[19] Consequently per capita figures are not used in Table 9.3, though the findings are so clear that this is no hardship.

London's importance to gross customs receipts was even greater than that for the excise, and out of all proportion to its share of Britain's population (about 8–9 per cent through the period) and shipping (24 per cent in 1775).[20] Necessarily this meant that the contributions from elsewhere were relatively small, notably so in the case of Wales, but also of East Anglia and Scotland. In fact, only seven ports provided 1 per cent or more of the total customs receipts in this period, but together they accounted for about 90 per cent of the total (Table 9.4).

---

[18] Beckett, 'Land tax or excise'; Colin Brooks, 'Public finance and political stability: the administration of the land tax, 1688–1720', *Historical Journal*, 17.2 (1974), pp. 281–300.
[19] In fact, Bristol and Hull were important ports for the midlands region through the period and Liverpool became so.
[20] Ralph Davis, *The rise of the English shipping industry in the seventeenth and eighteenth centuries* (Newton Abbot, 1972), p. 27.

Table 9.2 *Regional distribution of land tax assessments, 1744 – rank order by per capita, £*

	Per capita	% share absolute total	% national per capita
South East	0.49	34	219
East Anglia	0.36	10	160
Midlands	0.25	17	112
London	0.25	9	110
South West	0.25	17	103
North	0.10	8	44
Wales	0.10	3	37
Scotland	0.03	2	16

Source: Anon., *Land tax at 4s in ye pound paid by England & Wales in 1702, & 1744, proportion'd and compar'd by 513 parts, according to ye no. of Members of Parliament, and ye square miles in each county* (1745); BL, Harleian 4226, ff. 15–16; for population see note 17

Table 9.3 *Gross customs receipts, by region, 1710–1780 – percentage share at given dates, rank order 1780*

	1710	1750	1780	Change 1710–80
London	80.3	67.2	68.2	−12.1
North	4.8	15.4	10.5	5.7
South West	11.7	9.6	9.1	−2.6
South East	0.9	2.6	5.1	4.2
Scotland	1.5	2.9	3.6	2.1
East Anglia	0.6	2.0	3.1	2.5
Wales	0.2	0.1	0.2	0.0
Midlands	0.0	0.2	0.1	0.1
	100.0	100.0	100.0	

Note: figures are of money receipts, ignoring payment by bonds for mainly duty-neutral re-exports.

Source: England and Wales, BL Add Mss 8133A, Musgrave papers, 'The gross and neat produce of the revenue of customs at the several ports in England and Wales, 'ranged alphabetically in two parts. Part I. The account stated annually from the year 1778. Part II. The account taken every tenth year from the year 1700' [c. 1788]. Scottish figures have kindly been provided by Dr Philip Rössner.

Table 9.4 *Gross customs receipts of ports producing 1 per cent or more of the total, 1710–1780 – percentage share of total, rank order*

	Total collected, £	% share
London	19,382,315	71
Bristol	1,874,447	7
Liverpool	1,253,126	5
Whitehaven	829,824	3
Glasgow	479,543	2
Hull	461,394	2
King's Lynn	271,883	1

Source: as for Table 9.3.

Many ports provided little revenue. For the eight years studied, in England and Wales eleven ports produced under £5,000 and fifty-one of the seventy-eight ports under £50,000.[21] Seventeen of England and Wales' seventy-two customs ports produced no net revenue, with management charges exceeding gross receipts. Such a skewed distribution was not static, but it is worth noting from Table 9.3 that London's share was higher in 1780 than in 1750 (receipts at Whitehaven were in sharp structural decline from 1750, and those at Bristol, Glasgow, and Liverpool had been more severely affected by the American War).

Two clear points have emerged from this evidence of the relative burdens of the excise, land tax, and customs: of the enormous amounts collected across the period in London specifically and the south-east more generally; and secondly of the consistently small amounts collected from Scotland and Wales, and occasionally from some of England's regions. It is helpful to highlight aspects of these two main findings a little.

In the middle of the eighteenth century London's share of Britain's tax take was 33 per cent of the excise and 67 per cent of the customs. Given that the collection of the excise was more evenly spread, one might have expected London's share to decline across the century as the early industrial revolution took hold in other parts of the island, even if Hammond's 1925 statement that the industrial revolution 'was like a storm that passed over London and broke elsewhere' is no longer tenable.[22] Yet that plainly did not happen as Table 9.5 shows.

[21] The eleven ports were Cardigan (£276), Cardiff, Aberdovey, Carlisle, Ilfracombe, Gweek, Padstow, Llanelli, Arundel, Aldeburgh, and Looe (£4,661). Over this period, 76 per cent of gross customs collected in Scotland was at Glasgow (56 per cent) and Leith (20 per cent). The source is as for Table 9.3.

[22] J. L. Hammond, 'Eighteenth-century London', *New Statesman*, 24.621 (21 March 1925), p. 693.

Table 9.5 *Per capita gross excise receipts, 1685–1796 – as a percentage of London, by rank order 1796*

	1685	1796	Change
London	100	100	
South East	35	29	−6
North	25	24	−1
East Anglia	34	22	−12
South West	20	18	−2
Midlands	23	18	−6
Scotland	n.a.	9	certainly +ve
Wales	15	6	−10

Source: as for Table 9.1.

A key feature of London's contribution to Britain's fiscal state in this period is that it was always very large, out of all proportion to its population, and remained so, excises collected there growing faster from a much higher base than other parts of England and Wales. Only Scotland closed the gap on it in the eighteenth century, but from paltry levels and to a small degree.

No concerted study exists of Scotland's contribution to the British fiscal state for the century after the parliamentary Union of 1707.[23] In the Union negotiations the national debt was held to be English and Welsh only, despite the fact that it had been contracted to fund a foreign policy formally conducted by a crown under the regnal Union of 1603. Moreover, it was generally recognized that the population and economy of England and Wales was much larger and more productive than Scotland's. Similarly, England and Wales were known to be more heavily taxed. Political arithmetic was employed to help settle public finance arrangements under the Union, with figures produced of the revenues of the two fiscal systems immediately before 1707. The absolute differences in amounts raised in England and Wales on the one hand and Scotland on the other hand were recognized by both sets of negotiators and addressed by some of the terms of the Union.[24]

At the Union a single framework of common customs duties, allowances, bounties, and drawbacks was applied to the overseas trade of all

[23] There is a lot of useful information in Ian Donnachie, *A history of the brewing industry in Scotland* (Edinburgh, 1979).

[24] Aided by the tercentenary there is a very large literature on the Union negotiations. Two excellent overviews are Clare Jackson, 'Union historiographies', in T. M. Devine and Jenny Wormald, eds., *The Oxford handbook of modern Scottish history* (Oxford,

parts of Britain, though full union of the customs systems did not take place until the nineteenth century. Something similar happened with the excise, save that some existing duties were excluded or particular provisions made, at least for a while, notably in the case of malt and salt. The thrust of this was that Scotland was not immediately expected to have to pay the excise at English and Welsh rates on all commodities. A period of adjustment of about seven years was expected, while gradually new British duties would be introduced that would lead to further fiscal convergence across the island. Thirdly, Scotland's contribution to the land tax was fixed at £48,000, and could rise only in proportion to the growth of the land tax in England and Wales above its current figure. It is notable that fixing the ratio in this way was only done with regard to the land tax and not to customs and excise; otherwise the assumption surely was that gradually Scottish customs and excise rates would converge with those in England and Wales. Finally, as is well known, Scotland received compensation, the so-called Equivalent, to cover the costs of the national debts of south Britain, the adjustment of the Scottish coinage, and losses in the failed Darien scheme which had consumed so much of Scotland's liquid capital.[25]

From the statistics already provided it is clear that taxes collected in Scotland were very low compared to England and that if the gap narrowed, especially after 1775, it remained substantial in 1800. Table 9.6 summarizes the position.

Given such figures, it is hardly surprising that in 1799 Pitt the younger put Scotland's share of British national income at just 4 per cent, which was exactly its share of the income tax in the following year.[26] Still, as has been seen, the contribution of Wales to British public revenues was even smaller in the eighteenth century, though unlike Scotland it had far fewer immediate calls on what little money was raised there.

2012), pp. 338–54 and Bob Harris, 'The Anglo–Scottish treaty of Union, 1707 in 2007: defending the Revolution, defeating the Jacobites', *Journal of British Studies*, 49.1 (2010), pp. 28–46. On the financial aspects particularly, see Douglas Watt, *The price of Scotland: Darien, Union and the wealth of nations* (Edinburgh, 2007) and William Peter Deringer, 'Calculated values: the politics and epistemology of economic numbers in Britain, 1688–1738' (Princeton University PhD thesis, 2012), ch. 2. Scotland's fiscal state before the Union 'was fragile, limited, and increasingly unable to guarantee its own security', with revenues being farmed until 1707. Laura A. M. Stewart, 'The "rise" of the state', in Devine and Wormald, eds., *Modern Scottish history*, p. 233.

25 A so-called rising equivalent was intended to keep in Scotland any increases in revenue above those calculated in 1706. In practice this was impossible to administer and was formally abandoned in 1720 by 5 George I, c. 20.

26 George Rose, *A brief examination into the increase of the revenue, commerce, and manufactures of Great Britain from 1792 to 1799* (5th edn., 1799), Appendix 7; TNA, CUST17/21.

Table 9.6 *Scottish per capita gross revenue receipts, 1708–1800 – as a percentage of England and Wales*

	Excise	Customs
1708	13	11
1755	14	15
1800	42	38

Note: English customs data is for 1710 and 1750.
Sources: Excise: CUST145/4–13 (online from the European State Finance Database, www.esfdb.org); NAS E554/3. Customs: Philip Rössner, personal communication; TNA CUST17/21; BL Add Mss 8133A, Musgrave papers. Population: see note 17.

From Gross Receipts to Exchequer Receipts

Exploring the amounts of tax collected gives a good sense of the actual burdens on society of the British fiscal state. But not all gross receipts were passed on to the Exchequer in London: everywhere money was spent on management charges, bounties, drawbacks, allowances, and pensions, and in Scotland also on the equivalent, civil government, and the central kirk. Because of accounting conventions at the time, this is spending which most studies of the British fiscal state have ignored, but whose consideration helps to bring out some new features of its priorities and dynamics. The evidence is a little patchy, but nonetheless very clear (Table 9.7).

As Table 9.7 shows, the English and Welsh excise had the least immediate charges placed on gross revenue, with net receipts very nearly 90 per cent.[27] But the Scottish excise was very different, with management costs more than double those of England and Wales and significant other sums being spent within Scotland. Between 1707 and 1800 some £3.21 million of Scottish excise receipts were spent on civil government and the kirk there, £0.65 million on the equivalent, and £0.43 million on fish bounties, or together more than 24 per cent of gross receipts.[28]

Just as patterns of collecting customs revenue were very different to the excise, so in the main were the immediate charges on gross receipts. Customs management charges in England and Wales were very slightly lower than its excise service – qualifying some of the usual arguments about the relative efficiency of the excise – but were very much higher in

[27] TNA, CUST145/4–14.
[28] NAS, E554/3.

Table 9.7 *Spending from gross tax receipts before remittance to London,*
1684–1800 – as percentage of gross

	Management	Other	Total
Excise			
England and Wales, 1684–1787	7	3	10
Scotland, 1708–1800	18	33	51
Customs			
England and Wales, 1710–80	7	38	45
Scotland, 1707–48	38	58	96
Scotland, 1788	19	49	68
Scotland, 1800	10	31	41
England and Wales, 1800	5	20	25

Sources: as for Table 9.6; Clements Library, Shelburne Mss, vol. 109, f. 57; 'A state of the
general account of the customs ... for the year ending 5th of January 1789', in Lambert,
Sessional papers, vol. 66, p. 299.

Scotland, and if on a sharp downward path after mid-century were still
much higher in 1800.

Across Britain, a lot of gross customs revenue was spent on other
items, almost wholly on drawbacks and bounties. Unfortunately for
England and Wales, the source does not distinguish between them, and
to include drawbacks, which repaid import duties on foreign goods when
they were re-exported, is rather distracting given they were often duty-
neutral – though they were important in other ways. Fortunately, another
source provides statistics on bounties only (for 1710–60), which were
just more than 4 per cent of gross customs receipts in England and Wales
and drawbacks nearly 37 per cent.[29] Given the nature of drawbacks, it
might be better to say that bounties were nearly 9 per cent of gross customs minus drawbacks in those years. In Scotland between 1707 and
1748 drawbacks accounted for 33 per cent of gross customs receipts and
bounties 16 per cent (or 23 per cent of receipts excluding drawbacks).
Relatively, in the first half of the century bounties were at least two and a
half times as costly in Scotland as in England and Wales for this period,
and arguably as much as four times as costly. These gaps had almost
completely disappeared by 1800: bounties in Scotland were 11 per cent
of gross customs revenue and 9 per cent in England and Wales, while
across Britain drawbacks were now much less important.[30]

[29] Data on bounties are in the Clements Library, Townshend papers, 8/21/8.
[30] TNA, CUST17/21.

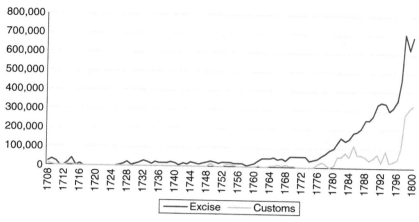

Figure 9.1 Scottish customs and excise remittances to London, 1708–1800 (£).
Source: see note 31

As has become clear, public finances were raised and spent in England and Wales very differently to Scotland. This was especially so regarding levels of remittances to London. Put most simply, between 1708 and 1800 Scotland provided less than 2 per cent of the total customs and excise receipts at the Exchequer in London, though as Figure 9.1 suggests almost all of this came in the last twenty years of the century.[31] For most of the eighteenth century, Scottish public revenues, which were in any case very low on a per capita basis, were mainly spent there, with pretty small amounts being remitted to London.

Understanding the Geography of the British Fiscal State

So far, attention has been focused on describing some of the general patterns of raising public revenue and the immediate purposes to which it was put. Some attempts have been made to put the numbers in context, particularly regarding population size, but the numbers have been rather taken on trust. It is time to qualify and explain them.

A convenient way to introduce the issues is to turn to Scottish replies to the English MP's 1790 complaint noted earlier (p. 280) about collecting

---

[31] Clements Library, Shelburne papers, vol. 109, f. 57 and Townshend papers, 8/21/8; NAS, E554/3; David Macpherson, *Annals of commerce* (4 vols., 1802), vols. 3–4, passim; Mitchell, *British historical statistics*, pp. 575–9.

the excise in Scotland. Unsurprisingly, the Excise Board in Edinburgh immediately and vigorously refuted his views. They pointed out that there had been an eight-fold rise in the excise collected in Scotland since 1708 (and that he had used net, not gross figures), that many goods bought in Scotland came from England, such that 'the Duties on which ... tho' put to the credit of the English Revenue, yet in fact are paid by the Inhabitants of Scotland', and that Scotland's population was under a third that of England's and her exports just one-seventeenth. So considering the 'disproportion betwixt the opulence & consumption of the two countries, it will appear that the amount of the Scotch excise is by no means short of the full proportion it ought to yield'. In their eyes, one proof of this was that their efforts had generated 'not a little odium' in Scotland, leading to 'complaints of too great rigor & severity ... not only by Traders ... but some times from the landed interest, & particularly of Incorporated bodies in Scotland'.[32] Simultaneously another Scot, a well-connected merchant, argued similarly that 'every tax is levied regularly, and full as strictly as in England, by careful, attentive boards and officers.' In this view, the problem was that England had not tailored its funding system to Scotland's distinctive environment and economy: English politicians 'have not been good œconomists, nor lenient masters'.[33]

To the Scottish Excise Board, their administration was as strong as anywhere, but the Scottish economy certainly was not and was also naturally difficult to collect taxes from. Even this was arguably an incomplete assessment. Schematically six fundamental and interlinked factors effect levels of revenue, both over time and between regions: which economic activities were or were not subject to duties; the extent to which such activities were within the view of the state by being marketed rather than household based; the levels of economic activity subject to duties; differences in the cost-effectiveness of collecting revenue because of the natural environment and the distribution of taxpayers; the efficiency of the revenue administration; and levels of fraud and smuggling.

---

[32] NAS, CE8/3, ff. 87–92. A similar analysis from about 1800 noted Scotland's relatively low population, poorer climate, and scarcity of money – i.e., lower level of economic activity. National Library of Scotland (NLS), Melville papers, MS640, ff. 147–8.

[33] Anon., *Considerations on the Union between England and Scotland, and on some commercial matters in both kingdoms* (1790), pp. 66–7, 6. This was by a merchant and member of Edinburgh Chamber of Commerce, probably therefore George Chalmers, who was active on behalf of it and others on such matters about then. See Edinburgh City Archives, Edinburgh Chamber of Commerce minute book, ED005/1, ff. 60, 172–5. He appears not to be the George Chalmers who authored *An estimate of the comparative strength of Great Britain during the present and four preceding reigns* (1782). Sir John Sinclair also argued that taxes were well collected in Scotland by 1800 in *The history of the public revenue of the British empire* (3rd edn., 3 vols., 1805), vol. 3, p. 143.

Table 9.8 *Main sources of London's gross excise revenue, 1741 and 1796 – % share raised by five most lucrative duties*

1741 (18 categories)		1796 (28 categories)	
Beer	25	Tea*	24
Tea*	20	Foreign spirits*	20
Imported liquors*	14	Beer	19
Low wines	13	Wine*	11
Soap	10	Tobacco and snuff*	9
Sub-total	82	Sub-total	83

Note: * are imported goods
Sources: Sandon Hall, Harrowby Trust Mss 525, f. 22; TNA, PRO 30/8/288, f. 56

Obviously a key factor of the geography of revenue collection was deter-mining the commodities on which the customs and excise should fall. Most importantly, the thirty-five years after the Glorious Revolution saw most duties on exported goods removed to try to improve Britain's balance of payments and manufacturing base.[34] Consequently, the enormous growth through much of the eighteenth century of manufactured exports from the midlands and north had a trivial direct effect on revenues. Similarly important was the extension of the excise from its almost complete focus on beer, ale, and malt in the seventeenth century to a range of other manu-factured products, to some services, and to imported commodities. If the intent of some of these developments was clearly to try to collect more revenue outside of the greater London region, the growing importance of the excise on imported commodities in the second half of the eighteenth century was a major countervailing change. The growth of excise duties on imported tobacco, tea, and wine led to greater amounts of excise being paid at the ports, London especially, as Table 9.8 shows.

Moreover, it was all very well for Glasgow to have driven a huge trade in re-exported tobacco, as it certainly did, but in revenue terms this was fairly unproductive. Scotland's smokers were fiscally much less signifi-cant than those supplied by London's tobacco merchants.[35]

London's strong showing in excise collection was partly, therefore, a consequence of the great size and continuing vitality of its market

[34] N. A. Brisco, *The economic policy of Robert Walpole* (New York, 1907), chs. 2–4.
[35] Philipp Robinson Rössner, *Scottish trade in the wake of the Union (1700–1760): the rise of a warehouse economy* (Stuttgart, 2008). In 1796 the excise on tobacco produced gross receipts of £49,011 in Scotland and £286,601 in London. NAS, E554/3; TNA, PRO 30/8/288, f. 56. That is, 14 per cent of the British total was collected in Scotland.

economy, but it was also a consequence of important political decisions about what to tax and how, especially excising some imported goods (tea, tobacco, foreign spirits, and cocoa). For example, tea duties could have been charged to the customs, but they came under the excise. Tea could have been imported by anyone, but in fact was a monopoly of the London-based East India Company. Thus 99 per cent of British tea excise was collected in London, but in the late eighteenth century the capital had only 7 per cent of Britain's 53,000 licensed tea dealers.[36] Such decisions favoured revenue collection in the capital, with inevitable consequences for the apparent productivity of revenue collection elsewhere. Not, as will become clear in the next section, that taxation policies did not seek to increase revenues from other parts of Britain.

In framing tax policies, administrators and politicians were dealing with a moving target, an economy evolving more profoundly than at any point since the changes wrought by the Black Death in the fourteenth century. It was bound to be difficult for them to keep up. Moreover, aspects of economic change were profound yet very subtle, especially the shift of economic activity from the household to the market and, hence, potentially within the reach of the state. For example, Mathias estimated that in the 1710s home brewing, none of which was exciseable, may have accounted for 50 per cent of total English beer output, and was still 40 per cent by the 1780s.[37] That meant that even if levels of overall production and duties were static between those dates, that shift alone would have raised excise receipts on beer by up to 20 per cent. How far there was a shift in economic activity from the household to the market is, therefore, an important consideration for a few products (beer, soap, and candles especially).[38] Generally domestic production was much less common in towns than the countryside, helping to explain London's importance to excise receipts. Consequently, increasing urbanization provides a rough proxy for the decline of household production. In this regard, however, it is notable that many Scottish towns grew rapidly in the period, with the proportion of Scotland's population living in towns of 5,000 or more rising from 8 per cent in 1691 to 27 per cent in 1801, compared to figures for England of about 17 per cent in 1700 and 28 per cent in 1801. Clearly levels of urbanization in 1801 were very similar in north and south Britain, with Edinburgh and Glasgow Britain's fourth

---

[36] Hoh-Cheung Mui and Lorna H. Mui, *Shops and shopkeeping in eighteenth-century England* (Kingston, Montreal, 1989), pp. 301–3.
[37] Peter Mathias, *The brewing industry in England, 1700–1830* (Cambridge, 1959), p. 377.
[38] Fine, 'Production and excise', pp. 165–6.

and fifth largest cities.[39] This must have helped excise receipts to rise as a whole, but obviously other factors must explain why amounts collected in Scotland were so much lower even in 1800.

If urbanization in Scotland was probably associated with the growing relative importance of the market economy, and hence of potential revenue collection, it must also have aided collection, with a lower proportion of the population coming to live beyond the great glen where the natural terrain and low population density made the cost-effectiveness of collection questionable. Such natural difficulties surely help to explain some of the patterns set out earlier. As Davenant noted in the late seventeenth century, parts of the English north and west were 'so wild, and the houses lie so dispersed, that the retailers cannot be so well watched as in the home counties, where the dealers are in a narrower compass, and have less opportunities to deceive the king's officers'. He also noted, however, that in and about London people bought their beer in the capital which 'swells the excise of the home counties'.[40] If that was true of parts of England and Wales, then such a situation was felt even more keenly in significant parts of Scotland: as Lord Kames put it, 'in a country thinly populated ... the expence of collecting makes too great a proportion of the sums collected'.[41] Even in the late eighteenth century, the Excise Board in Edinburgh thought that 'the remote situation and uncultivated state' of parts of Scotland rendered it uneconomic for revenue officers to be based there. Year after year they proposed that the collection of duties there be contracted out.[42] Such calls fell on deaf ears, in part presumably because revenue officers served other purposes, especially as positions of patronage, as agents for other elements of economic regulation (such as the ban on the export of wool), and as figures of authority more generally (such as checks to Jacobitism). It is worth recalling, after all, that in many

---

[39] Ian D. Whyte, 'Urbanization in eighteenth-century Scotland', in T. M. Devine and J. R. Young, eds., *Eighteenth-century Scotland: new perspectives* (East Lothian, 1999), pp. 178–9; E. A. Wrigley, *People, cities and wealth: the transformation of traditional society* (Oxford, 1987), p. 162; Joyce Ellis, 'Regional and county centres, 1700–1840', in Clark, ed., *Cambridge urban history*, p. 679.

[40] Joan Thirsk and J. P. Cooper, eds., *Seventeenth-century economic documents* (Oxford, 1972), p. 806. Charles Davenant, who served in the excise then, likely had a hand in producing the data on excise by English and Welsh collections in the 1670s and 1680s used earlier. He reflected on the question in BL Harleian Mss 5120, f. 9r and later showed an interest in the regional incidence of taxation in *An essay upon ways and means* (1695).

[41] Henry Homes, Lord Kames, *Sketches of the history of man*, ed. James A. Harris (3 vols., Indianapolis, IN, 2006), vol. 2, p. 445.

[42] NAS, CE8/1, f. 27. From at least 1780 the Board produced an annual report for the Treasury in London, recommending improvements to the excise laws.

Table 9.9 *Excise officers, territories, and population size in mid-eighteenth-century Britain*

	Officers	Acres per officer	Population per officer
England	3,299	9,860	1,755
Scotland	444	42,938	2,770
Wales	194	24,290	2,268

Note: numbers of officers is for 1741 for England and Wales, and 1743 for Scotland. Acreages in millions: England 32.5, Scotland 19.1, Wales 4.7. Population in millions taken to be: England 5.79, Scotland 1.23, Wales 0.44.
Sources: Sandon Hall, Harrowby Trust Mss 525, ff. 1–50; NAS, GD1/54/10; population as for note 17.

English and Welsh ports customs receipts fell well short of management charges.[43]

Some places were simply too poor and too inaccessible to warrant a lot of effort to collect revenue, regions that were especially common in Scotland and Wales. Consequently, England was much more closely scrutinized by revenue officers, as a snapshot of the excise from the 1740s in Table 9.9 shows.

The key measure in Table 9.9 is of population per officer, where the differences between the three nations, while significant, were much less than those found earlier of the amounts of revenue raised: in 1741 gross excise per capita was £0.44 in England, £0.06 in Scotland, and £0.12 in Wales. Different 'densities' of revenue officers can only partly explain geographical variations in the amounts collected that were detailed earlier.

Rising numbers of productive revenue officers were a major development of the eighteenth-century British fiscal state. There were 2,525 excise officers in 1708 and 7,500 in 1797, with the average gross amount collected per officer increasing from £678 to £1,625.[44] Costs of collection shrank everywhere, but especially in Scotland from around mid-century, bringing them much closer to levels in England and Wales. How far such developments were due to administrative rearrangements on the one hand, and on the other to scale economies

---

[43] This was probably true in many Scottish ports also, though figures have not yet been found to settle the matter.

[44] Numbers of officers are from: Brewer, *Sinews of power*, p. 66; Norman Chester, *The English administrative system, 1780–1870* (Oxford, 1981), p. 167; TNA, T45/1, T45/4/9B. Rates of increase were slightly faster in Scotland than in England and Wales.

generated by the exogenous growth of the revenue base, is impossible to say with certainty. But the latter certainly needs more weight than it has tended to receive. Britain's growing and urbanizing economy provided an increasingly easy target for tax gatherers. Yet countervailing forces were sometimes at work, making it hard to collect all the revenues that were due. Indeed, smuggling and fraud were inherent and inescapable features of Britain's fiscal state at the time, albeit ones that waxed and waned.

When all is said and done, smuggling is a business, usually depending on getting goods and services to consumers more cheaply than those paying duties – called 'fair traders' at the time. If that cannot be done, the business will fold. Smugglers might be motivated by anti-authoritarian sentiments (such as Jacobites or so-called social criminals), but unless the business pays, such sentiments are unlikely to count for much.[45] Moreover, if avoiding duties gives smugglers a competitive advantage, this involves distinctive costs and risks. Resources had to be spent and trading restricted to avoid detection, seizure of goods, personal capture, and punishment. Goods had to be found to fill holds on return voyages, both to maximize shipping resources and to provide vital ballast. Obviously, such costs and risks are only worth it if the duties are high enough (relative to what consumers have to pay). In fact, because of the government's pressing need for money to wage frequent wars in the eighteenth century and its heavy dependence on indirect taxes, pressures to create high duties were often hard for it to resist. In 1790, a member of the central excise office in Edinburgh undertook a thorough-going critique of what he saw as a self-defeating system of 'over-taxing'.[46]

Revenue defrauders operated under similar conditions to smugglers, but the drawbacks and bounties introduced in the century or so after 1660 as part of the mercantile system created distinctive opportunities for illicit activity. Goods might be landed (or re-landed) secretly so as to be able to claim such incentives more than once on the same shipment. Various frauds were resorted to in an attempt to diminish duties, such as inaccurate manifests, adulteration, and false weighing. Differences in duties and administration for spirits produced in England and Scotland even created

---

[45] For a good introduction to the scholarly literature on the topic for eighteenth-century Britain see Paul Monod, 'Dangerous merchandise: smuggling, Jacobitism, and commercial culture in southeast England, 1690–1760', *Journal of British Studies*, 30.2 (1991), pp. 150–82. The major study is Paul Muskett, 'English smuggling in the eighteenth century' (Open University PhD thesis, 1997).

[46] Hamilton, *Principles of taxation*.

the conditions for internal smuggling.[47] English manufacturers more generally doubted that their Scottish brethren were being fully taxed.[48]

It is impossible accurately to know how much smuggling or revenue fraud there is today, let alone the period covered by this book.[49] By definition, it is hidden from view, coming into plain sight only occasionally. Seizures of smuggled goods and changing levels of revenue receipts following alterations of duties, especially after significant cuts, can hint at the scale of evasion, allowing some approximations to be proposed.[50] But it is impossible to go further; any 'estimate must in great measure depend upon conjecture'.[51] Even so, it is notable that while briefly prime minister in 1782–3, Lord Shelburne was advised by the Excise Board that 40 per cent of potential revenue was lost to smugglers.[52] Whether that was right is unknown and unknowable, but what is clear is that many at the time thought that smuggling periodically surged, especially towards the end of and immediately after major wars of the middle of the century – in the mid-to-late 1740s,[53] the early and mid-1760s,[54] and the early and mid-1780s.[55] It certainly existed at other times, but in these periods higher duties increased potential rates of return on smuggling, while the authorities were especially exercised about its existence then, in part because of a

---

[47] J. A. Chartres, 'Spirits in the north-east? Gin and other vices in the long eighteenth century', in Helen Berry and Jeremy Gregory, eds., *Creating and consuming culture in north-east England, 1660–1830* (Aldershot, 2004), p. 53; John Philipson, 'Whisky smuggling on the border in the early nineteenth century', *Archaeologia Aeliana*, 4th series, 39 (1961), pp. 151–63.

[48] NAS, CE8/1, f. 34; CE8/2, ff. 45–7, 93–4, 160–2. Complaints related to tea, soap, and distilling, all but one coming from London, the exception being Newcastle.

[49] H. M. Revenue Service, *Measuring tax gaps 2015 edition: methodological annex* (2015).

[50] A major attempt to estimate the extent of tea smuggling was made by W. A. Cole, 'Trends in eighteenth-century smuggling', *Economic History Review*, 10.3 (1958), pp. 395–410. This was criticized in Hoh-Cheung Mui and Lorna H. Mui, 'Smuggling and the British tea trade before 1784', *American Historical Review*, 74.1 (1968), pp. 44–73, and their '"Trends in eighteenth-century smuggling" reconsidered', *Economic History Review*, 28.1 (1975), pp. 28–43. Replied to in W. A. Cole, 'The arithmetic of eighteenth-century smuggling', *Economic History Review*, 28.1 (1975), pp. 44–9. For an estimate of tobacco smuggling see Robert C. Nash, 'The English and Scottish tobacco trades in the seventeenth and eighteenth centuries: legal and illegal trade', *Economic History Review*, 35.3 (1982), pp. 354–72.

[51] Clements Library, Shelburne papers, vol. 119, f. 106.

[52] Ibid., f. 95.

[53] *JHC*, 25 (1745–50), pp. 101–10 (24 March 1746).

[54] For example, 'the smuggling trade is as much carryed on, and practised on the Coast of England as ever I knew it'. Warren Lisle, Guernsey, 20 August 1764. Clements Library, Townshend papers, 297/2/10.

[55] The Excise Commissioners reported in 1783 that smuggling had 'become an evil of so great magnitude & enormity ... to require an immediate remedy'. Clements Library, Shelburne papers, vol. 119, f. 63.

belief that privateers were inclined to turn to smuggling in the transition from war to peace.[56]

If the scale of smuggling and fraud is impossible to determine, it is equally impossible to say certainly that it was more common in parts of Britain than others. That said, the authorities believed that it tended to be more prevalent in Devon and Cornwall, Kent and Sussex, the Channel Islands, around the Irish Sea, and across Scotland more generally, at least before 1750. What impact smuggling and fraud in these areas had on tax collected is impossible to say. But there were well-established views that it was significant in Scotland that are worth considering briefly.

In the four decades after 1707, fiscal convergence between the three nations made limited headway, with attempts to speed the process often being thwarted.[57] In 1713 the extension of the malt tax to Scotland almost led to the collapse of the Union and more generally it naturally suited many Scots, Jacobites particularly, to decry the public revenue regime under the Union. At the extreme was the lament of Robert Freebairn in 1716:

Before the Union we had no Taxes but were laid on by our own Parliaments, and those very easie, and spent within our own Country. Now we have not only the ... Land Tax, and Customs conform to the English Book of Rates, near the Triple what we formerly pay'd, and Excise, both most rigorously exacted by a Parcel of Strangers, sent down to us from England, but also the Malt-Tax, the Salt-Tax, the Leather-Tax, the Window-Tax, and Taxes upon Candles, Soap, Stearch ... the Tax upon stamped Paper and Parchments ... most of ... which are bound upon us for 64, and some of them for 99 years to come.[58]

Given the paltry levels of taxes collected in Scotland before the 1770s, this was plainly a gross exaggeration.[59] Nonetheless, there were clear signs of resistance to the new fiscal regime, with renewed attempts to levy the malt tax in Scotland in 1725 leading to rioting in Glasgow and wider discontent.[60] In 1729 the actions of revenue officers in Scotland were denounced at length in print for infringing liberty and trade, prefiguring

---

[56] It was then linked to 'crime waves'. Douglas Hay, 'War, dearth and theft in the eighteenth century: the record of the English courts', *Past and Present*, 95 (1982), pp. 117–60.

[57] R. H. Campbell, 'The Anglo–Scottish Union of 1707. II. The economic consequences', *Economic History Review*, 16.3 (1964), pp. 472–4.

[58] Quoted in Christopher A. Whatley, *Scottish society, 1707–1830: beyond Jacobitism, towards industrialisation* (Manchester, 2000), p. 188.

[59] The claim regarding the 'parcel of strangers' is examined in J. F. Mitchell, 'Englishmen in the Scottish excise department, 1707–1832', *Scottish Genealogist*, 13.2 (1966), pp. 16–28. Over that period 30 per cent of the Scottish Excise Board's commissioners were English, but only 3 per cent of collectors. See also John Stuart Shaw, *The management of Scottish society, 1707–1764: power, nobles, lawyers, Edinburgh agents and English influences* (Edinburgh, 1983), p. 67.

[60] *Culloden papers*, [ed. H. R. Duff] (1815), p. 82.

some of the Scottish complaints of the excise scheme in 1733.[61] Most famously, in 1736 Edinburgh erupted, climaxing in the lynching of Captain John Porteous, whose troops had shot dead members of a disorderly crowd watching a smuggler's execution for robbing a customs house. Such conflict between the authorities and the people is often held to characterize Scotland's position towards Britain's fiscal state, not least because of the immortalization of the Porteous riot early in Walter Scott's 1818 novel, *The heart of mid-Lothian*. As he put it, 'Smuggling was almost universal in Scotland in the reigns of George I. and II.; for the people, unaccustomed to imposts, and regarding them as an unjust aggression upon their ancient liberties, made no scruple to elude them wherever it was possible to do so.'[62] In fact, Walpole had been told as much in 1724, that even the 'well affected' embraced the black economy in Scotland, and from about 1730 London received repeated warnings from Duncan Forbes, a Scot through and through, that public revenues in Scotland were ill-collected.[63]

Scott carefully confined his comments to the period before 1760. Certainly no especial importance was attached to smuggling by the Excise Board in Edinburgh in 1790 when they defended their administration. In fact, smuggling was known still to be a significant problem in spirit distilling, stamp duties were said to be 'openly evaded' in Scotland in 1790, and there was no incentive to collect the land tax more efficiently. But the statistics of revenue collection certainly suggest that smuggling in Scotland had diminished from around 1750, especially after 1775.[64] Likely that was particularly because of measures taken by the authorities: weeding Jacobites from the revenue services between 1746 and 1752;[65] setting up a pension scheme for loyal excise officers in

---

[61] Reay Sabourn, *Oppression exposed, or liberty and property maintained: being an enquiry into the several mismanagements of persons concerned in the revenues of customs and excise in Scotland* (Edinburgh, 1729); Paul Langford, *The excise crisis: society and politics in the age of Walpole* (Oxford, 1975).

[62] Walter Scott, *The heart of mid-Lothian*, ed. David Hewitt and Alison Lumsden (Edinburgh, 2004), p. 22.

[63] Cambridge University Library, Ch(H) 40/16 – see also /18 for a report on the growth of smuggling after 1707. [Duncan Forbes], *Some considerations on the present state of Scotland* (Edinburgh, 1744); see his 'State of the revenue of Scotland', in *Culloden papers*, pp. 188–95. In 1744 Forbes met with Pelham, Scrope from the Treasury, and Lord Tweedale, the Scottish secretary, to discuss Scottish public revenues: *More Culloden papers*, ed. Duncan Warrand (5 vols., Inverness, 1923–9), vol. 3, p. 198.

[64] NLS, Melville papers, Mss 640, f. 39r. W. R. Ward, 'The land tax in Scotland, 1707–98', *Bulletin of the John Rylands Library*, 37 (1954–5), pp. 288–308.

[65] BL Add Mss 33,050, Newcastle papers, ff. 110–87 [c. 1752?]. Also William Coxe, ed., *Memoirs of the administration of the right honourable Henry Pelham* (2 vols., 1829), vol. 2, pp. 412–17, 439–40. A remarkably detailed list of the Scottish customs officers in 1752

1748;[66] purchasing for £70,000 the rights of the Duke of Atholl to collect customs duties on in the Isle of Man in 1765 so as to end its role as an entrepôt for smuggling in the Irish Sea;[67] in the 1780s several extraordinary exemptions from duties were compounded, including compensation payments of £40,000 and £21,580;[68] investing in more revenue officers; and administrative rearrangements, including closer oversight of those at the sharp end of the customs and excise.[69] Taken together, that was no small effort or cost. Smuggling certainly remained a problem in Scotland in 1800, but so it did elsewhere in Britain, and it probably only partly explains Scotland's much lower levels of gross tax receipts.

Conclusion

This chapter has tested the view that the British fiscal state – which ultimately rested on legislative foundations – was keenly felt everywhere by exploring the fundamental outcome of tax legislation, how much money was raised. It has provided plenty of evidence that the 'British' experience involves averaging widely divergent national and regional experiences, experiences which were not simply a consequence of the distribution of natural resources and circumstances. That is, the gap between prescription and practice varied from place to place and the excise officers praised in many accounts of the fiscal-military state were much more successful in some places than others – as indeed were the customs officers so often written out of their accounts.

---

is in the Clements Library, Shelburne papers, vol. 109. The purge was probably associated with the efforts of Corbyn Morris, who in 1748 was sent by Pelham to Scotland 'to introduce greater efficiency into revenue collection north of the border'. Bob Harris, *Politics and the nation: Britain in the mid-eighteenth century* (Oxford, 2002), p. 29. NLS, MS 1918 lists some of those involved in the rising in Scotland, compiled from information supplied from various ports. Those named include, ff. 3–4, Sir John Wederbury, collector of the excise for Angus, along with other former revenue officers as well as, f. 11, John Ferrier, reputedly a notorious smuggler.

[66] Established by royal charter and referred to in 5 & 6 William IV, c. 72. For a list of charters, see http://privycouncil.independent.gov.uk/royal-charters/chartered-bodies/.

[67] Ros Stott, 'Revolution? What revolution? Some thoughts about revestment', *Proceedings of the Isle of Man Natural and Antiquarian Society*, 11.4 (2003–5), pp. 541–52; Ros Stott, 'A brief encounter: the Duke of Atholl and the Isle of Man, 1736–1764', in Peter Davey and David Finlayson, eds., *Mannin revisited: twelve essays on Manx culture and environment* (Edinburgh, 2002), pp. 105–13.

[68] NAS, CE8/1, ff. 58, 76–85; CE8/2, ff. 32, 59–60. These are noted briefly in Binney, *British public finance*, pp. 24 and 39–40.

[69] Particularly important appears to have been the appointment in 1785 of two 'General Surveyors' of Excise in Scotland. NAS, E561/3. Reports of their activities are scattered within NAS, CE8/2.

This was something which worried leading ministers. In many cases the statistics used in this chapter derive from investigations at the time into which parts of Britain appeared to be heavily taxed, which parts lightly taxed. It was certainly a pressing issue in the final decades of the seventeenth century, both within government and amongst the wider political nation, including Charles Davenant, Edmond Halley, and John Houghton. Walpole investigated the situation in Scotland in the 1720s. In the 1740s Pelham obtained reports on levels of revenue collection in Scotland and Wales, presumably sensing that relatively little was being raised there. Few leading ministers thereafter could ignore this aspect of Britain's fiscal state. Relevant reports can be found in the papers of Townshend, North, Shelburne, and Pitt the younger – as well as among those of their aides such as Charles Jenkinson, Sir William Musgrave, and George Rose. Their concerns require that some modifications be made to our understanding of the British fiscal state so much lauded by a generation of historians.

Firstly, it is absolutely vital to appreciate that at the national level the paths of England, Scotland, and Wales differed markedly. In particular, there was no seamless expansion of the English system into Scotland at the Union. Put most simply, the negotiators in 1706 grossly underestimated the differences between the economies, environments, and public finance administrations of the two partners. Extracting public revenue from Scotland was never going to be easy and only modest headway was made over the next forty years. With some justification in 1752 Lord Chancellor Hardwicke complained of 'the insufficient manner in which the taxes had been collected in that northern quarter of the kingdom: some method should be taken to make Scotland pay her taxes; but could any ministry ever hit upon that method?'[70] It is telling that when he complained, the costs of collecting the excise in Scotland expressed as a share of gross receipts were more than three times those of south of the border and had actually grown since the Union. Using this measure of efficiency, England and Wales had made significant strides in the seventeenth century, but Scotland initially went backwards after the Union, erratically inched forward from about 1746–1774, and only then moved forward decisively (see Figure 9.2).

The substantial rise in taxes collected in Scotland after 1775 was doubtless due to a number of factors: a decline of smuggling and fraud, greater administrative efficiency, urbanization, and economic growth. Yet the extent of change must not be exaggerated. In 1800 much less

---

[70] Horace Walpole, *Memoirs of King George II*, ed. John Brooke (3 vols., New Haven, CT, 1985), vol. 1, p. 184.

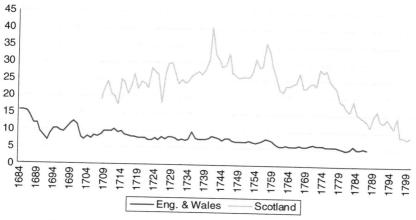

Figure 9.2 Excise management charges, as % of gross receipts, 1684–1800.

Note: data for England and Wales available to 1787 only and for Scotland from 1708 only.

Source: European State Finance Database (TNA, CUST145/4–13) at www.esfdb.org/table.aspx?resourceid=12081, accessed 16 August 2015; NAS, E554/3.

customs, excise, and income taxes were collected in Scotland than in England and Wales. The consistency of this evidence from different revenue streams suggests that Scotland's economy was still markedly less productive and that smuggling and fraud remained relatively more significant. More widely, it may be telling that criticisms by Scots of the national debt, which taxes underwrote, were frequent and potent. Hume and Smith were the best known of these, but the Earls of Eglinton and Stair, Lord Elibank, and William Pulteney also went in to print on the matter.[71] That is, a key section of Scottish society questioned a main use to which taxes were put.

Yet Wales appears to have had an even weaker economy, with very little customs and excise being collected there in the period. Doubtless that was

---

[71] David Hume, 'Of public credit', especially pp. 360–1 in his *Essays, moral, political and literary*, ed. Eugene F. Miller (Indianapolis, IN, 1987); Smith, *Wealth of nations*, vol. 2, pp. 928–9; [Alexander Montgomerie, Earl of Eglinton], *An inquiry into the original and consequences of the public debt* (Edinburgh, 1753); [Patrick Murray, Lord Elibank], *Thoughts on money, circulation and paper currency* (Edinburgh, 1758), pp. 32–3; John Dalrymple, Earl of Stair, *The state of the national debt, the national income, and the national expenditure* (1776); William Pulteney, *Considerations on the present state of public affairs, and the means of raising the necessary supplies* (1779), pp. 21–3.

partly because of the significance of Bristol (and Chester and Liverpool) to the principality, as well as the ability to send Welsh produce through the marches to English consumers.[72] Even so, Wales's very small population, which grew more slowly than that of England and Scotland in the eighteenth century, fundamentally constrained what it could contribute to the British fiscal state. Policy makers in London consequently paid little attention to Wales, but strongly believed that more money could be raised from Scotland, with the Jacobite rising of 1745–6 killing off lingering ideas of letting sleeping dogs lie.

If one major finding of this chapter has been to uncover important three-nation elements within the British fiscal state, another has been of the huge importance of London. It certainly mattered that revenue officers were spread out across the land, but many excise collections and customs ports produced very little revenue. By contrast, London's producers and consumers were major contributors to the public purse, though no less important was that the Treasury was able to exploit the numerous strong internal trading ties that linked the capital and Britain's regions. By collecting so much customs and excise in the capital, the fiscal state was indirectly drawing on provincial resources in a highly cost-effective way. Indeed, it is no exaggeration to say that London's continuing importance to the development of England's society and economy, brilliantly conceptualized by Wrigley, was a key reason for the success of the fiscal state in Britain.[73] The vitality of London's own economy, including developing trading links with Europe, America, and Asia, was associated with the constant evolution of its service sector connections with the rest of Britain – roads, waterways, banking, insurance, and the law.[74] Those connections were vital to the fruitfulness of Britain's fiscal state. No other European city (capital or otherwise) functioned similarly for its nation-state – in 1787 Arthur Young was very struck by how quiet were

---

[72] In 1745 it was guessed that £100,000 worth of woollen goods was sent from Wales to England overland. BL Lansdowne Mss, 1215, f. 172v: 'The annuall trade of south and north Wales compared in exports, imports and coast goods inwards and outwards – a medium for three years' [1742–5]. W. E. Minchinton, 'Bristol – metropolis of the west in the eighteenth century', *Transactions of the Royal Historical Society*, 5th series, 4 (1954), pp. 69–89.

[73] E. A. Wrigley, 'A simple model of London's importance in changing English society and economy, 1650–1750', *Past and Present*, 37 (1967), pp. 44–70. Britain's 'bloody code', hanging property offenders, was also implemented much more often in and around London. Peter King and Richard Ward, 'Rethinking the bloody code in eighteenth-century Britain: capital punishment at the centre and on the periphery', *Past and Present*, 228 (2015), pp. 159–205.

[74] Emphasized by Braudel and others. See the discussion in David Ormrod, *The rise of commercial empires: England and the Netherlands in the age of mercantilism, 1650–1770* (Cambridge, 2002), pp. 337–8.

the roads around Paris compared to London – though it led to anxieties about London's excessive size and influence. Andrew Fletcher's complaint from 1703, 'That London should draw the riches and government of the three kingdoms to the south-east corner of this island, is in some degree as unnatural, as for one city to possess the riches and government of the world', was reiterated by Hume in mid-century and, famously, taken up by Cobbett in the early nineteenth-century English context.[75]

A third key finding of this chapter has been to make clear that, contrary to what is often assumed, a very porous line separated customs and excise at the time. In 1796 30 per cent of the excise was raised on just five imported goods: foreign spirits, tobacco, wine, cocoa, and tea.[76] Britain's fiscal state depended rather more on overseas trade than is generally appreciated. A key reason for collecting duties on imports via the excise was to try to negate some of the incentives to smuggle. The more general point here is that smuggling and fraud were much larger problems than has generally been appreciated and provided a vital dynamic for the evolution of fiscal policy. Yet this chapter has also shown that the costs of collecting the customs were low, at least in England and Wales. By being concentrated on certain ports it escaped some of the costly overheads inherent to the excise, which had to cover the whole country, if to varying degrees.[77]

The final major point of this chapter has been to show the need to recognize that contemporary public finance accounting practices were irregular, with important items of expenditure having been handled in such a way that they do not feature in the standard statistical compendium. It is certainly true that direct expenditure on the military, and indirect expenditure on it via servicing the national debt, overwhelmingly dominated central government expenditure. But it is clear that spending on bounties directly from customs duties before money was remitted to London, considered in the previous chapter, was an important minor strand of expenditure that has been neglected within the fiscal-military state literature.

[75] Arthur Young, *Travels in France during the years 1787, 1788 and 1789*, ed. Constantia Maxwell (Cambridge, 1929), pp. 14, 49, 72, 79; Andrew Fletcher, *Political works*, ed. John Robertson (Cambridge, 1997), p. 213; Hume, 'Of public credit', p. 354; William Cobbett, 'To Mr Canning', *Cobbett's Weekly Political Register*, 22 February 1823, p. 481.

[76] TNA, PRO 30/8/288. f. 56.

[77] There is no modern history of the customs service in Britain. But see Elizabeth Evelynola Hoon, *The organization of the English customs system, 1696–1786* (New York, 1938); Eric J. Graham, *A maritime history of Scotland, 1650–1790* (East Linton, 2002).

10   Conclusion

'The spirit of English legislation is an incomprehensible mixture of the spirits of innovation and of routine, which perfects the details of laws without noting their principles; which always goes ahead in a straight line, taking step after step in the direction it happens to be in, without looking to right or to left to make connections between the different roads it is following.'

Alexis de Tocqueville, 1833[1]

History is always in tension between the pressure to generalize and the pressure to refine. But this is not a tension between equals: generalizations tend to have a greater impact than refinements. How then, to generalize from the material in Chapters 2–9? To do so, it is helpful to bear in mind some key historiographical and conceptual issues that frame this book.

In the case of Britain's political economies, the labels and aggregates discussed in Chapter 1 reflect, as much as anything, differences in perspective and, consequently, choices about the selection of evidence. Those who resort to 'mercantilism' tend to focus on certain actions such as the navigation acts as representative of a wider whole and as expressions of a more-or-less conscious policy. Those who prefer to think in terms of the 'fiscal-military' state concentrate instead on patterns of expenditure by central government as the crucial determinant of how political power affected economic life. Those two approaches are not mutually exclusive because they share a belief in the significance of central government itself wielding power, while for neither is the gap between prescription and practice usually given much weight. By contrast, those who emphasize the importance of liberty and property to the economic order largely do so with reference to the impact of constitutional considerations. And finally, those who see the British state as especially 'reactive' focus their

---

[1] *Journeys to England and Ireland*, ed. J. P. Mayer (1958), pp. 82–3.

attention on how wider pressures for action developed in society at large rather than central government.

In this historiographical light it is important to stress that the starting point of this book was to use a comprehensive and systematic exploration of Acts of Parliament as a way of capturing the key means by which political power was applied to economic life. Certainly not all political actions affecting economic life in Britain in this period were expressed through Acts of Parliament, but most were, at least in part. Consequently, this book has explored Britain's political economies in the round, without privileging one area over another: due weight has been given to domestic and overseas considerations in their full richness. Amongst other things, Acts of Parliament set taxes, organized and underwrote the national debt, hedged and prompted overseas trade, limited company formation, set maximum interest rates, defined weights and measures, sought to balance the interests of creditors and debtors, and put in place many requirements about skills, labour relations, quality control, and markets. But such general efforts sat alongside even greater numbers of specific economic acts especially relating to the piecemeal enclosure of much land and improving the nation's infrastructure. Together, the scale of this richly varied effort was enormous, comprising more than 7,500 acts. What were the key characteristics of this legislative fertility?

In addressing that question it is helpful to bear in mind the sorts of general characteristics or concepts important when considering political influences on economic decisions. One aspect is the extent of protection provided from threats to life and property, that is, the nature of security. Those threats might be from without, but they could also be from within, including not just basic issues of law and order, but questions of property rights and access (including customary expectations). Second, is the degree to which the liberty of individuals and groups was impinged on by governmental regulation or direction. That is, what part political authorities played in economic life, both through direct intervention, including taxation, and indirect oversight. Thirdly, is the issue of the extent to which political power was imperial, national, regional, or local in its reach. For all three of those considerations, fourthly, it is important to ask how far prescription and practice diverged. Finally, it is helpful to adapt Montesquieu's distinction between laws and mores: Britain's political economies in this period are to be judged not only by their forms, but also by their temper.

Unquestionably, the volume of economic legislation considered in this period is critical to understanding the relationship of politics to economic life. Few if any other European states were as prolific. Yet if the French Estates General did not meet between 1615 and 1789, representative assemblies survived in the Dutch Republic, the Holy Roman Empire, Hungary, Poland, Sweden, and Switzerland. The roles that all these institutions played and the powers that they exercised varied, but they could be very active. In Sweden all legislation required the consent of its Riksdag, leading historians to identify an 'age of liberty' from 1719–72.[2] The permanent diet of the Holy Roman Empire 'acquired a broad range of competences and activities in matters of imperial business and politics' and was a place where 'members could articulate, negotiate, and reconcile their interests and policies, mediate and display conflicts, conduct information politics'.[3]

Westminster was clearly but one of a number of such assemblies in Europe in this period. But there were certainly important differences between it and them. Many assemblies did not meet as regularly, frequently, or at such length as Westminster, restricting the amount of business they could conduct. The Hungarian diet met in only sixteen years between 1712 and 1796, and so was a site for occasional bargaining rather than concerted legislative action.[4] The imperial Reichstag met much more often than that and agreed some 2,000 resolutions between 1663 and 1740, but turned only 10 per cent into laws – in the same period Westminster passed nearly 3,800 acts. Critical here was the extent of independence and authority of assemblies. Ultimately Westminster's authority rested on the Commons' control over public finances, taxation particularly, ensuring an effective balance between Parliament's three parts: Commons, Lords, and monarch. Such an authority was unusual. The imperial Reichstag, for example, could not consider tax business, significantly limiting its authority.[5] In many German states too 'parliaments' were reluctant to check executive government and declined.[6]

A related feature was the extent to which central legislative bodies had to work with regional powers. In the Dutch republic its seven provinces enjoyed a significant degree of autonomy, limiting the power of the States

---

[2] Michael Roberts, *Swedish and English parliamentarianism in the eighteenth century* (Belfast, 1973), pp. 3 and 5; Julian Swann, 'Politics and the state' in T. C. W. Blanning, ed., *Short Oxford history of Europe: the eighteenth century* (Oxford, 2000), p. 36.

[3] Karl Härter, 'The permanent imperial diet in European context, 1663–1806', in R. J. W. Evans, Michael Schaich, and Peter H. Wilson, eds., *The Holy Roman Empire, 1495–1806* (Oxford, 2011), pp. 124, 132. See also Joachim Whaley, *Germany and the Holy Roman Empire* (2 vols., Oxford, 2012), vol. 2, ch. 7.

[4] Orsolya Szakály, 'Managing a composite monarchy: the Hungarian diet and the Habsburgs in the eighteenth century', in D. W. Hayton, James Kelly, and John Bergin, eds., *The eighteenth-century composite state: representative institutions in Ireland and Europe, 1689–1800* (Basingstoke, 2010), p. 210.

[5] Härter, 'The permanent imperial diet', p. 134.

[6] F. L. Carsten, *Princes and parliaments in Germany from the fifteenth to the eighteenth century* (Oxford, 1959), p. v.

General.[7] Even stronger veto powers considerably hampered the work of the Polish Sejm and the Swiss Tagsatzung.[8] An important element of Westminster's legislative fertility was its jurisdictional reach, of its capacity to legislate for the whole of Britain and its empire, in both general terms and, within Britain, local ones as well. This was a more centralized system, where counties were small enough not to be able to mount serious opposition or resistance, at least after the mid-seventeenth century. It is telling that the Council of the Welsh Marches was abolished in 1689, a move strongly supported in Wales.[9] Despite the strength of local identities, the weakness of regional blocs in Britain was an important characteristic of the nature of state action.

It might finally be noted that the size and composition of assemblies in Europe in this period varied. Importantly, though dominated by landowners, Westminster was not formally composed of 'estates', meaning that its membership was less rigidly defined and enjoyed few legal privileges. (And its landowners were fairly commercially minded.) The Swedish diet comprised four estates – the nobility, clergy, burghers, and peasants – numbering as many as 1,000, though dominated by the nobles, and by the middle of its age of liberty often ground to a halt.[10] This pattern, and the growing power of aristocrats, was a common one among assemblies in Europe, though distinctively the Dutch States General comprised just twenty-four men, mostly cut from the same cloth – Calvinist civic leaders, a commercial elite.[11]

If the volume of economic legislation considered at Westminster was impressive, that was partly because general legislation tended to move forward by frequent refinements. A striking feature was that central government made so many laws within the same two broad subject areas of public finances and overseas trade. Long chains and dense networks of laws resulted. Three key reasons were at work: the requirement to renew the statutory basis of many parts of public finances annually as a means of ensuring Parliament was a regular part of the governmental process; the incremental nature of policy making; and the difficulties of creating

---

[7] Maarten Prak, *The Dutch Republic in the seventeenth century: the golden age* (Cambridge, 2005), p. 4; Thomas Poell, 'Local particularism challenged, 1795–1813', in Oscar Gelderblom, ed., *The political economy of the Dutch republic* (Farnham, 2009), p. 291.

[8] Härter, 'The permanent imperial diet', p. 128; Jerzy Lukowski, *Liberty's folly: the Polish-Lithuanian commonwealth in the eighteenth century, 1697–1795* (1991), p. 92.

[9] C. Skeel, *The Council in the Marches of Wales: a study of local government during the sixteenth and seventeenth centuries* (1904); Philip Loft, 'Peers, Parliament and power under the revolution constitution, 1685–1720' (UCL PhD thesis, 2015), pp. 262–4. The Council in the North had been abolished in 1641.

[10] Roberts, *Swedish and English parliamentarianism*, p. 12.

[11] A. R. Myers, *Parliaments and estates in Europe to 1789* (1975), pp. 129–30.

acts that worked – because of lack of ambition, poor drafting, misjudged objectives (arising from poor information or ideas), maladministration, and evasion. The first of these reasons was largely a legacy of the constitutional battles of the seventeenth century. But the others, which were closely related, were of lasting significance in this period.

Long chains and intricate networks of governmental economic legislation speak powerfully of the nature of policy at the time, particularly of a degree of hesitancy and uncertainty in identifying and defining measures that were acceptable both within Parliament and without. Cautious, piecemeal, and incremental legislation resulted, driven more by common but evolving assumptions than some grand plan. Critical here was that such legislation usually emanated from relatively small departments of central government supported by very limited manpower at their direct disposal to enforce acts. Striking efforts were made to escape from those constraints, but there was only so much that could be done. Although central government in Britain was lavishly funded compared to its European counterparts, and although overseas trade in general and imperial trade in particular were corralled to a degree, smuggling, evasion, and fraud were periodically very common. The previous three chapters have brought out aspects of this clearly. Bounties were liable to fraud and, even when successful, over-stretched payment systems. Similarly, attempts to institute an effective administration to implement the ban on the export of wool came to nought. The costs, financial and political, were deemed to outweigh the benefits. And in Chapter 9 a sense was gained of how the administration of national tax laws varied somewhat within Britain from nation to nation and region to region, in part because of the need to take account of varied circumstances and attitudes.

To work governmental economic legislation had to have a high degree of legitimacy, that is be acceptable to enough of the population to be easily enforced or self-enforcing by expressing widely held norms or aims – and had, therefore, to be somewhat unambitious. Fundamental therefore was the view people took of the uses to which taxes were put and the aim of much trade regulation. On the first while there was general acceptance, indeed often enthusiasm, for many wars fought by Britain, taxes are rarely popular and anti-war sentiment became more widely and powerfully expressed in the wars against revolutionary America and France in the final quarter of the eighteenth century.[12] And trade regulations were often but not always seen as necessary to heighten national well-being.

---

[12] John Sainsbury, *Disaffected patriots: London supporters of Revolutionary America 1769–1782* (Kingston, Ontario, 1987); J. E. Cookson, *The friends of peace: anti-war liberalism in England, 1793–1815* (Cambridge, 1982).

As has been seen, free trade sentiment was being expressed from at least the early seventeenth century.

It is important to remember that in any period taxes and regulations create economic opportunities, both legal and not. Those illegal opportunities ('regulatory arbitrage' in the jargon) grow as taxes rise, restrictions become more onerous, or incentives like bounties proliferate. As Ogilvie has put it,

> Limiting economic access affects not only distribution but efficiency. It reduces the volume of economic activity in the formal sector and creates incentives for the excluded to violate institutional rules by moving into the informal sector. ... So a key feature of any formal institution is the size and nature of the informal sector it creates.[13]

Governments naturally decry the black economy, but their actions create the conditions for its existence. How large it is at any time is by definition impossible to tell, but we have seen that it was believed to be a structural problem regarding the export of wool, revenue frauds, and the collection of taxes in certain areas, including Scotland. Lacking sufficient wherewithal, central government struggled through the period to address such problems. This struggle was recognized early, yet for a long time the response was reiteration, tweaking, and, often enough, harsher penalties. But usually this failed to address the fundamental issue, the chances of participants in the informal economy being caught and prosecuted. In 1779 it was argued that

> Visionary and speculative politicians, may conceive that acts of Parliament may force rogues to be honest even against their interest, but experience and common sense proves, that temptation to gain, opperates [sic] stronger upon the minds of bad men, than any laws human or divine. The consequence is clear and incontestable, that nothing can prevent smuggling and illicit trade, but removing the temptation. Portable articles subject to high duties will be smuggled; large drawbacks will encourage the relanding such articles, and selling them here for home consumption after the drawbacks are received.[14]

Such realizations and the ever-growing complexity, indeed perplexity, of governmental economic legislation created the conditions in which moves towards consolidation, rationalization, and liberalization began to take place from the 1780s. The *Wealth of nations* helped with that shift, but often made points that had been made many times before. The great growth of governmental economic legislation in the period 1689–1775

---

[13] Sheilagh Ogilvie, *Institutions and European trade: merchant guilds, 1000–1800* (Cambridge, 2011), p. 420.

[14] *Morning Chronicle*, 18 May 1779. I am grateful to Shane Horwell for this reference.

put in place the conditions for a radical rethinking of the place of such legislation in managing society as a consequence of the American crisis. It is telling that the language of 'political economy', 'reform', and 'liberal' all prospered from the 1770s.[15]

The dynamics behind and consequences of specific economic legislation were quite different. Because their scope was usually local or personal they were quite unlike general measures – if sometimes working alongside or within general laws, as in specific acts relating to turnpikes and general acts relating to highways.[16] As Maitland put it, many specific acts might better be viewed as privileges, special rights, or liberties rather than laws, albeit with the force of law.[17] These allowed their proponents to escape or transcend existing forms (often themselves granted as privileges), usually for their own betterment, if justified in the language of the wider public good. As such, it is interesting to note that much the same was being done in France at the time, if in different sectors, trades, and industries than Britain and by crown diktat rather than the deliberations of a representative assembly.[18]

Profit motives lay behind much specific economic legislation and as such show the responsiveness of Parliament to broader changes, especially to the needs of propertied society regarding agriculture and inland trade. In this way frequent close connections were made between market conditions and political power, allowing the redrawing of many property rights and the creation of new authorities to transcend the limitations of old ones. In a sense this was a commercialization of political power leading to an intensification of market relations within society. It also meant that much better links were established between central government and provincial society, though as Chapters 4 and 9 showed, relations that were much stronger in England than Scotland. In this way, geographical patterns of specific economic legislation throw up another element in the composite nature of the British state in this period. Even by 1800 marked differences remained in the political economies of England and Scotland.

---

[15] Joanna Innes, '"Reform" in English public life: the fortunes of a word', in Arthur Burns and Joanna Innes, eds., *Rethinking the age of reform: Britain 1780–1850* (Cambridge, 2003), pp. 71–97; Daniel B. Klein, 'The origin of "liberalism"', *Atlantic*, 13 February 2014, online at www.theatlantic.com/politics/archive/2014/02/the-origin-of-liberalism/ 283780/.

[16] Crisply summarized in Richard Price, *British society, 1680–1880: dynamism, containment, and change* (Cambridge, 1999), p. 129.

[17] F. W. Maitland, *The constitutional history of England* (Cambridge, 1908), p. 382; Magnus Ryan, 'Freedom, law, and the medieval state', in Quentin Skinner and Bo Stråth, eds., *States and citizens: history, theory, prospects* (Cambridge, 2003), pp. 51–62.

[18] Jeff Horn, *Economic development in early modern France: the privilege of liberty, 1650–1820* (Cambridge, 2015).

A key aspect of Britain's political economies was that its statutory basis meant that it was subject to a significant degree of scrutiny, both inside and outside Parliament. The cases studied in Part Two showed that clearly, with petitions, pamphlets, and lobbying taking place alongside deliberations at Westminster, all framed by the formal structures for turning bills into acts. The contrast with France here is telling.

To Horn 'The Bourbon state was no enemy of capitalism. State-sponsored economic reform in the eighteenth century exhibited a vibrancy, a creativity that has been downplayed'.[19] In a related vein, Peter Jones has concluded that 'By European standards France was an impressively well-ordered state.'[20] Perhaps, but it was arranged very differently to the other states often said to have been well-ordered, Prussia and Britain.[21] Certainly the monarchy was active. Louis XV, monarch from 1714–74, issued 4,000 arrêts du Conseil, of which around 1,000 were of a general nature.[22] The contrôleur général des finances provided a central point of contact, but one that operated in a much less public way than the Westminster parliament, and where, consequently, connection, patronage, corruption, and cronyism lacked much of an external check.[23] Not only, therefore, did small local economic interests turn to the focal point of sovereign power more readily in Britain than in France, and not only did executive government have publicly to negotiate with propertied society, but the legitimacy of the outcomes, Acts of Parliament, was, it seems likely, wider and deeper than the decisions of the contrôleur general and the Conseil royal des finances.

France comprised a complicated mix of central and regional authorities – provincial assemblies operated in only one-third of the country while in the region of the 'grand gabelle', centring on Paris, higher duties meant that salt was six times more expensive than in the 'pays rédimés des gabelles' in the south-west.[24] By contrast, Britain was a relatively unified and centralized state and economy, with London absolutely

---

[19] Horn, Economic development, p. 9.

[20] P. M. Jones, Reform and revolution in France: the politics of transition, 1774–1791 (Cambridge, 1995), p. 45.

[21] Marc Raeff, The well-ordered police state: social and institutional change through law in the Germanies and Russia, 1600–1800 (New Haven, CT, 1983), challenged by Andre Wakefield, The disordered police state: German Cameralism as science and practice (Chicago, IL, 2009).

[22] Jean-Louis Halpérin, Five legal revolutions since the seventeenth century: an analysis of a global legal history (Cham, 2014), p. 14.

[23] Roland E. Mousnier, The institutions of France under the absolute monarchy, 1598–1789 (2 vols., Chicago, IL, 1979), vol. 2, ch. 12.

[24] Myers, Parliaments and estates in Europe, pp. 102–5; J. F. Bosher, The single duty project: a study of the movement for a French customs union in the eighteenth century (1964).

pivotal.[25] (Indeed, the role of London has been seen (in Chapter 9) to have been even greater than has previously been thought, even if it did not itself require much specific economic legislation.) Certainly Britain comprised the largest single market in Europe at the time, if one hampered by the illegal survival of local weights and measures and a frequently inadequate coinage. Yet a key finding of this book is that central government had a limited administration, necessarily devolving considerable practical authority to the localities. Central government had some means to act, and in emergencies, as in dealing with cattle plague, could get a lot done locally, but the failed plans to register the wool clip discussed in Chapter 7 point up some key limitations. Few wanted the manpower of central government to grow at the time.[26] Thus in 1833 John Bowring, an enthusiastic free trader, asserted that 'England is a country of decentralisation. We have got a government, but we have not got a central administration. Each county, each town, each parish looks after its own interests. Industry is left to itself'.[27]

One response to that was the heaping up of economic legislation, and sometimes heaping new institutions on top of or amidst old ones. Hindle has stressed the 'sedimentary' nature of this, of the laying down of one layer of authority on top of another, again and again.[28] But frequently new ones only partially covered the old, leading to ever richer and confusing landscapes of authority. Old ones thrived in places, lingered in others, but died elsewhere. Similarly, often enough old laws remained on the statute book, gradually becoming less observed. Consequently, while this book has stressed the 'creative' aspects of legislation, this period saw a decline, if not a smooth one, in the significance of manor courts, guilds, clerks of markets, wage regulation, statute labour for road repair, the assize of bread and ale, and Scottish heritable jurisdictions.[29] This was a liberalization of sorts.

---

[25] Interesting reflections on this point are made by G. E. Aylmer, 'The peculiarities of the English state', *Journal of Historical Sociology*, 3.2 (1990), pp. 91–108.

[26] This is given too little weight in interpretations which stress the dirigisme of Britain's political economies, e.g.: William J. Ashworth, 'The intersection of industry and the state in eighteenth-century Britain', in Lissa Roberts, Simon Schaffer, and Peter Dear, eds., *The mindful hand: sites, artefacts and the rise of modern science and technology* (Chicago, IL, 2007), pp. 349–77; Joanna Guldi, *Roads to power: Britain invents the infrastructure state* (Cambridge, MA, 2012). Guldi's argument is expertly criticized in Dorian Gerhold's review in *Victorian Studies*, 56.2 (2014), pp. 291–3.

[27] Tocqueville, *Journeys to England and Ireland*, pp. 61–2.

[28] Steve Hindle, *The state and social change in early modern England, c. 1550–1640* (Basingstoke, 2000), p. ix.

[29] Because sources usually dwindle, studying such declines is difficult and thus the literature available is patchy, but see: Michael John Walker, 'The extent of the guild control

Laws that fell into abeyance, largely reiterated old ones, or were always ineffective were an important fraction of economic legislation. But if that is one significant qualification to the enormous volume of such efforts in this period, it must also be remembered that key areas of economic life received little attention from Parliament. The relative absence of laws with regards to certain walks of economic life is in certain respects as meaningful as their presence. Notably, given their general importance, little legislative attention was directed towards manufacturing, labour relations, or mining. They were subject to some acts (especially through the revenue laws affecting established industries like beer, soap, candles, leather, bricks, and coal), but under 200 in total otherwise addressed these or other industries, a small fraction of the number passed in the major areas of economic legislation – there were 279 relating to the much smaller sector of money and banking, for example.[30] This relative autonomy was relished by many manufacturers, especially in rapidly developing industries in the last quarter of the eighteenth century, particularly given central government's intense need to find more income. Adam Smith played on this, while chambers of commerce gave such views increasingly formal expression from the era of the American Revolution.

It would be easy to assume that the amassing of more than 7,500 economic acts in this period constituted a great erosion of liberty and certainly in a profound sense there was a marked 'thickening' of the legal framework of economic life in Britain in this period.[31] But a key finding of this book is of the very ambiguous or uncertain nature of many such acts. Clearly some economic legislation sought to constrain behaviour or reduced its rewards. But the gap between prescription and practice meant this did not grate as much as it might have. Moreover, some economic legislation removed constraints on the behaviour of some people and increased the rewards of such behaviour, such as parliamentary enclosure. But in such cases if the liberty of landowners after enclosure was enhanced, plenty of villagers complained that they had become

---

of trades in England, c.1660–1820: a study based on a sample of provincial towns and London companies' (University of Cambridge PhD thesis, 1986); Brodie Waddell, 'Governing England through the manor courts, 1550–1850', *Historical Journal*, 55.2 (2012), pp. 279–315; Sidney Webb and Beatrice Webb, 'The assize of bread', *Economic Journal*, 14.54 (1904), pp. 196–218; W. E. Minchinton, ed., *Wage regulation in pre-industrial England* (Newton Abbot, 1972); Joanna Innes, 'Regulating wages in eighteenth and early nineteenth-century England: arguments in context', in Perry Gauci, ed., *Regulating the British economy, 1660–1850* (Farnham, 2011), pp. 195–215.

[30] The statistics are set out in Table 3.3 in Chapter 3.

[31] David Lemmings, *Law and government in England during the long eighteenth century: from consent to command* (Basingstoke, 2011), p. 11, argues that statute law eroded common law during the period, thereby narrowing the nature of governance.

slaves to the vicissitudes of free labour markets. There is a very real sense in which liberty and freedom – and, in the context of political economy, their antonyms regulation and protectionism – lie in the eye of the beholder. Vexed conceptual issues – to Burke 'Abstract Liberty, like other mere abstractions, is not to be found' – are often riddled with essentially political presumptions about the justness or not of free markets and the rule of law, at least when economic historians declaim on the subject.[32]

Nonetheless, it is clear that enthusiasm for 'liberal' sentiments and measures grew from around 1770. The 'liberal arts' (grammar, logic, rhetoric, music, arithmetic, geometry, and astronomy) had long been seen as the fundamentals of a good education, but the term 'liberal' began to resonate in different ways as thinking about political economy developed. 'Liberal' and 'liberality' were used in various senses, not just in association with openness and freedom. In 1651, for example, Hobbes tied it to character: 'Riches joined with liberality, is Power; because it procureth friends, and servants; Without liberality, not so'.[33] Smith in the *Wealth of nations* wrote of the liberal professions and liberal rewards to labour, for example, but did write in favour of a 'liberal system' of free trade.[34] Here the old definition of liberality as generosity was hitched to the new notion that economic affairs between nations might be better ordered similarly, rather than spurred by jealousy. This was a European development, with scepticism towards protectionism, empire, and slavery all playing a part.[35] It was far from only an intellectual development. Thus in 1784 the Birmingham businessman Samuel Garbett wrote in praise of the 'liberal Principles of Barter', 'liberal designs', and the benefits of a 'much more liberal Plan of Commerce than exists at present'.[36] It was this more particular way, rather than broader notions of liberty or liberalism, that began to affect some economic legislation from around 1770, in part because they aligned well with fiscal and administrative imperatives. Some hesitant steps towards a more liberal state were taken in the 1780s.

---

[32] Edmund Burke, *The writings and speeches of Edmund Burke, vol. 3: party, Parliament, and the American war, 1774–1780*, ed. Warren M. Elofson, and John A. Woods (Oxford, 1996), p. 120; Quentin Skinner, *Liberty before liberalism* (Cambridge, 1998), which challenged Isaiah Berlin's famous *Two concepts of liberty* (Oxford, 1958). As to the sorts of conceptual differences involved, Berlin wrote to Bernard Crick that 'I think that what you call freedom ... I prefer to call power'. Isaiah Berlin, *Building: letters, 1960–1975*, ed. Henry Hardy and Mark Pottle (2013), p. 273.

[33] Thomas Hobbes, *The leviathan*, ed. Richard Tuck (Cambridge, 1991), p. 62.

[34] Smith, *Wealth of nations*, vol. 1, p. 538.

[35] Jennifer Pitts, *A turn to empire: the rise of imperial liberalism in Britain and France* (Princeton, NJ, 2005); Sankar Muthu, *Enlightenment against empire* (Princeton, NJ, 2003).

[36] BL, Add Mss 88,906/1/11, Bowood papers, ff. 67, 68, 109.

Britain's political economies were multi-faceted. Simultaneously mercantilist, fiscal-military, composite state, and reactive elements operated. The degree of regulation waxed and waned, confused by the gap between prescription and practice. At one level property became more secure, but taxes mounted along with the compulsory redistribution of property rights. It is very telling that Lord Chancellor Mansfield denied 'the proposition that parliament takes no man's property without his consent: it frequently takes private property without making what the owner thinks a compensation'.[37] Much the same was true regarding liberty. The waning of some regulations and the failure to perpetuate others increased economic freedoms, but to others Acts of Parliament involved unwelcome exactions and restrictions. It is this variegated or Janus nature of Britain's political economies which stands out. It is worth remembering that while Adam Smith lambasted Britain's 'mercantile system' at considerable length, he ultimately concluded that 'In Great Britain industry is perfectly secure; and though it is far from being perfectly free, it is as free or freer than in any other part of Europe.'[38]

Centrally, in the end the supremacy of the Westminster parliament as an arbiter of the proper uses of political power was accepted by many within Britain, if less so in its empire. Its legitimacy was born of negotiation, a degree of transparency, and opportunities for engagement with a wider public, all in the context of approaching law-making cautiously and flexibly. This enabled central government to pursue its aims with a high degree of authority and considerable resources. But it also meant that local concerns turned to Westminster in huge numbers, seeking sovereign powers with which to enhance their economic prospects. This was a key aspect of the state's centralization, of local interests using central powers. By contrast, central powers had, aside from the collection of revenue, to depend heavily on local propertied society to implement its measures. In this essentially bifurcated way political power and economic life were closely related and functioned reasonably well, providing sufficient authority for those seeking it, without that authority being overbearing to them. An important part of that was the relatively public nature of law-making and the real chance for many proposals that Parliament would reject them. Numbers of fails, more than 3,300, were high and highly significant. Moreover, while the great growth of law-making after

---

[37] Quoted in P. J. Marshall, 'Parliament and property rights in the late eighteenth-century British empire', in John Brewer and Susan Staves, eds., *Early modern conceptions of property* (1995), p. 535. I have discussed this wider point in 'Compulsion, compensation and property rights in Britain, 1688–1833', *Past and Present*, 210 (2011), pp. 93–128.
[38] Smith, *Wealth of nations*, vol. 1, p. 540.

1688 lacked coordination, ways were found to stop the resulting edifice from becoming too heavy for its foundations or self-defeating. At times its credibility was questioned, but parliamentarians, while sure of their institution's primacy, found the ways to move with the times, if far too slowly and slightly for some. The Westminster parliament was no *ancien régime* institution.[39]

How did this matter? It is important to restate that this book has studied a context of the early industrial revolution, but not its causes. As was noted earlier, a few have denied the significance of institutions as a cause of British economic growth at the time (pp. 33–4). But if nothing else this book has shown that politics mattered a lot to people at the time. It was a vital part of their economic life. But can more be said? Some economic historians certainly think so. Two examples will suffice. David Landes particularly emphasized among Britain's institutional advantages secure property rights, enforceable rights of contract, and stable, honest, and responsive government operating within publicly known rules.[40] By contrast, Patrick O'Brien will have nothing of such 'Whiggish rhetoric that highlights Parliamentary government, private enterprise, liberalism and *laissez-faire*'. For him what was critical was the success of central government in raising revenue to support a large military, the Royal Navy particularly, which carved out and supported new, distant markets for British goods. The fiscal-military state, warfare, empire, and the mercantile system significantly advantaged Britain's merchants and manufacturers.[41]

Despite their differences Landes and O'Brien agree that Britain's economic performance was internationally exceptional in the eighteenth century, that institutional considerations were a critical causal factor of that, and, though they put no great weight on it, that in institutional terms the fount of British exceptionalism was Parliament. Moreover, they both establish the causal relationship at work by stressing the contemporaneous development of parliamentary supremacy and Britain's economic precocity. The difficulty here is distinguishing between coincidence and causation. Simply because the output and productivity of Britain's economy and Parliament both rose in the eighteenth century

[39] Julian Hoppit, 'Reformed and unreformed Britain, 1689–1801', in William Doyle, ed., *The Oxford handbook of the ancien régime* (Oxford, 2012), pp. 506–21.

[40] David S. Landes, *The wealth and poverty of nations: why some are so rich and some so poor* (New York, 1998), pp. 217–18. Landes also stressed the importance of social, cultural, and ideological factors.

[41] Patrick Karl O'Brien, 'State formation and the construction of the institutions for the first industrial nation', in Ha-Joon Chang, ed., *Institutional change and economic development* (New York, 2007), p. 194.

does not mean that there was a clear causal relationship at work. Links, which there surely were, might flow in either or both directions (and so be iterative), and range from weak to strong.[42]

At the general level the heterogeneity of political power renders meaningless any single measure of that power, while depending on GDP estimates as an index of economic performance is beset with significant problems, evidential and conceptual.[43] There is simply no way of capturing the relationships at work in a neat and meaningful way. Moreover, assessing the effects of Britain's political economies ultimately depends on assessing alternative arrangements, counterfactuals, for which evidence obviously is unavailable.[44]

One point about chronology is worth emphasizing. Work by Wrigley over several decades has pointed to significant developments in the structure and productivity of England's economy since around 1600, more than 150 years before the classic start date of the industrial revolution.[45] This chimes well with studies by the likes of Joan Thirsk and Paul Slack, along with recent per capita GDP estimates.[46] What is clear is that prolonged if slow economic growth began before the resolution of Britain's constitutional crises discussed in Chapter 1. It might be tempting to conclude from this that political arrangements were neither a prime mover nor a brake on developments, that other factors – economic, social, cultural, environmental – were more important. That may be. But three points are worth stressing. First, it is clear that the regularization of the meetings of Parliament as a consequence of the Glorious Revolution of 1688–9 released pent-up demand for legislation. Second, the causes of economic growth in Britain were different at the end of the

---

[42] For some important reflections on identifying such relationships see Sheilagh Ogilvie, '"Whatever is, is right"? Economic institutions in pre-industrial Europe', *Economic History Review*, 60.4 (2007), pp. 649–84.

[43] The most recent estimates are rough approximations: Stephen Broadberry, Bruce M. S. Campbell, Alexander Klein, Mark Overton, and Bas van Leeuwen, *British economic growth, 1270–1870* (Cambridge, 2015). For a recent criticism of the concept and uses of GDP see Dirk Philipsen, *The little big number: how GDP came to rule the world and what to do about it* (Princeton, NJ, 2015). I discussed some of the problems of earlier GDP estimates for Britain in 'Counting the industrial revolution', *Economic History Review*, 43.2 (1990), pp. 173–93.

[44] Patrick Karl O'Brien and Leandro Prados de la Escosura, 'The costs and benefits for Europeans from their empires overseas', *Revista de Historia Económica*, 16.1 (1998), p. 31.

[45] For his most recent statement see E. A. Wrigley, *The path to sustained growth: England's transition from an organic economy to an industrial revolution* (Cambridge, 2016).

[46] Joan Thirsk, *Economic policy and projects: the development of a consumer society in early modern England* (Oxford, 1978); Paul Slack, *The invention of improvement: information and material progress in seventeenth-century England* (Oxford, 2015); Broadberry et al., *British economic growth*, p. 204.

eighteenth century than 100 years before. The growth of economic Acts of Parliament after 1760 or so showed how responsive Parliament was to the financial needs of both central government and propertied society. Finally, it is far more historically accurate to emphasize multi-causality rather than mono-causality. As Wrigley has put it, 'The temptation to seek a cause is strong, but it is seldom possible to establish with certainty that it is demonstrable.'[47]

Assessments of the impact of economic legislation must often be qualitative and give due weight to both general and specific measures and material and non-material consequences. But an important starting point is to repeat that the value of economic legislation is demonstrated by the vast numbers sought both by government and by specific, local, and personal interests. A large amount of effort was put into this because it was believed to be necessary for prosperity or order. Ultimately, despite the criticisms that were periodically made of the profligacy of such law-making, this was sustained – indeed numbers of acts grew enormously in the late eighteenth century. Thus Parliament was highly responsive to economic needs, large and small, and the key focal point where ways of improving the economy were deliberated on and decided. Parliament played an important role in the generation, debate, and promulgation of views about ways of improving economic life. It may not always have generated effective laws as a consequence, but it tried hard to do so. To disregard that is to take a very limited view of what was at issue. Parliament was a highly active participant in Britain's economic fortunes.

Turning to general economic legislation, plainly such acts provided fundamental frameworks for economic life: a high degree of internal security, a national market (with in theory common taxes, weights, measures, and money), a common if porous imperial market, and a medley of encouragements to do this and discouragements to do that. Within this Britain's economy did relatively well. Or more accurately some parts of it did – which speaks of the need to place economic legislation alongside other causal factors of Britain's economic fortunes: that at the general level such acts provided a framework for private enterprise but not, save in very few cases, a pathway to be followed.[48] But detailing more precisely the effects is very difficult. For example, the importance of internal security is usually emphasized by recourse to the necessity of such conditions for market activity – essentially Hobbes' point – while the national

---

[47] Wrigley, *The path to sustained growth*, pp. 201–3, the quote is at 202.
[48] Pat Hudson, 'The regional perspective', in Pat Hudson, ed., *Regions and industries: a perspective on the industrial revolution in Britain* (Cambridge, 1989), pp. 5–38.

market is related to Smith's observation that the division of labour, a key determinant of productivity, is determined by the extent of the market.[49] That is, such arguments are inductive and probable, not deductive and certain.

It is possible to speculate on the effects of some general economic legislation, such as public finances, if rather crudely. On the income side, it is clear that Britain's central government taxed and borrowed more effectively than all other states in eighteenth-century Europe.[50] Yet as was seen in Chapter 9, tax gathering was focused markedly on London and the south-east. Effects elsewhere were certainly not negligible, but they were less direct. On the expenditure side, central government spending relative to rough estimates of GDP fluctuated heavily between periods of war (10–24 per cent) and of peace (8–14 per cent), averaging perhaps 15 per cent between 1689 and 1800.[51] This falls well short of modern levels. In Chapter 8 it was shown that these figures miss spending on bounties and drawbacks, though the latter were largely duty neutral. There certainly was a developmental aspect to Britain's public finances in this period, albeit a fairly modest one in the grand scheme of things and much more important in Scotland than England. Moreover, with so much of governmental spending on the military and national debts, it is the effects of war that loom large in assessing its consequences. A number of historians have addressed this question, pointing out both the positive and negative economic consequences of war, but there is no question that spending on the military was a small but important element of the domestic economy – in terms of provisioning, financial markets, and stability – and in establishing or keeping open access to some overseas markets.[52] But it seems best to stress the reciprocal links between such spending and

---

[49] Hobbes, *Leviathan*, p. 89: without security 'there is no place for Industry; because the fruit thereof is uncertain; and consequently no Culture of the Earth; no Navigation, nor use of the commodities that may be imported by Sea; no commodious Building ... And the life of man, solitary, nasty, brutish, and short'. Smith, *Wealth of nations*, vol. 1, p. 31: 'As it is the power of exchanging that gives occasion to the division of labour, so the extent of this division must always be limited by the extent of that power, or, in other words, by the extent of the market.'

[50] K. Kivanç Karaman and Şevket Pamuk, 'Ottoman state finances in European perspective, 1500–1914', *Journal of Economic History*, 70.3 (2010), p. 611. On a per capita basis Dutch taxes were a bit higher in the eighteenth century, but the Dutch state had gone bankrupt in 1715.

[51] Julian Hoppit, 'Checking the leviathan, 1688–1832', in Donald Winch and Patrick K. O'Brien, eds., *The political economy of British historical experience, 1688–1914* (Oxford, 2002), p. 282.

[52] For a summary see H. V. Bowen, *War and British society, 1688–1815* (Cambridge, 1998). These effects reached the greatest heights in the Revolutionary and Napoleonic wars. See Roger Knight, *Britain against Napoleon: the organization of victory, 1793–1815* (2013).

economic life in Britain, that both depended on the other, rather than to assert that the influences flowed in one direction only.

Attempts to measure the effects of general economic legislation have only made much headway with regard to the navigation acts and empire. One strand of this has been to consider the effects of the navigation acts, though the focus has usually been on colonial America rather than Britain.[53] But the effects on Britain were clearly ambiguous, for there were many costs involved.[54] It is also worth repeating the earlier point that Britain's trade with America was only briefly disrupted by the American Revolution. Another major strand has been the debate over the contribution of slavery to Britain's industrialization. In 1944 Williams argued that the effects were very large, with the monopoly of the navigation acts a significant part in that.[55] This part of Williams' thesis has been little explored by others, but Eltis and Engerman have attempted to measure the effects, concluding that they were contributory but not determining, with the West Indian colonies making the sort of impact that a single English county made.[56] This seems right: in a relatively complex economy such as Britain's in the eighteenth century, multi-causality and complex interrelations operated, such that any one major factor sat alongside many others and yet was a requirement for the whole to operate as well as it did.

Plainly, the navigation acts and the use of taxes to finance Britain's imperial endeavours were important in a general way. But Chapter 8 showed that bounties and drawbacks were an important (but evidentially hidden) element of public expenditure that often sat within or alongside the navigation acts. Some bounties had a direct effect on economic activity (especially on the agriculture of East Anglia and around London, Scottish fisheries, and linen production everywhere), others were supportive, while it is very unlikely that Glasgow would have risen to the extent that it did in this period to become a great entrepôt without tobacco being an enumerated product whose import duties could be reclaimed on re-exportation.[57] But certainly these significant influences

---

[53] For late contributions to the debate, which reference key earlier works, see: Gary M. Walton, 'The new economic history and the burdens of the navigation acts', *Economic History Review*, 24.4 (1971), pp. 533–42; Larry Sawyers, 'The navigation acts revisited', *Economic History Review*, 45.2 (1992), pp. 262–84.

[54] Stanley L. Engerman, 'British imperialism in a mercantilist age, 1492–1849: conceptual issues and empirical problems', *Revista de Historia Económica*, 16.1 (1998), pp. 206–7.

[55] Eric Williams, *Capitalism and slavery* (1944).

[56] David Eltis and Stanley L. Engerman, 'The importance of slavery and the slave trade to industrialising Britain', *Journal of Economic History*, 60.1 (2000), pp. 123–44.

[57] T. M. Devine, *The tobacco lords: a study of the tobacco merchants of Glasgow and their trading activities, c. 1740–1790* (Edinburgh, 1975); Philipp Robinson Rössner, *Scottish trade in the wake of the Union (1700–1760): the rise of a warehouse economy* (Stuttgart, 2008).

were not felt by all such efforts to stimulate or restrain activity, not least because evasion and fraud were never far away.

At first blush, the effects of specific economic legislation seem altogether clearer. All of those enclosure acts led to the distribution of thousands upon thousands of acres of land. This was done to make money in the belief that heightened productivity would more than off-set the costs involved. It is implausible to believe that landowners would have turned to Parliament time and again had this not usually been the case. Much the same can be said of acts to improve rivers, turnpike roads, and dig canals, though here the key consideration was often the reduction of transaction costs (both in time and money), thereby widening available markets. Using rough and ready data, Bogart has estimated that the resulting productivity gains were impressive compared to the economy as a whole.[58] Sometimes the returns fell short of expectations, perhaps because the project ran into unanticipated obstacles, but what the case of fen drainage showed in Chapter 6 is how persistent local propertied society was in pursuing improvement and seeking the legislation to aid them in that. If one approach did not work, then another would often be tried. To them, statutory authority mattered, and mattered a lot; Parliament was responsive to, if not uncritical of, their requests.

It is important, especially for specific economic legislation, to view impacts not merely through the eyes of its proponents, but also on wider society. The approach of this book has certainly been to look from Westminster out across Britain and beyond. But had the reference point been the individual in her or his community, then the resulting picture would have been very different. Here it is important to recall the coercive elements inherent to much economic legislation. Acts empowered central government to tax its people, whether they liked it or not; acts stopped people from accessing certain resources, such as common land; acts put a charge on using main roads beyond one's locality; and acts hindered or disallowed access to a range of economic opportunities, including the free movement of labour because of the poor laws. Given the restricted parliamentary franchise of the period, and given the huge numbers of economic acts, many people viewed Parliament and its laws as invasive, oppressive, bewildering, and unfair: to some these were 'lawless laws', benefitting 'little tyrants', that trampled on 'the grave of labours rights

---

[58] Dan Bogart, 'The transport revolution in industrialising Britain', in Roderick Floud, Jane Humphries, and Paul Johnson, eds., *The Cambridge economic history of modern Britain: vol. 1, 1700–1870* (Cambridge, 2014), p. 385. Better-based figures with regard to road transportation only have been made by Dorian Gerhold, 'The development of stage coaching and the impact of turnpike roads, 1653–1840', *Economic History Review*, 67.3 (2014), pp. 818–45.

and left the poor a slave'.[59] Economic legislation frequently intruded into social relations in eighteenth-century Britain, if more often expressed in terms of conflicting interests than of classes.

Near the start of this conclusion five headings were identified with which to consider the nature of Britain's political economies: protection and security; regulation and liberty; geopolitical reach; the gap between prescription and practice; and the distinction between legal forms and temper. In the main, the British state provided a high degree of protection and security in this period; its brilliance at raising revenue was a key means of enabling that. But a crucial development was the ease with which legislation empowered the compulsory redistribution of property rights, albeit depending on compensation payments. This usually took place at the level of specific legislation, but was collectively highly significant. With regard to regulation and liberty it is clear that political power was utilized variously. Conscious deregulation took place in some areas, the transatlantic slave trade for example for a time, and in many other areas through disuse of existing institutions and powers, sometimes consciously, sometimes not. Yet many new regulations were introduced along with some targeted spending on stimulating economic activity, producing altogether a complex patchwork, with no clear pattern. It is also clear that Britain's political economies were, thirdly, felt differently in different parts of Britain and its empire. Closest to home, there were marked differences between England and Scotland, both in terms of how they engaged with Parliament and central government for economic ends, but also in terms of the impact of economic legislation on them. Thirdly, this book has pointed up how difficult it was to turn laws into actions, and of the importance of understanding how those laws created opportunities for the black economy to develop. Most notably, 'mercantilism' is vitiated as a concept not only because it was a hodgepodge of measures and because much economic legislation cannot be thought of as mercantilist at all, but also because at the sharp end the regulations central to it were often avoided. Finally, the temper of Britain's political economies is suggested by their form. The huge numbers of economic statutes say much about the availability of Parliament to a wide body of interests, but also of the reluctance of legislators to pass acts that were too general. Britain's political economies rested heavily on how propertied society accessed sovereign power and of how that power was generally used in fairly small bits and pieces. Even central government found it hard not to pass act

---

[59] John Clare, 'The mores', in his *Major works*, ed. Eric Robinson and David Powell (Oxford, 2004), pp. 168–9.

after act about much the same thing. Hesitancy went hand in hand with no little effort.

To conclude. It is the scale and heterogeneity of Britain's political economies in this period which must be stressed. Legislatively this took four main forms: there was considerable variation within Britain, not only between England and Scotland, but also within the former; legislative action was so large and varied that it is nonsensical to credit this as a coherent 'economic policy'; applying a single label to this effort – be it 'mercantilist', 'fiscal-military', or whatever, is too limiting; and there was often a considerable gap between the letter of the law and the practice of the law, especially relating to general economic legislation. At the heart of this was the fact that propertied society had good access to sovereign power but was reluctant to countenance a more powerful government at home. That was a balance that suited most landowners, merchants, and manufacturers and, as such, gave them confidence to try to seize the opportunities that were developing. Voluminous and usually bespoke legislation was to them usually more desirable than executive action. Moreover, although Parliament was a highly unrepresentative institution, its insistence on ordering its business according to well-known rules, as well as a willingness to allow the wider public to play its part, helped to legitimate statutes. Far from all were happy with the outcomes, but the piecemeal and essentially cautious nature of law-making ultimately suited economic life well enough, though by the end of the eighteenth century the mountain of acts was becoming increasingly unworkable in certain respects. Reform began to have an effect, just as Britain's early industrial revolution threw up major new problems for Parliament to tackle, as well as creating the economic might to make free trade an increasingly realizable, even necessary, economic policy.[60]

---

[60] For a brief introduction Julian Hoppit, 'Political power and economic life, 1650–1870', in Floud, Humphries, and Johnson, eds., *The Cambridge economic history of modern Britain*, pp. 361–6.

Appendix 1: Legislation Subject Scheme

All acts and fails have been subject coded using the scheme outlined here, which is very slightly revised from that used in Hoppit, *Failed legislation*. Acts and fails have been given detailed codes, but they are then grouped under sub-headings and main headings. There is a subjective element to the scheme; placing measures in the most suitable category is not always easy, in which case they have been given two codes. Economic legislation comprises subject codes: 200–19, 301–3, 610–19, 700–69, 800–19.

0 – PERSONAL

WEALTH – 00
> 000 ESTATES BROADLY DEFINED (including settlements, specific leases, jointures)
> 001 WILLS, INHERITANCE
> 002 GUARDIANSHIP, MINORS
> 003 PATENTS
> 004 DIVORCE AND ALLOWING TO MARRY
> 005 ILLEGITIMATE, LEGITIMATE
> 006 BANKRUPTCY, DEBT OF INDIVIDUAL
> 009 MISCELLANEOUS

STATUS – 01
> 010 NAME CHANGE
> 011 NATURALIZATION (individual or small groups only)
> 012 DIGNITIES (peerage creation, rewards for public service)
> 019 MISCELLANEOUS

1 – GOVERNMENT

EXECUTIVE – 10
> 100 THE CROWN
> 101 FORFEITED ESTATES, CROWN GRANTS, CROWN LANDS
> 102 DEPARTMENTS AND OFFICES

103 ECONOMIC REFORM
109 MISCELLANEOUS

LEGISLATURE – 11

110 PARLIAMENTARY ELECTIONS, REFORM
111 PARLIAMENTARY BUSINESS
112 PARLIAMENTARY PRIVILEGE
119 MISCELLANEOUS

LOCAL – 12

120 COUNTY
121 PARISH
122 BOROUGH
123 OTHER LOCAL JURISDICTION
124 COLONIES AND PLANTATIONS (including Ireland pre-1801)
129 MISCELLANEOUS

FOREIGN POLICY – 13

130 TREATIES, DIPLOMACY
139 MISCELLANEOUS

2 – FINANCE

PUBLIC FINANCE – 20
200 LAND TAX, INCOME TAX
201 CUSTOMS AND EXCISE
202 SMUGGLING AND FRAUD
203 PUBLIC LOTTERIES, ANNUITIES
204 SUPPLY UNSPECIFIED
205 LOANS AND NATIONAL DEBT MANAGEMENT (Bank of England)
206 OTHER DIRECT TAXES (e.g. windows, carriages, stamp duties)
207 DEBTS TO CROWN
208 CIVIL LIST
209 MISCELLANEOUS (including Exchequer administration)

MONEY AND BANKING – 21

210 COINAGE AND CLIPPING
211 BULLION
212 STOCK EXCHANGE AND SHARE MARKET
213 BANKS, LENDERS (e.g. pawnbrokers)

214 USURY

215 NOTES, BILLS OF EXCHANGE AND OTHER PAPER MONEY

216 INSURANCE, ASSURANCE

217 BANKRUPTCY AND DEBT (not individuals)

219 MISCELLANEOUS (including private lotteries)

3 – LAW AND ORDER

LAW – 30

300 CRIMINAL LAW

301 LAW OF PROPERTY (including land registry)

302 INTELLECTUAL PROPERTY (e.g. rewards, patents, copyright)

303 COMMON LAW, CUSTOMARY RIGHTS

304 MARRIAGE LAW

305 GAME LAW

309 MISCELLANEOUS

ORDER – 31

310 LEGAL ADMINISTRATION AND PROCEDURE

311 CIVIL ORDER, RIOTS, SEDITION

312 TREASON, OATHS OF ALLEGIANCE, IMPEACHMENTS

313 PUNISHMENTS (including outlawry), PARDONS, INDEMNITY

314 PRISONS AND PRISONERS

315 POLICING, LAW ENFORCEMENT

319 MISCELLANEOUS

4 – RELIGION

ESTABLISHED CHURCHES – 40

400 LIVINGS, ENTITLEMENTS, TITHES

401 PARISHES, CHURCHES, CATHEDRALS (building fabric, creating parishes)

402 HIERARCHY AND ADMINISTRATION

403 THEOLOGY, RITUAL

404 FASTS, CELEBRATIONS

405 AUTHORITY, CHURCH COURTS

406 TEST AND CORPORATION ACT, INDEMNITY

409 MISCELLANEOUS

NON-ESTABLISHED RELIGIONS – 41

410 GENERAL TOLERATION, GENERAL
NATURALIZATION
411 PROTESTANT DISSENT
412 POPERY
413 BLASPHEMY, SABBATH BREAKING, SWEARING,
ATHEISM (see 606)
419 MISCELLANEOUS

5 – ARMED SERVICES

ARMY – 50 (excluding Marines)
500 RECRUITMENT AND DISBANDING
501 PAY AND ARREARS
502 PROVISIONS, EQUIPMENT, ORDNANCE,
VICTUALLING, DEBTS
503 ORGANIZATION AND DISCIPLINE
504 FORTIFICATIONS
505 PENSIONS, RETIREMENT, FAMILY SUPPORT,
HOSPITALS (e.g. Chelsea)
509 MISCELLANEOUS (including promotions)

NAVY – 51 (including Marines)
510 RECRUITMENT AND DISBANDING
511 PAY AND ARREARS
512 PROVISIONS, EQUIPMENT, ORDNANCE,
VICTUALLING, DEBTS
513 ORGANIZATION AND DISCIPLINE
514 FORTIFICATIONS AND CONVOYS
515 PENSIONS, RETIREMENT, FAMILY SUPPORT,
HOSPITAL (e.g. Greenwich)
516 PRIZES, PRIVATEERS, AND PIRACY
519 MISCELLANEOUS (including promotions)

MILITIA – 52 (including Volunteers)
520 RECRUITMENT AND DISBANDING
521 PAY AND ARREARS
522 PROVISIONS, EQUIPMENT, ORDNANCE,
VICTUALLING, DEBTS
523 ORGANIZATION AND DISCIPLINE
524 FORTIFICATIONS
525 PENSIONS, RETIREMENT, FAMILY SUPPORT,
HOSPITALS
529 MISCELLANEOUS (including promotions)

6 – SOCIAL ISSUES

HEALTH AND COMMUNITY – 60

600 PHYSICAL AND MENTAL HEALTH (e.g. hospitals, apothecaries, quarantine)

601 WATER SUPPLY AND SEWAGE

602 STREETS, PAVEMENTS, AND CLEANSING

603 LIGHTING AND WATCH

604 BUILDING REGULATIONS AND HOUSING

605 FIRE

606 MORAL REGULATION (including prostitution, gambling)

607 CEMETERIES AND DEATH

608 GENERAL PUBLIC WORKS

609 MISCELLANEOUS

LABOUR – 61

610 WAGES (including truck)

611 HOURS AND CONDITIONS

612 APPRENTICESHIP AND SKILLS

613 COMBINATIONS, FRIENDLY SOCIETIES

614 EMIGRATION AND IMMIGRATION (not poor relief settlement regulations)

615 LABOUR RELATIONS

619 MISCELLANEOUS

POOR LAW AND POVERTY – 62

620 POOR LAW RELIEF (including bastardy and settlement)

621 VAGRANCY

622 WORKHOUSES, BRIDEWELLS, IDLENESS, PUTTING TO WORK

623 CHARITIES FOR POOR (including orphans, prostitutes)

629 MISCELLANEOUS

EDUCATION AND KNOWLEDGE – 63

630 SCHOOLS

631 UNIVERSITIES, COLLEGES

632 LIBRARIES

633 SCIENCE AND THE USEFUL ARTS

634 THE WRITTEN WORD (e.g. press, censorship)

639 MISCELLANEOUS

CULTURE – 64

640 THEATRE, MUSIC, ENTERTAINMENT
641 MUSEUMS, EXHIBITIONS, ART etc.
642 SPORT
643 MISCELLANEOUS (including monuments)

7 – ECONOMY

THE LAND – 70

700 ENCLOSURE AND WASTELANDS
701 LEASES, GENERAL
702 STEWARDSHIP
703 DRAINAGE AND FLOODING
704 GENERAL IMPROVEMENTS
709 MISCELLANEOUS

AGRICULTURAL PRODUCTION – 71

710 CORN
711 OTHER CROPS (including market gardening)
712 LIVESTOCK AND DAIRY PRODUCTION
713 WOODS AND FORESTS
714 FISHERIES (including whaling)
719 MISCELLANEOUS

MINES AND QUARRIES – 72

720 COAL
721 METALS
722 OTHER (including salt)
723 QUARRIES
729 MISCELLANEOUS

FOOD AND DRINK MANUFACTURES – 73

730 BREWING, DISTILLING, MALT
731 FOOD PROCESSING (e.g. baking, butchery)
739 MISCELLANEOUS

OTHER MANUFACTURES – 74

740 WOOL
741 OTHER TEXTILES
742 METAL
743 LEATHER
744 WOOD
745 CONSTRUCTION
746 PRECIOUS METAL AND JEWELLERY

747 SHIPBUILDING
749 MISCELLANEOUS

INTERNAL TRADE – 75

750 CONSUMPTION RESTRICTIONS-ENCOURAGEMENT (sumptuary laws)
751 COMPANIES AND BUSINESS LAW (including guilds)
752 WEIGHTS, MEASURES, STANDARDS, FRAUDS
753 PRICE REGULATION
754 WHOLESALERS – MERCHANTS, JOBBERS, BADGERS
755 RETAILERS – SHOPS, MARKETS, AND FAIRS, HAWKERS
759 MISCELLANEOUS (including coasting, local tolls)

EXTERNAL TRADE – 76

760 IMPORT, EXPORT REGULATIONS (including navigation acts)
761 FOOD AND DRINK (including tobacco and sugar)
762 TEXTILES
763 SLAVES
764 OTHER RAW MATERIALS
765 OTHER FINISHED PRODUCTS
769 MISCELLANEOUS

8 – COMMUNICATIONS

WATER – 80

800 RIVERS
801 CANALS
802 BRIDGES, FERRIES, AND TUNNELS
803 PORTS, HARBOURS, DOCKS, PIERS, QUAYS (including pilots)
804 SHIPPING
805 LIGHTHOUSES AND SAFETY AT SEA
809 MISCELLANEOUS (including coastal defence)

ROADS – 81

810 ROADS, GENERAL
811 ROADS, SPECIFIC (largely turnpikes)
812 POST OFFICE
813 ROAD VEHICLES
819 MISCELLANEOUS

9 – MISCELLANEOUS

UNKNOWN – 900
MULTIPURPOSE – 910
UNCERTAIN – 920

Appendix 2: Specific Economic Legislation by English and Scottish Counties, 1707–1800

County	1750/5 pop.	Acts	Fails	Success %	Index
					Acts/Pop
Aberdeenshire	116,168	7	0	100	10
Argyllshire	66,286	6	1	86	15
Ayrshire	59,009	0	3	0	0
Banffshire	38,478	0	0	N.A.	0
Bedfordshire	53,102	85	31	73	261
Berkshire	92,162	86	25	77	152
Berwickshire	23,987	8	1	89	54
Buckinghamshire	86,912	94	11	90	176
Buteshire	7,125	1	0	100	23
Caithness	22,215	1	1	50	7
Cambridgeshire	73,764	81	28	74	179
Cheshire	124,893	58	13	82	76
Clackmannanshire	9,003	3	1	75	54
Cornwall	130,302	32	9	78	40
Cumberland	83,370	49	28	64	96
Derbyshire	105,261	148	29	84	229
Devon	293,337	55	37	60	31
Dorset	92,194	53	18	75	94
Dumfriesshire	39,788	10	1	91	41
Dunbartonshire	13,857	0	1	0	0
Durham	127,646	66	24	73	84
East Lothian	29,709	4	0	100	22
Elginshire	30,604	1	0	100	5
Essex	188,508	34	13	72	29
Fifeshire	81,570	8	1	89	16
Forfarshire (Angus)	68,883	4	1	80	9
Gloucestershire	206,599	173	27	87	136
Hampshire	144,633	102	32	76	115
Herefordshire	74,313	48	3	94	105
Hertfordshire	84,099	60	14	81	116
Huntingdonshire	32,004	66	17	80	336
Inverness-shire	59,563	1	1	50	3

(cont.)

County	1750/5 pop.	Acts	Fails	Success %	Index Acts/Pop
Kent	183,701	117	25	82	104
Kincardineshire	23,057	2	1	67	14
Kinross-shire	4,889	1	1	50	33
Kirkcudbrightshire	21,205	2	0	100	15
Lanarkshire	81,726	34	0	100	68
Lancashire	317,157	148	38	80	76
Leicestershire	97,088	190	39	83	319
Lincolnshire	163,607	301	78	79	300
Linlithgowshire	16,829	13	1	93	126
London	670,000	95	117	45	23
Middlesex	584,571	114	27	81	32
Midlothian	90,412	16	3	84	29
Nairnshire	5,694	0	0	N.A.	0
Norfolk	233,585	141	24	85	98
Northamptonshire	116,079	184	40	82	258
Northumberland	134,539	68	24	74	82
Nottinghamshire	88,427	135	33	80	249
Orkney	23,381	0	0	N.A.	0
Oxfordshire	94,893	119	36	77	204
Peebles-shire	8,908	4	0	100	73
Perthshire	120,116	8	2	80	11
Renfrewshire	26,645	6	2	75	37
Ross and Cromarty	48,084	1	0	100	3
Roxburghshire	34,704	6	2	75	28
Rutland	13,251	22	3	88	271
Selkirkshire	4,021	2	1	67	81
Shetland	15,210	0	0	N.A.	0
Shropshire	137,461	82	16	84	97
Somerset	231,958	142	40	78	100
Staffordshire	150,819	120	25	83	130
Stirlingshire	37,014	10	2	83	44
Suffolk	166,650	120	11	92	117
Surrey	151,015	72	36	67	78
Sussex	98,376	65	20	76	108
Sutherland	20,774	0	0	N.A.	0
Warwickshire	132,472	183	54	77	225
Westmorland	35,468	33	24	58	152
Wigtownshire	16,466	1	0	100	10
Wiltshire	166,798	149	48	76	146
Worcestershire	109,703	123	29	81	183
Yorkshire	521,188	648	201	76	203
Total	7,857,285	4,821	1,374	78	100

Source: see Chapter 4, note 38.

Bibliography

ARCHIVES

Bedfordshire Archives and Record Services

> Franklin Papers, FN1255, FN1265/1275, 1319–22, 1327–9.
> Duke of Bedford Thorney Abbey estate papers, R/4508/13 and
> R Fens (uncatalogued), Boxes 1–2.

British Library, London

> Add Mss, 4761, Milles collection.
> Add Mss, 4880, Strahan papers.
> Add Mss, 8133, Musgrave papers.
> Add Mss, 88,906/1/11, Bowood papers.
> Add Mss, 33,050, Newcastle papers.
> Add Mss, 35,906, 35,910, Hardwicke papers.
> Add Mss, 38,217, 38,339, Liverpool papers.
> Egerton Mss, 2985.
> Harleian Mss, 5120, 7021.
> Lansdowne Mss, 1049, 1215
> Stowe Mss, 354.

Cambridge University Library

> Walpole papers, Ch(H) 40/16, 18, 41/1/1–64, 80/486.

Cambridgeshire Archives

> Accounts of Conservators of the River Cam, Q/S9/1 (1751–92),
> 2 (1793–1824).
> Order book 1722–7, Bedford Level Corporation, R59/31/11/20.
> Petitions to the Bedford Level Corporation, S/B/SP/1–790.

Edinburgh City Archives

Edinburgh Chamber of Commerce minute book, ED005/1.

Huntington Library, San Marino, California

Ellesmere papers, EL9609, 9855.

Lincolnshire Archives Office

Quarter sessions, LQS B/7/2–8.
Spalding Sewers 488/A-E, 493–6, 500/77–8, 500/101.

The National Archives, Kew

Board of Trade, BT6/99, BT6/230.
Colonial Office, CO389/14/9, CO390/4.
Customs, CUST17/21, CUST24/19, CUST37/62 CUST145/4–14.
Privy Council, PC1/1/171PC/1/16/11, 25.
Pitt papers, PRO 30/8/288.
State papers, SP34/2/23.
Treasury, T1/332/41–2, T1/351/47, 49, 59, T1/361/21 and 38, T1/425/286–7, T1/462/43–4, T1/487, T1/506/52, T36/13, T45/1, T45/4/9B, T64/274/67, T64/278, 281, T64/282/1–2.

The National Archives of Scotland, Edinburgh

CE8/1–3, Scottish Excise to Treasury.
E554/3, Excise accounts, 1707–1807.
E561/3, Excise officials, 1707–c. 1800.

National Library of Scotland, Edinburgh

Melville papers, Mss 640.
MS 1918, 'Copys of original papers delivered to the Lord Justice Clerk'.

Northamptonshire Record Office

W(A) Box 4/parcel XIII, no. 9, 'A survey of the river Nine'.

Parliamentary Archives, London

House of Lords main papers, HL/PO/JO/10/3/213/37; HL/PO/JO/10/3/218/8; HL/PO/JO/10/7/681, 703, 740, 760, 849, 867, 894, 921, 945, 974, 1006.

Sutro Library, San Francisco, California

Sir Joseph Banks collection, Fens, F5, 6, 8, and 9.

West Yorkshire Archives Service, Bradford

Worsted Committee minute book, 56D88/1/1.

William L. Clements Library, Ann Arbor, Michigan

Shelburne Papers, vols. 109, 114, 119, 135i.
Townshend Papers, 8/17/3–11, 16–17, 22, 8/21/8, 297/2/10.

PRINTED PRIMARY SOURCES

Joseph Addison and Richard Steele, *The Spectator* ed. Donald F. Bond (5 vols. Oxford, 1965).

James Anderson, *Observations on the means of exciting a spirit of national industry; chiefly intended to promote the agriculture, commerce, manufactures, and fisheries of Scotland* (Edinburgh, 1777).

Annals of Agriculture (46 vols., 1784–1815).

Anon., *A collection of all the statutes now in force, against the transportation of wooll* (1714).

A collection of statutes concerning Rochester Bridge (1733).

A collection of statutes concerning the incorporation, trade, and commerce of the East India Company (1786).

A list of goods prohibited to be imported into or exported from Great Britain (1775).

A narrative of the proceedings and resolutions of a general meeting of the delegates from the manufacturers of wool, held at the Crown and Anchor tavern, in the Strand, the 28th of November, 1787 (1787).

A plan for obtaining an Act of Parliament for the better draining the North-Level, part of the Great Level of the fens [1753?].

A refutation of the charges brought forward by Mr. Coltman, at a meeting held at Spilsby, against Sir Joseph Banks, and his steward, Mr. Parkinson (1803).

A result of a meeting at Wisbech, December 17, 1768 (1768).

A short state of facts; tending to shew the utility of the proposed plan of navigation from the town of Bishops Stortford, to join the Cambridge River (1788).

A state of the revenue and debt of the Corporation of Bedford-Levels [1753?].

A view of the taxes, funds and public revenues of England ... from the year 1702, to the year 1712 inclusive (1743).

A word or two to the South Holland proprietors, and the Fleet commoners (1796).

Abstract of several Acts of Parliament, now in force, to prevent the exportation of wool, sheep, & c. [1740?].

Account of nature, &c. of oil from beech-tree (1714).

An abstract of the ancient and present state of the navigation of Lynn, Cambridge, &c [1775?].

An account of the late design of buying up the wooll of Ireland in company. In a letter to J. L. (1674).

An ample disquisition into the nature of regalities and other heretable jurisdictions (1747).

An answer, paragraph by paragraph, to A report of the present state of the great level of the fens [1724].

An epitome of the bill now depending in Parliament, the better to prevent the exportations of live, sheep, wool, &c. (1788).

Angliae tutamen: or, the safety of England (1695).

Answer to the observations on, intitled Bedford Level [1778].

Bedford Level [1778].

Calculations and remarks, shewing the utility of extending the Cambridge navigation, so as to communicate with the City of London (n.d.).

Calculations on the navigation proposed to be made in order to extend the communication between London and Cambridgeshire, by water carriage [1788?].

Case of the commoners in the Soke of Bolingbroke (1810).

Considerations on the Union between England and Scotland, and on some commercial matters in both kingdoms (1790).

Considerations upon the present state of the wool trade, the laws made concerning that article, and how far the same are consistent with true policy, and the real interest of the state (1781).

Directions for raising flax ... re-printed by order of the Lords Commissioners for Trade and Plantations (1781).

Directions for the sowing and preparing of flax (Dublin, 1711).

Free and candid remarks on the plan of taxation, as resolved on by the Eau-Brink Cut Committee (Kings Lynn, [1794?]).

Gephyralogia: an historical account of bridges, antient and modern (1751).

'Observations of London merchants on American trade, 1783', *American Historical Review*, 18.4 (1913), pp. 769–80.

Reasons attempting to shew the necessity of the proposed cut from Eau Brink to Lynn (1793).

Reasons for a limited exportation of wooll (1677).

Reasons humbly offered, to bring in a bill to confirm the decrees for draining of Lindsey-level, in the county of Lincoln [1660?].

Remembrances: or, a compleat collection of the standing orders of the House of Lords in England (1744).

Some general observations on the petitions now before the honourable House of Commons, praying a remedy against the running of wool [1741?].

State of the revenue and debt of the Corporation of the Bedford-Levels [1753?].

Superiorities display'd: or, Scotland's grievance, by reason of the slavish dependence of the people upon their great men (Edinburgh, 1746).

The ancient trades decayed, repaired again (1678).

The claim of taxing the navigations and free lands for the drainage and preservation of the fens (1793).

The deplorable case of the chief and other agents or officers that have been deputed and concerned in the preventing the carrying away and the exportation of wool of this kingdom [1702].

The fisheries revived: or, Britain's hidden treasures discovered (1750).
The laws of sewers; or the office and authority of Commissioners of Sewers (2nd edn., 1732).
The legal claim of the British sugar-colonies to enjoy an exclusive right of supplying this kingdom with sugars, in return for sundry restrictions laid upon these colonies in favour of the products, manufactures, commerce, revenue, and and [sic] navigation, of Great-Britain; demonstrated by proofs extracted from the statute-book [1792].
The Liverpool tractate: an eighteenth-century manual on the procedure of the House of Commons, ed. Catherine Strateman (New York, 1937).
View of the conduct of parties, respecting the proposal of accommodation offered by the merchants of Lynn, to the promoters of the bill for making the cut from Eau Brink to Lynn (1794).
John Anstie, *A general view of the bill presented to Parliament during the last session, for preventing the illicit exportation of British wool and live sheep* (1787).
A letter addressed to Edward Phelips, esq. member for the county of Somerset, containing general observations on the advantages of manufacturing the combing wool of England, which is smuggled to France (1788).
John Anstie *To the land-owners, wool-growers, and wool-dealers, in the county of Sussex* ([n.p.], 1786).
J.W. Archenholz, *A picture of England* (2 vols., 1789).
John Armstrong, *Colonel Armstrong's report, with proposals for draining the fenns and amending the harbour of Lynn, 1724* (1724).
James Ashley, *A seventh letter from the Rev. James Ashley, Rector of Fleet, to Mr. George Maxwell, respecting the Fleet inclosure* (Wisbech, 1802).
Thomas Badeslade, *The history of the ancient and present state of the navigation of the port of King's Lyn, and of Cambridge* (1725).
A scheme for draining the great level of the fens, called Bedford-Level (1729).
Samuel Baldwin, *A survey of British customs* (1770).
[Joseph Banks], *The propriety of allowing a qualified exportation of wool discussed historically* (1782).
[Cesar Beccaria], *An essay on crimes and punishments* (1767).
[Jean Bertrand, Benjamin Samuel Georges Carrard, and Gabriel Seigneux de Correvon], *Essays on the spirit of legislation, in the encouragement of agriculture, population, manufactures, and commerce* (1772).
Theodore Besterman, ed., *Voltaire's correspondence* (107 vols., Geneva, 1953–65).
Thomas Birch, *The history of the Royal Society of London* (4 vols., 1756–7).
James Bischoff, *A comprehensive history of the woollen and worsted manufactures* (2 vols., 1842).
Reasons for the immediate repeal of the tax on foreign wool (3rd edn., 1820).
William Blackstone, *Commentaries on the laws of England* (4 vols., Oxford, 1765–9).
Walter Blith, *England's improver, or a new survey of husbandry* (1649).
Charles Bridgman [i.e., Bridgeman], *A report of the present state of the Great Level of the fens, called Bedford-Level, and of the port of Lynn; and of the Rivers Ouse and Nean* (1724).

British Parliamentary Papers.

William Bunyon, ... *or, strange news from the fenns. Being a full and true account of a [p]owerful and tumultuous riot, near Spalding in Lincolnshire* (1700).

Edmund Burke, *The writings and speeches of Edmund Burke, vol. 3: Party, Parliament, and the American War, 1774–1780.* Edited by Warren M. Elofson and John A. Woods (Oxford, 1996).

Richard Burn, *The justice of the peace, and the parish officer* (2 vols., 1755).

R. H. Campbell, ed., *States of the annual progress of the linen manufacture, 1727–1754* (Edinburgh, 1964).

Benjamin Pitts Capper, *A statistical account of the population and cultivation, produce and consumption, of England and Wales, compiled from the accounts laid before the House of Commons, and the Board of Agriculture* (1801).

Harold B. Carter, ed., *The sheep and wool correspondence of Sir Joseph Banks, 1781–1820* (New South Wales and London, 1979).

Richard Carter and Peter Ellers, *A scheme for preventing the exportation of wool* (1713).

[William Carter], *England's interest asserted: in the improvement of its native commodities; and more especially the manufacture of wool* (1669).

[William Carter] *The proverb crossed, or a new paradox maintained, (viz.) that it is not at all times true, that interest cannot lye* (1677).

James J. Cartwright, ed., *The Wentworth papers 1705–1739: selected from the private and family correspondence of Thomas Wentworth, Lord Raby, created in 1711 Earl of Strafford* (1883).

George Chalmers, *An estimate of the comparative strength of Great Britain during the present and four preceding reigns* (1782).

[Edward Chamberlayne], *Englands wants: or several proposals probably beneficial for England* (1668).

E. Chambers, *Cyclopædia: or, an universal dictionary of arts and sciences* (2 vols., 1728).

John Clare, *The major works.* Edited by Eric Robinson and David Powell (Oxford, 2004).

The parish: a satire. Edited by Eric Robinson (Harmondsworth, 1986).

'Sir John Clerk's observations on the present circumstances of Scotland, 1730', ed. T. C. Smout, *Miscellany of the Scottish History Society*, 10 (1965), pp. 175–212.

W. Cobbett, ed., *The parliamentary history of England, from the earliest times to the year 1803* (36 vols., 1806–20).

Cobbett's Weekly Political Register.

Roger Coke, *A discourse of trade* (1670).

Charles Nalson Cole, *A collection of laws which form the constitution of the Bedford Level Corporation* (1761; 2nd edn., 1803).

Patrick Colquhoun, *A treatise on the wealth, power, and resources, of the British empire* (1814).

William Coxe, ed., *Memoirs of the administration of the right honourable Henry Pelham* (2 vols., 1829).

Earl of Crawford, *A bibliography of royal proclamations of the Tudor and Stuart sovereigns and of others published under authority, 1485–1714* (2 vols., Oxford, 1910).

Bibliotheca Lindesiana: vol. VIII, handlist of proclamations issued by royal and other constitutional authorities, 1714–1910 (Wigan, 1913).

Culloden papers [ed. H. R. Duff] (1815).

Timothy Cunningham, *The history of the customs, aids, subsidies, national debts, and taxes ... The third edition corrected. With several improvements suggested by Sir Charles Whitworth* (1778).

John Dalrymple, Earl of Stair, *The state of the national debt, the national income, and the national expenditure* (1776).

John Dalrymple, *The question considered, whether wool should be allowed to be exported, when the price is low at home, on paying a duty to the public?* (1781).

Charles Davenant, *An essay on the East-India-trade* (1696).

An essay upon ways and means (1695).

The political and commercial works of that celebrated writer Charles D'Avenant. Edited by Sir Charles Whitworth (5 vols., 1771).

Thomas Day, *A letter to Arthur Young, esq. on a bill now depending in Parliament to prevent the exportation of wool* (1788).

Alexis de Tocqueville, *Journeys to England and Ireland.* Edited by J. P. Mayer (1958).

[Matthew Decker], *An essay on the causes of the decline of foreign trade* (1744).

Daniel Defoe, *An essay upon projects* (1697).

A tour through the whole island of Great Britain. Edited by Pat Rogers (Harmondsworth, 1971).

John Dickinson, *Letters from a farmer in Pennsylvania* (New York, 1768).

John Dryden, *King Arthur* (1691), in *The works of John Dryden, vol. 16.* Edited by Vinton A. Dearing (Berkeley, CA, 1996).

William Dugdale, *The history of imbanking and drayning of divers fens and marshes* (1662).

James Earnshaw, *An abstract of various penal statutes relating to the revenue of customs* (2 vols., 1793).

Edinburgh Monthly Review.

Bryan Edwards, *The history, civil and commercial, of the British colonies in the West Indies* (2 vols., 1793).

George Eliot, *Middlemarch: a story of provincial life* (1871–2).

W. Ellis, *The modern husbandman, or the practice of farming* (4 vols., 1744).

Extracts from the records of the Convention of the Royal Burghs of Scotland, 1759–79 (Edinburgh, 1918).

Robert Filmer, *Patriarcha and other writings.* Edited by Johann P. Somerville (Cambridge, 1991).

Andrew Fletcher, *Political works.* Edited by John Robertson (Cambridge, 1997).

[Duncan Forbes], *Some considerations on the present state of Scotland* (Edinburgh, 1744).

[Joseph Galloway], *Cool thoughts on the consequences to Great Britain of American independence* (1780).

J. Gee, *An abstract of reasons for encouraging the linen manufactory* [1767].

Considerations on the expediency of a bounty upon hemp and flax of home growth [1767].

Observations on the growth of hemp and flax in Great Britain (1765).

Joshua Gee, *The trade and navigation of Great-Britain considered: a new edition with many interesting notes and additions, by a merchant* (1767).

Gentleman's Magazine.

Isaac Gervaise, *The system or theory of the trade of the world* (1720).

Gloucester Journal.

Anchitell Grey, ed., *Debates of the House of Commons, from the year 1667 to the year 1694* (13 vols., 1769).

Alexander Hamilton, James Madison, and John Jay, *The federalist.* Edited by Terence Ball (Cambridge, 2003).

[Andrew Hamilton], *An enquiry into the principles of taxation* (1790).

Hansard, *Commons debates.*

[Joseph Harris], *An essay upon money and coins* (1757).

[David Hartley], *The budget* (1764).

John Hatsall, *Precedents and proceedings in the House of Commons: under separate titles, with observations* (4 vols., 1818).

John Haynes, *Great Britain's glory, or an account of the great numbers of poor employ'd in the woollen and silk manufacturies ... with the reasons for the decay of those trades* (1715).

Cecil Headlam, ed., *Calendar of state papers, colonial series, 1706–1708, June.* (1916).

[Robert Heron], *A letter from Ralph Anderson, esq. to Sir John Sinclair* (Edinburgh, 1797).

HMC, *Eighth report* (1881).

Eleventh report, appendix, part 4. The manuscripts of the Marquess of Townshend (1887).

House of Lords manuscripts, vol. 2 (new series). *The manuscripts of the House of Lords, 1697–1699* (1905).

Thomas Hobbes, *The leviathan.* Edited by Richard Tuck (Cambridge, 1991).

William Holmes, *A digest of the Acts of Parliament, (now in force) for preventing the exportation of sheep, wool, & c.* (Exeter, 1786).

John Baker Holroyd, *Lord Sheffield's report at Lewes wool fair, July 26th, 1819* (1819).

Julian Hoppit, ed., *Nehemiah Grew and England's economic development* (Oxford, 2012).

David Hume, *Essays, moral, political, and literary.* Edited by Eugene F. Miller (Indianapolis, IN, 1987).

The letters of David Hume. Edited by J. Y. T. Greig (2 vols., Oxford, 1932).

[Stephen Theodore Janssen], *Smuggling laid open, in all its extensive and destructive branches* (1763).

[Theodore Janssen], *General maxims in trade, particularly applied to the commerce between Great Britain and France* (1713).

Samuel Johnson, *A dictionary of the English language* (1755).

Samuel Johnson and James Boswell, *Johnson's journey to the western islands of Scotland and Boswell's journal of a tour to the Hebrides with Samuel Johnson, LL.D.* Edited by R. W. Chapman (Oxford, 1978).

Journal of the Commissioners for Trade and Plantations, vol. 7 from January 1734–5 to December 1741 (1930).

Journal of the Commissioners for Trade and Plantations, vol. 8 from January 1741–2 to December 1749 (1931).

Journals of the Commons ... of Ireland, vols. 18–19 (1796–1800).

Journals of the House of Commons, vols. 8 (1660–7) to 55 (1799–1800).

Journals of the House of Lords, vols. 9 (1660–6) to 42 (1798–1800).

[Henry Home, Lord Kames], *Progress of flax-husbandry in Scotland* (Edinburgh, 1766).

[Henry Home, Lord Kames], *Sketches of the history of man*. Edited by James A. Harris (3 vols., Indianapolis, IN, 2007).

[J. Keymor], *A cleare and evident way for enriching the nations of England and Ireland* (1650).

William Killigrew, *The property of all English-men asserted, in the history of Lindsey Level* (1705).

[Nathaniel Kinderley], *The present state of the navigation of the towns of Lyn, Wisbeech, Spalding, and Boston* (Bury St Edmunds, 1721).

Nathaniel Kinderley [son of the above], *The ancient and present state of the navigation of the towns of Lyn, Wisbeach, Spalding, and Boston* (2nd edn., 1751).

Charles King, *British merchant; or commerce preserv'd* (3 vols., 1721).

David Lagomarsino and Charles T. Wood, ed., *The trial of Charles I: a documentary history* (Hanover, NH, 1989).

Sheila Lambert, ed., *The House of Commons session papers of the eighteenth century* (147 vols., Wilmington, DE, 1975).

George S. Lamoines, ed., *Charges to the Grand Jury, 1689–1803*, Camden, Fourth Series, 43 (1992).

John Locke, *Two treatises of government*. Edited by Peter Laslett (Cambridge, 1991).

Jean Louis de Lolme, *The constitution of England*. Edited by David Lieberman (1784 edn., Indianapolis, IN, 2007).

John London, *Some considerations on the importance of the woollen manufactures* (1740).

London Gazette.

A. M'Donald, *An essay upon the raising and dressing of flax and hemp* (Edinburgh, 1784).

David Macpherson, *Annals of commerce* (4 vols., 1802).

John Maitland, *Observations on the impolicy of permitting the exportation of British wool, and of preventing the free importation of foreign wool* (1818).

Thomas Manly, *A discourse shewing that the exportation of wooll is destructive to this kingdom* (1677).

[Joseph Massie], *An essay on the many advantages accruing to the community from the superior neatness, conveniences, decorations and embellishments of great and capital cities* (1754).

[Joseph Massie], *Observations on the new cyder-tax* [1764?].

Joseph Massie], *A representation concerning the knowledge of commerce as a national concern; pointing out the proper means of promoting such knowledge in this kingdom* (1760).

George Maxwell, *General view of the agriculture of the county of Huntingdon* (1793).

Robert Maxwell, *Select transactions of the Honourable Society of Improvers in the Knowledge of Agriculture in Scotland* (Edinburgh, 1743).

M. W. McCahill, ed., *The correspondence of Stephen Fuller, 1788–1795: Jamaica, the West India interest at Westminster and the campaign to preserve the slave trade. Parliamentary History*, Special Issue: Texts and Studies Series 9, 33, Supplement 1 (2014).

J. R. McCulloch, *The literature of political economy: a classified catalogue* (1845).

Diary of John Milward, esq. Member of Parliament for Derbyshire September 1666 to May 1668. Edited by Caroline Robbins (Cambridge, 1938).

W. E. Minchinton, ed., *Politics and the port of Bristol in the eighteenth century. The petitions of the Society of Merchant Venturers, 1698–1803* (Bristol Record Society, 23, 1963).

William Molyneux, *The case of Ireland's being bound by Acts of Parliament in England stated* (Dublin, 1698).

[Alexander Montgomerie, Earl of of Eglinton], *An inquiry into the original and consequences of the public debt* (Edinburgh, 1753).

Jonas Moore, *The history or narrative of the Great Level of the fenns* (1685).

Morning Chronicle.

[Patrick Murray, Lord Elibank], *Thoughts on money, circulation and paper currency* (Edinburgh, 1758).

Thomas Neale, *The ruinous state of the parish of Manea in the Isle of Ely, with the causes and remedy of it* (n.p., 1748).

William Nicholson, *An abstract of such Acts of Parliament as are now in force for preventing the exportation of wool* (1786).

[Dudley North], *Discourses upon trade: principally directed to the cases of interest, coynage, clipping, increase of money* (1691).

The Oakes diaries: business, politics and the family in Bury St Edmunds, 1778–1827. Edited by Jane Fiske. Suffolk Records Society, 32 (2 vols., Woodbridge, 1990).

Thomas Hyde Page, *Minutes of the evidence of Sir Thomas Hyde Page, Knight, on the second reading of the Eau Brink drainage bill* (1794).

Parliamentary Register (1790).

P. Paxton, *A discourse concerning the nature, advantage, and improvement of trade* (1704).

Joshua Peart, Henry Boulton, and Nathaniel Kent, *South Holland embankment* (1791).

Christopher Pemberton, *Eau Brink accounts: copy of statement of account made up to the 25th August, 1817* (1817).

W. Pennington, *Reflections on the various advantages resulting from the draining, inclosing, and allotting of large commons and common fields* (1769).

John Phillips, *A treatise on inland navigation: illustrated with a whole-sheet plan, delineating the course of an intended navigable canal from London to Norwich and Lynn* (1785).

William Playfair, *The commercial and political atlas; representing, by means of stained copper-plate charts, the exports, imports, and general trade of England; the national debt, and other public accounts* (1786).

James Postlethwayt, *The history of the public revenue, from the revolution in 1688, to Christmas 1753* (1759).

[Malachy Postlethwayt], *A dissertation on the plan, use, and importance of the universal dictionary of trade and commerce* (1749).

[Malachy Postlethwayt], *The universal dictionary of trade and commerce* (2 vols., 1751–5).

T. Pownall, *A letter from Governor Pownall to Adam Smith* (1776).

Live and let live; a treatise on the hostile rivalships between the manufacturer and land-worker [1787].

A memoir entituled drainage and navigation but one united work ... addressed to the corporations of Lynn-Regis and Bedford Level (1775).

[William Pulteney], *The budget opened. Or an answer to a pamphlet intitled, a letter from a Member of Parliament to his friends in the country* (1733).

[William Pulteney], *Considerations on the present state of public affairs, and the means of raising the necessary supplies* (1779).

Ferdinand Pulton and Thomas Manby, *A collection of statutes now in use* (1670).

Reports from the committees of the House of Commons 1715–1801, vol. 6 (1782–1802).

Carew Reynell, *The true English interest* (1674).

George Rose, *A brief examination into the increase of the revenue, commerce, and manufactures of Great Britain from 1792 to 1799* (5th edn., 1799).

Jean Jacques Rousseau, 'Political economy', in *The social contract*. Edited by Christopher Betts (Oxford, 1994).

Nathaniel Ryder, 'Parliamentary diaries of Nathaniel Ryder, 1764–7', ed. P. D. G. Thomas, *Camden Miscellany*, 23 (1969), pp. 229–372.

Reay Sabourn, *Oppression exposed, or liberty and property maintained: being an enquiry into the several mismanagements of persons concerned in the revenues of customs and excise in Scotland* (Edinburgh, 1729).

H. Saxby, *The British customs* (1757).

Walter Scott, *The heart of mid-Lothian*. Edited by David Hewitt and Alison Lumsden (Edinburgh, 2004).

William A. Shaw, ed., *Bibliography of the collection of books and tracts on commerce, currency, and poor law (1557 to 1763) formed by Joseph Massie* (1937).

[Thomas Sheridan], *A discourse of the rise and power of parliaments* (1677).

R. C. Simmons and P. D. G. Thomas, eds., *Proceedings and debates of the British parliaments respecting North America, 1754–1783* (6 vols., Millwood, NY, 1982–7).

John Sinclair, *Address to the landed interest, on the corn bill now depending in Parliament* (1791).

Address to the Society for the Improvement of British Wool, constituted at Edinburgh, on Monday, January 31, 1791 (1791).

The history of the public revenue of the British empire (3rd edn., 3 vols., 1805).

Plan for establishing a Board of Agriculture and internal improvement (1793).

John Sinclair [son of the above], *Memoirs of the life and works of the late right honourable Sir John Sinclair* (2 vols., Edinburgh, 1837).

Adam Smith, *Additions and corrections to the first and second editions of Dr. Adam Smith's Inquiry into the nature and causes of the wealth of nations* (1784).

The correspondence of Adam Smith. Edited by Ernest Campell Mossner and Ian Simpson Ross (Oxford, 1987).

An inquiry into the nature and causes of the wealth of nations. Edited by William Playfair. Introduction by William Rees-Mogg (3 vols., 1995).

An inquiry into the nature and causes of the wealth of nations. Edited by R. H. Campbell and A. S. Skinner (2 vols., Oxford, 1976).

John Smith, *Chronicon rusticum-commerciale; or, memoirs of wool* (2 vols., 1747).

St James's Chronicle.

The statutes at large, passed in the parliaments held in Ireland (21 vols., Dublin, 1786–1804).

Robert Steele, ed., *Tudor and Stuart royal proclamations, 1485–1714* (2 vols., Oxford, 1910).

James Steuart, *An inquiry into the principles of political oeconomy* (2 vols., 1767).

The letter-book of John Steuart of Inverness, 1715–1752. Edited by William Mackay, Scottish History Society Publications, second series, vol. 9 (1915).

Dugald Stewart, 'Account of the life and writings of Adam Smith, LL.D', in Adam Smith, *Essays on philosophical subjects*. Edited by W. P. D. Wightman, J. C. Bryce, and I. S. Ross (Oxford, 1980), pp. 269–351.

William Stout, *The autobiography of William Stout of Lancaster, 1665–1752*. Edited by J. D. Marshall (Manchester, 1967).

John Swinton, *An abridgment of the public statutes in force and use relative to Scotland* (2 vols., Edinburgh, 1755).

Joan Thirsk and J. P. Cooper, eds., *Seventeenth-century economic documents* (Oxford, 1972).

[Charles Townshend], *National thoughts, recommended to the serious attention of the public: with an appendix, shewing the damages arising from a bounty on corn* [1751].

[Josiah Tucker], *A brief essay on the advantages and disadvantages which respectively attend France and Great Britain, with regard to trade* (1749).

[Josiah Tucker], *The elements of commerce and theory of taxes* [Bristol?, 1755].

[Josiah Tucker], *Reflections on the present low price of coarse wools* (1782).

[Edmund Turnor], *A short view of the proceedings of the several committees and meetings held in consequence of the intended petition to Parliament, from the county of Lincoln, for a limited exportation of wool* (1782).

[William Vaughan], *Reasons in favour of the London-docks* (1795).

Cornelius Vermuyden, *A discourse touching the drayning the great fennes* (1642).

Neil Walker and Thomas Craddock, *The history of Wisbech and the fens* (1849).

Edward Walls, *A letter to the right honourable Sir Joseph Banks* (1803; 2nd edn., 1804.

Horace Walpole, *Memoirs of King George II*. Edited by John Brooke (3 vols., New Haven, CT, 1985).

[Daniel Webb], *An enquiry how far the declining state of the British woollen manufactures for exportation does affect the English landed interest* [1732?].

[William Webster], *The consequences of trade, as to the wealth and strength of any nation; of the woollen trade in particular, and the great superiority of it over all other branches of trade* (1740).

[William Webster], *The draper confuted; or, a candid and impartial, but full answer to the consequences of trade: humbly offer'd to the consideration of both houses of Parliament* (1740).

Samuel Wells, *The history of the drainage of the great level of the fens, called Bedford Level* (2 vols., 1828–30).

[Philip Wharton], *The true Briton* (2 vols., 1723).

[George Whatley], *Reflections on the principles of trade in general* (1769).

Anne Whiteman, ed., *The Compton census of 1676: a critical edition* (Oxford, 1986).

[Charles Whitworth], *A collection of the supplies, and ways and means, from the Revolution to the present time* (1763).

[Charles Whitworth], *A register of the trade of the Port of London* (1777).

[Charles Whitworth], ed., *Scarce tracts on trade and commerce, serving as a supplement to Davenant's works* (2 vols., 1776).

[Charles Whitworth], ed., *Select dissertations on colonies and plantations. By those celebrated authors, Sir Josiah Child, Charles D'Avenant, LL. D. and Mr. William Wood.* (1775).

[Charles Whitworth], *State of the trade of Great Britain, in its imports and exports* (1776).

Orlo Cyprian Williams, ed., 'The minute book of James Courthope', *Camden Miscellany*, 20 (1953).

T.W.Williams, *A compendious digest of statute law, comprising the substance and effect of all the public Acts of Parliament in force, from Magna Charta ... to the twenty-seventh year of ... George III* (1787).

Joseph Wimpey, *Thoughts upon several interesting subjects, viz. on the exportation of corn, on the high price of provisions, on manufactures, commerce, &c.* [1770].

Arthur Young, *The autobiography of Arthur Young*. Edited by M. Betham-Edwards (1898).

General view of the agriculture of Lincolnshire (2nd edn 1813).

Political arithmetic (1774).

The question of wool truly stated (1788).

A speech on the wool bill, that might have been spoken in the House of Commons, Thursday, May the 1st, 1788 (1788).

Travels in France during the years 1787, 1788 and 1789. Edited by Constantia Maxwell (Cambridge, 1929).

E. A. W. Zimmermann, *A political survey of the present state of Europe, in sixteen tables* (1787).

SECONDARY SOURCES

Daron Acemoglu, Simon Johnson, and James A. Robinson, 'Institutions as a fundamental cause of long-run growth', in Philippe Aghion and Steven N. Durlauf, eds., *Handbook of economic growth*, vol. 1a (Amsterdam, 2005), pp. 385–472.

Daron Acemoglu and James A. Robinson, 'Paths of economic and political development', in Barry R. Weingast and Donald A. Wittman, eds., *The Oxford handbook of political economy* (Oxford, 2006), pp. 673–92.

Frances Acomb, *Anglophobia in France, 1763–1789: an essay in the history of constitutionalism and nationalism* (Durham, NC, 1950).

Doohwan Ahn and Brendan Simms, 'European great power politics in British public discourse, 1714–1763', in William Mulligan and Brendan Simms, eds., *The primacy of foreign policy in British history, 1660–2000: how strategic concerns shaped modern Britain* (Basingstoke, 2010), pp. 79–101.

William Albert, *The turnpike road system in England, 1663–1840* (Cambridge, 1972).

Robert C. Allen, *The British industrial revolution in global perspective* (Cambridge, 2009).

L. J. Alson, 'New institutional economics', in Steven N. Durlauf and Lawrence E. Blume, eds., *The new Palgrave dictionary of economics* (2nd edn., 8 vols., 2008), vol. 6, pp. 32–9.

Michael Anderson, 'Guesses, estimates and adjustments: Webster's 1755 "census" of Scotland revisited again', *Journal of Scottish Historical Studies*, 31.1 (2011), pp. 26–45.

Charles M. Andrews, *British committees, commissions, and councils of trade and plantations, 1622–1675* (Baltimore, 1908).

The colonial background of the American Revolution (New Haven, CT, 1931).

England's commercial and colonial policy (New Haven, CT, 1938).

David Armitage, *The ideological origins of the British empire* (Cambridge, 2000).

Frances Armytage, *The free port system in the British West Indies: a study in commercial policy, 1766–1822* (1953).

Robert Ashton, 'The parliamentary agitation for free trade in the opening years of the reign of James I', *Past and Present*, 38 (1967), pp. 40–55.

T. S. Ashton, *Economic fluctuations in England, 1700–1800* (Oxford, 1959).

An economic history of England: the eighteenth century (1972)

William J. Ashworth, *Customs and excise: trade, production, and consumption in England, 1640–1845* (Oxford, 2003).

'The intersection of industry and the state in eighteenth-century Britain', in Lissa Roberts, Simon Schaffer, and Peter Dear, eds., *The mindful hand: sites, artefacts and the rise of modern science and technology* (Chicago, IL, 2007), pp. 349–77.

Tony Aspromourgos, 'The mind of the oeconomist: an overview of the "Petty papers" archive', *History of Economic Ideas*, 9.1 (2001), pp. 39–101.

Raymond Astbury, 'The renewal of the Licensing Act in 1693 and its lapse in 1695', *The Library*, 5th series, 33.4 (1978), pp. 296–322.

G. E. Aylmer, 'The peculiarities of the English state', *Journal of Historical Sociology*, 3.2 (1990), pp. 91–108.

Bernard Bailyn, *Voyagers to the west: a passage in the peopling of America on the eve of revolution* (New York, 1986).

Stephen Banks, *Informal justice in England and Wales, 1760–1914: the courts of public opinion* (Woodbridge, 2014).

Toby C. Barnard, *Improving Ireland? Projectors, prophets and profiteers, 1641–1786* (Dublin, 2008).

The kingdom of Ireland, 1641–1760 (Basingstoke, 2004).

Donald Grove Barnes, *A history of the English corn laws, 1660–1846* (1930).

John M. Barney, 'Shipping in the port of King's Lynn, 1702–1800', *Journal of Transport History*, 20.2 (1999), pp. 126–40.

Thomas C. Barrow, *Trade and empire: the British customs service in colonial America, 1660–1775* (Cambridge, MA, 1967).

Arthur Herbert Basye, *The Lords commissioners of trade and plantations, commonly known as the Board of Trade, 1748–1782* (New Haven, CT, 1925).

Robert H. Bates, 'Lessons from history, or the perfidy of English exceptionalism and the historical significance of France', *World Politics*, 15.4 (1988), pp. 499–516.

J. A. G. Baverstock, '"A chief standard work": the rise and fall of David Hume's *History of England* 1754 – c.1900' (University of London PhD, 1997).

S. B. Baxter, *The development of the Treasury, 1660–1702* (1957).

T. W. Beastall, *The agricultural revolution in Lincolnshire* (Lincoln, 1978).

Andrew D. M. Beaumont, *Colonial America and the Earl of Halifax, 1748–1761* (Oxford, 2014).

J. V. Beckett, 'Land tax or excise: the levying of taxation in seventeenth- and eighteenth-century England', *English Historical Review*, 100.395 (1985), pp. 285–308.

John G. A. Beckett, *The urgent hour: the drainage of the Burnt Fen district in the South Level of the fens, 1760–1981* (Ely, 1983).

David A. Bell, *The cult of the nation in France: inventing nationalism, 1680–1800* (Cambridge, MA, 2001).

Robert J. Bennett, *Local business voice: the history of chambers of commerce in Britain, Ireland, and revolutionary America, 1760–2011* (Oxford, 2011).

'Malachy Postlethwayt: genealogy and influence of an early economist and spin doctor', *Genealogists' Magazine*, 31 (June 2011), pp. 1–7.

Maurice W. Beresford, 'The common informer, the penal statutes and economic regulation', *Economic History Review*, 10.2 (1957), pp. 222–38.

'The decree rolls of Chancery as a source for economic history, 1547–c. 1700', *Economic History Review*, 32.1 (1979), pp. 1–10.

'Habitation versus improvement: the debate on enclosure by agreement', in F. J. Fisher, ed., *Essays in the economic and social history of Tudor and Stuart England in honour of R. H. Tawney* (Cambridge, 1961), pp. 40–69.

Isaiah Berlin, *Building: letters, 1960–1975*. Edited by Henry Hardy and Mark Pottle (2013).

Two concepts of liberty (Oxford, 1958).

Mary Sarah Bilder, *The transatlantic constitution: colonial legal culture and the empire* (Cambridge, MA, 2004).

J. E. D. Binney, *British public finance and administration, 1774–1792* (Oxford, 1958).

E. C. Black, *The association: British extra-parliamentary organisation, 1769–1793* (Cambridge, MA, 1963).

R. D. Collison Black, 'Theory and policy in Anglo–Irish trade relations', *Journal of the Statistical and Social Inquiry Society of Ireland*, 18.3 (1950), pp. 312–26.

T. C. W. Blanning, *The culture of power and the power of culture: old regime Europe, 1660–1789* (Oxford, 2002).

Alan Bloom, *The fens* (1953).

Dan Bogart, 'Did the Glorious Revolution contribute to the transport revolution? Evidence from investment in roads and rivers', *Economic History Review*, 64.4 (2011), pp. 1073–112.

'The transport revolution in industrialising Britain', in Roderick Floud, Jane Humphries, and Paul Johnson, eds., *The Cambridge economic history of modern Britain: vol. 1, 1700–1870* (Cambridge, 2014), pp. 368–91.

Dan Bogart and Gary Richardson, 'Making property productive: reorganizing rights to real and equitable estates in Britain, 1660 to 1830', *European Review of Economic History*, 13.1 (2009), pp. 3–30.

'Property rights and parliament in industrializing Britain', *Journal of Law and Economics*, 54.2 (2011), pp. 241–74.

Francesco Boldizzoni, *The poverty of Clio: resurrecting economic history* (Princeton, NJ, 2011).

Maurice F. Bond, *Guide to the records of Parliament* (1971).

Brian Bonnyman, 'Agrarian patriotism and the landed interest: the Scottish "Society of Improvers in the Knowledge of Agriculture", 1723–1746', in Koen Stapelbroek and Jani Marjanen, eds., *The rise of economic societies in the eighteenth century: patriotic reform in Europe and North America* (Basingstoke, 2012), pp. 26–51.

The third Duke of Buccleuch and Adam Smith: estate management and improvement in enlightenment Scotland (Edinburgh, 2014).

J. F. Bosher, *The single duty project: a study of the movement for a French customs union in the eighteenth century* (1964).

Peter J. Bowden, *The wool trade of Tudor and Stuart England* (1962).

H. V. Bowen, *War and British society, 1688–1815* (Cambridge, 1998).

Julie Bowring, 'Between the Corporation and Captain Flood: the fens and drainage after 1663', in Richard W. Hoyle, ed., *Custom, improvement and landscape in early modern Britain* (Farnham, 2011), pp. 235–61.

T. H. Bowyer, 'The published forms of Sir Josiah Child's *A new discourse of trade*', *The Library*, 5th series, 11.2 (1956), pp. 95–102.

Michael Braddick, *The nerves of state: taxation and the financing of the English state, 1558–1714* (Manchester, 1996).

'State formation and the historiography of early modern England', *History Compass*, 2.1 (2004), pp. 1–17.

H. L. Bradfer-Lawrence, 'The merchants of Lynn', in Clement Ingleby, ed., *A supplement to Blomefield's Norfolk* (1929), pp. 143–203.

Betty Brammer, 'The Holland Fen: social and topographical changes in a fenland environment, 1750–1914' (University of Leicester PhD thesis, 2009).

Charles Brears, *Lincolnshire in the seventeenth and eighteenth centuries* (1940).

John Brewer, *Party ideology and popular politics at the accession of George III* (Cambridge, 1976).

The sinews of power: war, money and the English state, 1688–1783 (1989).

John Brewer and Eckhard Hellmuth, eds., *Rethinking Leviathan: the eighteenth-century state in Britain and Germany* (Oxford, 1999).

'Introduction: rethinking Leviathan', in Brewer and Hellmuth, eds., *Rethinking Leviathan: the eighteenth-century state in Britain and Germany* (Oxford, 1999), pp. 1–21.

Asa Briggs, 'Middle class consciousness in English politics, 1780–1846', *Past and Present*, 9 (1956), pp. 65–74.

N. A. Brisco, *The economic policy of Robert Walpole* (New York, 1907).

John Broad, 'Cattle plague in eighteenth-century England', *Agricultural History Review*, 31.2 (1983), pp. 104–15.

Stephen Broadberry, Bruce M. S. Campbell, Alexander Klein, Mark Overton, and Bas van Leeuwen, *British economic growth, 1270–1870* (Cambridge, 2015).

David Broderick, *The first toll-roads: Ireland's turnpike roads, 1729–1858* (Cork, 2002).

John Brooke, 'Namier and Namierism', *History and Theory*, 3.3 (1963–4), pp. 331–47.

C. W. Brooks, 'Interpersonal conflict and social tension: civil litigation in England, 1640–1830', in A. L. Beier, David Cannadine, and James M. Rosenheim, eds., *The first modern society: essays in English history in honour of Lawrence Stone* (Cambridge, 1989), pp. 357–99.

Colin Brooks, 'Public finance and political stability: the administration of the land tax, 1688–1720', *Historical Journal*, 17.2 (1974), pp. 281–300.

Liam Brunt and Edmund Cannon, 'The truth, the whole truth, and nothing but the truth: the English corn returns as a data source in economic history, 1770–1914', *European Review of Economic History*, 17.3 (2013), pp. 318–39.

Glenn Burgess, ed., *The new British history: founding a modern state, 1603–1715* (1999).

Robin A. Butlin, 'Images of the fenland region', in Edward Royle, ed., *Issues of regional identity in honour of John Marshall* (Manchester, 1998), pp. 25–43.

H. Butterfield, *The whig interpretation of history* (1931).

J. W. Cairns, 'Knight v. Wedderburn', in David Dabydeen, John Gilmore, and Cecily Jones, eds., *The Oxford companion to black British history* (Oxford, 2007), pp. 244–6.

R. H. Campbell, 'The Anglo–Scottish Union of 1707. II. The economic consequences', *Economic History Review*, 16.3 (1964), pp. 468–77.

John Cannon, *Aristocratic century: the peerage of eighteenth-century England* (Cambridge, 1984).

Kenneth E. Carpenter, *Dialogue in political economy: translations from and into German in the eighteenth century* (Boston, MA, 1977).

F. L. Carsten, *Princes and parliaments in Germany from the fifteenth to the eighteenth century* (Oxford, 1959).

H. B. Carter, *His Majesty's flock: Sir Joseph Banks and the merinos of George III of England* (Sydney, 1964).

J. D. Chambers, 'The Worshipful Company of Framework Knitters (1657–1778)', *Economica*, 27 (1929), pp. 296–329.

C. D. Chandaman, *The English public revenue, 1660–1688* (Oxford, 1975).

Andrew Charlesworth, ed., *An atlas of rural protest in Britain, 1548–1900* (1983).

John Chartres, 'English landed society and the servants tax of 1777', in N. Harte and R. Quinault, eds., *Land and society in Britain, 1700–1914: essays in honour of F. M. L. Thompson* (Manchester, 1996), pp. 34–56.

'Spirits in the north-east? Gin and other vices in the long eighteenth century', in Helen Berry and Jeremy Gregory, eds., *Creating and consuming culture in north-east England, 1660–1830* (Aldershot, 2004), pp. 37–56.

S. G. Checkland, *Scottish banking: a history, 1695–1973* (Glasgow, 1973).

George L. Cherry, 'The development of the English free-trade movement in Parliament, 1689–1702', *Journal of Modern History*, 25.2 (1953), pp. 103–19.

Norman Chester, *The English administrative system, 1780–1870* (Oxford, 1981).

Michael Chisholm, 'Locks, sluices and staunches: confusing terminology', *Transactions of the Newcomen Society*, 75.2 (2005), pp. 305–16.

'Navigation and the seventeenth-century draining of the fens', *Journal of Historical Geography*, 32.4 (2006), pp. 731–51.

G. N. Clark, *Guide to English commercial statistics, 1696–1782* (1938).

Science and social welfare in the age of Newton (Oxford, 1937).

The seventeenth century (2nd edn., Oxford, 1972).

Gregory Clark, 'The political foundations of modern economic growth: England, 1540–1800', *Journal of Interdisciplinary History*, 26.4 (1996), pp. 563–88.

Peter Clark, ed., *The Cambridge urban history of Britain: vol. 2, 1540–1840* (Cambridge, 2000).

Frederick C. Clifford, *A history of private bill legislation* (2 vols., 1885–7).

Hugh D. Clout, 'Reclamation of coastal marshland', in Hugh D. Clout, ed., *Themes in the historical geography of France* (1977), pp. 184–213.

R. H. Coase, 'The nature of the firm', *Economica*, 4 (1937), pp. 386–405.

D'Maris Coffman and David Ormrod, 'Corn prices, corn models and corn rents: what can we learn from the English corn returns?', in Martin Allen and D'Maris Coffman, eds., *Money, prices, and wages: essays in honour of Professor Nicholas Mayhew* (Basingstoke, 2014), pp. 196–210.

W. A. Cole, 'The arithmetic of eighteenth-century smuggling', *Economic History Review*, 28.1 (1975), pp. 44–9.

'Trends in eighteenth-century smuggling', *Economic History Review*, 10.3 (1958), pp. 395–410.

D. C. Coleman, *The economy of England, 1450–1750* (Oxford, 1978).

'Mercantilism revisited', *Historical Journal*, 23.4 (1980), pp. 773–91.

Myth, history and the industrial revolution (1992)

'Politics and economics in the age of Anne: the case of the Anglo–French trade treaty of 1713', in D. C. Coleman and A. H. John, eds., *Trade, government and economy in pre-industrial England: essays presented to F. J. Fisher* (1976), pp. 187–211.

ed., *Revisions in mercantilism* (1969).

Linda Colley, *Britons: forging the nation, 1707–1837* (New Haven, CT, 1992).

Lewis Namier (1989).

Michael J. Conlon, 'Anonymity and authority in the poetry of Jonathan Swift', in Howard D. Weinbrot, Peter J. Schakel, and Stephen E. Karian, eds., *Eighteenth-century contexts: historical inquiries in honor of Phillip Hart* (Madison, 2001), pp. 133–46.

S. J. Connolly, R. A. Houston, and R. J. Morris, 'Identity, conflict and economic change: themes and issues', in Connolly, Houston, and Morris, eds., *Conflict, identity and economic development: Ireland and Scotland, 1600–1939* (Preston, 1995), pp. 1–13.

Richard Connors, '"The grand inquest of the nation": parliamentary committees and social policy in mid-eighteenth-century England', *Parliamentary History*, 14.3 (1995), pp. 285–313.

Stephen Conway, 'British governments, colonial consumers, and continental European goods in the British Atlantic empire, 1763–1775', *Historical Journal*, 58.3 (2015), pp. 711–32.

J. E. Cookson, *The friends of peace: anti-war liberalism in England, 1793–1815* (Cambridge, 1982).

J. P. Cooper, 'Economic regulation and the cloth industry in seventeenth-century England', *Transactions of the Royal Historical Society*, 5th series, 20 (1970), pp. 73–99.

Penelope J. Corfield, *Power and the professions in Britain, 1700–1850* (1995).

James R. Coull, 'Fishery development in Scotland in the eighteenth century', *Scottish Economic and Social History*, 21.1 (2001), pp. 1–21.

N. F. R. Crafts, *British economic growth during the industrial revolution* (Oxford, 1985).

Maurice Cranston, *John Locke: a biography* (1957).

Michael Craton, 'The role of the Caribbean vice admiralty courts in British imperialism', *Caribbean Studies*, 11.2 (1971), pp. 5–20.

Pauline Croft, 'Free trade and the House of Commons, 1605–6', *Economic History Review*, 28.1 (1975), pp. 17–27.

Alan Cromartie, *Sir Matthew Hale 1609–1676: law, religion and natural philosophy* (Cambridge, 1995).

Eveline Cruickshanks and Howard Erskine-Hill, 'The Waltham black act and Jacobitism', *Journal of British Studies*, 24.3 (1985), pp. 358–65.

Piet van Cruyningen, 'Dealing with drainage: state regulation of drainage projects in the Dutch Republic, France, and England during the sixteenth and seventeenth centuries', *Economic History Review*, 68.2 (2015), pp. 420–40.

Karen Cullen, *Famine in Scotland – the 'Ill Years' of the 1690s* (Edinburgh, 2010).

L. M. Cullen, *Anglo–Irish trade, 1660–1800* (Manchester, 1969).

An economic history of Ireland since 1660 (2nd edn., 1981).

Susan Dale, 'Sir William Petty's "ten tooles": a programme for the transformation of England and Ireland during the reign of James II' (Birkbeck College, London, PhD thesis, 2011).

D. d'Avray, 'Max Weber and comparative legal history', in A. Lewis and M. Lobban, eds., *Law and history: current legal issues 2003*, vol. 6 (2004), pp. 189–99.

H. C. Darby, *The draining of the fens* (2nd edn., Cambridge, 1956).

K. G. Davies, *The Royal African Company* (1957).

Ralph Davis, 'English foreign trade, 1660–1700', *Economic History Review*, 7.2 (1954), pp. 150–66.

'English foreign trade, 1700–1774', *Economic History Review*, 15.2 (1962), pp. 285–303.

The industrial revolution and British overseas trade (Leicester, 1979).

The rise of the English shipping industry in the seventeenth and eighteenth centuries (Newton Abbot, 1972).

'The rise of protection in England, 1689–1786', *Economic History Review*, 19.2 (1966), pp. 306–17.

Lee Davison, Tim Hitchcock, Tim Keirn, and Robert B. Shoemaker, 'The reactive state: English governance and society, 1689–1714', in Davison, Hitchcock, Keirn, and Shoemaker, eds., *Stilling the grumbling hive: the response to social and economic problems in England, 1689–1750* (Stroud, 1992), pp. xi–liv.

Gary Stuart de Krey, *A fractured society: the politics of London in the first age of party, 1688–1715* (Oxford, 1985).

G. P. van de Ven, ed., *Man-made lowlands: history of water management and land reclamation in the Netherlands* (Utrecht, 1994).

Phyllis Deane, 'The output of the British woolen industry in the eighteenth century', *Journal of Economic History*, 17.2 (1957), pp. 207–23.

Phyllis Deane and W. A. Cole, *British economic growth, 1688–1959: trends and structures* (2nd edn., Cambridge, 1969).

William Peter Deringer, 'Calculated values: the politics and epistemology of economic numbers in Britain, 1688–1738' (Princeton University, PhD thesis, 2012).

Simon Devereaux, 'The historiography of the English State during "the long eighteenth century": Part I – decentralized perspectives/Part II – fiscal-military and nationalist perspectives', *History Compass*, 7.3 (2009), pp. 742–64; 8.8 (2010), pp. 843–65.

'The promulgation of statutes in late Hanoverian Britain', in David Lemmings, ed., *The British and their laws in the eighteenth century* (Woodbridge, 2005), pp. 80–101.

T. M. Devine, 'The great landowners of lowland Scotland and agrarian change in the eighteenth century', in Sally Foster, Allan Macinnes, and Ranald MacInnes, eds., *Scottish power centres from the early Middle Ages to the twentieth century* (Glasgow, 1998), pp. 147–61.

The tobacco lords: a study of the tobacco merchants of Glasgow and their trading activities, c. 1740–1790 (Edinburgh, 1975).

'The Union of 1707 and Scottish development', *Scottish Economic and Social History*, 5.1 (1985), pp. 23–40.

Oliver M. Dickerson, *The navigation acts and the American Revolution* (Philadelphia, PA, 1951).

H. T. Dickinson, 'The eighteenth-century debate on the sovereignty of parliament', *Transactions of the Royal Historical Society*, 5th series, 26 (1976), pp. 189–210.

P. G. M. Dickson, *The financial revolution in England: a study in the development of public credit, 1688–1756* (1967).

V. E. Dietz, 'Before the age of capital: manufacturing interests and the British State, 1780–1800' (Princeton University, PhD thesis, 1991).

G. M. Ditchfield, David Hayton, and Clyve Jones, eds., *British parliamentary lists, 1660–1800: a register* (1995).

Ian Donnachie, *A history of the brewing industry in Scotland* (Edinburgh, 1979).

Mary Douglas, *How institutions think* (1987).

J. A. Downie, 'The Commission of Public Accounts and the formation of the Country Party', *English Historical Review*, 91.358 (1976), pp. 33–51.

Robert Harley and the press: propaganda and public opinion in the age of Swift and Defoe (Cambridge, 1979).

John N. Drobak and John V. C. Nye, 'Introduction', to Drobak and Nye, eds., *The frontiers of the new institutional economics* (San Diego, CA, and London, 1997), pp. xv–xx.

Alastair J. Durie, ed., *The British Linen Company, 1745–1775* (Edinburgh, 1996).

The Scottish linen industry in the eighteenth century (Edinburgh, 1979).

Early Modern Research Group, 'Commonwealth: the social, cultural, and conceptual contexts of an early modern keyword', *Historical Journal*, 54.3 (2011), pp. 659–87.

David Eastwood and Laurence Brockliss, eds., *A union of multiple identities, the British Isles c. 1750–c. 1850* (Manchester, 1997).

Carolyn A. Edie, 'The Irish cattle bills: a study in Restoration politics', *Transactions of the American Philosophical Society*, 60.2 (1970), pp. 1–66.

J. H. Elliott, *Empires of the Atlantic world: Britain and Spain in America, 1492–1830* (New Haven, CT, 2006).

'A Europe of composite monarchies', *Past and Present*, 137 (1992), pp. 48–71.

Joyce Ellis, 'Regional and county centres, 1700–1840', in Peter Clark, ed., *The Cambridge urban history of Britain: vol. 2, 1540–1840* (Cambridge, 2000), pp. 573–704.

Kathryn M. Ellis, 'The practice and procedure of the House of Commons 1660–1714' (University of Aberystwyth, PhD thesis, 1993).

Steven G. Ellis and Sarah Barber, eds., *Conquest and union: fashioning a British state, 1485–1725* (Harlow, 1995).

David Eltis and Stanley L. Engerman, 'The importance of slavery and the slave trade to industrialising Britain', *Journal of Economic History*, 60.1 (2000), pp. 123–44.

G. R. Elton, *Reform and renewal: Thomas Cromwell and the common weal* (Cambridge, 1973).

Stanley L. Engerman, 'British imperialism in a mercantilist age, 1492–1849: conceptual issues and empirical problems', *Revista de Historia Económica*, 16.1 (1998), pp. 195–231.

S. R. Epstein, *Freedom and growth: the rise of states and markets in Europe, 1300–1750* (Abingdon, 2000).

Eric J. Evans, *The contentious tithe: the tithe problem and English agriculture, 1750–1850* (1976).

'Tithes', in Joan Thirsk, ed., *The agrarian history of England and Wales, vol. 5.2, 1640–1750: agrarian change* (Cambridge, 1985), pp. 389–405.

Niall Ferguson, *The cash nexus: money and power in the modern world, 1700–2000* (2002).

Ellen Sallie Filor, 'Complicit colonials: border Scots and the Indian empire, c. 1780–1857' (UCL, PhD thesis, 2014).

Ronald Findley and Kevin H. O'Rourke, *Power and plenty: trade, war, and the world economy in the second millennium* (Princeton, NJ, 2007).

Selma E. Fine, 'Production and excise in England, 1643–1825' (Radcliffe College, PhD thesis, 1937).

S. E. Finer, *Anonymous empire: a study of the lobby in Great Britain* (2nd edn., 1966).

John Finlay, *The community of the College of Justice: Edinburgh and the Court of Session, 1687–1808* (Edinburgh, 2012).

Lord Fitzmaurice, *Life of William Shelburne afterwards first Marquess of Lansdowne* (2nd edn., 2 vols., 1912).

M. W. Flinn, *The history of the British coal industry: vol. 2, 1700–1830, the industrial revolution* (Oxford, 1984).

Roderick Floud, Jane Humphries, and Paul Johnson, eds., *The Cambridge economic history of modern Britain: vol. 1, 1700–1870* (Cambridge, 2014).

Pierre Force, *Self-interest before Adam Smith: a genealogy of economic science* (Cambridge, 2003).

Michel Foucault, 'What is an author?', in Foucault, *Language, counter-memory, practice: selected essays and interviews*. Edited by Donald F. Bouchard (Oxford, 1977), pp. 113–38.

Peter Fraser, 'Public petitioning and Parliament before 1832', *History*, 46.158 (1961), pp. 195–211.

H. R. French, 'Social status, localism and the "middle sort of people" in England 1620–1750', *Past and Present*, 166 (2000), pp. 66–99.

C. E. Fryer, 'The royal veto under Charles II', *English Historical Review*, 32.125 (1917), pp. 103–11.

Mary O. Furner and Barry Supple, 'Ideas, institutions, and state in the United States and Britain: an introduction', in Furner and Supple, eds., *The state and economic knowledge* (Cambridge, 1990), pp. 3–39.

Anna Gambles, 'Free trade and state formation: the political economy of fisheries policy in Britain and the United Kingdom, circa 1750–1850', *Journal of British Studies*, 39.3 (2000), pp. 288–316.

John Gascoigne, *Joseph Banks and the English Enlightenment: useful knowledge and polite culture* (Cambridge, 1994).

Science in the service of empire: Joseph Banks, the British state and the uses of science in the age of revolution (Cambridge, 1998).

Perry Gauci, 'The clash of interests: commerce and the politics of trade in the age of Anne', *Parliamentary History*, 28.1 (2009), pp. 115–25.

'Learning the ropes of sand: the West India lobby, 1714–1760', in Gauci, ed., *Regulating the British economy, 1660–1850* (Farnham, 2011), pp. 107–21.

The politics of trade: the overseas merchant in state and society, 1660–1720 (Oxford, 2001).

John G. Gazley, *The life of Arthur Young, 1741–1820* (Philadelphia, PA, 1973).

Dorian Gerhold, 'The development of stage coaching and the impact of turnpike roads, 1653–1840', *Economic History Review*, 67.3 (2014), pp. 818–45.

'Review of Guldi, *Roads to power*', *Victorian Studies*, 56.2 (2014), pp. 291–3.

Joshua Getzler, *A history of water rights at common law* (Oxford, 2004).

'Theories of property and economic development', *Journal of Interdisciplinary History*, 26.4 (1996), pp. 639–69.

Conrad Gill, *The rise of the Irish linen industry* (Oxford, 1925).

Donald E. Ginter, *Voting records of the British House of Commons, 1761–1820* (6 vols., 1995).

D. V. Glass, *Numbering the people: the eighteenth-century population controversy and the development of census and vital statistics in Britain* (Farnborough, 1973).

Nicholas Goddard, 'Agricultural literature and societies', in G. E. Mingay, ed., *The agrarian history of England and Wales, 6: 1750–1850* (Cambridge, 1989), pp. 361–83.

Harry Godwin, *Fenland: its ancient past and uncertain future* (Cambridge, 1978).

Tal Golan, *Laws of men and laws of nature: the history of scientific expert testimony in England and America* (Cambridge, MA, 2004).

Eric J. Graham, *A maritime history of Scotland, 1650–1790* (East Linton, 2002).

Jack P. Greene, *Evaluating empire and confronting colonialism in eighteenth-century Britain* (Cambridge, 2013).

Negotiated authorities: essays in colonial political and constitutional history (Charlottesville, VA, 1994).

Peripheries and center: constitutional development in the extended polities of the British empire and the United States, 1607–1788 (New York, 1990).

Liah Greenfeld, *The spirit of capitalism: nationalism and economic growth* (Cambridge, MA, 2001).

Alan Greenspan, *The age of turbulence: adventures in a new world* (New York, 2007).

Harry Gribbon, 'The Irish Linen Board, 1711–1828', in Marilyn Cohen, ed., *The warp of Ulster's past: interdisciplinary perspectives on the Irish linen industry, 1700–1920* (Basingstoke, 1997), pp. 71–91.

Robert J. Griffin, 'Introduction', to Griffin, ed., *The faces of anonymity: anonymous and pseudonymous publication from the sixteenth to the twentieth century* (Basingstoke, 2003), pp. 1–17.

Trevor Griffiths, Philip Hunt, and Patrick O'Brien, 'Scottish, Irish, and imperial connections: Parliament, the three kingdoms, and the mechanization of cotton spinning in eighteenth-century Britain', *Economic History Review*, 61.3 (2008), pp. 625–50.

David Grigg, *The agricultural revolution in south Lincolnshire* (Cambridge, 1966).

Andrew Gritt, 'Making good land from bad: the drainage of West Lancashire, c. 1650–1850', *Rural History*, 19.1 (2008), pp. 1–27.

Vivian R. Gruder, *The royal provincial intendants: a governing elite in eighteenth-century France* (Ithaca, NY, 1968).

Joanna Guldi, *Roads to power: Britain invents the infrastructure state* (Cambridge, MA, 2012).

J. A. W. Gunn, '"Interest will not lie": a seventeenth-century political maxim', *Journal of the History of Ideas*, 29.4 (1968), pp. 551–64.

Politics and the public interest in the seventeenth century (Toronto, 1969).

H. M. Revenue Service, *Measuring tax gaps 2015 edition: methodological annex* (2015).

Paul H. Haagen, 'Eighteenth-century English society and the debt law', in Stanley Cohen and Andrew Scull, eds., *Social control and the state* (Oxford, 1983), pp. 222–47.

John Habakkuk, 'Economic history and economic theory', *Daedalus*, 100.2 (1971), pp. 305–22.

Jürgen Habermas, *The structural transformation of the public sphere: an inquiry into a category of bourgeois society*. Translated by Thomas Burger with the assistance of Frederick Lawrence (Cambridge, 1989; original German edn., 1962).

Samuel Halkett and John Laing, *A dictionary of the anonymous and pseudonymous literature of Great Britain* (4 vols., Edinburgh, 1882–8).

Jean-Louis Halpérin, *Five legal revolutions since the seventeenth century: an analysis of a global legal history* (Cham, 2014).

Henry Hamilton, *An economic history of Scotland in the eighteenth century* (Oxford, 1963).

J. L. Hammond, 'Eighteenth-century London', *New Statesman*, 24.621 (21 March 1925), pp. 693–4.

Norman Hampson, *The perfidy of Albion: French perceptions of England during the French Revolution* (Basingstoke, 1998).

Stuart Handley, 'Local legislative initiatives for social and economic development in Lancashire, 1689–1731', *Parliamentary History*, 9.1 (1990), pp. 14–37.

'Provincial influence on general legislation: the case of Lancashire, 1689–1731', *Parliamentary History*, 16.2 (1997), pp. 171–84.

A. A. Hanham, 'Whig opposition to Sir Robert Walpole in the House of Commons, 1727–1734' (University of Leicester, PhD thesis, 1992).

L. W. Hanson, *Contemporary printed sources for British and Irish economic history, 1701–1750* (Cambridge, 1963).

Vanessa Harding, 'The population of early modern London: a review of the published evidence', *London Journal*, 15.2 (1990), pp. 111–28.

Vincent T. Harlow, *The founding of the second British empire, 1763–1793* (2 vols., 1964).

Lawrence A. Harper, *The English navigation laws: a seventeenth-century experiment in social engineering* (New York, 1939).

Bob Harris, 'The Anglo–Scottish treaty of Union, 1707 in 2007: defending the Revolution, defeating the Jacobites', *Journal of British Studies*, 49.1 (2010), pp. 28–46.

'Patriotic commerce and national revival: the Free British Fishery Society and British politics, c. 1749–58', *English Historical Review*, 114.456 (1999), pp. 285–313.

Politics and the nation: Britain in the mid-eighteenth century (Oxford, 2002).

'Scotland's herring fisheries and the prosperity of the nation, c. 1660–1760', *Scottish Historical Review*, 79.1 (2000), pp. 39–60.

'The Scots, the Westminster parliament and the British state in the eighteenth century', in Julian Hoppit, ed., *Parliaments, nations and identities in Britain and Ireland, 1660–1850* (Manchester, 2003), 124–45.

Bob Harris and Charles McKean, *The Scottish town in the age of the Enlightenment, 1740–1820* (Edinburgh, 2014).

Michael Harris, 'Print and politics in the age of Walpole', in Jeremy Black, ed., *Britain in the age of Walpole* (Basingstoke, 1984), pp. 189–210.

Ron Harris, 'The encounters of economic history and legal history', *Law and History Review*, 21.2 (2003), pp. 297–346.

David Harrison, *The bridges of medieval England, 1300–1800* (Oxford, 2004).

N. B. Harte, 'The rise of protection and the English linen trade, 1690–1790', in N. B. Harte and K. G. Ponting, eds., *Textile history and economic history: essays in honour of Miss Julia de Lacy Mann* (Manchester, 1973), pp. 74–112.

Karl Härter, 'The permanent imperial diet in European context, 1663–1806', in R. J. W. Evans, Michael Schaich, and Peter H. Wilson, eds., *The Holy Roman Empire, 1495–1806* (Oxford, 2011), pp. 115–35.

Douglas Hay, 'The state and the market in 1800: Lord Kenyon and Mr Waddington', *Past and Present*, 162 (1999), pp. 101–62.

'War, dearth and theft in the eighteenth century: the record of the English courts', *Past and Present*, 95 (1982), pp. 117–60.

Douglas Hay and Nicholas Rogers, *Eighteenth-century English society: shuttles and swords* (Oxford, 1997).

David Hayton, 'Constitutional experiments and political expediency, 1689–1725', in Steven G. Ellis and Sarah Barber, eds., *Conquest and union: fashioning a British state, 1485–1725* (Harlow, 1995), pp. 276–305.

C. Robert Haywood, 'Mercantilism and South Carolina agriculture, 1700–1763', *South Carolina Historical Magazine*, 60.1 (1959), pp. 15–27.

Herbert Heaton, *The Yorkshire woollen and worsted industries from the earliest times up to the industrial revolution* (2nd edn., Oxford, 1965).

Michael Hechter, *Internal colonialism: the Celtic fringe in British national development 1536–1966* (1975).

James A. Henretta, *'Salutary neglect': colonial administration under the Duke of Newcastle* (Princeton, NJ, 1972).

Philip Hicks, *Neoclassical history and English culture: from Clarendon to Hume* (Basingstoke, 1996).

Henry Higgs, *Bibliography of economics, 1751–1775* (Cambridge, 1935).

Christopher Hill, *Reformation to industrial revolution: a social and economic history of Britain, 1530–1780* (1967).

Jacqueline Hill, 'Ireland without Union: Molyneux and his legacy', in John Robertson, ed., *A union for empire: political thought and the British Union of 1707* (Cambridge, 1995), pp. 271–96.

Richard L. Hills, *Machines, mills, and other uncountable costly necessities: a short history of the drainage of the fens* (Norwich, 1967).

Gertrude Himmelfarb, *The roads to modernity: the British, French and American Enlightenments* (2008).

Steve Hindle, 'Power, poor relief, and social relations in Holland Fen, c. 1600–1800', *Historical Journal*, 41.1 (1998), pp. 67–96.

   The state and social change in early modern England, c. 1550–1640 (Basingstoke, 2000).

Otto Hintze, 'Calvinism and raison d'etat in early seventeenth-century Brandenburg', in *The historical essays of Otto Hintze*, ed. Felix Gilbert (New York, 1975), pp. 88–154.

Albert O. Hirschman, *The passions and the interests: political arguments for capitalism before its triumph* (Princeton, NJ, 1977).

Derek Hirst, 'Making contact: petitions and the English republic', *Journal of British Studies*, 45.1 (2006), pp. 26–50.

B. A. Holderness, 'The English land market in the eighteenth century: the case of Lincolnshire', *Economic History Review*, 27.4 (1974), pp. 557–76.

Clive Holmes, 'Drainers and fenmen: the problem of popular political consciousness in the seventeenth century', in Anthony Fletcher and John Stevenson, eds., *Order and disorder in early modern England* (Cambridge, 1985), pp. 166–95.

   'The trial and execution of Charles I', *Historical Journal*, 53.2 (2010), pp. 289–316.

Istvan Hont, *Jealousy of trade: international competition and the nation-state in historical perspective* (Cambridge, MA, 2005).

Elizabeth Evelynola Hoon, *The organization of the English customs system, 1696–1786* (New York, 1938).

Julian Hoppit, 'Checking the leviathan, 1688–1832', in Donald Winch and Patrick K. O'Brien, eds., *The political economy of British historical experience, 1688–1914* (Oxford, 2002), pp. 267–94.

   'Compulsion, compensation and property rights in Britain, 1688–1833', *Past and Present*, 210 (2011), pp. 93–128.

   'The contexts and contours of British economic literature, 1660–1760', *Historical Journal*, 49.1 (2006), pp. 79–110.

   'Counting the industrial revolution', *Economic History Review*, 43.2 (1990), pp. 173–93.

   'Economical reform and the Mint, 1780–1816', *British Numismatic Journal*, 84 (2014), pp. 177–90.

   ed., *Failed legislation, 1660–1800, extracted from the Commons and Lords journals* (1997).

'Financial crises in eighteenth-century England', *Economic History Review*, 39.1 (1986), pp. 39–58.

'The landed interest and the national interest, 1660–1800', in Julian Hoppit, ed., *Parliaments, nations and identities in Britain and Ireland, 1660–1850* (Manchester, 2003), pp. 83–102.

'The nation, the state, and the first industrial revolution', *Journal of British Studies*, 50.2 (2011), pp. 307–31.

'Patterns of parliamentary legislation, 1660–1800', *Historical Journal*, 39.1 (1996), pp. 109–31.

'Petitions, economic legislation and interest groups in Britain, 1660–1800', in Richard Huzzey, ed., *Pressure on parliament* (Oxford, 2017).

'Political arithmetic in eighteenth-century England', *Economic History Review*, 49.3 (1996), pp. 516–40.

'Political power and economic life, 1650–1870', in Roderick Floud, Jane Humphries, and Paul Johnson, eds., *The Cambridge economic history of modern Britain: vol. 1, 1700–1870* (Cambridge, 2014), pp. 344–67.

'Reformed and unreformed Britain, 1689–1801', in William Doyle, ed., *The Oxford handbook of the ancien régime* (Oxford, 2012), pp. 506–21.

'Reforming Britain's weights and measures, 1660–1824', *English Historical Review*, 108.426 (1993), pp. 82–104.

Risk and failure in English business, 1700–1800 (Cambridge, 1987).

Jeff Horn, *Economic development in early modern France: the privilege of liberty, 1650–1820* (Cambridge, 2015).

The path not taken: French industrialization in the age of revolution, 1750–1830 (Cambridge, MA, 2006).

Henry Horwitz, 'Changes in the law and reform of the legal order: England (and Wales) 1689–1760', *Parliamentary History*, 21.3 (2002), pp. 301–24.

'The East India trade, the politicians and the constitution, 1689–1702', *Journal of British Studies*, 17.2 (1978), pp. 1–18.

Henry Horwitz and Patrick Polden, 'Continuity of change in the court of Chancery in the seventeenth and eighteenth centuries?', *Journal of British Studies*, 35.1 (1996), pp. 24–57.

Walter E. Houghton, 'The history of trades: its relation to seventeenth-century thought, as seen in Bacon, Petty, Evelyn and Boyle', *Journal of the History of Ideas*, 2.1 (1941), pp. 33–60.

R. A. Houston, *Peasant petitions: social relations and economic life on landed estates, 1600–1850* (Basingstoke, 2014).

The population history of Britain and Ireland, 1500–1750 (Basingstoke, 1992).

Anthony Howe, 'Restoring free trade: the British experience, 1776–1873', in Donald Winch and Patrick K. O'Brien, eds., *The political economy of British historical experience, 1688–1914* (Oxford, 2002), pp. 193–213.

Richard S. Howey, *A bibliography of general histories of economics, 1692–1975* (Lawrence, KS, 1982).

Pat Hudson, 'The limits of wool and the potential of cotton in the eighteenth and early nineteenth centuries', in Giorgio Riello and Prasannan Parthasarathi, eds., *The spinning world: a global history of cotton textiles, 1200–1850* (Oxford, 2009), pp. 327–50.

'The regional perspective', in Hudson, ed., *Regions and industries: a perspective on the industrial revolution in Britain* (Cambridge, 1989), pp. 5–38.

ed., *Regions and industries: a perspective on the industrial revolution in Britain* (Cambridge, 1989).

Edward Hughes, *Studies in administration and finance, 1558–1825 with special reference to the history of salt taxation in England* (Manchester, 1934).

Joel Hurstfield, *Freedom, corruption and government in Elizabethan England* (1973).

Terence W. Hutchison, *On revolutions and progress in economic knowledge* (Cambridge, 1978).

Before Adam Smith: the emergence of political economy, 1662–1776 (Oxford, 1988).

Joanna Innes, 'Central government "interference": changing conceptions, practices, and concerns, c. 1700–1850', in Jose Harris, ed., *Civil society in British history: ideas, identities, institutions* (Oxford, 2003), pp. 39–60.

Inferior politics: social problems and social policies in eighteenth-century Britain (Oxford, 2009).

'Legislating for three kingdoms: how the Westminster parliament legislated for England, Scotland and Ireland, 1707–1830', in Julian Hoppit, ed., *Parliaments, nations and identities in Britain and Ireland, 1660–1850* (Manchester, 2003), pp. 15–47.

'Legislation and public participation, 1760–1830', in David Lemmings, ed., *The British and their laws in the eighteenth century* (Woodbridge, 2005), pp. 102–32.

'"Reform" in English public life: the fortunes of a word', in Arthur Burns and Joanna Innes, eds., *Rethinking the age of reform: Britain 1780–1850* (Cambridge, 2003), pp. 71–97.

'Regulating wages in eighteenth and early nineteenth-century England: arguments in context', in Perry Gauci, ed., *Regulating the British economy, 1660–1850* (Farnham, 2011), pp. 195–215.

'The state and the poor: eighteenth-century England in European perspective', in John Brewer and Eckhard Hellmuth, eds., *Rethinking Leviathan: the eighteenth-century state in Britain and Germany* (Oxford, 1999), pp. 225–80.

Joanna Innes and Arthur Burns, 'Introduction', to Innes and Burns, eds., *Rethinking the age of reform: Britain, 1780–1850* (Cambridge, 2003), pp. 1–70.

Joanna Innes and Nicholas Rogers, 'Politics and government, 1700–1840', in Peter Clark, ed., *The Cambridge urban history of Britain, vol. 2, 1550–1840* (Cambridge, 2000), pp. 529–74.

Jonathan I. Israel, 'England's mercantilist response to Dutch world trade primacy, 1647–1674', in S. Groenveld and M. Wintle, eds., *Britain and the Netherlands, vol. 10: Government and the economy in Britain and the Netherlands since the Middle Ages* (Zutphen, 1992), pp. 50–61.

Robin Ives, 'Political publicity and political economy in eighteenth-century France', *French History*, 17.1 (2003), pp. 1–18.

W. T. Jackman, *The development of transportation in modern England* (3rd edn., 1966).

Clare Jackson, 'Union historiographies', in T. M. Devine and Jenny Wormald, eds., *The Oxford handbook of modern Scottish history* (Oxford, 2012), pp. 338–54.

G. Jackson, *The British whaling trade* (1978).

'Government bounties and the establishment of the Scottish whaling trade, 1750–1800', in John Butt and J. T. Ward, eds., *Scottish themes: essays in honour of Professor S. G. E. Lythe* (Edinburgh, 1976), pp. 46–66.

Margaret James, *Social problems and policy during the Puritan revolution, 1640–1660* (1930).

Rupert C. Jarvis, 'Illicit trade with the Isle of Man, 1671–1765', *Transactions of the Lancashire and Cheshire Antiquarian Society*, 58 (1947 for 1945–6).

D. T. Jenkins and K. G. Ponting, *The British wool textile industry, 1770–1914* (Aldershot, 1982).

Bob Jessop, *The capitalist state: Marxist theories and methods* (Oxford, 1982).

Byron Frank Jewell, 'The legislation relating to Scotland after the Forty-Five' (University of North Carolina, PhD thesis, 1975).

A. H. John, 'English agricultural improvement and grain exports, 1660–1765', in D. C. Coleman and A. H. John, eds., *Trade, government and economy in pre-industrial England: essays presented to F. J. Fisher* (1976), pp. 45–67.

'Statistical appendix' in G. E. Mingay, ed., *The agrarian history of England and Wales, vol. VI, 1750–1850* (Cambridge, 1989), pp. 972–1155.

E. A. J. Johnson, *Predecessors of Adam Smith: the growth of British economic thought* (1937).

Edith Mary Johnston-Liik, *History of the Irish parliament, 1692–1800* (6 vols., Belfast, 2002).

Colin Jones, *The great nation: France from Louis XIV to Napoleon* (2002).

P. M. Jones, *Reform and revolution in France: the politics of transition, 1774–1791* (Cambridge, 1995).

Gerrit P. Judd, *Members of Parliament, 1734–1832* (New Haven, CT, 1955).

M. R. Julian, 'English economic legislation, 1660–1714' (London School of Economics, MPhil thesis, 1979).

Peter Jupp, *The governing of Britain, 1688–1848: the executive, Parliament and the people* (Abingdon, 2006).

Michael Kammen, *Empire and interest: the American colonies and the politics of mercantilism* (Philadelphia, PA, 1970).

K. Kivanç Karaman and Şevket Pamuk, 'Ottoman state finances in European perspective, 1500–1914', *Journal of Economic History*, 70.3 (2010), pp. 593–629.

H. F. Kearney, 'The political background to English mercantilism, 1695–1700', *Economic History Review*, 11.3 (1959), pp. 484–96.

Tim Keirn, 'Monopoly, economic thought, and the Royal African Company', in John Brewer and Susan Staves, eds., *Early modern conceptions of property* (1995), pp. 427–66.

B. Keith-Lucas, 'County meetings', *Law Quarterly Review*, 70 (1954), 109–14.

James Kelly, *Poynings' law and the making of law in Ireland, 1660–1800* (Dublin, 2007).

Patrick Kelly, 'The Irish woollen export prohibition act of 1699: Kearney revisited', *Irish Economic and Social History*, 7 (1980), pp. 22–44.

Paul Kelly, 'British and Irish politics in 1785', *English Historical Review*, 90.356 (1975), pp. 536–63.

Betty Kemp, *Votes and standing orders of the House of Commons: the beginning* (1971).

James Kennedy, W. A. Smith, and A. F. Johnson, eds., *Dictionary of anonymous and pseudonymous English literature* (9 vols., Edinburgh and London, 1926–62).

Mark E. Kennedy, 'Fen drainage, the central government, and local interest: Carleton and the gentlemen of South Holland', *Historical Journal*, 26.1 (1983), pp. 15–37.

George T. Kenyon, *The life of Lloyd, first Lord Kenyon* (1873).

J. P. Kenyon, ed., *The Stuart constitution, 1603–1688: documents and commentary* (2nd edn., Cambridge, 1986).

John Maynard Keynes, *The general theory of employment, money, and interest.* Edited by Donald Moggridge (Cambridge, 1979).

Colin Kidd, 'North Britishness and the nature of eighteenth-century British patriotisms', *Historical Journal*, 39.2 (1996), pp. 361–82.

'The Phillipsonian Enlightenment', *Modern Intellectual History*, 11.1 (2014), pp. 175–90.

Subverting Scotland's past: Scottish Whig historians and the creation of an Anglo-British identity, 1689–c. 1830 (Cambridge, 1993).

Union and unionisms: political thought in Scotland, 1500–2000 (Cambridge, 2008).

T. J. Kiernan, *History of the financial administration of Ireland to 1817* (1930).

Daeryoon Kim, 'Political convention and the merchant in the later eighteenth century', in Perry Gauci, ed., *Regulating the British economy, 1660–1850* (Farnham, 2011), pp. 123–37.

Peter King and Richard Ward, 'Rethinking the bloody code in eighteenth-century Britain: capital punishment at the centre and on the periphery', *Past and Present*, 228 (2015), pp. 204–5.

Daniel B. Klein, 'The origin of "liberalism"', *Atlantic*, 13 February 2014, online at www.theatlantic.com/politics/archive/2014/02/the-origin-of-liberalism/283780/.

Denis Stephen Klinge, 'Edmund Burke, economical reform and the Board of Trade, 1777–1780', *Journal of Modern History* (1979), 51.3 on demand supplement, D1185-1200.

Wim Klooster, 'Inter-imperial smuggling in the Americas, 1600–1800', in Bernard Bailyn and Patricia L. Denault, eds., *Soundings in Atlantic history: latent structures and intellectual currents, 1500–1830* (Cambridge, MA, 2009), pp. 141–80.

Roger Knight, *Britain against Napoleon: the organization of victory, 1793–1815* (2013).

Mark Knights, 'Regulation and rival interests in the 1690s', in Perry Gauci, ed., *Regulating the British economy, 1660–1850* (Farnham, 2011), pp. 63–81.

Representation and misrepresentation in later Stuart Britain (Oxford, 2005).

'The Tory interpretation of history in the rage of parties', *Huntington Library Quarterly*, 68.1-2 (2005), pp. 353–73.

Nancy F. Koehn, *The power of commerce: economy and governance in the first British empire* (Ithaca, NY, 1994).

H. G. Koenigsberger, 'Composite states, representative institutions and the American revolution', *Historical Research*, 62.148 (1989), pp. 135–53.

Paul Kosmetatos, 'The winding-up of the Ayr bank, 1772–1827', *Financial History Review*, 21.2 (2014), pp. 165–90.

Thomas Kuhn, *The structure of scientific revolutions* (3rd edn., Chicago, IL, 1996).

Simon Kuznets, 'The state as a unit in the study of economic growth', *Journal of Economic History* 11.1 (1951), pp. 25–41.

Kwasi Kwarteng, 'The political thought of the recoinage crisis of 1695–7' (University of Cambridge, PhD thesis, 2000).

James Gray Kyd, *Scottish population statistics, including Webster's analysis of population 1755* (Edinburgh, 1952).

Leonard Woods Labaree, *Royal instructions to British colonial governors* (2 vols., New York, 1935).

Peter Lake and Steve Pincus, 'Rethinking the public sphere in seventeenth-century England', *Journal of British Studies*, 45.2 (2006), pp. 270–92.

Sheila Lambert, *Bills and acts: legislative procedure in eighteenth-century England* (Cambridge, 1971).

John Landers, *Death and the metropolis: studies in the demographic history of London 1670–1830* (Cambridge, 1993).

David S. Landes, *The wealth and poverty of nations: why some are so rich and some so poor* (New York, 1998).

Paul Langford, *The excise crisis: society and politics in the age of Walpole* (Oxford, 1975).

'Introduction: time and space', in Langford, ed., *The eighteenth century: 1688–1815* (Oxford, 2002), pp. 1–32.

Public life and the propertied Englishman, 1689–1798 (Oxford, 1991).

John Langton, 'Urban growth and economic change: from the late seventeenth century to 1841', in Peter Clark, ed., *The Cambridge urban history of Britain: vol. 2, 1540–1840* (Cambridge, 2000), pp. 453–90.

Robert M. Lees, 'The constitutional importance of the "Commissioners for Wool" of 1689: an administrative experiment of the reign of William III' [in two parts], *Economica*, 40 and 41 (1933), pp. 147–68, 264–74.

'Parliament and the proposal for a Council of Trade, 1695–6', *English Historical Review*, 54.213 (1939), pp. 38–66.

David Lemmings, 'The independence of the judiciary in eighteenth-century England', in Peter Birks, ed., *The life of the law: proceedings of the tenth British legal history conference Oxford 1991* (1993), pp. 125–49.

Law and government in England during the long eighteenth century: from consent to command (Basingstoke, 2011).

E. M. Leonard, 'The enclosure of common fields in the seventeenth century', *Transactions of the Royal Historical Society*, 19 (1905), pp. 101–46.

Marie Léoutre, 'Contesting and upholding the rights of the Irish parliament in 1698: the arguments of William Molyneux and Simon Clement', *Parliaments, Estates, and Representations*, 34.1 (2014), pp. 22–39.

David Lieberman, *The province of legislation determined: legal theory in eighteenth-century Britain* (Cambridge, 1989).

Keith Lindley, *Fenland riots and the English revolution* (1982).

E. Lipson, *A short history of wool and its manufacture* (1953).

Philip Loft, 'Peers, Parliament and power under the Revolution constitution, 1685–1720' (UCL, PhD thesis, 2015).

Jerzy Lukowski, *Liberty's folly: the Polish-Lithuanian commonwealth in the eighteenth century, 1697–1795* (1991).

D. S. Macmillan, 'The Russia Company of London in the eighteenth century: the effective survival of a "regulated" chartered company', *Guildhall Miscellany*, 4 (1971–3), pp. 222–36.

Eoin Magennis, 'Coal, corn and canals: Parliament and the dispersal of public moneys 1695–1772', *Parliamentary History*, 20.1 (2001), pp. 71–86.

Lars Magnusson, *Mercantilism: the shaping of an economic language* (1994).

F. W. Maitland, *The constitutional history of England* (Cambridge, 1908).

Robert Malcolmson. '"A set of ungovernable people": the Kingswood colliers in the eighteenth century', in John Brewer and John Styles, eds., *An ungovernable people: the English and their law in the seventeenth and eighteenth centuries* (1980), pp. 85–127.

Joseph J. Malone, *Pine trees and politics: the naval stores and forest policy in colonial New England, 1691–1775* (1964).

Julia de L. Mann, *The cloth industry in the west of England from 1640 to 1880* (1971).
    ed., *Documents illustrating the Wiltshire textile trades in the eighteenth century* (Wiltshire Archaeological and Natural History Society, 19, for 1963 (1964)).

P. J. Marshall, *The making and unmaking of empires: Britain, India, and America, c. 1750–1783* (Oxford, 2005).
    ed., *The Oxford history of the British empire, vol. 2, The eighteenth century* (Oxford, 1998).
    'Parliament and property rights in the late eighteenth-century British empire', in John Brewer and Susan Staves, eds., *Early modern conceptions of property* (1995), pp. 530–44.
    Remaking the British Atlantic: the United States and the British empire after American independence (Oxford, 2012).

Peter Mathias, *The brewing industry in England, 1700–1830* (Cambridge, 1959).
    The transformation of England: essays in the economic and social history of England in the eighteenth century (1979).

Peter Mathias and Patrick O'Brien, 'Taxation in England and France, 1715–1810: a comparison of the social and economic incidence of taxes collected for central governments', *Journal of European Economic History*, 5.3 (1976), pp. 601–50.

Michael McCahill, 'Estate Acts of Parliament, 1740–1800', in Clyve Jones, ed., *Institutional practice and memory: parliamentary people, records and histories. Essays in honour of Sir John Sainty* (Chichester, 2013), pp. 148–68.

Deirdre N. McCloskey, *Bourgeois equality: how ideas, not capital or institutions, enriched the world* (Chicago, IL, 2016).

Davis D. McElroy, 'The literary clubs and societies of eighteenth century Scotland, and their influence on the literary productions of the period from 1700 to 1800' (University of Edinburgh, PhD thesis, 1952).
    Scotland's age of improvement: a survey of eighteenth-century literary clubs and societies (Washington, DC, 1969).

W. R. McKay, *Clerks in the House of Commons, 1363–1989: a biographical list* (House of Lords Record Office occasional publications, no. 3, 1989).

Patrick McNally, 'Wood's halfpence, Carteret, and the government of Ireland, 1723–6', *Irish Historical Studies*, 30.119 (1997), pp. 354–76.

James Van Horn Melton, *The rise of the public in Enlightenment Europe* (Cambridge, 2001).

Judith A. Miller, 'Economic ideologies, 1750–1800: the creation of the modern political economy?', *French Historical Studies*, 23.3 (2000), pp. 497–511.

Samuel H. Miller and Sydney B. J. Skertchly, *The fenland, past and present* (Wisbech and London, 1878).

W. E. Minchinton, 'Agricultural returns and the government during the Napoleonic wars', *Agricultural History Review*, 1.1 (1953), pp. 29–43.

'Bristol – metropolis of the west in the eighteenth century', *Transactions of the Royal Historical Society*, 5th series, 4 (1954), pp. 69–89.

'The petitions of weavers and clothiers of Gloucestershire in 1756', *Transactions of the Bristol and Gloucestershire Archaeological Society for 1954*, 73 (1955), pp. 216–27.

ed., *Wage regulation in pre-industrial England* (Newton Abbot, 1972).

B. R. Mitchell, *British historical statistics* (Cambridge, 1988).

J. F. Mitchell, 'Englishmen in the Scottish excise department, 1707–1832', *Scottish Genealogist*, 13.2 (1966), pp. 16–28.

Rosalind Mitchison, *Agricultural Sir John: the life of Sir John Sinclair of Ulbster, 1754–1835* (1962).

'The old Board of Agriculture (1793–1822)', *English Historical Review*, 74.290 (1959), pp. 41–69.

Joel Mokyr, *The enlightened economy: an economic history of Britain, 1700–1850* (2009).

Paul Monod, 'Dangerous merchandise: smuggling, Jacobitism, and commercial culture in southeast England, 1690–1760', *Journal of British Studies*, 30.2 (1991), pp. 150–82.

Florence M. Montgomery, *Textiles in America, 1650–1870* (New York, 1985).

T. K. Moore and H. Horwitz, 'Who runs the house? Aspects of parliamentary organization in the later seventeenth century', *Journal of Modern History*, 43.2 (1971), pp. 205–27.

More Culloden papers, ed. Duncan Warrand, (5 vols., Inverness, 1923–9).

Raphaël Morera, *L'assèchement des marais en France au XVIIe siècle* (Rennes, 2011).

Renaud Morieux, *The Channel: England, France and the construction of a maritime border in the eighteenth century* (Cambridge, 2016).

P. Vander Motten, *Sir William Killigrew (1606–1695): his life and dramatic works* (Gent, 1980).

Roland E. Mousnier, *The institutions of France under the absolute monarchy, 1598–1789* (2 vols., Chicago, IL, 1979).

Hoh-Cheung Mui and Lorna H. Mui, *Shops and shopkeeping in eighteenth-century England* (Kingston, Montreal, 1989).

'Smuggling and the British tea trade before 1784', *American Historical Review*, 74.1 (1968), pp. 44–73.

'"Trends in eighteenth-century smuggling" reconsidered', *Economic History Review*, 28.1 (1975), pp. 28–43.

'William Pitt and the enforcement of the Commutation Act, 1784–1788', *English Historical Review*, 76.300 (1961), pp. 447–65.

Anne Murphy, *The origins of English financial markets: investment and speculation before the South Sea Bubble* (Cambridge, 2009).

Antoine Murphy, 'Le développment des idées économicas en France (1750–1756)', *Revue d'histoire Moderne et Contemporaine*, 33.4 (1986), pp. 521–41.

Paul Muskett, 'English smuggling in the eighteenth century' (Open University, PhD thesis, 1997).

Sankar Muthu, *Enlightenment against empire* (Princeton, NJ, 2003).

A. R. Myers, *Parliaments and estates in Europe to 1789* (1975).

Tom Nairn, *Gordon Brown: bard of Britishness* (Cardiff, 2006).

Robert C. Nash, 'The English and Scottish tobacco trades in the seventeenth and eighteenth centuries: legal and illegal trade', *Economic History Review*, 35.3 (1982), pp. 354–72.

'South Carolina indigo, European textiles, and the British Atlantic economy in the eighteenth century', *Economic History Review*, 63.2 (2010), pp. 362–92.

J. M. Neeson, *Commoners: common right, enclosure and social change in England, 1700–1820* (Cambridge, 1993).

John Norris, *Shelburne and reform* (1963).

Douglass C. North, 'The paradox of the West', in R. W. Davis, ed., *The origins of modern freedom in the West* (Stanford, CA, 1995), pp. 7–34.

Understanding the process of economic change (Princeton, NJ, 2005).

Douglass C. North and Barry R. Weingast, 'Constitutions and commitment: the evolution of institutions governing public choice in seventeenth-century England', *Journal of Economic History*, 49.4 (1989), pp. 803–32.

John V. C. Nye, *War, wine, and taxes: the political economy of Anglo–French trade, 1689–1900* (Princeton, NJ, 2007).

Patrick Karl O'Brien, 'Agriculture and the home market for English industry, 1660–1820', *English Historical Review*, 100.397 (1985), pp. 773–800.

'The Britishness of the first industrial revolution and the British contribution to the industrialization of "follower countries" on the mainland, 1756–1914', *Diplomacy and Statecraft*, 8.3 (1997), pp. 48–67.

'The political economy of British taxation, 1660–1815', *Economic History Review*, 41.1 (1988), pp. 1–32.

'Political preconditions for the industrial revolution', in P. K. O'Brien and R. Quinault, eds., *The industrial revolution and British society* (Cambridge, 1993), pp. 124–55.

'Political structures and grand strategies for the growth of the British economy, 1688–1815', in Alice Teichova and Herbert Matis, eds., *Nation, state and the economy in history* (Cambridge, 2003), p. 11–31.

'Public finance in the wars with France, 1793–1815', in H. T. Dickinson, ed., *Britain and the French Revolution, 1789–1815* (Basingstoke, 1989), pp. 165–87.

'State formation and the construction of the institutions for the first industrial nation', in Ha-Joon Chang, ed., *Institutional change and economic development* (New York, 2007), pp. 177–97.

Patrick Karl O'Brien and Leandro Prados de la Escosura, 'The costs and benefits for Europeans from their empires overseas', *Revista de Historia Económica*, 16.1 (1998), pp. 29–89.

P. K. O'Brien and P. A. Hunt, 'The rise of a fiscal state in England, 1485–1815', *Historical Research*, 66.160 (1993), pp. 129–76.

Frank O'Gorman, *Voters, patrons and parties: the unreformed electorate of Hanoverian England, 1734–1832* (Oxford, 1989).

Andrew Jackson O'Shaughnessy, *An empire divided: the American Revolution and the British Caribbean* (Philadelphia, PA, 2000).

'The formation of a commercial lobby: the West India interest, British colonial policy and the American revolution', *Historical Journal*, 40.1 (1997), 71–95.

Miles Ogborn, *Spaces of modernity: London's geographies, 1680–1780* (New York, 1998).

Sheilagh Ogilvie, *Institutions and European trade: merchant guilds, 1000–1800* (Cambridge, 2011).

'"Whatever is, is right"? Economic institutions in pre-industrial Europe', *Economic History Review*, 60.4 (2007), pp. 649–84.

Alison Gilbert Olson, 'Eighteenth-century colonial legislatures and their constituents', *Journal of American History*, 79.2 (1992), pp. 543–67.

Making the empire work: London and American interest groups, 1690–1790 (Cambridge, MA, 1992).

'Parliament, the London lobbies, and provincial interests in England and America', *Historical Reflections*, 6.2 (1979), pp. 367–86.

Mancur Olson, *The rise and decline of nations: economic growth, stagflation, and social rigidities* (New Haven, CT, 1982).

David Ormrod, *English grain exports and the structure of agrarian capitalism, 1700–1760* (Hull, 1985).

The rise of commercial empires: England and the Netherlands in the age of mercantilism, 1650–1770 (Cambridge, 2002).

Mark Overton, *Agricultural revolution in England: the transformation of the agrarian economy, 1500–1850* (Cambridge, 1996).

Gabriel B. Paquette, *Enlightenment, governance, and reform in Spain and its empire, 1759–1808* (Basingstoke, 2008).

Eric Pawson, *Transport and economy: the turnpike roads of eighteenth-century Britain* (1977).

Lillian M. Penson, *The colonial agents of the British West Indies: a study in colonial administration, mainly in the eighteenth century* (1924).

Jean-Claude Perrot, *Une historire intellectuell de l'économie politique, XVIIe–XVIIIe siècle* (Paris, 1992).

William A. Pettigrew, 'Constitutional change in England and the diffusion of regulatory initiative, 1660–1714', *History*, 99.338 (2014), pp. 839–63.

'Free to enslave: politics and the escalation of Britain's transatlantic slave trade, 1688–1714', *William and Mary Quarterly*, 3rd Series, 64.1 (2007), pp. 3–38.

Freedom's debt: the Royal African Company and the politics of the Atlantic slave trade, 1672–1752 (Chapel Hill, NC, 2013).

Dirk Philipsen, *The little big number: how GDP came to rule the world and what to do about it* (Princeton, NJ, 2015).

John Philipson, 'Whisky smuggling on the border in the early nineteenth century', *Archaeologia Aeliana*, 4th series, 39 (1961), pp. 151–63.

J. A. Phillips, 'The structure of electoral politics in unreformed England', *Journal of British Studies*, 19.1 (1979), pp. 76–100.

Nicholas Phillipson, *Adam Smith: an enlightened life* (2010).

'Towards a definition of the Scottish Enlightenment', in Paul Fritz and David Williams, eds., *City and society in the eighteenth century* (Toronto, 1973), pp. 125–47.

Steve Pincus, *1688: the first modern revolution* (New Haven, CT, 2009).

'From holy cause to economic interest: the study of population and the invention of the state', in Alan Houston and Steve Pincus, eds., *A nation transformed: England after the Restoration* (Cambridge, 2001), pp. 271–98.

'Rethinking mercantilism: political economy, the British empire, and the Atlantic world in the seventeenth and eighteenth centuries', *William and Mary Quarterly*, 3rd series, 69.1 (2012), pp. 3–34.

Steve Pincus and James Robinson. 'Challenging the fiscal-military hegemony: the British case', in Aaron Graham and Patrick Walsh, eds., *The British fiscal-military states, 1660–c. 1783* (2016), pp. 229–61.

Jennifer Pitts, *A turn to empire: the rise of imperial liberalism in Britain and France* (Princeton, NJ, 2005).

J. H. Plumb, *The growth of political stability in England, 1675–1725* (1967).

J. G. A. Pocock, *The discovery of islands: essays in British history* (Cambridge, 2005).

Thomas Poell, 'Local particularism challenged, 1795–1813', in Oscar Gelderblom, ed., *The political economy of the Dutch republic* (Farnham, 2009), pp. 291–320.

Mary Poovey, *A history of the modern fact: problems of knowledge in the sciences of wealth and society* (Chicago, IL, 1998).

Stephen Porter, ed., *Survey of London*, vol. 43: *Poplar, Blackwall and Isle of Dogs* (1994).

Maarten Prak, *The Dutch Republic in the seventeenth century: the golden age* (Cambridge, 2005).

Jacob M. Price, 'Who cared about the colonies? The impact of the thirteen colonies on British society and politics, circa 1714–1775', in Bernard Bailyn and Philip D. Morgan, eds., *Strangers within the realm: cultural margins of the first British empire* (Chapel Hill, NC, 1991), pp. 395–436.

Richard Price, *British society, 1680–1880: dynamism, containment, and change* (Cambridge, 1999).

R. B. Pugh, ed., *A history of the county of Cambridge and the Isle of Ely: volume 4: City of Ely; Ely, N. and S. Witchford and Wisbech hundreds* (2002).

Humphrey Quill, *John Harrison: the man who found longitude* (1966).

Theodore K. Rabb, 'Sir Edwin Sandys and the Parliament of 1604', *American Historical Review*, 69.3 (1964), pp. 646–70.

John Rae, *Life of Adam Smith* (1895).

Marc Raeff, *The well-ordered police state: social and institutional change through law in the Germanies and Russia, 1600–1800* (New Haven, CT, 1983).

Helen W. Randall, 'The rise and fall of martyrology: the sermons on Charles I', *Huntington Library Quarterly*, 10.2 (1947), pp. 135–67.

Salim Rashid, 'Adam Smith's acknowledgements: neo-plagiarism and *The wealth of nations*', *Journal of Libertarian Studies*, 9.2 (1990), pp. 1–24.

'Adam Smith's rise to fame: a re-examination of the evidence', *The Eighteenth Century: Theory and Interpretation*, 23.1 (1982), pp. 64–85.

James Raven, *The business of books: booksellers and the English book trade* (New Haven, CT, 2007).

'New reading histories, print culture and the identification of change: the case of eighteenth-century England', *Social History*, 23.3 (1998), pp. 268–87.

Joad Raymond, *Pamphlets and pamphleteering in early modern Britain* (Cambridge, 2003).

Anita Jane Rees, 'The practice and procedure of the House of Lords, 1714–1784' (University of Aberystwyth, PhD thesis, 1987).

Erik S. Reinert, 'Emulating success: contemporary views of the Dutch economy before 1800', in Oscar Gelderblom, ed., *The political economy of the Dutch republic* (Farnham, 2009), pp. 19–39.

Sophus A. Reinert, 'Blaming the Medici: footnotes, falsification, and the fate of the "English model" in eighteenth-century Italy', *History of European Ideas*, 32.4 (2006), pp. 430–55.

'The empire of emulation: a quantitative analysis of economic translations in the European world, 1500–1849', in Sophus A. Reinert and Pernille Røge, eds., *The political economy of empire in the early modern world* (Basingstoke, 2013), pp. 105–28.

Translating empire: emulation and the origins of political economy (Cambridge, MA, 2011).

Max Rheinstein, ed., *Max Weber on law in economy and society* (Cambridge, MA, 1954).

Honor Ridout, *Cambridge and Stourbridge Fair* (Cambridge, 2011).

Giorgio Riello, 'Nature, production and regulation in eighteenth-century France and England: the case of the leather industry', *Historical Research*, 81.211 (2008), pp. 75–99.

Giorgio Riello and Patrick K. O'Brien, 'The future is another country: offshore views of the British industrial revolution', *Journal of Historical Sociology*, 22.1 (2009), pp. 1–29.

Clayton Roberts, *The growth of responsible government in Stuart England* (Cambridge, 1966).

Michael Roberts, *Swedish and English parliamentarianism in the eighteenth century* (Belfast, 1973).

David N. Robinson, 'Sir Joseph Banks and the East Fen', in Christopher Sturman, ed., *Lincolnshire people and places: essays in memory of Terence R. Leach* (Lincoln, 1996), pp. 97–105.

Joan Robinson, *The economics of imperfect competition* (1933).

Nicholas Rogers, *Whigs and cities: popular politics in the age of Walpole and Pitt* (Oxford, 1989).

Pat Rogers, 'Nameless names: Pope, Curll, and the uses of anonymity', *New Literary History*, 33.2 (2002), pp. 233–45.

Jean-Laurent Rosenthal, *The fruits of revolution: property rights, litigation, and French agriculture, 1700–1860* (Cambridge, 1992).

Henry Roseveare, *The financial revolution, 1660–1760* (Harlow, 1991).

'Prejudice and policy: Sir George Downing as parliamentary entrepreneur', in D. C. Coleman and Peter Mathias, eds., *Enterprise and history: essays in honour of Charles Wilson* (Cambridge, 1984).

The Treasury: the evolution of a British institution (1969).

Philipp Robinson Rössner. 'The 1738–41 harvest crisis in Scotland', *Scottish Historical Review*, 90.1 (2011), pp. 27–63.

Scottish trade in the wake of the Union (1700–1760): the rise of a warehouse economy (Stuttgart, 2008).

Emma Rothschild, 'Adam Smith and the invisible hand', *American Economic Review*, 84.2 (1995), pp. 319–22.

George Rudé, *Hanoverian London, 1714–1808* (1971).

Julia Rudolph, *Common law and enlightenment in England, 1689–1750* (Woodbridge, 2013).

Andrea A. Rusnock, *Vital accounts: quantifying health and population in eighteenth-century England and France* (Cambridge, 2002).

Magnus Ryan, 'Freedom, law, and the medieval state', in Quentin Skinner and Bo Stråth, eds., *States and citizens: history, theory, prospects* (Cambridge, 2003), pp. 51–62.

David Harris Sacks and Michael Lynch, 'Ports, 1540–1700', in Peter Clark, ed., *The Cambridge urban history of Britain, vol. 2, 1540–1840* (Cambridge, 2000), pp. 377–424.

John Sainsbury, *Disaffected patriots: London supporters of Revolutionary America 1769–1782* (Kingston, Ontario, 1987).

J. C. Sainty and D. Dewar, *Divisions in the House of Lords: an analytical list 1685 to 1857* (House of Lords Record Office occasional publications, no. 2, 1976).

Rafael Torres Sánchez, 'The triumph of the fiscal-military state in the eighteenth century: war and mercantilism', in Rafael Torres Sánchez, ed., *War, state and development: fiscal-military states in the eighteenth century* (Pamplona, 2007), pp. 13–44.

Shinsuke Satsuma, *Britain and colonial maritime war in the early eighteenth century: silver, seapower and the Atlantic* (Woodbridge, 2013).

Richard Saville, *Bank of Scotland: a history, 1695–1995* (Edinburgh, 1995).

Larry Sawyers, 'The navigation acts revisited', *Economic History Review*, 45.2 (1992), pp. 262–84.

Dorothy L. Sayers, *The nine tailors* (1934).

Margaret Schabas, *The natural origins of economics* (Chicago, IL, 2005).

H. D. Schmidt, 'The idea and slogan of "perfidious Albion"', *Journal of the History of Ideas*, 14.4 (1953), pp. 604–16.

Gustav Schmoller, *The mercantile system and its historical significance* (1896).

Elizabeth Boody Schumpeter, *English overseas trade statistics, 1697–1808* (Oxford, 1960).

Leonard Schwartz, 'London 1700–1840', in Peter Clark, ed., *The Cambridge urban history of Britain: vol. 2, 1540–1840* (Cambridge, 2000), pp. 641–71.

David R. Schweitzer, 'The failure of William Pitt's Irish trade propositions 1785', *Parliamentary History*, 3.1 (1984), pp. 129–45.

James C. Scott, *Seeing like a state: how certain schemes to improve the human condition have failed* (New Haven, CT, 1998).

John Scott, *Digests of the general highway and turnpike laws* (1778).

W. C. Sellar and R. J. Yeatman, *1066 and all that* (1930).

Barbara Shapiro, 'Law reform in seventeenth-century England', *American Journal of Legal History*, 19.4 (1975), pp. 280–312.

Kevin Sharpe, *Reading revolutions: the politics of reading in early modern England* (New Haven, CT, 2000).

John Stuart Shaw, *The management of Scottish society 1707–1764: power, nobles, lawyers, Edinburgh agents and English influences* (Edinburgh, 1983).

Leigh Shaw-Taylor, 'Labourers, cows, common rights and parliamentary enclosure: the evidence of contemporary comment c. 1760–1810', *Past and Present*, 171 (2001), pp. 95–126.

'The management of common land in the lowlands of southern England circa 1500 to circa 1850', in Martina de Moor, Leigh Shaw-Taylor, and Paul Warde, eds., *The management of common land in north west Europe, c. 1500–1850* (Turnhout, 2002), pp. 59–85.

Richard Sheldon, 'Practical economics in eighteenth-century England: Charles Smith on the grain trade and the corn laws, 1756–72', *Historical Research*, 81.124 (2008), pp. 636–62.

Richard B. Sheridan, 'The Molasses Act and the market strategy of the British sugar planters', *Journal of Economic History*, 17.1 (1957), pp. 62–83.

Raymond L. Sickinger, 'Regulation or ruination: Parliament's consistent pattern of mercantilist regulation of the English textile trade, 1660–1800', *Parliamentary History*, 19.2 (2000), pp. 211–32.

A. W. B. Simpson, 'The rise and fall of the legal treatise: legal principles and the forms of legal literature', *University of Chicago Law Review*, 48.3 (1981), pp. 632–79.

C. Skeel, *The Council in the Marches of Wales: a study of local government during the sixteenth and seventeenth centuries* (1904).

A. W. Skempton, *British civil engineering, 1640–1840: a bibliography of contemporary printed reports, plans and books* (1987).

A. W. Skempton et al., eds., *A biographical dictionary of civil engineers in Great Britain and Ireland, vol. 1: 1500–1830* (2002).

Quentin Skinner, 'A genealogy of the modern state', *Proceedings of the British Academy*, 162 (2009), pp. 325–70.

Liberty before liberalism (Cambridge, 1998).

'The principles and practice of opposition: the case of Bolingbroke versus Walpole', in Neil McKendrick, ed., *Historical perspectives: studies in English thought and society in honour of J. H. Plumb* (1974), pp. 93–128.

Paul Slack, 'Government and information in seventeenth-century England', *Past and Present*, 184 (2004), pp. 33–68.

The invention of improvement: information and material progress in seventeenth-century England (Oxford, 2015).

Annette M. Smith, *Jacobite estates of the forty-five* (Edinburgh, 1982).

T. C. Smout, 'The Anglo–Scottish Union, 1707, 1: the economic background', *Economic History Review*, 16.3 (1964), pp. 455–67.

'Scottish landowners and economic growth, 1650–1850', *Scottish Journal of Political Economy*, 9.3 (1962), pp. 218–34.

Peter M. Solar, 'Poor relief and English economic development before the industrial revolution', *Economic History Review*, 48.1 (1995), pp. 1–22.

J. M. Sosin, *English America and imperial inconstancy: the rise of provincial autonomy, 1696–1715* (Lincoln, NE, 1985).

Thomas Sowell, *Conquests and cultures: an international history* (New York, 1998).

J. G. Sperling, 'Godolphin and the organization of public credit, 1702 to 1710' (University of Cambridge, PhD, 1955).

The South Sea Company: an historical essay and bibliographical finding list (Boston, MA, 1962).

Donna J. Spindle, 'The Stamp Act crisis in the British West Indies', *Journal of American Studies*, 11.2 (1977), pp. 203–21.

Hendrik Spruyt, *The sovereign state and its competitors: an analysis of systems change* (Princeton, NJ, 1994).

Peverill Squire, *The evolution of American legislatures: colonies, territories, and states, 1619–2009* (Ann Arbor, MI, 2012).

David Stasavage, *Public debt and the birth of the democratic state: France and Great Britain, 1688–1789* (Cambridge, 2003).

Ian K. Steele, 'The British parliament and the Atlantic colonies to 1760: new approaches to enduring questions', *Parliamentary History*, 14.1 (1995), pp. 29–46.

Politics of colonial policy: the Board of Trade in colonial administration, 1696–1720 (Oxford, 1968).

Tony Stephens, 'The Birtwhistles of Craven and Galloway: "the greatest graziers and dealers in the kingdom?"', *North Craven Heritage Trust Journal*, no vol. (2008), pp. 13–17.

Philip J. Stern, *The company-state: corporate sovereignty and the early modern foundations of the British empire in India* (New York, 2011).

Philip J. Stern and Carl Wennerlind, eds., *Mercantilism reimagined: political economy in early modern Britain and its empire* (Oxford, 2014).

Walter M. Stern, 'The first London dock boom and the growth of the West India docks', *Economica*, 19 (1952), pp. 59–77.

Byron S. Stewart, 'The cult of the royal martyr', *Church History*, 38.2 (1969), pp. 175–87.

Laura A. M. Stewart, 'The "rise" of the state', in T. M. Devine and Jenny Wormald, eds., *The Oxford handbook of modern Scottish history* (Oxford, 2012), pp. 220–35.

Lawrence Stone, ed., *An imperial state at war: Britain from 1688 to 1815* (1994).

Christopher Storrs, 'Introduction: the fiscal-military state in the "long" eighteenth century', in Christopher Storrs, ed., *The fiscal-military state in eighteenth-century Europe: essays in honour of P. G. M. Dickson* (Aldershot, 2009), pp. 1–22.

Ros Stott, 'A brief encounter: the Duke of Atholl and the Isle of Man, 1736–1764', in Peter Davey and David Finlayson, eds., *Mannin revisited: twelve essays on Manx culture and environment* (Edinburgh, 2002), pp. 105–13.

'Revolution? What revolution? Some thoughts about revestment', *Proceedings of the Isle of Man Natural and Antiquarian Society*, 11.4 (2003–5), pp. 541–52.

P. Studenski, *The income of nations, part 1, history* (New York, 1958).

John Styles, 'Spinners and the law: regulating yarn standards in the English worsted industries, 1550–1800', *Textile History*, 44.2 (2013), pp. 145–70.

Michael F. Suarez, 'Towards a bibliometric analysis of the surviving record, 1701–1800', in Michael F. Suarez and Michael L. Turner, eds., *The Cambridge history of the book in Britain: vol. 5, 1695–1830* (Cambridge, 2009), pp. 39–65.

Dorothy Summers, *The great level: a history of draining and land reclamation in the fens* (Newton Abbot, 1976).

Barry E. Supple, *Commercial crisis and change in England, 1600–1642* (Cambridge, 1959).

'The state and the industrial revolution, 1700–1914', in *The Fontana economic history of Europe, vol. 3.* Edited by Carlo M. Cipolla (1971), pp. 301–57.

Lawrence Susskind, 'Arguing, bargaining, and getting agreement', in Michael Moran, Martin Rein, and Robert E. Goodin, eds., *The Oxford handbook of public policy* (Oxford, 2006), pp. 269–95.

Lucy Sutherland, *Politics and finance in the eighteenth century.* Edited by Aubrey Newman (1984).

D. Swann, 'The pace and progress of port investment in England, 1660–1830', *Yorkshire Bulletin of Economic and Social Research*, 12.1 (1960), pp. 32–44.

Julian Swann, 'Politics and the state' in T. C. W. Blanning, ed., *Short Oxford history of Europe: the eighteenth century* (Oxford, 2000), pp. 11–51.

Andrew Swatland, *The House of Lords in the reign of Charles II* (Cambridge, 1996).

Roey Sweet, 'Local identities and a national parliament', in Julian Hoppit, ed., *Parliaments, nations and identities in Britain and Ireland, 1660–1850* (Manchester, 2003), pp. 48–63.

Orsolya Szakály, 'Managing a composite monarchy: the Hungarian diet and the Habsburgs in the eighteenth century', in D. W. Hayton, James Kelly, and John Bergin, eds., *The eighteenth-century composite state: representative institutions in Ireland and Europe, 1689–1800* (Basingstoke, 2010), pp. 205–20.

W. E. Tate, 'The cost of parliamentary enclosure in England (with special reference to the county of Oxford)', *Economic History Review*, 5.2 (1952), pp. 258–65.

A domesday of English enclosure acts and awards. Edited by Michael Turner (Reading, 1978).

'Members of Parliament and their personal relations to enclosure: a study with reference to Oxfordshire enclosures, 1757–1843', *Agricultural History*, 23.3 (1949), pp. 213–20.

Richard F. Teichgraeber, '"Less abused than I had reason to expect": the reception of *The wealth of nations* in Britain, 1776–1790', *Historical Journal*, 30.2 (1987), pp. 337–64.

Christine Théré, 'Economic publishing and authors, 1566–1789', in Gilbert Faccarello, ed., *Studies in the history of French political economy: from Bodin to Walras* (London and New York, 1998), pp. 1–56.

Joan Thirsk, 'Agricultural policy: public debate and legislation', in Joan Thirsk, ed., *The agrarian history of England and Wales, V, 1640–1750: II, Agrarian change* (Cambridge, 1985), pp. 298–388.

'The crown as projector on its own estates from Elizabeth I to Charles I', in R. W. Hoyle, ed., *The estates of the English crown, 1558–1640* (Cambridge, 1992), pp. 297–352.

Economic policy and projects: the development of a consumer society in early modern England (Oxford, 1978).

English peasant farming: the agrarian history of Lincolnshire from Tudor to recent times (1957).

The Restoration (1976).

Keith Thomas, 'Age and authority in early modern England, *Proceedings of the British Academy*, 62 (1976), pp. 205–48.

P. D. G. Thomas, *British politics and the Stamp Act crisis: the first phase of the American Revolution, 1763–1767* (Oxford, 1975).

The House of Commons in the eighteenth century (Oxford, 1971).

E. P. Thompson, 'The crime of anonymity', in Thompson et al., *Albion's fatal tree: crime and society in eighteenth-century England* (Harmondsworth, 1977), pp. 255–308.

Customs in common (1988).

Whigs and hunters: the origin of the Black Act (Harmondsworth, 1977).

Stephen John Thompson, 'Census-taking, political economy and state formation in Britain, c. 1790–1840' (University of Cambridge, PhD thesis, 2010).

'Parliamentary enclosure, property, and the decline of classical republicanism in eighteenth-century Britain', *Historical Journal*, 51.3 (2008), pp. 621–42.

John Torrance, 'Social class and bureaucratic innovation: the commissioners for examining the public accounts, 1780–1787', *Past and Present*, 78 (1978), pp. 56–81.

James D. Tracey, ed., *The political economy of merchant empires: state power and world trade, 1350–1750* (Cambridge, 1991).

Hugh Trevor-Roper, 'The general crisis of the seventeenth century', *Past and Present*, 16 (1959), pp. 31–64.

Keith Tribe, *Strategies of economic order: German economic discourse, 1750–1950* (Cambridge, 1995).

Thomas M. Truxes, *Defying empire: trading with the enemy in colonial New York* (New Haven, CT, 2008).

Michael Turner, *English parliamentary enclosure: its historical geography and economic history* (Folkestone, 1980).

M. E. Turner, J. V. Beckett, and B. Afton, *Agricultural rent in England, 1690–1914* (Cambridge, 1997).

Michael Turner and Trevor Wray, 'A survey of sources for parliamentary enclosure: the House of Commons' Journal and commissioners' working papers', *Archives*, 19.85 (1991), pp. 267–88.

Isolde Victory, 'The making of the 1720 Declaratory Act', in Gerard O'Brien, ed., *Parliament, politics and people: essays in eighteenth-century Irish history* (Dublin, 1989), pp. 9–29.

Jacob Viner, *Essays on the intellectual history of economics*. Edited by Douglas A. Irwin (Princeton, NJ, 1991).

'Power versus plenty as objectives of foreign policy in the seventeenth and eighteenth centuries', in D. C. Coleman, ed., *Revisions in mercantilism* (1969), pp. 61–91.

Studies in the theory of international trade (New York, 1937).

Peer Vries, *State, economy and the great divergence: Great Britain and China, 1680s–1850s* (2015).

Brodie Waddell, *God, duty and community in English economic life, 1660–1720* (Woodbridge, 2012).

'Governing England through the manor courts, 1550–1850', *Historical Journal*, 55.2 (2012), pp. 279–315.

Michael Wagner, 'The Levant Company under attack in Parliament, 1720–53', *Parliamentary History*, 34.3 (2015), pp. 295–313.

Dror Wahrman, *Imagining the middle class: the political representation of class in Britain, c. 1780–1840* (Cambridge, 1995).

Andre Wakefield, *The disordered police state: German Cameralism as science and practice* (Chicago, IL, 2009).

Michael John Walker, 'The extent of the guild control of trades in England, c.1660–1820: a study based on a sample of provincial towns and London companies' (University of Cambridge, PhD thesis, 1986).

Gary M. Walton, 'The new economic history and the burdens of the navigation acts', *Economic History Review*, 24.4 (1971), pp. 533–42.

J. R. Ward, *The finance of canal building in eighteenth-century England* (Oxford, 1974).

W. R. Ward, 'The land tax in Scotland, 1707–98', *Bulletin of the John Rylands Library*, 37 (1954–5), pp. 288–308.

Paul Warde, 'The idea of improvement, c.1520–1700', in Richard W. Hoyle, ed., *Custom, improvement and landscape in early modern Britain* (Farnham, 2011), pp. 127–48.

Jessica Warner and Frank J. Ivis, '"Damn you, you informing bitch": vox populi and the unmaking of the Gin Act of 1736', *Journal of Social History*, 33.2 (1999), pp. 299–330.

Douglas Watt, *The price of Scotland: Darien, Union and the wealth of nations* (Edinburgh, 2007).

Sidney Webb and Beatrice Webb, 'The assize of bread', *Economic Journal*, 14.54 (1904), pp. 196–218.

   English local government: the story of the king's highway (1913).

   Statutory authority for special purposes, with a summary of the development of local government structure (1922).

Brian Weiser, *Charles II and the politics of access* (Woodbridge, 2003).

Joachim Whaley, *Germany and the Holy Roman Empire* (2 vols., Oxford, 2012).

C. A. Whatley, 'Economic causes and consequences of the Union of 1707: a survey', *Scottish Historical Review*, 68.2 (1989), pp. 150–81.

   'Salt, coal and the Union of 1707: a revision article', *Scottish Historical Review*, 66.1 (1987), pp. 26–45.

   Scottish society, 1707–1830: beyond Jacobitism, towards industrialisation (Manchester, 2000).

W. H. Wheeler, *A history of the fens of south Lincolnshire* (2nd edn., Boston, 1896).

Ann E. Whetstone, *Scottish county government in the eighteenth and nineteenth centuries* (Edinburgh, 1981).

Edward White, *Law in American history: vol. 1, From the colonial years through the civil wars* (Oxford, 2012).

Ian D. Whyte, 'Urbanization in eighteenth-century Scotland', in T. M. Devine and J. R. Young, eds., *Eighteenth-century Scotland: new perspectives* (East Lothian, 1999), pp. 176–94.

T. S. Willan, *The early history of the Don navigation* (Manchester, 1965).

   The English coasting trade, 1600–1750 (1938).

   'The justices of the peace and the rates of land carriage, 1692–1827', *Journal of Transport History*, 5.4 (1962), pp. 197–204.

   River navigation in England, 1600–1750 (Oxford, 1936).

Eric Williams, *Capitalism and slavery* (1944).

Glyndwr Williams, 'The Hudson's Bay Company and its critics in the eighteenth century', *Transactions of the Royal Historical Society*, 20 (1970), pp. 149–71.

John Williams, *Digest of Welsh historical statistics* (2 vols., Cardiff, 1985).

Judith Blow Williams, *British commercial policy and trade expansion, 1750–1850* (Oxford, 1972).

Orlo Cyprian Williams, *The clerical organization of the House of Commons, 1661–1851* (Oxford, 1954).

The historical development of private bill procedure and standing orders in the House of Commons (2 vols., 1948–9).

Oliver E. Williamson, 'The new institutional economics: taking stock, looking ahead', *Journal of Economic Literature*, 38.3 (2000), pp. 595–613.

Kirk Willis, 'The role in Parliament of the economic ideas of Adam Smith, 1776–1800', *History of Political Economy*, 11.4 (1979), pp. 505–44.

Frances Willmoth, *Sir Jonas Moore: practical mathematics and Restoration science* (Woodbridge, 1993).

Charles H. Wilson, *Economic history and the historian: collected essays* (1969).

'Trade, society and the state', in *The Cambridge economic history of Europe, vol. 4. The economy of expanding Europe in the sixteenth and seventeenth centuries.* Edited by E. E. Rich and C. H. Wilson (Cambridge, 1967), pp. 487–575.

R. G. Wilson, 'Newspapers and industry: the export of wool controversy in the 1780s', in Michael Harris and Alan Lees, eds., *The press in English society from the seventeenth to nineteenth centuries* (Cranbury, NJ, London, and Ontario, 1986), pp. 80–104.

'The supremacy of the Yorkshire cloth industry in the eighteenth century', in N. B. Harte and K. G. Ponting, eds., *Textile history and economic history: essays in honour of Miss Julia de Lacy Mann* (Manchester, 1973), pp. 225–46.

Robin W. Winks, *The Oxford history of the British empire, vol. 5 Historiography* (Oxford, 1999).

Alfred C. Wood, *A history of the Levant Company* (Oxford, 1935).

Fiona Jean Wood, 'Inland transportation and distribution in the hinterland of King's Lynn, 1760–1840' (University of Cambridge, PhD thesis, 1992).

Patrick Woodland, 'Political atomization and regional interests in the 1761 Parliament: the impact of the cider debates 1763–1766', *Parliamentary History*, 8.1 (1989), pp. 63–89.

J. R. Wordie, 'The chronology of English enclosure, 1500–1914', *Economic History Review*, 36.4 (1983), pp. 483–505.

E. A. Wrigley, *The early English censuses* (Oxford, 2011).

Energy and the English industrial revolution (Cambridge, 2010).

'English county populations in the later eighteenth century', *Economic History Review*, 60.1 (2007), pp. 35–69.

The path to sustained growth: England's transition from an organic economy to an industrial revolution (Cambridge, 2016).

People, cities and wealth: the transformation of traditional society (Oxford, 1987).

'Rickman revisited: the population growth rates of English counties in the early modern period', *Economic History Review*, 62.3 (2009), pp. 711–35.

'A simple model of London's importance in changing English society and economy, 1650–1750', *Past and Present*, 37 (1967), pp. 44–70.

'The supply of raw materials in the industrial revolution', *Economic History Review*, 15.1 (1962), pp. 1–16.

E. A. Wrigley and R. S. Schofield, *The population history of England, 1541–1871: a reconstruction* (1981).

Nuala Zahedieh, *The capital and the colonies: London and the Atlantic economy, 1660–1700* (Cambridge, 2010).

'Regulation, rent-seeking and the Glorious Revolution in the English Atlantic economy', *Economic History Review*, 63.4 (2010), pp. 865–90.

J. van der Zande, 'Statistik and history in the German Enlightenment', *Journal of the History of Ideas*, 71.3 (2010), pp. 411–32.

David Zaret, 'Petitions and the "invention" of public opinion in the English revolution', *American Journal of Sociology*, 101.6 (1996), pp. 1497–555.

ONLINE RESOURCES

English Short Title Catalogue, http://estc.bl.uk.

The European State Finance Database, www.esfdb.org.

The History of Parliament, www.historyofparliamentonline.org.

Irish Legislation Database, www.qub.ac.uk/ild.

Office for National Statistics, www.ons.gov.uk.

The Oxford Dictionary of National Biography, www.oxforddnb.com.

Records of the Parliament of Scotland to 1707, www.rps.ac.uk.

Royal Charters, http://privycouncil.independent.gov.uk/royal-charters/chartered-bodies.

Index